Simon Kelly and April M. Watson

with Maura Coughlin and Neil McWilliam

IMPRESSIONIST FRANCE

Visions of Nation from Le Gray to Monet

Saint Louis Art Museum The Nelson-Atkins Museum of Art

This book is published in conjunction with the exhibition ***Impressionist France: Visions of Nation from Le Gray to Monet***, presented at The Nelson-Atkins Museum of Art from October 19, 2013, to February 9, 2014, and the Saint Louis Art Museum from March 16 to July 6, 2014.

Financial assistance has been provided by the Missouri Arts Council, a state agency.

Published by Saint Louis Art Museum, Saint Louis, Missouri, and The Nelson-Atkins Museum of Art, Kansas City, Missouri

Distributed by Yale University Press

Produced by Marquand Books, Inc., Seattle
www.marquand.com

Edited by Fronia W. Simpson
Designed by Jeff Wincapaw
Typesetting and layout by Marie Weiler
Typesetting assistance by Brynn Warriner
Proofread by Laura Iwasaki
Indexed by Candace Hyatt
Map on page 10 by Jeremy Linden
Color management by iocolor, Seattle
Printed and bound in China by C&C Color Printing Co., Ltd.

Library of Congress Cataloging-in-Publication Data
Impressionist France : visions of nation from Le Gray to Monet / Simon Kelly and April M. Watson ; with Maura Coughlin and Neil McWilliam.
pages cm
Summary: "Between 1850 and 1880, Impressionist landscape painting and early forms of photography flourished within the arts in France. In the context of massive social and political change that also marked this era, painters and photographers composed competing visions of France as modern and industrialized or as rural and anti-modern. *Impressionist France* explores the resonances between landscape art and national identity as reflected in the paintings and photographs made during this period, examining and illustrating in particular the works of key artists such as Édouard Baldus, Gustave Le Gray, the Bisson frères, Édouard Manet, Jean-François Millet, Claude Monet, Charles Nègre, and Camille Pissarro. This ambitious premise focuses on the whole of France, exploring the relationship between landscape art and the notion of French nationhood across the country's varied and spectacular landscapes in seven geographical sections and four scholarly essays, which provide new information regarding the production and impact of French Impressionism." —Provided by publisher.
"This book is published in conjunction with the exhibition *Impressionist France: Visions of Nation from Le Gray to Monet*, presented at The Nelson-Atkins Museum of Art from October 19, 2013, to February 9, 2014, and the Saint Louis Art Museum from March 16 to July 6, 2014."
Includes bibliographical references.
ISBN 978-0-300-19695-5 (pbk.)
1. Landscapes in art—Exhibitions. 2. Nationalism and art—France—History—19th century—Exhibitions. 3. National characteristics, French, in art—Exhibitions. 4. Art, French—19th century—Exhibitions. 5. Landscape photography—France—History—19th century—Exhibitions. I. Kelly, Simon (Simon R.) II. Watson, April M. III. Nelson-Atkins Museum of Art. IV. St. Louis Art Museum.
N8214.5.F8147 2013
709.44'09034—dc23 2013023234

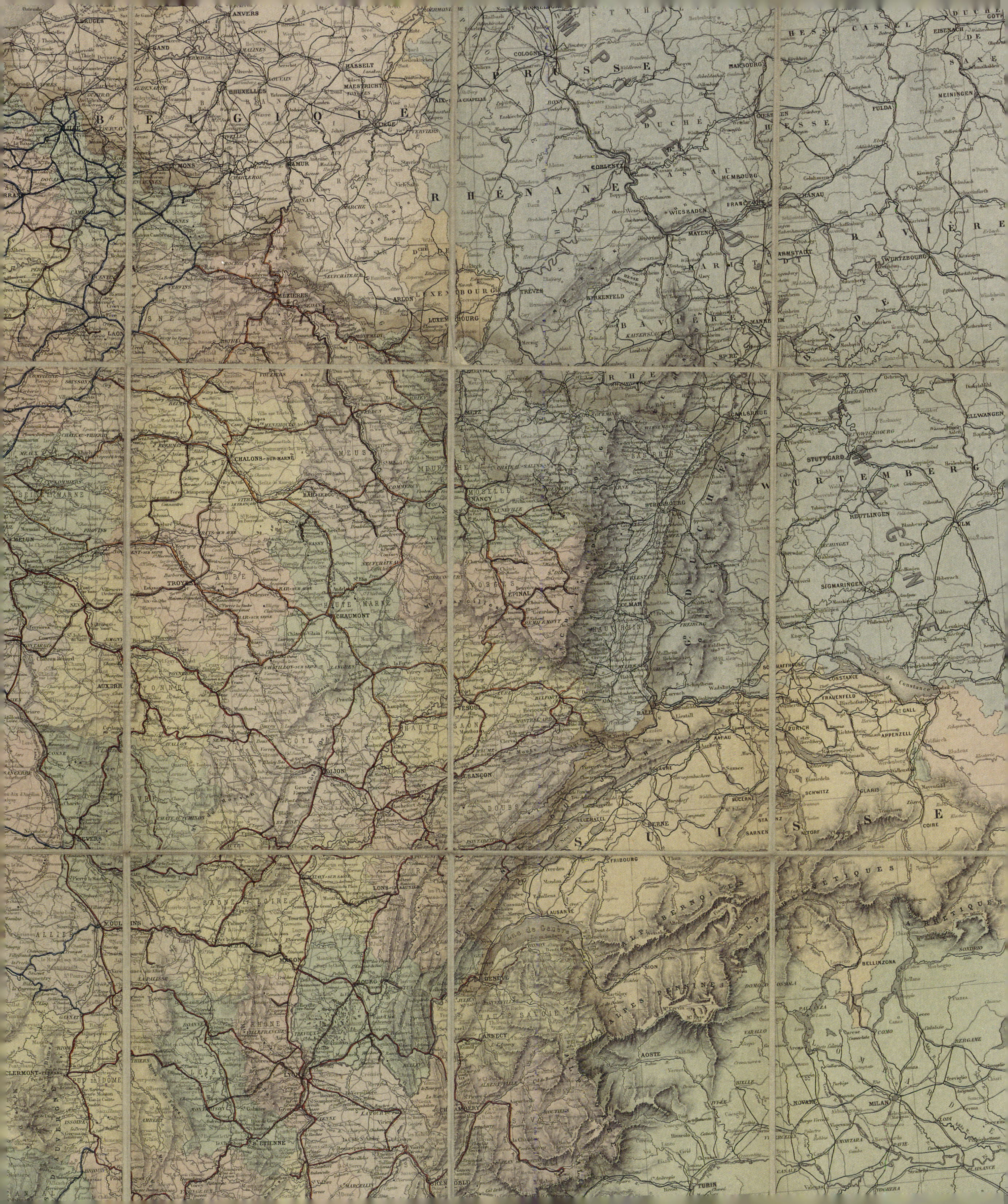

BELGIQUE
ANVERS
BRUXELLES
HASSELT
MAESTRICHT
NAMUR
MONS
CHARLEROI
DINANT
ARLON
LUXEMBOURG
MEZIERES
LAON
PRUSSE
RHÉNANE
COLOGNE
COBLENTZ
NASSAU
WIESBADEN
MAYENCE
HESSE
MARBOURG
FULDA
MEININGEN
EISENACH
SAXE
HANAU
BAVIERE
WURTZBOURG
TRÈVES
CHALONS-SUR-MARNE
BAR-LE-DUC
TROYES
AUBE
HAUTE MARNE
CHAUMONT
NANCY
METZ
STRASBOURG
COLMAR
EPINAL
VOSGES
BELFORT
VESOUL
BESANÇON
DIJON
AUXERRE
NEVERS
STUTTGARD
WURTEMBERG
REUTLINGEN
ULM
SIGMARINGEN
CONSTANCE
FRAUENFELD
ZURICH
S^T GALL
APPENZELL
AARAU
ZUG
SCHWITZ
GLARIS
LUCERNE
BERNE
COIRE
SUISSE
FRIBOURG
LAUSANNE
GENÈVE
SION
ALPES BERNOISES
ALPES PENNINES
HAUTE SAVOIE
ANNECY
AOSTE
BELLINZONA
COMO
BERGAME
NOVARE
MILAN
TURIN
MOULINS
ALLIER
CLERMONT-FERRAND
LYON
S^T ETIENNE

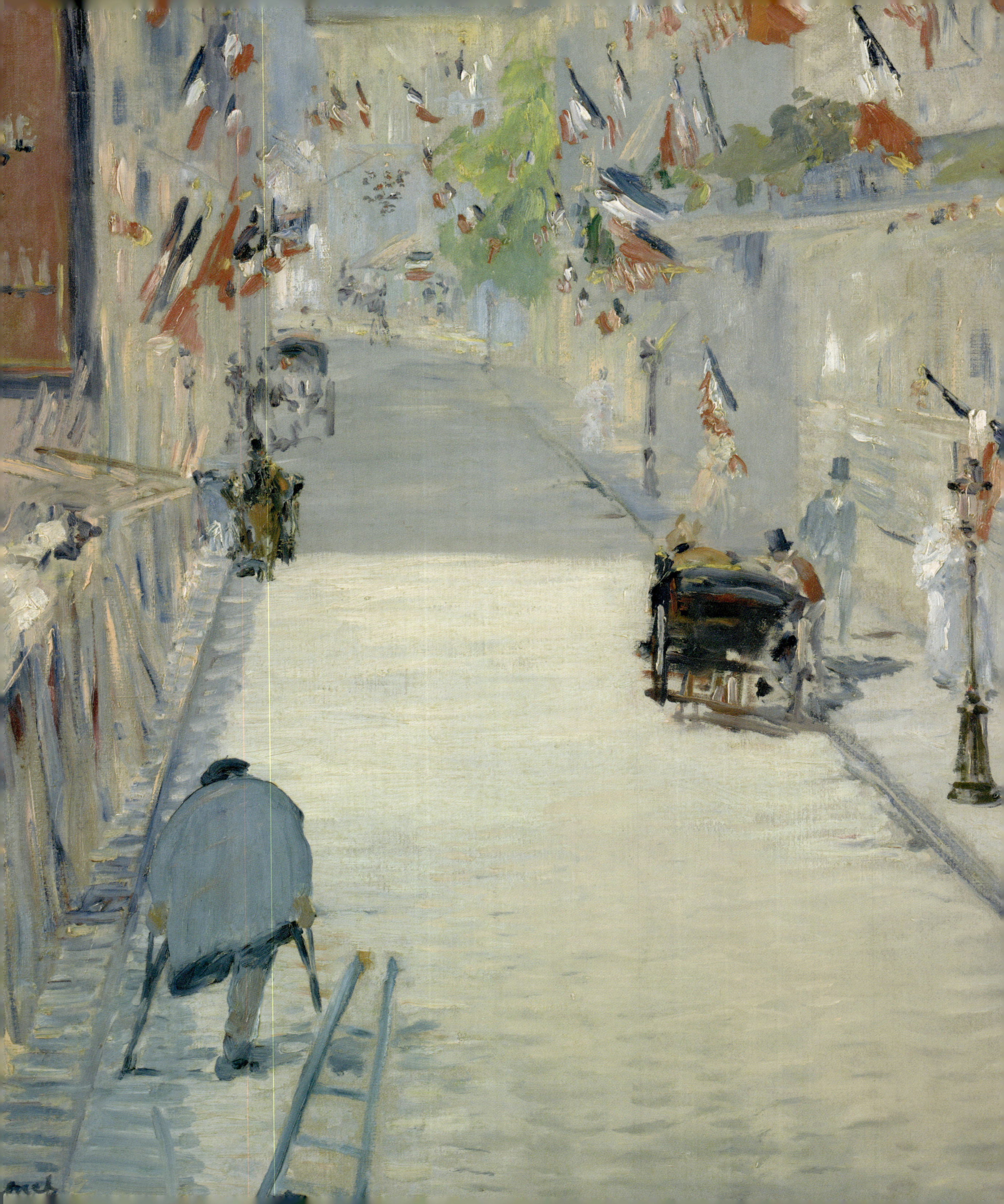

Contents

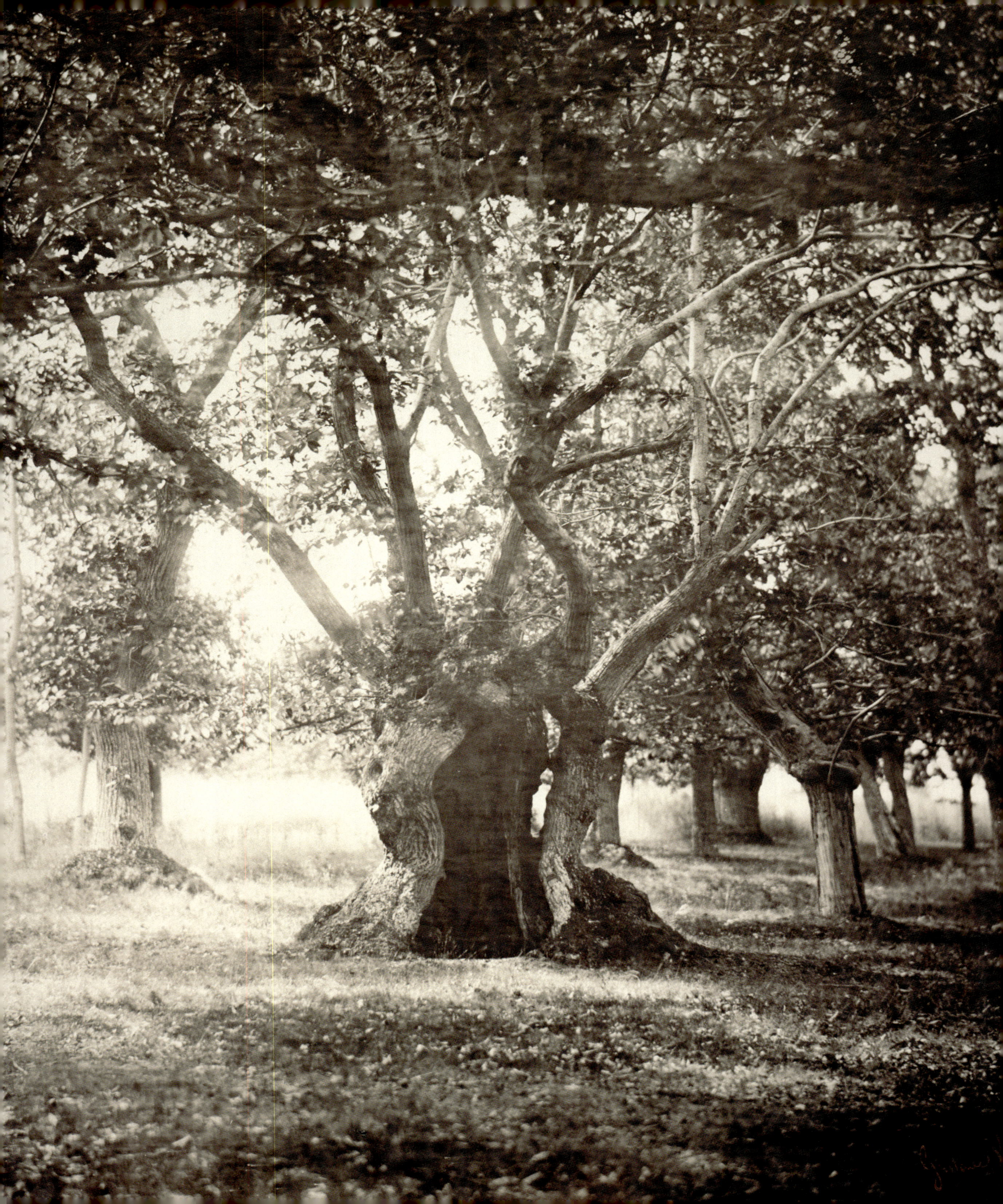

Directors' Foreword

THE EXHIBITION *Impressionist France: Visions of Nation from Le Gray to Monet* presents a fresh perspective on landscape imagery in mid-nineteenth-century France. Through paintings and photographs, this exhibition explores for the first time the rich and varied connections between landscape and national identity during a period in which France was fundamentally transformed and modernized.

Driven by the expansionist policies of the Second Empire (1852–70), the mid-nineteenth century saw massive social, political, and structural change in France with the emergence of an extensive rail network, improved roads, and the expansion of a canal system. Painters and photographers composed competing visions of France as modern and industrialized or, in equally potent terms, as rural and antimodern. This imagery was produced under a variety of auspices, both artistic and state sponsored.

It is within this historical context that key artists emerged, including Claude Monet, Édouard Manet, Camille Pissarro, and others from the Impressionist generation. During this same period, influential photographers, such as Gustave Le Gray, the Bisson frères, and Édouard Baldus, advanced the practice of photography from amateur experimentation to artistic mastery, while also demonstrating its value as a tool for state-sponsored agendas.

On behalf of the boards and staff of The Nelson-Akins Museum of Art and the Saint Louis Art Museum, we offer sincere thanks to the organizations and individuals whose generosity made this project possible. We would like to thank the National Endowment for the Arts, which provided two major grants for the research and development of the catalogue and exhibition, as well as the Federal Council on the Arts and the Humanities for the grant of United States Government indemnity. Financial assistance for both venues has been provided by the Missouri Arts Council, a state agency. In Kansas City, we are especially grateful to the Hall Family Foundation, which provided a major contribution for the exhibition's presentation at The Nelson-Atkins Museum of Art. Additional support for the Kansas City presentation was provided by The Manuel Rivera-Ortiz Foundation for Documentary Photography & Film and by the Campbell-Calvin Fund and Elizabeth C. Bonner Charitable Trust for exhibitions.

We are grateful as well to the many lenders in the United States and Europe who kindly agreed to lend important works to the exhibition. Their generosity has been essential for the realization of this project.

The exhibition was conceived by Simon Kelly, Curator of Modern and Contemporary Art at the Saint Louis Art Museum, and developed in collaboration with co-curator April M. Watson, Associate Curator of Photography at The Nelson-Atkins Museum of Art. We thank them for their vision and scholarship, which have brought to fruition this exploration of the correlation between landscape and national identity during a fascinating period in France's artistic and cultural history.

Brent R. Benjamin	Julián Zugazagoitia
Director	*Menefee D. and Mary Louise*
Saint Louis Art Museum	*Blackwell Director/CEO*
	The Nelson-Atkins Museum of Art

Acknowledgments

THIS CATALOGUE AND ACCOMPANYING EXHIBITION are the results of a collaborative effort between our two museums as well as numerous others. We are tremendously thankful to those directors, curatorial colleagues, museum professionals, and private collectors who enthusiastically supported this project, granting requests for loans of key works with which it was, at times, difficult to part: Douglas Druick, Gloria Groom, Matthew Witkovsky, and Elizabeth Siegel (The Art Institute of Chicago); Arnold L. Lehman and Richard Aste (Brooklyn Museum); Mirko Zardini, Louise Désy, and Iglika Avramova (Canadian Centre for Architecture, Montreal); Lynn Zelevansky and Louise Lippincott (Carnegie Museum of Art, Pittsburgh); Aaron Betsky and Esther Bell (Cincinnati Art Museum); David Franklin, William Robinson, and Barbara Tannenbaum (The Cleveland Museum of Art); J. David Farmer (Dahesh Museum of Art, New York); Christoph Heinrich and Timothy J. Standring (Denver Art Museum); Bill Bodine and Sarah J. Hall (Frick Art & Historical Center, Pittsburgh); Wataru Okada, Joseph Struble, Travis Johansen, and Taina Meller (George Eastman House, Rochester); James R. Kieselburg II (Grohmann Museum at Milwaukee School of Engineering); Stephanie Wiles and Andrew Weislogel (Herbert F. Johnson Museum of Art, Cornell University); Michael E. Shapiro and David Brenneman (The High Museum of Art, Atlanta); Charles Venable and Ellen W. Lee (Indianapolis Museum of Art); Timothy Potts, Scott Schaefer, Scott Allan, Judith Keller, Virginia Heckert, and Arpad Kovacs (The J. Paul Getty Museum, Los Angeles); Jack Becker and Toby Jurovics (Joslyn Art Museum, Omaha); Thomas P. Campbell, Stijn Alsteens, Keith Christiansen, Cora Michael, Susan Stein, Jeff Rosenheim, and Malcolm Daniel (The Metropolitan Museum of Art, New York City); Heather Haskell and Julia Courtney (Michele and Donald D'Amour Museum of Fine Arts, Springfield, Mass.); Kaywin Feldman and Patrick Noon (The Minneapolis Institute of Arts); Brigitte Gaillard (Musée d'art de Toulon); Joel Smith (The Morgan Library and Museum, New York City); Marianne Mathieu and Patrick de Carolis (Musée Marmottan Monet, Paris); Guy Cogeval, Sylvie Patry, Stéphane Guégan, and Xavier Rey (Musée d'Orsay, Paris); Chantal Fernex de Mongex (Musée des beaux-arts de Chambéry); Emmanuel Starcky and Laure Chabanne (Musées nationaux du Palais de Compiègne); Gary Tinterow, Anne Wilkes Tucker, and Del Zogg (Museum of Fine Arts, Houston); Earl A. Powell III, Kimberly A. Jones, Mary G. Morton, Ann Hoeningswald, Sarah Greenough, and Sarah Kennel (National Gallery of Art, Washington, D.C.); Timothy Rub, Joseph Rishel, Jennifer Thompson, and Peter Barberie (Philadelphia Museum of Art); Dorothy Kosinski (The Phillips Collection, Washington, D.C.); Brian J. Ferriso and Bruce Guenther (Portland Art Museum, Oregon); James Christen Steward and Katherine Bussard (Princeton University Art Museum); Larry J. Feinberg and Eik Kahng (Santa Barbara Museum of Art); Saralyn Reece Hardy and Stephen Goddard (Spencer Museum of Art, The University of Kansas, Lawrence); Michael Conforti and Richard Rand (The Sterling and Francine Clark Art Institute, Williamstown); Brian Kennedy and Lawrence W. Nichols (Toledo Museum of Art); Martin Roth and Martin Barnes (Victoria and Albert Museum, London); Alex Nyerges and Mitchell Merling (Virginia Museum of Fine Arts, Richmond); Robert L. and Barbara Bloch; Jay McDonald and Hans P. Kraus Jr.; Don Nice; and Mark Osterman and France Scully Osterman. For their generous assistance during the grant application process, we thank Wendy Clark, Robert Frankel, and the late David Bancroft at the National Endowment for the Arts, and Patricia Loiko and Laura Cunningham at the Federal Council on the Arts and the Humanities. We also thank Urs Bucher and Andre Pfanner of Swiss Re, Zurich, Switzerland, and The Manuel Rivera-Ortiz Foundation for Documentary Photography & Film.

At our two museums, we wish to thank above all our directors, Julián Zugazagoitia, Menefee D. and Mary Louise Blackwell Director/CEO, The Nelson-Atkins Museum of Art, and Brent R. Benjamin, Director, Saint Louis Art Museum, for their support and enthusiasm. We would also like to thank our curatorial colleagues: Nicole Myers, associate curator of European painting and sculpture at the Nelson-Atkins, provided invaluable assistance and insight with the installation at the Nelson-Atkins; and Eric Lutz, associate curator of prints, drawings, and photographs, was gracious with his help in the Saint Louis venue.

At the Nelson-Atkins, this exhibition marks the first major presentation of our nineteenth-century French photographs. For their essential and ongoing support of the museum's photography program and for their contribution toward the Kansas City presentation of this exhibition, we deeply appreciate the generosity of the Hall Family Foundation. In particular, sincere thanks go to Stacie J. Bohnsack, private controller; Terri R. Maybee, director; William A. Hall, president; and Donald J. Hall, chairman. We would also like to thank for their invaluable assistance Karen Christiansen, chief operating officer; Cindy Cart, curator, exhibitions management; Janet Mark, senior development director, corporate and foundation support; Ann Friedman, manager of grants and foundations; Julie Mattsson, associate registrar, loans and exhibitions; Emily Black Fry, interpretive planner; Tim O'Neill, exhibition designer; Keith F. Davis, senior curator, photography; Jane L. Aspinwall, associate curator, photography; Natalie Boten, department coordinator, photography; and Emily Henson, intern, photography. Kaitlyn Bunch, research and project assistant, photography, deserves special praise for her meticulous oversight of the project's many details. We also thank MacKenzie Mallon, department assistant, European painting and sculpture; Tara Brungardt, collections coordinator, photography; Elisabeth Batchelor, director, conservation and collections management; Scott Heffley, senior conservator, paintings; Mary Schafer, associate conservator, paintings; Saori Lewis, assistant conservator, photography; Judith Koke, director, education and interpretive programs; Marilyn Carbonell, head, library services; Roberta Wagener, library assistant; Steve Waterman, director, presentation; Michele Boeckholt, manager, graphic design; Beth Byers, Matthew Kemp, and Susan Patterson, graphic designers; Toni Wood, manager, marketing and communication; Kathleen Leighton, communications and media-relations officer; and the many contributors from our imaging services, fabrication and preparation, and information technology departments.

At the Saint Louis Art Museum, we would like to thank Carolyn Schmidt, deputy director and controller; Carl Hamm, deputy director; and Linda Thomas, assistant director for exhibitions and collections. We would also like to recognize the following staff members for their logistical help with the exhibition and catalogue: Philip Atkinson, exhibition designer; Ann Burroughs, associate educator; Marianne Cavanaugh, head librarian; Jon Cournoyer, senior graphic designer; Jeanette Fausz, registrar; Brigid Flynn, director, institutional giving; Paul Haner, director of conservation; Claire Walker, assistant paintings conservator; Matthew Hathaway, press officer; Nancy Heugh, paper conservator; Sabrena Nelson, educator; Molly Perse, exhibitions coordinator; Aliya Reich, former research assistant; Jeanne Rosen, administrative assistant; Ella Rothgangel, collections information and imaging administrator; Jennifer Stoffel, director of external affairs; Rachel Swiston, collections database assistant; Clare Vasquez, public services librarian; and Bryan Young, serials and interlibrary loan coordinator.

We thank scholars Maura Coughlin and Neil McWilliam for their expertise in writing the catalogue's essays, and Sydney Norton, researcher at the Saint Louis Art Museum, for her thoughtful chronology and valuable research. We thank Fronia W. Simpson, whose excellent editing and great patience helped bring this catalogue to fruition. We are grateful to Yale University Press, and particularly Patricia J. Fidler, publisher, Art and Architecture, for the distribution of the catalogue, and to Marquand Books for their guidance in the design and production of an elegant book, particularly Ed Marquand, partner, creative director; Adrian Lucia, partner, managing director; Jeff Wincapaw, design director; Ryan Polich, design and production assistant; Melissa Duffes, managing editor; Brielyn Flones, editorial assistant; Leah Finger, production manager; and Jeremy Linden, production artist.

Several individuals contributed their knowledge and expertise during the conception and research of this project. We thank Sylvie Aubenas, Richard Brettell, Malcolm Daniel, Thomas Galifot, Mike Heffernan, Laurent Herschtritt, Robert Hershkowitz, the late John House, Charles Isaacs, Ken Jacobson, Serge Kakou, Ian Kennedy, Sarah Kennel, Robert Koch, Hans P. Kraus Jr., Mack Lee, Alexander Novak, Serge Plantureux, Christopher Riopelle, Paul-Louis Roubert, Ann Thomas, William Schaeffer, Timothy Standring, and Richard Thomson. For inspiring a love for this period many years ago, April Watson would like to thank Eugenia Parry.

Finally, for their patience and steadfast moral support, April Watson would like to thank her family, Elijah, Fiona, and Violet Gewin.

Simon Kelly
Curator of Modern and Contemporary Art
Saint Louis Art Museum

April M. Watson
Associate Curator, Photography
The Nelson-Atkins Museum of Art

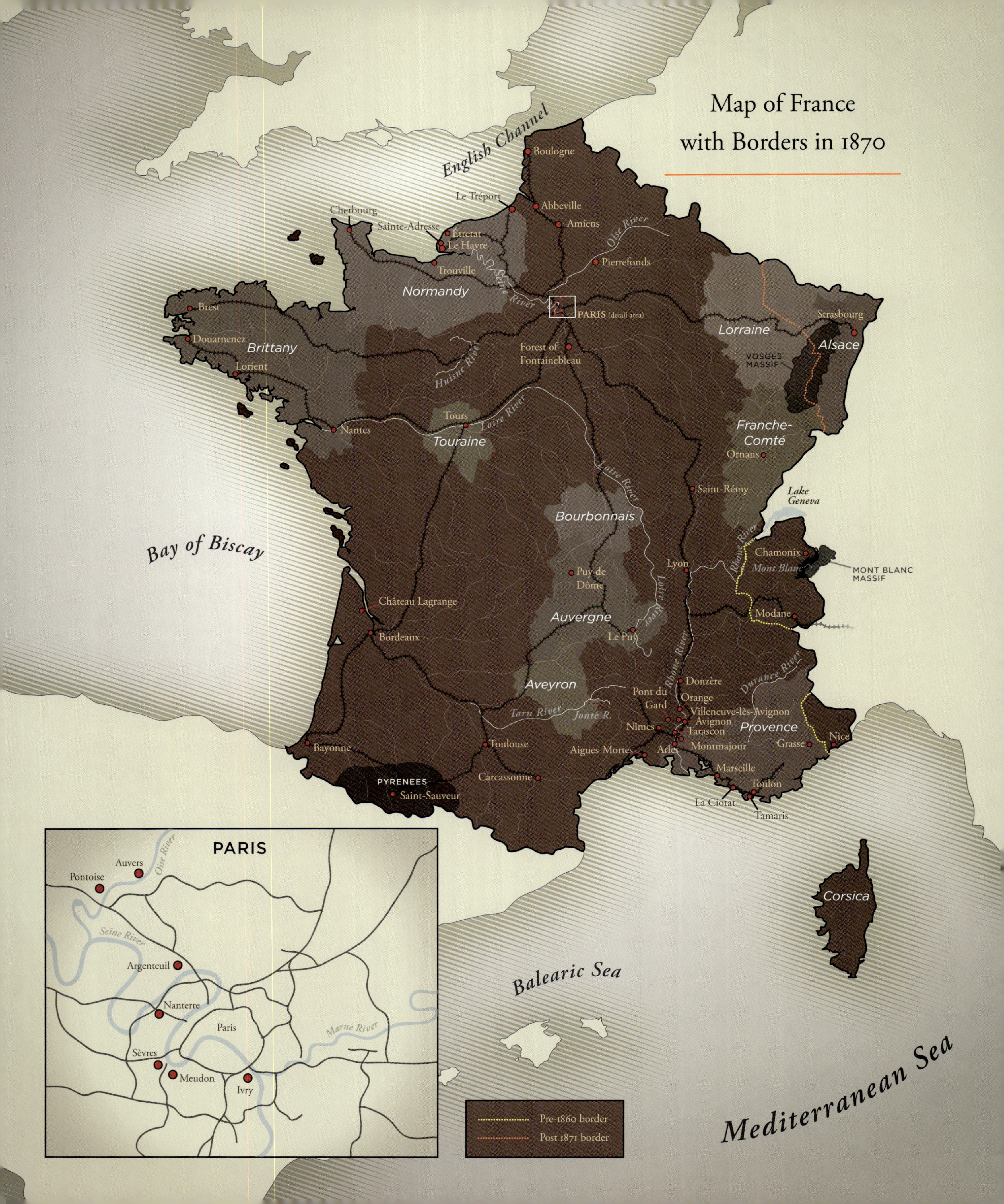
Map of France
with Borders in 1870
English Channel
Boulogne
Le Tréport
Abbeville
Amiens
Cherbourg
Sainte-Adresse
Étretat
Le Havre
Trouville
Oise River
Pierrefonds
Normandy
Seine River
Brest
PARIS (detail area)
Lorraine
Strasbourg
Alsace
VOSGES MASSIF
Douarnenez
Brittany
Lorient
Forest of Fontainebleau
Huisne River
Tours
Loire River
Nantes
Touraine
Franche-Comté
Ornans
Loire River
Saint-Rémy
Lake Geneva
Bourbonnais
Bay of Biscay
Puy de Dôme
Lyon
Rhone River
Chamonix
Mont Blanc
MONT BLANC MASSIF
Château Lagrange
Auvergne
Loire River
Modane
Bordeaux
Le Puy
Rhone River
Durance River
Donzère
Aveyron
Pont du Gard
Orange
Tarn River
Jonte R.
Villeneuve-lès-Avignon
Avignon
Tarascon
Nîmes
Provence
Nice
Grasse
Bayonne
Toulouse
Aigues-Mortes
Arles
Montmajour
Marseille
Toulon
La Ciotat
Tamaris
Carcassonne
PYRENEES
Saint-Sauveur
PARIS
Auvers
Oise River
Pontoise
Seine River
Argenteuil
Nanterre
Paris
Marne River
Sèvres
Meudon
Ivry
Corsica
Balearic Sea
Pre-1860 border
Post 1871 border
Mediterranean Sea

Introduction

SIMON KELLY AND APRIL M. WATSON

THIS EXHIBITION AND ACCOMPANYING CATALOGUE are about the idea of nation, specifically, the ways in which art constructs a sense of nation. Why organize a show about the idea of nation and nationhood today? In an age of growing globalization, as well as heightened mobility and migration, the concept of nation may seem increasingly outmoded. In Europe, for example, there is growing discussion of a European superstate. Yet the idea of national belonging persists. Communities and individuals continue to be wedded to the notion of national identity: they are deeply attached to their Frenchness, their Americanness, their Englishness. National identity remains a central mode of establishing individual identity. On an academic level, the very idea of nation persists as a touchstone of debate among philosophers, historians, and social theorists.[1]

In exploring nationhood, our project focuses on France, where debates around the idea of nation remain particularly relevant. In the fall of 2009, then-president Nicolas Sarkozy instigated a national debate, complete with an online survey, about what it meant to be French, asking questions ranging from French cuisine to such archetypically republican values as liberty, equality, and fraternity. The survey indicated that many elements combine to construct national identity, from perceived shared values to everyday food and drink. Our exhibition and book focus on one centrally important factor within the idea of nationhood: landscape. We argue that the geography of a nation—and especially that of France—is essential to its self-definition. The Alps, the cathedral of Notre-Dame in Paris, the châteaux of the Loire River valley, the Normandy coast, and the French Riviera all symbolize France to this day.[2] Our project explores these locations and more, defining landscape in the broadest sense to include townscapes as well as figurative images—particularly peasant scenes—in which figures are prominently represented within the landscape.

In examining the resonances between landscape and national identity, we focus on a pivotal period in French history—1850 until 1880. Why this period? It is well known that the nineteenth century was a time when the idea of nationhood became increasingly important across Europe. The era witnessed the creation of Italy in 1861 and the formal unification of Germany in 1871. The concept of nation was also essential in France and strongly promoted by the imperial regime of Napoléon III (1851–70) as well as the governments of the first decade of the Third Republic (1870–1940).[3] In the mid-nineteenth century, France was the most populous country in Europe; by 1851 the population had grown to approximately thirty-six million, more than either England and Germany.[4] It also had the largest square mileage of any country in Western Europe, encompassing, in 1870, approximately 208,500 square miles.[5] This period saw a new recognition of the geographic distinctiveness of the French landscape and its ancient monuments. At the same time, the years 1850–80 were ones of pivotal change in the modernization of France, during which the transformations in the landscape—from the reconstruction of Paris to modern viaducts and tunnels—were celebrated. These decades witnessed the expansion of the railroad, extensive urbanization, the rise of tourism, and the growth of industrialization. Concurrently, and in reaction to modernization, there arose an increased interest in and reverence for rural traditions and customs, as well as pastoral ideals. The exhibition and catalogue explore these competing visions of the nation, as modern and industrial on the one hand and ancient and rural on the other. Much of France's population, indeed, remained in rural locations during the nineteenth century—to a greater extent than its neighbors, England and Germany, where the pace of urbanization and industrialization was faster. The story of France during the mid- to late nineteenth century is often told as one of centralization, and it can be viewed as the colonization of the often remote rural regions of the country.[6] At the same time, our project emphasizes the importance of continuing regional and local differences and particularities.

Within this broader historical context, the years between 1850 and 1880 saw the confluence of painting and photography in defining national identity. These decades witnessed the culminating production of the artists of the Barbizon school and the high point of Impressionist painting. They also encompassed the golden age of early French photography. The works of art in this book and on the walls of the exhibition demonstrate the varied ways in which landscape painters and photographers represented the geography of their nation and, in so doing, served as crucial agents in developing a new idea of France through visual culture. Édouard Baldus, the Bisson frères, Jean-Baptiste-Camille Corot, Gustave Le Gray, Édouard Manet, Jean-François Millet, Claude Monet, Charles Nègre, and Camille Pissarro, among many others, all explored the diversity of the French landscape, its cities, its varied geographic features, and its agricultural production.

How does this exhibition differ from earlier shows? In investigating the idea of landscape and its relation to the French nation, it resembles two major previous displays of paintings: Richard Brettell and Scott Schaefer's *A Day in the Country: Impressionism and the French Landscape* (Los Angeles County Museum of Art, The Art Institute of Chicago, and Grand Palais, Paris, 1984–85) and John House's *Landscapes of France: Impressionism and Its Rivals* (Hayward Gallery, London, and Museum of Fine Arts, Boston, 1995–96).[7] Like them, our exhibition explores the range of Impressionist painting at midcentury while, like House's, it recognizes the importance of official Salon painting as a counterpoint to the avant-garde work of the Impressionists. Our show, however, distinguishes itself from those two earlier exhibitions by studying a broader range of the visual culture of the period, and particularly in ascribing to photography an importance equal to that of painting.[8] Painting and photography—together with print culture—were crucial in constructing an idea of France. Two more recent exhibitions have considered the relationship between paintings and photographs in the mid-nineteenth century, focusing on specific regions of France. Kimberly Jones explored the Forest of Fontainebleau in *In the Forest of Fontainebleau: Paintings and Photographs from Corot to Monet* (National Gallery of Art, Washington, D.C., 2008), while Carole McNamara concentrated on the Normandy coast in *The Lens of Impressionism: Photography and Painting along the Normandy Coast, 1850–1874* (University of Michigan Museum of Art, Ann Arbor, 2009). Our exhibition differs from those two shows in its broader conceptual focus on the whole of France and the idea of nation rather than a particular region.

The exhibition catalogue is organized around four essays, dealing with the overall emergence of nation as a theme in the arts, the role of photography, a developing sense of place in France, and the case study of one region, Brittany. Seven sections—Paris and the Modern Cityscape, Monuments, Forests and Rivers, Rural and Agricultural Life, Railroads and Factories, Mountains, and Marine Views: Ports and Tourism—discuss types of landscape, allowing thought-provoking juxtapositions of images as well as a focus on particular motifs, treated often in paintings and photographs. Within this organizational structure, we see the emergence of distinctive regional identities in such areas as Provence, Brittany, the Franche-Comté, Alsace-Lorraine, and Auvergne. Our project explores the relationship between nation and region as well as between center, that is, Paris, and periphery, within the developing idea of a greater France of infinite geographic variety. It strives to expand an appreciation for a range of rich landscape imagery that reflected and contributed to a growing sense of collective national belonging.

1. See Chantal Bax "A Forward-Looking France: Jean-Luc Nancy on National Identity," *Teloscope*, January 14, 2013.

2. This exhibition and catalogue deal with France, but the concept could equally well be applied to other European nations or to the United States. The Mississippi River, for example, embodies America; the Gateway Arch in Saint Louis, the idea of westward expansion; the midwestern plains, the American heartland; the Rockies Mountains, the idea of manifest destiny.

3. This is not to say, of course, that the process of nationhood did not develop outside these dates. The Third Republic's project of secular education to instill a sense of Frenchness in the population took place principally in the 1880s and 1890s, continuing into the early twentieth century. The last two decades of the nineteenth century were also crucial to the ongoing expansion of the railroad before a leveling off in railroad building in the early twentieth century.

4. In 1851 France had a population of 35.8 million. Great Britain and Ireland contained 27.5 million in 1851, and Germany, 35.3 million that same year. See Ministère du Commerce, *Annuaire statistique de la France*, 5e année (Paris: Imprimerie Nationale, 1882), 7.

5. After 1871, with the loss of Alsace-Lorraine, France was made smaller by approximately 5,600 square miles, approximately the size of the state of Connecticut. See Ministère du Commerce, *Annuaire statistique de la France*, 4ème année (Paris: Imprimerie Nationale, 1881), 13.

6. See Eugen Weber, *Peasants into Frenchmen: The Modernization of Rural France, 1870–1914* (Stanford: Stanford University Press, 1976). For a recent examination of the nineteenth-century exploration of France, see Graham Robb, *The Discovery of France: A Historical Geography from the Revolution to the First World War* (New York: W. W. Norton & Company, 2007).

7. See also Richard Thomson, ed., *Monet to Matisse: Landscape Painting in France, 1874–1914*, exh. cat. (Edinburgh: National Gallery of Scotland, 1994).

8. Stephen F. Eisenman, ed., *From Corot to Monet: The Ecology of Impressionism*, exh. cat. (Milan: Skira, 2010), explored the relation between painting and photography through the lens of "ecology."

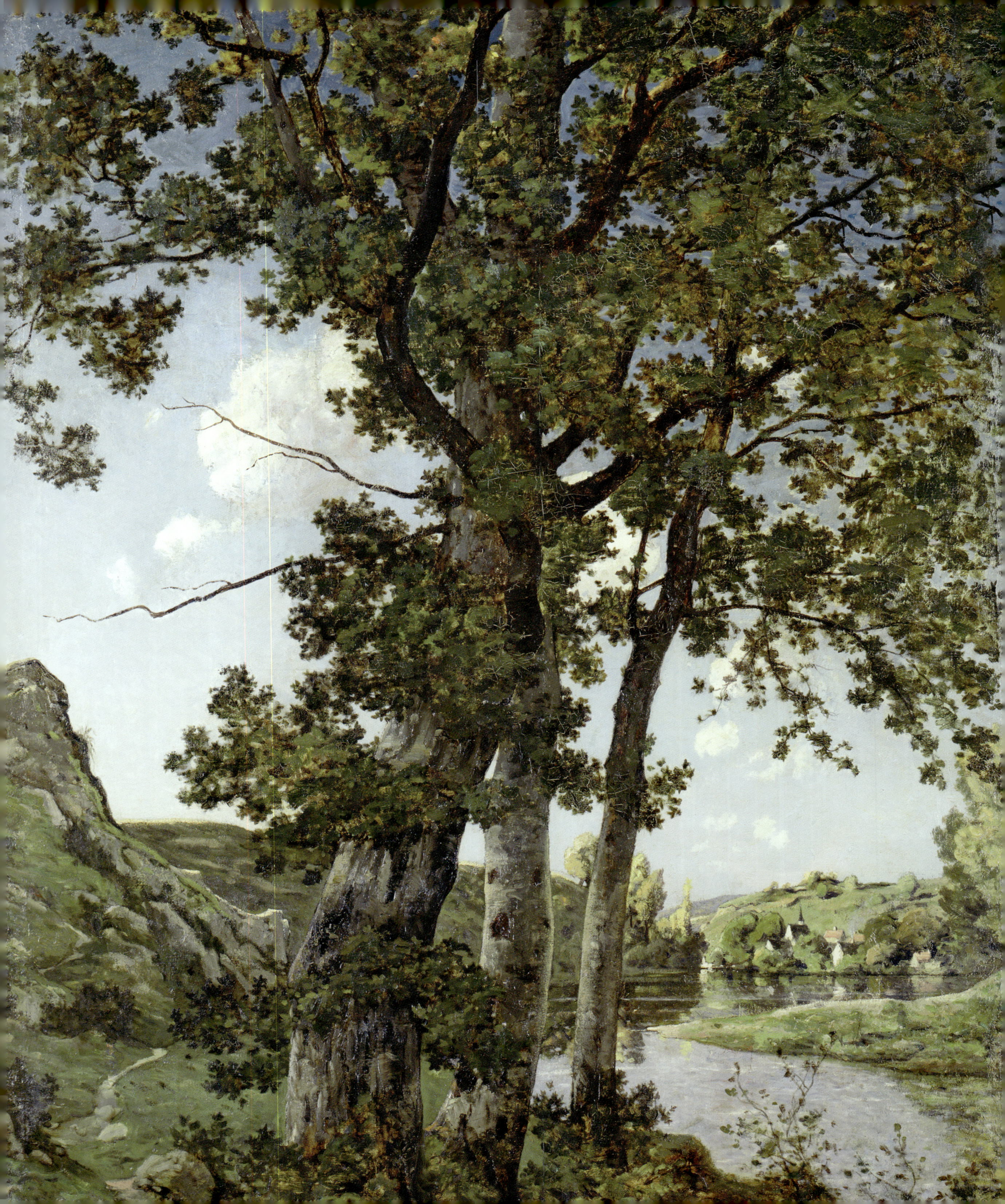

Landscape as "National Art": Visions of France, 1851–1878

SIMON KELLY

"LANDSCAPE," affirmed the radical critic Jules-Antoine Castagnary in 1878, "has been for a long time the pride of the French school, its originality is undeniable, and its superiority evident and accepted."[1] For this writer, the most distinctive aspect of the country's art was its landscape painting. Artists focused on the representation of their homeland, and the nature of their country was indeed impressive. France then, as today, was the largest nation in western Europe. Its diverse and spectacular geography ranged from the lush Normandy countryside to the light-filled expanses of Provence, from the rugged coastline of Brittany to the high peaks of the Alps. The fact of the exceptional diversity of the country's scenery was a commonplace by the end of the nineteenth century, frequently repeated in popular literature and school textbooks. Ernest Lavisse, in his best-selling history of France, described the nation as "this privileged land, bathed by three seas, flanked by the two highest mountain chains in Europe, watered by beautiful rivers, enjoying all the nuances of a temperate climate."[2] Paul Vidal de la Blache, the founder of the French school of modern geography, affirmed, "France has a wealth of variety that we do not find elsewhere."[3] Representations of this unique topography played a central role in building national identity during the nineteenth century, especially in the crucial years from 1851 to 1878. These years span the Second Empire and the first phase of the Third Republic, ending with the 1878 Paris Exposition universelle and the subsequent proclamation of "La Marseillaise" as the French national anthem and the naming of Bastille Day (July 14) as a public holiday.[4] They were also decades of exceptional richness in landscape imagery, which saw the culmination of the Barbizon school movement, the rise of Impressionism, and the golden age of early photography.

Landscape imagery became an important component within a broad-ranging campaign to construct a new sense of nation in France in the nineteenth century. That campaign also included the emergence of a single language, a clearly defined national history, a folklore with national heroes and founding ancestors, and the establishment of national monuments.[5] The idea of nation was not a given; instead,

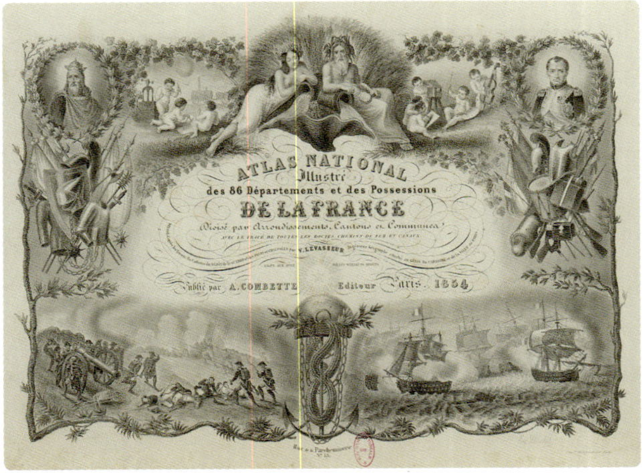

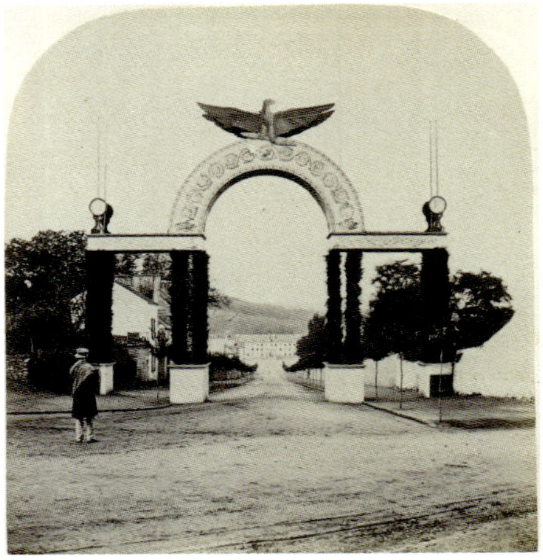

FIG. 1 Victor Levasseur, *Atlas national illustré des 86 départements et des possessions de la France* (Paris, 1854), title page

FIG. 2 Augustus Lovell Reeve and Henry Taylor, *Napoléonville—Triumphal Arch Erected to Celebrate the Emperor's Visit.* From *Narrative of a Walking Tour in Brittany* (London, 1859)

it was consciously constructed in the late eighteenth and nineteenth centuries with the rise of the democratic nation-state.[6] Such a construction was not, of course, unique to France. This period can be seen as the age of the nation across Europe as well as in the United States, where the modern political idea of nation—an entity based on universal suffrage—first came into being. Within this broader context, landscape came to symbolize nationhood. In America, the landscapes of the Hudson River school represented the vast wilderness of the continent and embodied a sense of manifest destiny through western expansion.[7] In England, the rustic landscapes of John Constable pictured a pastoral national vision.[8] The landscapes explored in this essay were also emblematic of nation and, like their Euro-American counterparts, often reflected wider political aspirations.

Visions of nation were constructed using landscape imagery in a wide range of visual media, including paintings, photographs, prints, and touristic ephemera. Landscape painting was most widely seen at the official exhibition space of the Salon, the most popular exhibition in nineteenth-century France, but was also viewed in alternative spaces such as dealers' galleries and exhibiting societies like that founded by the Impressionists. The period also saw the rise of photography, which was shown most notably at the Société française de la photographie, the largest French photographic society, and at the Salon from 1859. Print media also played a crucial role—more important than painting and photography—in defining a sense of nation. Atlases, illustrated newspapers and magazines, and touristic ephemera—especially tourist guides, posters, souvenir fans, and ribbons—were widely disseminated around the country and are of particular significance here. At this pivotal moment in French history, two principal readings of landscape emerged: a perception of France as rural and antimodern, looking back to its exceptionally rich history; and a notion of the nation as modern and industrialized, taking advantage of technology and looking to the future. These twin visions of France—like a Janus-faced nation, looking both back and forward—are crucial to an understanding of this period. They were not, of course, necessarily mutually exclusive. The title page of the most famous atlas of France at this time by Victor Levasseur, for example, shows the great national figures from the country's history—Charlemagne and Napoléon—alongside vignettes highlighting the nation's recent contributions to technology: the railroad and photography (fig. 1). At the top, tiny putti frolic in front of a steam train and examine a camera. Within this context of a rapidly expanding visual culture, artists, too, constructed a new idea of nation. The imagery of Gustave Le Gray—like that of many of his photographic colleagues—embraced both ancient and modern elements within France. Claude Monet's work pictured a utopian vision of a modern nation, representing industry, the railroad, and technology, and recording the most remarkable changes to the configuration of the landscape in centuries.[9]

Napoléon III and Building a Nation (1851–1870)

In the mid-nineteenth century, France, although built around a powerful capital, had strongly decentralized regions. In 1850 half of the nation did not speak French but, instead, used regional dialects such as Breton (in Brittany) or Occitan (in the South). A strong sense of division existed between the more industrialized North of the country and the less developed South. In December 1851 Napoléon III—nephew of Napoléon Bonaparte—seized power in a dramatic coup d'état. Within a year, he had proclaimed himself

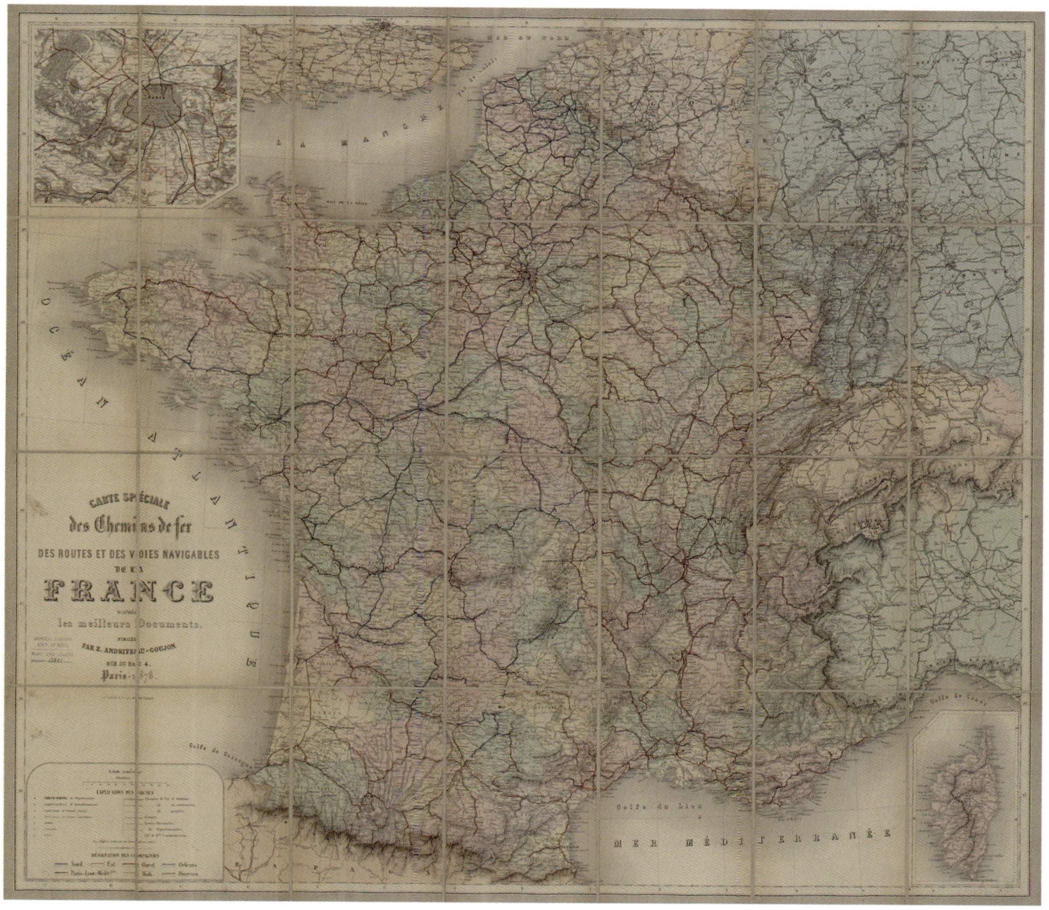

FIG. 3 Eugène Andriveau-Goujon, *Map of the Railways and Waterways of France According to the Best Documents*, 1878. Steel engraving with hand coloring mounted on linen, 33½ × 37½ in. (85.1 × 95.3 cm) Clark Library Map Collection, University of Michigan

emperor and soon focused on the encouragement of a sense of collective national belonging as a central part of his policy. Previous regimes—such as that of Louis-Philippe (1830–48)—had also encouraged national pride within the population, but Napoléon III set about this task with a new intensity. In his first decade in power, he traveled extensively around the provinces, seeking to inculcate regional loyalty. The rise of local consciousness—a sense of local patriotism—has often been seen as antithetical to the idea of a unified France.[10] Yet the traditions of regional separatism in France have not in general been as extreme as in other countries around Europe. The different provinces embraced their own identities but also saw themselves as part of a wider idea of France.[11] As Anne-Marie Thiesse has shown, during the nineteenth century the state government in Paris sought to support rather than suppress local customs, language, and folklore.[12] The emperor promoted the idea of a varied and diverse France of many indigenous cultures. His efforts to assimilate the provinces are particularly evident in his visits to Provence and Brittany in 1852 and 1858 (see the essay by Neil McWilliam in this volume). The emperor's trip to Brittany was memorably recorded by the British photographers Augustus Lovell Reeve and Henry Taylor. Their image of the imperial eagle atop the gateway to the newly created town of Napoléonville emphasizes the powerful imperial presence in the region (fig. 2). The official chronicler of this visit, Jean-Marie Poulain Corbion, noted that many such triumphal arches were specially constructed, including this "triple portico surmounted by an eagle with outspread wings and by bundles of flags in the middle of which you could read inscriptions in praise of their Majesties."[13]

France lagged behind England in its Industrial Revolution but was nevertheless the second-largest industrial nation in the world in the mid-nineteenth century.[14] Napoléon III promoted a vision of France as a modern economy—a vision shaped by his interest in the utopian thought of the Saint-Simonians,[15] as well as his experience of the more advanced manufacturing of Great Britain—the first fully industrialized nation—which he experienced during his time in England in the 1840s. Crucial to his vision was the rise of the railroad, which, by speeding up communications, brought different areas of the nation closer together and aided unification. France's rail system was unique in the context of other major rail systems such as those in Britain and the United States because of its public-private partnership between the state and the six independent railroad

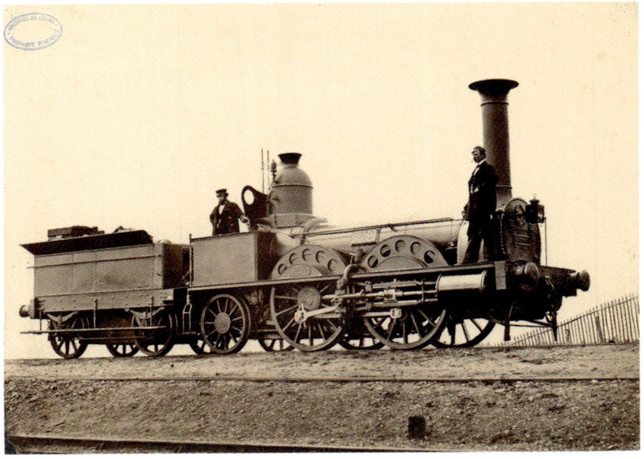

FIG. 4 Jules Camus, *Locomotive du Chemin [de fer] de l'Ouest, Évreux*. Albumen print from collodion glass negative. Archives départementales de l'Eure, France, cote 39 Fi 101

companies that operated rail lines in the various regions of France. In the first half of the century, railroad building in France was much slower than in Britain and America but accelerated considerably when Napoléon III came to power. In 1851 there were 2,018 miles of railroad in France; by 1870 this number had increased fivefold, to 9,658 miles. This in turn encouraged a new idea of nation. As the engineer Eugène Flachat noted, "We used to be Breton, Gascon, Norman, Picard, Lorrain, Alsatian, Provençal, but it was only in the top-level professions, in the large towns, in the army and navy that we understood and loved France. . . . The railroads have spread a more equal political life everywhere."[16] The remarkable expansion of the railroad during the Second Empire was charted by the mapmaker Eugène Andriveau-Goujon; the tracks of the railroad can be seen spreading across the nation, resembling a finely spun spiderweb (fig. 3).

How was this new vision of France as industrial nation represented in landscape imagery? Photography played a central role here. The railway companies that had emerged at midcentury commissioned albums of photographs that celebrated the country's architectural heritage as well as the engineering feats of aqueducts and tunnels that had been built for the railroads. Édouard Baldus, for example, was commissioned by two railroad companies to produce such albums. The first extolled the landscape along the rail line from Paris to Boulogne—a landscape of new railway stations and spectacular viaducts—and was given as a propagandistic gift to Queen Victoria on her visit to Paris in 1855, the first visit to France by an English monarch since the early sixteenth century. The second album, commissioned by the Paris–Lyon–Méditerranée railroad in 1861, represented the landscape around the rail line from Lyon to Toulon, again highlighting recent engineering feats, from the new bridges across the river Rhone to the three-mile-long Nerthe tunnel, one of the longest in Europe. Lesser-known photographic albums also promoted industrial prowess. Among these was the commission of some three hundred photographs by the *département* of the Eure in Upper Normandy from the photographer Jules Camus in 1861.[17] These images again foreground newly constructed viaducts and bridges as well as the trains themselves. One remarkable image shows a locomotive arriving at a station (fig. 4). Taken from below, the photograph shows the train looming above the spectator. Numerous prints of new railroads and factories appeared in print media and particularly in such widely distributed illustrated magazines as *L'illustration* and *Le monde illustré*.[18] The impact of the wood engravings in these magazines cannot be overestimated and can be seen as playing a prominent role in the emergent vision of France as a modern, industrialized nation.[19] Tourist guidebooks also expanded greatly as a genre and encouraged a sense of collective national belonging. The Joanne guides—the most widely known ones—were initially framed as a Library for the Railways and funded by the rail companies who saw their commercial potential in encouraging travel. Extensively illustrated, they promoted itineraries following the new rail lines and were sold cheaply at rail stations, and their texts were filled with a wide variety of information including economic, geographic, and geologic history. By 1869 there were ten regional guides in the series, *Itinéraire général de la France*, covering all areas of the country. They were all written in French (rather than regional dialects), gave measurements in the metric system, and quoted prices in a single currency (the franc, in a country in which money of the ancien régime was often still used), thus encouraging a sense of French nationhood.[20]

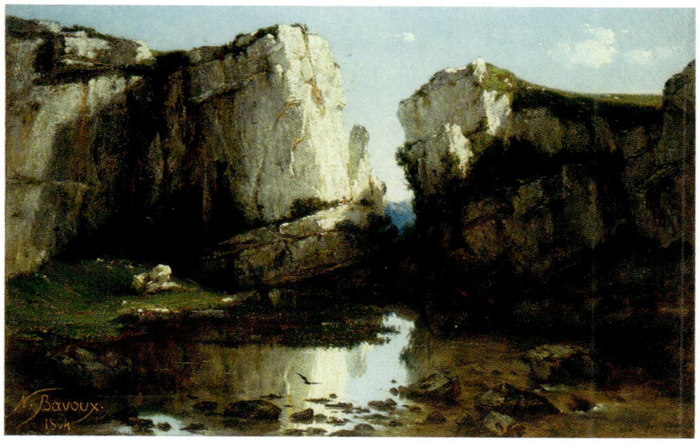

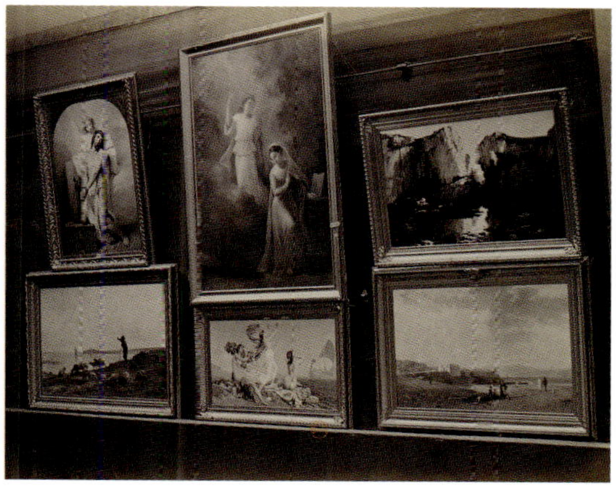

FIG. 5 Charles Bavoux, *Entre-Roches on the Doubs*, 1864. Oil on canvas, 48⅞ × 78¾ in. (124 × 200 cm). Musée des beaux-arts et d'archéologie, Besançon/Dépôt du Centre national des arts plastiques, Paris

FIG. 6 Charles Michelez, Album of photographs of works bought by the state, titled *Salon de 1864: Palais des Champs-Élysées; Tableaux commandés ou achetés par le Service des Beaux-Arts*. Bibliothèque nationale de France, Paris

Napoléon III made the exploration of France's history a central element of the state's cultural policy. Often focusing on the nation's Catholic and medieval past, the emperor patronized the extensive restoration of historical monuments—the château of Pierrefonds, the medieval abbey of Vézelay, the ancient fortified town of Carcassonne, and the cathedral of Notre-Dame. The state-sponsored Mission héliographique, dating to 1851, was here central, representing an important moment in the rediscovery of France's history (see the essay by Watson in this volume). Five photographers were commissioned by the government to travel the length and breadth of the country to record the variety of its cultural patrimony.[21] Their photographs provide a record of France as historical palimpsest, a nation whose land has been built up over time with layers of rich history. Napoléon III patronized paintings of the nation's monuments, including four pictures of the château of Pierrefonds in the 1860s, most notably two views by Paul Huet (cats. 27, 28).[22] Huet's pendant paintings celebrate the transformation of the château from medieval ruin to a glittering and completely refurbished monument. In his desire to discover the origins of the nation, Napoléon III also supported extensive archaeological excavations and the foundation of a new and pioneering archaeological museum at Saint-Germain-en-Laye extolling France's Gallo-Roman history. He even authored a two-volume history of Julius Caesar, focusing on Caesar's invasion of Gaul.[23] One further important state initiative was the imperial foundation in 1852 of the Comité de la langue, de l'histoire et des arts de la France, a body with the aim of rediscovering regional traditions of poetry as well as local patois dialects.

State patronage of landscape imagery thus played a central role within a much broader official approach intended to create a new sense of nationhood. A survey of state patronage underscores the degree to which the official position encouraged the imaging of the provinces in the 1850s and 1860s. About 20 percent of the works acquired at the Salon during the 1850s were landscapes of France, mainly views of the Forest of Fontainebleau, Normandy, and Brittany.[24] This number increased to about 25 percent by the 1860s—about thirty at each Salon—and evidenced a growing interest in France's outlying regions.[25] During the 1850s the painter Philippe-Auguste Jeanron was particularly favored with state support.[26] In the following decade, the artists Huet, Jeanron, Eugène Lavieille, Adolphe Appian, Antoine Chintreuil, and Camille Bernier were supported. From the Salon of 1864, for example, the state acquired views of the Alps, Provence, the Franche-Comté, and Brittany as well as of the ports of Marseille, Bordeaux, and Brest.[27] Charles Bavoux's *Entre-Roches on the Doubs*, purchased that year, features the enormous limestone cliffs that are characteristic of the landscape of the Franche-Comté in eastern France (fig. 5). His use of the palette knife produced a texture that mimics the actual surface of the rocks. Beginning in 1864, state purchases were photographically recorded; Bavoux's landscape can be seen surrounded by

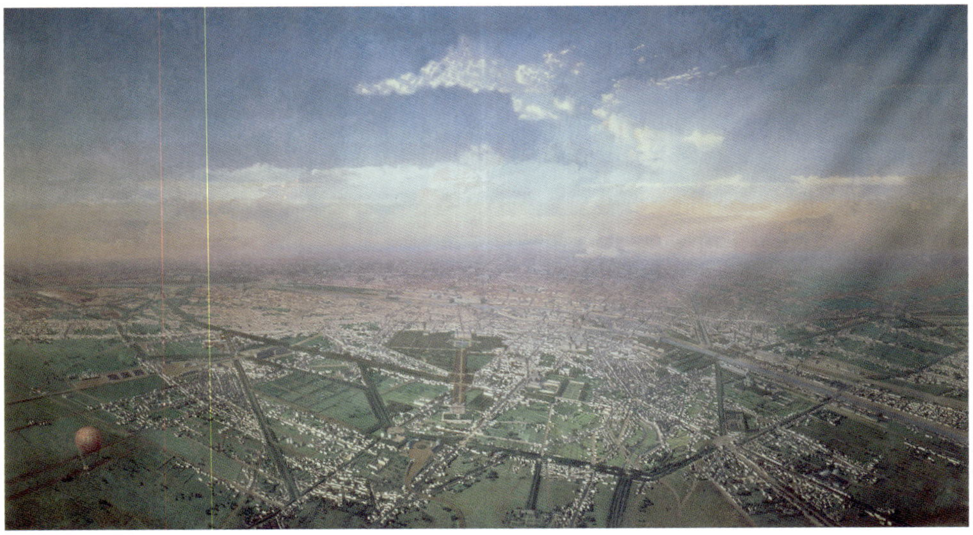

FIG. 7 Victor Navlet, *General View of Paris, Taken from the Observatoire, in a Balloon*, 1855. Oil on canvas, 12 ft. 9½ in. × 23 ft. 2¾ in. (3.9 × 7.1 m). Musée d'Orsay, Paris

other acquisitions (fig. 6). Purchases from the Salon were deposited at the Musée du Luxembourg, France's museum of contemporary art, which expanded considerably at mid-century.[28] Also sent to regional museums and town halls, they encouraged a sense of national belonging. Paintings were not necessarily sent to the regions that were depicted in them. Breton subjects, for example, were dispersed widely around the provinces in both the North and the South of the country.[29] The emperor and empress also privileged the acquisition of landscape through their enormous budget—some twenty-five million francs a year—through the Civil List. Landscape paintings made up 18 percent of their acquisitions. They were open-minded in their purchases, buying work not only by establishment artists but also by such avant-garde figures as Gustave Courbet, Jean-Baptiste-Camille Corot, and Théodore Rousseau.[30] Their acquisitions were shown in their imperial palaces—such as the Tuileries and Compiègne—but also often ended up in regional museums or at the Luxembourg.

State patronage also reflected the importance of Paris to Napoléon III's ideology. In the nineteenth century, Paris was by far the largest French city. No other regional center came close in terms of population; Lyon and Marseille were the next largest, but each could count only about two hundred thousand residents.[31] The capital's population, by contrast, doubled during the period of the Second Empire to about two million, as large numbers of people moved there from the provinces.[32] The emergence of a new idea of France in the Second Empire was inextricably linked to the rise of a new idea of Paris. As is well known, Paris was transformed at this time by Napoléon III and the prefect of the Seine, Baron Georges-Eugène Haussmann, into the city of expansive boulevards that we know today, which has served as a planning model for cities from Washington, D.C., to Mexico City. For Napoléon III, this transformation was informed by his admiration for the ancient world and specifically the belief that the capital could be the new Rome. In the early 1850s he commissioned from Victor Navlet the enormous painting *General View of Paris, Taken from the Observatoire, in a Balloon* (fig. 7), which was exhibited to acclaim at the 1855 Exposition universelle.[33] Navlet's painting, imagined from an extremely high viewpoint, highlights the huge size of the capital, showing the extensive network of streets with the Palais de l'Industrie (built specially for the 1855 exposition) and the Champs-Élysées in the distance. It served a propagandistic function at a time when Napoléon was promoting his capital on an international stage. The medieval history of the capital, however, remained important, and the emperor patronized images of Notre-Dame, the twelfth-century Gothic cathedral that remains to this day France's most visited attraction. During this period, the Gothic style was claimed as an inherently French expression, particularly by Napoléon's protégé, Eugène-Emmanuel Viollet-le-Duc, who had made the restoration of Notre-Dame a centerpiece of his efforts in the 1850s.[34] Paintings of Paris were still relatively rare in the Second Empire, however; only in the 1870s did a vogue for Parisian views emerge, most evident in the increasing number of works on view at the Salon that featured such urban scenes.[35]

For all his support of industrial expansion, Napoléon III did not encourage the depiction of industry in landscape

FIG. 8 Charles-François Daubigny. *View of Barentin Viaduct*. Wood engraving. From Jules Janin, *Voyage de Paris à la mer* (Paris, 1847)

FIG. 9 Théodore Gudin, *The French Fleet Traveling from Cherbourg to Brest*, 1858. Oil on canvas. Musée national de la Marine, Paris

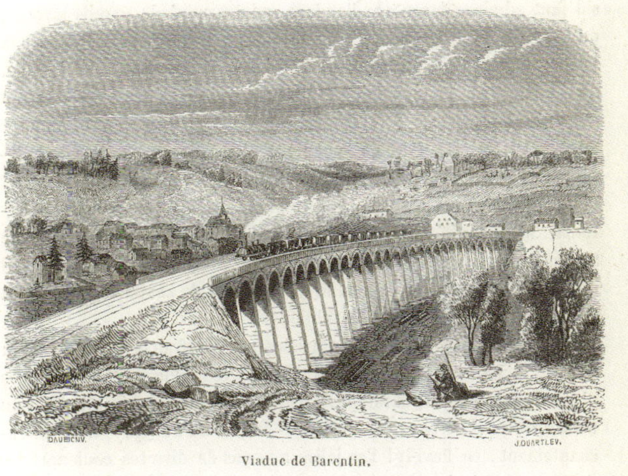

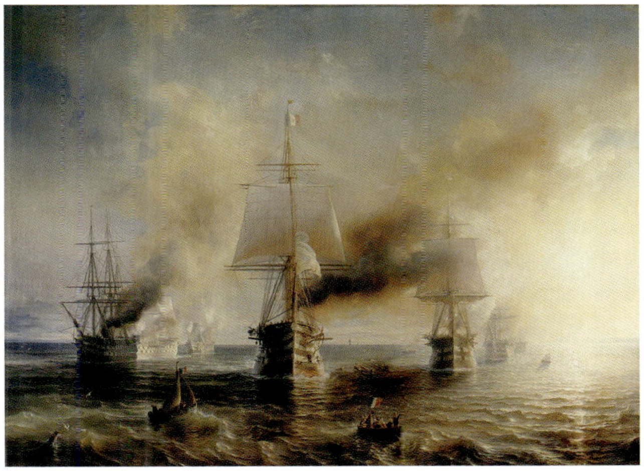

painting. The state acquired very few paintings of industry. This was in part due to the fact that landscapists themselves rarely painted industrial themes. During this period, landscape paintings—especially at the Salon but also at the auction houses and dealers' galleries—are conspicuous for their lack of representation of the most modern elements in the landscape, whether the railroads and factories or tunnels and viaducts that were transforming the face of the countryside at midcentury. Painters self-consciously screened out these dramatic changes in the landscape. Why they did so is unclear, but it is probable that such subjects were seen as unworthy for treatment in the more elevated art form of painting. Charles-François Daubigny is a salutary example since, as early as the 1840s, he had produced prints of the railroad line from Paris to Le Havre—prints that showed examples of feats of engineering such as the Barentin viaduct (fig. 8). His view of this recently constructed structure—which had collapsed in 1846, only to be immediately rebuilt—highlights its great span across the Normandy valley.[36] Daubigny, however, never represented such subjects in his painting, preferring pastoral, idyllic views, specifically of France's rivers (cat. 50). Only on rare occasions did a painter represent the subject of industry at the official Salons of the Second Empire. François Bonhommé, for example, produced a series of watercolors of the factories at Le Creusot—the largest industrial complex in France and one of the largest in Europe—which was shown at the 1867 Salon following a commission from the factory owners, the Schneider family.

France's industrial expansion in the Second Empire was evident not only on the land, in its railroads and factories, but also at sea, with the growth of its ports and commercial and military fleets. In contrast to the rarity of paintings of factories, pictures of France's marine strength were common. In 1858 the emperor commissioned a group of large-scale propagandistic works from Théodore Gudin, including *The French Fleet Traveling from Cherbourg to Brest* (fig. 9), which alone cost the huge sum of twenty thousand francs, one of the highest prices that the emperor paid for any painting during his reign.[37] Enormous three-masted ships—bearing witness to France's military might—are accompanied by a flotilla of tiny boats flying the French flag. Le Gray, too, produced a series of photographs of the same French fleet, also commissioned by the emperor (cat. 105). The state regularly acquired images of France's ports, tapping into a long tradition of marine imagery dating back to Claude-Joseph Vernet's eighteenth-century Ports of France.[38] Napoléon III also supported the expansion of the tourist industry on the Normandy coast, following the opening of the railroad from Paris to Le Havre in 1847. Not only was he a regular visitor to new coastal resorts—principally Trouville and

FIG. 10 Charles-Paul Desavary, *Corot at Arras*, 1871. George Eastman House, International Museum of Photography and Film, Rochester, New York

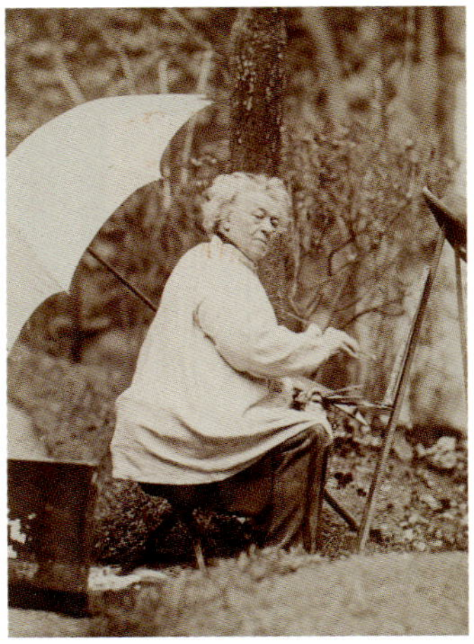

Deauville—with the empress Eugénie, but he also supported the new vision of leisured France in his landscape acquisitions.[39]

Independent Artistic Visions of Nation (1851–1870)

Within this broader cultural environment promoting nationhood, artists also developed their ideas of nation, independently of state support. The development of the railroad system encouraged artists to explore their homeland. As Louis Auvray noted in 1867:

> France has never been better appreciated by landscapists than since the routes of communication, so multiplied through the whole of the empire, have made travel within the range of all budgets. In the *départements* of the North, painters find the vast plains and hazy sky of Belgium, Holland, and Germany; in Provence, the beautiful sky and gilded hills of Italy; in Brittany and Normandy, pastures that England envies, and in the center of France, around Paris, attractive motifs that we don't find in any other country. That's why many artists are happy to depict the appearance of our beautiful country that is so varied.[40]

Auvray's proud comment reflects his sense of the exceptional variety of France's landscape. The representation of this range of imagery was a crucial element in the developing idea of nation.

An overview of the titles of paintings in the catalogues of the Paris Salon highlights the numerical increase in representations of France during the Second Empire.[41] Artists had traveled around France from the end of the eighteenth century—if not earlier—but Italy had always been the principal location that artists explored. Artists now painted the landscape of France for a wide range of reasons, which were not, of course, exclusively linked to nationalism. The rise of the art market, for example, played a crucial role in the rise of landscape imagery in the mid-nineteenth century. Landscape paintings—often of small scale—represented an important part of dealer stock, and artists responded to growing economic demand. Landscape, too, served as a primary site for formal experiment—generally to a greater degree than other genres, perhaps because of its relatively lowly role in the conventional hierarchy of genres, making artists more willing to take risks. For their part, collectors bought images of French landscape for a variety of causes, of which an allegiance to France might be only one factor. It was, for example, a critical commonplace at the time that collectors bought rural landscapes as an antidote to increasing urbanization.[42] Sophisticated patrons such as the Alsatian industrialist Frédéric Hartmann might also buy for formal considerations, such as the particular level of "finish" in a landscape painting.[43] Nonetheless, emerging ideas of nation represented an important factor in both the production and consumption of imagery of France.

Among the most peripatetic travelers around France was Corot, who was still painting *en plein air* in his homeland into his seventies. In a staged photograph by his friend Charles-Paul Desavary, the seventy-five-year-old Corot is shown painting outdoors at Arras in the midst of an extensive tour around France, despite being ravaged by gout at this time (fig. 10).[44] For an early commentator, Philippe Burty, Corot was above all a painter of his homeland: "He was a painter, a simple painter, a French painter. Italy and fashionable studio conversation in his youth had awakened his taste for grand lines. But he especially loved France, which also offers beautiful lines, as well as blue-tinged

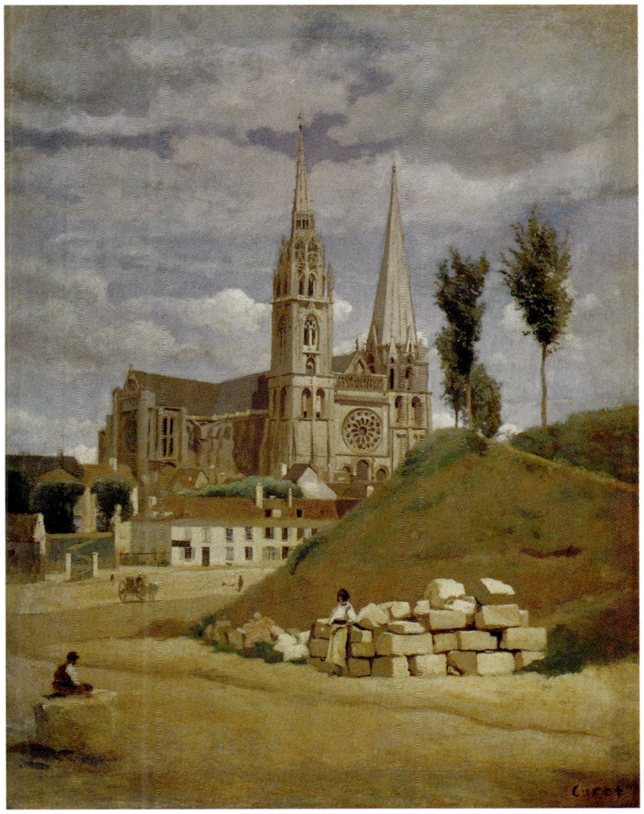

FIG. 11 Jean-Baptiste-Camille Corot, *Chartres Cathedral*, 1830, retouched 1872. Oil on canvas. 25¼ × 20¼ in. (64 × 51.5 cm). Musée du Louvre, Paris

hazes, broken skies, attractive foliage, and above all varied seasons and long dusks."[45] Corot also showed a deep interest in medieval architecture (cat. 29).[46] Early in his career, he had represented Chartres Cathedral; in the early 1870s he returned to the canvas, making minor changes by adding foreground figures (fig. 11). His fascination with Gothic architecture is further suggested by his late views of the belfry at Douai, the interior of Sens Cathedral, and a series of paintings of Mantes Cathedral.[47] Corot demonstrated a horror of industry and technology and focused on rustic imagery: his early biographer Théophile Silvestre visited the 1867 Exposition universelle with the artist and recorded his disdain on viewing the industrial—and particularly British—exhibits:

> We found ourselves in the middle of the Whitford cannons, besieged by the curiosity of the English. "Ah! For God's sake," said Corot, putting on an English accent to fits of laughter, "here are the inventors of these amazing things! That's nice! Nice!" Then, suddenly horrified by these engines of war . . . : "Is it possible to exhibit these terrible machines at the same time and in the same place as our landscapes and sheep? The world is mad . . . and cruel. And look, the inventors have a very pleased look! My God, what do they want to do with these things?"—"Put a hole in your canvases and kill your little sheep". . . On seeing a small cathedral of cotton reels of all colors from Manchester, "Ah! A beautiful factory to put in the background of my landscapes!"[48]

The later term *Barbizon school*—now used to describe principally Corot, Rousseau, Jean-François Millet, and Daubigny, who were at the forefront of avant-garde landscape painting in the mid-nineteenth century—is in fact misleading, since, although these artists certainly did form an important artistic colony at Barbizon, they also traveled the length and breadth of France.[49] Rousseau painted not only Barbizon but also Normandy, Brittany, Berry, the Loire valley, Auvergne, the Franche-Comté, the Alps, and the Pyrenees. Despite his international fame, he painted outside France only once, briefly, on a visit to Switzerland in 1860. Photographers, too, explored the country; the titles of works in the exhibitions of the Société française de la photographie highlight the variety of French landscapes on view.[50] The German-born Baldus was the photographer who perhaps journeyed most extensively around France. Paris undoubtedly remained the center of the French art world, but the midcentury also saw the rise of regional centers such as Marseille, Bordeaux, Besançon, Nantes, and Lyon, each with its own exhibition societies. Landscapists such as Corot regularly sent their work around this growing regional exhibition circuit.[51]

Rousseau protested strongly about being overlooked for state patronage during the Second Empire. Nonetheless, he invested his landscapes with nationalistic resonances. At midcentury Rousseau was perhaps the best-known painter of the Forest of Fontainebleau, regularly submitting

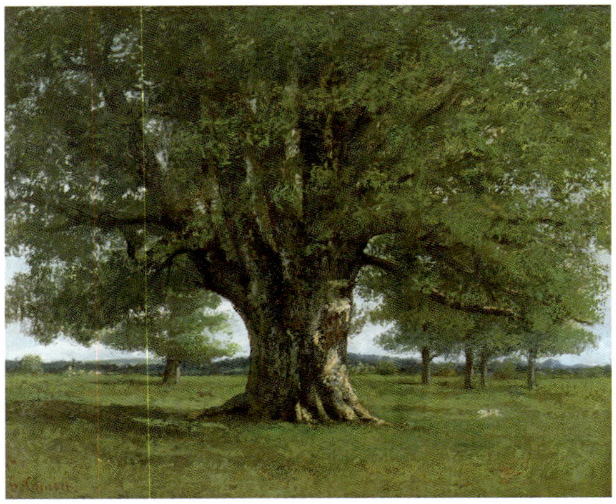

FIG. 12 Gustave Courbet, *Oak of Vercingetorix, Caesar's Camp near Alesia, Franche-Comté*, 1864. Oil on canvas, 35 × 43¼ in. (89 × 110 cm). Musée Courbet, Ornans

forest views to the Salon in the 1850s and 1860s. In 1852 he described the forest as "the most ancient in France . . . the only living souvenir that remains from the heroic times of the Fatherland from Charlemagne to Napoleon."[52] For Rousseau, the forest was filled with layers of history; the new follies and asphalt pavements for tourists were, in contrast, anathema. Rousseau represented primeval oaks (cat. 40) and rocky expanses, screening out the changes in the forest arising from midcentury tourism. Rousseau's friend and early biographer, Alfred Sensier, developed this nationalistic reading, linking the artist's work to Gallic history. For Sensier, Rousseau was "the painter of the forests of the druids, who brings back to life for us the time of the ancient Gauls."[53]

The photographer Charles Nègre also responded strongly to his nation's historical tradition. Only a year after the Mission héliographique (and in what one can see as an act of historical competition since he had been overlooked as one of those chosen for the mission), Nègre embarked on an ambitious photographic project to record the remarkably diverse Roman and medieval monuments of the South of France. In a rare example of an artist's statement explicitly ascribing nationalistic intention to his imagery, Nègre affirmed his wish to document the great "national art" in the South:

> Apart from the Roman antiquities scattered throughout certain (other) localities, almost all of the cities provided me with archaeological riches that are little known; the precious remains of Christian art of the eleventh, twelfth and thirteenth centuries. It is to the reproduction of these works of national art that I have paid special heed.[54]

Nègre's album, however, was never published—despite the production of a title page—and thus had limited impact.

Regional schools of painting also emerged in the Second Empire, which sought to promote—but also preserve—a sense of regional identity within the context of the wider nation. In the 1850s a landscape school grew up in Provence,[55] a region with a strong independent tradition and where a majority of the population spoke Occitan rather than French. Members of this emergent Provençal school—most notably Paul Guigou—showed their works regularly at the Paris Salon (cat. 58). For many who had never traveled to the South—and in an age before cinema and television—these paintings shaped national perceptions of the impressive, rugged expanses and intense light of Provence.[56] Artists also pictured Brittany—unique among French regions because of its Celtic identity—and focused on its distinctive peasant culture (see the essay by Coughlin in this volume).[57] In eastern France, painters—most significantly, Courbet—represented the mountainous landscapes of the Franche-Comté, an area with a history of independence. Courbet's art engaged with the Gallic history of France. In 1864 he painted *Oak of Vercingetorix, Caesar's Camp near Alesia, Franche-Comté* (fig. 12), a view of an enormous oak that was thought to be on the site of the battle of Alesia in 52 BC, when the Gallic chieftain Vercingetorix had stood up to the Roman invader, Julius Caesar. Courbet's work thus celebrated a crucial figure from France's ancient past.[58] In a lighthearted touch, a hound chasing a hare to either side of the tree offsets the gravitas of the massive oak. Despite receiving imperial patronage in 1865, the radical Courbet insisted on his opposition to imperial government. Republican critics also saw oppositional value in his work. For the radical republican Théophile Thoré, Courbet's rugged

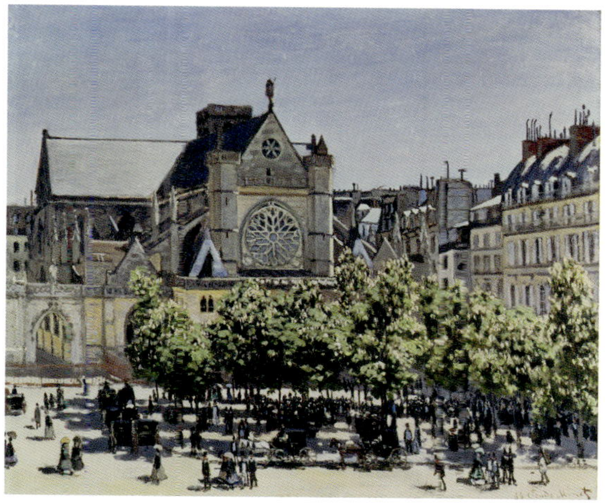

FIG. 13 Claude Monet, *Saint-Germain l'Auxerrois*, 1867. Oil on canvas, 31⅛ × 38½ in. (79 × 98 cm). Nationalgalerie, Staatliche Museen, Berlin

views—as well as those of Millet—offered a moral model for the rest of France, which contrasted with the decadence that he associated with the capital of Paris, and implicitly with the lavish regime of Napoléon III. Thoré wrote:

> In certain immoral periods, renewal can only happen by heroic means. A little savagery or rather wildness would not be out of place in these times of weakness. . . . Art in France is sick and it does not like these doctors from the Danube [German painters] who arrive with solid formulae and imperturbable health. Where will [doctors] come from? Well, they come from the forests and mountains. Millet lives among the rocks of Fontainebleau and Courbet in the gorges of Jura. That's why they don't have the same taste as those charming artists who paint rose-tinted scenes in the midst of boudoirs.[59]

Painters also focused on motifs of acknowledged national and international significance. The Second Empire, for example, saw a vogue for views at the Salon of the volcanic mountain of Le Puy, the highest peak in Auvergne and a site that attracted growing interest with the rise of geological history and the concomitant debates around France's prehistoric origins.[60] The annexation of the Alps from the Kingdom of Sardinia in 1860 also led to a spate of images, ranging from the photographs of the Bisson frères (see the essay by Watson in this volume, and cats. 92, 93) to the expansive, panoramic views of Rousseau and François-Louis Français (cats. 88, 89). In a display of national pride, these artists gave special attention to the newly acquired peak of Mont Blanc, Europe's highest mountain. Français's works, as many critics noted playfully, were nationalistic by the very nature of the artist's name. Le Guillois, for example, wrote in 1861, "The king of landscape in France is Français."[61] Perhaps surprisingly, however, few painters represented France's great Renaissance châteaux of the Loire during the Second Empire, despite the significance of those structures to the country's cultural patrimony. The print market, however—an important factor in encouraging images of nation—played a role by publishing a major volume on these châteaux in 1854 featuring prints by a range of artists including Français.[62]

During the 1860s, the young Impressionists pursued their visions of nation independently of state patronage. Frédéric Bazille, for example, devoted around half of the paintings in his brief career to images of the South of France around his native Montpellier (cats. 38, 39). For all their formal innovation, the Impressionists actually did not travel around France much in their early years, concentrating on Paris and its suburbs and the Normandy coast. When they embraced industry as a subject for painting in the 1860s, they were the first artistic group to systematically engage with the industrial landscape. Camille Pissarro was the first Impressionist to represent factories in the mid-1860s (cats. 82–84); his example would be followed by his friend Armand Guillaumin (cat. 85). Monet, for his part, engaged with the nation's history, painting three views of Paris that represent a significant early engagement with the imaging of the city. His *Saint-Germain l'Auxerrois* depicts this fifteenth-century church in the heart of Paris, resonant with historical association (it was the Parisian church attended by the kings of France) and is an unusual example of his early interest in medieval architecture (fig. 13).[63] His focus of these years, however, was on France's maritime tradition. Within the context of the strong interest in imagery of France's ports, Monet's views of Le Havre (the only main competitor to Marseille in terms of port trade in France)

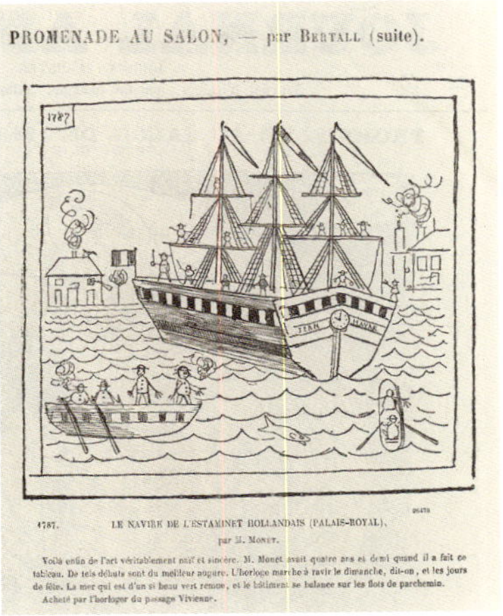

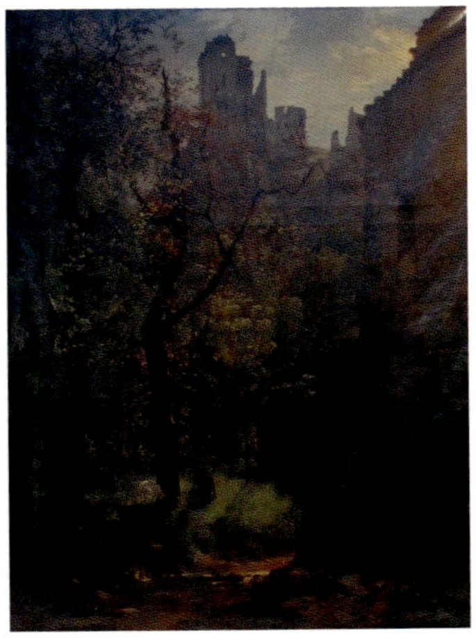

FIG. 14 Bertall, *The Dutch Tavern Ship.* From *Le journal amusant*, June 6, 1868

FIG. 15 Charles Busson, *The Old Moats of the Château of Lavardin, near Montoire.* Oil on canvas, 83½ × 63 in. (212 × 160 cm). Corcieux Town Hall, France, on loan from the Musée d'Orsay

can be seen as a reflection of his pride in this city, where he grew up. During the 1860s, he produced several large-scale views of the port for the Salon. The importance of this aspect of his work is overlooked today since his largest example in this mode—*Boats Leaving the Port of Le Havre*, shown at the 1868 Salon—has been lost and is known only from descriptions and caricatures (fig. 14). Émile Zola described the picture thus: "A three-master fills the canvas, pulled along by a tugboat. The black, monstrous shell rises above the greenish water; the sea billows and swells in the foreground, still rippling from the impact of the enormous mass which has cut through it."[64] Monet's work articulates a vision of France as a powerful trading nation.

Monet's images also suggest a nationalistic pride in new tourist resorts, which attracted visitors not only from France but also from England, aided by an expanded cross-channel ferry system. During the 1860s Monet regularly represented coastal resorts from Étretat to Trouville in several luminous views, highlighting these sites as important cosmopolitan destinations. In the summer of 1870, he produced a series of works of the busy boardwalk at Trouville, filled with tourists and animated by the colors of international flags (e.g., Wadsworth Atheneum Museum of Art, Hartford, Conn.). The ostensible optimism of these images, however, cloaked a wider historical reality: the very identity of France's nationhood was now under threat. Following Napoléon III's hubristic and ill-advised declaration of war on Prussia on July 19, 1870, the nation faced imminent defeat and the humiliation of invasion.

The 1870s: The Early Years of the Third Republic

Ideas of nation are shaped particularly in response to the trauma of war. In the summer of 1870, the French army was defeated by Prussia at the battle of Sedan after a brief military campaign. This event marked the end of the Second Empire when Napoléon III fled to England; it also led to the proclamation of the Third Republic. Paris would subsequently be besieged by the Prussians, while the important industrialized region of Alsace-Lorraine—a vital engine for France's economy—would be ceded to Prussia. The humiliating defeat in the Franco-Prussian War of 1870–71 had a deep impact on French ideas of nation in the following years. It is difficult to overemphasize the significance of this conflict for the French psyche, and it would become a signal factor in the origins of World War I.[65] The emergence of the Commune in the spring of 1871 and its subsequent brutal repression, in which up to thirty-five thousand French citizens were killed in the streets of Paris by their own countrymen, also had a profound effect on the national character.

Despite the foundation of the Third Republic, the years from 1873 to 1879 witnessed the repressive regime of the monarchist Marshal Patrice de MacMahon. During the years of MacMahon's presidency, state patronage was controlled by the ultraclerical aristocrat the marquis Philippe de Chennevières, director of the École des beaux-arts from 1873 to 1878. The numbers of state-acquired landscapes now diminished as Chennevières sought to promote principally history painting. The images of rural France supported by the state—and prevalent at the official Salon in the 1870s—offered a conservative vision of timeless stability, a kind of *rappel à l'ordre* (return to order)—similar to the situation after World War I. Landscape painters at the Salon—their names generally little known today—produced large-scale

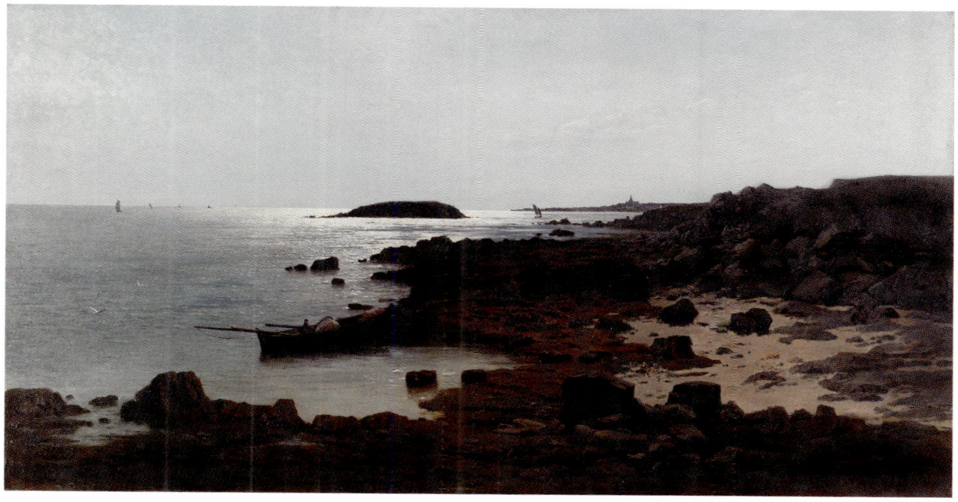

FIG. 16 Élodie La Villette, *The Shore of Lohic and the Île des Souris, near Lorient—the Sea Stretches Out*, 1875. Oil on canvas, 51⅛ × 98½ in. (130 × 250.3 cm). Musée des beaux-arts et d'archéologie, Besançon, on loan from the Musée d'Orsay, Paris, inv. Lux 167

works of *la France profonde* (deep France), focusing on the representation of small, rural communities and areas invested with centuries of history.[66] The state sanctioned such work in its purchases at the Salon.[67] It acquired, for example, several views of the village of Lavardin in Touraine, in the heart of rural France, by Charles Busson. Among these was a dramatically lit and meticulously rendered depiction of the ruins of the village's ancient twelfth-century castle (fig. 15), bought by the state in 1874, the year of the first Impressionist exhibition, for the large sum of four thousand francs.[68] The scene is animated by a deer, while the ruins loom above the castle's moats. The work remained on display at the Musée du Luxembourg for the rest of the century. Other little-known artists such as Eugène Lavieille and Camille Bernier were also favored by the administration.[69] Marine views were also prevalent at the Salon in the 1870s and extensively patronized by the state. Élodie La Villette, the only woman to exhibit large-scale landscapes at the Salon in the 1870s in what was a male-dominated environment, produced work that won the state's approval. Her *Shore of Lohic and the Île des Souris, near Lorient—the Sea Stretches Out* (fig. 16), acquired at the 1876 Salon and sent to the Musée de Besançon, is a vision of shimmering light, presenting a seemingly remote cove animated by intricate rock formations. La Villette's work self-consciously edits out the nearby busy, commercial harbor of Lorient. Her turn away from modernity contrasts with the work of her fellow artist Berthe Morisot, whose own rendition of Lorient reflects the emergence of the site not only as a commercial harbor but also as a tourist destination (cat. 116).

The 1870s also saw the continuation of a strong republican tradition in France, focused around radicals such as Léon Gambetta. The idea of nation had always been a central part of republicanism dating back to the time of the 1789 Revolution and the foundation of the country's system of *départements* as a means of overcoming regional differences and encouraging a sense of national unity. In 1872 Gambetta had even affirmed that France was not a "meeting of associated provinces . . . No! This whole, this unity, it is the French Republic."[70] In practice, as Thiesse has shown, republicanism remained open to the preservation of regional tradition while also, above all, recognizing the importance of developing a national system of lay education as a means of unifying the country.[71] Print media here played a crucial role. No book was more influential than the educational primer *Le tour de la France par deux enfants*, first published in 1877, which conflated the pastoral and industrial visions of nation. This book, organized as a journey around France by two children and profusely illustrated, sold approximately six million copies in the late nineteenth century and was vital in framing a sense of nation for millions of French schoolchildren, even acquiring the nickname "the little red book of the Republic." A patriotic text was accompanied by numerous wood engravings with images highlighting the country's natural wonders (such as Mont Blanc) and history (such as the town of Carcassonne). Other images represented the country's railways, showing, for example, the long tunnel of Nerthe, near Marseille, previously photographed by Baldus but here seen by a far larger audience (fig. 17).[72]

As has been noted by Philip Nord, the output of the Impressionists in the 1870s can be closely related to republicanism, and particularly the republican vision of a modern, secular France, embracing technological progress.[73] The industrial vision of France was a crucial part of the

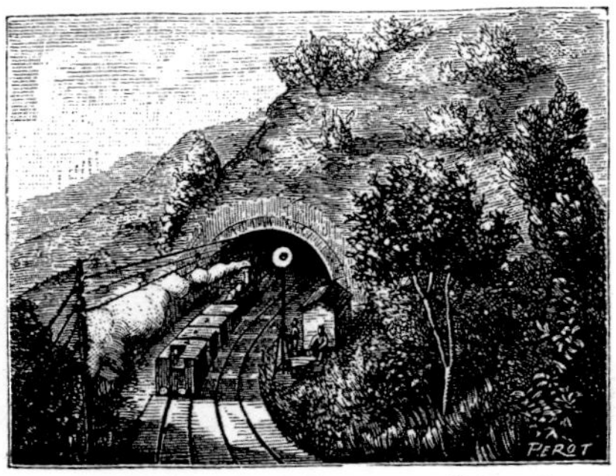

TUNNEL DE LA NERTHE, PRÈS DE MARSEILLE. — Un *tunnel* est un passage pratiqué sous terre ou à travers une montagne, dans lequel s'engagent les trains de chemin de fer. Le plus grand tunnel de France a été longtemps celui de la Nerthe, qui a près de 5 kilomètres de longueur. Un autre tunnel plus grand encore a été construit récemment pour mettre en communication la France et l'Italie : c'est celui du mont Cenis, dont la longueur dépasse 12 kilomètres.

FIG. 17 Perot, *La Nerthe Tunnel, near Marseille.* From G. Bruno, *Le tour de la France par deux enfants* (Paris, 1877), 180. Wood engraving

Impressionists' project alongside their better-known images of leisure.[74] Pissarro and Guillaumin painted the factories around Paris extensively. Morisot painted factories on the Gennevilliers plain just outside the capital, representing a transformed industrial landscape, newly irrigated with Parisian sewage water. Edgar Degas, too, who had stayed in Paris during the Franco-Prussian War and experienced at firsthand the invasion of the Prussians, produced work that embodied the new industrial confidence of the nation (cat. 86). The canvases of these artists can best be compared with the prints that regularly appeared in illustrated magazines, as well as in books like Julien Turgan's multivolume *Les grandes usines de France* (*Great Factories of France*), that were liberally illustrated with engravings of the factories of France. The industrial, modern vision of landscape is particularly evident in the work of Monet, who was generally seen by contemporary critics as the leader of the Impressionist group. As Paul Hayes Tucker first noted, Monet's industrial iconography of the 1870s can be viewed as a nationalistic celebration of France's new confidence after the humiliation of the Franco-Prussian War.[75] In the Parisian suburb of Argenteuil, Monet concentrated on representations of the newly reconstructed bridges across the Seine (cats. 77, 78). In Le Havre, he celebrated the central importance of this port to the commerce of the nation. *Grand Quai at Le Havre* (fig. 18) is one of several pictures that highlight the site's bustling energy. Cotton bales, perhaps having arrived from the United States, are lined up on the dock, while the quay itself is filled with a range of large three-masted ships and steamboats, referencing this transitional moment when steam increasingly supplanted sail as a mode of transport. Monet also represented the railroad and factories around the Normandy capital of Rouen. *The Cargo Convoy* (fig. 19) is a dramatic image of a freight train racing through the landscape, set against the many textile factories and iron foundries of the Rouennais suburb of Deville. Tiny figures in the foreground are dwarfed by the surrounding mass of factories, as they would once have been by the presence of mountains, making Monet's view an example of the "industrial sublime."[76] Monet's later paintings of the Gare Saint-Lazare (cat. 16) represent the culmination of his engagement with the railroad and focused on a station that was the hub for communications to Normandy and the West and, as such, at the center of France's new transportation network.

1878: The Paris Exposition Universelle

In the modern era, world's fairs played a central role in constructing a sense of nationhood. These spectacular displays of artistic and industrial prowess showcased the singular achievements of individual nations. The first world's fair had been held in London in 1851, and the fairs were subsequently mounted in an array of international venues. French artists—and particularly landscape painters—promoted their work and nation at fairs such as those in London in 1862, Vienna in 1873, and Philadelphia in 1876. Daubigny, for example, enjoyed considerable success with his pastoral views of France shown in Vienna. In the nineteenth century, Paris most frequently hosted the fair (on five occasions from 1855 until 1900).

The 1878 fair, the largest to date, attracted approximately six million international visitors and played a crucial role in finally cementing national confidence after the Franco-Prussian War. The republicans were now increasingly powerful, and Jules Grévy was elected the first truly republican president at the start of 1879, following the resignation of

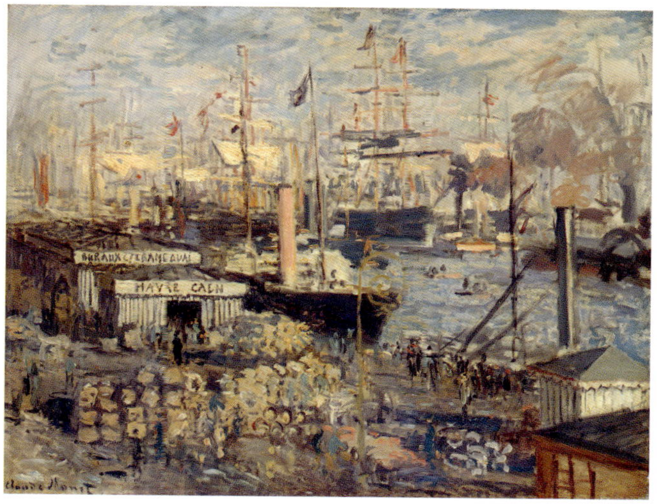

FIG. 18 Claude Monet, *Grand Quai at Le Havre*, 1874. Oil on canvas, 24 × 31⅞ in. (61 × 81 cm). The State Hermitage Museum, Saint Petersburg

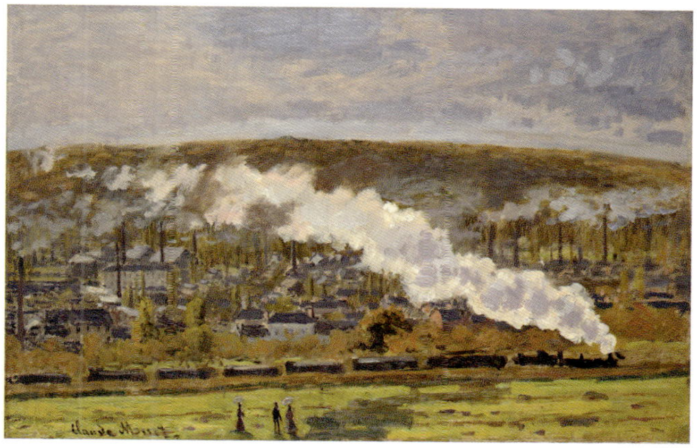

FIG. 19 Claude Monet, *The Cargo Convoy*, 1872. Oil on canvas, 19 × 29½ in. (48.1 × 75 cm). Pola Museum of Art, Japan

MacMahon. As Robert Simpson Cassatt, the father of the American artist Mary, noted,

> Paris is a wonder to behold—Such universal movement in every part of the city I am sure does not exist in any other city in the world not except London. The Exhibition is a continued success and its success has helped to establish the Republic—The Monarchists cannot conceal their spite at this. . . . In short the Republic is to show that there is no need of a Monarchy to make Paris the gayest city in the world.[77]

Despite these words, the official beaux-arts display of French painting was a conservative exhibition, filled with rural landscape imagery. Corot was the dominating presence; he was represented by ten works, while several of his friends and pupils also had prominent displays. Lavieille, one of his leading pupils, had the largest landscape exhibition with thirteen paintings. Daubigny showed nine works (cat. 50); Henri-Joseph Harpignies, five (cat. 56); Français, three (cat. 89); and Huet, also three (cats. 27, 28).[78] More controversial artists were, however, barely to be seen. Courbet showed only a single work, and there was no painting by Millet.[79] Nor were there any works by Édouard Manet or any of the Impressionists. The pictures on view reflected the vision of the marquis de Chennevières, head of the Paintings Jury.[80] Chennevières's notion of France was presented in a range of pastoral imagery, wedded to the country's distinctive layers of history, both man-made and natural. An image by Harpignies is characteristic (fig. 20), showcasing ancient oaks and a picturesque village with a medieval church spire. This construction of the Old World of France can be contrasted with that of the United States, a country with far less architectural history, where the emphasis was instead placed on the sublime scale and wilderness of the New World landscape. The work of Sanford Gifford, for example, was emblematic.[81]

The vision of nation—and in particular the French landscape school—presented at the 1878 Exposition universelle was not, however, uncontested. At the same time as the fair, the major dealer Paul Durand-Ruel—the most important supporter of both the Barbizon school and the Impressionists—boldly organized a spectacular exhibition of landscape painting of the French school that foregrounded the work of those artists such as Millet and Courbet whose works had been marginalized in the official show. Durand-Ruel's display was enormous, with 382 works[82]—Corot's work was highlighted (it was uniquely able to satisfy both conservative and avant-garde tastes)—and the dealer affirmed that, despite having relatively few visitors, the show was more impressive than that at the exposition.[83] Durand-Ruel's exhibition tapped into a much wider discourse surrounding the rise of the French school at this moment, a discourse that represented a further

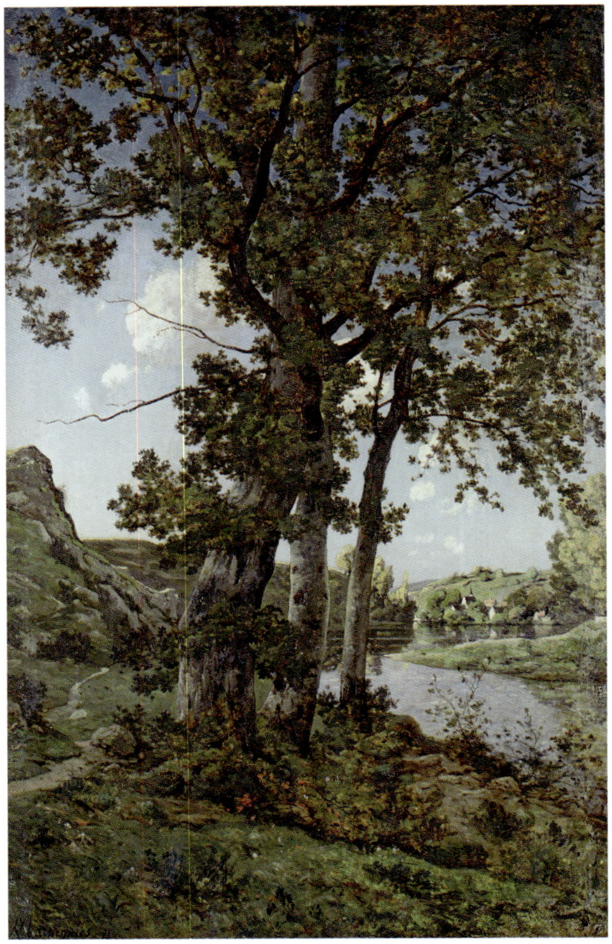

FIG. 20 Henri-Joseph Harpignies,
The Oaks of Château-Renard (Allier), 1875.
Oil on canvas, 65¾ × 43 in. (167 × 109 cm).
Musée des Beaux-Arts, Orléans, France

component crucial to the rise of nationhood.[84] In this very year, the critic Théodore Duret published the first synthetic overview of the officially marginalized Impressionist movement, legitimizing the work by presenting the artists as the inheritors of an indigenous French school of landscape painting. For Duret, the core group of Impressionist painters—Monet, Alfred Sisley, Pierre-Auguste Renoir, and Morisot—inherited the mantle of Corot, Courbet, and Manet as the principal avant-garde artists of their day.[85]

Few Impressionist paintings were on view in 1878—there was no Impressionist group show that year—but Monet produced the most memorable records of the Exposition universelle. In celebration of the success of the fair, the French government declared June 30, 1878, a national holiday, the Fête de la Paix. This holiday was also a celebration of the country's rebirth after the Franco-Prussian War and was planned on a massive scale. Three hundred thousand flags were unfurled around the capital in a remarkable display of patriotism. Monet painted two views of the flag-bedecked streets in the old center of Paris. These flag scenes can be seen more broadly within Monet's career as the culmination of his engagement with utopian modern-life themes. After 1878, perhaps disillusioned by a lack of patronage for his modern iconography, he turned to exclusively pastoral, antimodern imagery.[86] Monet's images reinforced the republican administration—now supplanting the repressive MacMahon—and, as such, reflected the artist's own liberal, republican beliefs.[87] Monet later remembered the circumstances surrounding the creation of the flag pictures: "I'm very fond of flags. On the first national holiday on June 30th, I went out with my working equipment to the rue Montorgueil; the street was decked out with flags and the crowd was going wild. I noticed a balcony, I went up and asked permission to paint, which was granted me."[88] If Monet's description is laconic, his images are euphoric. The most dramatic of the two shows rue Saint-Denis with flags—most unfurled, some curled up like lances—forming a dynamic pattern (fig. 21). A crowd moves in the street below, and a single umbrella can be seen—also in the national colors—but the flags dominate the composition. A flag to the right is inscribed "Vive la République" (Long Live the Republic). Monet's work is a celebratory, intoxicating image heralding the emergence of a newly confident nation.

Conclusion

In the final decades of the nineteenth century, new symbols of nation would emerge and be repeatedly imaged. Perhaps most notably, the Eiffel Tower was constructed in 1889 for the Exposition universelle of that year and would soon become an emblem of the modern nation.[89] In the 1890s Monet focused on the medieval cathedral of Rouen in a series of iconic images, while his views of poplar trees represent a

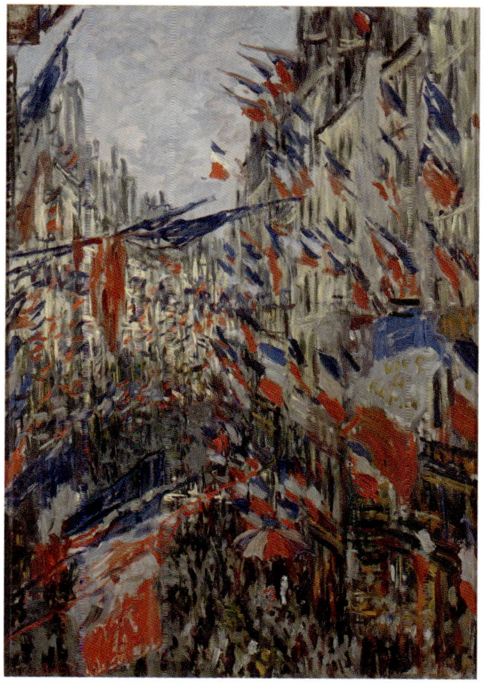

FIG. 21 Claude Monet, *The Rue Saint-Denis*, 1878. Oil on canvas, 29⅞ × 20½ in. (76 × 52 cm). Musée des beaux-arts, Rouen, France

subject that had been a symbol of the republican tradition since its selection as the tree of liberty in the 1789 Revolution.[90] Monet's nationalism remained strong until the end of his career, when he gave *Water Lilies* paintings to the French state as, in the words of his biographer Gustave Geffroy, a "bouquet of flowers" to celebrate the victory of World War I.[91] Other images, such as those of Millet, would take on new meaning as emblems of French tradition and timeless rural values.[92] Landscape and nation remained connected in the France imagination through the twentieth century—particularly in the genre of film[93]—and continues until this day. The landscape of the nation is celebrated in postmodern fashion at the Futuroscope near Poitiers and, outside France, at the Epcot Center in Florida. Issues of nationhood remain central, even as the very idea of nation is threatened in Europe by the concept of the supranational state.

Within this broader chronology, the years between 1851 and 1878 were crucial to the construction of nation, and especially for the links between landscape and nationhood. The very geographic boundaries of France changed during this time, evident particularly in the addition of the Alps and the Alpes-Maritimes (including the town of Nice) in 1860, and the loss of the industrial region of Alsace-Lorraine in 1870–71. These decades represent a transitional moment in the history of France, largely because of the transformative arrival of the railroad and the shift from an ancient, rural world toward a new age of scientific and industrial progress. Landscape—more than figurative imagery—now emerged as the genre most suited to articulate a new idea of France. The degree of success of state-supported efforts to promote landscape imagery can be debated. State-supported landscape photography, for example, was often little disseminated and largely unknown in the years after its production. The names of state-patronized landscape painters—despite their undoubted merit and historical importance—have often been lost to posterity. Nonetheless, during these years, the Barbizon school painters provided visions of France's varied geography in a rich tradition that ended with the deaths of Corot and Millet in 1875, Courbet in 1877, and Daubigny in 1878. Pioneering photographers, too, created their own landscape tradition in the 1850s and 1860s before this largely died out in the following decade, as landscape photography was supplanted by the rise of the commercial carte de visite industry. The Impressionists engaged with a range of modern iconography—especially railroads and factories—in a way that would rarely be repeated in their later work. Landscape imagery during these three decades thus played a crucial role in the construction of the idea of France, whether as a space of historical richness, of agricultural bounty, or of industrial strength. In 1878 the novelist and critic Émile Zola provided an overview of the nation's recent artistic history in which he focused on landscapists as those who "always walked ahead and constituted the force and beauty of our school." Poignantly, however—and affected by the recent deaths of the great landscape masters—he noted that after this "glorious past . . . alas! our school of landscape is not flourishing . . . at the moment."[94] For this critic, at least, landscape imagery would never embody the aspirations of the nation in quite the same way again.

Thanks to Neil McWilliam, Steven C. Hause, Elizabeth Childs, and Bradley Fratello for their support.

1. Jules-Antoine Castagnary, *Le siècle*, May 10, 1878: "Le paysage est depuis longtemps l'orgueil de l'école française, son originalité incontestable, sa supériorité évidente et acceptée."

2. Ernest Lavisse, *Deuxième année d'histoire de France* (Paris: Librairie Armand Colin, 1884), 2: "cette terre privilégiée, baignée par trois mers, flanquée des deux plus hautes chaînes de montagnes de l'Europe, arrosée par de beaux fleuves, jouissant de toutes les nuances d'un climat tempéré."

3. Quoted in Anne-Marie Thiesse, *Ils apprenaient la France: L'exaltation des regions dans le discours patriotique* (Paris: Maison des Sciences de l'Homme, 1997), 3: "la France a une richesse de gammes qu'on ne trouve pas ailleurs."

4. France became a republican (as opposed to nominal) republic in early 1879. On January 5, 1879, the Republicans won control of the Senate, and on January 30 President Patrice de MacMahon resigned; Jules Grévy was elected president to replace him. On March 14, 1879, "La Marseillaise" was restored as the French national anthem. On July 6, 1880, Bastille Day was declared a national holiday.

5. Thiesse, *Ils apprenaient la France*; and Anne-Marie Thiesse, *La création des identités nationales: Europe XVIIIe–XXe siècle* (Paris: Éditions du Seuil, 1999). See also Neil McWilliam and June Hargrove, eds., *Nationalism and French Visual Culture, 1870–1914*, Studies in the History of Art 68, Center for Advanced Study in the Visual Arts, Symposium Papers 45 (Washington, D.C.: National Gallery of Art, 2005).

6. For wider theories around the idea of nation, see Benedict Anderson, *Imagined Communities: Reflections on the Origin and Spread of Nationalism* (London: Verso, 1991); and Ernst Gellner, *Nations and Nationalism* (Ithaca, N.Y.: Cornell University Press, 1983; Oxford: Blackwell, 2006). It is worth noting that, although universal male suffrage was instituted in France in 1848, it was not until 1944 that women were also granted the right to vote.

7. See Tim Barringer, "The Course of Empires: Landscape and Identity in America and Britain, 1820–1880," in Andrew Wilton and Tim Barringer, *American Sublime: Landscape Painting in the United States, 1820–1880*, exh. cat. (London: Tate, 2002), 38–65.

8. See Stephen Daniels, *Fields of Vision: Landscape Imagery and National Identity in England and the United States* (Princeton: Princeton University Press, 1993). Daniels's work highlights the contributions of cultural geography to the discourse around nationhood.

9. Virginia Spate, in *Claude Monet: Life and Work* (New York: Rizzoli, 1992), has noted this utopian element (128): "Although they were rooted in perceptual experience, the paintings of Monet's first twenty years as a painter were Utopian, their endless beauties generated by a longing for some ideal, sensuous plenitude."

10. See Eugen Weber, *Peasants into Frenchmen: The Modernization of Rural France, 1870–1914* (Stanford: Stanford University Press, 1976). At midcentury, Weber notes (67), for example, that the populations of twenty-four of France's eighty-six *départements* did not speak French.

11. For other regions, see Viktoria von der Bruggen and Christine Peltre, eds., *L'Alsace pittoresque: L'invention d'un paysage, 1770–1870*, exh. cat. (Paris: Hazan; Colmar: Musée Unterlinden, 2011); and *1860–1960: L'annexion de la Savoie à la France; Histoires et connexions*, ed. Sylvain Milbach, exh. cat. (Milan: Silvana Editoriale Spa, 2010).

12. Thiesse, *Ils apprenaient la France*, subtitles her book "the exaltation of the regions in the patriotic discourse" (l'exaltation des régions dans le discours patriotique). It is, however, worth noting that Napoléon III did repress the Association bretonne in 1853, a body that had to sought to promote Breton customs and identity.

13. *Récit du voyage de Leurs majesties l'empereur et l'impératrice en Normandie et en Bretagne (août, 1858)*; quoted in *La Bretagne en relief: Premiers voyages photographiques en Bretagne*, exh. cat. (Quimper: Musée Départemental Breton, 2000), 48: "triple portique surmonté de l'aigle aux ailes déployés et de faisceaux de drapeaux au milieu desquels se lisaient des inscriptions à la louange de Leurs Majestés."

14. Germany was not yet a single state at midcentury but had achieved some economic unity through the creation of the Zollverein (German Customs Union) in 1818. That union surpassed France in many areas: in 1851, for example, the Zollverein produced 8.6 million tons of coal as opposed to 4.9 million tons in France. See Brian R. Mitchell, *European Historical Statistics, 1750–1975* (Ann Arbor: Facts on File, University of Michigan, 1980).

15. Saint-Simonianism was a utopian political movement of the first half of the nineteenth century, inspired by the writings of Claude-Henri de Rouvroy, comte de Saint-Simon, advocating the centrality of science and industry in the regeneration of society.

16. Eugène Flachat, *Les chemins de fer en 1862 et en 1863* (Paris: Hachette, 1863), 80: "On était donc Breton, Gascon, Normand, Picard, Lorrain, Alsacien, Provençal, mais ce n'était que dans les hautes professions, dans les grandes villes, à l'armée sur la flotte qu'on comprenait et qu'on aimait la France. . . . Les chemins de fer ont répandu partout une vie politique plus égale."

17. See Frédéric Laux et al., *Une campagne photographique dans l'Eure: Au temps de l'impressionisme*, exh. cat. (Bonsecours: Éditions Point de Vues; Département de l'Eure; Ville d'Evreux; Ville de Vernon, 2010).

18. To cite one example of many, an article in *L'illustration* in 1867 celebrated the opening of a new railroad through the Jura in 1867.

19. *L'illustration*, for example, enjoyed a weekly circulation of 37,500 by 1890. See James R. Lehning, *To Be a Citizen: The Political Culture of the Early French Republic* (Ithaca, N.Y.: Cornell University Press, 2001), 167.

20. See Hélène Morlier, "Les Guides Joanne: Invention d'une collection," *In Situ: Revue des patrimoines*, no. 15 (2011), http://insitu.revues.org/524.

21. See Anne de Mondenard, *La Mission héliographique: Cinq photographes parcourent la France en 1851* (Paris: Centre des Monuments Nationaux/Monum, Éditions du Patrimoine, 2002).

22. In 1865 the state acquired Pierre Justin Ouvrié's *Château of Pierrefonds in 1864*, in 1867 and 1868 Huet's two views, and in 1869 Lansyer's *Château of Pierrefonds*. For an overview of the photographs by Ch. Michelez of the works acquired by the state from 1864 to 1886, see ARCHIM website (http://www.culture.gouv.fr/public/mistral/caran_fr), F/21/*7635- F/21/*7655.

23. The Gallo-Roman museum was created by imperial decree at Saint-Germain-en-Laye in 1862. At its formal opening in 1867, it had 8,300 objects. It would later become the Musée des antiquités nationales. See Catherine Granger, *L'empereur at les arts: La liste civile de Napoléon III* (Paris: École de Chartes, 2005), 354–66. The emperor's interest in Gaul also affected his patronage, encouraging his acquisition of Penguilly l'Haridon's view of Provence from Gallic times (Musée d'Orsay, Paris) from the 1869 Salon.

24. See Pierre Angrand, "L'état mécène: Période autoritaire du Second Empire (1851–1860)," *Gazette des beaux-arts* 71, nos. 1192–93 (May–June 1968): 303–48. No comparably in-depth study exists for state patronage of the 1860s.

25. John House indicates that a third of state acquisitions were landscapes—about forty. But an overview of images of France acquired by the state (in the photographs of Michelez) indicates in fact a smaller number of approximately thirty (20 in 1864, 30 in 1865, 30 in 1866, 20 in 1867, 30 in 1868, 20 in 1869, 30 in 1870). House's number probably includes landscapes showing sites outside France. See House, "Authority versus Independence: The Position of French Landscape in the 1870s," in *Framing France: The Representation of Landscape, 1870–1914*, ed. Richard Thomson (Manchester: Manchester University Press, 1998), 15–34.

26. Ten landscapes by Jeanron were acquired by the state between 1851 and 1860. The focus on Jeanron shows that politics was obviously not an overriding factor in decisions regarding state patronage: he had been a prominent left-wing politician during the Second Republic. Formal elements were probably most important here; Jeanron's works are both highly finished in style and picturesque in subject matter. See Angrand, "L'état mécène."

27. *The Glacier of Mont Blanc* by Sébastien Hugard, *Entre-Roches on the Doubs* by Charles Bavoux, *The Lighthouse of Marseille* by Jeanron, *A View of Dauphiné* by Bellel, *View of the Port of Bordeaux* by Adolphe Couveley, and *Souvenir of Cap Frehel (Brittany)* by Francis Blin.

28. In 1849, 147 works were in the Luxembourg, and 240 by 1875. See Geneviève Lacambre, *Le Musée du Luxembourg en 1874*, exh. cat. (Paris: Éditions des Musées Nationaux, 1974), 8.

29. Octave Penguilly l'Haridon's *The Little Seagulls, Shore of Belle-Île-en-Mer*—a view of the Breton island of Belle-Île—was acquired for two thousand francs at the 1859 Salon and sent to the museum in Rennes (Brittany). As House ("Authority versus Independence," 32) has noted, Yan Dargent's *La roche Meurice, Evening*, shown at the Salon of 1868, was sent to Béziers in the South; Emmanuel Lansyer's *Rocks at Arvéchen (Finistère)* was sent to Lille in the North.

30. Napoléon III and Empress Eugénie acquired two works by Corot (including *Solitude: Souvenir of Vigen (Limousin)* [Thyssen-Bornemisza Collection, Madrid] for 18,000 francs in 1866) and Daubigny's *The Wide Valley at Optevoz* (Musée des Beaux-Arts, Compiègne) for five thousand francs in 1857. They also purchased Courbet's *Le puits noir (Black Well)* (Musée d'Orsay, Paris) in 1865 for two thousand francs. Eugénie was also an important supporter of Rosa Bonheur, acquiring her work in 1864, following a visit to the artist's studio. For an excellent, in-depth examination of Napoléon III's patronage, see Granger, *L'empereur at les arts*. For Eugénie's patronage, see Alison McQueen, *Empress Eugénie and the Arts: Politics and Visual Culture in the Nineteenth Century* (Farnham: Ashgate, 2011).

31. In other European countries, there were very large regional towns (such as Manchester in England and Munich in Germany, each with populations of about 500,000), but there was no regional town of comparable size in France.

32. See David H. Pinkney, *Napoleon III and the Rebuilding of Paris* (Princeton: Princeton University Press, 1972).

33. The work was officially purchased for six thousand francs on November 13, 1855, by Napoléon III. It was displayed for the rest of the nineteenth century at the Musée du Louvre (where it remained until 1986). At the 1853 Salon Navlet showed two other Parisian views, *Paris on the East Side: View Seen from the Roofs of the Louvre* and *Paris on the West Side: View Seen from the Southern Tower of Notre-Dame* (both Musée Carnavalet, Paris), both of which were acquired by Napoléon III and sent to Versailles. See Granger, *L'empereur et les arts*, 591–92.

34. In 1854 Viollet-le-Duc affirmed that the Gothic style was "the symbol of French nationality and the most powerful attempt towards unity" (le symbole de la nationalité française et la plus puissante tentative vers l'unité). Eugène-Emmanuel Viollet-le-Duc, *Dictionnaire raisonné de l'architecture française du XIe au XVIe siècle* (Paris: B. Bance, 1854), 2:281.

35. See Jules Castagnary, "Salon de 1876," in Castagnary, *Salons (1872–79)* (Paris: Bibliothèque Charpentier, 1892), 2:270. Official patronage of urban views was also rare, but there were exceptions, such as Antoine Guillemet's *View of Bercy*, acquired by the state in 1874.

36. The nationalistic reading of this image is complicated by the fact that British engineers had been largely responsible for the construction of the bridge in the 1840s. See Ian Kennedy and Julian Treuherz, *The Railway: Art in the Age of Steam*, exh. cat. (New Haven: Yale University Press, 2008), 70.

37. Two other maritime paintings—one showing Napoléon III at Genoa, where he had signed a treaty with Italy, leading to the acquisition of new land—were commissioned by the emperor for twenty thousand francs each, amounting to a total of sixty thousand francs. These works were shown at the London International Exhibition in 1862 and again in Paris at the Exposition universelle of 1867. The view of Napoléon III at Genoa caused a minor sensation when it was shown at the Gambart Gallery in London in 1864. See Granger, *L'empereur at les arts*, 537.

38. Among these was Jules Noël's *View of Brest*, acquired at the 1864 Salon. Claude-Joseph Vernet's series of fifteen paintings of the ports of France (1754–65) provides a valuable record of the maritime industry in eighteenth-century France. See Philip Conisbee, *Painting in Eighteenth-Century France* (Ithaca, N.Y.: Cornell University Press, 1981), 181–84.

39. The emperor acquired Eugène Le Poittevin's view of bathers at the resort of Étretat (Musée des beaux-arts, Troyes) for seven thousand francs in the mid-1860s. See Granger, *L'empereur et les arts*, 575.

40. Louis Auvray, *Exposition des beaux-arts: Salon de 1867* (Paris: Ve Jules Renouard, 1867), 53: "La France n'a jamais été mieux appreciée des paysagistes que depuis que les voies de communication, tellement multipliés sur tous les points de l'empire, mettent les voyages à la portee de toutes les bourses. Les peintres trouvent dans les départements du Nord les vastes plaines et le ciel brumeux de la Belgique, de la Hollande et de l'Allemagne; dans le Provence, le beau ciel et les coteaux dorés de l'Italie; en Bretagne et en Normandie, une vegetation de pâturage que l'Angleterre nous envie, et au centre de la France, aux environs de Paris, des sites riants qu'on ne rencontre dans aucun autre pays. Voilà pourquoi beaucoup d'artistes se plaisent à reproduire les aspects si variés de notre belle patrie."

41. See Jon Whiteley, "Subject Index to Paintings Exhibited at the Paris Salon, 1673–1881," Sackler Library, Oxford.

42. Anne Wagner emphasizes this aspect in the Parisian collector's interest in Courbet's landscapes. See Anne M. Wagner, "Courbet's Landscapes and Their Market," *Art History* 4, no. 4 (December 1981): 410–31.

43. See Simon Kelly, "The Patronage of Frédéric Hartmann and the Question of 'Finish,'" *Burlington Magazine* 142 (September 2000): 549–60.

44. Corot's nationalism at this time is also evident in his donation of his large *Saint Sebastian* (Walters Art Museum, Baltimore) to a lottery in 1871 to raise money for the orphans of war victims. See Alfred Robaut, *L'oeuvre de Corot: Catalogue raisonné et illustré* (Paris: H. Floury, 1905), 2:330.

45. Philippe Burty, introduction in the catalogue for the retrospective at the École des beaux-arts after Corot's death, *Corot*, exh. cat. (Paris: Jules Juteau et Fils, 1875), 24–25: "Il était un peintre, un simple peintre, un peintre français. L'Italie et les conversations à la mode dans les ateliers durant sa jeunesse, avaient éveillé en lui le goût pour les grandes lignes. Mais il aima singulièrement la France qui offre de belles lignes aussi, et des vapeurs bleutées et des ciels rompus, et de fines verdures, et surtout les saisons alternées, et les longs crépuscules."

46. See Josine Eikelenboom Smits, "Le role de l'architecture dans les paysages de Corot," in *Corot: Un artiste et son temps, Actes du colloque organisés au musée du Louvre, 1996* (Paris: Klincksieck and Musée du Louvre; Rome: Académie de France à Rome, Villa Médicis, 1998), 229–46.

47. *The Belfry at Douai* (Musée du Louvre, Paris), *View of the Interior of Sens Cathedral* (Musée du Louvre, Paris), and *View of the Cathedral and Town of Mantes* (Musée des beaux-arts, Reims).

48. Cited in Robaut, *L'oeuvre de Corot*, 1:238: "D'abord, nous nous trouvâmes . . . au milieu des canons Whitford, assiégés par la curiosité des Anglais. 'Ah! Goddam,' fit Corot, imitant l'accent des Anglais à faire pouffer de rire, 'voici les inventeurs de ces jolies choses! C'est-il gentil! C'est-il gentil!' Puis, tout à coup, horrifié par tous ces engins de guerre, par ces boulets ronds et ces boulets coniques, pittance future de ces énormes gueules rayées: 'Est-il possible, dit-il, d'exposer ces affreuses machines en même temps et dans le même lieu que nos paysages et nos petits moutons? Le monde est fou . . . et atroce. Et voyez les inventeurs ont l'air enchantés! Mon Dieu, que veulent-ils faire de

ça?'—'Trouer vos paysages et tuer vos petits moutons.' . . . A la vue d'une petite cathédrale de bobines de cotton omnicolore de Manchester: 'Ah! La belle fabrique à mettre au fond de mes paysages!'"

49. As is often noted, this term is anachronistic and was not used by the artists themselves. It was coined by the British art historian and dealer David Croal Thomson in 1890. See David Croal Thomson, *The Barbizon School of Painters* (London: Chapman and Hall, 1890).

50. The 1861 exhibition, for example, included views by the Bisson frères of Mont Blanc and the Alps and views of the Forest of Fontainebleau by Olympe Aguado and Paul Delondre.

51. Corot sent his *View of La Rochelle* (Yale University Art Gallery) to several regional shows, including those at Rouen, Bordeaux, Saintes, Toulouse, Amiens, and Arras.

52. See "Petition to Napoleon III [1852]," in Greg M. Thomas, *Art and Ecology in Nineteenth-Century France: The Landscapes of Théodore Rousseau* (Princeton: Princeton University Press, 2000), 214.

53. Jean Ravenel [Alfred Sensier], "Salon de 1865," *L'époque*, May 17, 1865: "le peintre des forêts des druides, qui fait revivre en nous le temps des vieux Gaulois." For Sensier, the planting of Russian pines in the forest was also a sacrilegious dishonoring of native soil. In an unpublished manuscript, he remembered the original rocky expanses of the forest: "Le stupide Bois d'Hiver le Forestier destructeur n'avait pas encore empoisonné les Landes et les plaines mousseuses de ses pins Russes qui déshonorent notre sol gaulois. Les Gorges d'Apremont étaient nues de leur venerable nudité, sous leur poil de bruyères, sous leur bure des siècles. On y voyaient alors sous son ensemble majestueux le grand Cirque Gaelique ou les géants nos ancêtres assemblaient leurs tribus." (The stupid, destructive forest manager Bois d'Hiver had not yet poisoned the Landes and the mossy plains with Russian pines that dishonor our Gallic soil. The Gorges d'Apremont were truly bare for all to see, beneath their coat of heather, beneath their centuries-old cloak. One saw there then, in its majestic whole, the great Gallic amphitheater where the giants, our ancestors, assembled their tribes.) See Alfred Sensier, "Notes pour l'histoire de la Forêt de Fontainebleau," Archives Sensier, M35, no. 37, Fontainebleau, Bibliothèque municipale.

54. Charles Nègre, *Le Midi de la France: Sites et monuments historiques*: "Indépendamment des antiquités romaines répandues dans certains endroits, presque toutes ces villes m'ont fourni des richesses d'archéologie peu connues: ce sont des restes précieux de l'art chrétien aux XIe, XIIe et XIIIe siècles; c'est à la reproduction des oeuvres d'art de cet art national qui je me suis plus particulièrement attaché." See both French and translation in André Jammes and Eugenia Parry Janis, *The Art of French Calotype with a Critical Dictionary of Photographers, 1845–1870* (Princeton: Princeton University Press, 1983), 262. About seventy-four plates survive.

55. See Jean-Roger Soubiran, *Le paysage provençal et l'école de Marseille avant l'impressionisme, 1845–1874*, exh. cat. (Paris: Réunion des Musées Nationaux; Toulon: Musée de Toulon, 1992).

56. Guigou's works came to embody the region of Provence in the 1860s, just as would those of Paul Cézanne in the succeeding generation. Even Cézanne's iconic motif, Mont Sainte-Victoire, as has been recently noted, had not only regional but also national resonance as a site of Gallic resistance to Julius Caesar. Cézanne's technique of *passage* may also have been informed by his interest in the archaeology of the region and particularly the appearance of prehistoric flints. See Nina Maria Athanassoglou-Kallmyer, *Cézanne and Provence: The Painter in His Culture* (Chicago: University of Chicago Press, 2003).

57. See André Cariou, *De Turner à Monet: La découverte de la Bretagne par les paysagistes au XIXe siècle*, exh. cat. (Quimper: Musée des Beaux-Arts de Quimper; Palantines, 2011).

58. Courbet's work entered a debate regarding the correct location of the ancient site of Alesia. While Courbet argued that this site was at Alaise, near Flagey (the village where he was born), opinion in the 1860s increasingly identified the site as Alise-Sainte-Reine in Burgundy. In his *History of Julius Caesar*, the emperor argued for the latter location.

59. Théophile Thoré, "Salon de 1861," in W. Bürger, *Salons de W. Bürger, 1861 à 1868* (Paris: Ve Jules Renouard, 1870), 1:93: "A de certaines époques immorales, la rénovation ne peut s'opérer que par des moyens héroiques. Un peu de sauvagerie ou plutôt de barbarie ne disconviendrait point dans les temps de défaillance. . . . L'art en France est malade, et il n'aime pas ces médecins du Danube qui arrivent avec des recettes solides et une santé imperturbable. D'où viennent-ils? Eh bien, ils viennent des forêts et des montagnes. Millet vit dans les roches de Fontainebleau et Courbet dans les gorges du Jura. C'est pourquoi ils n'ont pas le meme goût que les charmants artistes qui peignent rose au milieu des boudoirs."

60. One hundred sixteen views of Le Puy were exhibited at the Salon between 1852 and 1870. See Whiteley, "Subject Index to Paintings Exhibited at the Paris Salon, 1673–1881."

61. Le Guillois, "Le Salon en quatrains," *Diogène*, no. 65 (June 9, 1861):

Français
C'est franc, c'est poétique et sage:
Trois toiles, trois succès!
C'est que le roi du paysage
En France est Français.

62. The Tours entrepreneur Alfred Mame commissioned artists to produce prints of these châteaux, including Chenonceau, Blois, and Ambroise. The painter Louis Français spent twenty months in the region; his resulting prints included a view of the picturesque Renaissance château of Azay-le-Rideau.

63. In focusing on this medieval structure, Monet screened out the recently constructed medievalizing tower and town hall next to it, suggesting his attraction to original architecture rather than contemporary imitations. See Christopher Riopelle, "Renoir in the City," in *Renoir Landscapes, 1865–1883*, exh. cat. (London: National Gallery, 2007), 42.

64. Émile Zola, "Salon de 1868," in *Émile Zola: Salons*, ed. F. W. J. Hemmings and Robert J. Niess (Geneva: Librairie E. Droz; Paris: Librairie Minard, 1959), 130: "Un trois-mâts emplit la toile, remorqué par un vapeur. La coque noire, monstrueuse, s'élève au-dessus de l'eau verdâtre; la mer s'enfle et se creuse au premier plan, frémissant encore sous la heurt de la masse énorme qui vient de la couper."

65. See Rachel Chrastil, *Organizing for War: France, 1870–1914* (Baton Rouge: Louisiana State University Press, 2010).

66. For several images, see John House, ed., *Landscapes of France: Impressionism and Its Rivals*, exh. cat. (London: Hayward Gallery, 1995), for example, Henri-Joseph Harpignies, *Ruins of the Château of Hérisson*, 116–17, cat. 26, and Charles Busson, *The Village of Lavardin (Loir-et-Cher)*, 128–29, cat. 32. See also his *Impressionism: Paint and Politics* (New Haven: Yale University Press, 2004).

67. The arts administration during these years was run by the artistically conservative figures Charles Blanc (1871–73) and Philippe de Chennevières (1873–78). In 1872–73 Blanc acquired large numbers of landscapes at the Salon (34 in 1872), but the numbers declined under Chennevières's leadership (29 in 1874, 12 in 1875, 6 in 1876, only 3 in 1877, and 21 in 1878). These figures are based on House (*Landscapes of France*, 24). An overview of the photographs by Michelez of state acquisitions suggests slightly different figures (28 in 1872, 4 in 1873, 31 in 1874, 7 in 1875, 5 in 1876, 3 in 1877, 20 in 1878). Favored artists included Guillemet, Léon Pelouse, Français, Lansyer, and Élodie La Villette.

68. See Lacambre, *Le Musée du Luxembourg en 1874*, 44.

69. Bernier's views of Brittany included *January, Brittany* (Musée d'Orsay, Paris), acquired for two thousand francs in 1872, in which Breton farmers plow the land in age-old rituals. The critic Gabriel Monod noted in 1878 ("Les beaux-arts à l'Exposition universelle de 1878," 34): "M. Bernier has become the painter of Brittany; nobody has better represented this harsh granite land, its sad marshes, its knotted and strong trees, its soft and veiled sky." (M. Bernier

s'est fait le peintre de la Bretagne; personne n'a mieux rendu cette dure terre granitique, ses landes mélancoliques, ses arbres noueux et forts, son ciel doux et voilé.)

70. Quoted in James F. McMillan, "La France Profonde, Modernity, and National Identity," in House, *Landscapes of France*, 57.

71. See Thiesse, *Ils apprenaient la France*.

72. G. Bruno [Augustine Fouillée], *Le tour de la France par deux enfants* (Paris: Belin, 1877), 85 (Mont Blanc), 181 (tunnel of Nerthe), 209 (Carcassonne).

73. See Philip Nord, *The Republican Moment: Struggles for Democracy in Nineteenth-Century France* (Cambridge, Mass.: Harvard University Press, 1995).

74. See James H. Rubin, *Impressionism and the Modern Landscape: Productivity, Technology, and Urbanization from Manet to Van Gogh* (Berkeley: University of California Press, 2008). The Impressionists' images of leisure can also be seen as articulating a new republican view of the French nation: see Tricia Cusack, *Riverscapes and National Identities* (Syracuse, N.Y.: Syracuse University Press, 2010). For the politics of the Impressionists in the 1870s, see also Philip Nord, *Impressionists and Politics: Art and Democracy in the Nineteenth Century* (London: Routledge, 2000).

75. See esp. Paul Hayes Tucker, *Monet at Argenteuil* (New Haven: Yale University Press, 1982).

76. James H. Rubin, "Rouen's Industrial Sublime: Monet, Pissarro, and Modernity," in *A City for Impressionism: Monet, Pissarro and Gauguin in Rouen*, exh. cat. (Milan: Skira, 2010), 96–122. As Rubin notes (108), by 1850 forty-three factories had been established in the area, and that number grew in the 1870s.

77. Robert Simpson Cassatt to Alexander Cassatt, October 4, 1878, in *Cassatt and Her Circle: Selected Letters*, ed. Nancy Mowll Mathews (New York: Abbeville, 1984), 140.

78. *Exposition universelle internationale de 1878. Catalogue officiel. Tome 1. Groupe I.* (Paris: Imprimerie Nationale, 1878), Class I, Oil Paintings (Classe I, Peintures à l'huile).

79. Pierre Vaisse, *La Troisième République et les peintres* (Paris: Flammarion, 1995), 123–25. Vaisse argues that there were a significant number of realist artists in the show, and that Millet's work did not appear because he no longer had someone to argue the case for his inclusion. Millet had died in 1875, and his great apologist, Alfred Sensier, had died in 1877. In contrast, Corot's prominence in the show was secured by the insistent support of Alfred Robaut.

80. For Chennevières, see J. Foucart and L.-A. Prat, eds., *P. de Chennevières, Souvenirs d'un directeur des beaux-arts*, new ed. (Paris: Arthéna, 1979). For a more negative view of Chennevières's role as *directeur des beaux-arts*, see Jane Mayo Roos, "Aristocracy and the Arts: Philippe de Chennevières and the Salons of the Mid-1870s," *Art Journal* 48 (Spring 1989): 53–62.

81. For Gifford, see *Exposition universelle internationale de 1878. Catalogue officiel. Tome 1. Groupe I.*

82. *Exposition retrospective de tableaux et dessins des maîtres modernes* (Paris: Galeries Durand-Ruel, 1878).

83. "Mémoires de Paul Durand-Ruel," in Lionello Venturi, *Les archives de l'impressionisme* (Paris: Durand-Ruel, Éditeurs, 1939), 2:209–10: "l'exposition surpassa en importance et en beauté celle qu'Antonin Proust eut après moi l'idée d'organiser en 1889. . . . cette exposition a laissé une profonde impression à tous ceux qui vinrent y admirer les oeuvres de nos grands artistes, mais elle manquait du prestige officiel et son success fut fort restreint." (the exhibition surpassed in importance and beauty the one that Antonin Proust had the idea of organizing after me in 1889 [the French artists' exhibition at the 1889 Exposition universelle]. . . . this exhibition left a profound impression on all those who came to admire there the works of our great artists, but it lacked official prestige and its success was very limited.)

84. A prominent figure in promulgating the notion of a French landscape school was Alfred Sensier. In his "Lecture on Landscape," delivered in 1870 in Durand-Ruel's gallery (Sensier, "Conférence sur le paysage," reprinted in Sensier, *Souvenirs sur Théodore Rousseau* [Paris: Techener, 1872]), he developed a narrative around an indigenous school of landscape painting, culminating in the work of Rousseau and Millet. He defined the art of Millet (XV) as "an art robust, frank, sincere, where he has unveiled the epic of rustic life with the courage of a Gaul" (un art robuste, franc, sincere, où il a déroulé avec un courage de Gaulois l'épopée de la vie rustique). He defined the unique characteristics of this school (VII) as its closeness to nature and devotion to an "art original, autochtone, plein d'esprit, de rudesse et de loyauté" (an original art, native, full of spirit, toughness and loyalty). Sensier argued that the Renaissance initiated a long period of decline in French art (VII), since it saw an influx of Italian work "eminently city-dwelling, refined" (éminemment citadin, raffiné), which "scorns outdoor beauties, invigorating air, to be shut away in sanctuaries and palaces" (dédaigne les beautés extérieures, l'air vivifiant, pour se renfermer dans les sanctuaires et les palais).

85. See Théodore Duret, *Les peintres impressionistes* (Paris, 1878; repr., Whitefish, Mont.: Kessinger, 2010).

86. Monet expanded the geographic range of his imagery around France just as he moved away from a self-consciously modern iconography. This shift in his practice may have been informed by his failure to find a consistent market for his modern-life subjects by the end of the 1870s.

87. Monet's republicanism is evident in a letter from 1871, expressing his disgust at the treatment of the suppression of the Commune; Monet to Pissarro, May 27, 1871, in Daniel Wildenstein, *Claude Monet: Biographie et catalogue raisonné* (Lausanne: La Bibliothèque des Arts, 1974), 1:427: "Vous avez appris sans doute la mort de ce pauvre Courbet fusillé sans jugement. Quelle ignoble conduite que celle de Versailles, tout cela est affreux et rend malade. Je n'ai de coeur à rien. Tout cela est navrant." (You have doubtless heard about the death of this poor Courbet, shot without trial. What kind of shameful conduct is this by Versailles, all this is terrible and makes me sick. I don't have the heart for anything. It's all distressing.)

88. The comment was made during the visit of the dealers René Gimpel and Georges Bernheim to Monet in October 1920. Quoted in René Gimpel, *Diary of an Art Dealer*, trans. John Rosenberg with intro. by Herbert Read (New York: Farrar, Straus and Giroux, 1966), 152.

89. See paintings such as those by Georges Seurat (*Eiffel Tower*, 1889, Fine Arts Museums of San Francisco) and Robert Delaunay (*Eiffel Tower*, 1924, Saint Louis Art Museum).

90. See Paul Hayes Tucker, *Monet in the '90s: The Series Paintings*, exh. cat. (Boston: Museum of Fine Arts, Boston, 1989).

91. Gustave Geffroy, *Claude Monet: Sa vie, son oeuvre* (Paris: Éditions G. Crès et Cie, 1924), 2:190.

92. Bradley Fratello, "France Embraces Millet: The Intertwined Fates of *The Gleaners* and *The Angelus*," *Art Bulletin* 85, no. 4 (December 2003): 685–701.

93. In the twentieth century, filmmakers increasingly appropriated the themes treated by painters and photographers of the previous century. Jean Renoir's *A Day in the Country* engages with the theme of Impressionist leisure, while Jean Vigo's *L'Atalante* speaks to the theme of industry. *Jean de Florette* evokes the rural landscape of Provence.

94. Émile Zola, "L'école française de peinture à l'Exposition de 1878," in *Émile Zola: Salons*, 199, 217: "marchèrent toujours à l'avant et constituèrent la force et la beauté de notre école" (199), "glorieux passé" (199), "Hélas! notre école de paysage n'est guère florissante . . . à l'heure actuelle" (217).

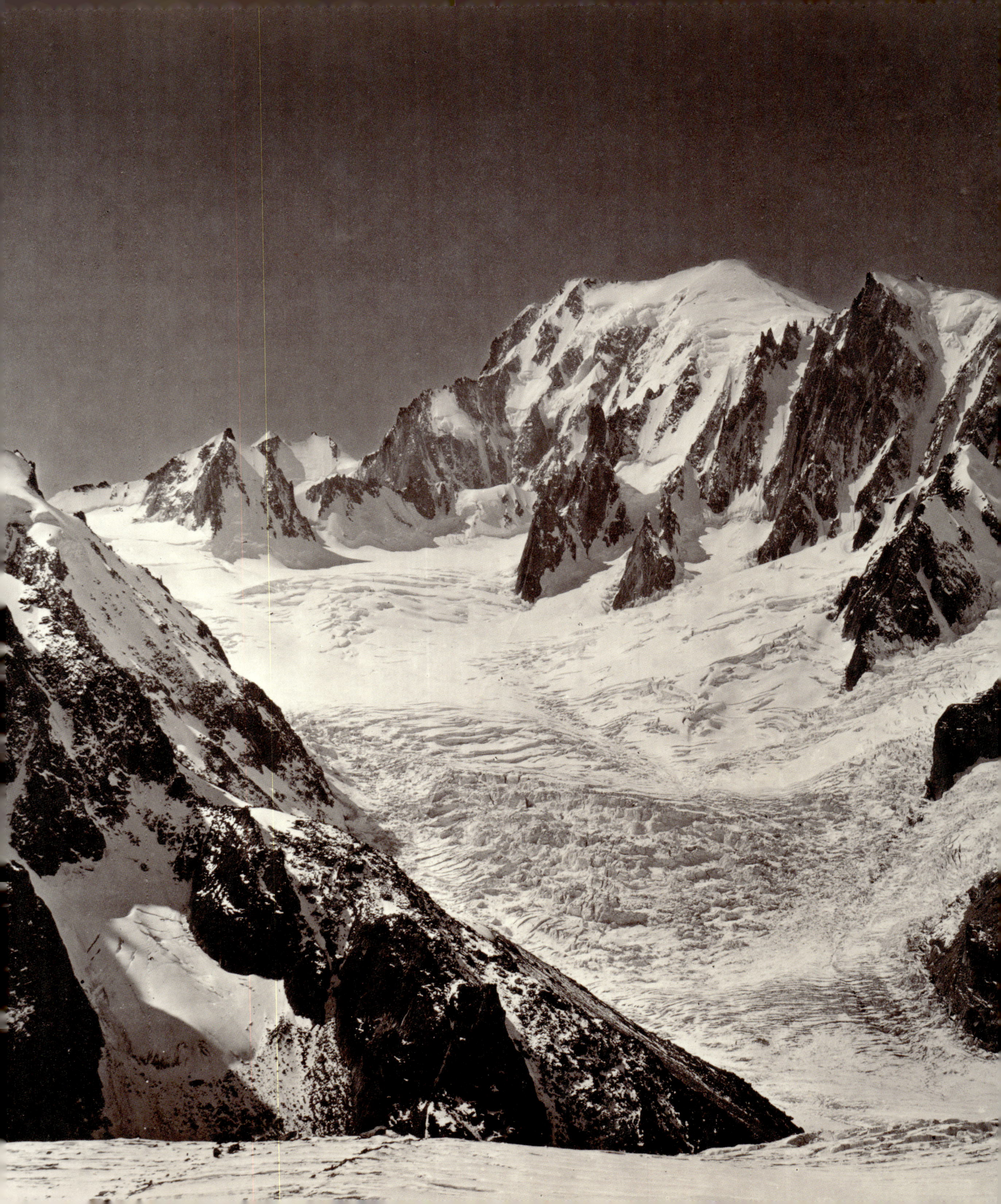

Between Past and Progress, Empire and Enchantment: Photography, Landscape, and National Identity in Mid-Nineteenth-Century France

APRIL M. WATSON

ON AUGUST 23, 1860, the emperor Napoléon III, the empress Eugénie, and an imperial entourage of prominent government officials, members of court, and numerous servants and soldiers began a five-week voyage through southeastern France and to Corsica and Algiers.[1] This was no leisurely vacation but, rather, a tour de force of propaganda. Along the way, the imperial couple was greeted by dignitaries and the social elite and welcomed by local inhabitants, who regaled them with cannon salutes, masquerade balls, and fireworks displays, among other festivities.[2] As they traveled from region to region, Eugénie visited hospitals and orphanages, while Napoléon III inspected military barracks. They also took in the scenery: on the route from Annecy to Thonon, the group encountered a road bordered by pine trees, on whose branches the local residents had hung the French tricolor flag, offering the couple "a quick glance of the picturesque."[3] Parisians followed details of the imperial trek in newspapers and illustrated journals, vicariously experiencing a journey through the French countryside that few had made themselves. Empress Eugénie summarized the experience thus: "This wasn't a voyage, but a triumphal march. . . . It was like living in a dream, in enchantment."[4]

One highlight of that journey was the couple's visit to the newly annexed Savoy region (Haute-Savoie), which, along with the port city of Nice, had been ceded to France in March of that year by the Kingdom of Sardinia, as outlined in the Treaty of Turin (1860).[5] The most visible symbol of the Savoy was the towering peak of Mont Blanc. At 15,781 feet above sea level, the great white mountain was still a Romantic symbol of sublime grandeur. In 1860 it also became a precious new jewel in the royal crown. To ascend the mountain was to encounter the most extreme forces of nature. The view from its summit also implied a kind of territorial declaration. As one reporter noted in *Le monde illustré*: "To dominate the delicious Chamonix Valley, and admire a marvelous spectacle, the traveler must climb the *Grands mulets*, isolated rocks two hundred cubits high, which form the obligatory stop for the night for intrepid tourists who confront fatigue from an ascension of

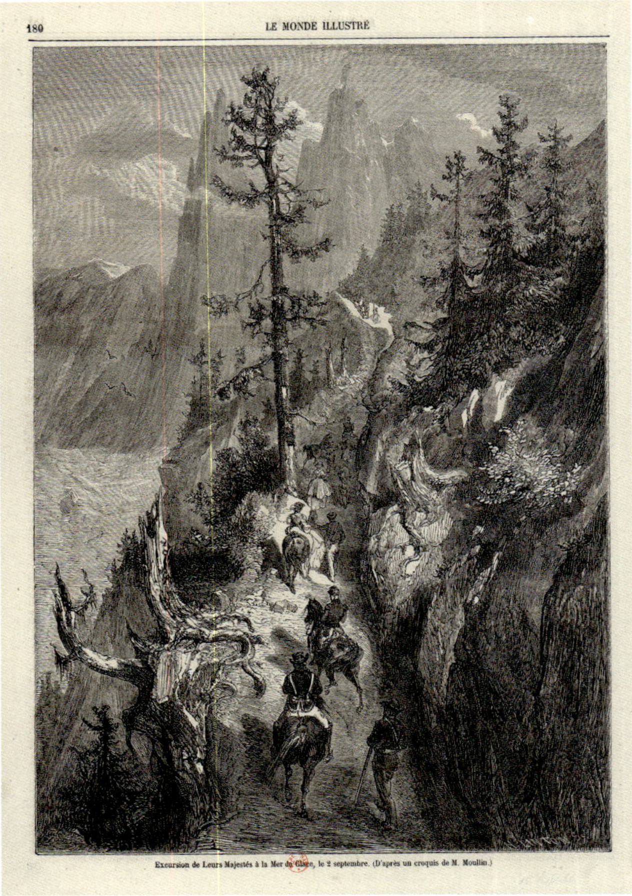

FIG. 22 Gustave Doré (illustrator), Henri Linton (engraver). *Excursion de Leurs Majestés à la Mer de Glace, le 2 Septembre*, from *Le monde illustré*, September 2, 1860

Mont Blanc. From the *Grands mulets*, the view extends over all the Chamonix Valley. . . . These grandiose panoramas move all hearts, and we do not doubt that the intrepid travelers . . . have been struck with admiration by the view of nature's grandeurs."[6]

Newspaper accounts of the imperial journey were often accompanied by wood engravings (fig. 22). While these illustrations—though often derived from photographs—conveyed some sense of the scenery, they failed to provide full evidentiary "proof" or the rich visual details that photography could achieve. It is not surprising, therefore, that the imperial entourage was accompanied for this mountainous leg of the journey by either one or both of the Bisson frères, the Paris-based photographic team consisting of the brothers Louis-Auguste Bisson and Auguste-Rosalie Bisson.[7] By 1860 the Bissons were well known for their Alpine views, having made several successful photographic ventures between 1854 and 1860.[8] The technical and aesthetic mastery of their large-format wet-collodion photographs had been broadly celebrated. As Ernest Lacan wrote in the April 1859 issue of *La lumière*: "The richness of details, the beauty of lines, the intelligent choice of light effects, the truth of aerial perspective, so difficult to render in photography, makes these prints among the most complete that have been produced."[9]

When the entourage arrived in Chamonix on September 2, 1860, at least one of the brothers (Auguste-Rosalie, or Bisson jeune) was with them.[10] The group attempted the ascent of Mont Blanc the following morning, embarking with cheers of "Vive l'empereur! Vive l'impératrice!" but inclement weather and the imperial couple's low tolerance for the extreme cold prevented them from reaching the summit. Auguste-Rosalie nonetheless succeeded in exposing several glass negatives during the climb. Albumen prints from these negatives, along with prints made from later ventures, were assembled into seven similar albums titled *Haute-Savoie, le Mont Blanc et ses glaciers: Souvenir du voyage de LL. MM. l'Empereur et l'Impératrice*, with the Bissons frères credited on the title page as "photographes de sa majesté l'Empereur" (fig. 23).[11]

Most of the album's photographs feature the region's glacial terrain without any overt reference to the imperial entourage.[12] In only one plate, *Pyramide de l'Impératrice (Mer de Glace)*, is a small French flag—an emblem of national identity and sovereignty—clearly evident on the Mer de Glace glacier (fig. 24). Even the presence of human figures is minimal in these views. People appear only once, in a photograph of the Bissons' climbing party: the figures are pictured as small, antlike forms silhouetted against a horizonless backdrop of jagged, glacial terrain. Though a few photographs depict the village of Chamonix, most concentrate on the region's natural topography: the glaciers, crevasses, and peaks that would have been familiar to climbers through earlier publications and firsthand scientific accounts.

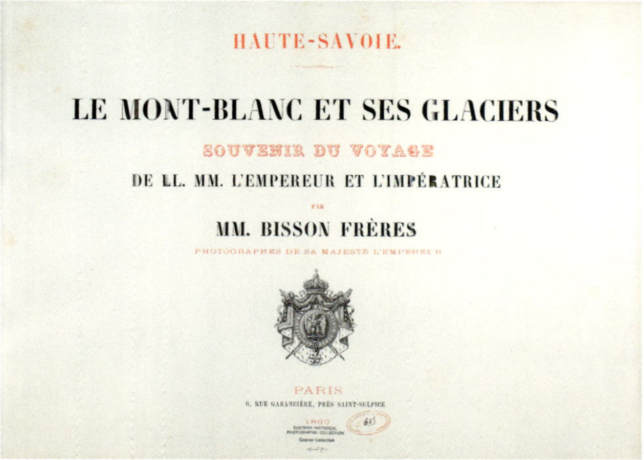
HAUTE-SAVOIE.

LE MONT-BLANC ET SES GLACIERS

SOUVENIR DU VOYAGE

DE LL. MM. L'EMPEREUR ET L'IMPÉRATRICE

PAR

MM. BISSON FRÈRES

PHOTOGRAPHES DE SA MAJESTÉ L'EMPEREUR

PARIS

8, RUE GARANCIÈRE, PRÈS SAINT-SULPICE

FIG. 23 Auguste-Rosalie Bisson and Louis-Auguste Bisson, *Haute-Savoie, le Mont Blanc et ses glaciers: Souvenir du voyage de LL. MM. l'Empereur et l'Impératrice* (Paris: Henri Plon, 1860), title page. George Eastman House, 81:1014:24

The photographs from the 1860 Savoy expedition increased the Bissons' fame and stature. However, it was in July 1861 that they truly made history. Auguste-Rosalie succeeded in reaching the summit of Mont Blanc with a party of twenty-five porters and the guide Auguste Balmat.[13] Bisson jeune made at least three known views. One of the most stunning of these photographs depicts a group of figures posed as if ascending toward the summit, standing next to a deep crevasse, carrying their ice picks, ropes, and other equipment (cat. 92). Auguste-Rosalie Bisson returned to the Alps in 1862 and again reached the summit, making six new negatives.[14]

The photographs of 1860 and 1861 secured for the Bisson frères an international reputation for unparalleled large-format Alpine views, placing them at the forefront of what was fast becoming a competitive tourist and collector market. These photographs, as well as the heroic travails of Auguste-Rosalie himself,[15] were praised in the photographic press. In 1861 prints were exhibited in Paris, Toulouse, and Marseille.[16] One 1861 panorama of Mont Blanc earned the Bissons a first-place medal at the 1862 London International Exhibition.[17] The brothers' photographs both benefited from and inspired a surge of tourism to the French-speaking Savoy region. It was an industry facilitated by a burgeoning rail system as well as the publication in 1860 of Auguste Marc's *Le voyage de leurs majestés impérials dans le sud-est de la France, en Corse et en Algérie* and Adolphe Joanne's guidebook to the Savoy. The Bissons no doubt capitalized on this public zeal, selling numerous prints through their Paris studio at 35, boulevard des Capucines.

Given the circumstances of the production and dissemination of these landscape views, the Bissons' photographs satisfied a number of interests: aesthetic, scientific, commercial, and imperial. Though ostensibly made for a market eager to obtain detailed visual documentation of the glacial and geologic features of the region, the striking photographs of unpeopled glacial fields, mountain peaks, icy crags, precipitous ravines, and raw rock formations also had an aesthetic appeal that harked back to Romantic notions of the sublime.[18] While the novelty of seeing imagery of a terrain never before photographed was highly lauded, the images stood in marked contrast to landscape photographs of industrial "progress" being produced by such contemporaries as Édouard Baldus, who was commissioned to make views of newly constructed rail stations and railway bridges (cat. 75, pls. 25, 27, 43; cat. 76, pls. 3, 52, 69). Additionally, by picturing a prized new territorial possession, the photographs celebrated the emperor's perceived political might and were thus seen as a valuable tool by the state.

In many ways, the Bissons' Alpine views provide an excellent case study for considering the myriad ways in which photography in mid-nineteenth-century France helped coalesce a burgeoning sense of national identity as read in the landscape, particularly during the 1850s and early 1860s. The Bissons were working during an especially rich and exciting time in the history of French photography. The technology for positive-negative paper photography (as opposed to daguerreotypy, which produced unique, highly detailed images on polished, silver-coated metal plates) had advanced to a point that a desirable degree of informational detail, greater portability, and reduced exposure time had been achieved, thus rendering photography easier to practice in the field. Amateurs and a select group of aesthetically minded professionals, who were drawn to the medium from a variety of disciplines, came together to share images and techniques and to establish a serious

FIG. 24 Auguste-Rosalie Bisson and Louis-Auguste Bisson, *Pyramide de l'Impératrice (Mer de Glace)*. Albumen print from collodion glass negative, 8⅞ × 15⅞ in. (22.5 × 39.3 cm). From *Haute-Savoie, le Mont Blanc et ses glaciers: Souvenir du voyage de LL. MM. l'Empereur et l'Impératrice* (Paris: Henri Plon, 1860), pl. 15. George Eastman House, 81:1014:24

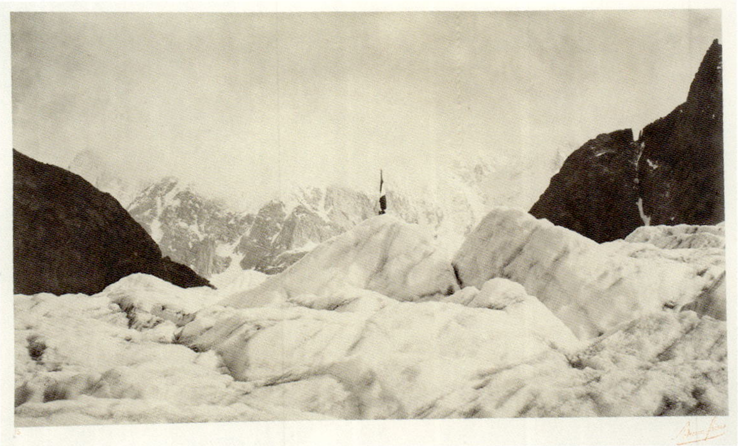

discourse for the advancement of the medium as both an art and a science. At a time when landscape paintings depicting French subjects were being regularly exhibited at the annual Salons, as Simon Kelly discusses in his essay in this volume, landscape photography was being produced under a variety of auspices and shown within photographic circles—most notably the Société héliographique, founded in 1851, and the longer-lived Société française de la photographie, founded in 1854. It was also gaining a foothold, if not exactly being granted a high art status, in international exhibition venues, such as the Great Exhibition of 1851 in London and the Exposition universelle of 1855 in Paris. During this period, state-funded and -supported initiatives were also an integral component of photographic practice, particularly during the 1850s before the policies of the Second Empire began to encounter a rising tide of opposition. This essay will broadly map the key practitioners and relevant subjects from this period, emphasizing throughout the connections between past aesthetic traditions and Second Empire politics and between art, science, industry, and commerce.

The golden age of nineteenth-century French photography roughly coincided with the growth of industry and centralization of state power under Napoléon III during the Second Empire. The emperor also evinced an interest in preserving the country's patrimony and creating a cohesive narrative of France's past (see the essay by Kelly in this volume). These forces, however, had developed well before either photography's invention in 1839 or Napoléon III's coup d'état in 1851 and official appointment as emperor the following year. As the urban historian M. Christine Boyer has suggested, the imperative to document and preserve France's artifacts and monuments to compile an archive of collective cultural memory began in the late eighteenth century. These impetuses evolved from the Enlightenment embrace of scientific classification, cataloguing, and indexing as sources of knowledge and from the desire to restore structures that had been damaged during the Revolution.[19] Numerous antiquarian and archaeological societies were formed during the 1820s and 1830s to identify, inventory, and preserve artifacts and monuments of aesthetic worth, and to guard against vandalism by monitoring their condition and assessing the need for restoration. Romantic writers such as Victor Hugo contributed to this preservationist spirit by regularly decrying acts of vandalism. His famous novel *Notre-Dame de Paris* (1831), in which the cathedral itself is a central character, brought attention to the building at a time when it had fallen into great disrepair. The architect Eugène-Emmanuel Viollet-le-Duc, who would become an important figure in overseeing restoration projects determined by the Commission des monuments historiques of 1837, initiated neo-Gothic "restorations" to Notre-Dame between 1845 and 1864. At the end of his campaign, the famed cathedral bore little trace of previous alterations or the deterioration and destruction that had occurred over the preceding six centuries.[20] The fervor for the historical preservation of monuments was no guarantee of objective historical authenticity.

Concurrently, there was a movement within intellectual circles to formulate the history of France, rather than continue a traditional focus on ancient Greece and Rome. Central to crafting this "new" history was the experience of traveling throughout France, to savor the country's diverse terrain, customs, languages, and monuments. Local and regional histories could then be woven into a rich, panoramic tapestry of collective national memory. Local and

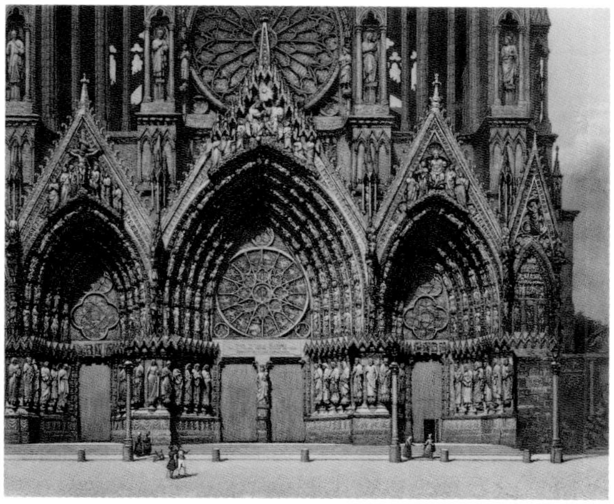

FIG. 25 Noël-Marie-Paymal Lerebours, *Portal de Notre-Dame de Reims*, ca. 1843. Aquatint and etching after a daguerreotype, 8¼ × 10¼ in. (21 × 26 cm). From *Excursions daguerriennes*, vol. 2. Spencer Museum of Art, The University of Kansas, 1979.0079

provincial structures, sites, and landscapes began to coalesce in a broader history of the French nation.[21]

By the time the invention of photography was officially announced in 1839, the climate was ripe for using the medium's fact-gathering potential to help shape a history of France, one in which the visualization of landscape played a significant role. An early example of using photography to document city scenes and landscapes, both in France and abroad, was the Excursions daguerriennes. This venture, which resulted in two bound volumes of engravings copied from daguerreotypes, was organized by Noël-Marie-Paymal Lerebours (fig. 25). Lerebours sent artists and journalists equipped with cameras all over the world to record various sites. The equipment was both fragile and heavy, however, and the daguerreotype, as a unique image, could not be reproduced in multiples except through photomechanical translations like aquatint or wood engraving. Due to patent restrictions on William Henry Fox Talbot's calotype process, positive-negative paper photography—which allowed for easier portability and mass reproduction—developed more slowly in France.[22] However, by 1847 Louis-Désiré Blanquart-Evrard successfully circumvented Talbot's patent and introduced the calotype in France. Blanquart-Evrard published his recipes, resulting in a surge of interest in the process on the part of French photographers. Technical improvements continued throughout the early 1850s. In 1850–51 Gustave Le Gray introduced the waxed paper negative process, which revolutionized the practice for photographers wishing to travel by eliminating the onerous step of preparing negatives on-site. In 1851 the wet-collodion glass-negative process, introduced by the English artist-photographer Frederick Scott Archer, further advanced the medium. Thus by 1851 and the dawning of the Second Empire, photographers were able to use larger-format cameras and lighter loads of equipment and perform simpler chemical operations in the field. Perhaps most important, they had the ability to make numerous original prints from a paper or glass negative, as distinguished from daguerreotypy. Photography had progressed to the point that its potential as a recording medium was both eminently viable and highly desirable.

The first significant state-funded photographic initiative in France was aimed at amassing an archive of photographic documentation of the nation's architectural patrimony. The Mission héliographique of 1851 was funded and organized by the Commission des monuments historiques and engaged the talents of five photographers: Édouard Baldus, Hippolyte Bayard, Henri Le Secq, Gustave Le Gray, and Auguste Mestral (Le Gray and Mestral worked largely as a team). Each photographer was given a loosely scripted itinerary and a list of monuments, determined from the regional inventories of restoration societies and the on-site visits of the inspector general of the Monuments historiques, Prosper Mérimée. All of the photographers, based in Paris, left for different parts of France. Baldus was sent to the central and southern part of the country, to the Loire and Rhone valleys; Bayard traveled north to Normandy; Le Secq went northeast to Champagne and Alsace; and Le Gray and Mestral headed south and west, toward Orléans and the valley of the Loire, among other areas. By the end of 1851 the photographers had traveled to more than half of France's *départements*.[23]

Though ostensibly produced to make accurate records for a historical archive, many of these images failed to conform to any single fact-gathering formula. As the art historian Eugenia Parry Janis asserts, some of the photographers—

Le Gray and Mestral in particular—at times seemed to follow their own artistic whims to create Romantic conceptions of these buildings as ruins in the landscape, akin to the precedent set in Baron Isidore Taylor and Charles Nodier's *Voyages pittoresques et romantiques dans l'ancienne France*.[24] As such, these views were often as much about the landscape settings as they were about the structures themselves. Anne de Modenard's definitive research on the Mission héliographique indicates that though the commission favored images that were made close enough to the subjects to ensure rich informational detail, it did not entirely dismiss photographs with unconventional compositions or vantage points. Further, while the original intention may have been to create an archive, the final collection was far from exhaustive. None of the five photographers adhered strictly to his checklist. There is no record that Bayard turned in his negatives or proofs.[25] Finally, there is the question of the work's ultimate fate. When the project came to an end, the commission selected 258 negatives and proof prints, possibly as early as May 1852, and stored them in drawers, without exhibiting or publishing them. This act did not go unnoticed by the critic Francis Wey and other members of the Société héliographique, who had a vested interest in the project.[26] Wey noted, with deep regret, that the failure to use and promote the photographs was a matter of national interest: "the photographers have been deprived of the publicity that they had expected, and our country will be unable to reap the rewards of the most beautiful work that had yet been produced."[27]

Despite the fact that the photographs were not made public, the significance of the Mission héliographique was profound. It gave many of those involved a degree of public stature they would not otherwise have achieved and offered a working model that could be used for future projects.[28] Baldus, perhaps more than any other photographer during this period, benefited from several state-funded projects as well as privately financed ventures that celebrated Second Empire ideals of industrial progress. The technical and aesthetic mastery of Baldus's photographs won him government support to record the architecture and monuments of Paris and the Roman remnants in the South of France.[29] Titled *Villes des France photographiées*, the portfolio consisted of twenty installments of at least three photographs each. These installments were delivered to the government from 1852 through 1856.[30] Realizing the popularity of such subjects, Baldus continued to develop his stock, traveling again to the Midi in 1853. As Malcolm Daniel notes in his formative research on Baldus, the photographer employed a tripartite artistic strategy (a general view, close-up details, and a more poetic interpretation) for each subject to satisfy as wide an audience as possible: architects, sculptors, and painters, each of whom had different interests.[31]

Baldus earned two major commissions in 1855. He was hired by the architect Hector Lefuel to document the construction of the new Louvre, Napoléon III's massive project to link the old Louvre and the Tuileries. The largest such commission given to a photographer at that time, it occupied Baldus for two years, during which time he produced more than two thousand photographs (cats. 6, 7).[32] Also in 1855, the wealthy industrialist Baron James de Rothschild, president of the Chemin de fer du Nord, commissioned Baldus to produce an album documenting the Northern Rail line from Boulogne to Paris, to be presented as a souvenir to Queen Victoria and Prince Albert on the occasion of their eagerly anticipated visit to France in August 1855.

The commission of this railway album reflected multiple intentions. Though certainly aimed at highlighting the significance of the Chemin de fer du Nord and the Second Empire's advances in rail travel, it also celebrated the new economic and political alliance between France and Great Britain. Additionally, while the album did include some views along the rail line that the queen and prince took from Boulogne to Paris, it was not meant to be a systematic survey of the sites the queen would have seen along the way. Nor was it meant to focus exclusively on newly constructed rail stations and the tracks themselves. Though these subjects do appear in the queen's album, they are interspersed with views of cathedrals, bridges, viaducts, and towns nestled in the landscape.[33]

In July 1861 Baldus was commissioned by the Conseil d'administration of the Southern Region to produce an album focusing on the southern Paris–Lyon–Méditerranée rail line (PLM; established in 1857). This work, comprising sixty-nine images, is even more majestic in scope, with a more masterfully composed sequence of images. Combining his own existing images with new views, Baldus crafted a journey that begins in the region of Lyon and passes through the ancient and medieval villages of Provence to the industrial port city of Marseille. The album ends in Toulon, on the Côte d'Azur, with a view of the newly constructed rail station (cat. 76, pl. 69).

To a greater degree than the Chemin de fer du Nord album, the album for the PLM celebrates the railway's achievement in connecting past with present, through the juxtaposition of old structures and new engineering feats (cat. 76, pls. 32, 33). The PLM rail line linked its northern terminus, Paris, with France's southernmost extremities. The resulting bonds between city and provinces were not merely geographic, industrial, or economic. Perhaps more than any other unifying feat in mid-nineteenth-century France, the development of a major rail system had a radical impact on reshaping notions of time, distance, and place, as people and goods traveled more rapidly and in greater numbers between Paris and the provinces. The PLM specifically joined the nation's capital to its largest and most important southern industrial port, Marseille, considered the gateway to the Orient and Africa. In the other direction, the line went directly to Paris, from which travelers could take the northern line to Boulogne, on the Normandy coast, facilitating trade with Great Britain and beyond.

Another important photographer in this period, Charles Nègre, produced a significant body of work reflecting the increased interest in France's architectural patrimony beyond the capital city. Nègre, a painter turned photographer from Grasse, set out in August 1852 through the Midi. Unlike Baldus, Nègre financed his own trip and marketed his work himself. He created more than three hundred photographs on this trip, choosing seventy-four for publication in his primary work, *Le Midi de la France, sites et monuments historiques photographiés par Charles Nègre, peintre*.[34] Though his portfolio was commercially unsuccessful, Nègre's work was praised by the critic Henri de Lacretelle, who wrote poetically about Nègre's vision of the Midi as it contrasted with the confusion of modern times: "The Midi is, in its most intimate corners, within these pages. . . . Traverse it. It consoles us in the fog of today."[35]

Nègre was also lauded for his genre and Paris street scenes, which he began as early as 1851. Some of these views, such as his market scenes, feature unposed groupings of street vendors and their customers outside the Hôtel de Ville (cat. 4). At the time, these works were considered remarkable technical achievements: "instantaneous" exposures of perhaps a second or less. De Lacretelle praised this seeming spontaneity in *La lumière*, noting: "This is life itself, and Nègre has stopped it with a marvel, in a hundredth of a second."[36] Made, at least in part, as studies for paintings, Nègre's street pictures speak to a broader modern artistic interest in the daily life of the capital city, at a moment when Paris was on the cusp of radical transformations at the hand of Baron Georges-Eugène Haussmann.

In many ways, the reconstruction of Paris was at the core of Napoléon III's political agenda. A centralized state required a more centralized capital city, one that symbolized modernity and efficiency. Haussmann, appointed prefect of the Seine in 1853, wholeheartedly upheld this policy. He worked closely with the emperor to transform the quasi-medieval center of old Paris, with its overcrowded and unsanitary living conditions, unnavigable and crime-riddled streets, into an open, hygienic, and orderly capital. Haussmann's tactics were aggressive and controversial, especially among the poor and working classes that were displaced as old neighborhoods were dismantled, particularly in the eastern part of the city. In his own words, Haussmann aimed to raze the "sordid, filthy, crowded houses which were, for the most part, but entry ways to misery and disease, and subjects of shame for a great country like France."[37]

Haussmann's ultimate plan was to transform Paris into an interconnected city of zones and to increase the efficiency of traffic circulation by broadening boulevards and linking them through existing monuments and *places*. To achieve this, he completely demolished the cramped and insalubrious neighborhoods filled with internal immigrants who had come to the city from the provinces seeking work and cheap rents.[38] In addition, Hausmann added more than four thousand acres of open park space and completely revamped the sewer and water supply systems.[39] In 1859 he extended the boundaries of Paris to incorporate the surrounding suburbs, thus doubling the city's area and increasing the number of inhabitants by two hundred thousand. This maneuver, which ran counter to the policies of all previous governments, brought an outlying population considered angry, dangerous, and sympathetic to insurrection under the city's authority and on to its tax rolls.[40] By 1870, when Haussman was forced aside, Paris was no longer a crowded, disjointed city of medieval streets and alleys that recalled "the torturous paths of insects in the heart of a piece of fruit."[41] It had become a modern metropolis, zoned according to function and class distinctions.

At some point during the early stages of Haussmann's process, and certainly by the early 1860s, Charles Marville was hired to record the city's transformations.[42] After early direction under Haussmann's prefecture of the Seine,

Marville's activities were likely overseen by the Service des Travaux historiques, a committee established in 1865, which was responsible for organizing and publishing a multivolume series titled *Histoire générale de Paris*. As the historian Marie de Thézy has determined, Marville seems to have worked systematically, according to Haussmann's plans, to photograph those areas slated for imminent demolition (cats. 13, 14).[43] He also documented Hausmann's new constructions—such as the place de l'Étoile (cat. 12)—and made an extensive series of the Bois de Boulogne (cat. 11). Marville's use of the medium suggests no distinction or preference for one aspect of Haussman's plan over another. The spaces and structures of old and new Paris alike are seen with a similar, detached vantage point, with neither receiving preferential aesthetic treatment.

Paris was a locus for artistic and commercial activity during this period. Virtually all of the major photographers were based in Paris, and the professionals were producing works to sell to urban audiences. This situation factored into a conception of nature and countryside that was in many ways defined by an urban sensibility. Bourgeois Parisians (especially) who could increasingly afford to travel via railway thought of nature as a healthy, rejuvenating escape, particularly after the cholera outbreak of 1849. They sought spiritual and physical renewal along the seaside or in the forest or found solace from urban chaos in the traditional ways of provincial towns. As Nicholas Green has argued in his study of Paris and its environs during the decades leading up to the Second Empire, urban bourgeois culture produced a particular vision of "natural nature, or *natura naturans*," that was informed less by the reality of deep traditions in French provincial culture (*la France profonde*) than by an idyllic vision. As Green notes, "such a vision of nature was deeply bound into the crystallization of a powerful metropolitan ideology."[44] Definitions and expectations of rural or unpopulated landscapes and the people who resided there were thus informed by a bourgeois urban sensibility and class biases. Photography, with its ability to project a sense of verisimilitude, was a convincing tool in helping both to shape these conceptions for popular consumption and/or to complicate them. For example, to create his figure studies of "peasant" girls, a photographer known only as Giraudon's artist (act. 1870s) posed models in traditional garb as if they were engaged in a variety of mundane activities—carrying a bundle of sticks, gathering hay, or hanging out laundry (cats. 63–65). He then sold them to painters—such as Jean-François Millet—who regularly incorporated such imagery in his canvases.

The Forest of Fontainebleau, located approximately thirty miles southeast of the capital city, was a popular destination for Parisians wishing to experience nature, despite the fact that by the 1860s, the forest was far from untamed. The forty-two thousand acres surrounding the sixteenth-century Renaissance palace at Fontainebleau were former royal hunting grounds, which had been placed under direct jurisdiction of the state in 1858.[45] In 1839 Claude-François Denecourt published his first guidebook to the forest, with variations and later editions continuing until his death in 1878. Denecourt's books were not simply guides to navigating the forest. Rather, they were part of his elaborate transformation of the place through the creation of extensive trails. Trees, rocks, and scenic vistas were assigned names, many referencing French historical figures such as Charlemagne and King Clovis (cat. 48). Aided enormously by the completion of a rail line from Paris in 1849, which stopped at Fontainebleau en route to Tonnerre, Denecourt fueled a thriving tourist industry by sensationalizing the natural landscape and at times even fabricating sites to illustrate a version of history culled more from imagination than fact.

The increase in tourism during the 1850s and 1860s offended those artists and writers who had gone to the forest's glades to experience its tranquil splendors a few decades earlier.[46] Another source of contention was the logging industry, which destroyed large swaths of old-growth trees and replanted new species—particularly pine, considered more suitable for building materials. The painter Théodore Rousseau was one of the most outspoken critics of this practice, petitioning the emperor himself in 1852 to preserve and protect the forest from such incursions. Typical for many of the Barbizon painters who had regularly visited or established permanent residency in Fontainebleau from the 1830s through the 1850s, Rousseau conceived of the forest as a sanctuary, the antithesis of and an antidote to modern urban life.[47]

Of the many photographers who made pictures in Fontainebleau, none was more dedicated to exploring its varied natural topography than Eugène Cuvelier. Cuvelier's oeuvre is composed almost entirely of landscape views in and around the village of Barbizon, on the northwest edge of the forest. Born in Arras, Cuvelier learned the art of photography from his father, Adalbert, a successful merchant

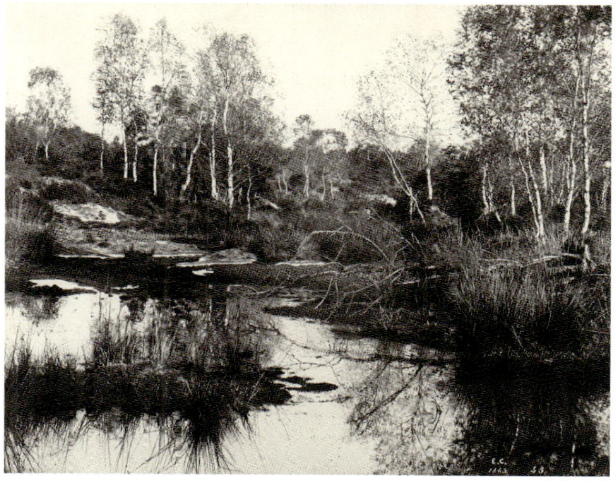

FIG. 26 Eugène Cuvelier, *Franchard*, 1863. Albumen print from collodion glass negative. 8 × 10⅜ in. (20.3 × 26.4 cm). The Nelson-Atkins Museum of Art, Kansas City, Missouri, Gift of the Hall Family Foundation, 2008.13.7

as well as a painter and accomplished amateur photographer. The young Cuvelier had trained as a painter with Constant Dutilleux and through him met such artists as Jean-Baptiste-Camille Corot, Charles-François Daubigny, Paul Huet, Millet, and Rousseau.[48]

Cuvelier's landscape photographs are diverse in technique and composition. He crafted exquisite prints in limited quantities, reflecting an amateur's fascination with photographic materials and an interest in artistic experimentation for its own sake. His intimate compositions explore the range of the forest's terrain, from its gnarled oak trees and the thick foliage of the Bas-Bréau, to the rocky gorges of Franchard and Apremont, and the spare, otherworldly beauty of the boulders at Macherin (fig. 26; cats. 46–48). Though figures and traces of the roads and hundreds of trails that tourists had begun to frequent are occasionally included, most of his images present the forest as a refuge, focusing on the overall experience of the place. Cuvelier's forest, like Rousseau's (cat. 40), is a moody, evocative place, shaped by light and shadow and far removed from urban hustle and bustle.

Gustave Le Gray first made photographs in Fontainebleau in 1849, recording the forest's natural drama on regular excursions throughout the 1850s. His earliest prints were made using his waxed paper negative process.[49] He later made a series of albumen prints that focused on the magnificence of the forest's old trees, particularly the venerated oaks, which had stood on the grounds for centuries. France's national tree, the oak was seen as a sacred, stalwart species, a silent witness to the passage of time, from the age of the Gauls to the present day. In one stunning photograph of 1856, Le Gray features a great hollow oak, splayed open with branches curving upward in a corona of foliage (cat. 44).[50] He also included an element of artistic self-reflexivity: visible in the left background is the cart Le Gray used to transport his equipment, giving a nod to the photographer's presence in the scene. His view of a semi-uprooted beech tree (cat. 45), another of the forest's oldest and most admired species, is an unusual and striking composition. Clearly attracted by the drama of this singular subject, Le Gray took advantage of the intense sunlight to create bold contrasts between highlights and shadows, especially where the tree has begun to separate from the forest floor. The tension inherent in this single recorded moment—between the tree's longevity and its apparently imminent demise—alludes to a host of metaphors pertinent to the artistic depiction of the forest. This picture invites no vicarious escape into the forest's verdant depths. Rather, it arrests the viewer with a startling record of change, whether the result of natural forces or human intervention.

The tourist trade in Fontainebleau encouraged the marketing of nature for urban visitors in the decades leading up to and continuing throughout the Second Empire. The photographs by Cuvelier and Le Gray circulated very differently, however, within Parisian circles. Though both men exhibited their Fontainebleau photographs at the annual exhibitions of the Société française de la photographie, of which they were members, Cuvelier was always considered an artistic amateur. He exhibited only occasionally, sharing photographs within a close circle of friends, including, likely, Corot, who may well have used Cuvelier's photographs as inspiration for some of his paintings.[51] In contrast, Le Gray—also trained as a painter, in the studio of Paul Delaroche—was a professional who, by 1855, had established a studio at 35, boulevard des Capucines. Janis has suggested that Le Gray was, in fact, making images in Fontainebleau

FIG. 27 Olympe Aguado, *Crossroads in the Bois de Boulogne*, ca. 1856. Albumen or coated salt print from paper negative, 11³⁄₁₆ × 15¾ in. (28.4 × 40 cm). The Nelson-Atkins Museum of Art, Kansas City, Missouri, Gift of the Hall Family Foundation, 2008.25.1

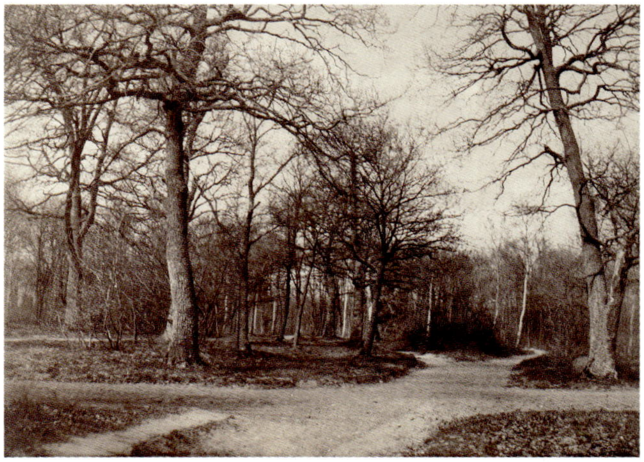

with the intention of selling them to a Parisian public well versed in Denecourt's enterprise.[52] Although his precise commercial mechanisms are not known, Le Gray would no doubt have tried to market his photographs beyond the annual exhibition venues of the photography societies or such major public attractions as the 1855 Exposition universelle in Paris. As Sylvie Aubenas has asserted, Le Gray likely sold prints from his studio and also offered them on consignment to specialized print sellers.[53]

Amateur photographers—those who did not own or operate a commercial studio—were vital to this history of early French landscape photography. Often from the upper classes, they had the resources to pursue photography as an avocation. These men often had distinguished backgrounds in art and science and were not mere hobbyists. They had a fervent desire to advance the medium's technical aspects and its scientific and documentary capacities and to establish its credentials as an art form. They were founding members of the nation's two most significant photography societies: the Société héliographique and the Société française de la photographie (SFP). Through annual exhibitions, which were extensively reviewed in *La lumière* and the *Bulletin* (the organs of the Société héliographique and the SFP, respectively),[54] these amateurs created some of the most accomplished photographs of the 1850s and 1860s.[55]

Several photographers, including Henri Le Secq, Charles Nègre, Olympe Aguado, and Joseph Vigier, learned the photographic process from Le Gray, who from 1850 to 1855 taught from his studio in the barrière de Clichy. Le Secq and Nègre, like Le Gray, had trained as painters, and Le Secq, like Aguado and Vigier, came from privileged backgrounds. Each became adept calotypists, preferring the paper negative for its painterly, suggestive rendition of texture, light, and shadow (fig. 27). The light weight of paper made this technique, at least through the mid-1850s, more desirable than glass for photographers working in the field. Some, like Le Secq, worked almost exclusively with the calotype, abandoning photography completely about 1860 rather than taking up the newly dominant wet-collodion glass method. Others oscillated between paper and glass negatives. The painter André Giroux, who practiced photography for about ten years beginning about 1850, used both techniques, often focusing on agrarian subjects and vernacular architecture in the center of France (cat. 55). He systematically retouched his negatives—particularly the skies—with ink washes and other drawing techniques.

Given Le Gray's influence, it is not surprising that many of his students adopted a painterly approach, choosing the calotype technique to convey the textures and atmosphere of provincial subjects. Often, their landscapes included the kinds of picturesque motifs—rural cottages with thatched roofs, old bridges, pastoral river scenes—that Barbizon painters regularly depicted (cats. 50, 56). Some, like Le Secq, whose mastery of the calotype process was virtually unparalleled, pushed the process's ability to sculpt form through a sophisticated use of chiaroscuro. This effect is particularly evident in a rare, large-format view of a troglodyte dwelling, one of a series he took in France's Loire valley region (cat. 69). The deep recess of the building's arched entranceway is plunged into complete blackness, adding an unusual element of mystery to this vernacular structure. This subject would also have been of historical interest to Le Secq, only two years after he completed his Mission héliographique work. The term *troglodyte*, which originally meant "cave dweller," in the fifteenth century came to refer to a group of political activists who lived underground to avoid taxation,

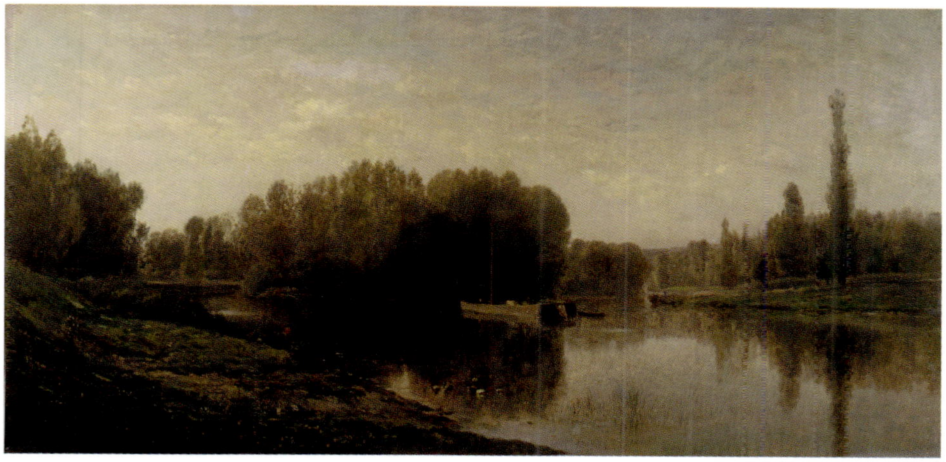

FIG. 28 Charles-François Daubigny, *Banks of the Oise*, 1859. Oil on canvas, 35½ × 71⅝ in. (90 × 182 cm). Musée des beaux-arts, Bordeaux, France

often in limestone dwellings that had been carved out during the Middle Ages. In both its materiality and subject matter, Le Secq's photograph looks back in time, celebrating past traditions and regional French histories rather than embracing modern processes or architectural subjects.

While many early amateurs (and professionals) made landscape photographs that presented an idyllic, preindustrial view of rural life, the industrialized landscape was a rarer subject. Baldus's railway images—as well as Adolphe Terris's views of Marseille (cats. 22, 23)—serve as examples. Factories, too, appear in photographs, though to a much lesser degree. In the early 1850s Le Gray made two views of a factory at Terre-Noire, in southeastern France, near Saint-Étienne (cat. 80).[56] Though little is known about the factory itself or the circumstances surrounding Le Gray's decision to photograph it (it may well have been a commission), the image pictures the kind of industrial subject that would figure more regularly in the significantly later paintings of Camille Pissarro and Claude Monet (cats. 82–84, 87). Another early amateur photographer of industrial subjects was the chemist Henri-Victor Regnault, who made several views of the buildings and grounds of the Manufacture impériale de Sèvres, where he served as director (cat. 81). Though no direct correlations can be drawn between these photographs and the Impressionists, the fact that such images existed in the early 1850s suggests that among early practitioners rural landscape imagery was not exclusively picturesque, nor did it always hark back to Romantic precedents. Instead, images such as these presented a more complicated notion of landscape, as an industrialized, human-altered terrain.

Though photography was often hailed as being true to nature, some of the most celebrated landscape photographs were produced using overt manipulations to emulate painterly effects. Le Gray was a master of this practice, as was Camille Silvy. They often combined and altered negatives to ensure the desired atmospheric effects in both sky and land. Silvy's *River Scene* of 1858 (cat. 57), commended by one critic as "one of the finest landscapes that we ever remember to have seen reproduced by photography," was compared to seventeenth-century Dutch landscape painting.[57] As Mark Haworth-Booth has noted, *River Scene* also garnered an unintended political interpretation from one reviewer who wrote that the picture's "dark thundercloud, ready to burst . . . yet [is] clear and transparent in the shadows. Is this a true portrait of that country? Is it a method of speaking out, yet escaping the fate of a political martyr?"[58] Silvy's composition, with its open foreground, dramatic reflections, and tree-lined shores, recalls Daubigny's landscapes of the Oise River, one of which—*Banks of the Oise*—drew great critical attention at the Salon of 1859 (fig. 28).[59] Silvy composed his scene such that the river recedes from an expansive foreground into the background, inviting the viewer—who might identify with the assorted figures along the riverbank—into the space. If there were political or class critiques implicit in the composition or in the choice of figures depicted, as some have suggested, these intentions were well hidden. Silvy's aim was high art, and he unabashedly employed techniques to assure the painterly effects that a "straight" photograph could not at that time achieve on its own.[60] Only a short train ride away from Paris, this actual river, the Huisne, was geographically accessible and aesthetically alluring to Parisians eager to consume such sanguine visions of nature. Though illusory, the photograph's naturalistic details and connection to an actual location would surely have rendered it all the more appealing for such

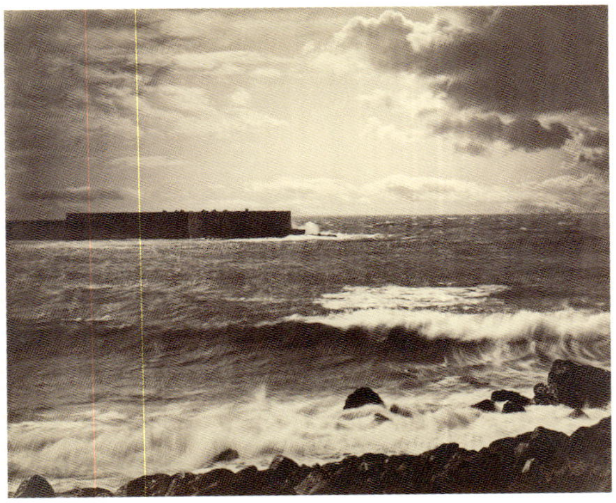

FIG. 29 Gustave Le Gray, *The Great Wave, Sète*, ca. 1857. Albumen print from collodion glass negative, 13½ × 16½ in. (34.3 × 41.9 cm). The J. Paul Getty Museum, 84.XM.637.1

urban audiences who would have been familiar with these kinds of pastoral river scenes shown regularly in the annual painting Salons.

The most commercially, technically, and aesthetically successful photographs of the mid-1850s—and, arguably, of the entire nineteenth century—were the seascapes of Gustave Le Gray. As was the case with Silvy's later *River Scene*, English audiences were the first to view Le Gray's *Brig upon the Water*, the most widely disseminated of his marine views (cat. 103). It was first shown at a private meeting of the Photographic Society of London in November 1856, causing a great buzz within British photographic circles. Its appearance in Paris early the following year excited similar commentary and acclaim. Though *Brig upon the Water* itself was ostensibly composed from one negative, several of his other seascapes were produced using multiple negatives to allow both the sky and foreground areas to be rendered with equal aesthetic force. This was an extremely difficult feat to achieve, let alone master, given the technical limitations of the medium, which rarely allowed even exposures of sea (or landscape) and sky. Le Gray further enhanced his reputation in 1857, on a trip to the Mediterranean coast, where he produced two so-called instantaneous pictures of waves breaking along the rocky shoreline at Sète, *The Breaking Wave* (cat. 108) and *The Great Wave, Sète* (fig. 29). The latter in particular was celebrated for its unprecedented recording of a wave at the moment it unfurls. Of all the seascapes Le Gray produced between 1856 and 1858, these two photographs, along with *Brig upon the Water*, firmly established the medium as a form of high art, on a level with painting. Their enormous critical and commercial success thus set a new standard for the artistic potential of landscape photography while establishing Le Gray's public renown.

Le Gray's seascapes, much like the Bissons' views of Mont Blanc, represent the pinnacle of careers cemented by, if not exclusively dependent on, unprecedented achievements in landscape photography in mid-nineteenth-century France. Both bodies of work reflect the influence of artistic precedents, commercial desires, and imperial interests. If the spare, glacial summit of Mont Blanc and the vast waters of the Atlantic Ocean or Mediterranean Sea represented the awesome grandeur of the nation's natural geographic extremes, the photographs also suggested, through their technical ability to record those limits and their dissemination en masse, a capacity to claim sublime territory as the nation's own. There are, of course, many reasons that Napoléon III might have taken delight in looking down at the Chamonix Valley from Mont Blanc or gazing out to sea as he sailed the Mediterranean toward the French territories of Corsica and Algiers. But given his voracious (and ultimately disastrous) imperialist appetite, one cannot help but speculate that the emperor might have been just as interested in envisioning territories beyond the horizons of these stunning photographs as he was delighting in what had already been claimed by the camera.

Despite the great success of their photographs, neither Le Gray nor the Bisson frères faced bright financial futures. Le Gray's demise was swift and tragic. Forced to close his lavish studio at 35, boulevard des Capucines in February 1860 after his financial backers dissolved the firm Le Gray et Cie, Le Gray set sail with the writer Alexandre Dumas in May of that year. Hopelessly indebted, he left France as a fugitive, abandoning his wife and two children in Marseille, eventually settling in Egypt. Though he continued to photograph, setting up a studio in Alexandria, Le Gray never returned to France. The Bissons, though in far better straits

FIG. 30 Félix Nadar, *Nadar's Studio, 35, boulevard des Capucines*, ca. 1850. Bibliothèque nationale de France

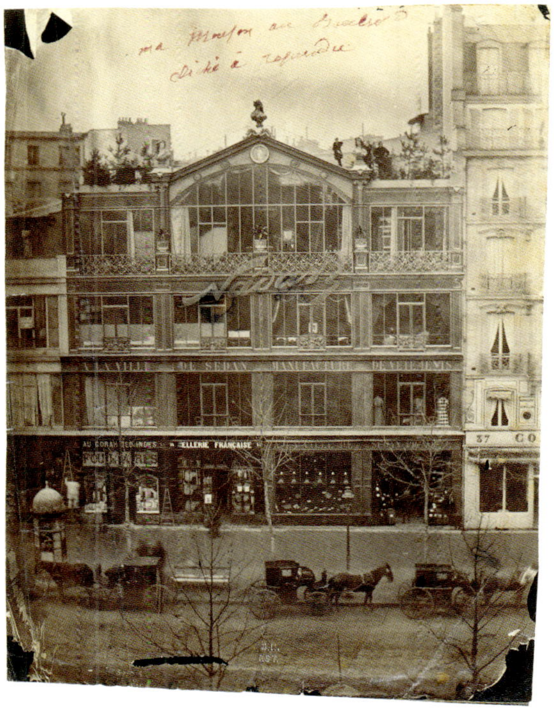

than their colleague, dissolved their business in 1864, just four years after their momentous scaling of Mont Blanc. Even Baldus, who had firmly established himself as a favorite with the state, filed for bankruptcy in 1887. These artistic professionals, who took pride in their expertly crafted, large-format views and who had great success during the 1850s, stood little chance against the onslaught of cartes de visite, stereographic views, and *cartes postales* that were disseminating in vaster and far more affordable quantities the kinds of photographs eagerly sought by the expanding middle class.[61] The artistic significance of amateurs was also on the wane by 1860. Though some, like Cuvelier, continued to produce and exhibit landscapes throughout the early part of that decade, many simply pursued other interests. For all intents and purposes, the golden age of French photography and the flourishing of landscape views produced for artistic and state-sponsored uses came to a close by the 1860s.

In April 1860, precisely two months after Le Gray's firm was dissolved and four years before the Bissons closed their studio, the portrait photographer Nadar signed a twenty-three-year lease for his studio at 35, boulevard des Capucines (fig. 30). His friend the painter Claude Monet went to his studio in 1873, looking for a venue for the first Impressionist exhibition, which took place there April 15–May 15, 1874. Monet painted two canvases from Nadar's studio, looking down on the bustling boulevard des Capucines toward the place de l'Opéra, one of Paris's newly transformed squares (cat. 15, fig. 54).[62] Second Empire France, which ended in 1871 with France's humiliating defeat in the Franco-Prussian War, was no more, and Le Gray and the Bissons had, quite literally, long since left the building. However, one cannot help but imagine the specter of their glorious contributions to French landscape imagery lingering in memory, as a valuable precursor to what would become the Impressionist revolution.

1. This summation is indebted to Robin Louis Thorne Ptacek, "Bisson frères: Two Pioneers of Photography" (PhD diss., University of California, Santa Barbara, 1989), esp. 88–93. As Ptacek notes, the imperial entourage traveled from Paris to Lyon, to Annecy, and then to Chamonix and Mont Blanc in the recently annexed Savoy region. They continued through Provence to Nice and Villefranche (also recently acquired) and then sailed on the imperial yacht to Corsica. Their final destination, before returning to Paris, was Algeria, which had become, under the Second Empire, an official French *département*. By September 20 the entourage was back on the French mainland, in the city of Perpignan near the Pyrenees and the Franco-Spanish border. By September 21 the emperor and empress had returned to the palace of Saint-Cloud.

2. See Maurice Paléologue, *Les entretiens de l'Impératrice Eugénie* (Paris: Librairie Plon, 1923), 19–21.

3. Maxime Vauvert, "Voyage de L.L. M.M. l'empereur et l'impératrice," *Le monde illustré*, September 8, 1860, 158: "La route bordée par une range de sapins, aux branches desquels les habitants du bourg avaient suspendu des drapeaux tricolors, offrait un coup d'oeil des plus pittoresques."

4. Quoted in Paléologue, *Les entretiens de l'Impératrice Eugénie*, 19: "Ce ne fut pas un voyage, mais une marche triomphale . . . il semblait vivre dans un rêve, dans un enchantement."

5. The Treaty of Turin, between France and the Kingdom of Sardinia (Piedmont), ceded Savoy and Nice to France in exchange for France's cooperation in the effort to liberate Lombardy and the Veneto from Austrian oppression.

6. Vauvert, in *Le monde illustré*, 158: "Pour dominer la délicieuse vallée de Chamounix, et admirer un merveilleux spectacle, le voyageur doit monter aux *Grands mulets*, rochers isolés, haut de deux cents coudées, et qui forment la halte de nuit obligée pour les touristes intrépides qui affrontent les fatigues d'une ascension au Mont-Blanc. Des Grands mulets, la vue sétend sur toute la vallée de Chamounix. . . . Ces panoramas grandioses émeuvent tous les cœurs, et nous ne doutons pas que les augustes voyageurs . . . n'aient été frappés d'admirations à la vue de ces grandeurs de la nature."

7. It is not known for certain how the Bissons came to the attention of the emperor. Napoléon and the empress Eugénie had visited the Bissons' studio in December 1856, on the one-year anniversary of the opening of their studio at 35, boulevard des Capucines. The Bissons may have also won imperial favor in the summer of 1859, during the Franco-Italian campaign against Austria, when they photographically reproduced maps of the Lombardy-Venice area, which significantly aided the French soldiers. See Ptacek, "Bisson frères," 79. For more on the Bissons' involvement with map reproduction, see "Nouvelle application de la photographie," *La lumière*, June 4, 1859, 90; and "Reproduction des cartes géographiques par la photographie par MM. Bisson frères," *Revue photographique* 3 (1859): 182–83.

8. Auguste-Rosalie Bisson made his first photograph of the Alps—which he called an *Étude de montagne*—in June 1854. In 1855, with the financial assistance of the Bissons' patron, the wealthy Mulhouse textile manufacturer Daniel Dollfus-Ausset, Bisson jeune traveled to the Swiss Alps to photograph the aftereffects of a recent earthquake. Auguste-Rosalie made subsequent trips to the region in 1858 and 1859. See Milan Chlumsky, "Une victoire des Bisson: La conquête des Alps," in *Les frères Bisson photographes de flèche en cime, 1840–1870*, exh. cat. (Paris: Bibliothèque Nationale de France; Essen: Museum Folkwang, 1999), 159–62.

9. Ernest Lacan, "Revue photographique," *La lumière*, April 2, 1859, 55: "La richesse de des détails, la beauté des lignes, le choix intelligent des effets de lumière, la vérité de la perspective aérienne, si difficile à rendre en photographie, mettent ces épreuves au rang des plus complètes qui aient été produites." Lacan was referring specifically to prints made during a trip to the region in the summer of 1858.

10. It is known that Auguste-Rosalie was with the imperial couple on this leg of the journey, whereas Louis-Auguste's presence is unconfirmed. While an album bearing the stamp of imperial approval was produced, it is likely that it was a self-generated venture aimed at making a profit. Auguste-Rosalie had proposed a souvenir album consisting of twelve or twenty-four prints before the 1860 ascent, and on March 23, 1861, the periodical *L'illustration* announced the availability of a souvenir album by the Bissons. See Chlumsky, "Une victoire des Bisson," 163; and http://expositions.bnf.fr/napol/grand/054.htm.

11. Among the individuals who received an album were Victor Emmanuel II (the king of Sardinia and later of Italy), Eugène-Emmanuel Viollet-le-Duc, and the photographer Louis-Alphonse Davanne. The state ordered three copies.

12. This assessment is based on the Haute-Savoie albums in the collections of the George Eastman House, Rochester, New York, and the Bibliothèque nationale de France, Paris. Chlumsky's research has shown ("Une victoire des Bisson," 169n37) that though Napoléon and Eugénie do not appear in the photographs included in the albums, at least one photograph (Bibliothèque nationale de France) was taken of the imperial couple with the entourage during this venture.

13. Auguste Balmat was a direct descendant of Jacques Balmat, the first man credited with having reached Mont Blanc's summit in 1786, along with Michel-Gabriel Paccard. For a full account of Auguste-Rosalie's ascent, see "Ascension de Mont-Blanc par un photograph," *Revue photographique* 6 (1861): 249–52.

14. Ptacek, "Bisson frères," 102; and Chlumsky, "Une victoire des Bisson," 166.

15. The travails included high winds, heavy snows, the threat of avalanche and frostbite, and the immense difficulties of coating glass plates in freezing temperatures. See *Revue photographique* 6 (1861): 249–52.

16. *Les frères Bisson photographes de flèche en cime*, 196–97.

17. Ibid., 197.

18. Such conceptions are evident in Baron Isidore Taylor and Charles Nodier's *Voyages pittoresque et romantiques dans l'ancienne France* and as described in literary accounts by Jean-Jacques Rousseau (*La nouvelle Héloïse*, 1761) and Percy Bysshe Shelly (*Mont Blanc*, 1817). Romantic travel writing also perpetuated these notions: François-René de Chateaubriand's *Voyage au Mont Blanc, et réflexion sur les paysages de montagne* (1805) and Victor Hugo's *Voyages aux Alpes* (1829) were both widely read accounts of the authors' travels in the region.

19. This research is indebted to M. Christine Boyer's essay "La Mission Héliographique: Architectural Photography, Collective Memory and the Patrimony of France, 1851," in *Picturing Place: Photography and the Geographical Imagination*, ed. Joan M. Schwartz and James R. Ryan (London: I. B. Tauris, 2003), 21–54.

20. See Daniel D. Reiff, "Viollet-le-Duc and Historic Restoration: The West Portals of Notre-Dame," *Journal of the Society of Architectural Historians* 30, no. 1 (March 1971): 17–30.

21. After 1789 the state assumed responsibility for protecting church possessions and the properties of those aristocrats and royalty that had been confiscated. The French naturalist and antiquarian Aubin-Louis Millin is credited with first articulating the expression "historic monuments" in 1790, when describing his collection of national antiquities. See André Chastel, "The Notion of Patrimony," in *Rethinking France: Les lieux de mémoire*, ed. Pierre Nora, vol. 3, *Legacies* (Chicago: University of Chicago Press, 1992), 19.

22. For a detailed account of the often heated exchanges between Talbot and the French photographic community during this period, see Paul-Louis Roubert, "Cendrillon ranimée: Émergence de la photographie sur papier en France," in Sylvie Aubenas and Paul-Louis Roubert, *Primitifs de la photographie: Le calotype en France, 1843–1860*, exh. cat. (Paris: Gallimard; Bibliothèque Nationale de France, 2010), 36–51.

23. Boyer, "La Mission Héliographique," 44.

24. See Anne de Modenard, *La Mission héliographique: Cinq photographes parcourent la France en 1851* (Paris: Centre des Monuments Nationaux; Monum, Éditions du Patrimoine, 2002), 205. De Modenard notes that no documentation exists to verify exactly when or how the selection was made, though there are references in *La lumière* that suggest that by May 22 the work of at least one of the photographers, Le Secq, had been selected by the commission. André Jammes and Eugenia Parry Janis, *The Art of French Calotype with a Critical Dictionary of Photographers, 1845–1870* (Princeton: Princeton University Press, 1983), 60–66.

25. De Modenard, *La Mission héliographique*, 30.

26. The Mission héliographique and the Société héliographique were intimately connected. Key society members—Léon de Laborde and Prosper Mérimée—played a role in the mission, and all five of the photographers chosen for the mission were society members. *La lumière* also gave extensive coverage to the mission.

27. Francis Wey, "Comment le soleil est devenu peintre," *Musée des familles*, July 20, 1853, 291–98; quoted in Sylvie Aubenas, *Gustave Le Gray, 1820–1884*, exh. cat. (Los Angeles: J. Paul Getty Museum, 2002), 66: "Le public est donc privé de ces estampes que chacun se disputerait; les photographes sont frustrés de la publicité qu'ils avaient espérée, et notre pays ne peut se faire honneur de la plus belle oeuvre qui se soit produite jusqu'ici. Nous avions demandé davantage et nous espérions mieux."

28. De Modenard, *La Mission héliographique*, 208–13.

29. Ibid., 210. Baldus won rapid approval from the Ministry of the Interior, which underwrote twenty copies of this work in advance for a total of twelve thousand francs.

30. Malcolm Daniel, *The Photographs of Édouard Baldus*, exh. cat. (New York: Metropolitan Museum of Art; Montreal: Canadian Centre for Architecture, 1994), 28.

31. Ibid., 32.

32. Ibid., 56–57.

33. At Rothschild's request, the Nord album was later produced, likely about 1859–60, in an edition of twenty-five, meant to be given to the company's board of directors. As Malcolm Daniel notes, these later editions were related to the queen's album and share approximately two-thirds of the same photographs. They differ, however, in terms of the total number of images, the attribution of additional photographs, and the addition of images depicting a second, newer branch of the rail line from Saint-Denis to Creil (via Chantilly). Daniel speculates that Baldus did not assemble the albums; rather, one of Rothschild's agents may have done so, selecting images from a wider pool of photographers. See Daniel, "Édouard-Denis Baldus and the Chemin de Fer du Nord Albums," *Image* 35, nos. 3–4 (Fall–Winter 1992): 3–38.

34. Aubenas and Roubert, *Primitifs de la photographie*, 297.

35. Henri de Lacretelle, "Albums photographiques," *La lumière* 3 (February 12, 1853): 26: "Le Midi est, par ses coins les plus intimes, dans ces pages. . . . Parcourons-le. Il nous consolera du brouillard d'aujourd'hui."

36. *La lumière* 2, no. 28 (February 28, 1852): 37: "C'est la vie elle-même, et M. Nègre l'a arrêtée par un prodige, dans un centième de seconde." De Lacretelle's estimate of the exposure time cannot have been accurate.

37. Haussman, as translated and quoted in David P. Jordan, *Transforming Paris: The Life and Labors of Baron Haussmann* (Chicago: University of Chicago Press, 1995), 220.

38. Between 1800 and 1850, the population within the old city walls had doubled; outside the city walls, it had quadrupled. See Jordan, Transforming Paris, 95.

39. This achievement won Haussmann worldwide acclaim, and by 1867 the administration gave public tours to such dignitaries as the Russian czar and the king of Portugal. See ibid., 276.

40. Ibid., 285–86.

41. From Charles Merruau, *Souvenirs de l'Hôtel de Ville de Paris (1848–1852)*; translated and quoted in Jordan, *Transforming Paris*, 93.

42. The exact dates of Marville's employ are unknown. Many city records from this period, housed in the Hôtel de Ville, were destroyed in a fire set by Communards during the Commune in 1871, which completely gutted the building's interior.

43. Marie de Thézy, *Charles Marville: Photographs of Paris, 1852–1878* (New York: Alliance Française, 1981), 67.

44. Nicholas Green, *The Spectacle of Nature: Landscape and Bourgeois Culture in Nineteenth-Century France* (Manchester: Manchester University Press, 1990), 11.

45. For an excellent and thorough discussion of the literary, artistic, and political history and geology of the forest, see Kimberly Jones, "Landscapes, Legends, Souvenirs, Fantasies: The Forest of Fontainebleau in the Nineteenth Century," in Kimberly Jones et al., *In the Forest of Fontainebleau: Painters and Photographers from Corot to Monet*, exh. cat. (Washington, D.C.: National Gallery of Art, 2008), 4–27.

46. Millet eventually set up permanent residence there, in 1849, and by 1856 Rousseau had acquired a summer cottage, though always keeping studios and apartments in Paris. See Green, *Spectacle of Nature*, 117–18.

47. Rousseau first visited the forest in 1820 and in 1847 began renting a house in Barbizon, which would become his residence when not in Paris. See chronology in Jones et al., *In the Forest of Fontainebleau*, 185; Green, *Spectacle of Nature*, 117–18.

48. On March 7, 1859, Eugène Cuvelier married Louise Ganne, the daughter of an enterprising innkeeper who had established the Auberge Ganne in the mid-1820s to accommodate the influx of artists and students who had begun to come to the forest to sketch and paint. This union brought the young artist-photographer into more frequent contact with these artists, whose paintings were undoubtedly an influence on his own aesthetic. Both Corot and Rousseau were witnesses to the marriage.

49. As Aubenas has determined (*Gustave Le Gray*, 46), Le Gray was probably not working alone but in the company of others, including one of his students, the American-born, Paris-based John Beasley Greene, who likely joined him on a trip in 1852.

50. Sarah Kennel proposes that this oak may have been La Reine Blanche (The White Queen), which was popular with artists who often stowed easels and other equipment inside the tree's hollow. See Kennel, "An Infinite Museum: Photography in the Forest of Fontainebleau," in Jones et al., *In the Forest of Fontainebleau*, 158.

51. Malcolm Daniel, *Eugène Cuvelier: Photographer in the Circle of Corot*, exh. cat. (New York: Metropolitan Museum of Art, 1996), 14.

52. Eugenia Parry Janis, *The Photography of Gustave Le Gray*, exh. cat. (Chicago: Art Institute of Chicago; University of Chicago Press, 1987), 47.

53. Aubenas, *Gustave Le Gray*, 56.

54. The writer and critic Ernest Lacan played a central role in shaping early debates about photography as they appeared in the pages of *La lumière* and other significant photography journals. Lacan was a regular contributor throughout the 1850s and served as editor in chief. In 1860 he left *La lumière* because of disagreements with its publisher, Alexis Gaudin, but continued to write for *Le moniteur de photographie*, another journal he cofounded with the German publisher Paul Liesegang. Lacan also reviewed photography when it was shown at international exhibitions such as the Exposition universelle in Paris in 1855, eager to promote its significance as both an art and a science, while distinguishing it from more commercial uses. "Ernest Lacan (1828–1879)," in *Encyclopedia of Nineteenth-Century Photography*, ed. John Hannavy (New York: Routledge, 2008), 2:811–12.

55. Though their interest began to wane by the end of the 1850s, as photography was increasingly seen as an investment opportunity, the efforts of these early elite practitioners were crucial, particularly in the period 1850–55.

56. See Aubenas, *Gustave Le Gray*, 83n103.

57. Quoted in Mark Haworth-Booth, *Camille Silvy, River Scene* (Malibu, Calif.: J. Paul Getty Museum, 1992), 15.

58. Quoted in ibid., 17.

59. Quoted in ibid., 37.

60. He used at least two negatives for the print in the collection of the Victoria and Albert Museum, London. He adjusted tonal values by altering the negatives and drew clouds along the horizon by hand.

61. See the extensive study by Elizabeth Anne McCauley, *Industrial Madness: Commercial Photography in Paris, 1848–1871* (New Haven: Yale University Press, 1994).

62. Daniel Wildenstein, *Monet: Catalogue Raisonné*, vol. 3, *Nos. 1–968* (Cologne: Taschen, 1994), 125.

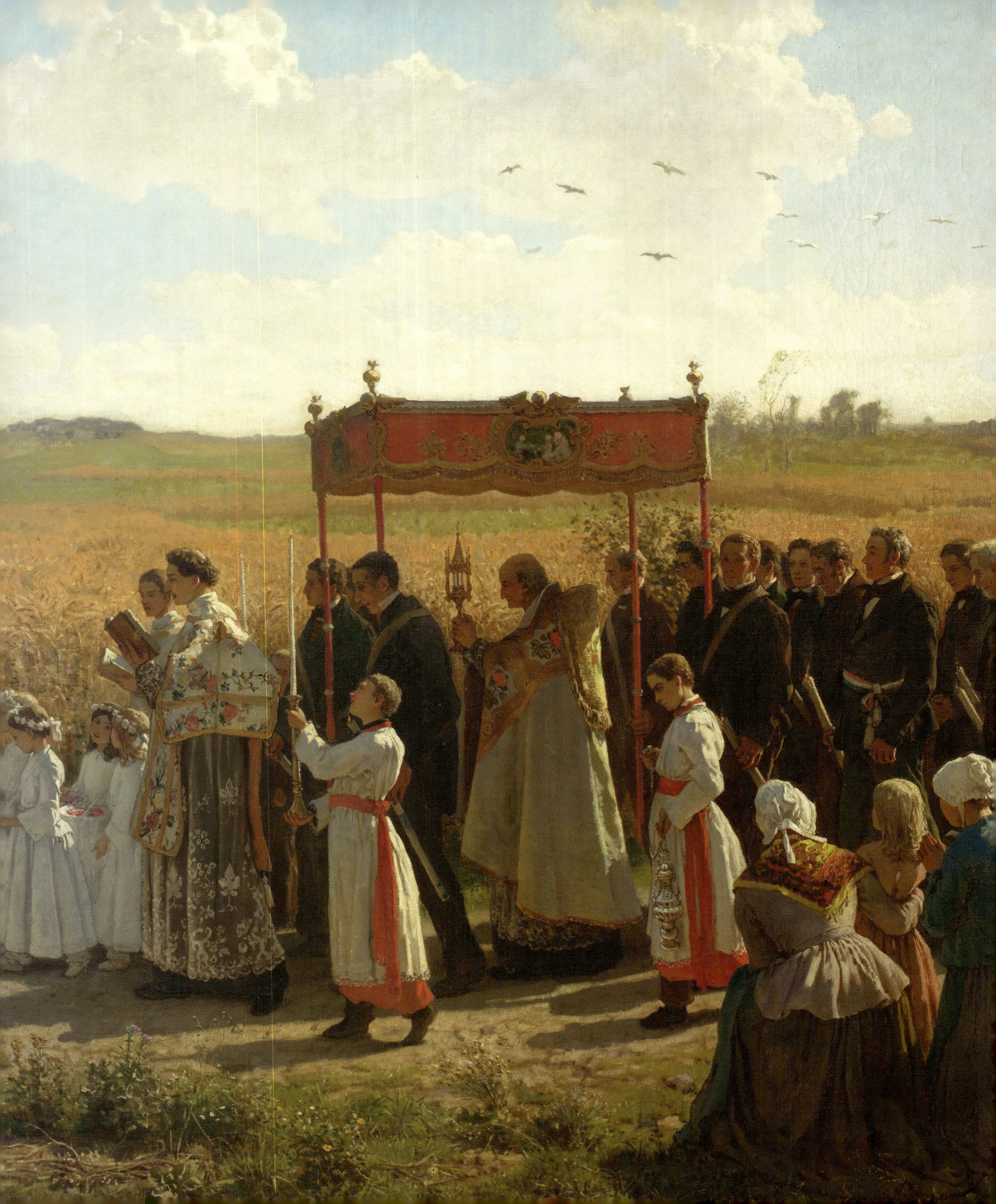

A Sense of Place: Representing the Region in Nineteenth-Century France

NEIL McWILLIAM

IN 1878 A JOURNEY AROUND FRANCE that had begun almost sixty years earlier came to an end. The *Voyages pittoresques et romantiques dans l'ancienne France* had been conceived in 1820 as a comprehensive and luxuriously produced inventory of the nation's monumental heritage. Its principal backers, the writer Charles Nodier and the cultural impresario Baron Isidore Taylor, were committed royalists horrified by the damage exacted on the country's churches and châteaux by the French Revolution and the continuing threat posed by entrepreneurs who pillaged the vestiges of the past for building material. Their twenty-four folio volumes offered a richly illustrated panorama of the natural and built environment constituting the national patrimony, organized in series dedicated to the historical regions that made up *l'ancienne France*. These provinces—Franche-Comté, Languedoc, Auvergne, and the like—were a reminder of a world that had existed before the Revolution and its efforts to fortify a sense of national belonging by replacing traditional territorial divisions with a rational, historically unmarked network of eighty-six administrative *départements*.[1]

The journey ended where it had begun, with a volume on Normandy, and followed a format that had characterized the series since its inception. Sections devoted to towns such as Bayeux or sites like the castle at Falaise (fig. 31) were accompanied by lithographs that positioned monuments within the surrounding landscape before offering more focused illustrations of interiors, architectural details, and ground plans. Émile Sagot's depiction of the twelfth-century *château-fort* embraces a formula that was unchanged for more than half a century and remains indebted to the Romantic topographical style perfected in the series' early volumes.[2] The print is dominated by the castle keep, which looms over a cluster of characteristically Norman half-timbered dwellings. In the foreground, two smartly dressed city gents admire the view, while all around locals in regional costume go about their business, oblivious to the beauty and significance of their surroundings. Confronted with Sagot's sleepy scene of provincial life, it would be easy

FIG. 31 Émile Sagot, *The Castle of Falaise 1*. Lithograph. From Baron Isidore Taylor and Charles Nodier, *Voyages pittoresques et romantiques dans l'ancienne France, Normandie*, vol. 3 (Paris: Firmin-Didot, 1878)

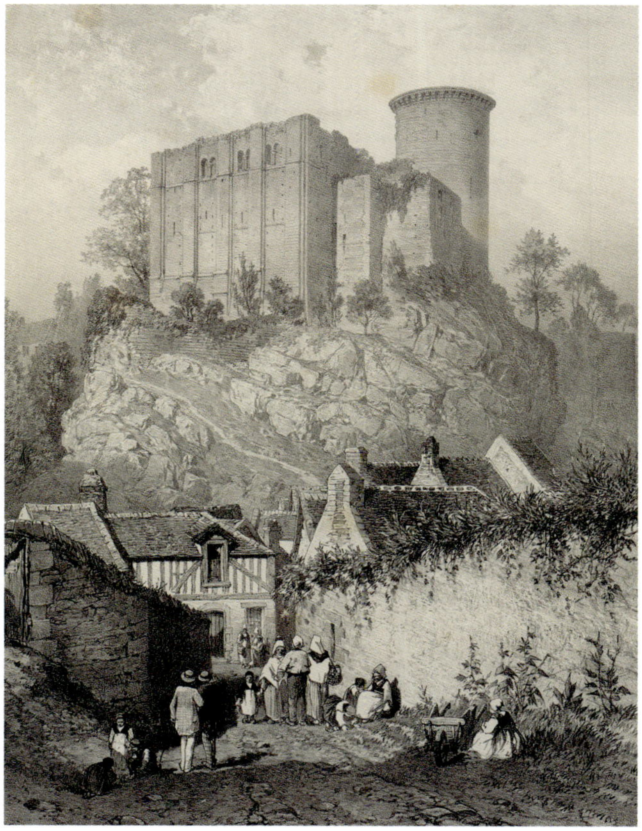

to imagine that the nineteenth century had passed Falaise by, yet the town was not only a local administrative center but also had an important textile industry, employing some four thousand workers, and since 1859 was connected to the outside world by train. The town's heritage had also become part of its fortune, as visitors to Normandy were drawn to its picturesque streets and its reputation as the birthplace of William the Conqueror, whose memory was preserved by a local museum that rather improbably proclaimed itself a former home of the Norman duke.[3]

If anything, then, it was the *Voyages pittoresques* that had been outpaced by the century, and its founders' nostalgia for an *ancienne France*, sustained on the dual pillars of church and crown, that had become increasingly anachronistic. Since the publication of the first volume in 1820, France had experienced four regime changes, three revolutions, and a major invasion. Though still predominantly an agrarian economy, it had undergone extensive industrial growth that encouraged a transfer of population to urban centers and ended the isolation of even the remotest region through the improvement of roads and the development of rail travel. Better communications not only facilitated individual movement but also laid the foundations of a truly national culture, by gradually introducing communities to standardized products, such as ready-made clothing, and to print media, which themselves became increasingly accessible as a system of elementary education was extended across France. Such developments slowly effected a form of cultural convergence in a country that had long been characterized by deep-seated diversity, rooted in regional particularism and manifested in linguistic differences, indigenous traditions, isolation from metropolitan control, and an attenuated sense of national belonging.[4]

If the political and economic forces shaping life in the French regions had changed vastly since the debut of the *Voyages pittoresques* in 1820, cultural representations of provincial France and its peasant population had also undergone significant transformation. After an initial breakthrough in the 1830s, landscape painting, a genre traditionally attracting little prestige and dominated by carefully manicured views of Italy or entirely fictive *paysages historiques* fabricated in the studio, made substantial inroads commercially and aesthetically. The Paris Salon exhibition, where artists vied to attract critical attention and sell their work to private clients or the state, featured ever-expanding numbers of landscapes, most of which celebrated the French countryside rather than idealized vistas far removed in time or space.[5] While most landscape painters favored intimately evocative depictions of rural calm over more topographically distinctive scenic views,[6] this current continued to flourish in the graphic arts, as locally specific variants of the *Voyages pittoresques* accompanied a burgeoning tourist industry that developed around improved communications in the second half of the century.[7] At the same time, the rural population, previously an object of disdain among urban elites, began to exert a fascination registered on the walls of the Salon

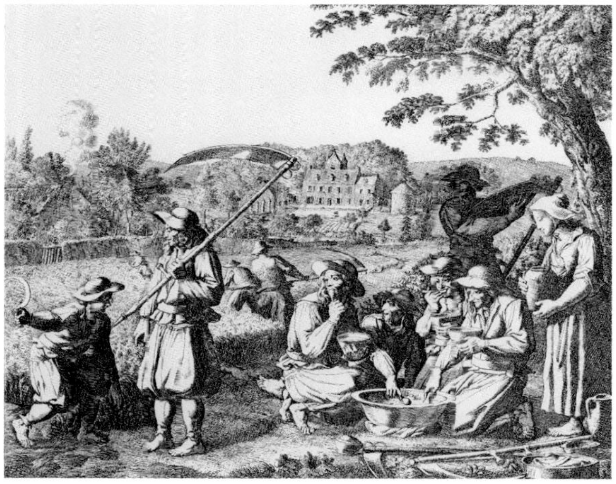

FIG. 32 Olivier Perrin, *La Moisson* (*La Coupe des foins*), 1808. Engraving. Bibliothèque nationale de France, Paris

and in the fictional portrayals of peasant life pioneered in the 1840s by George Sand. Even works in regional patois and languages such as Breton or Provençal began to attract metropolitan readers who sought in such sources a point of entry to the nation's ancestral roots or a vision of pastoral innocence far removed from the tribulations of city life.

This creeping commodification of the landscape and traditional cultures of rural France was not a seamless process, however, and certainly not one that can be unproblematically equated with a maturing national consciousness. Though such a factor comes into play, there is little to suggest the more overt instrumentalization of landscape as an emblem of collective value such as can be found in American manifest destiny imagery during this period, or in the cult of *Heimat* in postunification German landscape.[8] Critical commentary in midcentury France is more inclined to appraise landscape in terms of the artist's success in evoking mood or conveying emotion, and concern for the specific associations of the site portrayed was, at best, a secondary consideration. The riverside scenes of an artist such as Charles-François Daubigny or the forest clearings favored by the colony at Barbizon acquire an imprecise, generic quality that typically trades on the countryside's appeal to the urban viewer as a place of physical ease and psychological well-being. The gradual shift from this vernacular style of landscape to early Impressionism's more prosaic and actualized vision of rural France and its suburban fringes challenged this appealingly expressive mode of representation. In directly confronting the spectator with evidence of the incursions of contemporary life into the supposedly unchanging French scene, its exponents stood accused of distorting nature rather than offering a more topical view of provincial life that could appeal to a metropolitan public. The critic Charles Bigot made the charge most forcefully at the 1877 Impressionist show:

> In the final analysis, it is not true nature that they have looked at and tried to render, but rather the nature that one encounters on outings in the great city or its surroundings, where the harsh notes of the houses, with their white, red, or yellow walls and their green shutters, come up against the vegetation of the trees and form violent contrasts with it. How much better have . . . our modern landscapists, the Rousseaus, the Corots, and the Daubignys, understood how to express not only the poetry but also the truth of nature! How much better have they represented the countryside, with its waters, its woods, its fields, and its meadows, with its distant and calm horizons![9]

None of this is to say, however, that the Frenchness of French landscape remained an entirely peripheral issue. Indeed, in 1867 the liberal critic Jules-Antoine Castagnary was moved to declare: "Through landscape painting, art becomes national . . . it takes possession of France, of the soil, the air, the sky, the landscape of France. This earth that has borne us up, this air we breathe, this harmonious and gentle whole which constitutes as it were the face of our mother country, we carry it in our soul."[10] If landscape was primarily understood as a literal or representational space for the exploration of subjectivity, the individual's status as a national subject, drawing sustenance from a sense of belonging to a suprasubjective, communal space, could certainly be reconciled with such priorities. Yet a sense of belonging begged the question of precisely what it was that the individual was being invited to identify with, and it is here that the historical tensions between region and nation could

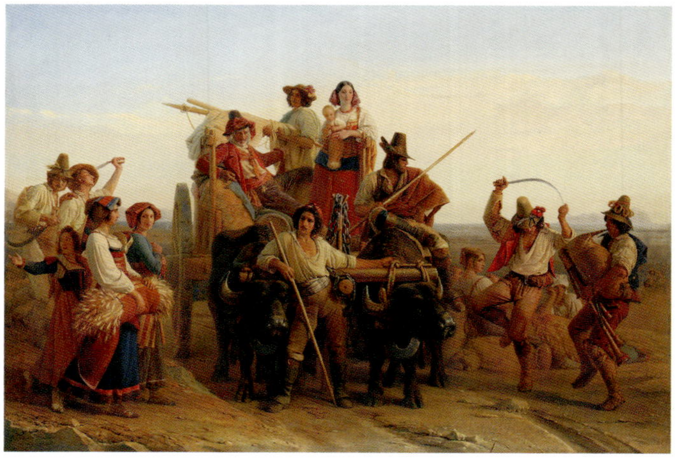

FIG. 33 Léopold Robert, *Arrival of the Harvesters in the Pontine Marshes*, 1831. Oil on canvas, 55½ × 83½ in. (141 × 212 cm). Musée du Louvre, Paris

complicate untroubled mediation between the two. Cultural representations of local life and landscape could thus potentially carry a range of meanings, not all of which were compatible with a desire to forge a sense of unity through an evocation of the diverse constituencies that made up the national family.

If, in the words of the great historian Jules Michelet, "history is above all entirely geographical,"[11] the interplay between time and space had left particularly indelible traces on the character and culture of the French nation. Unlike Italy and Germany, its neighbors immediately to the east, France had been a unitary state since the late Middle Ages, though until 1789 various regions continued to enjoy a range of statutory privileges. Dismissed by the revolutionary leader Honoré Mirabeau as an "unformed aggregate of disunited people,"[12] the nation was reconfigured in January 1790 in order to eradicate regional particularism and instill a sense of unity and cohesion. Though the new *départements* were initially understood as promoting a fundamental equality both between the various provinces and in the provinces' collective relationship with the capital, opponents quickly interpreted moves against the administrative geography of the ancien régime as little more than a centralist power grab by radicals intent on imposing their values on a reluctant nation. Suspicions intensified with an initiative coordinated by the priest-turned-politician the abbé Grégoire to replace local patois and regional tongues with a standardized French language, a move designed to undermine pockets of provincial resistance to the Revolution and generalize "the sole and invariable use of the language of freedom."[13] Combined with counterrevolutionary uprisings in Brittany and the Vendée and federalist revolts that swept the provinces in 1793, the Revolution's attempts to undermine regional prerogatives and cultures, together with its hostility to the Catholic Church, instilled lingering suspicion of Paris that persisted well into the nineteenth century and did much to shape cultural initiatives in regions such as Brittany and Provence. The historian Mona Ozouf has remarked on "the particular difficulties France [has had] in conceptualizing its regional differences."[14] These difficulties—reciprocated in regional ambivalence toward the sociocultural implications of integration within the nation-state—are a central legacy of the upheaval of the Revolutionary era.

The half century following the Revolution saw the emergence and consolidation of strongly defined regional differences within the national cultural imagination. Before 1789, commentators on the provinces rarely identified any specific features of tradition, dress, or daily life that marked out the inhabitants of particular localities or suggested continuities between present-day customs and the distant past. Initially inspired by Napoléon's desire to provide a martial pedigree for the imperial Grande Armée, enthusiasts in 1804 established a Celtic Academy, which claimed to find in Brittany the remnants of an ancient warrior nation whose descendants were today extending French dominion across the continent.[15] Although occasionally tinged with condescension toward what was seen as popular irrationalism, the academy's investigations of traditional lore and everyday life introduced a metropolitan audience to an exotic community apparently surviving unchanged in rural isolation. Inspired by ambitions to access a primitive past that had in fact largely disappeared, early investigators of Breton life sketched in the outlines of an image of the province that hardened into a stereotype over the course of the century.[16] For its champions, the Celtic populations of Brittany represented "the senior branch in the great family of

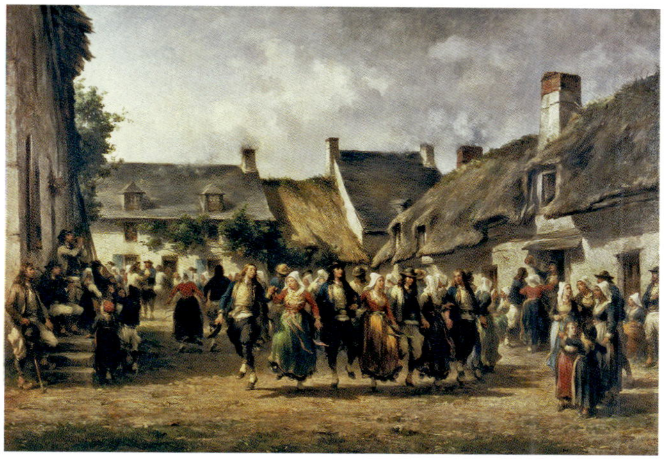

FIG. 34 Adolphe Leleux, *Breton Wedding*, 1863. Oil on canvas, 54½ × 80⅛ in. (138.5 × 203.5 cm). Musée des beaux-arts de Quimper, France

nations," "the fathers of so many warlike peoples,"[17] whose sons remained true to their heritage. Hardy, independent, deeply pious, the Breton came to epitomize a rugged simplicity untouched by the spurious sophistication of the city. The region's distinctive, and highly varied, local costume—mistakenly believed to date back to ancient times—became one of the most immediately recognizable symbols of regional alterity and offered a staple subject for painters at the Salon well into the twentieth century.[18]

The pedigree for such work can itself be traced back to the Celtic Academy and to the work one of its members, the painter and engraver Olivier Perrin. A native of Brittany based in the town of Quimper, Perrin published an album of engravings, *La galerie des moeurs, usages et costumes des Bretons de l'Armorique*, in 1808. The project proved short-lived, but Perrin himself was conscientious in recording the community in the countryside outside his hometown. Other than a series of genre paintings of village life, Perrin produced a substantial number of sketches that, following his death, were collected as *La galerie bretonne ou vie des Bretons de l'Armorique* (1835); illustrated and published serially with a text by Alexandre Bouët, it organized Perrin's scenes into a fictional biography following the young peasant Corentin from birth to marriage.[19] Other than their marked sensitivity to the details of popular material culture, Perrin's engravings are untypical in the prominence they accord to the depiction of labor (fig. 32). Eschewing the pastoral mode that the eighteenth century perfected to mystify the physical effort of agricultural work, Perrin's scenes (and Bouët's commentary) unusually insist on the hardships of rural life. Contrasting the energy of the young Corentin who labors enthusiastically while his older companions stop to eat, Bouët remarks: "Haymaking is hard work that demands even more strength than skill: while it lasts, meals take place whenever exhaustion sets in."[20]

Perrin's work, though it failed to reach a broad public, offers a precocious—and unusually nuanced—example of a pictorial genre that would exert wide appeal from the 1830s onward. The ground had been laid toward the end of the previous decade with the popularity of scenes of Italian peasant life, a genre that attracted artists across Europe but reached its apogee with the success at the Paris Salon of the Swiss painter Léopold Robert. Paintings such as *Arrival of the Harvesters in the Pontine Marshes*, exhibited in 1831 (fig. 33), suggest an elegance and ease far removed from the laboring Breton rustics, though the artist himself emphasized his concern to achieve an appropriate balance between authenticity and the ideal. "What I pursue with the greatest pleasure," Robert confided to his mother in 1823, "is giving to the least of my figures, to the simplest of my subjects, a charming polish that does not sacrifice truth to nature, for that is the essential thing."[21] Robert was widely praised for achieving precisely this mix, though critics were doubtful that representations of the French peasantry could attain a comparable dignity. Despite such misgivings, the 1830s and 1840s witnessed a significant growth in rural genre scenes at the Paris Salon, as artists began to explore the provinces in search of subject matter that was both convincingly contemporary yet reassuringly timeless in its evocation of the unchanging rhythms of country life. Brittany once again attracted the earliest and most widespread attention. Foremost among a generation of artists who gravitated to the province in the late 1830s, Adolphe Leleux acquired a reputation for the unvarnished authenticity of his work—a quality that occasionally provoked censure as contravening aesthetic proprieties and social decorum. Yet Leleux led

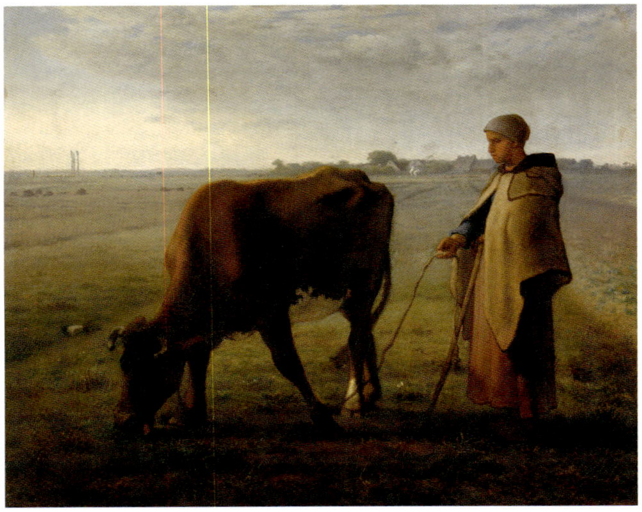

FIG. 35 Jean-François Millet, *Peasant Pasturing Her Cow*, 1858. Oil on canvas, 28¾ × 36⅝ in. (73 × 93 cm). Musée du monastère royal de Brou, Bourg-en-Bresse

the way in shaping rural life for an urban public and was rewarded with state purchases of works such as *Breton Wedding*, which was commissioned in 1859 for the national collection of contemporary art at the Musée du Luxembourg in Paris and displayed at the 1863 Salon (fig. 34). His essentially formulaic depictions of Lower Brittany, which varied little over the years, satisfied broadly generic expectations for portrayals of the region (though Leleux never specified the precise location of his scenes). Colorful costumes are worn by wholesome, somewhat theatrical figures whose "primitivism" is studiedly picturesque and who are rarely shown engaged in the sort of labor that features in Perrin's earlier record of peasant life.[22]

By 1859 the writer and critic Maxime du Camp could single out a specialized cadre of *paysanistes* showing at that year's Salon, praising their success in overcoming pastoral clichés in favor of a naturalism that "shows us the unceasing communion of the peasant with the land, a communion that is so intimate and profound that often the two become as one."[23] Du Camp awarded pride of place to Jean-François Millet, whose *Peasant Pasturing Her Cow* (fig. 35) was otherwise generally criticized that year for the artist's alleged exaggeration of the young woman's morose appearance.[24] More representative of critical and official taste was Edmond Hédouin, a *paysaniste* admired for the "poetry" of his work in 1859 and whom du Camp had lavishly praised at the 1857 Salon for his *Gleaners at Chambaudouin* (fig. 36), declaring of the women running to escape an advancing storm, "true peasants they may be, disheveled and impetuous, but they possess great elegance."[25] Hédouin had emerged in the 1840s, initially specializing in scenes of the French Pyrenees (a region also favored by Leleux) before shifting focus to the province of Constantine in the recently acquired French colony of Algeria. Later, the painter relocated to the Beauce region south of Paris, memorializing different aspects of popular life in this richly agricultural area.

Hédouin's canvas was purchased by the state in 1857 and joined the national collection at the Musée du Luxembourg. Over the course of the Second Empire, from Napoléon III's seizure of power in 1851 until his abdication in 1870, the museum acquired a number of regional scenes that, though substantially outnumbered by the history paintings that dominated the collection, offered a glimpse both of the *paysanistes'* growing prestige and of the vision of rural France favored in official circles.[26] Portrayals of Brittany predominate, celebrating the apparent vitality of traditional village communities, while artists such as Jules Breton and Charles Marchal report from other parts of the nation. The work of a Parisian artist who settled in the Alsatian market town of Bouxwiller ("where the customs and costumes of the good old days have pretty well survived," according to the critic Edmond About), Marchal's *Choral of Luther* (fig. 37) is unusual in recalling France's Protestant population. Presenting "the simple, everyday religion of a people that is pious though cold, practical and hardworking,"[27] Marchal reports back from one of France's most distant provinces, part of the nation only since the seventeenth century. Alsatian customs and distinctive dress acquired particular resonance following annexation by Germany in the wake of the Franco-Prussian War in 1871, but the region had become an increasing object of curiosity during the Second Empire, thanks in no small part to the vogue for the rustic ghost stories produced by Erckmann-Chatrian.[28]

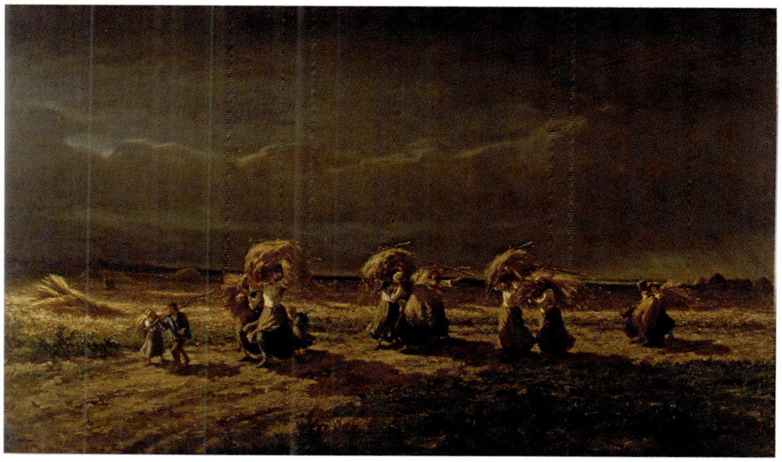

FIG. 36 Edmond Hédouin, *Gleaners at Chambaudouin*, 1857. Oil on canvas, 61¾ × 102⅜ in. (157 × 260 cm). Museé Paul Dini, Villefranche-sur-Saône, France

Like Marchal's painting, Breton's *The Blessing of the Wheat in Artois* (fig. 38), purchased in 1857 and one of three works by the artist in the Luxembourg's collection, also typifies the association between rural life and religiosity. Part of a long-running series that memorialized country ways in the painter's birthplace near the Belgian border, the canvas recalls an artist conspicuously absent from the Luxembourg—Gustave Courbet. Yet while Courbet's *Burial at Ornans* had caused consternation at the 1851 Salon because of its ambivalent evocation of small-town life in eastern France, Breton reassures where Courbet had sown doubt. Breton's canvas asserts the centrality of faith to the rural worldview. The priest displaying the host is the literal and figurative pivot of the composition, and the focus of veneration. In Courbet's work, by contrast, the crucifix held high above the officiant's head—and largely ignored by the assembled mourners—seems rather to underline the essentially secular character of the scene. In social terms, too, Breton implies a more settled, generally respected acceptance of rank, as the village elders follow the priest, while more modest villagers bring up the rear under the watchful authority of a *garde champêtre*.

The prominence in the Luxembourg of artists such as Breton, Hédouin, Marchal, and Leleux and the exclusion of the more critical perspectives offered by Courbet and Millet suggest a vision of rural life most congenial to those in power. Yet the overall paucity of such works (comparable in number to representations of Italian peasants in the collection), together with the relatively modest proportion of landscapes, implies a certain tentativeness regarding the representation of contemporary France. Though conservative aesthetic priorities that continued to favor history painting certainly help to account for this disproportion, struggles over the symbolic appropriation of the meanings of rural life and regional culture during the midcentury may also have played a role.

Provincial resistance to central government had been a persistent feature of relations between Paris and the provinces since the 1830s. Though the authoritarian rule of Napoléon I had imposed obedience throughout the Empire (1804–14), and the resurgent conservatism of the Bourbon monarchy won widespread sympathy among provincial elites during the Restoration (1815–30), the accession of Louis-Philippe following the July Revolution ignited smoldering resentment against the upstart Orléanist dynasty in many parts of rural France. Brittany, in particular, quickly emerged as a center of legitimist opposition to the new monarch, who aroused early suspicion thanks to his strained relations with the Catholic Church. Clergy, together with provincial nobles, projected Brittany as a haven of faith and stability rooted in a reverence for tradition that had been lost in the rest of France. According to the writer and philologist Théodore Hersart de la Villemarqué, "In our mountains . . . and deep valleys, sheltered from contact with the towns and all French influence, the past lives on in the present. Language, civilization, old memories and historic songs have been preserved there by poor folk."[29] Villemarqué, who frequented legitimist circles in Paris, infused the sleepy world of provincial erudition with unabashed militancy. In 1839 he published the first edition of a collection of verse, *Barzaz-Breiz*, which claimed to reveal the enduring vigor of an oral tradition that lived on in the isolated communities of Brittany and embodied the vitality of a millennial culture and its system of beliefs. The volume, whose authenticity was questioned by later specialists in Breton ethnography, was the linchpin of a campaign in which

FIG. 37 Charles Marchal, *Choral of Luther*, 1863. Oil on canvas, 43 × 68½ in. (109 × 174 cm). Musée départemental des Vosges, Épinal, France

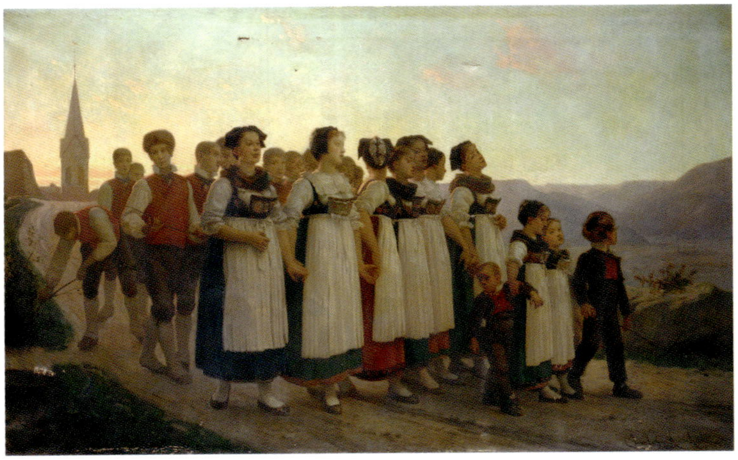

Villemarqué presented the province as a hapless victim of French aggression: "No, you are no longer free, oh my country! But we love you in your chains and our lives, this blood we have spilled over twenty centuries on the field of battle in your cause, are still yours! Ah! If we could spill our blood once more! If we could break the chains that burden your old age."[30]

Though rarely expressed with such vigor, similarly dissident sentiments appeared in conservative circles in Brittany and among the Breton diaspora in Paris. Catholic efforts in the province focused on fostering use of the Breton tongue, and catechisms and popular saints' lives were published in Breton dialects, while clergy encouraged members of their flock to resist the lure of the city and remain true to traditional ways. The bishop of Quimper's Lenten message of 1846, warning of the potentially harmful consequences of education, is unequivocal: "That you need to be polished by the modern civilization of this century we do not contest, but take care lest by polishing you civilization wears you out, weakens you, erases the imprint of your religious character. . . . That is why we are genuinely happy to see you uphold your old customs, your old costume, your old language."[31] Seen in such a way, regional particularity acted as a cordon sanitaire, protecting the local population from the moral and material lure of metropolitan culture and reinforcing the authority of local elites in the face of intrusion from outside. Defenders of traditional communities looked with horror at the ever-growing railway network, seeing it as an invasive agent of contagion, which would ultimately render the peasant every bit as intractable as his urban counterpart, prone to drink, godlessness, and dissent. For the moment, commentators viewed spots like the Breton coast around Tréguier with undisguised relief: "While elsewhere a single thought that is infiltrated in the midst of the masses can throw them into turbulent agitation, here all is calm and placid."[32]

Fear that external incursions would undermine and eventually eradicate differences in vernacular culture fostered efforts across France to celebrate the local and record its legacy before time ran out. Once again, Brittany took the lead, with the establishment in 1843 of the Association bretonne. Ostensibly a cultural organization, in reality the association attracted conservatives disenchanted with centralized government and its agents. The same was true in the North, where the Comité flamand de France was established to defend the Flemish tongue in 1853, and in Provence, where, in 1854, the poet Frédéric Mistral founded the Félibrige, a poetic society intended to restore luster to the language and culture of the *pays d'oc*. Mistral's initiative, which achieved national prominence following publication of his rural epic *Mirèio* in 1859, grew out of a politically varied interest in the vernacular fostered by worker-poets and regional enthusiasts during the 1840s. As early as 1852 the poet Joseph Roumanille was able to publish an anthology of Provençal verse, *Li Prouvençalo*, whose introduction adopted a decidedly anticentralist tone. Comparing Provence with other oppressed cultures across Europe, its author, Saint-René Taillandier, attacked the internationalist aspirations of the humanitarian left and celebrated "the awakening of racial feeling" that had generated a "sort of insurrection" across the continent.[33] Mistral himself, who emerged as a towering figure in the regionalist movement in the half century before his death in 1914, became an outspoken advocate of political and cultural decentralization, calling for the reassertion of local pride in the history, language, and traditions of Provence: "Instead of stagnating in

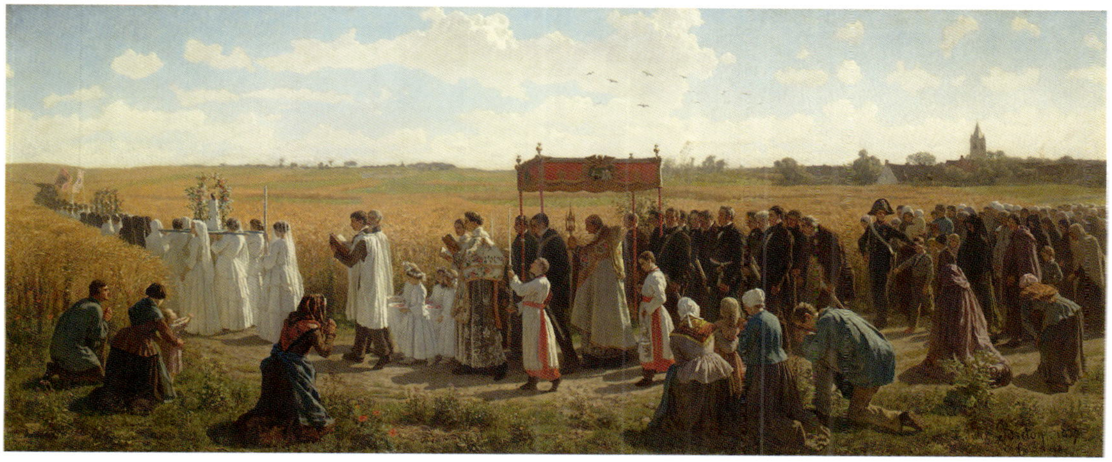

ignorance of their own history, of the grandeur of their past, and of their [shared] personality, we want our people to learn that their fathers always considered themselves a race, and that the old sons of Provence knew how to live as free men and always to defend themselves as such."[34]

Though by far the most successful and enduring of such initiatives, the Félibrige exemplifies a cultural awakening in the provinces that gathered pace in the second half of the century. If writers were the main actors and principal beneficiaries of such a trend,[35] the visual arts, too, benefited from a limited, though significant, challenge to the hegemony of Paris. The provinces had acquired a network of provincial art schools under the ancien régime, while Napoléon I laid the foundations for a system of regional museums, which received regular donations of work purchased by the state at the Paris Salon. At the grassroots level, provincial centers saw the development in midcentury of locally run artistic societies, Sociétés des amis des arts, which sponsored exhibitions that brought artists of national standing to the regions and helped foster a vigorous homegrown culture. Writing in 1865, the critic Philippe Burty noted that such groups "are uniquely able, in artistic terms, to peacefully decentralize France" and recognized their vital contribution in supporting provincial practitioners and promoting "the diffusion of ideas about art among the masses."[36] A more belligerent stance toward redressing the cultural imbalance between Paris and the regions was taken by the young art historian and future administrator Philippe de Chennevières. Contributing in 1849 to the legitimist *Revue provinciale*, Chennevières attacked the "imperious, all-consuming, uniform authority" emanating from the capital and called for an artistic repatriation that would favor "solid, naive, sublime, and personal inspiration," found only in the heartlands.

FIG. 38 Jules Breton, *The Blessing of the Wheat in Artois*, 1857. Oil on canvas, 50½ × 126 in. (128.5 × 320 cm). Musée des beaux-arts, Arras, France

This strategy, he asserted, was essential for the nation's ideological health: "contempt for the arts is the beginning of unreason in politics: with its naive instinct, the communist hydra, that the provincial movement took the lead in resolving to crush and eliminate, has always despised and rejected the arts."[37]

Such a Manichaean contrast between an all-consuming metropolis and the enervated regions overlooked the extent to which the state had itself attempted to intervene in collecting and interpreting the cultural patrimony of provincial France. In 1834 Minister of Education François Guizot established a committee to coordinate research by local scholarly societies concerned with national history and culture. These efforts were stepped up in 1840 with the creation of the Comité historique des arts et monuments, charged with recording and preserving material heritage, and in 1851 five photographers were selected to undertake a comprehensive inventory of nationally important sites in the Mission héliographique intended to facilitate decisions regarding the protection and renovation of threatened structures (cats. 24–26). This interest in material remains was matched by official sponsorship of efforts to record and promote the literary heritage, preserved both in unpublished manuscripts discovered in provincial libraries and in the oral tradition of rural communities. Villemarqué himself, though an object of sustained suspicion, benefited from official support and indeed was nominated to the philological section of the Comité de la langue, de l'histoire et des arts de la France

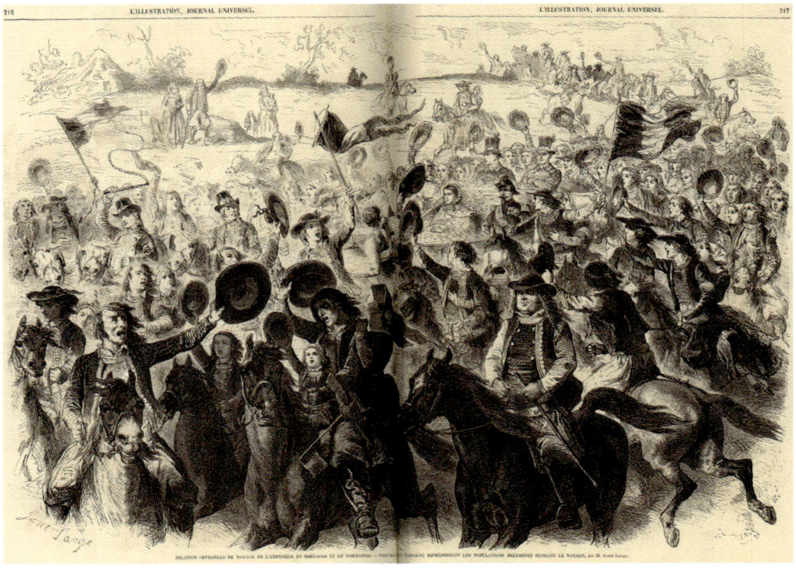

FIG. 39 Janet-Lange, *Relation officielle du voyage de l'Empereur en Bretagne et en Normandie—Esquisse d'un tableau représentant les populations bretonnes pendant la voyage.* From *L'illustration* 32, no. 814 (October 2, 1858): 216–17

established by Napoléon III in 1852. The committee's first undertaking was to be a collection of popular verse, whose publication, according to Education Minister Hippolyte Fortoul, would reveal an "unaffected genius" born of "the old French spirit" that would put contemporary writers to shame. Inspired by the emperor's desire to "respectfully preserve the songs that recall our fathers' heroic struggles and the peaceful joys of the domestic hearth,"[38] the committee charged local teachers with collecting appropriate examples. Their tepid response provoked a reproachful missive from Fortoul, who accused provincial schoolmasters of "a lack of patriotic zeal for the work to which they had been called," pointedly noting that France alone among European nations failed to value "the earliest efforts of their national genius" whose poetic relics were revered in neighboring countries.[39]

It is, of course, no surprise that teachers charged with extending the reach of the French language should be ambivalent about quizzing students on the use of patois, otherwise sedulously excluded from the classroom. Such an initiative does, however, reveal how the authorities sought to reconcile regional with national identity, to use a sense of place—with its attendant language, traditions, and beliefs—as a point of access to an image of France viewed as an aggregate of different, though mutually reinforcing, cultures. Though such a strategy was most fully realized after 1870,[40] its roots can be traced back to initiatives such as Fortoul's projected poetry collection. It emerges, too, in the ceremonial that surrounded Napoléon III's official tours of provincial France, and most strikingly in his visit to Brittany in 1858. Previous journeys around the South of France in 1852 and Alsace in 1853 had incorporated displays of peasants in regional dress, predominantly identified with the female population. In Brittany, however (where authorities had recently banned the Association bretonne as an allegedly subversive organization), Napoléon and his consort Eugénie were constantly met with traditional dances, gifts of regional costume, and speeches in the vernacular—an aspect highlighted in press coverage of the tour (fig. 39). In the province's capital of Rennes, the emperor delivered a speech in which he extolled the Bretons as "a people . . . that is above all royalist, catholic and martial." Implicitly acknowledging the region's federalist inclinations, he countered by underlining the nation's deeper bonds, asserting, "If France is not completely homogenous by nature, it is united in its feelings." To drive home his point, the emperor concluded by calling on Brittany to embrace progress while nurturing the past:

> While hastening its steps along the path of civilization, it preserves intact the tradition of noble feelings that have distinguished it over the centuries. May it retain these simple ways, this proverbial openness, this fidelity to sworn faith, this perseverance in duty, this submission to the will of God, who watches over the humblest hearth as over the highest destiny of empires![41]

The fall of Napoléon's Second Empire, Prussia's cataclysmic invasion of France, and Germany's subsequent annexation of the provinces of Alsace and Lorraine left

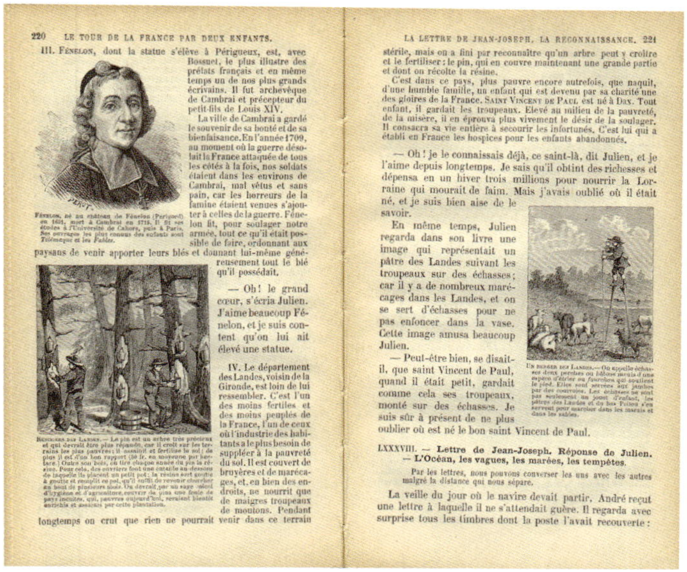

220 LE TOUR DE LA FRANCE PAR DEUX ENFANTS.

III. Fénelon, dont la statue s'élève à Périgueux, est, avec Bossuet, le plus illustre des prélats français et en même temps un de nos plus grands écrivains. Il fut archevêque de Cambrai et précepteur du petit-fils de Louis XIV.

La ville de Cambrai a gardé le souvenir de sa bonté et de sa bienfaisance. En l'année 1709, au moment où la guerre désolait la France attaquée de tous les côtés à la fois, nos soldats étaient dans les environs de Cambrai, mal vêtus et sans pain, car les horreurs de la famine étaient venues s'ajouter à celles de la guerre. Fénelon fit, pour soulager notre armée, tout ce qu'il était possible de faire, ordonnant aux paysans de venir apporter leurs blés et donnant lui-même généreusement tout le blé qu'il possédait.

Fénelon, né au château de Fénelon (Périgord) en 1651, mort à Cambrai en 1715. Il fit ses études à l'Université de Cahors, puis à Paris. Ses ouvrages les plus connus des enfants sont *Télémaque* et les *Fables*.

— Oh! le grand cœur, s'écria Julien. J'aime beaucoup Fénelon, et je suis content qu'on lui ait élevé une statue.

IV. Le département des Landes, voisin de la Gironde, est loin de lui ressembler. C'est l'un des moins fertiles et des moins peuplés de la France, l'un de ceux où l'industrie des habitants a le plus besoin de suppléer à la pauvreté du sol. Il est couvert de bruyères et de marécages, et, en bien des endroits, ne nourrit que de maigres troupeaux de moutons. Pendant longtemps on crut que rien ne pourrait venir dans ce terrain

Résiniers des Landes. — Le pin est un arbre très précieux et qui devrait être plus répandu, car il croît sur les terrains les plus pauvres; il assainit et fertilise le sol; de plus il est d'un bon rapport (36 fr. en moyenne par hectare.) Outre son bois, on tire chaque année du pin la résine. Pour cela, des ouvriers font une entaille au-dessous de laquelle ils placent un petit pot; la résine sort goutte à goutte et remplit ce pot, qu'il suffit de revenir chercher au bout de plusieurs mois. On devrait, par un sage calcul d'hygiène et d'agriculture, couvrir de pins une foule de pays incultes, qui, pauvres aujourd'hui, seraient bientôt enrichis et assainis par cette plantation.

LA LETTRE DE JEAN-JOSEPH. LA RECONNAISSANCE. 221

stérile, mais on a fini par reconnaître qu'un arbre peut y croître et le fertiliser: le pin, qui en couvre maintenant une grande partie et dont on récolte la résine.

C'est dans ce pays, plus pauvre encore autrefois, que naquit, d'une humble famille, un enfant qui est devenu par sa charité une des gloires de la France. Saint Vincent de Paul est né à Dax. Tout enfant, il gardait les troupeaux. Elevé au milieu de la pauvreté, de la misère, il en éprouva plus vivement le désir de la soulager. Il consacra sa vie entière à secourir les infortunés. C'est lui qui a établi en France les hospices pour les enfants abandonnés.

— Oh! je le connaissais déjà, ce saint-là, dit Julien, et je l'aime depuis longtemps. Je sais qu'il obtint des richesses et dépensa en un hiver trois millions pour nourrir la Lorraine qui mourait de faim. Mais j'avais oublié où il était né, et je suis bien aise de le savoir.

En même temps, Julien regarda dans son livre une image qui représentait un pâtre des Landes suivant les troupeaux sur des échasses; car il y a de nombreux marécages dans les Landes, et on se sert d'échasses pour ne pas enfoncer dans la vase. Cette image amusa beaucoup Julien.

— Peut-être bien, se disait-il, que saint Vincent de Paul, quand il était petit, gardait comme cela ses troupeaux, monté sur des échasses. Je suis sûr à présent de ne plus oublier où est né le bon saint Vincent de Paul.

Un berger des Landes. — On appelle échasses deux perches ou bâtons munis d'une espèce d'étrier ou *fourchon* qui soutient le pied. Elles sont serrées aux jambes par des courroies. Les échasses ne sont pas seulement un jouet d'enfant, les pâtres des Landes et du bas Poitou s'en servent pour marcher dans les marais et dans les sables.

LXXXVIII. — **Lettre de Jean-Joseph. Réponse de Julien. — L'Océan, les vagues, les marées, les tempêtes.**

Par les lettres, nous pouvons converser les uns avec les autres malgré la distance qui nous sépare.

La veille du jour où le navire devait partir, André reçut une lettre à laquelle il ne s'attendait guère. Il regarda avec surprise tous les timbres dont la poste l'avait recouverte:

FIG. 40 From G. Bruno, *Le tour de la France par deux enfants* (Paris: Librairie classique Eugène Belin, 1887), 220–21

traumatic scars on the nation's self-image and on the ways in which individual provinces—particularly those that had been lost—could be imagined as relating to the whole. In 1877, the year before the *Voyages pittoresques* came to an end, a new journey began that was firmly shaped by the temper of the times. *Le tour de la France par deux enfants*, by Augustine Fouillée (using the pseudonym G. Bruno), was directed at a rising generation implicitly charged with restoring the nation's honor. Selling three million copies in its first ten years alone, Fouillée's tale followed André and Julien, two young orphaned refugees from Lorraine who journey around France in search of their uncle. Along the way, they visit much of the nation, learning about the character of individual provinces, their local industries, great men, and notable monuments (fig. 40). Regional dress and local patois are treated slightingly, and relatively little is made of distinctive regional landscapes. Yet the work's subtitle—*Devoir et patrie* (Duty and Motherland)—and its final chapter, "J'aime la France," leave little doubt as to the pedagogical trajectory of this new journey. Weaving together part and whole, the local and the national, into a harmonious union, *Le tour de la France* leaves its youthful pilgrims initiated into the cult of the nation, proclaiming at the end: "Beloved France, we are your children, and we wish to become worthy of you!"[42]

1. See Marie-Vic Ozouf-Marignier, *La formation des départements: La représentation du territoire français à la fin du 18ème siècle* (Paris: Éditions de l'École des Hautes Études en Sciences Sociales, 1989).

2. Indeed, forty-three prints in this final volume by Charles Séchan, lithographed by Eugène Cicéri, were based on drawings made in 1842. See Anita Louise Spadafore, "Baron Taylor's 'Voyages pittoresques'" (PhD diss., Northwestern University, 1973), 253.

3. See, for example, Katharine S. Macquoid, *Through Normandy* (London, 1874), 415–33. The town had at least two hotels catering to tourists. Like most of Falaise, the Musée Malfilâtre was destroyed in August 1944.

4. For a discussion of cultural diversity during this period, see Graham Robb, *The Discovery of France* (New York: W. W. Norton and Co., 2007). Eugen Weber, however, in "Who Sang the *Marseillaise*?," in *My France: Politics, Culture, Myth* (Cambridge, Mass.: Harvard University Press, 1991), 95, notes, "In 1893, according to official figures, about a quarter of the 37,000-odd communes in France spoke no French"—some 7.5 million people.

5. During the 1860s, approximately one-third of state purchases at the Salon (an average of about forty paintings) consisted of landscapes. These works were distributed mainly to provincial museums and official buildings. See John House, "Authority versus Independence: The Position of French Landscape in the 1870s" in *Framing France: The Representation of Landscape in France, 1870–1914*, ed. Richard Thomson (Manchester: Manchester University Press, 1998), 17.

6. See Greg M. Thomas, "The Topographical Aesthetic in French Tourism and Landscape," *Nineteenth-Century Art Worldwide* (Spring 2002), http://www.19thc-artworldwide.org/index.php/spring02/198-the-topographical-aesthetic-in-french-tourism-and-landscape (accessed May 26, 2012).

7. As an example, see Lucie Goujard, *Voyages pittoresques: Normandie, 1820–2009*, exh. cat. (Milan: Silvana Editoriale, 2009), the catalogue of an exhibition held jointly in Rouen, Caen, and Le Havre.

8. See Albert Boime, *The Magisterial Gaze: Manifest Destiny and American Landscape Painting, c. 1830–1865* (Washington, D.C.: Smithsonian Institution Press, 1991); and Shearer West, *The Visual Arts in Germany, 1890–1937: Utopia and Despair* (New Brunswick, N.J.: Rutgers University Press, 2001), 33–58.

9. Quoted in House, "Authority versus Independence," 28: "Au fond, ce n'est pas la véritable nature qu'ils ont regardée et qu'ils s'efforcent de rendre, c'est surtout la nature telle qu'on l'entrevoit par échapées dans la grande ville ou dans les environs, là où les notes criardes des maisons, des murailles blanches, rouges ou jaunes, avec leurs volets verts, viennent se mêler à la végétation des arbres et former avec elle des contrastes violents. . . . Ah! que nos paysagistes modernes, les Rousseau, les Corot, les Daubigny, ont su mieux exprimer non pas seulement la poésie, mais aussi la vérité de la nature! qu'ils ont mieux représenté la campagne, avec ses eaux, ses bois, ses champs et ses prairies, avec ses lointains et calmes horizons!"

10. Jules-Antoine Castagnary, "Salon de 1867," in *Salons* (Paris, 1892), 235: "Par le paysage, l'art devient national . . . il prend possession de la France, du sol, de l'air, du ciel, du paysage français. Cette terre qui nous a portés, cette atmosphère que nous respirons, tout cet ensemble harmonieux et doux qui constitue comme le visage de la mère patrie, nous le portons dans notre âme." Quoted in Françoise Cachin, "The Painter's Landscape," in *Rethinking France: Les lieux de mémoire*, ed. Pierre Nora, vol. 2, *Space*, trans. David P. Jordan (Chicago: University of Chicago Press, 2006), 333.

11. Jules Michelet, *Tableau de la France* (1833) (Paris: Les Belles Lettres, 1949), 4: "l'histoire est avant tout géographique."

12. Quoted in Jacques Revel, "The Region," in Nora, *Space*, 154: "agrégat inconstitué de peuples désunis."

13. Abbé Henri Grégoire, "Rapport sur la nécessité et les moyens d'anéantir les patois et d'universaliser l'usage de la langue française," 16 Prairial, an II (1794), reprinted in *La Révolution française: Revue historique* 2 (1882): 653: "l'usage unique et invariable de la langue de la liberté."

14. Mona Ozouf, "La Révolution et la perception de l'espace national: Fédération, fédéralisme et stéréotypes régionaux," in *L'école de la France: Essai sur la révolution, l'utopie et l'enseignement* (Paris: Gallimard, 1984), 27: "la difficulté particulière de la France à penser les différences régionales."

15. See Nicole Belmont, "L'Académie celtique et George Sand: Les débuts des recherches folkloriques en France," *Romantisme* 5, no. 9 (1975): 29–38. Napoléon's Celtic enthusiasms were themselves inspired by his reading of James Macpherson's Ossian poems—a forged epic, ostensibly drawn on ancient oral verse collected in the Scottish Highlands and published in 1765.

16. For an excellent summary of this process, see Catherine Bertho, "L'invention de la Bretagne: Genèse sociale d'un stéréotype," *Actes de la recherche en sciences sociales*, no. 35 (1980): 45–62.

17. J. Lavallée, "Discours préliminaire," *Mémoires de l'Académie celtique* 1 (1807): 3: "la branche aînée de la grande famille des nations"; "les pères de tant de peuples belliqueux."

18. On later exponents of Breton subject matter, see Eric Storm, *The Culture of Regionalism: Art, Architecture and International Exhibitions in France, Germany, and Spain, 1890–1939* (Manchester: Manchester University Press, 2010), 29–41.

19. On Perrin, see Denise Delouche, *Peintres de la Bretagne: Découverte d'une province* (Paris: Librairie C. Klincksieck, 1977), 123–38.

20. Alexandre Bouët and Olivier Perrin, *Breiz-Izel ou Vie des Bretons de l'Armorique* (Paris: B. Dusillon, 1844), 1:166: "La coupe des foins est un travail pénible et qui exige encore plus de force que d'adresse; aussi tant qu'il dure, la nourriture se mesure-t-elle à la fatigue qu'il occasionne."

21. Quoted in Pierre Gassier, *Léopold Robert* (Neuchâtel: Ides et Calendes, 1983), 157: "Ce que je cherche avec le plus de plaisir, c'est de donner aux moindres figures, aux sujets les plus simples par eux-mêmes, une élévation qui charme, sans que la vérité de la nature soit sacrifiée, car c'est la première chose."

22. On Leleux, see, most recently, Denise Delouche, *Les peintres de la Bretagne* (Quimper: Palantines, 2011), 78–80.

23. Maxime du Camp, *Le Salon de 1859* (Paris: Librairie Nouvelle, 1859), 94–95: "nous montre l'incessante communion du paysan et de la terre, communion si intime et si profonde que bien souvent les deux êtres ne font plus qu'un."

24. See Neil McWilliam, "Le paysan au Salon: Critique d'art et construction d'une classe sous le Second Empire," in *La critique d'art en France, 1850–1900*, ed. Jean-Paul Bouillon (Saint-Étienne: Université de Saint-Étienne, 1989), 84–85.

25. Quoted in *Exigences de réalisme dans la peinture française entre 1830 et 1870*, exh. cat. (Chartres: Musée des Beaux-Arts, 1984), 137: "Toutes paysannes vraies qu'elles sont, débraillées et rapides, les faneuses ont une grande tournure."

26. The following remarks draw on the works presented in Geneviève Lacambre, *Le Musée du Luxembourg en 1874*, exh. cat. (Paris: Éditions des Musées Nationaux, 1974). The contents of the museum at this date were largely the result of purchases made during the Second Empire.

27. Edmond About, *Salon de 1864* (Paris: Hachette, 1864), 146–47: "où les usages et les costumes du bon temps se sont assez bien conservés"; "la religion simple et familière d'un peuple croyant, mais froid, pratique, laborieux."

28. On depictions of the region, see Viktoria von der Brüggen and Christine Peltre, *L'Alsace pittoresque: L'invention d'un paysage, 1770–1870*, exh. cat. (Paris: Hazan; Colmar: Musée Unterlinden, 2011).

29. Théodore Hersart de la Villemarqué, "Un débris du bardisme," *Écho de la jeune France*, April 15, 1836; quoted in Francis Gourvil, *Théodore-Claude-Henri Hersart de La Villemarqué (1815–1895) et le "Barzaz-Breiz" (1839–1845–1867): Origines, éditions, sources, critique, influences* (Paris: Oberthur, 1959), 50: "Dans nos montagnes . . . et nos vallées profondes, à l'abri du contact des villes et de

toute influence française, le passé revit dans le présent. La langue, la civilisation, les vieux souvenirs, les vieilles chansons historiques y ont été sauvés par un peuple pauvre."

30. Ibid., 24: "Non, tu n'es plus libre, ô ma patrie! mais nous t'adorons dans les fers, mais nos vies, mais ce sang que nous avons versé pendant vingt siècles pour ta cause sur les champs de bataille, est toujours à toi! Ah! si nous pouvions le verser encore! si nous pouvions briser les chaines dont on a chargé ta vieillesse."

31. Quoted in Robert Gildea, *The Past in French History* (New Haven: Yale University Press, 1994), 200: "Vous avez besoin, dit-on, d'être polis par la civilisation avancée du siècle, nous ne le disputerons pas, mais prenez garde qu'à force de vous polir la civilisation ne vous use, ne vous amoindrisse, n'efface l'empreinte de votre caractère religieux. . . . Voilà pourquoi nous voyons avec un contentement réel que vous teniez à vos vieux usages, à vos vieux costumes, à votre vieille langue."

32. Léon-Louis Buron, *La Bretagne catholique: Description historique et pittoresque* (Paris, 1856), 306: "Tandis qu'ailleurs une seule pensée infiltrée au milieu des masses les jette dans une turbulente agitation, là tout est calme et placide."

33. Saint-René Taillandier, introduction to *Li Prouvençalo: Poésies diverses*, ed. Joseph Roumanille (Avignon: Séguin Aîné, 1852), vi: "Le réveil du sentiment de race"; "espèce d'insurrection."

34. Frédéric Mistral, "Ce que nous voulons," speech delivered to an assembly of Catalan poets at Saint-Rémy, September 9, 1868; quoted in Eugène Garcin, "Croisade du Provençal contre le français," *Revue moderne* 50, no. 3 (February 10, 1869): 479: "Nous voulons que notre peuple, au lieu de croupir dans l'ignorance de sa propre histoire, de sa grandeur passée, de sa personnalité, apprenne enfin ses titres de noblesse; apprenne que ses pères se sont considérés toujours comme une race; apprenne qu'ils ont su, nos vieux Provençaux, vivre toujours en hommes libres, et en tout temps se défendre comme tels."

35. See Anne-Marie Thiesse, *Écrire la France: Le mouvement littéraire régionaliste de langue française entre la Belle Époque et la Libération* (Paris: PUF, 1991).

36. Philippe Burty, "L'exposition de Bordeaux," *Gazette des beaux-arts* 18, no. 5 (May 1, 1865): 465–66: "peuvent seules—pour ce qui concerne les artistes—décentraliser pacifiquement la France"; "la diffusion des idées d'art dans les masses." On provincial societies, see Nicolas Buchaniec, *Salons de province: Les expositions artistiques dans le nord de la France (1870–1914)* (Rennes: Presses Universitaires de Rennes, 2010); Ann-Doris Meyer, "Le paysage alsacien aux expositions de l'Association rhénane pour l'encouragement des beaux-arts (1837–1866)," in von der Brüggen and Peltre, *L'Alsace pittoresque*, 105–11; and Jean-Roger Soubiran, *Le paysage provençal et l'école de Marseille avant l'impressionnisme, 1845–1874*, exh. cat. (Paris: Réunion des Musées Nationaux; Toulon: Musée des Beaux-Arts, 1992), 70–83.

37. Philippe de Chennevières-Pointel, "Des beaux-arts en province, de leur histoire et de leur régénération," *Revue provinciale* 2 (March 1849): 57, 62, 64: "autorité impérieuse, absorbante, uniforme"; "l'inspiration solide, naïve, sublime, personnelle"; "le mépris des arts est le commencement de la déraison en politique; l'hydre communiste, que le movement provincial s'est tout d'abord donné pour but d'écraser et d'anéantir, a toujours, par un instinct naïf, méprisé et conspué les arts."

38. Hippolyte Fortoul to Napoléon III, September 13, 1852, reprinted in *Bulletin du Comité de la langue, de l'histoire et des arts de la France* 1 (1852): 22: "une fraîcheur de génie"; "vieil esprit français"; "conserver avec respect les chants qui rappellent les luttes héroïques de nos pères et les joies paisibles de leurs foyers domestiques."

39. Hippolyte Fortoul, December 5, 1853, reprinted in *Bulletin administratif de l'instruction publique* 4, no. 48 (December 1853): 602–3: "le moins de zèle pour l'oeuvre patriotique à laquelle ils sont conviés"; "[les] premiers efforts de leur génie nationale."

40. See Anne-Marie Thiesse, *Ils apprenaient la France: L'exaltation des régions dans le discours patriotique* (Paris: Maison des Sciences de l'Homme, 1997); and Stéphane Gerson *The Pride of Place: Local Memories and Political Culture in Nineteenth-Century France* (Ithaca, N.Y.: Cornell University Press, 2003). These works modify the arguments presented in Eugen Weber, *Peasants into Frenchmen: The Modernization of Rural France, 1870–1914* (Stanford: Stanford University Press, 1976).

41. Quoted in J. M. Poulain-Corbion, *Récit du voyage de l'Empereur et de l'Impératrice en Normandie et en Bretagne* (Paris, 1858), 244–45: "un peuple . . . qui est avant tout monarchique, catholique et soldat"; "Si la France n'est pas complètement homogène dans sa nature, elle est unanime dans ses sentiments"; "tout en hâtant sa marche dans les voies de la civilisation, elle conserve intacte la tradition des nobles sentiments qui l'ont distinguée depuis des siècles. Qu'elle conserve cette simplicité des moeurs, cette franchise proverbiale, cette fidélité à la foi jurée, cette persévérance dans le devoir, cette soumission à la volonté de Dieu qui veille sur le plus humble foyer domestique comme sur les plus hautes destinées des empires!"

42. G. Bruno [Augustine Fouillée], *Le tour de la France par deux enfants* (Paris: Belin, 1877), 308 "France aimée, nous sommes tes enfants, et nous voulons devenir dignes de toi!" See Jacques Ozouf and Mona Ozouf, "*Le Tour de la France par deux enfants*: The Little Red Book of the Republic," in *Realms of Memory. The Construction of the French Past*, ed. Pierre Nora, vol. 2, *Traditions* (New York: Columbia University Press, 1997), 125–50.

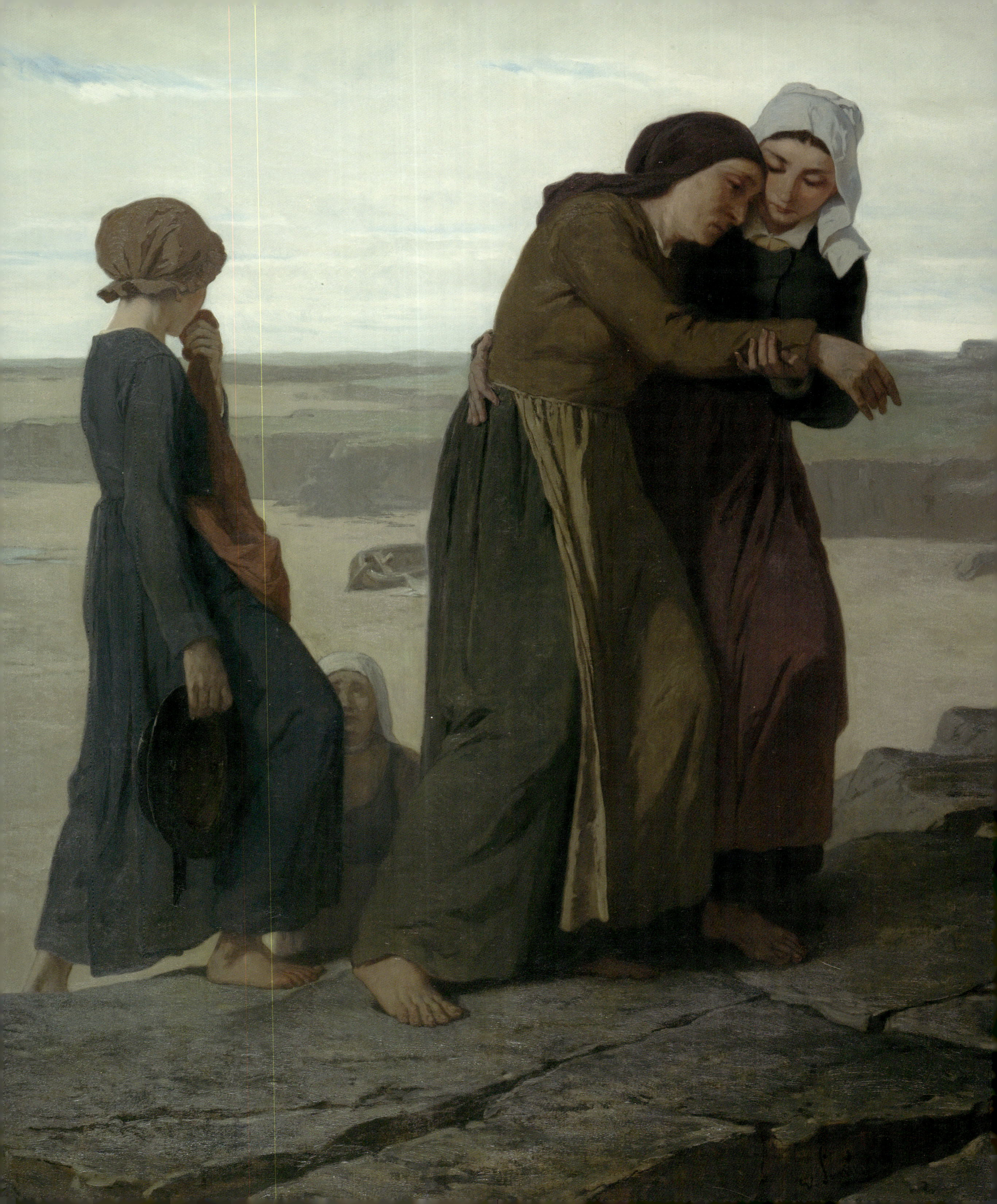

Place Myths of the Breton Landscape

MAURA COUGHLIN

OVER THE COURSE OF THE NINETEENTH CENTURY, the reputation of Brittany underwent dramatic change. Long considered a wild, Atlantic edge of Europe, this formerly remote province gradually became a desirably "authentic" and picturesque tourist destination in France. Nineteenth-century literary and visual representations presented Brittany as a place lost in time or as an open-air museum of the living past. Countless writers, illustrators, photographers, and painters (both French and foreign, as well as notable, educated Bretons) traveled the countryside to discover remnants of the region's Neolithic and Celtic histories.[1] In their images and texts, Brittany emerged as a vital yet ancient cultural landscape (fig. 41).

A sense of place, however, involves much more than visual and literary representation; the critical concept of "place" can also be understood as an ongoing process in which "the reproduction of social and cultural forms, the formation of biographies, and the transformation of nature ceaselessly become one another," to appropriate the words of the cultural geographer Allan Pred.[2] Bringing together a complex network of human experiences, creations, and expectations in the material landscape of Brittany, this cultural process of making and maintaining a sense of place was driven by the desire of tourists and artists to travel back in time, where they might discover and, alongside its residents, temporarily reinhabit this mythic landscape.

Although Brittany's mythic status or "place myth" seemingly excluded it from participating in modern history, Brittany had never been truly isolated.[3] Before it became a French province when Anne of Brittany married the French king in 1532, the allegiances of the duchy of Brittany shifted back and forth from England to France. Until the French Revolution, the province of Brittany retained some of its former political autonomy; this ended with the abolition of the duchy and its division into five *départements* in 1789. In spite or perhaps because of its gradual cultural integration into the modern French nation, visitors sought out aspects of the region that appeared to have retained the cultural heritage of the past. To many early nineteenth-century French

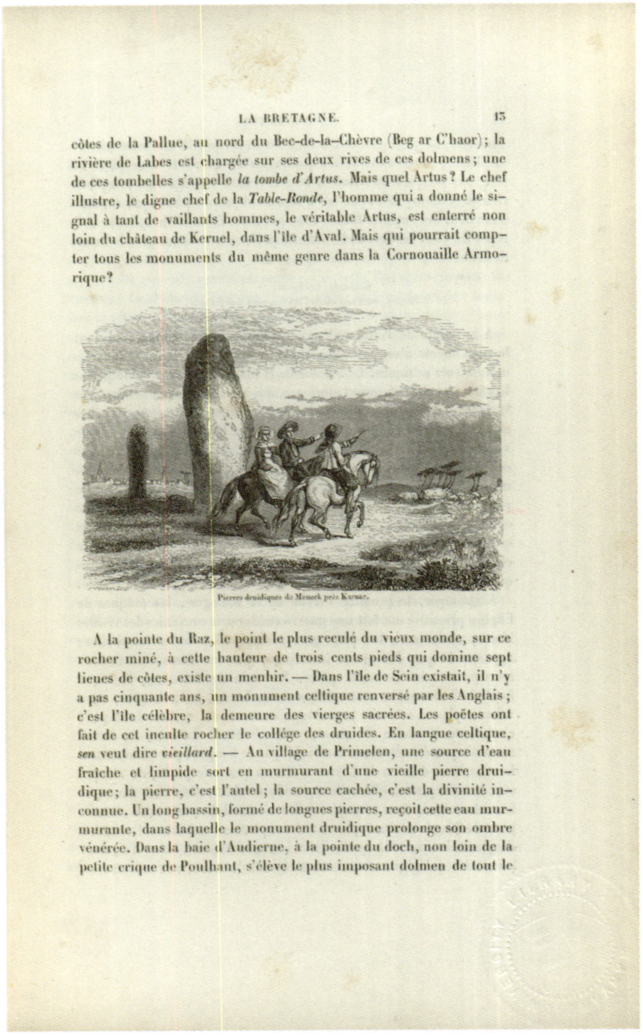
LA BRETAGNE. 13

côtes de la Pallue, au nord du Bec-de-la-Chèvre (Beg ar C'haor); la rivière de Labes est chargée sur ses deux rives de ces dolmens; une de ces tombelles s'appelle *la tombe d'Artus*. Mais quel Artus? Le chef illustre, le digne chef de la *Table-Ronde*, l'homme qui a donné le signal à tant de vaillants hommes, le véritable Artus, est enterré non loin du château de Keruel, dans l'île d'Aval. Mais qui pourrait compter tous les monuments du même genre dans la Cornouaille Armorique?

Pierres druidiques de Menock près Karnac.

A la pointe du Raz, le point le plus reculé du vieux monde, sur ce rocher miné, à cette hauteur de trois cents pieds qui domine sept lieues de côtes, existe un menhir. — Dans l'île de Sein existait, il n'y a pas cinquante ans, un monument celtique renversé par les Anglais; c'est l'île célèbre, la demeure des vierges sacrées. Les poëtes ont fait de cet inculte rocher le collége des druides. En langue celtique, *sen* veut dire *vieillard*. — Au village de Primelen, une source d'eau fraîche et limpide sort en murmurant d'une vieille pierre druidique; la pierre, c'est l'autel; la source cachée, c'est la divinité inconnue. Un long bassin, formé de longues pierres, reçoit cette eau murmurante, dans laquelle le monument druidique prolonge son ombre vénérée. Dans la baie d'Audierne, à la pointe du doch, non loin de la petite crique de Poulhant, s'élève le plus imposant dolmen de tout le

FIG. 41 Jules-Gabriel Janin, *Pierres druidiques*. From Janin, *La Bretagne* (Paris, 1845), 13

observers, Brittany—with few main roads, sea on three sides, and marshland to the east—was virtually isolated from the continent.[4] In the novel *Béatrix* (1839), Honoré de Balzac described provincial life as paralyzed in the past, noting that, without adequate roads, "especially in Brittany . . . certain towns [are] completely outside of the movement which gives to the nineteenth century its peculiar characteristics."[5] Echoing Balzac's sentiments, many overviews of landscape painting in Brittany emphasize the region's relative isolation from tourism, and hence from artists, until the national train line (the Orléans line from the Gare de Montparnasse) was extended to Quimper in the Second Empire.[6]

Undeniably, the expanded rail lines greatly reduced travel time for visitors to Brittany. But the changes brought by modern travel and transport technologies did not alter the landscape overnight or in a uniform pattern: Brittany in the nineteenth century was by no means homogeneous in terms of political allegiances, modernization, isolation of its communities, or relative prosperity of its workers. Migration within the province meant that the population of some large towns grew as the agricultural landscape emptied out. Cholera epidemics ravaged many small communities, even on the outer islands. Some exports boomed, as fish and shellfish were sent by train to the markets of Paris, but the trains also brought in cheaply manufactured goods with which local businesses could not compete. In the later nineteenth century, the new fish canneries in Douarnenez and Concarneau drew workers from the surrounding countryside; these large towns rapidly developed densely packed, squalid workers' quarters, whose residents had fled rural poverty.[7]

Before the train lines opened up the provinces of France to mass tourism, several notable series of lavishly illustrated travel texts were published on the subject of travel in Brittany. In books edited by Baron Isidore Taylor, Jules Janin, Léon Curmer, and others, France's provincial regions were catalogued with often-lengthy descriptions of climate, geography, and the effects of this local nature on the cultural character of the region and its inhabitants.[8] As the historian Stéphane Gerson has shown, these travel texts actively worked to inventory and critique all aspects of regional difference in the ultimate project of constructing a sense of national unity from the ruinous cultural disarray their authors found in the fragmented regions of post-Revolutionary France.[9] The illustrations in the volumes on Brittany both introduced the province to the French public and cemented visual stereotypes about Brittany in the general imagination.[10] From the 1790s onward, travelers described the people of Brittany as a remnant of a "pure" Celtic race, independent of France or any other culture. The

FIG. 42 From Jacques Cambry, *Voyage dans le Finistère* (Paris: Cercle-Social, 1799), frontispiece

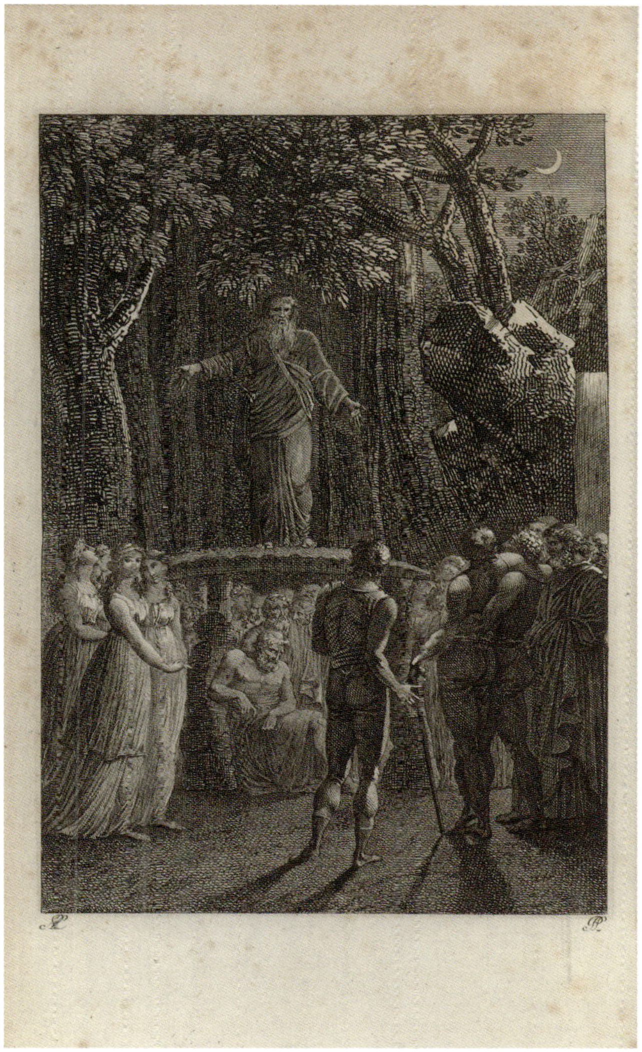

depopulated, rural landscape was viewed by many tourists as a "relic region," existing in a suspended state of cultural ruin, its prehistoric past at once mysteriously distant and uncannily alive.[11] Countless travelers to Brittany who had absorbed its powerful place myth through these texts eagerly sought to collect their own "authentic" views of the landscape of Celtic Brittany. Throughout the nineteenth century, French, British, and American visitors published travelogues, enthusiastically reporting on their observations of prehistoric dolmens, medieval pilgrimage sites and Calvary crosses (*calvaires*), rural coastal laborers, and women in traditional costume as well as religious events and women observing the "Celtic" cult of the dead.

Jacques Cambry, the founder of the antiquarian and archaeological society first known as the Celtic Academy, toured post-Revolutionary Brittany and published the first, and perhaps most influential, text on the region in 1799; *Voyage dans le Finistère* inspired generations of Celtomaniac travelers to seek out the traces of a Celtic and feudal past in the Romantic ruins of Brittany.[12] Cambry, for example, presented the Neolithic alignments of more than three thousand stones at Carnac as an undiscovered national legacy: "if the monument of Carnac had existed near London, how many times it would have been engraved and celebrated by the poets in England! How other nations could have been made to respect this temple of the Celtic nation!"[13]

Cambry had little doubt that prehistoric stone structures like Carnac had served sacrificial and funerary functions, and the illustrations to his text visualize this: the frontispiece of Cambry's travelogue, *Voyage dans le Finistère*, depicts a Druid speaking to a crowd from atop a table menhir, or passage tomb (fig. 42). Like many antiquarians and historians of his day, Cambry attributed Brittany's Neolithic stone monuments (ca. 5200–2200 BC) to the Celts and Druids, who settled in Brittany at least one thousand years later.[14] Writers, artists, and illustrators followed this Romantic, nationalist interpretation of Neolithic monuments as a native tradition of northern France that was resistant to the Roman Empire and unbeholden to Mediterranean classicism. There are no published works on Brittany's prehistoric stones before 1760, yet, by the mid-nineteenth century, menhirs, dolmens, and the Carnac alignments had become common themes of landscape description.[15] The republican historian Jules Michelet commented in 1851 that it is unlikely one could walk half an hour in some parts of Brittany "without encountering one of the formless monuments that are called druidic."[16]

Brittany's Neolithic standing stones are gray granite, the ubiquitous local stone that is the material of its geologic sense of place. Granite is also the stuff of its weather-beaten

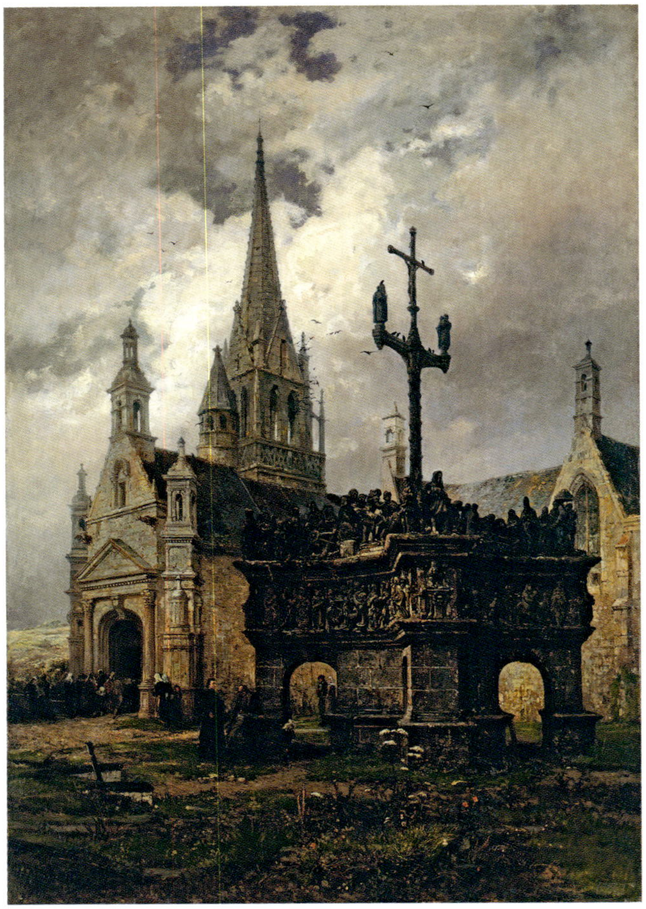

FIG. 43 Jacques Guiaud, *Church and Calvary at Guimiliau*, ca. 1873. Oil on canvas, 67¼ × 47⅝ in. (171 × 121 cm). Musée des beaux-arts de Quimper, France

craggy coastline and its lichen-covered, somber towns, sculptures, and churches. Writers often conflated the material qualities of this stone with the Breton landscape, the character of its people, and the many layers of their cultural histories. Balzac describes the residents of the area of Guérande as "old as the granite of Brittany . . . neither Frenchmen nor Gauls,—they are Bretons; or, to be more exact, they are Celts. Formerly, they must have been Druids, gathering mistletoe in the sacred forests and sacrificing men upon their dolmens."[17] Janin writes in his description of the islands off the coast of Finistère, "there is nothing as sad as this land of granite that is constantly beaten by wind, with neither a tree nor shelter."[18]

Tourists might have expected to find a "pure" Celtic or Druidic place, uncorrupted by outside contact, but Brittany had a long global history. For centuries Breton men had traveled widely on the world's oceans (as sailors, merchants, doctors, and naturalists), and Breton harbors were connecting points of a complex global network. In the fifteenth and sixteenth centuries, hundreds of vessels shipped out in the Bordeaux–England wine trade from the south coast of Finistère; in the seventeenth and eighteenth centuries, the French West India Company departed from the docks of Lorient for Asia; at the same time, Nantes (then part of Brittany) was the hub of the slave trade in France, outstripping the combined trade of Le Havre, Bordeaux, and La Rochelle. From the late eighteenth to the early twentieth century, cod fishing boats departed from Paimpol and other north coast harbors for Newfoundland and Iceland, and Saint-Brieuc was central to the global export of linen and hemp from the sixteenth to the nineteenth century. The wealth that flooded into (and through) Brittany from global trade between the fifteenth and eighteenth centuries built many of the fortified towns, castles, and religious compounds that still stand today.[19] These extensive trade networks connected Brittany to the Atlantic and beyond, yet the place myth of Brittany promised a static and insular Breton culture rather than a long heritage of maritime mobility. As the anthropologist Charles R. Menzies writes, Brittany's centuries of fishing and maritime trade are entirely continuous with our present globalized world; he cautions that it is myopic to look for a significant moment of modern, technological rupture with the past when the railroad arrived in Brittany.[20]

The elaborate architecture and sculpture of the parish closes (*enclos*) of Finistère are visible evidence of wealth derived from the international linen trade in the sixteenth and seventeenth centuries. These compounds built of granite contain ritual structures including pilgrimage churches, multifigured Calvary crosses, fountains, elaborate triumphal archways, ossuaries, and oratories (fig. 43).[21] Artists and writers from the time of Cambry onward were fascinated by this architectural and sculptural tradition, but they often presented these sites as provincial folk sculpture and

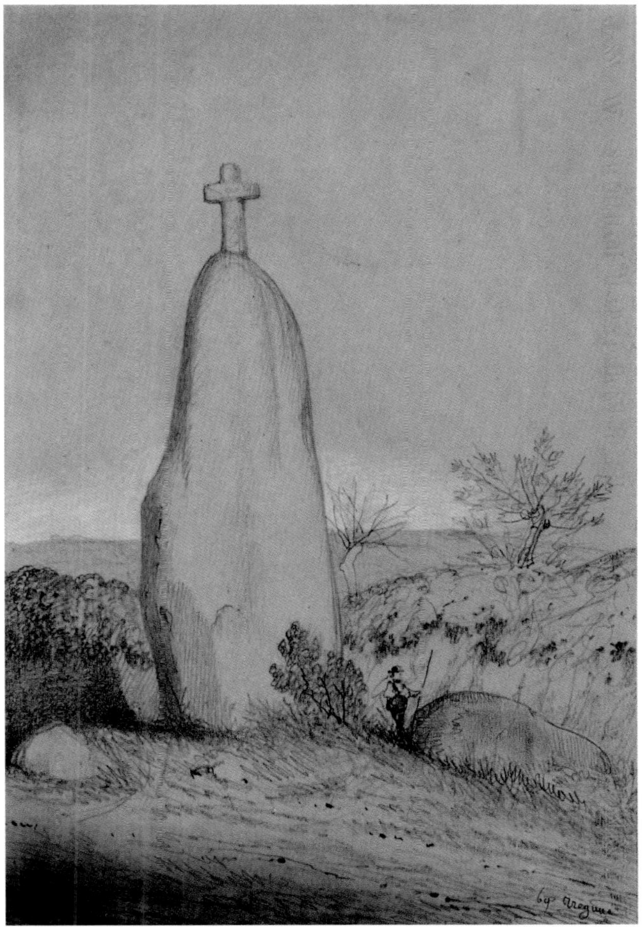

FIG. 44 Jean-Marie Sagot, *The Menhir at Trégunc*, 1869. 12¼ × 8½ in. (31.3 × 21.6 cm). Musée départemental Breton, Quimper, France

as vestiges of an isolated medieval past, instead of reading them as much more recent, competitive displays of early industrial wealth among the larger towns of Finistère. Because the closes continued to function as the focus of annual pilgrimages and pardon rituals, travel writers understood them as part of the (imagined) Celtic past kept alive by continuous devotion of the pious peasantry.

Jean-Marie Sagot, an illustrator who produced archaeological lithographs for the well-known series *Voyages pittoresques et romantiques dans l'ancienne France*, was trained as an architect, but he also worked as a traveling inspector and illustrator of historical monuments.[22] His drawing of 1869 depicts the megalithic menhir of Trégunc, a Neolithic standing stone that was appropriated and Christianized by being recarved, rendering the bulk of the granite an exaggerated base for a simple stone cross (fig. 44). Other menhirs, such as the famous standing stone of Saint-Uzec, had been recut this way after a series of Jesuit missions worked to "re-Christianize" Brittany in the seventeenth century.[23] In the 1890s, illustrations depicting Breton men recutting menhirs into ersatz calvaries emphasized rural Bretons' resistance to secular Third Republic policies.[24] Sagot's drawing, by including a diminutive peasant shepherd at the colossal menhir's base, depicts the present landscape of Brittany as having an emphatically Christian identity that has completely appropriated its pagan past.

As Karine Salomé's recent, extensive survey demonstrates, several of the Breton islands were imagined as spaces of unconverted pagan practice—even when there was no archaeological record to support it.[25] The tragic, suicidal Druid priestess Velleda is the sole survivor of nine virgins who inhabited the Île de Sein: the last refuge of the Druids in François-René de Chateaubriand's prose epic about the persecution of early Christians, *Les martyrs* (1809).[26] Michelet echoes the Romantic allure of this mythic Celtic past, describing the island as "the abode of the sacred virgins who gave the Celts fine weather or shipwreck. There they celebrated their gloomy and murderous orgies; and the seamen heard with terror, far off at sea, the clash of barbaric cymbals. This island is the traditional birth-place of Myrddyn, the Merlin of the middle age."[27] Velleda is, not surprisingly, a popular theme for Romantic painters of treacherous femmes fatales, such as André-Charles Voillemot (fig. 45), who theatrically positions his almost nude Druidess on an ambiguously Neolithic stone, again inhabiting the visible remains of the past.

By contrast, naturalist artists working on the French Atlantic coast developed a genre of images that focused on peasants working or looking to sea. Most influential were the conventions established by the Norman-born "peasant painter" Jean-François Millet in the 1850s. The eloquent gestures of his harvesters, milkmaids, washerwomen, gleaners, sowers, and wood gatherers are echoed in countless images

FIG. 45 André-Charles Voillemot, *Velleda*, 1869. Oil on canvas, 90½ × 58¼ in. (230 × 148 cm). Musée des beaux-arts, Rennes, France

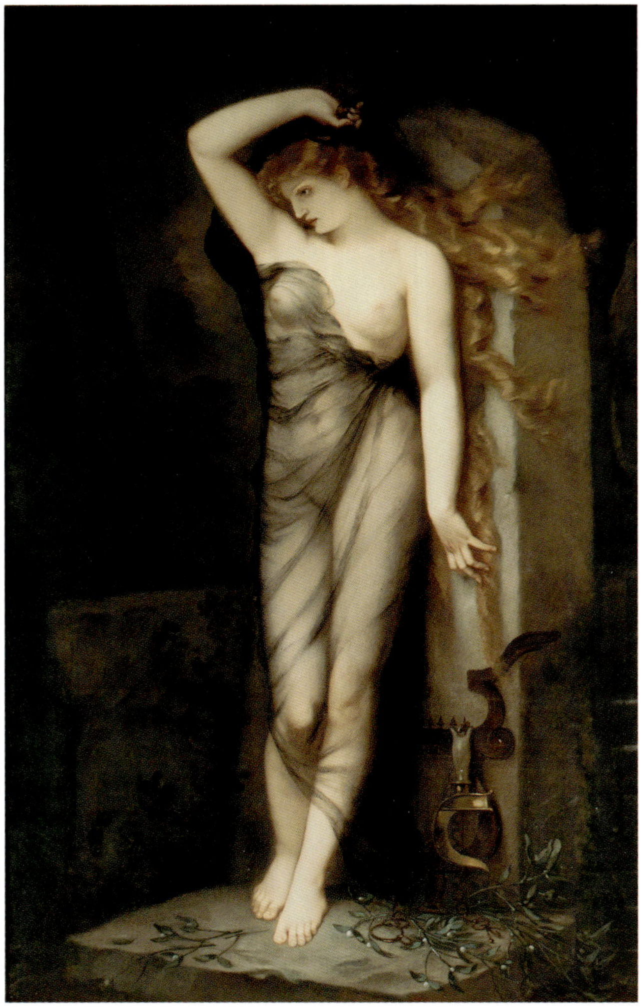

of seasonal labors painted by fellow artists working on the Brittany coast. Following Millet's lead, depictions of local Breton figures often show them from a low angle, a heroic compositional strategy, because it makes them seem to tower above the landscape. They gather seaweed, wash laundry at shoreline springs, harvest shellfish, or look to sea for signs of returning boats (fig. 46). Through these heroic figures, we perceive that the land is an ongoing place of work, of seasonal ritual, of unbroken continuity with its people. Like the images from travel texts that place Druids or peasants beside great stones, the physically robust peasant women depicted on the Brittany coast connect the landscape with its many histories.

In the 1850s, critics of Millet both attacked and validated the artist's unidealized vision of rural life and the French peasant's connection to "nature" through the rural landscape.[28] This attitude is best exemplified by the critic Jules-Antoine Castagnary's description of Millet's now iconic painting *The Gleaners* (Musée d'Orsay, Paris) in his review of the Salon of 1857:

> I find it difficult to admit that it is possible to separate the peasant from nature. He forms, one might say, an integral part of it, like a tree, like an ox. Individuality is certainly more pronounced in him than in an animal or plant, because he masters the one and uses the other. But from the artistic point of view, the peasant finds himself to be only the highest point in a series that begins with the vegetable and rises to him, a peasant, and proceeds in such a way that he is linked to nature by chains more solid than those of serfdom, I mean the laws of harmony. Like the oak whose strength he has, like the ox whose slowness he possesses, he is—by his gait, his dress, his attitude—in harmony with the nature that surrounds him. In the fields, whether he is working or resting, he is magnificent in color, form and action; elsewhere he is always grotesque and ugly.[29]

Breton peasants, especially peasant women, became a standard feature of naturalist landscapes of Brittany, presented in just this sense that Castagnary articulates: as part of an unbroken natural order. Whereas mid-nineteenth-century paintings that depict bourgeois men looking to sea from the shore (such as Gustave Courbet's *Sea at Palavas* [1854, Musée Fabre, Montpellier]) invite the viewer to ponder with them the infinite expanses of nature, Breton marine landscapes do not present peasant women as having the same aesthetic relationship with either the viewer or the sea. Following the influential model established by Millet's peasants, Breton peasant women are most often positioned as human aspects of the landscape, to be looked at as they

FIG. 46 Jean-François Millet, *Washerwomen*, ca. 1855.
Oil on canvas, 17⅛ × 21⅛ in. (43.5 × 53.7 cm).
Museum of Fine Arts, Boston,
Gift of Mrs. Martin Brimmer, 06.2422

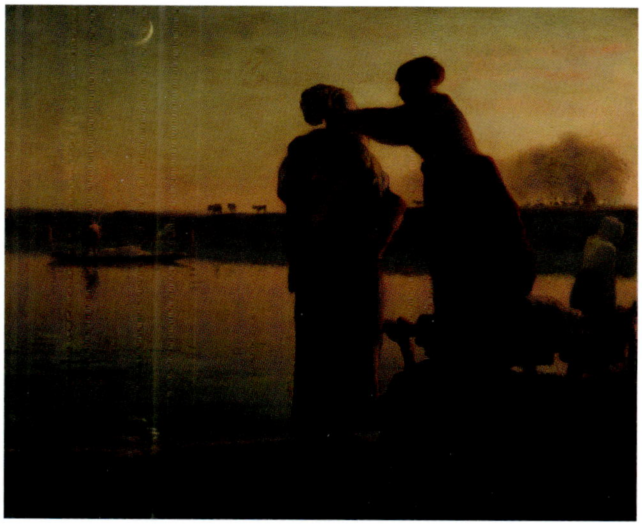

work, wait, watch, mourn, gossip, and, occasionally, take part in religious gatherings.

In Evariste-Vital Luminais's *The Widow* or *The Fisherman's Family* of 1865 (fig. 47), we can imagine that a tragedy has just transpired on the shore. Five female figures ascend a rocky cliff; the central figure, who wears a black cloth of mourning on her head, is held up in the arms of another woman, caught in a swoon of grief that echoes countless images of the Virgin Mary at the foot of the cross. Rather than watching the sea in hopes of a returning ship, she walks away from it: for her there is nothing more to look at.[30] Luminais, later a painter of grand historical genre paintings, shows us the everyday drama of life on the coast near his home city of Nantes.

The same year that Luminais's painting appeared at the Paris Salon, the naturalist painter Jules Breton first visited Brittany and was immediately drawn to its landscape and peasant culture. He returned many times to the town of Douarnenez, where one of his favorite themes was that of women washing clothing in a spring by the sea. A young sardine processor, Jeanne Calvet, posed for many of the female figures in *The Washerwomen of the Breton Coast* (cat. 61).[31] This scene of everyday labor has no trace of Douarnenez's pervasive presence of dead fish, waste, packaged food, or, for that matter, global trade, as a sardine worker is transformed into a timeless goddess, enacting a plein air ritual washing of white linen. Breton's images of peasant figures, like Millet's laundresses, bear heavy burdens on their heads, becoming statuesque caryatids, wedded to land, heroic above all. By locating the heavy and unpleasant work of washing laundry by hand in a spring on the coast, Breton perpetuates a celebration of "timeless" and "natural" female labor that had become a feature of the local landscape. Obdurate and stony in resolute devotion to their task, his washerwomen are as wedded to the landscape as are the granite cliffs surrounding them.

Marguerite Moreau, who posed for *The Wounded Seagull*, was another of Breton's favorite models from Douarnenez (cat. 62). The tips of her *penn-sardin* coiffe (the local costume of the women of Douarnenez) are caught by the wind, mimicking the wings of the bird in her arms and the one who flies above the sea behind her. Breton emulates the examples of both Millet's and Courbet's heroic peasants in this image of woman, sea, and creature. Moreau, with her dark hair and strong, working arms, seems a powerful female force, allied to coastal nature. Following the example of Breton, so many artists were drawn to Douarnenez in the later nineteenth century that it came to be called the "Breton Barbizon."[32] But in none of these coastal naturalist images do we have the least inkling that any tourists, artists, or other outsiders are present in the landscape.

With the exception of one painting by Berthe Morisot (discussed below), the Impressionists did not paint the Brittany coast as a space of modern tourism until Claude Monet worked at Belle-Île in 1886. This stands in marked contrast to images of the Normandy coast that proliferate from the 1860s onward. The art historian Robert Herbert has eloquently shown that the modern desires of tourists, like those of traveling artists, are lenses that significantly shape landscape representations.[33] In the seaside town of Trouville on the Lower Normandy coast, Courbet, Eugène Boudin, and Monet all spent summers in the 1860s, painting views of the shore and sea and portraits of the summer

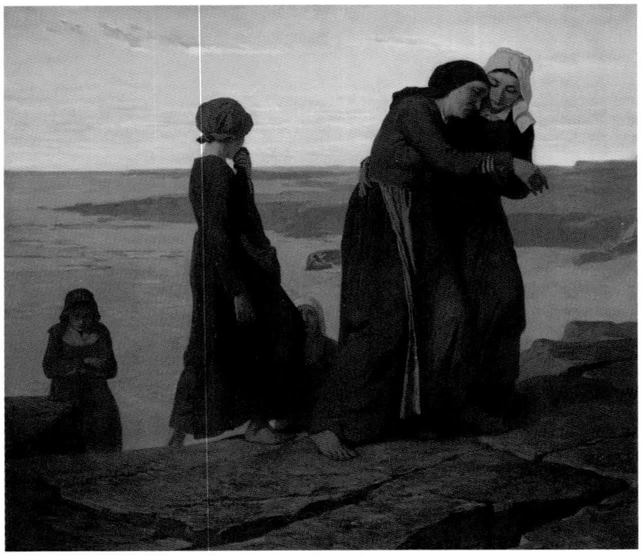

FIG. 47 Evariste-Vital Luminais, *The Widow* or *The Fisherman's Family*, 1865. Oil on canvas, 35¾ × 41⅛ in. (91 × 104.5 cm). Musée d'Orsay, Paris, France

residents and their friends and family; sometimes, they also turned their attention to the modern life of summer tourism. To describe this latter type of image, Herbert borrows the sociologist John Urry's term the "collective gaze": a view of the tourist experience that acknowledges the presence of tourism and the representation of different classes, from different places.[34] The resort at Étretat, farther north in the Seine-Maritime *département* of Upper Normandy and known for its dramatically pierced cliffs, had a similar appeal for all of these artists. In the 1870s and 1880s, Monet, who prided himself on his Norman roots, gradually moved away from including the presence of modern coastal tourism that had been so prominent in his works of the 1860s. In his celebrated series of paintings of waves and rocks, painted in 1886 on Belle-Île, there are no figures present at all. In these later works, Monet's "romantic gaze" erases the presence of tourism. As Herbert writes: "Giving primacy to the self, Monet's paintings communicate the reactions of a privileged individual who convinces the viewer of distance from the city and its crowds, from work and its corollaries of reason and community."[35]

Since Herbert published this carefully researched text in 1994, the field of tourism studies has expanded beyond the exclusively visual fascinations of the bourgeois urban flaneur, providing new critical approaches to representations of tourism. Rather than viewing the experience of tourism as a preexisting discourse that is imposed on the hapless traveler, Dean MacCannell and others have shown that tourists have participatory agency in generating their own narratives.[36] Tourism studies, more recently, also consider the embodied experience of the tourist: participatory, material, and bodily experiences such as walking, dancing, traveling, eating, and sea bathing.[37] Considering the many relationships forged by the practices of tourism, in which tourists, landscapes, locals, and many things, both natural and manufactured, are bound together—what one researcher has dubbed "tourismscapes"—I would like to propose some ways in which artists and other summer tourists who traveled by train to Brittany became intrigued by the networked summer culture, or tourismscape, of the Breton religious summer festivals, or pardons.

A full generation before the Impressionists, landscape painters of the Barbizon generation such as Jean-Baptiste-Camille Corot, Charles-François Daubigny, and Paul Huet painted the coasts, ports, peasants, fairs, and religious festivals of Brittany. Monet's friend and mentor Boudin, who made his career painting the bourgeois summer culture of resort towns on the Normandy coast, also worked extensively in Brittany, where he found the pardons of rural Brittany to be a countertype of summer festivity to the parade of bourgeois fashion on the beach at Trouville.[38]

Following the lead of Corot, who began painting images of Breton peasants in the 1830s, Boudin painted two types of peopled landscapes, both of which represent the participation of those gathered in particularly site-specific summer tourism performances of ritual and costume. The beaches of Trouville were the summer site of a year-round culture of fashion display (performed on the Paris boulevards, for instance) for French and British upper-class women (cat. 111). At Breton pardons, peasant women were likewise on display in holiday costume that signified very specifically

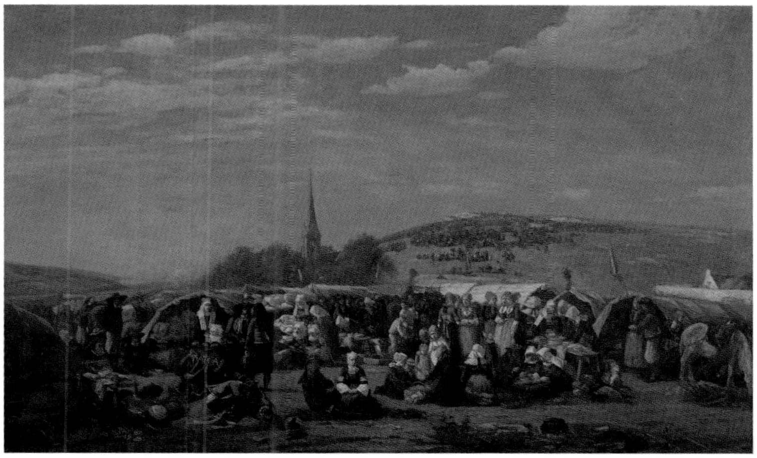

FIG. 48 Eugène Boudin, *Pardon of Sainte-Anne-la-Palud*, 1858. Oil on canvas. Musée Malraux, Le Havre

on the local level as to the village, family, wealth, and marital status of the wearer.

These popular religious practices were often framed in travel narratives as vestiges of Celtic or pagan-inflected medieval rites that had been hybridized with Catholicism.[39] Like Paris fashion display, Breton pardon spectacle had a specific temporal and geographic legibility for its participants who had, for the most part, traveled to attend the event. In the context of religious spectacle in Brittany, the term *pardon* is often used loosely for many types of events. Generally speaking, pardons were held on a saint's feast day and focused on a local site such as a church, chapel, or holy well. The saint might be further connected to the site by the presence of sacred relics (such as the finger of John the Baptist at Saint-Jean-du-Doigt, or Saint John of the Finger) or reports of a miraculous appearance there. The pardon at Sainte-Anne-la-Palud, depicted by Boudin in 1858, was one of the largest (fig. 48). According to Breton popular belief, St. Anne, patron saint of sailors, had been born a Breton queen in Douarnenez before she went to the Holy Land.[40] Other pardons had very local origins (sites such as holy wells were often pagan in origin), yet they partook equally of the fervor of the nineteenth-century religious revival that was gaining steam throughout rural France. Travel to the pardons was often construed as an act of penance and endurance in itself. As depicted in Alexandre Le Bihan's painting, participants came by foot or over water (see fig. 50): to attend Mass and perform a range of rituals—often including the circling of a holy building, well, or stone—in order to obtain grace or forgiveness. Thus, through travel, a very dispersed Breton population was temporarily united in its profession of faith to the local saint or site.[41]

Cambry's influential text describes a pardon as a bodily interaction with a specific place, such as

> a chapel, a fountain, a place devoted to the memory of some saint, of some miracle. There you confess, take communion, give alms, submit to superstitious practice; there you buy crosses, rosaries and images to touch to the statue of the demi-god; there you rub your face, your forehead, your paralytic arm on a miracle-working stone; there you throw coins and pins into the fountains; you soak a shirt in one in order to be cured, or a belt to assure child-bearing without pain. You leave after having danced, having gotten drunk, money all spent but full of hope.[42]

As Cambry notes, a pardon's festive social practices blurred the lines of sacred and profane. After the daytime penitential acts of circling the site, singing hymns, walking in procession, and attending High Mass, pardons often descended into festive celebration.[43] In Brittany, artists were most interested in the pious events of the daytime and did not, for the most part, include the secular or commercial aspects of these gatherings (fig. 49).

Representations of these events have long been interpreted by recourse to the notion of artistic "primitivism."[44] In an influential article on Paul Gauguin and the Pont-Aven school, the art historians Fred Orton and Griselda Pollock argue that the preferred subject matter of these painters—rural women in festive regional costume and images of subsistence farming and coastal harvesting—was in fact predicated by the new wealth accumulated through industrialized agriculture, manufactured goods, and trade with the rest of the continent.[45] Misunderstanding the

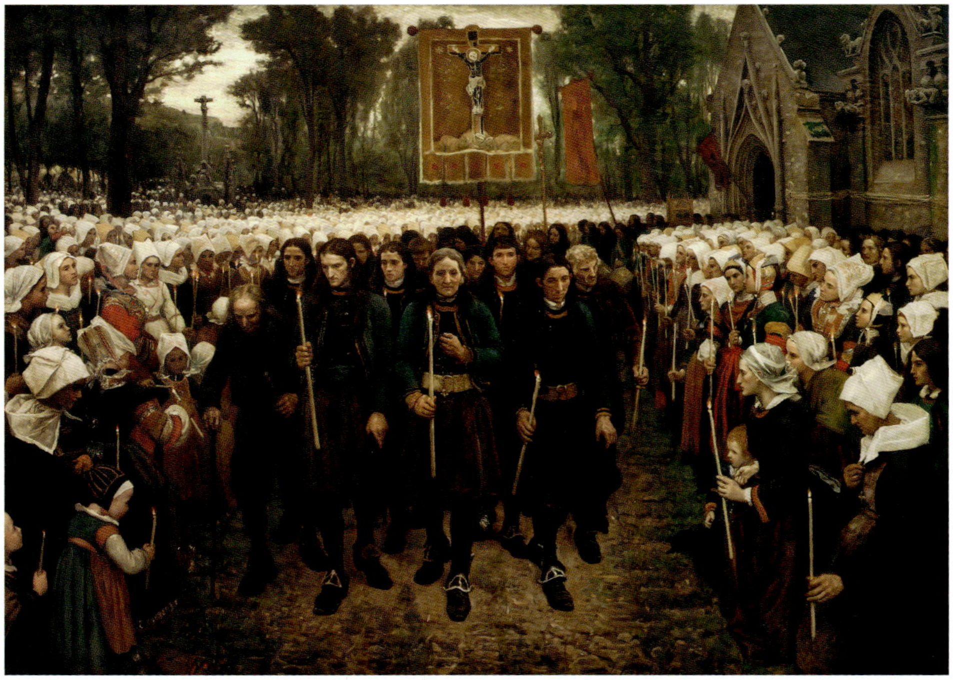

FIG. 49 Jules Breton, *A Pardon, Brittany*, 1869. Oil on canvas. Colección Museo Nacional de Belles Artes, Havana, Cuba

modernity of local costume, just as they misread the history of the *calvaires*, was all bound up in the pictorial romance of Brittany. However, reducing all imagery produced in Brittany to misguided primitivism denies, through the logic of the "tourist gaze," the profound knowledge of local culture that some artists gained through prolonged contact with the place. This influential concept of modern "primitivism" also assumes that a dramatic break with the past was effected by modernity and that this break was willfully ignored. Tourists who came from outside the region desired the myth of Brittany, and Bretons, on tour quite locally, played a part in the process of enacting and maintaining their living traditions as these shifted, grew, or died out.

Reading the visual spectacle of pardons with exclusive reference to the one-directional "tourist gaze" fails to acknowledge that almost everyone at a pardon was looking at the others as "strangers" and that being seen there was part of the attraction of participating, as much as it was for a fashionable bourgeois woman on the beach at Trouville. In addition to attracting tourists from elsewhere, the pardons brought together the infrequently mobile female population of islands and small villages that had little outside contact. These festive events provided a rare opportunity for peasant women to stop working and to travel (generally by foot or over water), but, unlike the international crowds who flocked to the Channel coast, this was a very local form of tourism within Brittany that was more akin to a medieval pilgrim's journey than a restful modern vacation (fig. 50). Viewing the pardon as a "tourismscape" helps us to understand that this spectacle of religious tourism was a collective performance that served to maintain Brittany's place myth.

Berthe Morisot's painting *The Harbor at Lorient* (cat. 116), as the curator André Cariou explains, is a singular early example of an Impressionist working in Brittany.[46] Morisot represents the Breton port as it might be encountered on a pleasurable summer day, including a fashionably dressed, modern Parisian woman (her sister, Edma) on the wall at the right. The clear, coastal light in her painting owes much to her teacher Corot's insistence on working from nature. Like Monet at Saint-Adresse or Boudin at Trouville in the 1860s, Morisot's interest in this place is entirely of her present moment. The port at Lorient was not a draw for tourists as was the channel coast at this time—Morisot's reason for visiting was that her sister Edma had just married a naval officer, Adolphe Pontillon, and he was stationed in Lorient.[47] In spite of these almost accidental circumstances, the artist's remarkably modern image does not interpret Lorient as France's former gateway to the Orient, nor does it people the landscape with recognizable provincials (as Corot did in Brittany); this stands in marked contrast to the allegorical image of the port of Marseille, painted about the same year by her dear friend Pierre Puvis de Chavannes

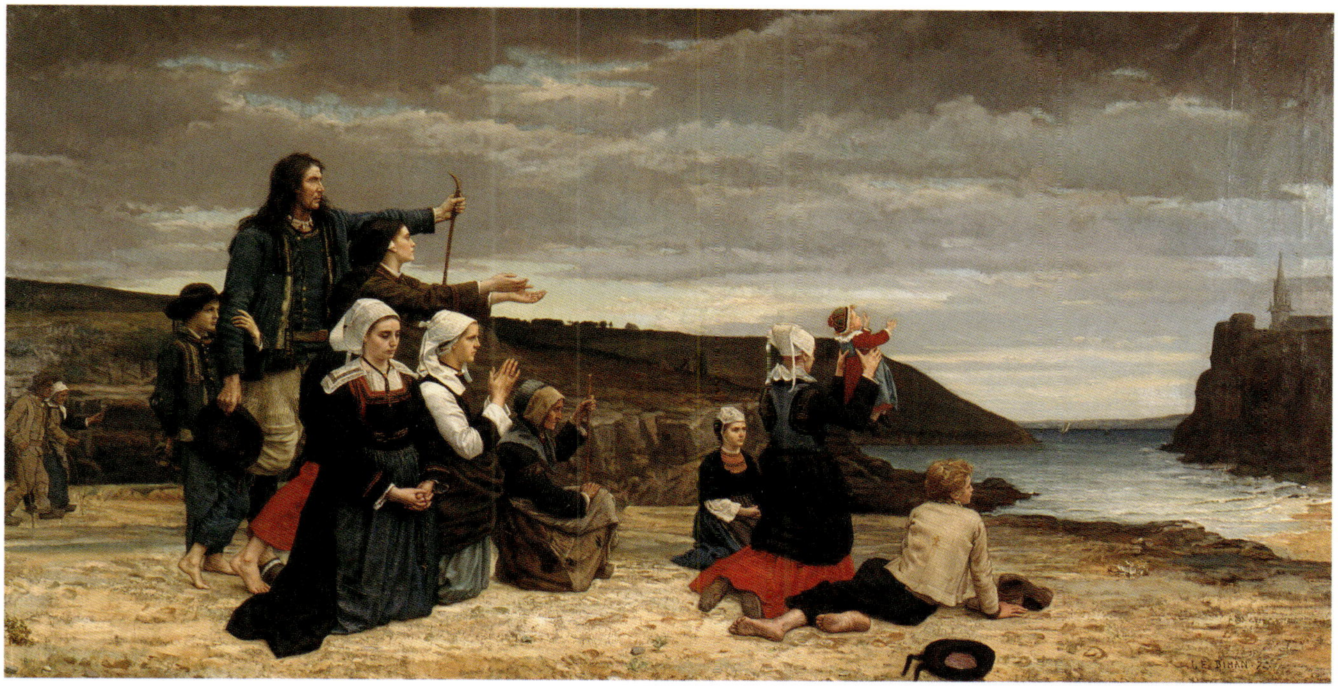

FIG. 50 Alexandre Le Bihan, *Pilgrimage in Brittany*, 1875. Oil on canvas, 50 × 99¼ in. (127 × 252 cm). Musée des beaux-arts, Rennes, France

(cat. 119). The once globally connected port of Lorient is remade as a generic modern French river landscape with boats, not so very different from Impressionist views of the Seine. For Morisot, this is a site that seems to have no place myth at all, a place that modern women now occupy as tourists, recent residents, and artists. This Impressionist representation of bourgeois tourism on the Brittany coast would remain unique, without offspring for the next few decades.

By the late 1870s the menhirs, calvaries, costumes, pardons, and ports that would fascinate fin de siècle naturalists as well as the artists of the Pont-Aven circle had become firmly entrenched elements of Brittany's visual place myth. The landscape of Brittany, both natural and cultural, was imagined by the French as carved out of ancient granite and inhabited by a living culture. Artists saw some of this, and invented some, becoming part of the extended network that built and maintained the place myth of the landscape of Brittany.

1. For overviews of the nineteenth-century discovery of Brittany by the Celtic Academy, see Catherine Bertho, "L'invention de la Bretagne: Genèse sociale d'un stéréotype,'" *Actes de la recherche en sciences sociales*, no. 35 (1980): 45–62; Nicole Belmont et al., "L'Académie celtique," in *Hier pour demain: Arts, traditions et patrimoine* (Paris: Réunion des Musées Nationaux, 1980), 54–77; Mona Ozouf, "L'invention de l'ethnographie française: Le questionnaire de l'Académie celtique," *Annales: Histoire, sciences sociales* 36, no. 2 (1981): 210–30. For recent surveys of landscape artists working in Brittany, see Denise Delouche and Jean-Marc Michaud, *Bretagne, terre des peintres* (Saint-Thonan: Cloître, 2003); André Cariou, *De Turner à Monet: La découverte de la Bretagne par les paysagistes au XIXe siècle*, exh. cat. (Quimper: Musée des Beaux-Arts de Quimper; Palantines, 2011); and Denise Delouche, *Les peintres de la Bretagne* (Quimper: Palantines, 2011).

2. Allan Pred, "Place as Historically Contingent Process: Structuration and the Time-Geography of Becoming Places," *Annals of the Association of American Geographers* 74, no. 2 (1984): 292.

3. The history and philosophy of the term "place myth" is elaborated in Nina Lübbren, *Rural Artists' Colonies in Europe, 1870–1910* (Manchester: Manchester University Press, 2001), 115. Whereas Lübbren outlines a Foucauldian interpretation of the term as it was most notably theorized in Nicholas Green, *The Spectacle of Nature: Landscape and Bourgeois Culture in Nineteenth-Century France* (Manchester: Manchester University Press, 1990), the present essay departs from an emphasis on purely visual modes of expressing tourist experience.

4. See Delouche and Michaud, *Bretagne, terre des peintres*, 11.

5. Honoré de Balzac, *Béatrix*, trans. Katharine Prescott Wormeley (Boston: Roberts, 1895), 1.

6. This is a common approach taken in many of the aforementioned surveys of art and tourism in Brittany. On the changes in modern tourism affected by train and motor travel in the late nineteenth and early twentieth centuries, see Patrick Young, "Of Pardons, Loss and Longing: The Tourist's Pursuit of Originality in Brittany, 1890–1935," *French Historical Studies* 30, no. 2 (2007): 269–304.

7. Charles R. Menzies, *Red Flags and Lace Coiffes: Identity and Survival in a Breton Fishing Village* (Toronto: University of Toronto Press, 2011), 17.

8. Isidore-Justin-Séverin Taylor and Charles Nodier, *Voyages pittoresques et romantiques dans l'ancienne France*, 24 vols. (Paris: J. Didot l'Ainé; Firmin Didot et Cie, 1820–78). Among the volumes are those dedicated to Ancienne Normandie, Bourgogne, Picardie, Champagne, Auvergne, Bretagne, Languedoc, and the Franche-Comté. Jules-Gabriel Janin, *La Bretagne* (Paris: E. Bourdin, 1844); and *Les français peints par eux-mêmes: Encyclopédie morale du dix-neuvième siècle* (Paris: L. Curmer, 1840). On the latter text and its patterns of description, see Luce Abélès, "La province vue par Les Français," in *Les français peints par eux-mêmes: Panorama social du XIXe siècle*, Dossiers du Musée d'Orsay, ed. Ségolène Le Men (Paris: Réunion des Musées Nationaux, 1993), 56. Also see Cariou, *De Turner à Monet*, 84–88.

9. Stéphane Gerson, "Parisian Litterateurs, Provincial Journeys and the Construction of National Unity in Post-Revolutionary France," *Past and Present*, no. 151 (May 1996): 141–73.

10. Cariou, *De Turner à Monet*, 82.

11. The phrase "relic region" comes from David M. Hopkin, *Voices of the People in Nineteenth-Century France* (Cambridge: Cambridge University Press, 2012), 33.

12. Jacques Cambry, *Voyage dans le Finistère; ou, État de ce département en 1794 et 1795* (Paris: Cercle-Social, 1799).

13. Jacques Cambry, *Monuments celtiques, ou recherches sur le culte des pierres* (Paris: Johanneau, 1805), xxx: "Si le monument de Carnac avoit [*sic*] existé près de Londres, combien de fois on l'eût fait graver. Comme il eût été célébré par les poètes de l'Angleterre! comme en eût force les nations à respecter ce temple métropolitain de la Celtique! Qu'on en juge par la multitude d'ouvrages imprimés avec tant de luxe, qui représentent le *stonehenge*." As Bertho, "L'invention de la Bretagne," outlines, the character of the landscape had a powerful function in the construction of Brittany's provincial identity in the wake of the Revolution.

14. In the preface to *Monuments celtiques*, Cambry outlines the study of this legacy as the agenda of the Celtic Academy as discussed in Krzysztof Pomain, "Franks and Gauls," in *Realms of Memory*, ed. Pierre Nora and Lawrence D. Kritzman (New York: Columbia University Press, 1996), 40.

15. The few traces of the Druids found in classical literature are Iron Age. The comte de Caylus in the 1760s was the first to suggest that Neolithic monuments such as Carnac were much older than the classical period. See Cariou, *De Turner à Monet*, 52–55, for an excellent overview of Romantic-era antiquarian and artistic representations of Brittany's prehistoric monuments.

16. Jules Michelet, *History of France*, trans. G. H. Smith (New York: Appleton, 1847), 271.

17. Balzac, *Béatrix*, 9.

18. Janin, *La Bretagne*, 595: "Rien n'égale la tristesse de ce séjour sans cesse battu par les vents; pas un arbre, pas un abri, sur cette terre de granit."

19. Menzies, *Red Flags and Lace Coiffes*, 21.

20. Ibid.

21. Stephen Walker, "Accommodating the Apocalypse: An Examination of the Relationships between the Economics of Salvation and the Architecture of the Breton Enclos," *Journal of Architecture* 6 (Autumn 2001): 249.

22. Musée Départemental Breton, Quimper, files.

23. See Daniel Giraudon, "Patrimoine de Pleumer-Bodoù: Le menhir de Saint Uzec," *Mythologie française*, no. 237 (December 2009): 11–23.

24. Catherine Puget, *Peintres de la Bretagne et quête spirituelle (1860–1960)*, exh. cat. (Pont-Aven: Musée de Pont-Aven, 2006), 19.

25. Karine Salomé, *Les îles bretonnes: Une image en construction, 1750–1914* (Rennes: Presses Universitaires de France, 2003), 221.

26. Ibid., 224. See Delouche, *Les peintres de la Bretagne*, 66.

27. Michelet, *History of France*, 152.

28. See Maura Coughlin, "The Artistic Origins of the French Peasant-Painter: Jean-François Millet; Between Normandy and Barbizon" (PhD diss., New York University, Institute of Fine Arts, 2001).

29. Jules-Antoine Castagnary, "Salon de 1857," first published in *Le Présent*, 1857; translated and quoted in Elizabeth Holt, *The Art of All Nations, 1850–73* (Princeton: Princeton University Press, 1982), 204.

30. This is an important naturalist theme in the later nineteenth century. For an overview of the theme of the widow on the seacoast, see Maura Coughlin, "Representing Heritage and Loss on the Brittany Coast: Sites, Things and Absence," *International Journal of Heritage Studies* 2 (2012): 1–16.

31. Annette Bourrut Lacouture, *Jules Breton, Painter of Peasant Life*, exh. cat. (New Haven: Yale University Press in association with the National Gallery of Ireland, 2002), 243.

32. Cariou, *De Turner à Monet*, 108.

33. Robert L. Herbert, *Monet on the Normandy Coast: Tourism and Painting, 1867–1886* (New Haven: Yale University Press, 1994).

34. Ibid., 11.

35. Ibid., 111.

36. See Dean Maccannell, "Tourist Agency," *Tourist Studies* 1 (2001): 23–37. Also see René van der Duim, "Tourismscapes: An Actor-Network Perspective," *Annals of Tourism Research* 34, no. 4 (2007): 961–76.

37. See David Crouch and Luke Desforges, "The Sensuous in the Tourist Encounter: Introduction; The Power of the Body in Tourist Studies," *Tourist Studies* 3 (2003): 7.

38. See John House and David Hopkin, *Impressionists by the Sea*, exh. cat. (London: Royal Academy of Arts, 2007), 49.

39. See Young, "Of Pardons, Loss and Longing," for an excellent discussion of the literature on pardons and tourism. Also see Cariou, *De Turner à Monet*; and Philippe Le Stum, *Pardons et pèlerinages de Bretagne* (Rennes: Ouest-France, 1997).

40. For example, see Peter Anson, *Fisher Folk-Lore: Old Customs, Taboos and Superstitions among Fisher Folk, Especially in Brittany and Normandy and on the East Coast of Scotland* (London: Faith Press, 1965), 69.

41. See Phillippe Lacombe, "The Breton Body in Culture and Religion" *Sport in Society* 4, no. 3 (2001): 32.

42. Cambry, *Voyage dans le Finistère*, 73–74: "On appelle pardons en Bretagne, une chapelle, une fontaine, un lieu consacré par le souvenir de quelque saint, de quelque miracle. On s'y confesse, on communie, on y donne l'aumône, on se soumet à quelque pratique superstitieuse, on achète des croix, des chapelets et des images qu'on fait toucher à la statue du saint; on frotte son front, son genou, son hras paralysé, contre une pierre merveilleuse; on jette des liards et des épingles dans les fontaines, on y trempe sa chemise pour se guérir, sa ceinture pour accoucher sans peine, son enfant, pour le rendre inaccessible à la douleur. On se retire après avoir dansé, après s'être enivré, vide d'argent, mais riche d'espérance."

43. Lacombe, "Breton Body," 35–38.

44. Hollister Sturges, *Jules Breton and the French Rural Tradition*, exh. cat. (Omaha, Nebr.: Joslyn Art Museum, 1982), 83, describes pardons as "[u]nchanged for two hundred years, these annual mystical penitential pilgrimages were the last vestiges of Feasts of the Dead."

45. Fred Orton and Griselda Pollock, "Les Données Bretonnantes: La Prairie de Représentation," in *Avant Gardes and Partisans Reviewed* (Manchester: Manchester University Press, 1996), 80.

46. Cariou, *De Turner à Monet*, 25.

47. Ibid.

1

PARIS AND THE MODERN CITYSCAPE

PARIS WAS SEMINALLY IMPORTANT in constructing French national identity. By far the largest city in France in the mid-nineteenth century, it was also the largest on mainland Europe, although smaller than London, at that time the world's most populous city. The population of Paris doubled from about one million in 1850 to two million in 1870.[1] Paris served as the economic, political, and cultural heart of the French nation. It was even famously described by the German Francophile Walter Benjamin as the "capital of the nineteenth century."[2] It remains to this day the leading tourist destination in the world.

The mid-nineteenth century saw the radical transformation of Paris as a result of the efforts of Napoléon III and the Prefect of the Seine, Baron Georges-Eugène Haussmann. Much of old, medieval Paris, with its tight, narrow streets and alleyways—as recorded in the photographs of Charles Marville—was swept away and replaced by an urban plan of expansive boulevards, parks, and a modern sewer system, as well as major buildings such as the Opéra and the new Louvre.[3] The very architecture of the city was seen as having nationalistic traits. The travel writer Adolphe Joanne argued that the boulevards were an emblem of France's democracy because there the full range of social classes intermingled: "Paris, the town of equality, the democratic town par excellence, wanted to have in its heart a promenade that represents, that serves the needs of the crowd, and that completely belongs to everyone. [I]t was created, with love, the true promenade of the future, the true garden of the freed nation, the Boulevards."[4]

Photographers were among the first to document the new Paris. Gustave Le Gray photographed new bridges and renowned architectural landmarks, while Édouard Baldus recorded the newly constructed Louvre, and Charles Marville, the renovated parks and squares of the capital. Stereoscopic views flourished during the Second Empire and played a crucial role in shaping the visual culture of Paris. Painters represented the transformed capital more rarely in the 1850s. Even as the city witnessed unprecedented new construction, the major monuments of the Middle Ages continued to be revered. The great medieval cathedral of Notre-Dame, for example, was extensively restored at midcentury.

A range of painters and photographers represented the structure at this time, including Johan-Barthold Jongkind, Baldus, and Charles Nègre. Paris's expansion was emulated in the nation's second city, Marseille, the reconstruction of which was documented in the photographs of Adolphe Terris.

The confidence surrounding Napoléon III's new Paris was profoundly shaken by the traumas of being besieged by the Prussians during the Franco-Prussian War and by the Commune in 1871. Nonetheless, the capital regenerated rapidly in the early years of the Third Republic. During the 1870s the Impressionists focused on representing the resurgence of the modern city. Claude Monet painted its newly developed boulevards and rail stations, while Pierre-Auguste Renoir explored the boulevards in richly colorful images. Paul Cézanne examined the importance of the wine market as a central element within the city's economy. The nation's renewed sense of pride culminated in the 1878 Exposition universelle. Millions of people flocked to the capital from across the globe. The nation's new sense of international stature was embodied by the exhibition of the enormous head of Frédéric-Auguste Bartholdi's Statue of Liberty, a future gift from the French nation to the United States, symbolizing the closeness between these two countries. Édouard Manet represented the patriotic fervor in the capital at this time.

1. David Pinkney, *Napoleon III and the Rebuilding of Paris* (Princeton: Princeton University Press, 1972), 151.

2. Walter Benjamin, *The Arcades Project*, trans. Howard Eiland and Kevin McLaughlin (Cambridge, Mass.: Belknap Press of Harvard University Press, 1999), 5.

3. The Paris sewers, for example, increased in length from 23.5 miles in 1830 to 373 miles in 1876. James H. Rubin, *Impressionism and the Modern Landscape: Productivity, Technology, and Urbanization from Manet to Van Gogh* (Berkeley: University of California Press, 2008), 67.

4. Adolphe Joanne, *Paris illustré* (Paris: Hachette, 1867), 45.

JOHAN-BARTHOLD JONGKIND
DUTCH, 1819–1891

1

The Cathedral of Notre-Dame de Paris, Seen from the Pont de l'Archevêché

1849

Oil on canvas

13¾ × 23⅞ in. (35 × 60.6 cm)

Santa Barbara Museum of Art, Museum purchase with funds provided by 19th-century Acquisition Fund, 1999.1

THE DUTCH PAINTER Johan-Barthold Jongkind arrived in Paris from Holland in 1846, funded by a grant from the Dutch government. In the ensuing decades, he emerged as an important painter of the capital, anticipating the Impressionists in his focus on urban subject matter. Jongkind produced several views of the city, including such structures as the Pont Neuf, the city's oldest bridge, as well as the barge traffic on the river and the new iron bridges. He served as an important mentor for several of the younger Impressionists, including particularly Claude Monet. The critic Émile Zola saw Jongkind as the archetypal painter of the modern city: "this deep love of modern Paris, I found in Jongkind . . . he understood that Paris remains picturesque even in its rubble."[1]

The Cathedral of Notre-Dame de Paris, Seen from the Pont de l'Archevêché shows the twelfth-century cathedral of Notre-Dame on the Île de la Cité in the center of Paris. In the mid-nineteenth century, the cathedral was often represented by such artists as Jean-Baptiste-Camille Corot and Charles-François Daubigny.[2] Jongkind's view is taken from the left bank of the Seine, looking downstream. The artist shows the scaffolding around the building's twin towers, a reference to the restoration work that was ongoing from 1845 until 1864 and orchestrated by the architect Eugène-Emmanuel Viollet-le-Duc (see cats. 2, 3).[3] The republican Viollet-le-Duc embraced the Gothic as a national French style, as opposed to Classical art, and emphasized the merits of France's medieval cathedrals as distinctive and unique indigenous architecture.[4] The restoration of Notre-Dame notably included the addition of a steeple, but Jongkind's view shows the cathedral before that construction took place. This is the earliest of the artist's twelve known paintings of Notre-Dame. A later view of the cathedral from the opposite direction shows the steeple clearly visible (fig. 51).[5] Jongkind's 1849 painting also shows the *bateaux-lavoirs*—washboats—that were a central part of city life at midcentury and fulfilled an important role in maintaining urban hygiene. Piles of laundry are visible in the boat at bottom right, while a washerwoman descends a plank. For the artist's early biographer, this work was "one of the most perfect that its author signed."[6] —SK

1. Émile Zola, "Jongkind," in "La cloche," January 23, 1872: "cet amour profond du Paris moderne, je l'ai trouvé dans Jongkind . . . il a compris que Paris reste pittoresque jusque dans ses décombres." Quoted in Victorine Hefting, *Jongkind, sa vie, son oeuvre, son époque* (Paris: Arts et Métiers Graphiques, 1974), 369.

2. See Corot's *Notre-Dame et le Quai des Orfèvres*, 1833 (Musée Carnavalet, Paris). Daubigny made his debut at the 1838 Salon with *Notre-Dame and Île Saint Louis* (private collection).

3. Jongkind's view is based on two related drawings, one in black chalk dated September 28, 1848, and the other in red chalk. Étienne Moreau-Nélaton, *Jongkind raconté par lui-même* (Paris: Henri Laurens, 1918), 14–15.

4. See Eugène-Emmanuel Viollet-le-Duc, "Du style gothique au XIXe siècle," *Annales archéologiques* 4 (1846): 334.

5. Adolphe Stein, Sylvie Brame, François Lorençeau, and Janine Sinizergues, *Johan-Barthold Jongkind: Catalogue critique de l'oeuvre; Peintures*, vol. 1 (Paris: Brame & Lorenceau Éditions, 2003), nos. 65, 66, 69, 70, 91, 123, 124, 125, 126, 329, 330, 331.

6. Moreau-Nélaton, *Jongkind raconté par lui-même*, 14: "l'un des plus parfaits que son auteur ait signés."

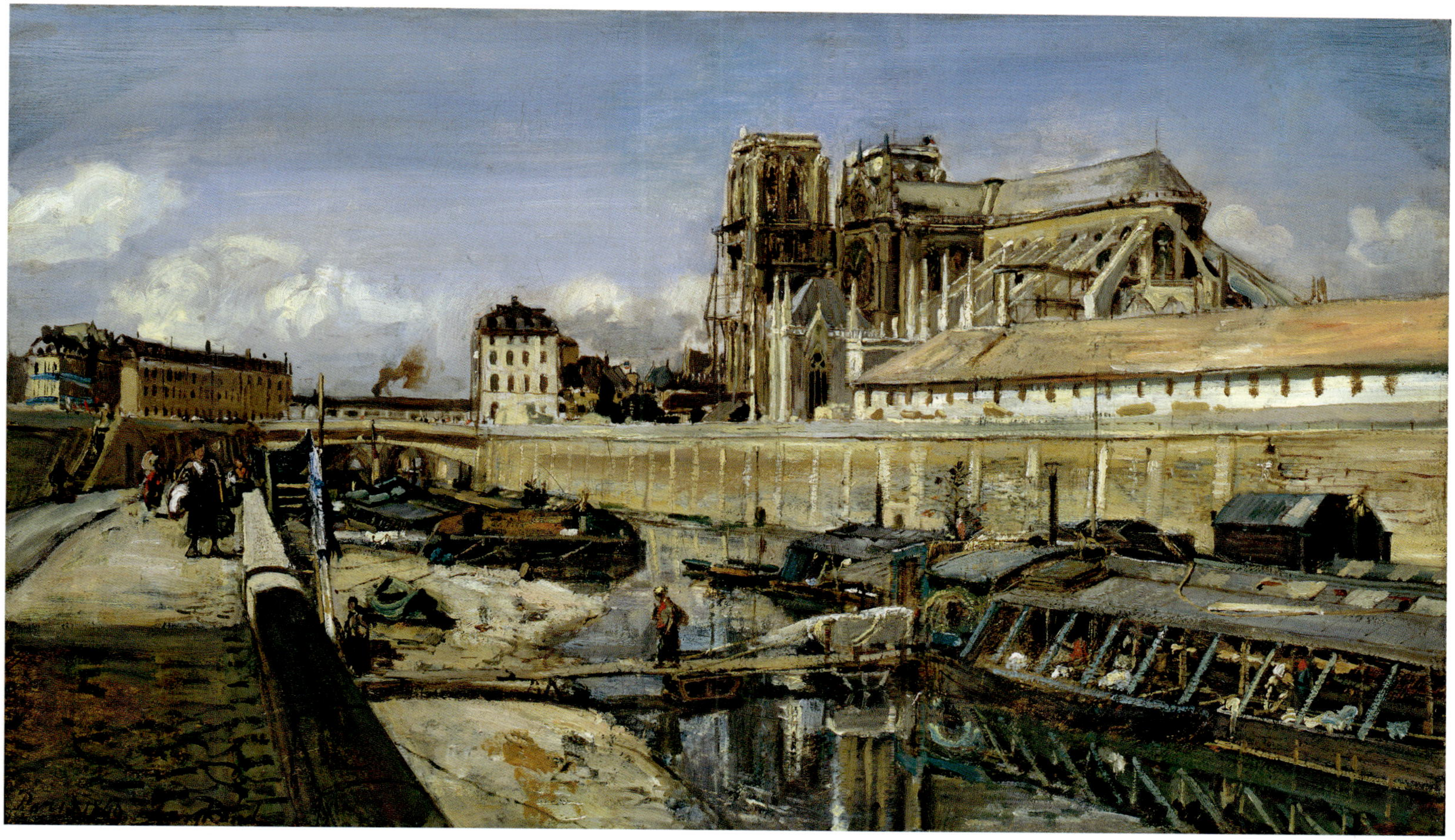

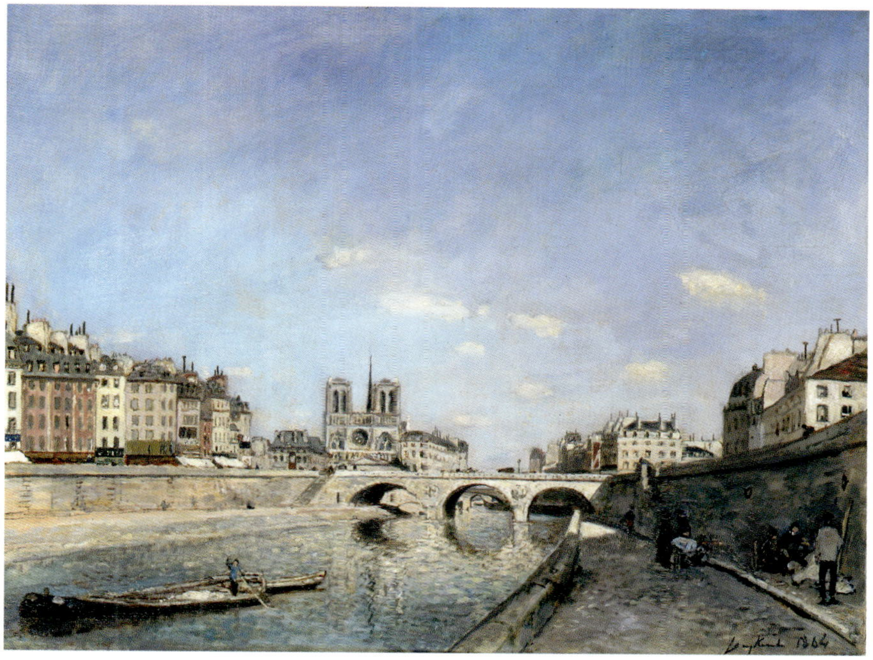

FIG. 51 Johan-Barthold Jongkind, *The Seine and Notre-Dame, Seen from the Quai des Grands Augustins and the Pont Saint-Michel*, 1864. Oil on canvas, 16½ × 22¼ in. (42 × 56.5 cm). Musée d'Orsay, Paris

2

ÉDOUARD BALDUS
FRENCH, 1813–1889

Notre-Dame, Paris

1852–53

Salt print from collodion glass negative

11⁹⁄₁₆ × 17⁹⁄₁₆ in. (29.5 × 44.7 cm)

The Cleveland Museum of Art, Edwin R. and Harriet Pelton Perkins Memorial Fund, 1991.35

LOCATED ON THE ÎLE DE LA CITÉ in the center of Paris—the city's founding site—the original Gothic cathedral of Notre-Dame (built between 1163 and 1250) stood for centuries as a symbol of both royal and religious authority. During the Revolutionary era of the late eighteenth century, Notre-Dame became a prime target for Revolutionaries, who defaced many of its facade statues and interior decor. More than one hundred statues from the west facade—those that bore "Gothic semblances of the kings of France," in particular—were beheaded with a sledgehammer, while crowns, scepters, and other monarchic symbols were either pillaged or vandalized.[1]

Throughout the first half of the nineteenth century, Notre-Dame was alternately venerated and reviled according to shifting political regimes and the strength of their religious affiliations. During the post-Revolutionary period, the cathedral fell into a state of neglect. Passionate public sentiment to restore the cathedral arose during the 1830s and early 1840s, spurred in no small part by the publication of Victor Hugo's popular novel *Notre-Dame de Paris* in 1831. On March 11, 1844, the architects Eugène-Emmanuel Viollet-le-Duc and Jean-Baptiste Antoine Lassus won a competition to restore Notre-Dame—referred to by the architects as a "ruin"—and construct a sacristy.[2] Lassus died in 1857, leaving the specifics of their collaboration ambiguous and whatever blame that resulted in the controversial changes on the shoulders of Viollet-le-Duc, who persevered for seven more years.

Viollet-le-Duc was a fervent proponent of a Gothic revival. His definition of "restoration" was a self-admittedly modern conception: one that confounded critics who accused him of rewriting history. "To restore a building is not to preserve it, to repair or rebuild it," he wrote in one report to the Minister of Justice and Religious Rites. "It is to reinstate it in a condition of completeness that could never have existed at any given time."[3] Viollet-le-Duc and Lassus's plan for Notre-Dame resulted in a new steeple, a restructuring of both transepts and the flying buttresses of the nave and choir, a change in the cathedral's interior elevation, and a restored sculptural plan for the west portals. They also reinstituted a sculptural program of gargoyles, many of which had served as drainpipes during the Middle Ages but had been removed during the eighteenth century owing to their propensity to deteriorate. The renovated cathedral was officially dedicated on May 31, 1864.

The renovation of Notre-Dame attracted widespread public attention throughout Paris and beyond. The structure became a symbol for all of France, symbolizing as it did a direct connection with the country's medieval past. Several photographers made images of the cathedral during the 1850s, including Édouard Baldus, Henri Le Secq, Charles Marville, the Bisson frères, and Charles Nègre. By about 1852 and 1853, when Baldus and Nègre photographed the edifice, Viollet-le Duc and Lassus were approximately halfway through their renovations, and Baron Georges-Eugène Haussmann had yet to begin his unsparing demolitions of the Île de la Cité.[4] In this early salt print of Notre-Dame, before the addition of Viollet-le-Duc's spire in 1859–60, Baldus opted for an oblique view featuring the apse and sacristy. He would photograph the edifice multiple times, earning praise from Ernest Lacan in September 1853 for a large print of the cathedral that demonstrated the photographer's mastery of tones and finesse with details.[5] His frontal views of Notre-Dame from the mid-1850s, which highlight the west portal, reflect a bolder, more mature style that bears an affinity with renderings of architectural elevations.

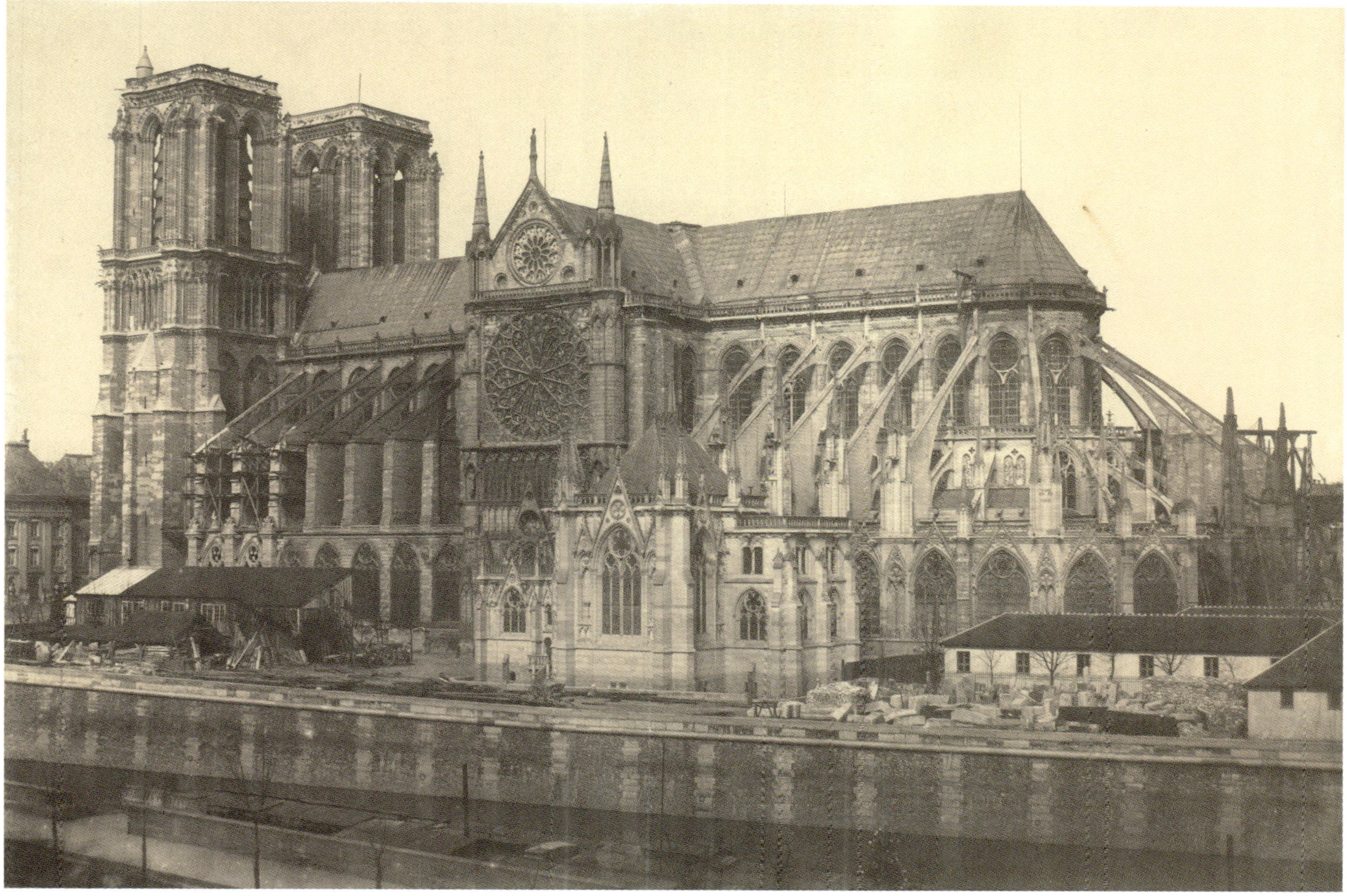

3

CHARLES NÈGRE
FRENCH, 1820–1880

West Facade, Notre-Dame, Paris

ca. 1853

Salt print from waxed paper negative

12 15/16 × 9 1/8 in. (32.8 × 23.1 cm)

Jay McDonald, courtesy of Hans P. Kraus Jr., New York

A very similar vantage point was taken by Nègre in 1853, in one of a series of views of the cathedral he made between 1852 and about 1856. Nègre's most famous photograph of Notre-Dame, of 1853, however, is not a straightforward document of the architecture. Instead, it features Viollet-le-Duc's most well-known north tower gargoyle, which came to be known as Le Stryge (The Vampire), and his friend the photographer Le Secq, standing on the balustrade just behind the creature, with his elbow cocked, wearing the top hat of a flaneur (fig. 52). By pulling back from the gargoyle, Nègre foregrounds the formal affinity between Le Secq and the fantastic creature, one described in Hugo's 1831 novel as an uncanny guardian of sacred space, existing somewhere between fantasy and real life.[6] —AMW

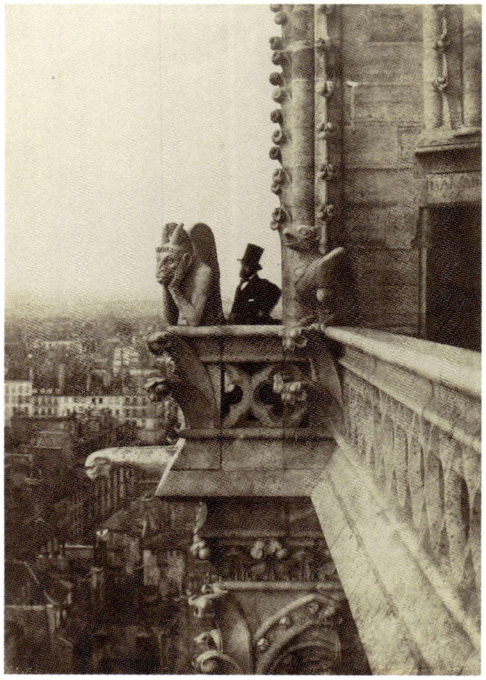

FIG. 52 Charles Nègre, *Le Stryge*, 1853. Salt print from waxed paper negative, 12¾ × 9 in. (32.5 × 23 cm). Musée d'Orsay, Paris

1. Alain Erlande-Brandenburg, "Notre Dame of Paris," in *Rethinking France*, ed. Pierre Nora, vol. 3, *Legacies* (Chicago: University of Chicago Press, 2009), 400.

2. This description of Notre-Dame derives from the architects' report to the Minister of Justice and Culture on January 31, 1843. Quoted in Michael Camille, *The Gargoyles of Notre-Dame: Medievalism and the Monsters of Modernity* (Chicago: University of Chicago Press, 2009), 3.

3. Quoted in M. F. Hearn, ed., *The Architectural Theory of Viollet-le-Duc: Readings and Commentary* (Cambridge, Mass.: Massachusetts Institute of Technology, 1990), 269.

4. Most of Haussmann's demolitions took place during the 1860s. In what was the city's most densely populated medieval core, he left only Notre-Dame, the Conciergerie, the Palais de Justice, and the Sainte-Chapelle untouched. Wine merchants, brothel proprietors, and tanners, among others, were forced off the island to make way for this new legal and administrative center, which became less a distinct neighborhood than a midway passage between the right and left banks of Paris. Some fifteen thousand residents were forced out of their homes, which were replaced by three civic structures: the Tribunal de Commerce (1860), the Caserne de la Cité, a police barracks (1865), and the Hôtel-Dieu, a hospital (1869). Haussmann also constructed a park behind the apse of Notre-Dame and greatly expanded the parvis in front of the cathedral to forty times its original size, making it suitable as a parade ground for soldiers stationed in the nearby barracks. By setting the structure apart from its environs like a sculpture on a pedestal and situating it amid a newly constructed array of civic structures, Haussmann recontextualized Notre-Dame, diminishing its religious importance and celebrating its stature as a national, and more secularized, architectural symbol. See David P. Jordan, *Transforming Paris: The Life and Labors of Baron Haussmann* (Chicago: University of Chicago Press, 1995), 198–201.

5. Ernest Lacan, "Revue photographique," *La lumière*, September 24, 1853, 154.

6. For a lengthy and thoughtful discussion of this photograph, see Eugenia Parry Janis, "The Man on the Tower of Notre Dame: New Light on Henri Le Secq," *Image* 19, no. 4 (December 1976): 13–25; and Camille, *Gargoyles of Notre-Dame*, 234–37.

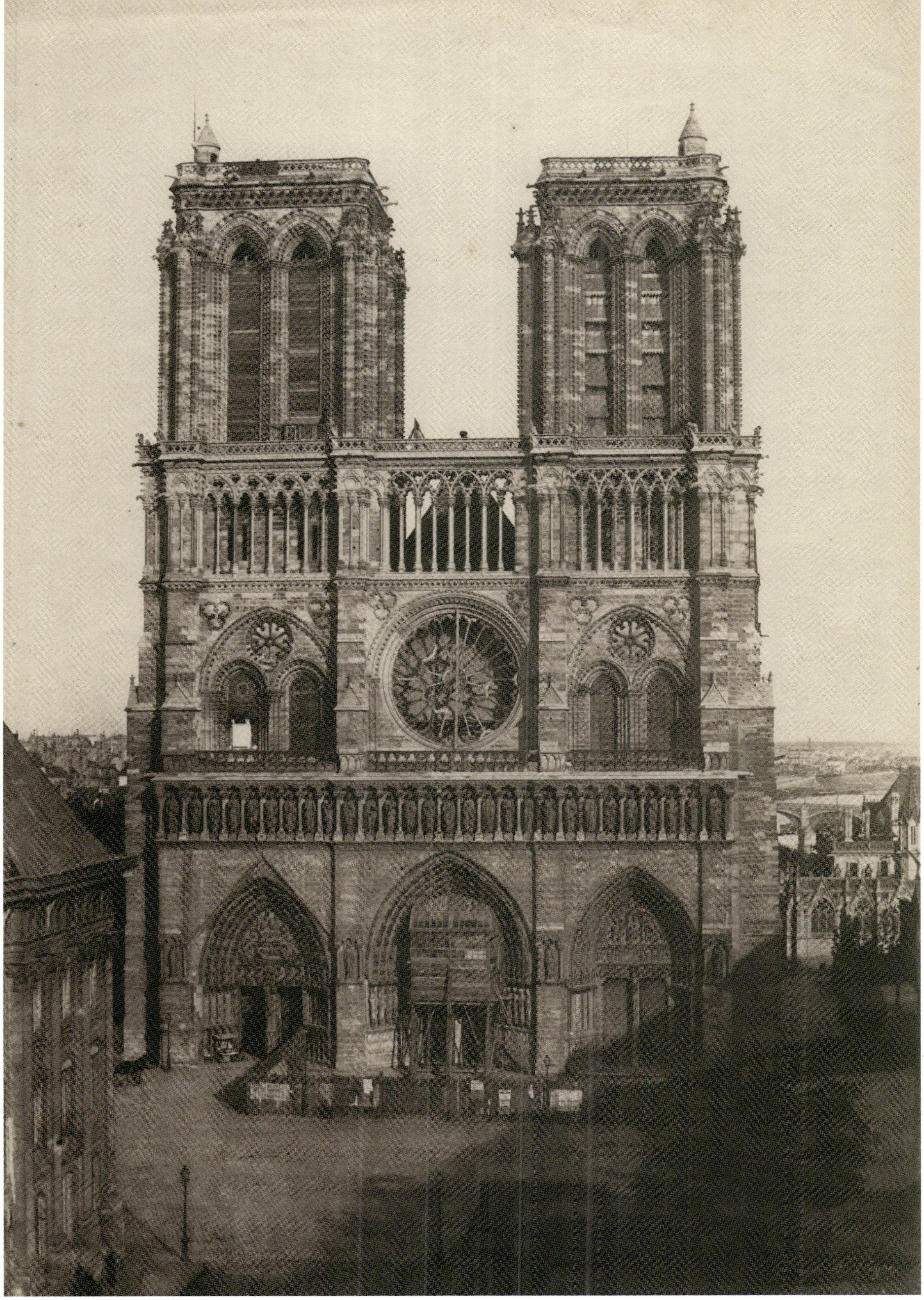

4

CHARLES NÈGRE
FRENCH, 1820–1880

Market Scene at the Port of the Hôtel de Ville, Paris

before February 1852

Salt print from paper negative

$5^{13}/_{16} \times 7^{13}/_{16}$ in. (14.7 × 19.9 cm)

National Gallery of Art, Washington, D.C., Patrons' Permanent Fund, 2003.74.1

CHARLES NÈGRE IS PERHAPS BEST KNOWN today for his genre scenes and motion studies, the majority of which were made between about 1851 and 1853. He was trained as a painter, in the studio of Paul Delaroche, and counted among his classmates the painter Charles-François Daubigny as well as fellow painters turned photographers Gustave Le Gray and Henri Le Secq. After Delaroche was forced to close his studio in 1843, Nègre continued his studies with Jean-Auguste-Dominique Ingres. He regularly exhibited in the annual painting Salons between 1843 and 1853, garnering praise from the noted art critic Théophile Gautier and earning a third-place medal for eight paintings shown in 1850.[1] Nègre took up photography as a means of making aids for his painting, starting with the daguerreotype process and moving to paper photography at some point in the late 1840s to early 1850s.

In the spring of 1851 Nègre experimented with a combination of lenses that allowed him to render street life with an unprecedented degree of instantaneity. In discussing one of his market scenes—quite possibly this one—the critic Henri de Lacretelle noted: "He has made with incredible daring a market scene that took place on the quay across from his own. Street porters walk, merchants raise an arm, and a chicken shivers beneath the hand that seizes it. They have all left their exact image in Nègre's camera, more quickly than their shadows on the pavement. This is life itself, and Nègre has stopped it with a marvel, in a hundredth of a second."[2] Though de Lacretelle must have exaggerated the brevity of the exposure (it would have been impossible to achieve it at the time given the materials and equipment available), the critic's astonishment attests to Nègre's innovation. The blurring of figures has been deemed "preimpressionist" by later historians, though it was an effect Nègre achieved involuntarily.[3] —AMW

1. This research is indebted to James Borcoman's formative study of Nègre's oeuvre, in *Charles Nègre, 1820–1880*, exh. cat. (Ottawa: National Gallery of Canada, 1976).

2. Henri de Lacretelle, "Revue photographique," *La lumière*, February 28, 1852, 37: "Il a saisi avec une hardiesse incroyable une scène de marché qui avait lieu sur le quai en face du sien. Les portefaix marchent, les marchandes élèvent le bras, le volaille frissonne sous le main qui la saisit. Ils ont tous laissé leur image exacte dans la chambre obscure de M. Nègre, plus rapidement que leur ombre sur le pavé. C'est la vie elle-même, et M. Nègre l'a arrêtée par une prodige, dans un centième de seconde."

3. Françoise Heilbrun, *Charles Nègre, Photographe, 1820–1880*, exh. cat. (Paris: Éditions des Musées Nationaux, 1980), 59.

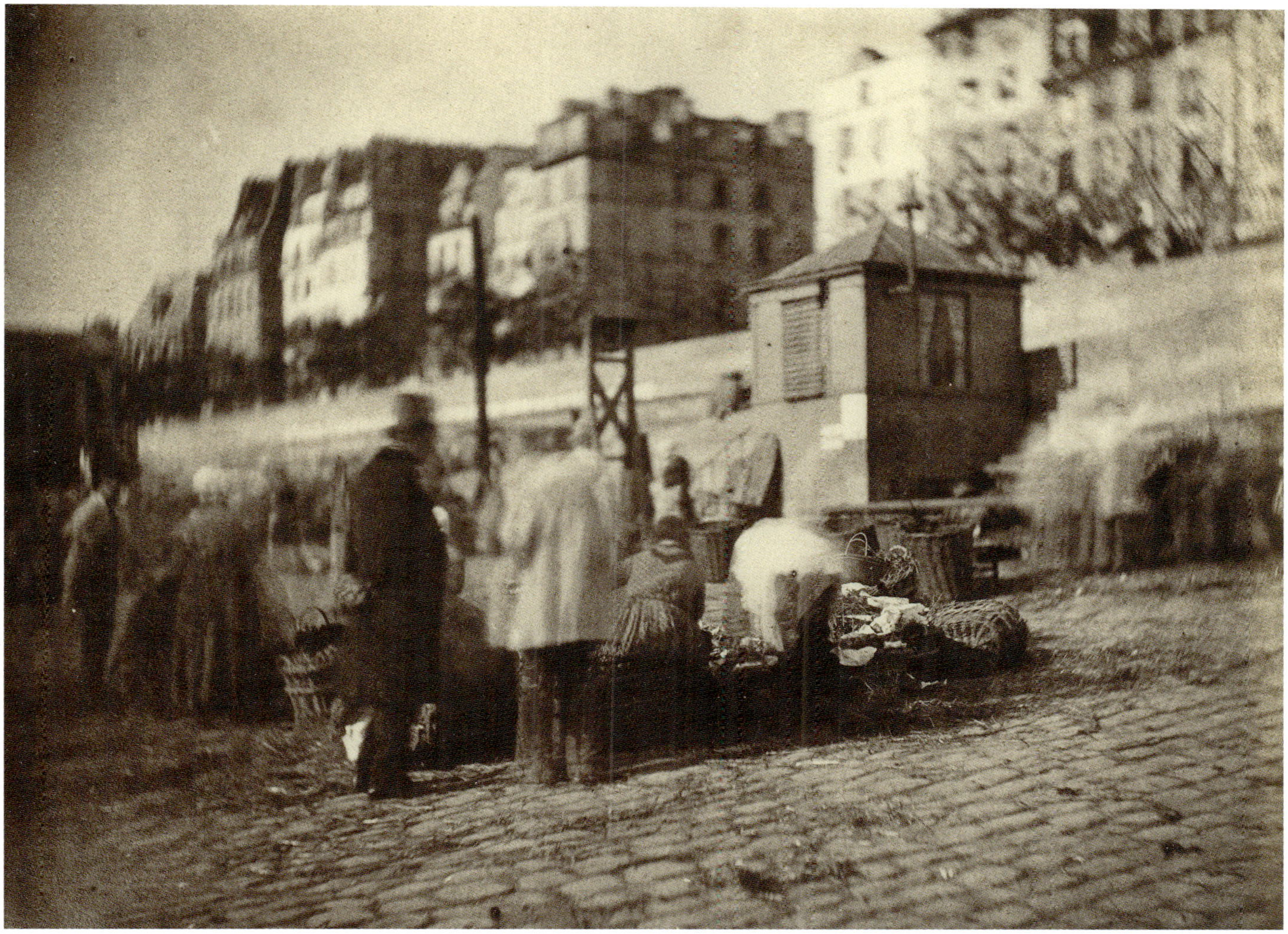

5

PAUL CÉZANNE
FRENCH, 1839–1906

The Wine Market at Jussieu

1872

Oil on canvas

28¾ × 36¼ in. (73 × 92.1 cm)

Portland Art Museum, Portland, Oregon, Museum Purchase: Private Donors' Fund, 1999.25

PAUL CÉZANNE IS PROBABLY BEST KNOWN for his deep attachment to his native region of Provence, but he also produced a significant body of work in Paris and its environs. The latter are principally landscapes around the capital—in sites such as Pontoise and the Forest of Fontainebleau—but there is also a small group of cityscapes.[1] Cézanne moved to Paris in 1861 and initially stayed until 1872, returning intermittently thereafter and retaining a studio in the capital. During his early years in Paris, he was an outsider figure whose work was consistently refused at the Salon and whose pictures treated dark and tormented themes such as murder and rape.

The Wine Market at Jussieu represents a warehouse of the city's wine market on the left bank with barrels piled up outside.[2] The red barrels to the right provide a rich color accent. Paris was home to several markets for the collection and distribution of produce from around the country, such as grain and oysters. Given the significance of the wine industry to France's economy, this market was among the most important. The wine market had been established in 1664 and was expanded by Napoléon Bonaparte between 1813 and 1819. As the Joanne guide noted, this market comprised five large warehouses as well as enormous underground cellars, able to store almost 26.5 million gallons of wine.[3] Barrels arrived from wine-growing regions such as Bordeaux (cat. 60), Burgundy, and the Midi by coach, rail, and barge, and the wine was distributed principally around Paris itself. In 1872 the capital's inhabitants consumed the enormous amount of 103 million gallons of wine, amounting to an average of more than 55 gallons for each Parisian over the year.[4]

Cézanne shows the view from his second-floor studio window at 45, rue de Jussieu, where he lived with his new wife, Hortense Fiquet, from December 1871 until June 1872 and where their son, Paul, was born.[5] The site was not ideal for a new family, as the artist's friend Achille Emperaire noted after a visit in early 1872: "Paul is not very well set up; also there is a noise which could awaken the dead."[6] According to Emperaire, this painting was made at a time of increasing isolation for the painter.[7] Nonetheless, Cézanne did receive the support of his good friend Camille Pissarro, to whom he presented the work. It was probably this picture that Pissarro was describing when he wrote: "Our Cézanne gives us some hope and I have seen some paintings: I have with me a picture with remarkable vigor and strength."[8] The dark palette and vigorous impasto are characteristic of the artist's early output before he adopted a more ordered approach to brushwork. With Pissarro's support, Cézanne exhibited at the Impressionist exhibitions of 1874 and 1877.

Cézanne showed interest in representing factories and industrial subjects intermittently throughout his career.[9] Here, he highlighted a wine market, which represented a crucial element in the broader Parisian, as well as French, economy. —SK

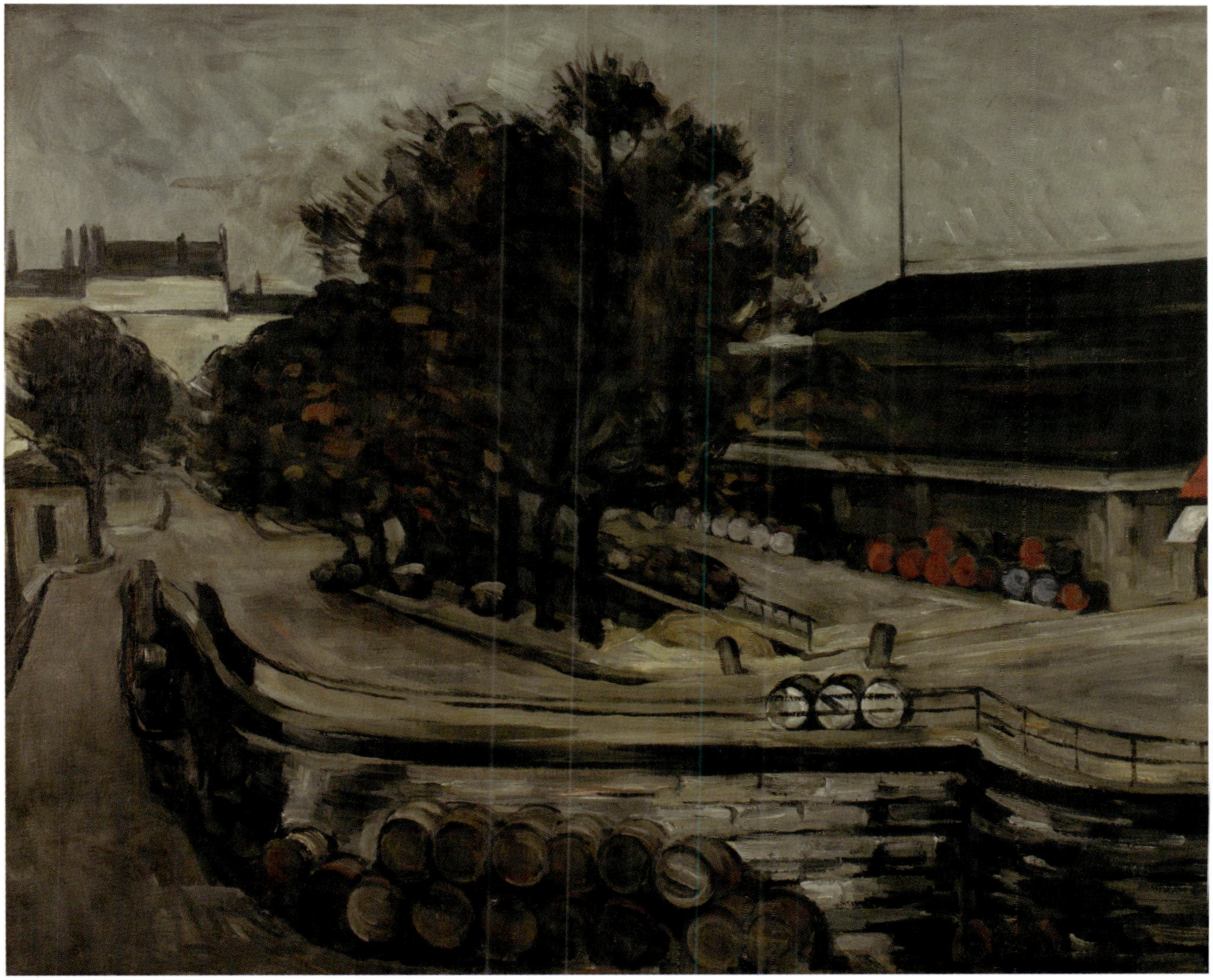

1. *The Roofs of Paris* (private collection), *The Quai de Bercy* (Kunsthalle, Hamburg), and *Rue de Saules, Montmartre* (private collection). See Denis Coutagne, ed., *Cézanne and Paris*, exh. cat. (Paris: Éditions de la Réunion des Musées Nationaux, 2011), 18, 66, 71.

2. Cézanne represented the old, established market and not, as has often been thought, the new wine entrepôt founded upstream on the other side of the river on the quai de Bercy in 1869. John Rewald gives the incorrect quai de Bercy location in *The Paintings of Paul Cézanne: A Catalogue Raisonné* (New York: Harry N. Abrams, 1996), 1:141; James Rubin notes the correct Jussieu site in *Impressionism and the Modern Landscape: Productivity, Technology, and Urbanization from Manet to Van Gogh* (Berkeley: University of California Press, 2008), 75, as does Coutagne, *Cézanne and Paris*, 217. The Jussieu market has been destroyed and replaced by a branch of Paris University. Cézanne's friend Armand Guillaumin represented the Jussieu wine market seen from across the river, showing horse-drawn carts unloading wine barrels from barges, in *The Seine: Rainy Weather* (Museum of Fine Arts, Houston).

3. Adolphe Joanne, *Paris illustré: Nouveau guide de l'étranger et du parisien* (Paris: Hachette, 1867), 964–66, at 965: "les caves et celliers peuvent contenir un million d'hectolitres de vin et 150,000 hectolitres d'eaux-de-vie."

4. See Pierre Gillet, "L'approvisionnement de Paris en vin," *Annales de géographie* 48, no. 274 (1939): 366.

5. Cézanne to Achille Emperaire, January 26, 1872: "I have just seen Zola who visited me at no. 45 rue de Jussieu. . . . I live in what used to be rue Saint-Victor, now rue de Jussieu, opposite the wine store, on the second floor." Quoted in John Rewald, ed., *Paul Cézanne, Letters* (Oxford: Bruno Cassirer, 1976), 134.

6. Emperaire, ibid., 135.

7. Ibid., 136: "I have left Cézanne—it was unavoidable, otherwise I would not have escaped the fate of the others. I found him here deserted by everybody. He hasn't got a single intelligent or close friend left. Zola, Solari and all the others are no longer mentioned. He is the strangest chap one can imagine."

8. Pissarro to Antoine Guillemet, September 3, 1872: "Notre Cézanne nous donne des espérances et j'ai vu des peintures; j'ai chez moi une peinture d'une vigueur, d'une force remarquables." Quoted in Janine Bailly-Herzberg, *Correspondance de Camille Pissarro*, vol. 1, *1865–1885* (Paris: Éditions du Valhermeil, 2003), 76–77.

9. See, for example, *Factories near the Mont Cengle*, 1867–69 (private collection), and *The Sea near l'Estaque*, ca. 1878–79 (Musée Picasso, Paris).

ÉDOUARD BALDUS
FRENCH, 1813–1889

6

Louvre, the Two Last North Bays of the Facade of the Gallery of Seven Meters, in the Cour Visconti

1856–57

Albumen print from collodion glass negative

13⅝ × 17⅝ in. (34.6 × 44.8 cm)

The Nelson-Atkins Museum of Art, Kansas City, Missouri, Gift of the Hall Family Foundation, 2011.12.46

7

Louvre, Pavillon Colbert

1855

Albumen print from collodion glass negative

16¹⁵⁄₁₆ × 13³⁄₁₆ in. (43 × 33.5 cm)

The Nelson-Atkins Museum of Art, Kansas City, Missouri, Gift of the Hall Family Foundation, 2007.21.1

THE CONSTRUCTION OF THE NEW LOUVRE, which linked the old Louvre and Tuileries palaces, was Napoléon III's most amibitious building project. French kings since the Renaissance had dreamed of such an achievement. For the emperor, the symbolic prestige of connecting the Second Empire to the legacies of such figures as Catherine de Médicis and Louis XIV was a driving impetus. The project also involved clearing slums that had arisen in the Louvre's courtyard; they were demolished in 1849.[1] The plans for construction began in 1848 under the architect Louis Visconti and were continued by Hector Lefuel after Visconti's death in December 1853. The endeavor relied on the skills of masons, sculptors, mural painters, and photographers—specifically, Édouard Baldus, who assumed the massive undertaking of documenting the entire process.[2] By the time the building was inaugurated in August 1857, Baldus had produced more than two thousand photographs at a cost of more than sixty thousand francs: it was the most lucrative state commission given to a photographer at that time.[3] By the end of 1857, twenty-five sets of albums, of four volumes each, were produced and distributed to the imperial couple and their children, high-ranking government officials, and foreign dignitaries, including Queen Victoria, the kings of Bavaria and Prussia, and the czar of Russia.[4]

The majority of Baldus's photographs for the project fell into two categories: intimate, detailed views of statuary and decorative stonework, printed using small-format paper negatives; and large-scale architectural views of the many pavilions and courts constituting the new Louvre. These larger views were made using glass negatives and the wet-collodion process. Baldus, using wet collodion for the first time during this project, demonstrated how perfectly this latest photographic technology was suited to architectural representation and documentation. His views are bold, geometric compositions rendered sharply and in an even light, to emphasize pattern, texture, volume, and form.

The two Baldus photographs featured here depict a portion of the Cour Visconti, in the southern limb, and the Pavillon Colbert, located on the interior court side of the northern wing. The close-up view of the Cour Visconti segment—a full-frame cropping of one section on the north facade of the building—is a particularly striking composition. Here, the building's geometry and textures transform the picture into something more artistically dynamic than a simple architectural record.

Baldus exhibited several of his large-scale architectural views of the Louvre numerous times in France and abroad between 1856 and 1862.[5] In his review of the 1861 exhibition of the Société française de la photographie, Ernest Lacan—Baldus's fervent and stalwart champion—reported that the photographer had "copied stone by stone all the new Louvre and contributed laboriously in pushing photography to a

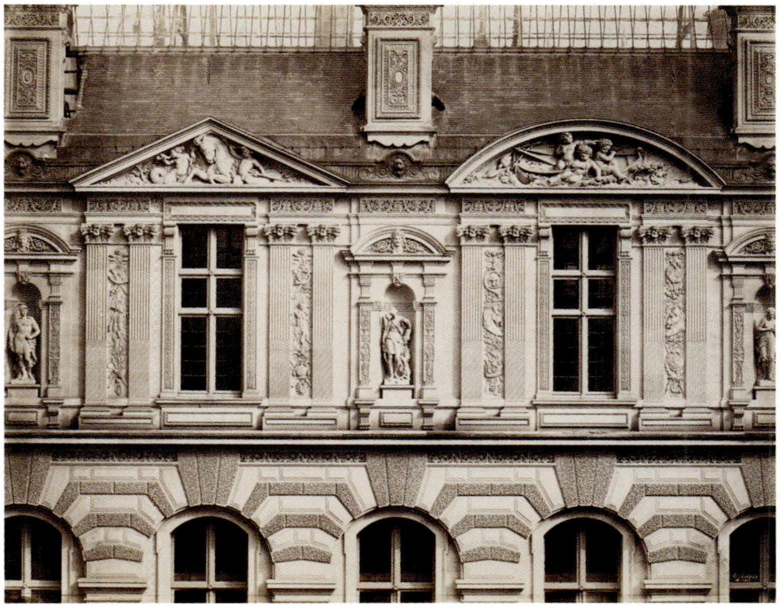

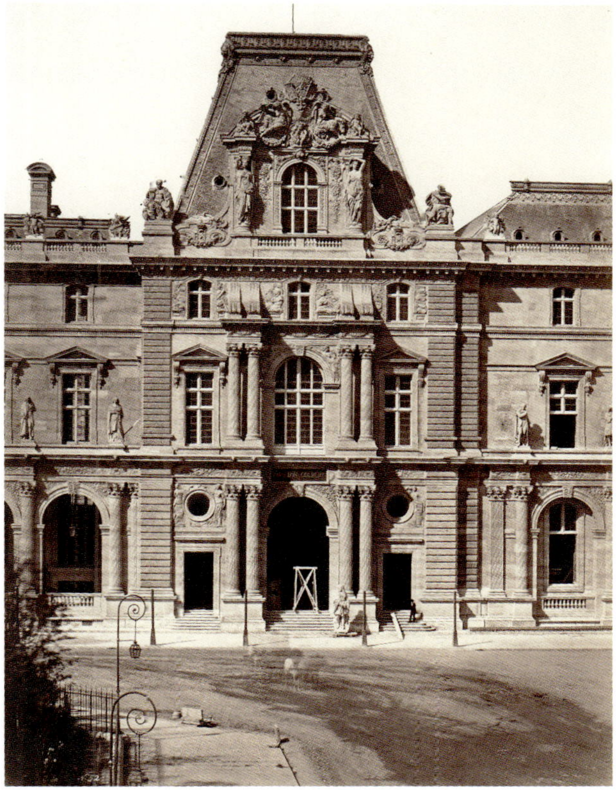

degree nearest perfection."[6] Baldus continued to photograph the Louvre for several years after the 1857 inauguration, both as a periodic official photographer and for his own personal sales.[7] Between 1869 and 1875 Baldus's Louvre photographs were published as gravures in two- and three-volume sets titled *Palais du Louvre et des Tuileries*. By 1875 these publications were particularly timely records of the buildings, as certain portions had been badly damaged during the Commune of 1871. —AMW

1. David P. Jordan, *Transforming Paris: The Life and Labors of Baron Haussmann* (Chicago: University of Chicago Press, 1995), 113.

2. Ernest Lacan, "Exposition photographique," *Le moniteur de la photographie* 7 (June 15, 1861): 49.

3. Malcolm Daniel, "'Stone by Stone': Édouard-Denis Baldus and the New Louvre," *History of Photography* 16, no. 2 (Summer 1992): 116.

4. For a complete listing of the recipients, see ibid., 121n7.

5. These included the Exhibition of Photographs of the Manchester Photographic Society (1856); the Exposition instituée par l'Association pour l'encouragement et le développement des arts industriels en Belgique, in Brussels (1856 and 1857); the second, third, and fourth exhibitions of the Société française de la photographie (1857, 1859, and 1861), in Paris; the first, second, and third annual exhibitions of the Architectural Photographic Association (1858, 1859, and 1860), in London; the Photographic Society of London (1858); the exhibition of the Société photographique de Marseille (1861); and the International Exhibition of Industry and Art in London (1862), where he was awarded a medal. See Malcolm Daniel, *The Photographs of Édouard Baldus*, exh. cat. (New York: Metropolitan Museum of Art; Montreal: Canadian Centre for Architecture, 1994), 242–45.

6. Ernest Lacan, "Exposition photographique," *Le moniteur de la photographie* 7 (June 15, 1861): 49: "Quand on a produit autant d'oeuvres que lui, quand on a copié pierre à pierre tout le nouveau Louvre, et contribue laborieusement à pousser la photographie jusqu'au degré le plus voisin de la perfection, on pourrait s'endormir sur les lauriers."

7. As Daniel has noted ("'Stone by Stone,'" 119) Baldus made images of the Louvre through at least the mid-1860s and sold photographs through various book and prints sellers in Italy, Germany, Austria, England, and France, including a dozen sellers in Paris alone.

8

ÉDOUARD BALDUS
FRENCH, 1813–1889

Hôtel de Ville and the Pont d'Arcole during Queen Victoria's Visit

1855
Albumen print from collodion glass negative
12$^{11}/_{16}$ × 17$^{9}/_{16}$ in. (32.2 × 44.5 cm)
The Nelson-Atkins Museum of Art, Kansas City, Missouri, Gift of the Hall Family Foundation, 2010.18.6

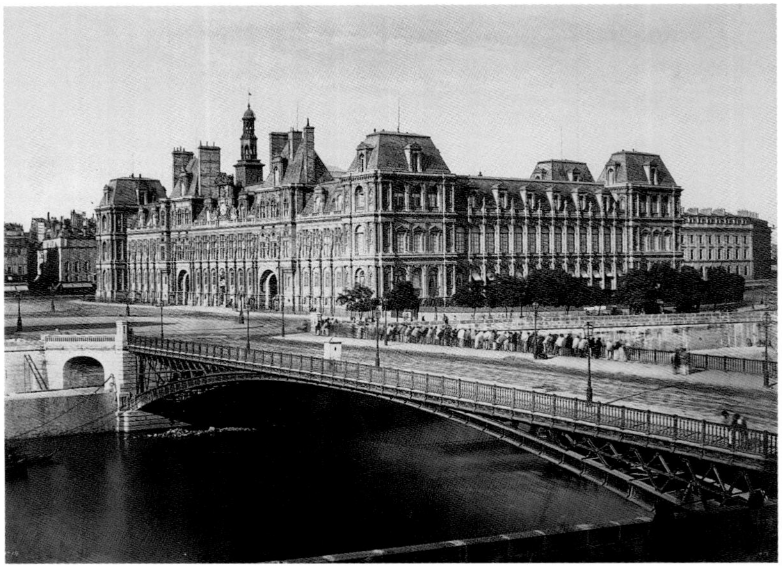

QUEEN VICTORIA WAS THOROUGHLY enchanted by Napoléon III's changes to Paris when she and Prince Albert toured the city during their widely celebrated visit to France in August 1855.[1] "The Emperor has done wonders for Paris, and for the Bois de Boulogne," she wrote to her uncle Leopold, the king of Belgium. "I am *delighted*, *enchanted*, *amused*, and *interested*, and think I never saw anything more beautiful and gay than Paris."[2] Baron Georges-Eugène Haussmann seemed to have spared no expense when hosting the queen at the Hôtel de Ville, where an immense ball was held in their honor. According to one report, the prefect's quarters were transformed into an exotic display, which included rare plant species, golden lattices, colorful lights, and a fabricated grotto.[3] Queen Victoria also graciously accepted the honor of having a street named after her.[4]

In 1835 the Hôtel de Ville was expanded to include two wings that connected to the existing facade. During the Second Empire, it became a popular subject for photographers. Baldus, who also created an album of photographs for the British monarchs commemorating their trip on the rail line from Boulogne to Paris (an album on which the Northern Railway album is based, cat. 75) made this view of the Hôtel de Ville and the Pont d'Arcole. —AMW

1. The royal visit was of enormous political and symbolic signficance for both England and France. It marked the first time an English monarch had made an official visit since 1520 and cemented the friendship of the royal couples while affirming the political alliance between their two countries. Victoria and Albert were met with great fanfare at almost every juncture of their journey: after arriving via steamship on August 18 at Boulogne, they received a military salute from forty thousand troops and were personally escorted by Napoléon III. Victoria and Albert immediately traveled from the coast to Paris aboard the imperial train, on France's fastest rail line, the Chemin de fer du Nord.

2. Queen Victoria to the king of Belgium, August 23, 1855, in *The Letters of Queen Victoria: A Selection of Her Majesty's Correspondence between the Years 1837 and 1861*, vol. 3, *1854–1861*, ed. Arthur Christopher Benson and Viscount Esher (London: John Murray, 1908), 135.

3. Patrice de Moncan, *Le Paris d'Haussmann* (Paris: Les Éditions du Mécène, 2009), 163.

4. Benson and Esher, *Letters of Queen Victoria*, 136.

9

GUSTAVE LE GRAY
FRENCH, 1820–1884

The Pont du Carrousel, Paris: View to the West from the Pont des Arts

1856–58

Albumen print from collodion glass negative

14⅞ × 19³⁄₁₆ in. (37.8 × 48.8 cm)

National Gallery of Art, Washington, D.C., Patrons' Permanent Fund, 1995.36.94

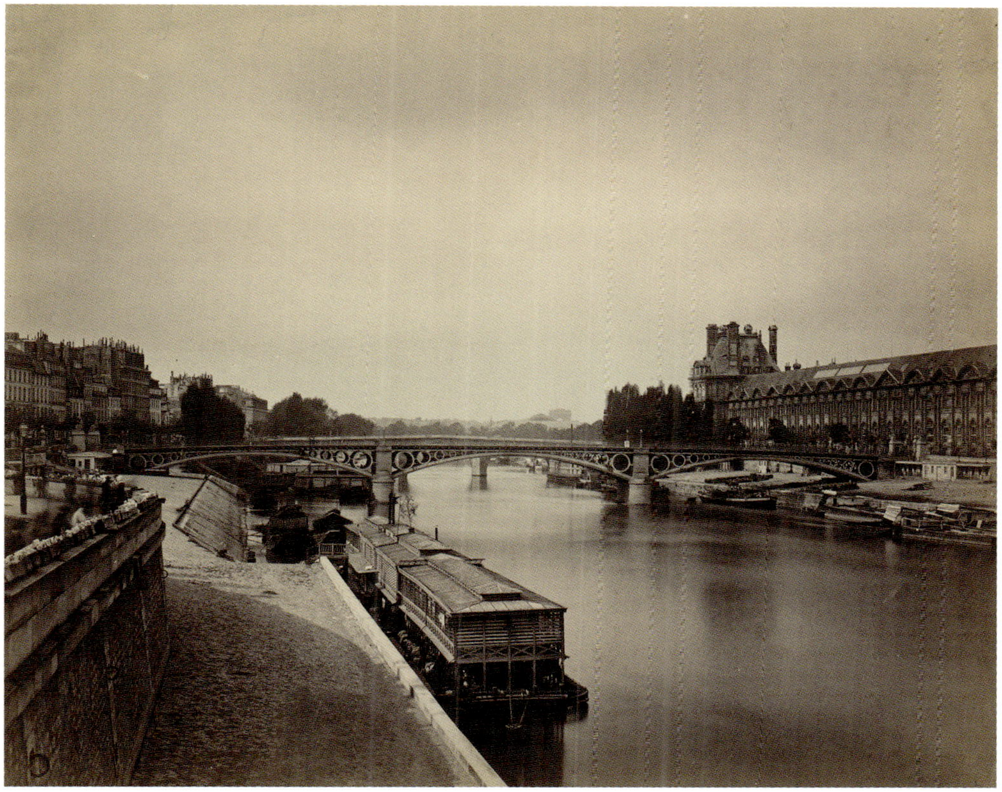

THE PONT DU CARROUSEL WAS DESIGNED by the architect Antoine-Rémy Polonceau in the early years of the July Monarchy (1830–48). Constructed between October 1832 and November 1834, it was considered the first major modern bridge in France made using metal.[1] The Pont du Carrousel differed from many such structures at the time, which were suspension bridges. It was composed of three arches of equal length, reinforced by a series of circular cast-iron supports above the spandrels, which became known as *ronds des serviettes* (napkin rings). Situated at the four corners of the bridge were allegorical statues representing the Seine, the City of Paris, Industry, and Abundance. These statues were set on hollow cast-iron pedestals, which served as toll booths for tax collectors.

This particular view of the bridge by Le Gray was one of at least two known views he made of the subject in 1859, during his final year in Paris. Le Gray, in fact, devoted much of 1859 to photographing the major monuments of the capital city—including the Louvre, the Tour Saint-Jacques, the Panthéon, and Notre-Dame.[2] —AMW

1. The Pont des Arts, constructed between 1801 and 1803, was made with cast iron, but it was used for pedestrian traffic, not for vehicles, as was the Pont du Carrousel.

2. As Sylvie Aubenas has speculated, this was perhaps Le Gray's final attempt to make a profit and keep his benefactors satisfied. If so, the effect was unsuccessful. Le Gray et Cie was dissolved on February 1, 1860, forcing Le Gray to close his studio at 35, boulevard des Capucines. Sylvie Aubenas, *Gustave Le Gray, 1820–1884*, exh. cat. (Los Angeles: J. Paul Getty Museum, 2002), 374.

10

JEAN-CHARLES CAZIN
FRENCH, 1841–1901

The Quarry of Monsieur Pascal near Nanterre

ca. 1875
Oil on canvas
28 × 36 in (71.1 × 91.4 cm)
Private Collection

JEAN-CHARLES CAZIN'S REPUTATION in his lifetime depended largely on biblical and mythological scenes as well as an extensive body of evocative, often mysterious landscapes.[1] He also, however, produced a small group of more realistic works in which he presented a vision of the French nation as modern and industrial. Among these were views of factories and quarries around Paris and boatyards around Boulogne.[2] These images of the country as enjoying a lively economy probably reflect his republican beliefs, also evident in his tender view of the deathbed of the radical republican Léon Gambetta (Musée national du château de Versailles).

In *The Quarry of Monsieur Pascal near Nanterre*, workers are shown extracting limestone blocks from a quarry in Nanterre, a suburb west of Paris. Cazin shows a view from below with an overcast sky and two-thirds of the picture space taken up by the large pit of the quarry. The men work with hammers and pickaxes to remove the stone and cut it into smaller blocks; these are then loaded on a horse-drawn carriage, inscribed in red, "M. Pascal, Nanterre." The suited man at the lower left may be Monsieur Pascal, presumably the owner of the quarry, who may have commissioned the picture. The work probably represents a site at the base of Mont Valérian at Nanterre, perhaps one of the three quarries located on the route de Suresnes.[3] This painting is directly related to the expansion of Paris, since these blocks were used for new construction in the capital: in all likelihood, they would have been transported by barge along the nearby river Seine. This was one of several quarries that operated on the outskirts of Paris; others were in the Forest of Fontainebleau and on Montmartre, where limestone, sandstone, and granite were extracted.[4] In 1869, for example, the enormous amount of almost nineteen million cubic feet of quarry stone and almost twelve million cubic feet of cut and shaped stone were used in Paris.[5] Limestone and sandstone were particularly crucial for the reconstruction of Paris, since they were the stones of choice for the city's pavements as well as the new apartments on the boulevards and major building projects such as the Paris Opéra (cat. 18).

Cazin lived in England from 1871 until 1875, having left France at the time of the Franco-Prussian War; this work was probably painted shortly after his return. He followed a working practice that relied on the importance of memory, so this picture was probably based on close visual study rather than any actual preliminary studies. The artist's blond palette reflects his training with Jean-Baptiste-Camille Corot, with whom he worked closely about 1870. Beyond its formal qualities, Cazin's work is emblematic of the enormous quarrying industry that existed around Paris to satisfy the great demands engendered by Baron Georges-Eugène Haussmann's urban rebuilding.[6] —SK

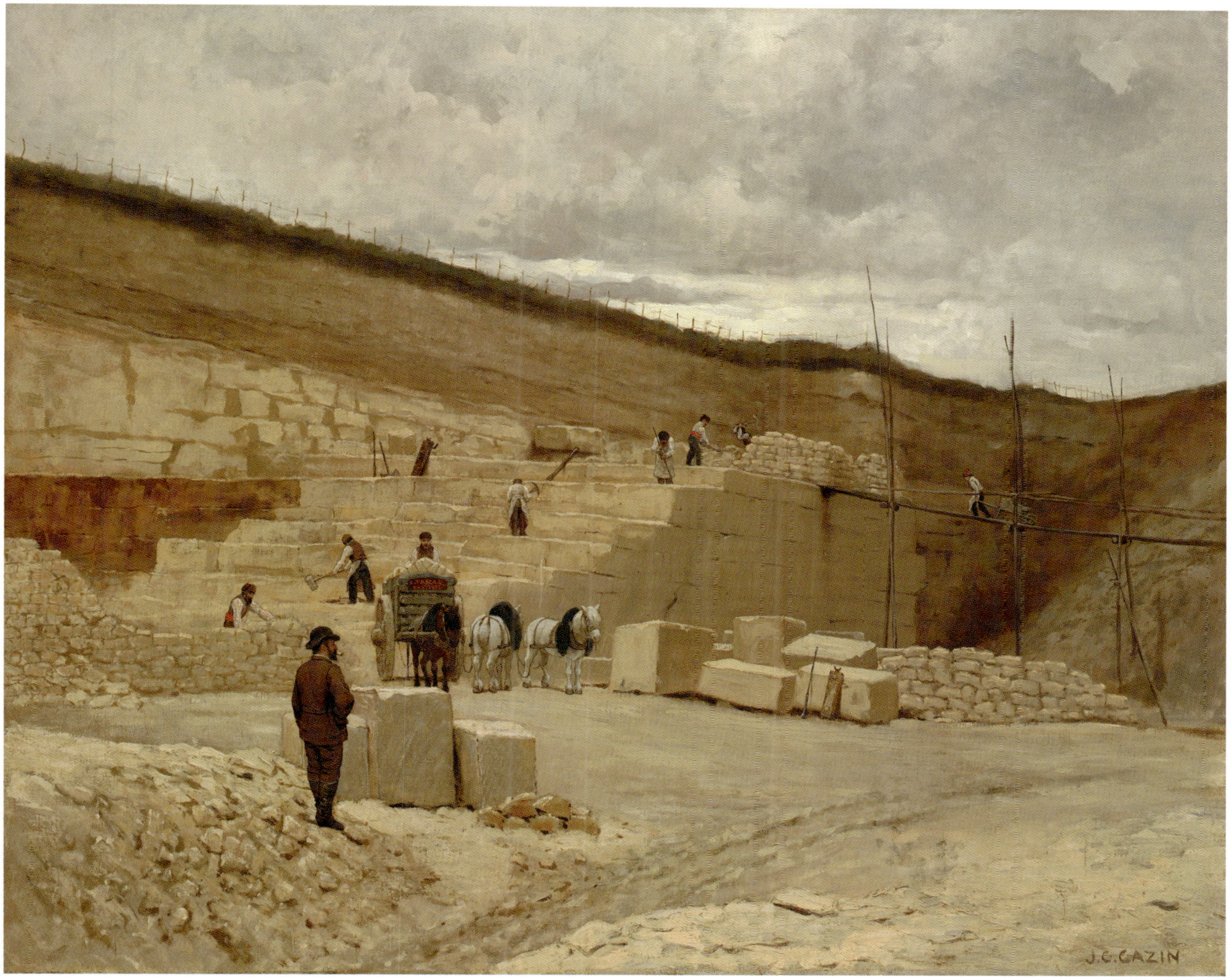

1. Léonce Bénédite, *Jean-Charles Cazin* (Paris: G. Baranger fils, 1902).

2. *The Boatyard (Le Chantier)* (The Cleveland Museum of Art), shown at the 1876 Salon, and *Les quais* (Musée d'Orsay, Paris). See also *The Stone Quarry* (location unknown), reproduced in Paul Desjardins, "En mémoire de Jean-Charles Cazin," *Gazette des beaux-arts* 43 (September 1901): 181. For discussion of *The Boatyard*, see Louise d'Argencourt, *European Paintings of the 19th Century* (Cleveland: Cleveland Museum of Art, 1999), 1:112–14.

3. These were the Carrière des Côtes d'Auty, Carrière aux Loups, and Carrière au Hameau de la Folie. See Michel Hébert and Jacques Delahaye, *Nanterre*, Mémoire en images (Joué-les-Tours: Éditions Alan Sutton, 1997), 62.

4. "Les carrières de Paris," in Louis Simonin, *Les merveilles du monde souterrain* (Paris: Hachette, 1868), 91–133.

5. *Annuaire pour l'an 1869, publié par le Bureau des longitudes* (Paris: Gauthier-Villars, 1869), 209: "Quarry stone of all kinds [Moellons de toute espèce]: 533,823 [cubic meters]. Cut stone, slabs and squares of stone [Pierre de taille, dalles et carreaux de pierre]: 328,437 [cubic meters]."

6. Even before Haussmann, some four million paving stones (*pavés*), weighing 100,213 tons, were quarried in the years before 1848 from the Forest of Fontainebleau. Adolphe Joanne, *Les environs de Paris* (Paris: Hachette, 1856), 657.

CHARLES MARVILLE
FRENCH, 1813–1879

11

View of the Kiosk of the Great Lake, Bois de Boulogne, Paris

ca. 1858–60
Albumen print from collodion glass negative
10³⁄16 × 14³⁄16 in. (25.9 × 36.1 cm)
Princeton University Art Museum, Museum purchase, Gift of the Florence Gould Foundation, x1994-52

12

Place de l'Arc de Triomphe (Place de l'Étoile, Paris)

ca. 1877
Albumen print from collodion glass negative
8¹⁵⁄16 × 14½ in. (22.7 × 36.8 cm)
The J. Paul Getty Museum, Los Angeles, 84.XM.505.3

DURING THE 1830S AND 1840S Charles Marville (born Charles-François Bossu) was a prolific illustrator,[1] producing hundreds of drawings for literary and geographic works, such as editions of the popular novel *Paul et Virginie* by Bernadin de Saint-Pierre (1832), Charles Nodier's *La Seine et ses bords* and *La Saône et ses bords* (1836), and the new publication of Paulin's *Géographie illustrée, cours complets de géographie* (1837). Like many artists turned photographers, he took up photography about 1850, at the time Louis-Désiré Blanquart-Evrard and Gustave Le Gray were publishing various treatises on paper photography. Recognizing the vast potential of this process, which allowed numerous positive prints to be made from a single negative, Blanquart-Evrard founded a printing establishment in Lille in September 1851. Through his Imprimerie photographique, which operated through 1855, he published numerous albums of photographic works by dozens of photographers, including more than one hundred architectural and landscape images by Marville.[2]

In the mid-1850s Marville switched from paper to glass negatives, working in the wet-collodion process from that point onward, likely for its ability to render architectural details with great precision and tonal range. In 1858 he received his first municipal commission from the city of Paris to produce a series of photographs of the newly transformed Bois de Boulogne, a former royal hunting ground at the western edge of Paris that became a part of the city on July 13, 1852.[3] The transformation of the Bois was of particular interest to Napoléon III, who was inspired by the design of London's Hyde Park. He granted millions of francs to the project, putting Baron Georges-Eugène Haussmann in charge of oversight. Haussmann hired the engineer Jean-Charles-Adolphe Alphand, who was well versed in the latest technologies of road construction and water systems management. The first phase of the project included the construction of two ornamental lakes. The larger lake was lined in cement to help maintain water flow. A cascade, a cement grotto, and thousands of yards of meandering pathways beneath which irrigation pipes were laid were also created. The second phase of construction involved the removal of a four-hundred-year-old wall separating the Bois from the Longchamp plain. A racecourse was built in Longchamp's southern portion. The Bois was completed in 1858. One writer in *Le monde illustré* remarked on its significance as compared with other notable European public parks: "Today the Bois is completely transformed . . . our readers will see with interest a picturesque topography of this grand Parisian promenade that is as great in importance as the Prado of Madrid, the Thiergarten of Berlin, the Cascines of Florence and the Prater of Vienna."[4]

Marville made approximately seventy negatives in the Bois de Boulogne. The exact intentions for the photographs

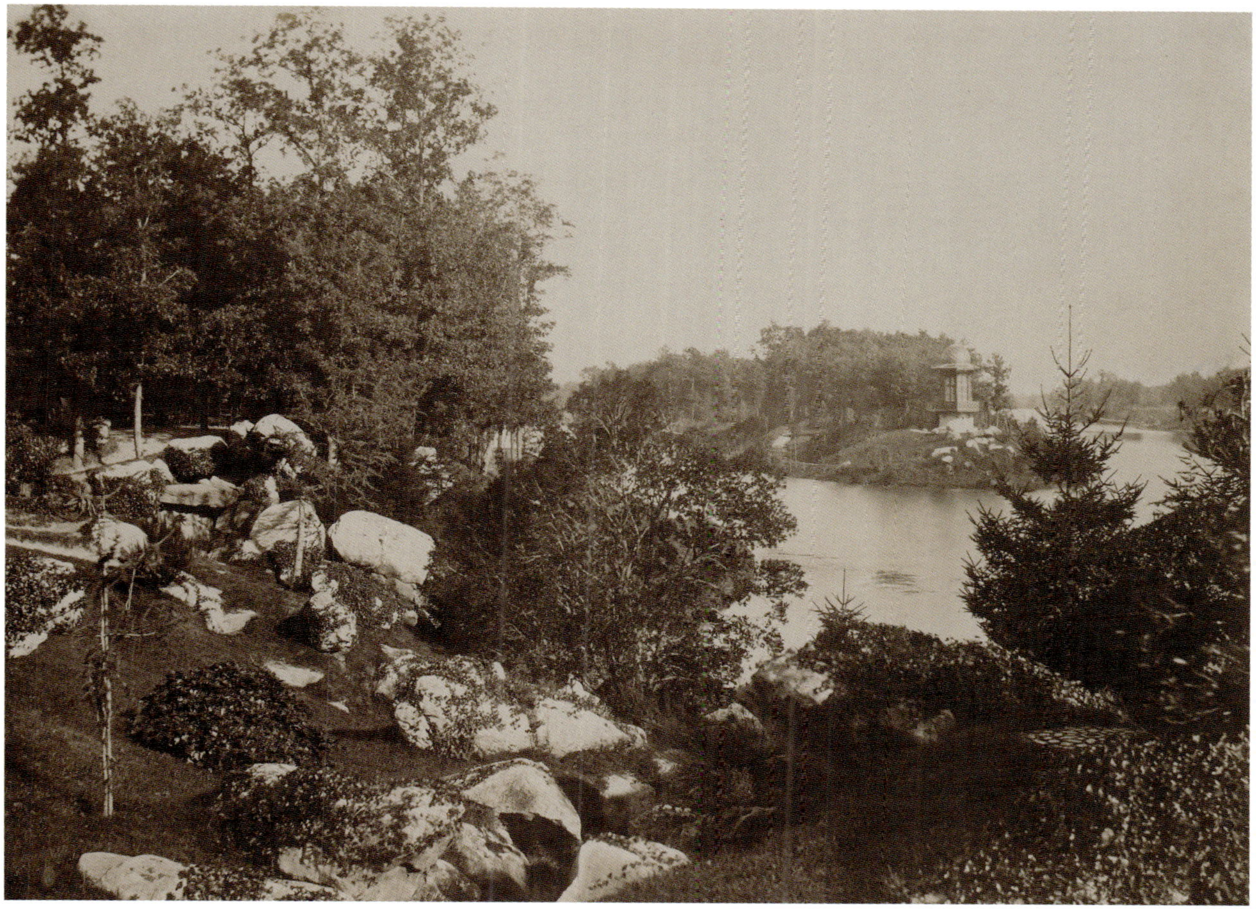

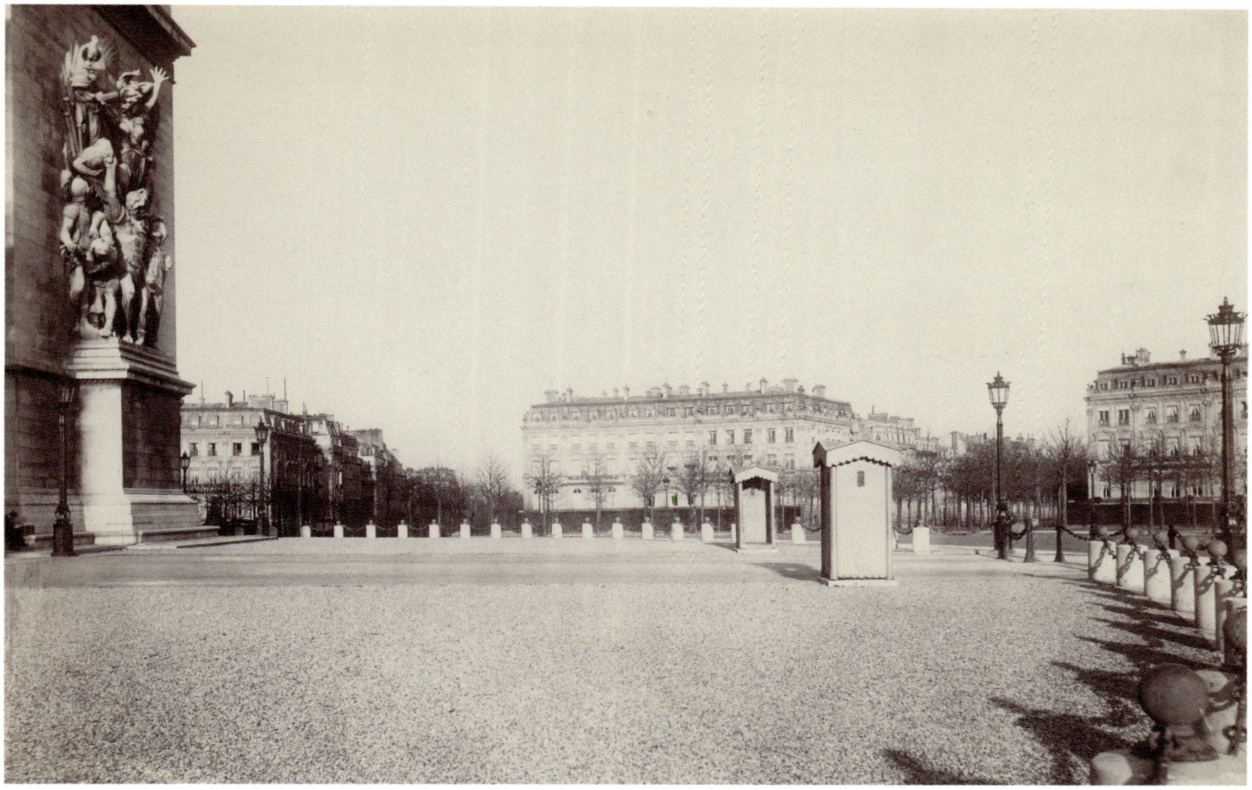

CHARLES MARVILLE

FRENCH, 1813–1879

13

Rue Tirechappe, View from the Rue Saint-Honoré

1860–70; printed later

Albumen print from collodion glass negative

14⅜ × 11 in. (36.5 × 27.9 cm)

The J. Paul Getty Museum, Los Angeles, 84.XM.346.13

14

Rue des Lavandières

ca. 1868

Albumen print from collodion glass negative

11¾ × 10¾ in. (29.9 × 27.3 cm)

The Nelson-Atkins Museum of Art, Kansas City, Missouri, Gift of the Hall Family Foundation, 2007.2.9

are not entirely clear: they may have been commissioned as archival documentation, for use in presentation albums and displays celebrating Haussmann's new Paris at international exhibitions, or perhaps for multiple purposes.[5] He recorded virtually all of the park's newest features, from its benches, lakes, grotto and waterfall, to its winding paths, popular Swiss chalet–style restaurant, and leisure boats for hire. While many of the photographs are relatively conventional in their straightforward recording of subjects, Marville's training as a painter and illustrator can be seen in select views (such as cat. 11). Marville framed the lake using the rocky foreground terrain as a *repoussoir*, drawing the viewer's attention to the Great Lake and kiosk in the background. Despite these picturesque compositional devices, the constructed nature of the landscape does not fully yield itself to illusionistic reverie. Visible in the right foreground is a manhole cover, calling attention to the constructed reality of this seemingly "natural" escape.

At some point in the early 1860s, Marville was officially given the title *photographe de la ville de Paris*, and it is the work produced under these auspices for which he is best known. From 1864 to 1868 Marville produced 425 photographs documenting the narrow streets and decrepit buildings slated for demolition according to Haussmann's plans (cats. 13, 14, and fig. 53) Some streets were completely demolished. Such was the case with the rue Tirechappe, formerly located in the central part of Paris, which was razed to create a wider, straighter street that could directly connect the markets at Les Halles with the Seine riverfront.

Before Marville completed his work recording old Paris, he was commissioned by the city to document the "new" Paris of Haussmann's creation, defined by its grand boulevards, renovated churches, and gas streetlights. The place de l'Étoile was one such subject. The most dramatic of Haussmann's *places*, it had at its center the Arc de Triomphe, which had been designed to celebrate Napoléon I's victory at Austerlitz. Haussmann enlarged the place de l'Étoile, adding seven streets to the existing five that radiated from the arch. To ensure a symmetrical arrangement, Haussmann positioned the radiating streets such that eight of them were identical in size, while the other four were twice their width. Marville's photograph, which features a portion of the arch at the left, offers a sense of the site's monumental vision as well as its rigorous plan.

Though Marville only infrequently exhibited his photographs at the Société française de la photographie, he did include his photographs of Paris in the Exposition universelle of 1867, a section of which was devoted to documenting Haussmann's achievements. In 1871 most of Marville's prints of old Paris were destroyed in the fire that consumed the Hôtel de Ville during the Paris Commune. —AMW

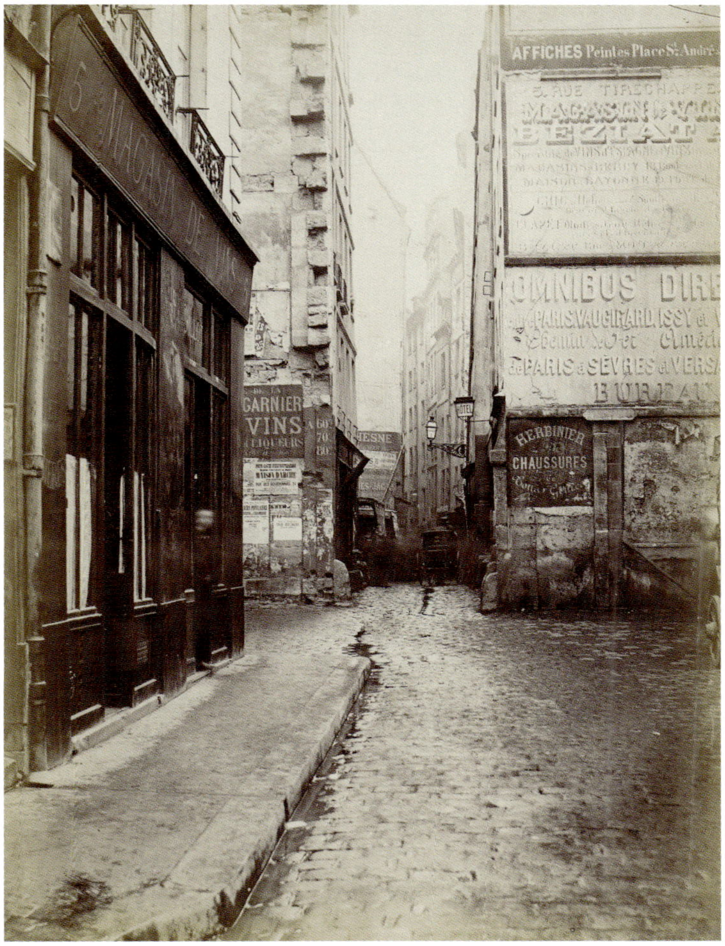

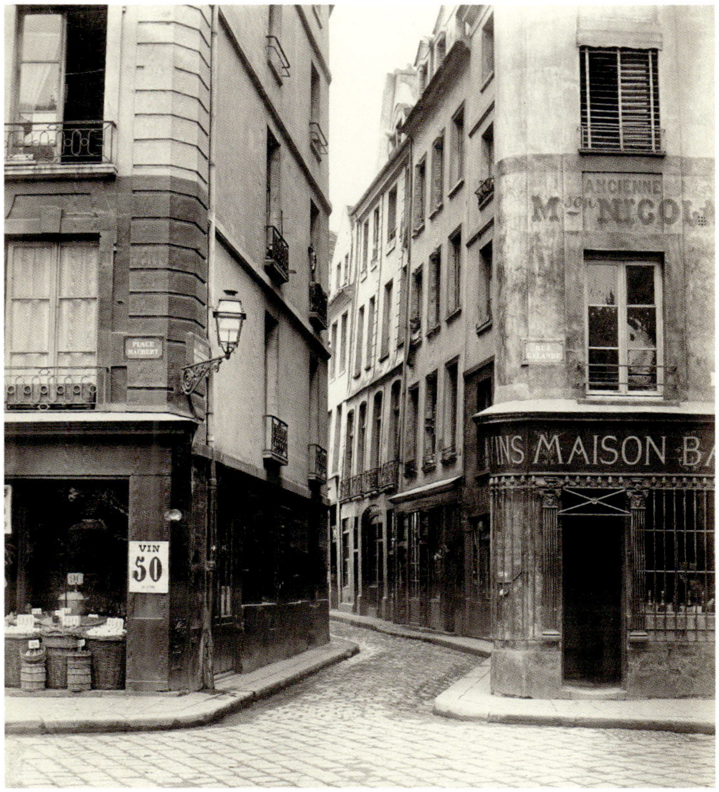

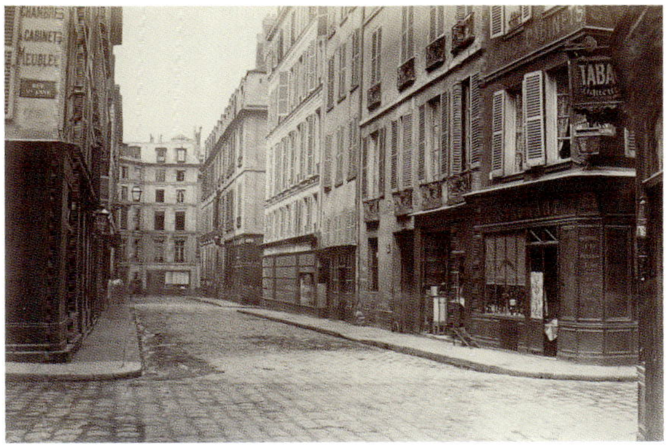

FIG. 53 Charles Marville, *Rue Thérèse (de la rue du Hasard)*, ca. 1870s. Albumen print from collodion glass negative, 9½ × 14¾ in. (24.1 × 37.5 cm). Spencer Museum of Art, The University of Kansas, Lawrence, Museum purchase: Friends of the Art Museum, 1997.0024

1. New details regarding Marville's early life, including his birth name and confirmed death date (Sarah Kennel, e-mail message to author, January 2013), have been discovered by Sarah Kennel and Daniel Catan and will be published in Sarah Kennel, *Charles Marville: Photographer of Paris*, exh. cat. (Washington, D.C.: National Gallery of Art in association with University of Chicago Press, 2013).

2. See Isabelle Jammes, *Blanquart-Evrard et les origines de l'édition photographique française: Catalogue raisonné des albums photographiques édités, 1851–1855* (Paris: Librairie Droz, 1981), 58. Marville's images appear in the albums *Album photographique de l'artiste et de l'amateur* (1851), *L'art religieux: Architecture, sculpture, peinture* (1853–54), *Les bords du Rhin et souvenirs des Pyrénées* (1853), *Études et paysages* (1853), *Études photographiques* (1853), *Mélanges photographiques* (1851), *Musée photographique* (1852), *Paris photographique* (1851 or 1853), *Souvenirs photographiques* (1853), and *Variétés photographiques* (1853–54).

3. This commission was announced in *La Lumière*, September 11, 1858, 147. Marville was also commissioned to photograph in the Bois de Vincennes, the eastern working-class counterpart to the Bois de Boulogne, though he produced far fewer views of this project, which had less political import for the emperor.

4. Émile Bourdelin, "Le Bois de Boulogne," *Le monde illustré*, June 2, 1860, 362: "Aujourd'hui que le bois est complétement transformé . . . nos lecteurs ne verront peut-être pas sans intérêt une topographie pittoresque de cette grande promenade parisienne qui laisse bien loin comme importance, le Prado de Madrid, le Thiergarten de Berlin, les Cascines de Florence et le Prater de Vienne."

5. For a thorough discussion of Marville's Bois de Boulogne photographs, see Peter D. Barberie, "Conventional Pictures: Charles Marville in the Bois de Boulogne" (PhD diss., Princeton University, 2007).

15

CLAUDE MONET
FRENCH, 1840–1926

Boulevard des Capucines

1873–74

Oil on canvas

31⅝ × 23¾ in. (80.3 × 60.3 cm)

The Nelson-Atkins Museum of Art, Kansas City, Missouri, Purchase: the Kenneth A. and Helen F. Spencer Foundation Acquisition Fund, F72-35

CLAUDE MONET WAS BORN in the north of Paris, at 45, rue Laffitte, and, of all the Impressionists, produced the most systematic exploration of the newly transformed capital. Between 1867 and 1878 he painted a large number of Parisian views, representing the new boulevards and the railroad station the Gare Saint-Lazare as well as older churches, monuments, and bridges, including the Panthéon and the Pont Neuf.

In the winter of 1873 Monet portrayed the boulevard des Capucines, a boulevard almost 550 yards long in the north of Paris, which dated back to the late seventeenth century; it was named after a convent that had stood on the street until 1790.[1] The boulevard had been largely rebuilt by Baron Georges-Eugène Haussmann in the Second Empire as part of the fashionable reconstruction of the city around the nearby Opéra.[2] Monet shows a lively, bustling street in winter. Snow-covered hansom cabs traverse the tree-lined street: twenty-three thousand horses were said to move along the thoroughfare each day.[3] The expansive pavement area is filled with crowds of people; a single Morris (advertising) column is rendered in brown and yellow: touches of red may be balloons for sale, perhaps for a festival. To the right, cropped, top-hatted silhouettes of men can be seen on a balcony; the space directly above their heads is the place de l'Opéra. To the left are Haussmann's elegant multistoried buildings. In the center is the prestigious Grand Hôtel, built in 1863 and described by Adolphe Joanne as "the largest and most beautiful hotel in Paris."[4] Monet's picture evokes the energy and flux of the modern city, particularly in the movement of the pedestrians. His treatment of their blurred forms may be indebted to the widely circulated stereoscopic views of the modern city (cat. 19). This association with photography is further suggested by the fact that he painted his scene from the studio of the prominent photographer Nadar, whose address was 35, boulevard des Capucines.[5]

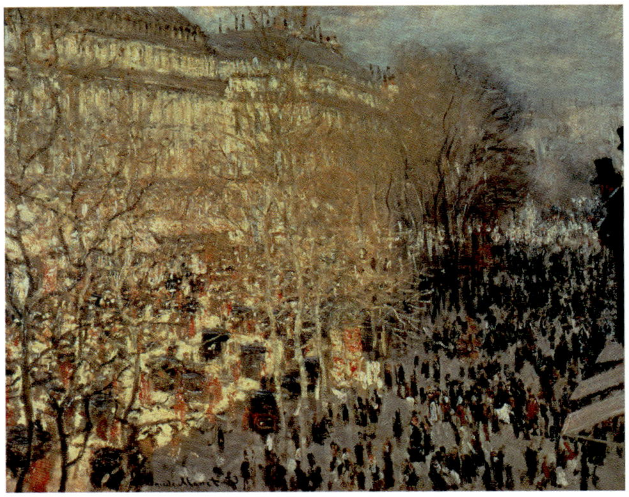

FIG. 54 Claude Monet, *Boulevard des Capucines*, 1873. Oil on canvas, 24 × 31½ in. (61 × 80 cm). Pushkin Museum, Moscow

Monet painted the same view in a pendant horizontal composition. In contrast to the cool, wintry light of the Nelson-Atkins picture, the street here is shown in warm sunlight, with the foreground in shadow (fig. 54). Whereas the winter scene is very sketchily painted—the gray ground is clearly visible—this work is more highly finished. The awnings, for example, are now clearly articulated and the men on the balcony more defined.

Monet showed a painting titled *Boulevard des Capucines* at the first Impressionist exhibition in 1874—also held at 35, boulevard des Capucines—and it is now generally accepted that this was the Pushkin picture. The painting was ridiculed for its sketchy technique, but some critics saw the artist's success in rendering the modern city. As Ernest Chesneau noted: "Never has the prodigious animation of the public street, the swarming of the crowd on the asphalt

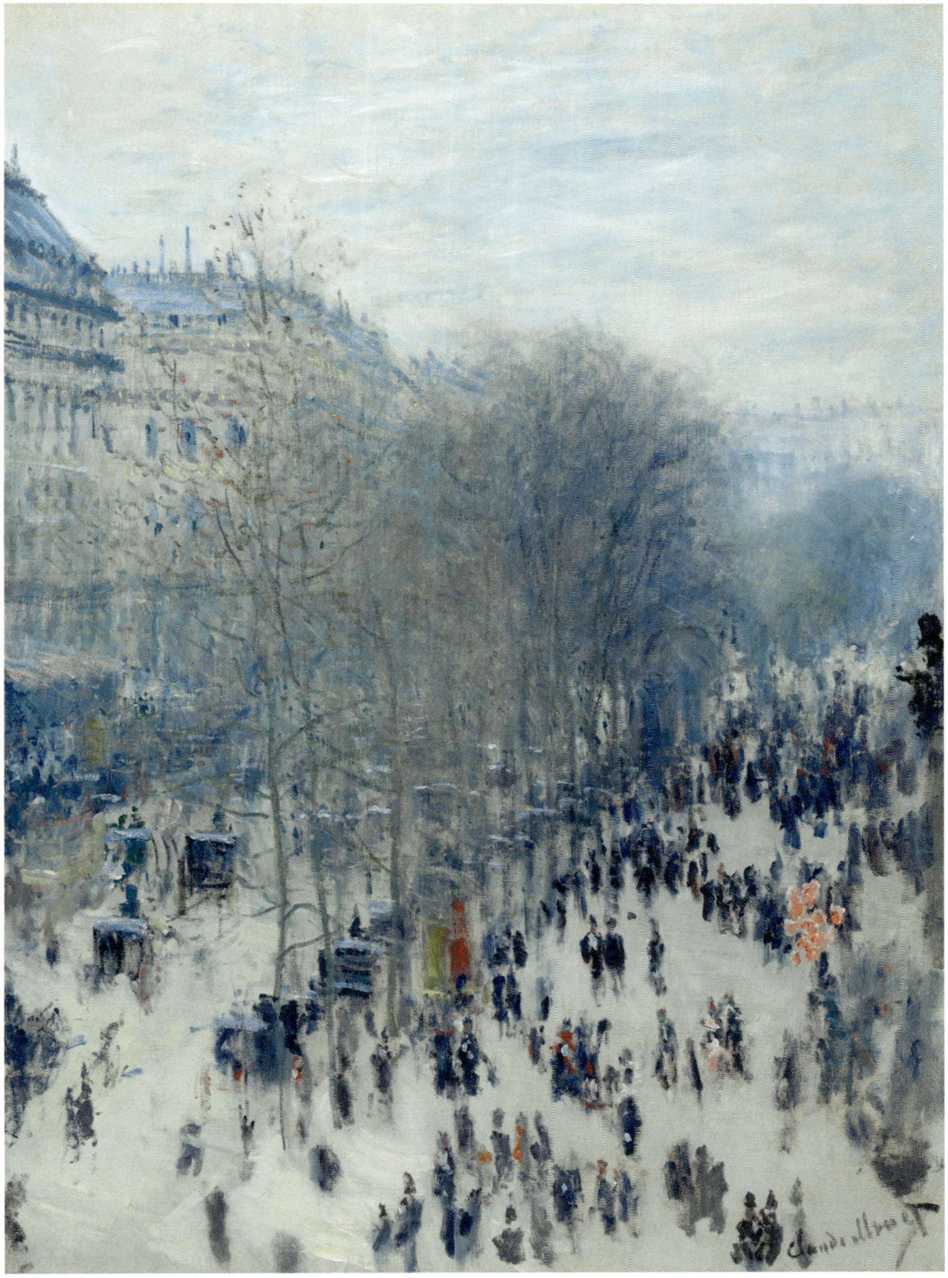

and the carriages on the highway, the movement of the trees in the dust and the light—never has the elusive, fugitive, instantaneousness of the movement been captured and fixed in its tremendous fluidity as in this extraordinary, marvelous sketch."[6]

Monet's exploration of the city continued with twelve views of the Gare Saint-Lazare, a large train station servicing the western part of the country, particularly Normandy. The station was built in the mid-1830s, and the engineer Eugène Flachat greatly expanded it in 1851–53 by adding an enormous roof and two more sets of tracks. In January 1877 Monet obtained permission from the director of the Western Railways to paint inside the station. As the critic Pierre Véron noted, Monet "wanted to convey the impression produced on travelers by the noise of these engines at arrival and departure times."[7] The majority of Monet's views show the station's interior, the spaces beneath its roof filled with dense plumes of steam (fig. 55). *Le Pont de l'Europe, Gare Saint-Lazare*, however, shows the rail tracks outside. Two railway workers in blue overalls are next to a locomotive that is probably arriving at the station. Monet emphasized the swirling smoke and steam and included the

16

CLAUDE MONET
FRENCH, 1840–1926

Le Pont de l'Europe, Gare Saint-Lazare

1877

Oil on canvas

$25\frac{5}{8} \times 31\frac{15}{16}$ in. (65 × 81 cm)

Musée Marmottan Monet, Paris, 4015

color accent of a red signal.[8] This is the only one of Monet's twelve views to show a close-up of the Pont de l'Europe, the star-shaped iron bridge constructed over the tracks between 1865 and 1868.[9] This steel-girdered structure was emblematic of French engineering prowess, anticipating the Eiffel Tower of two decades later.[10] It was favored by many other Impressionists—particularly Gustave Caillebotte—as a symbol of the modern city. Farther back, Monet painted the sunlit, elegant apartment buildings of the recently built rue de Rome, which stretched for approximately three-quarters of a mile. As Adolphe Joanne noted, this was one of those "new and fashionable" streets that had "transformed the quarter."[11]

Le Pont de l'Europe, Gare Saint-Lazare was shown at the third Impressionist exhibition in 1877. Most critics reviewed Monet's group of Saint-Lazare pictures as a group. The conservative Léon de Lora wrote: "Claude Monet . . . gives us five or six interior views of the Gare Saint-Lazare, filled with black, pink, gray, violet smoke which make ineffable scrawls." He noted that the *Pont de l'Europe* "is not without merit, but is absolutely without charm."[12] The liberal critic Jacques was more positive, pointing out that Monet's "brush has expressed not only the movement, color and activity [of the station] but also the clamor; it is unbelievable. Yet the station is full of din—grindings, whistles—that you make out through the colliding blue and gray clouds of dense smoke. It is a pictorial symphony."[13]

Monet's two paintings sum up the artist's early intoxication with the modern city of Paris, embodied in its new boulevards and railroad stations. After painting the flag-filled streets on the Fête de la Paix on June 30, 1878 (see fig. 57), he would turn away from such urban views to more pastoral subject matter. —SK

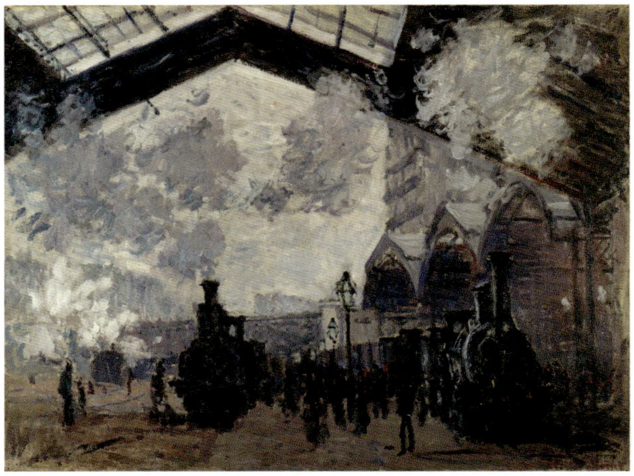

FIG. 55 Claude Monet, *The Gare Saint-Lazare*, 1877. Oil on canvas, $21\frac{3}{8} \times 29$ in. (54.3 × 73.6 cm). National Gallery, London, Bought 1982

1. James Rubin, *Impressionism and the Modern Landscape: Productivity, Technology and Urbanization from Manet to Van Gogh* (Berkeley: University of California Press, 2008), 30–32. See also *Les grands boulevards*, exh. cat. (Paris: Musées de la Ville de Paris, 1985); and Patrice de Moncan, *Les grands boulevards de Paris: De la Bastille à la Madeleine* (Paris: Les Éditions de Mécène, 1997), 348–63.

2. Pierre Larousse noted that the Hôtel des Capucines had been the site of an important 1848 barricade but had been replaced by "elegant buildings" (elégantes constructions). The other side of the street had been "demolished for the establishment of the Grand Hôtel and the reconstruction of the Opera." The street had become the "center of a new quarter" (le côté opposé, démoli pour l'établissement du Grand Hôtel et la reconstruction de l'Opéra, est devenu le centre d'un nouveau quartier). The Jockey Club and Grand Café, "the most fashionable café in Paris," were also on the street. See Larousse, *Grand dictionnaire universel du XIXe siècle* (Paris: Éditions Larousse, 1867), s.v. "boulevard."

3. David H. Pinkney, *Napoleon III and the Rebuilding of Paris* (Princeton: Princeton University Press, 1958), 71.

4. Adolphe Joanne, *Paris illustré* (Paris: Hachette, 1867), xxx: "le plus vaste et le plus bel hôtel de Paris." This seven-hundred-room hotel occupied the entire trapezoidal block between the place de l'Opéra and the rue Scribe. It was built by the Compagnie immobilière de Paris, owned by the Péreire brothers, Émile and Isaac, prominent Parisian financiers and rivals of the Rothschilds.

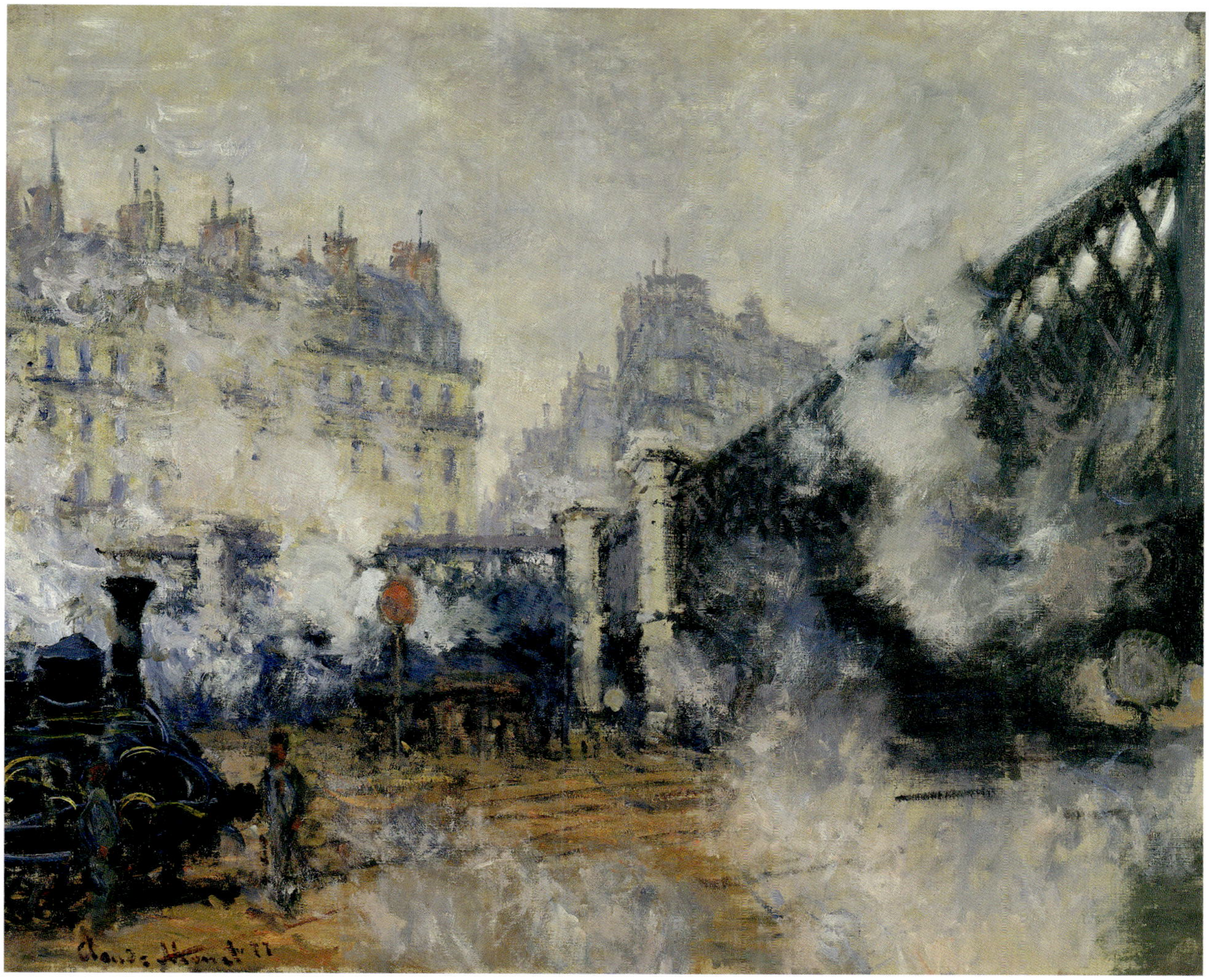

5. The studio was also well known as the space for the early exhibitions of the Société française de la photographie, the most prestigious French photographic society.

6. Ernest Chesneau, "A côté du Salon: II. Le plein air: Exposition du boulevard des Capucines," *Paris-Journal*, May 7, 1874: "Jamais l'animation prodigieuse de la voie publique, le fourmillement de la foule sur l'asphalte et des voitures sur la chaussée, l'agitation des arbres du boulevard dans la poussière et la lumière; jamais l'insaisissable, le fugitif, l'instantané du mouvement n'a été saisi et fixé dans sa prodigieuse fluidité, comme il l'est dans cette extraordinaire, dans cette merveilleuse ébauche." Quoted in Ruth Berson, *The New Painting: Impressionism, 1874–1886; Documentation*, vol. 1, *Reviews* (San Francisco: Fine Arts Museums of San Francisco, 1996), 18.

7. Pierre Véron, "Les impressionistes," *La petite presse*, April 9, 1877, 2; quoted in Anne Roquebert, "This Stunning Paris," in *Claude Monet, 1840–1926*, exh. cat. (Paris: Réunion des Musées Nationaux, 2010), 149.

8. Other views, such as *The Signal* (Niedersächsisches Landesmuseum, Hannover), also highlight the signals at the station.

9. Adolphe Joanne, *Guide de l'étranger dans Paris et ses environs* (Paris: Hachette, 1877), 52: "Le pont en fer qui la supporte a été construit sous la direction de M. Jullien. Il est entré dans sa construction 3500 tonnes de cette matière. De fortes culées en pierre en soutiennent les poutres et s'élèvent en grosses piles sur les angles de la place pour encadrer les balustrades, qui sont aussi en fer."

10. For an early view of the bridge, see Auguste Lamy's wood engraving in *L'illustration*, April 11, 1868. The bridge was demolished in 1930.

11. Joanne, *Guide de l'étranger dans Paris et ses environs*, 70: "Sur la rive droite, des rues nouvelles et commodes, aboutissant à de nombreux boulevards, ont métamorphosé les quartiers de Chaillot, des Champs-Élysées et de Monceaux. La rue de Rome (1200 mètres environ) relie le pont Cardinet (parc de Monceaux) aux rues Saint-Lazare et de la Pépinière prolongées."

12. Léon de Lora, "L'exposition des impressionistes," *Le gaulois*, April 10, 1877, 2: "Claude Monet . . . nous donne cinq ou six vues intérieures de la gare Saint-Lazare, emplis de fumées, noires, roses, grises, violacées, qui en font d'ineffables grimoires. Le *pont de Rome* . . . n'est pas sans mérite, mais c'est tout à fait sans agrément." Quoted in Berson, *Reviews*, 153.

13. See Jacques, "Menus propos: Salon impressioniste," *L'homme libre*, April 11, 1877, 2: "Le pinceau rendant, non-seulement le mouvement, la couleur, l'activité, mais le bruit, c'est invraisemblable; et pourtant cette gare est pleine de tapage, de grincements, de sifflements, qu'on distingue à travers la fumé intense, dont les nuages azurés et gris se heurtent. C'est une symphonie picturale." Quoted in Berson, *Reviews*, 155.

17

PIERRE-AUGUSTE RENOIR

FRENCH, 1841–1919

The Grands Boulevards

1875

Oil on canvas

20½ × 25 in. (52.1 × 63.5 cm)

Philadelphia Museum of Art, The Henry P. McIlhenny Collection in memory of Frances P. McIlhenny, 1986, 1986-26-29

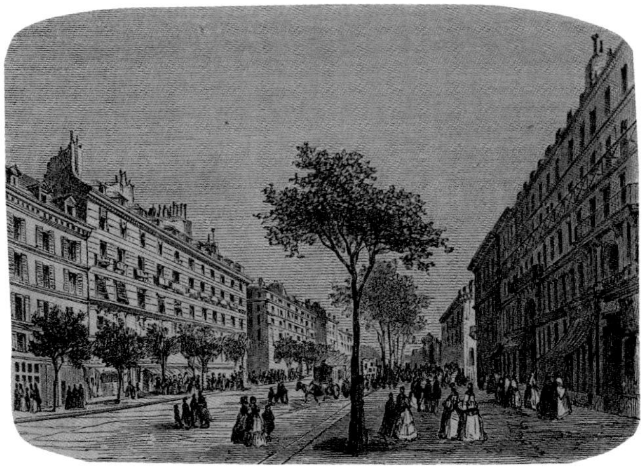

FIG. 56 *Boulevard des Italiens.* From Adolphe Joanne, *Paris illustré: Nouveau guide de l'étranger et du parisien* (Paris: Hachette, 1867), 65

PIERRE-AUGUSTE RENOIR, who grew up in Paris's third arrondissement, painted approximately ten views of the city during the 1860s and 1870s.[1] He first painted Paris in 1867, representing the Champs-Élysées at the time of the Exposition universelle (private collection), and subsequently depicted a range of sites, including the Bois de Boulogne and the Pont Neuf. Renoir published articles about the architecture of Paris in the late 1870s and in general was very opposed to the new buildings added by Baron Georges-Eugène Haussmann, despising, for example, Charles Garnier's new Opéra.[2] In general, his preference was for the older, more established medieval architecture around Paris. Indeed, in 1877 he complained that Paris's old buildings had been replaced by new structures "cold and lined up like soldiers at a review."[3] Nonetheless, his paintings counter his words by showing a more positive attitude toward the modern city.

The Grands Boulevards, a springtime view, represents one of the boulevards of Paris, redeveloped by Haussmann during the Second Empire. As John Zarobell has noted, the painting has in the past been titled both *Boulevard des Italiens* and *Place de la Trinité*, but the location has not been firmly identified.[4] The picture may be intended to be a generic, archetypical image, alluding to the four Grands Boulevards in northern Paris: the boulevard des Italiens, the boulevard des Capucines, the boulevard Montmartre, and the boulevard de la Madeleine. Renoir includes the essential elements of these boulevards, which were such a central part of the modern city of Paris: the wide street and sidewalk, the greenery to create an atmosphere that encouraged strolling, a gas lamp, a Morris advertising column, the tiered apartment blocks with ground-floor commercial stores fronted by brightly colored, striped awnings. Renoir's image is reminiscent of a print of the boulevard des Italiens that appeared in Adolphe Joanne's *Illustrated Paris* in 1867 (fig. 56). Joanne noted that this boulevard was particularly known for its elegant flaneurs: "under the pale sun which illuminates its asphalt roads, beneath the clarity of its gas lamps come to operate, day and night, indefinable beings in turn called refined, beautiful, marvelous, incredible, dandys, fashionistas, lions, fops."[5] We may imagine that Renoir represented similar figures in the seated man to the left as well as the men conversing in the street. A fashionable woman in a red hat crosses with her two young children; a tall nun also crosses the street, stopping before a rapidly moving horse-drawn carriage. Despite his disparaging words about Haussmann's architecture, Renoir presented an idyllic view of the city, softening the angular lines of the new buildings in a warm, embracing light.

The Grands Boulevards is characteristic of Renoir's images of modern Paris that highlight the energy and flux of Haussmann's new city. As Colin Bailey has noted, Renoir's pictures of the capital's restored bridges and new boulevards present a "benign and hopeful vision of urban sociability."[6]

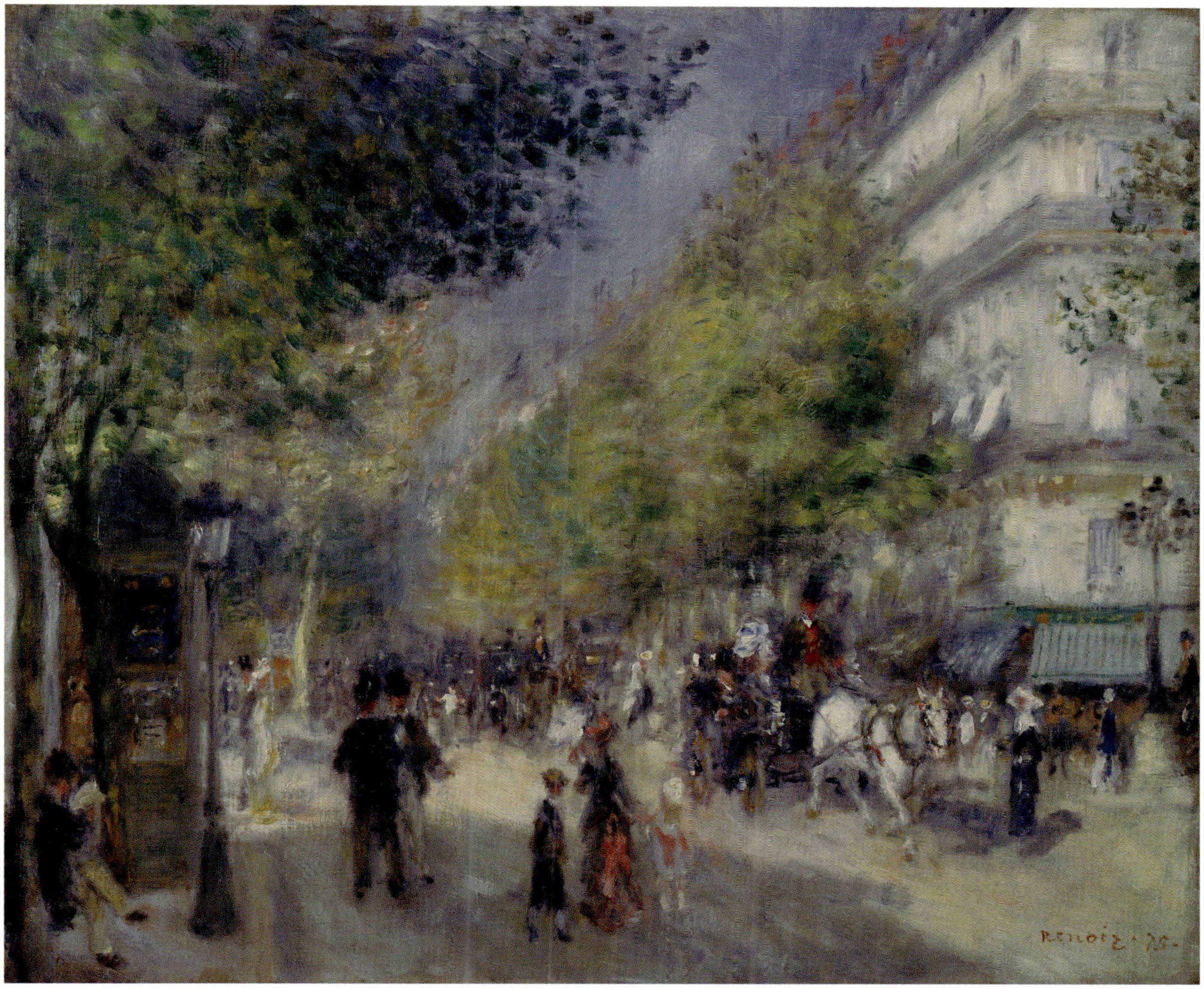

The artist seems to have imagined boulevards as sites for the intermingling of a range of classes and social types. Seen from this perspective, this view taps into Renoir's wider republican and egalitarian aspirations for the French nation.[7] —SK

1. Christopher Riopelle, "Renoir in the City," in *Renoir's Landscapes, 1865–1883*, ed. Colin B. Bailey and Christopher Riopelle, exh. cat. (London: National Gallery, 2007), 32–49.

2. See Robert L. Herbert, "Renoir's Writings, 1877–1884," in *Nature's Workshop: Renoir's Writings on the Decorative Arts* (New Haven: Yale University Press, 2000), 1–24.

3. Auguste Renoir, letter to the editor, *L'impressioniste* 3 (April 21, 1877); quoted in Robert L. Herbert, *Impressionism: Art, Leisure and Society* (New Haven: Yale University Press, 1988), 15.

4. See John Zarobell in Bailey and Riopelle, *Renoir's Landscapes*, 162–63. In 1905 Camille Mauclair titled the painting *Le boulevard des Italiens* in *L'art et la couleur: Les maîtres contemporains*, no. 1 (Paris, 1905). Renoir's friend Ambroise Vollard identified the location as the place de la Trinité. Vollard, *Tableaux, pastels et dessins de Pierre-Auguste Renoir* (Paris, 1918; repr., San Francisco: Alan Wofsy Fine Arts, 1989), 1:88, no. 352. Renoir produced two other images of the place de la Trinité in 1875: *Place de la Trinité* (private collection) and *Square de la Trinité* (Rhode Island School of Design, Providence). No boulevards, however, run off this square, only roads (the rue de Londres, rue Saint-Lazare, rue de Clichy, rue de la Chaussée d'Antin). James Rubin identifies Renoir's view as the boulevard des Capucines, recently treated by Claude Monet (cat. 15): Rubin, *Impressionism and the Modern Landscape: Productivity, Technology, and Urbanization from Manet to Van Gogh* (Berkeley: University of California Press, 2008), 32.

5. Adolphe Joanne, *Paris illustré* (Paris: Hachette, 1867), 64: "C'est sous le pâle soleil qui éclaire ses chaussées d'asphaltes, c'est à la clarté de ses becs de gaz que, chaque jour et chaque nuit, viennent manoeuvrer les êtres indéfinissables tour à tour appelés raffinés, beaux, merveilleux, incroyables, dandys, fashionables, lions, gandins."

6. Bailey, entry for *The Pont Neuf*, in Bailey and Riopelle, *Renoir's Landscapes*, 115.

7. The republican Renoir had remained in Paris during the Commune and had a genuine sympathy for insurrectionaries, whom he described as "brave fellows, full of good intentions." Renoir also felt an affinity for Léon Gambetta, calling him "the simplest and most courteous man I ever met." Quoted in Philip Nord, *The Republican Moment: Struggles for Democracy in Nineteenth-Century France* (Princeton: Princeton University Press, 1995), 164–65.

18

DELMAET & DURANDELLE
FRENCH, ACT. 1862–90

LOUIS-ÉMILE DURANDELLE
FRENCH, 1839–1917

HYACINTHE-CESAR DELMAET
FRENCH, 1828–1862

Work Yard in Front of the Paris Opéra

April–December 1866

Albumen print from collodion glass negative

11⅛ × 15³⁄₁₆ in. (28.3 × 38.7 cm)

George Eastman House, Rochester, New York, Gift of Eastman Kodak Company; ex-collection Gabriel Cromer, 1980:0099:0008

THE PLACE DE L'OPÉRA became the new center of fashionable Paris under Baron Georges-Eugène Haussmann's design. In March 1858 he maneuvered a deal between the city of Paris and the state to create two new streets—the rues Auber and Halévy—and the place de l'Opéra. Haussmann eventually worked with the architect Charles Rohault de Fleury, who drew up complete plans. By 1860 Haussmann proposed a new opera house to anchor the site and to become a focal point for the neighborhood, which since the eighteenth century had been populated by theaters, cafés, and promenades frequented by the wealthier sectors of Parisian society. A public competition for the designer of the new opera house attracted 170 submissions, from which seven finalists were chosen. The winner was thirty-six-year-old Charles Garnier, who had not previously completed a project in Paris.[1]

The Opéra itself was a lavish structure, harking back to French classicism but decidedly innovative in its use of modern building materials. The building took fourteen years to construct, at a cost of twenty-five million francs. It was the most expensive structure executed during the Second Empire. When it was finished, it represented the imperial ambitions of Napoléon III, as an architectural celebration of the art and culture of the elite who could afford such civilized pleasures.

Between 1865 and 1872 the commercial photographer Louis-Émile Durandelle, operating under the name of his firm Delmaet & Durandelle, produced approximately 115 photographs recording the construction and interior decoration of the Opéra, using glass-plate negatives and the wet-collodion process. The resulting albumen prints, most of which were made in a large format, record various phases of the massive project: excavations, internal elevations, and close-up views of the decorative ornamentation. As such, these photographs served multiple purposes: artistic, documentary, political. While several views, such as the one shown here, include the men hired to work on the site, others are devoid of figures, depicting the play of light and shadow on the architectural forms. Because many of his human subjects look back at the camera and were standing close to Durandelle, there is a palpable sense of human connection between the photographer and his subjects that is not apparent in similar commissions by other photographers, such as Baldus's recording of the new Louvre's construction (see cats. 6, 7). Many of Durandelle's photographs were later published, along with lithographs and engravings, in the album *Le Nouvel Opéra de Paris*, comprising four volumes—*Sculpture ornamentale*, *Statues décoratives*, *Peintures décoratives*, and *Bronzes*—which were distributed largely to a clientele of architects and designers. —AMW

1. Garnier's win did not please Empress Eugénie, who preferred Garnier's far more established competitor Eugène-Emmanuel Viollet-le-Duc, with whom Garnier had worked as a draftsman. David P. Jordan, *Transforming Paris: The Life and Labors of Baron Haussmann* (Chicago: University of Chicago Press, 1995), 208.

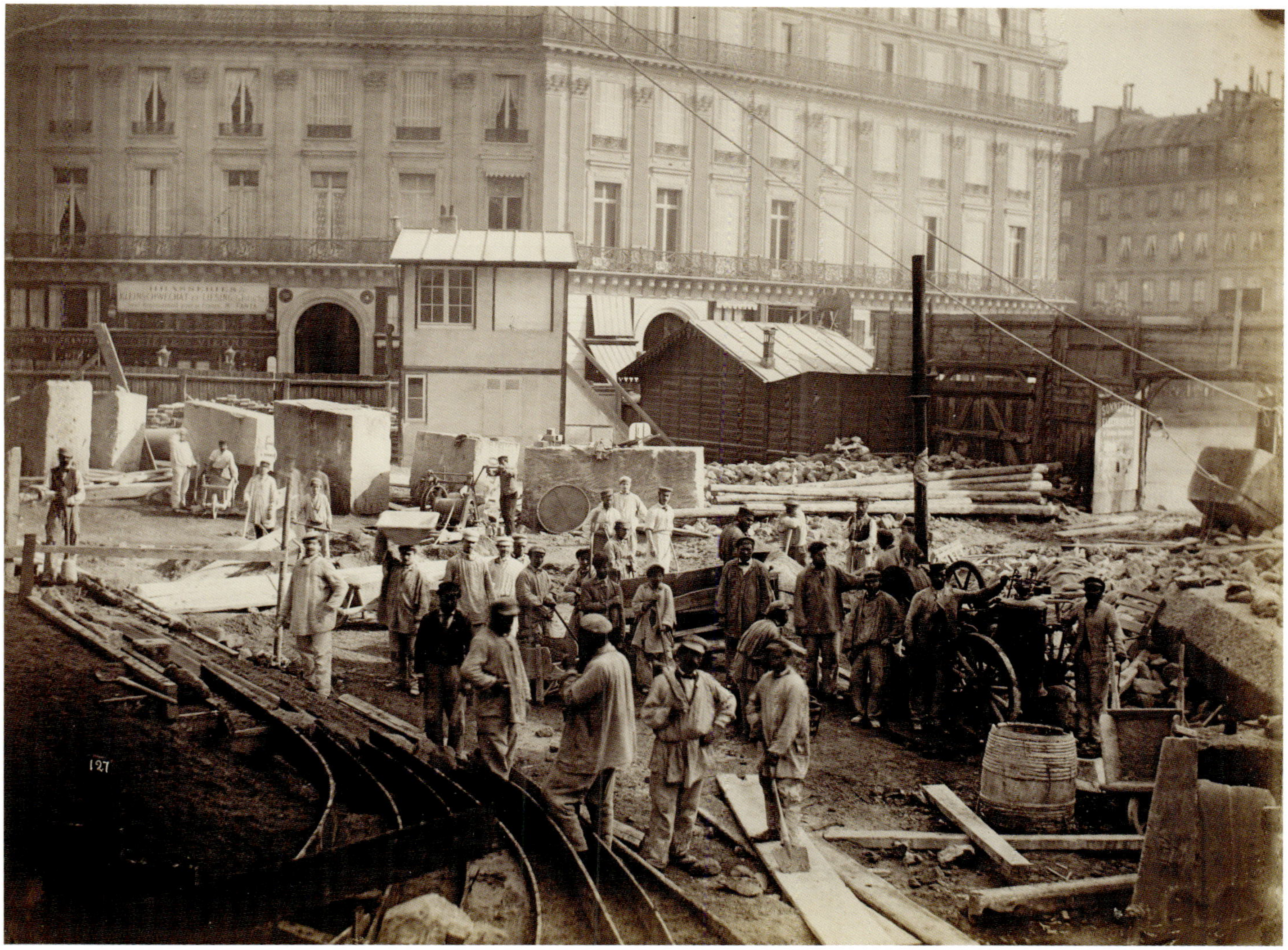
127

HIPPOLYTE JOUVIN (ATTRIBUTED)
FRENCH, 1825–CA. 1887

19

Rue de Rivoli and Hôtel du Louvre

ca. 1865

Stereograph; albumen prints from collodion glass negative

Each image 3⅛ × 3 in. (7.9 × 7.5 cm) on 3³⁄₁₆ × 6¹¹⁄₁₆ in. (8.1 × 17.1 cm) mount

George Eastman House, Rochester, New York, Purchased from Fred S. Lightfoot with funds provided by Eastman Kodak Company, 1981:7500:0001

HIPPOLYTE JOUVIN
FRENCH, 1825–CA. 1887

20

Pont and Place de la Concorde

ca. 1865

Stereograph; albumen prints from collodion glass negative

Each image 3⅛ × 3 in. (8 × 7.5 cm) on 3⅜ × 6¹¹⁄₁₆ in. (8.6 × 17 cm) mount

George Eastman House, Rochester, New York, Purchased from Fred S. Lightfoot with funds provided by Eastman Kodak Company, 1981:7500:0005

THE SURGE OF INTEREST in stereography after its introduction at the 1851 Great Exhibition in London propelled numerous entrepreneurs to establish commercial studios and capitalize on the public appetite for this affordable and collectible photographic format. During the 1860s stereographs and cartes de visite were the most popular type of commercial photographs. As Anne McCauley has noted, stereoscopic views accounted for just over 40 percent of all titles registered for copyright in Paris in 1868.[1] While American and British stereographers focused on dramatic landscape views, the French studios created a broad range of subjects, including theatrical genre scenes, erotica, landscapes, and views of Baron Georges-Eugène Haussmann's renovated Paris. The largest firms in Paris to produce stereo views included Alexandre Ferrier and Charles Soulier (which became Ferrier Père & Fils & Soulier), whose trade lists eventually exceeded 40,000 titles. Adolphe Braun began publishing stereographs in 1856, and by 1871 his list included 8,500 titles.[2] Lesser known was Hippolyte Jouvin, who seems to have issued his works in smaller series. His titles included *Voyage en Normandy*, *Voyage en Bretagne*, *Midi du France*, and *Vue instantanées*, the series of 189 stereo views from which these two Parisian street scenes derive. Here, Jouvin composed the city's grand boulevards like the rue de Rivoli or notable sites like the Pont and place de la Concorde in such a way that the strong diagonal recessionals helped to intensify a three-dimensional effect when the images were viewed through a stereoscope. The inclusion of people and carriages on the streets in these images also convey a sense of instantaneity, even if true snapshots would not proliferate until the 1880s, when advances in materials and camera equipment enabled faster exposures. Jouvin's rue de Rivoli stereograph nonetheless begins to give viewers a sense of the hustle and bustle of crowded Parisian street life that Monet depicts along the boulevard des Capucines (see cat. 15). —AMW

1. Elizabeth Anne McCauley, *Industrial Madness: Commercial Photography in Paris, 1848–1871* (New Haven: Yale University Press 1994), 98.

2. This information derives from William C. Darrah's formative study of the stereograph, Darrah, *The World of Stereographs* (Gettysburg, Pa.: W. C. Darrah, 1977), 113–15.

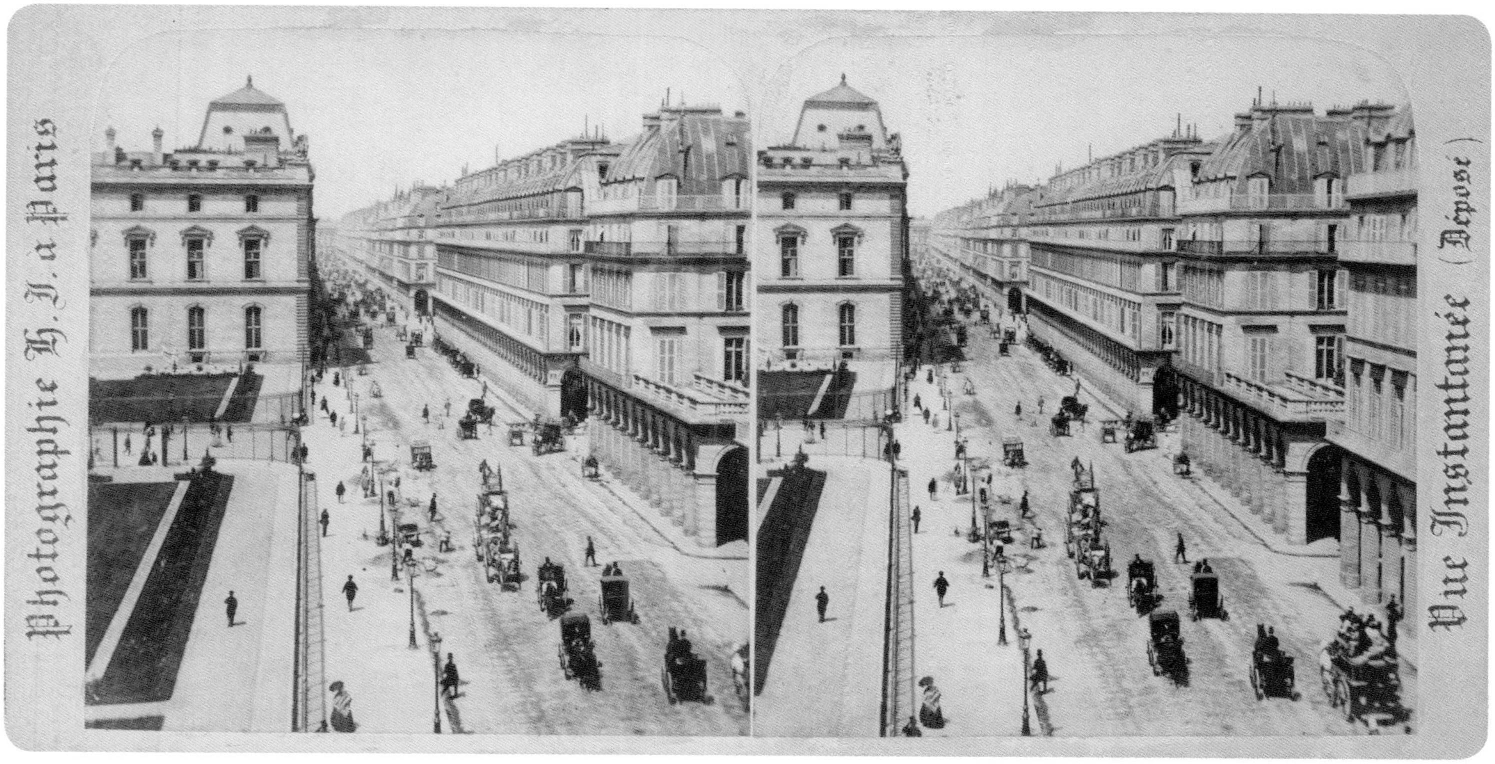
Photographie H. J. a Paris
Vue Instantanée (Déposé)

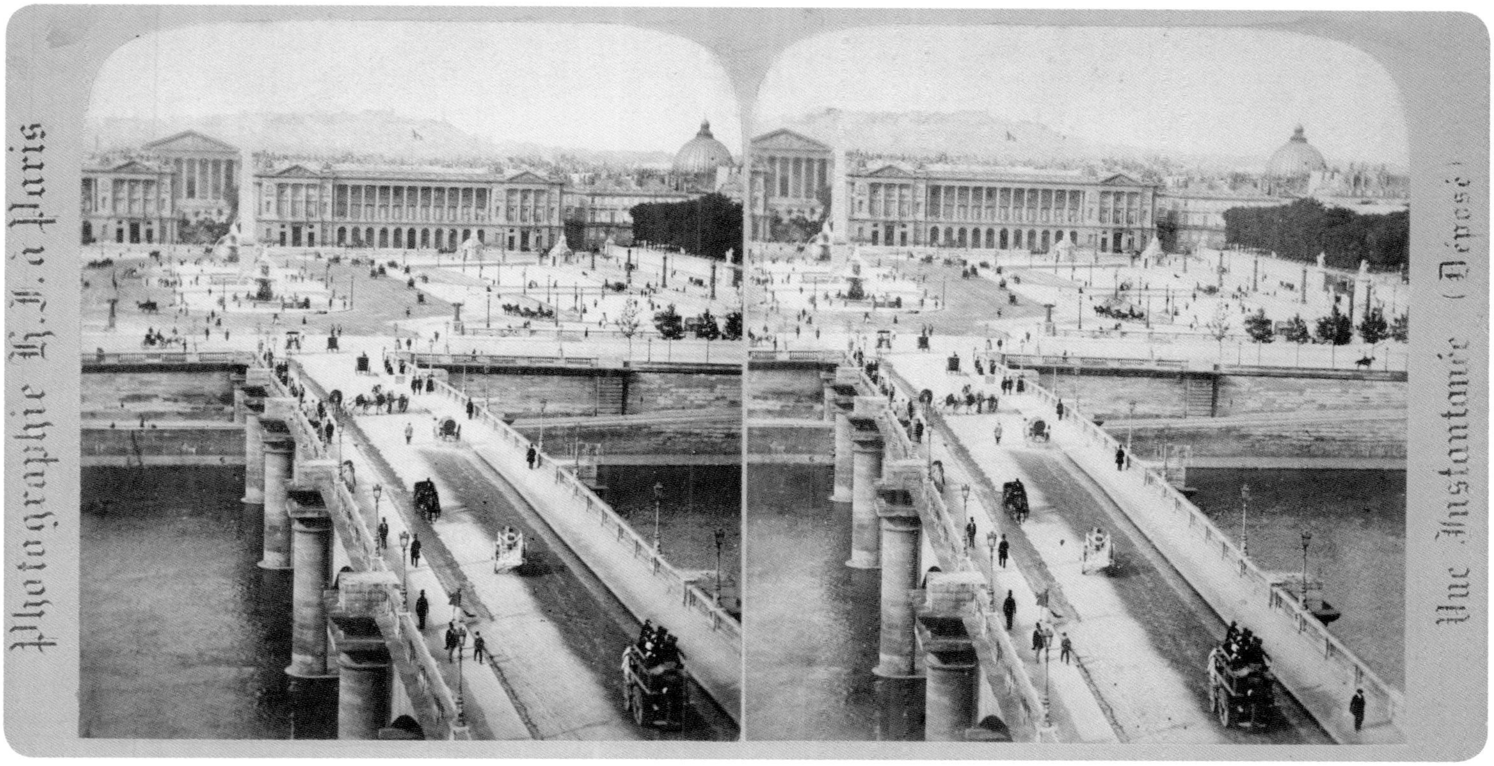
Photographie H. F. a Paris
Vue Instantanée (Déposé)

21

ÉDOUARD MANET

FRENCH, 1832–1883

The Rue Mosnier with Flags

1878

Oil on canvas

25¾ × 31¾ in. (65.4 × 80 cm)

The J. Paul Getty Museum, Los Angeles, 89.PA.71

ÉDOUARD MANET WAS BORN IN PARIS and represented the city often throughout his career, painting the capital's transformed panorama at the time of the 1867 Exposition universelle, the Gare Saint-Lazare, and Baron Georges-Eugène Haussmann's new boulevards.[1] The artist's patriotic embrace of the city is particularly evident in his enthusiastic proposal in 1879 to paint the ceiling of the rebuilt Hôtel de Ville (city hall) with images of "all the men now living who in civil life have contributed or are contributing to the greatness and wealth of Paris."[2] He proposed an accompanying series of paintings on the theme of "the belly of Paris": public markets, parks, racetracks, underground activities, railways, and bridges.

The Rue Mosnier with Flags shows a recently built street in the Batignolles quarter of northwestern Paris.[3] This street had been created in 1870–71 as part of the redevelopment around the Gare Saint-Lazare and ran parallel to the rail tracks: the rubble in the left foreground fills a space alongside the railway cutting. The residential road was described by Émile Zola in his novel *Nana* as "a new and quiet street in the quartier de l'Europe, without any shops, with fine houses of narrow little apartments."[4] Manet painted this work from his studio window at 4, rue de Saint-Petersbourg, where he had lived since 1872. The street is festooned with flags on the national holiday of June 30, the Fête de la Paix, in celebration of the 1878 Exposition universelle.[5] One newspaper, *Le constitutionnel*, suggested that as many as two million flags flew in Paris on that day.[6] The official government journal evoked the national spirit of unity that surrounded the festival: "In every arrondissement, in every neighborhood, even the poorest, the flowers, the illuminations, the banners, the flags of all nations, the concerts, the joyful songs gave to this demonstration of public confidence a character of general appeasement. Parisians, provincials, foreigners, seemed during that beautiful day, to form but one great family."[7]

Manet's work, however, has a strange sense of stillness and was probably painted in the late afternoon—as the longer shadows suggest—after the celebrations were over.[8] Three horse-drawn carriages are sparsely interspersed along the street, while figures move wraithlike along the pavement on the right. The cropped form of a workman carrying a ladder at the lower left probably alludes to the removal of the flags. The most striking figure in the composition is the amputee in a blue smock, hobbling along near the workman with the ladder. This is probably a victim of the Franco-Prussian War or Commune, and his inclusion undercuts the celebratory atmosphere evidenced by the display of the flags. As Robert Herbert has noted, this figure "exposes the realities that lay behind the showy displays of the MacMahon Government."[9] Juliet Wilson-Bareau has also pointed out that Manet included this same amputee in a related prints project, which endorsed a radical republican philosophy.[10] The republican Manet had frequently critiqued the repressive monarchist regime of Patrice de MacMahon in his works of the 1870s.

Manet's picture can be contrasted with Claude Monet's more celebratory view of the festivities at the nearby rue Montorgeuil on the same day, June 30, 1878 (fig. 57). The implicit critical charge in Manet's work contrasts with the more affirmative energy of Monet's picture. By 1879 a more liberal, truly republican government was in power. Manet's embrace of this new administration is evident in a watercolor from 1880—*Vive l'amnistie* (fig. 58)—in which he praised the return of political prisoners following a general amnesty. *The Rue Mosnier with Flags* sums up Manet's complex patriotism, which was of a decidedly republican, antimonarchist type. —SK

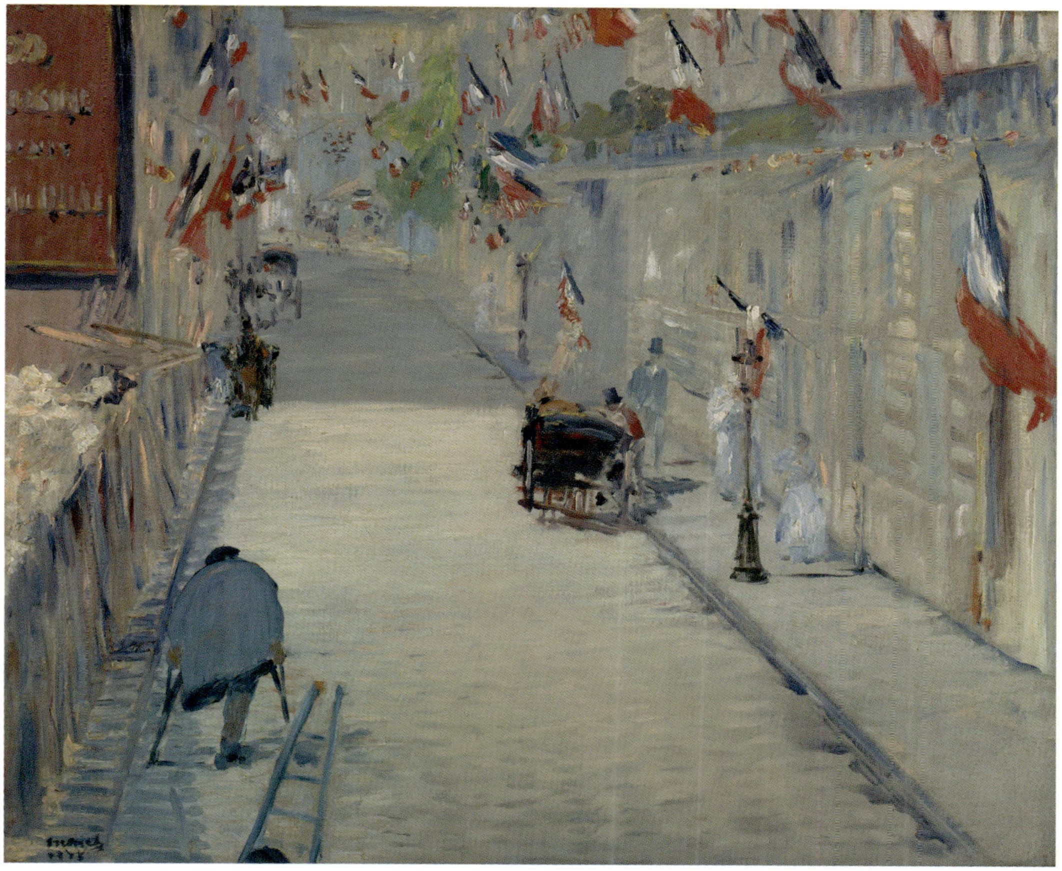

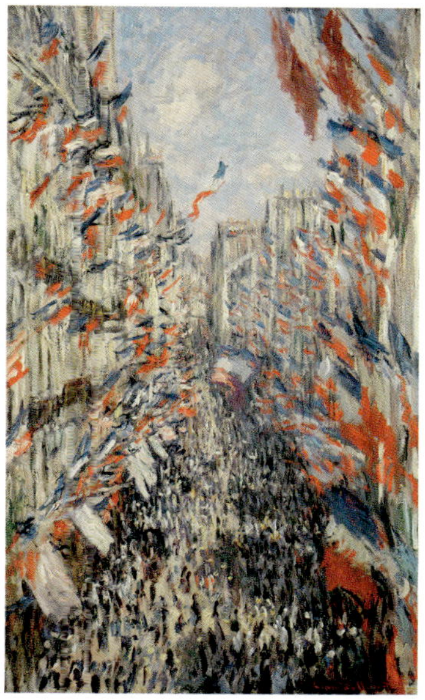

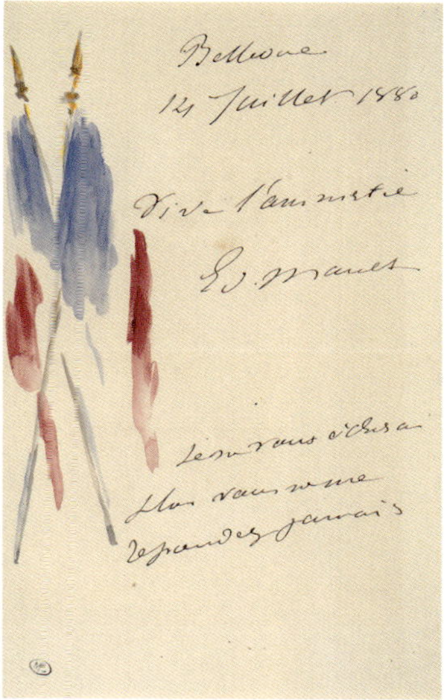

FIG. 57 Claude Monet, *The Rue Montorgueil in Paris: Celebration of June 30, 1878*, 1878. Oil on canvas, 31⅞ × 19¹¹⁄₁₆ in. (81 × 50 cm). Musee d'Orsay, Paris

FIG. 58 Édouard Manet, *Long Live the Amnesty* (*Vive l'amnistie*), letter written to Isabelle Lemonnier, July 14, 1880. Watercolor, 7 × 4½ in. (18 × 11.2 cm). Musée d'Orsay, Paris

1. *The Exposition Universelle in 1867* (National Gallery, Oslo) and *The Railroad* (National Gallery of Art, Washington, D.C.).

2. Juliet Wilson-Bareau, ed., *Manet by Himself* (London: MacDonald, 1991), 185.

3. In 1884 the street was renamed the rue de Berne and retains this name today. For a detailed overview of Manet's picture, see Juliet Wilson-Bareau, *Manet, Monet and the Gare Saint-Lazare*, exh. cat. (Washington, D.C.: National Gallery of Art; New Haven: Yale University Press, 1998), 131–43.

4. Émile Zola, *Nana* (Paris: G. Charpentier, 1880), 275–76: "une rue neuve et silencieuse du quartier de l'Europe, sans une boutique, dont les belles maisons, aux petit appartements étroits." The novel, although written in 1878–79, is set in the Paris of 1869–70, when the street was still unfinished.

5. Jane Mayo Roos, "Within the 'Zone of Silence': Monet and Manet in 1878," *Art History* 11 (September 1988): 372–407.

6. *Le siècle*, July 1–2, 1878, 1: "Nous n'exagérons certainement pas en évaluant à deux millions les drapeaux qui ont pavoisé les façades le jour." Quoted in ibid., 387. An estimate of three hundred thousand is probably more realistic.

7. *Journal officiel*, July 2, 1878, 7542: "Dans tous les arrondissements, dans tous les quartiers, même les plus pauvres, les fleurs, les illuminations, les bannières, les drapeaux de toutes les nations, les concerts, les chants joyeux donnaient à cette manifestation de la confiance publique un caractère d'apaisement general. Parisiens, provinciaux, étrangers semblaient, durant cette belle journée, ne former qu'une grande famille." Quoted in ibid.

8. Manet produced two other paintings of the rue Mosnier, which show pavers at work and a very sketchy scene of celebration on June 30, with a large flag in close-up by Manet's studio window: *Rue Mosnier with Pavers* (Kunsthaus, Zurich) and *Rue Mosnier Decorated with Flags* (private collection, Zurich). He also painted a related oil sketch, *Knife Grinder and Street Lamp* (Philadelphia Museum of Art, 1978.1.20), and two wash drawings, *Rue Mosnier with a Gaslamp* (The Art Institute of Chicago, 4515) and *Rue Mosnier in the Rain* (Szépművészeti Muzeum, Budapest, 1935-2735).

9. See Robert L. Herbert, *Impressionism: Art, Leisure and Parisian Society* (New Haven: Yale University Press, 1988), 30.

10. Manet showed the same amputee in a wash illustration, *Man on Crutches* (The Metropolitan Museum of Art, New York), for the cover design of a musical composition by Ernest Cabaner, "The Beggars" ("Les Mendiants"). This song put to music the radical socialist philosophy of Jean Richepin's "The Beggar's Song" ("La chanson des gueux"). See Wilson-Bareau, *Manet, Monet and the Gare Saint-Lazare*, 141–43.

ADOLPHE TERRIS
FRENCH, 1820–1900

22

Great Works of Marseille, Opening of the Rue Impériale, View of the Site Taken from the Boulevard des Dames

1863

Albumen print from collodion glass negative

14⅛ × 15¹¹⁄₁₆ in. (35.9 × 39.9 cm)

The Nelson-Atkins Museum of Art, Kansas City, Missouri,
Gift of the Hall Family Foundation, 2012.8.6

23

Great Works of Marseille, Boulevard Baille, View Taken from the Place Castellane

1863

Albumen print from collodion glass negative

14³⁄₁₆ × 15¹¹⁄₁₆ in. (36 × 39.9 cm)

The Nelson-Atkins Museum of Art, Kansas City, Missouri,
Gift of the Hall Family Foundation, 2008.47.7

FROM 1840 THROUGH 1920, the city of Marseille underwent major urban transformations. The changes occurred rapidly: in 1830 factories and manufacturers in Marseille employed almost 18,000 workers, most of whom were artisans and tradesmen. By 1840 that number had increased to 21,500, and by 1850, to between 35,000 and 40,000.[1] Between 1830 and 1870 the old port was considered the fifth largest in the world, and its traffic increased fivefold in these decades.[2] During these years, there was also a rise in factory industries, notably sugar refining, machine construction, oil pressing, tanning, and flour milling. Napoléon III, recognizing the city's rapidly growing potential as an industrial nexus, implemented several major projects during the 1850s and 1860s, modeled on Baron Georges-Eugène Haussmann's renovations in Paris. These included demolitions of the old city north of the old port, opening that area's overpopulated and insalubrious quarters and creating major arteries connecting commercially strategic points.

In 1862 construction began on the rue Impériale (today, the rue de la République), a major artery built to connect the docks of the old port to the docks of Joliette, located just to the north. This task involved moving massive amounts of earth as well as huge numbers of inhabitants: sixteen thousand people were displaced to accommodate the new road, which at the height of its construction necessitated trenches almost fifty feet deep.[3]

In 1863 the city commissioned Adolphe Terris to document the contruction of the rue Impériale in a series of photographs called *Grands travaux de Marseille*. These images focused on the site's excavations and the demolition of buildings. In 1866 the photographs were assembled into albums, destined for archival purposes. The city assigned Terris another commission in 1880, this time to document the streets that were slated for destruction to make way for the rue Colbert, on which construction began in 1882.

These two photographs derive from the same album and focus on Terris's first commission. One image depicts a view of the roadworks, featuring a small train, taken from the boulevard des Dames. The other shows the view looking down the boulevard Baille, from the place de Castellane, which is located approximately one mile southeast of the city's old port. Here, the shadowy vestiges of several figures appear along the street. Though technically a result of these figures moving during the long exposure, the blurred presences also suggest the passage of time and human displacement resulting from Marseille's transformation from a modest commercial and agricultural center to a major industrial port. —AMW

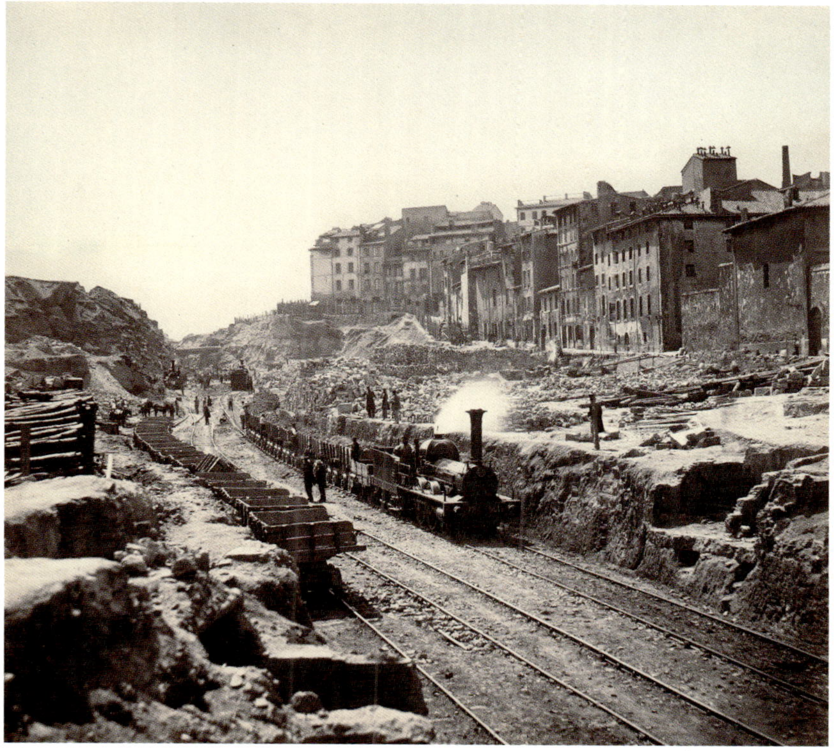

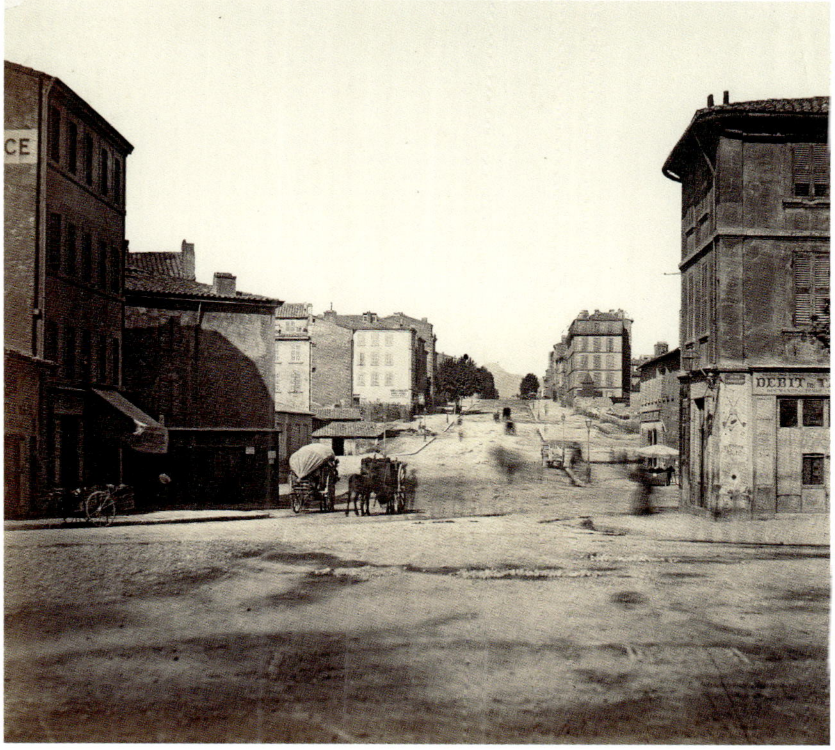

1. Xavier Daumalin and Olivier Raveux, "Marseille (1831–1865): Une révolution industrielle entre Europe du Nord et Méditerranée," *Annales: Histoire, sciences sociales, 56e année*, no. 1 (January–February 2001): 156.

2. William H. Sewell Jr., "Social Change and the Rise of Working-Class Politics in Nineteenth-Century Marseille," *Past and Present* 65 (November 1974): 77.

3. This information derives from the website for Les Archives de la Ville de Marseille, http://archivesenligne.marseille.fr, under Fonds photographique Adolphe Terris (1820–1899): épreuves photographiques des rues détruites pour les percements des rues Impériale et Colbert et monuments de Marseille (1862; 1880).

2
MONUMENTS

IN DEFINING THE IDEA OF NATIONHOOD, landscape imagery offered a journey not only through space but also through time. Monuments played a key symbolic role in the construction of nationhood and national identity during the mid-nineteenth century. Their physical presence in the landscape provided architectural evidence of France's rich and varied past, from its Roman ruins to its great Gothic cathedrals to its Renaissance châteaux. The importance of these structures was often overlooked, however, in the early part of the nineteenth century. Châteaux and cathedrals had been allowed to fall into ruin after suffering years of neglect or severe damage at the hands of Revolutionaries. Monasteries and churches were overgrown or dilapidated. By the mid-nineteenth century France's diverse architectural patrimony benefited from a new appreciation, fueled in part by the vivid descriptions of monuments and ruins by Romantic artists and travel writers, as well as the efforts of architects, antiquarians, archaeologists, and historians who sought to align France's present with its past. In the modern age of uncertainty and rapid change, monuments also provided a certain reassurance about France's capacity to endure through the centuries in addition to a degree of solace from the anxieties of the present.

Preservation and restoration came to be seen as a national duty. The Commission des monuments historiques, founded in 1837, affirmed that the state must preserve its monuments for posterity. One of the commission's key initiatives was the Mission héliographique of 1851. This was the first state-funded project to employ photographers. Five men—Édouard Baldus, Hippolyte Bayard, Gustave Le Gray, Henri Le Secq, and Auguste Mestral—were selected and sent with specific itineraries to different parts of France, tasked with documenting monuments to determine preservation priorities. Throughout the Second Empire, Napoléon III promoted the discovery and conservation of France's history as a crucial aspect of the state's cultural policy. The emperor patronized the extensive restoration of historical monuments, including the château of Pierrefonds, the ancient fortified town of Carcassonne, the medieval abbey of Vézelay, and the cathedral of Notre-Dame. All of these projects were overseen by the architect Eugène-Emmanuel

Viollet-le-Duc, whose controversial theory of restoration had as its goal not to return monuments to their original state but, rather, to reconstruct them according to how, in his estimation, they should have looked in the first place.

The heightened concern for preservation of France's architectural past coincided with an increased interest in the construction of France's history as a unified narrative. Between 1833 and 1867, for example, Jules Michelet documented the history of France in his seventeen-volume *Histoire de France*, which was arguably the first extensive history of the nation. Painters such as Frédéric Bazille and photographers like Baldus were drawn to such subjects as the medieval walled city of Aigues-Mortes in the South for both their historical resonances and their unique aesthetic appeal. The Roman ruins of the Midi, particularly those in Provence, were frequent subjects for the photographers Baldus and Charles Nègre, who sought both state-funded commissions and commercial clients, as well as artistic prestige among their contemporaries. Aligning the architectural symbols of France's past glories also served Second Empire agendas. During the 1860s, Napoléon III commissioned Paul Huet to paint the restored château at Pierrefonds and acquired his work after its exhibition at the Salon of 1867. Jean-Baptiste-Camille Corot was also drawn to this subject, a favored project of the emperor, who saw himself as the modern inheritor of the medieval power and prestige conveyed by the fourteenth-century edifice.

By the end of the Second Empire, with the expansion of the railroad and the rise of middle-class leisure and tourism, those monuments that had been unappreciated and infrequently visited at the start of the nineteenth century (except by those adventurous and hearty travelers, often Parisians, who sought them out) were easily accessible by train. As Viollet-le-Duc affirmed in 1862: "the railroad allows us to see more monuments in a week than it was previously possible to visit in a month."[1]

1. Eugène Viollet-le-Duc, "L'enseignement des arts: Il y a quelque chose à faire: IV," *Gazette des beaux-arts*, 4ème année, 13, no. 3 (September 1862): 254.

24

GUSTAVE LE GRAY
FRENCH, 1820–1884

AUGUSTE MESTRAL
FRENCH, 1812–1884

Apse of Saint-Sernin, Toulouse

1851; printed 1852
Salt print from paper negative
9¼ × 12¹³⁄₁₆ in. (23.5 × 32.5 cm)
The Nelson-Atkins Museum of Art, Kansas City, Missouri, Gift of the Hall Family Foundation, 2012.8.5

THE ARCHITECT EUGÈNE-EMMANUEL VIOLLET-LE-DUC was an early and enthusiastic proponent of photography's applications for architectural restoration. In 1843, just four years after Louis-Jacques-Mandé Daguerre and William Henry Fox Talbot announced their inventions, he wrote a report addressed to the Minister of Justice and Religious Rites, extolling the medium's virtues for record making: "Photography, which assumes every day a more important phase in scientific studies, seems to have appeared for the very purpose of aiding this grand work of restoration of ancient buildings, in which the whole of Europe has begun to take an interest."[1] In his estimation, using hand-drawn sketches as the basis for restoration work was ultimately unreliable, given their questionable accuracy. In his mind, drawing was not to be trusted for the "correctness of graphical reports," whereas the camera would ensure a subject's direct mechanical transcription from reality to image. In fact, he believed that photography superseded the human eye when it came to powers of observation. He noted that the medium "presents the advantage of supplying indisputable reports—documents that can be permanently consulted when restorations mask the traces left by the ruin. . . . Photography cannot be too sedulously used in restorations; for very frequently a photograph discovers what had not been perceived in the building itself."[2]

After his restoration of the basilica of Vézelay in the early 1840s, Viollet-le-Duc recommended the use of daguerreotypes to Prosper Mérimée, the head of the Commission des monuments historiques (a government agency established in September 1837). Both men felt that although the daguerreotype's extraordinary level of detail was useful for architectural records, its inability to be reproduced in multiples limited its applications. By the summer of 1851, after technical advances in calotype (paper) photography in France, the medium became even better suited to the type of fieldwork required of photographers who needed to travel long distances. A few months later, the Commission des monuments historiques decided to send five photographers on different itineraries throughout France to document the nation's architectural patrimony. The Mission héliographique was announced in *La lumière* on June 29:

> Five members of the Société héliographique, MM. Bayard, Lesecq [*sic*], Mestral, Le Gray and Baldus, are going to receive from the Commission des monuments historiques different important missions in the interior of France. It is to photographically reproduce our most beautiful monuments, those among them that are menaced by ruin and are in need of urgent restoration. One does not even have to say that France possesses more Gothic cathedrals, more beautiful cathedrals than all the rest of Europe. The letters of notice for the photographic mission are a novelty, and one proof that the direction of fine arts neglects nothing that relates to the art [of photography] and its progress.[3]

Gustave Le Gray and Auguste Mestral were initially assigned separate itineraries in the Southwest and Auvergne regions of France, but the two men, who had known each other and worked together since at least 1848, combined their assignments into one longer journey. They traveled together for most of the time and occasionally photographed sites included on the other's list. In many instances, the negatives were signed with the names of both photographers. Le Gray and Mestral left Paris on July 1 with two cameras and headed southwest into the Loire valley, making an extended stay in Blois. They continued more or less

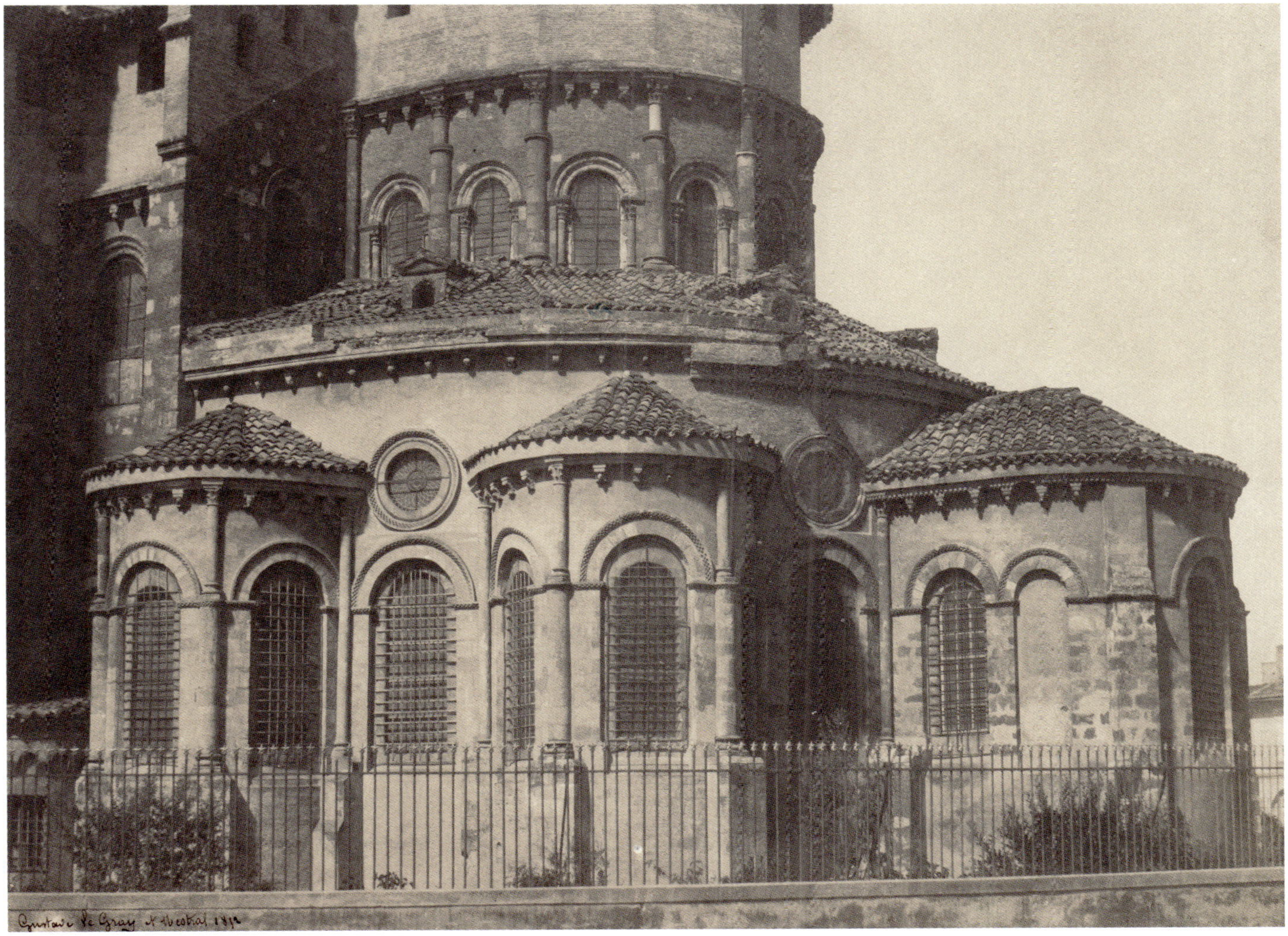

in a southerly direction, staying fifteen days in Samur and ten days in Poitiers. From there, they continued south to Bordeaux, Cahors, and Toulouse, where they made several photographs of the Romanesque pilgrimage church of Saint-Sernin (cat. 24) and spent eleven days in the great medieval walled city of Carcassonne, where they produced another extensive series of photographs (cat. 25). After a short trip to Perpignan, near the Spanish border, they headed north, through Narbonne and into Auvergne of south-central France, stopping in Le Puy to photograph the twelfth-century cloister of the pilgrimage church of Notre-Dame Le Puy (cat. 26), and then on to Clermont-Ferrand before returning to Paris. By the time they arrived back in the French capital sometime in September, they had covered approximately 1,996 miles and produced more than six hundred negatives.[4]

Saint-Sernin was a Romanesque structure that had been expanded in the eleventh century from a fourth-century basilica and established as a pilgrimage site during the Carolingian era. Saint-Sernin's restoration was considered imperative due to the damages incurred during and immediately following the Revolution at the end of the eighteenth century. Of particular significance was the apse, which was considered to be, before extensive damages to the roof, "the most perfect part" of the monument "in its relationship between art, construction, grace and effect," as stated in a document published by the Société archéologique du Midi de la France.[5] This view of the church by Le Gray and Mestral is composed to emphasize the apse's radiating chapels, suggesting that the commission deemed this portion of the edifice of particular interest. In 1845 the commission had assigned Viollet-le-Duc to make a complete study of the

25

GUSTAVE LE GRAY
FRENCH, 1820–1884

AUGUSTE MESTRAL
FRENCH, 1812–1884

The Ramparts of Carcassonne

1851

Salt print from waxed paper negative

9¼ × 13¹⁄₁₆ in. (23.5 × 33.2 cm)

The Metropolitan Museum of Art, New York, Gilman Collection, Purchase, Harriete and Noel Levine Gift, 2005, 2005.100.34

building, though various delays prevented him from actually beginning restorations until about 1860. Le Gray and Mestral's view thus depicts the structure before the architect's renovations, which included a complete rebuilding of the roof over the nave, transept, choir, and apse. Viollet-le-Duc's changes to the structure, which were based on his theory that restoration was less an act of repairing or rebuilding and more an effort to "reestablish a complete state that may never have existed at any given time," were highly controversial.[6] In 1874, five years before Viollet-le-Duc's death, the abbé Carrière, then president of the Société d'archéologie du Midi de la France, summarized the overall reaction as "a concert of blame and regret."[7]

The walled, hilltop city of Carcassonne, located in the country's Languedoc region overlooking the Aude River, was founded in Roman times. Over the centuries, it underwent various waves of modification, largely for defensive purposes, from the time of the Visigoths in the fifth century, to the eleventh-century Cathar occupation, to the late thirteenth-century fortifications. The cathedral of Sainte-Nazaire was begun in the Romanesque style during the eleventh century but was later rebuilt as an essentially Gothic structure. Even before the Revolutionary period, the city had begun to fall into great disrepair, such that the French government was on the brink of demolishing it, until various parties, including an impassioned Carcassonne resident and archaeological historian named Jean-Pierre Cross Mayrevieille, succeeded in bringing attention to the city's historical import. Viollet-le-Duc, who in 1844 had been tasked with restoring Saint-Nazaire, was eventually commissioned to restore the entire citadel by 1850. It was an enormous endeavor that lasted until his death.

At the time Le Gray and Mestral photographed the city in 1851, it had yet to undergo the architect's most enduring changes: covering the citadel's numerous, ruined towers with conical tiled roofs, in an effort to refashion them as an idealized version of their thirteenth-century state. They photographed the city in several ways, using distanced, general views; close-up studies of the city's main portals and passages; and middle-distance views such as this one, which features the imposing presence of the Tour de la Vade, one of the citadel's most impressive and impenetrable towers. This photograph is distinguished by its aesthetic sensitivity to light and shadow, as well as its composition, which monumentalizes the tower as it looms over the small grave markers at its base.

After leaving Carcassonne, Le Gray and Mestral moved north into Auvergne. They stayed approximately ten days in Le Puy, where they photographed the impressive cathedral of Notre-Dame, with its distinctive twelfth-century Romanesque cloister (cat. 26). In photographing this structure, they framed as broad a view of the cloister as possible, then homed in on a group of arcades. In this image, for which sole credit is given to Le Gray, the photographer concentrated on one complete span of an arch, framed between equal portions of adjacent arches. The alternating colors of the voussoirs add to the tonal dynamism of the image, which is a tight compositional play between surface and depth, light and dark.

In late September 1851, before Le Gray and Mestral officially returned from their trip, the photographers sent the first few examples of their photographs back to Paris. Impressed by their "enormous" size and accomplished artistry, Francis Wey wrote about them as exemplifying

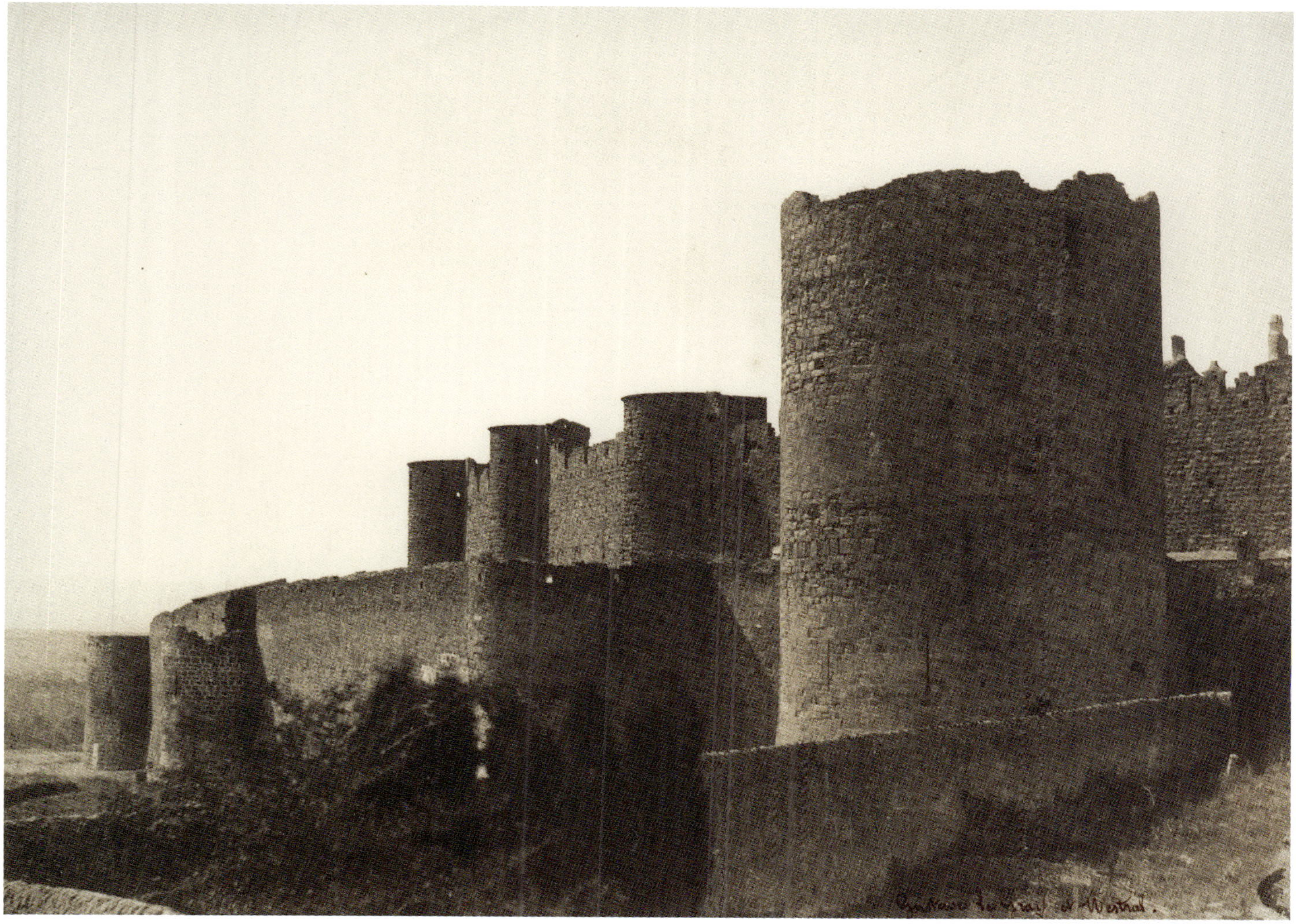

photography's potential: "Photography rises to a magic impression to which neither drawing nor painting is able to reach."[8] Despite this initial enthusiasm, many of Le Gray and Mestral's negatives and prints (and those of the other photographers as well) were never publicly exhibited by the commission. This was a great disappointment for many in the photographic community, because photographers and their critical supporters were expecting far more public exposure and personal publicity for the work that had been done. In point of fact, however, the commission's goal was to create an archive from which to determine restoration priorities, not to provide photographers with exhibition opportunities. Wey articulated his concerns in an 1853 article, in which he argued that the lack of public exposure for the Mission héliographique works was not simply a setback for the individual photographers, or even photography itself, though certainly these were concerns. More important, it inhibited national progress. Wey wrote: "The public is deprived of these prints, which have become an object of contention for all; the photographers have been deprived of the publicity that they had expected, and our country will be unable to reap the rewards of the most beautiful work that has yet been produced. We had asked for more and we had hoped for better."[9]

Despite the commission's decision, photographers like Le Gray and Mestral were not entirely without recourse. All five photographers were free to profit from any of the negatives and prints that did not become part of the mission's archive. Le Gray in particular took advantage of his work for the mission, regularly exhibiting views in Paris and

26

GUSTAVE LE GRAY

FRENCH, 1820–1884

Cathedral of Notre-Dame, Detail of the Cloister Arcade, Le Puy

1851; printed later

Albumen print from collodion glass negative

12¾ × 9⅜ in. (32.4 × 23.8 cm)

Saint Louis Art Museum, Museum Purchase, 194:1977

especially in London between 1852 and 1855.[10] Le Gray also printed from his negatives for commercial sale. For Le Gray, therefore, the work he did for the Mission héliographique was far from a futile endeavor, as it provided him with an opportunity to exploit fully his waxed paper technique and practice his art while exploring the country's architectural past. —AMW

1. Eugène-Emmanuel Viollet-le-Duc, "Rapport adressé à M. le Ministre de la Justice et des Cultes," 1843; quoted in *The Architectural Theory of Viollet-le-Duc: Readings and Commentary*, ed. M. F. Hearn (Cambridge, Mass.: Massachusetts Institute of Technology, 1990), 277–78.

2. Ibid., 278.

3. *La lumière*, June 29, 1851, 83: "Cinq membres de la Société Héliographiques, MM. Bayard, Lescq, Mesteral, Le Gray et Baldus, viennent de recevoir, du Comité des monuments historiques, diverses missions importantes dans l'intérieur de la France. Il s'agit de reproduire photographiquement nos plus beaux monuments, ceux surtout qui menacent ruine et qui exigent des réparations urgentes. L'on ne sait pas assez que la France possède à elle seule plus de cathédrales gothiques, plus de belles cathédrales que tout le reste de l'Europe. Les lettres d'avis ayant pour titre *Missions photographiques* sont une nouveauté, et une preuve que la direction des beaux-arts ne néglige rien de ce qui a rapport à l'art et à ses progrès."

4. This summary is deeply indebted to the formative research of Anne de Modenard, *Mission héliographique: Cinq photographes parcourent la France en 1851* (Paris: Centre des Monuments Nationaux; Monum, Éditions du Patrimoine, 2002), 151–57.

5. Quoted in *Viollet-le-Duc*, exh. cat. (Paris: Éditions de la Réunion des Musées Nationaux; the Ministère de la Culture et de la Communication, 1980), 102–3: "Personne n'ignore que cette partie du monument est la plus parfaite, sous le rapport de l'art, de la construction, de la grâce, et de l'effet."

6. Ibid., 105: "restaurer un édifice, ce n'est pas l'entretenir, le réparer ou le refaire, c'est le rétablir dans un état complet qui peur n'avoir jamais existé à un moment donné."

7. Ibid.: "un concert unanime de blâme et de regrets."

8. Francis Wey, "Des progrès et de l'avenir de la photographie," *La lumière*, October 5, 1851, 138: "La photographie s'élève à une magie d'impression à laquelle ni le dessin, ni la peinture n'avaient pu parvenir, surtout en ce qui concerne les édifices gothiques."

9. Francis Wey, "Comment le soleil est devenu peintre," *Musée de familles*, July 20, 1853, 294: "Le public est donc privé de ces estamps que chacun se disputerait; les photographes sont frustrés de la publicité qu'ils avaient espérée, et notre pays ne peut se faire honneur de la plus belle oeuvre qui se soit produite jusqu'ici. Nous avions demandé davantage et nous espérions mieux."

10. Sylvie Aubenas notes that Le Gray's prints of the Pont du Gard, the grand staircase at the château de Blois, and the bridge at Palada were particularly popular and were shown in London in 1852. Aubenas, *Gustave Le Gray, 1820–1884*, exh. cat. (Los Angeles: J. Paul Getty Museum, 2002), 67.

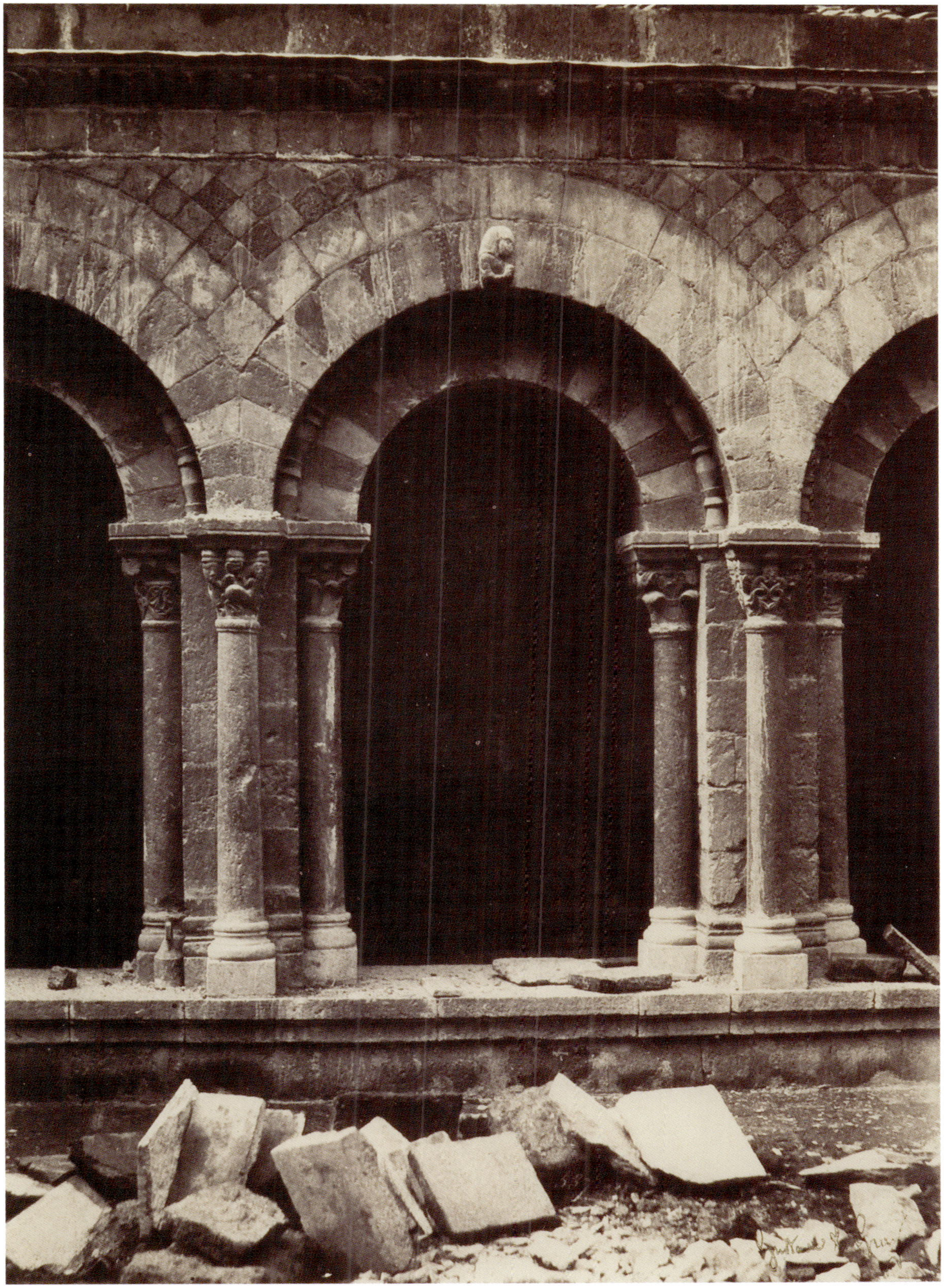

27

PAUL HUET
FRENCH, 1803–1869

The Château of Pierrefonds Restored

1865–67

Oil on canvas

$43\frac{5}{16} \times 63\frac{3}{16}$ in. (110 × 162 cm)

Musées nationaux du Palais de Compiègne, C.87.001

THE ROMANTIC LANDSCAPE PAINTER PAUL HUET produced pendant views of the enormous château of Pierrefonds both before and after it was restored. This château, located some sixty miles northeast of Paris, is among the most impressive of France's castles, an example of secular military architecture. Built at the end of the fourteenth century by Louis d'Orléans, it had been largely destroyed in the early seventeenth century and subsequently fell into ruin. During the Second Empire, Napoléon III ordered its restoration. This task was entrusted to the prominent architect Eugène-Emmanuel Viollet-le-Duc, who was thus provided another opportunity to focus on secular military architecture after his recent renovation of Carcassonne. Viollet-le-Duc began work in 1857. His initial plans were relatively modest, focusing on the keep and two of the towers but leaving the rest of the site in ruins. In 1861, however, Napoléon III ordered the restoration of the whole, intending to bring the building back to its former glory and, in so doing, create a prestigious royal residence close to the imperial palace at Compiègne. Viollet-le-Duc outlined his nationalistic vision for the entire château:

> The emperor recognized the importance of the ruins of Pierrefonds from the point of view of the history of art. The keep and nearly all the exterior defenses take on again their original appearance; thus, we will soon be able to see the most beautiful example of fifteenth-century feudal architecture in France come back to life through the august will of the sovereign. We have too many ruins in our country, and ruins scarcely provide an idea of the residences of the most enlightened lords of the Middle Ages, friends of the arts and letters, owners of immense riches. The castle of Pierrefonds, completely renovated, will make known this art both civil and military, which, from Charles V to Louis XI, was superior to everything else that was happening then in Europe. It's in fifteenth-century feudal architecture in France developed under the inspiration of the Valois that we find the origin of all the splendors of the Renaissance, much more than in the imitation of the Italian arts.[1]

For Viollet-le-Duc, the French fortified castle of the fourteenth and fifteenth centuries was among the most impressive examples of French art, "superior to everything else" in the late medieval world. The rebuilding went ahead through the 1860s, was interrupted by the fall of the emperor, and was ultimately completed by 1885, creating a turreted château, often described today as the archetypal "fairy-tale castle."[2] Nonetheless, the exterior remained close to the original medieval design.[3]

In the mid-1860s Napoléon III commissioned Huet to produce a painting of the refurbished château.[4] Huet was already well known as a painter of France's monuments and architectural heritage, having first come to prominence in the late 1820s. He also produced several images of châteaux for the *Voyages pittoresques* print albums in the 1830s and 1840s, thus acting as a direct link with that important precedent for the imaging of France's architectural patrimony. A good friend of Eugène Delacroix, Huet continued a Romantic tradition that emphasized the importance of picturesque, dramatic motifs. Huet was fiercely patriotic, nurturing left-wing republican beliefs, but these did not prevent him from receiving extensive state and imperial patronage in the Second Empire. To research his painting, Huet traveled to the

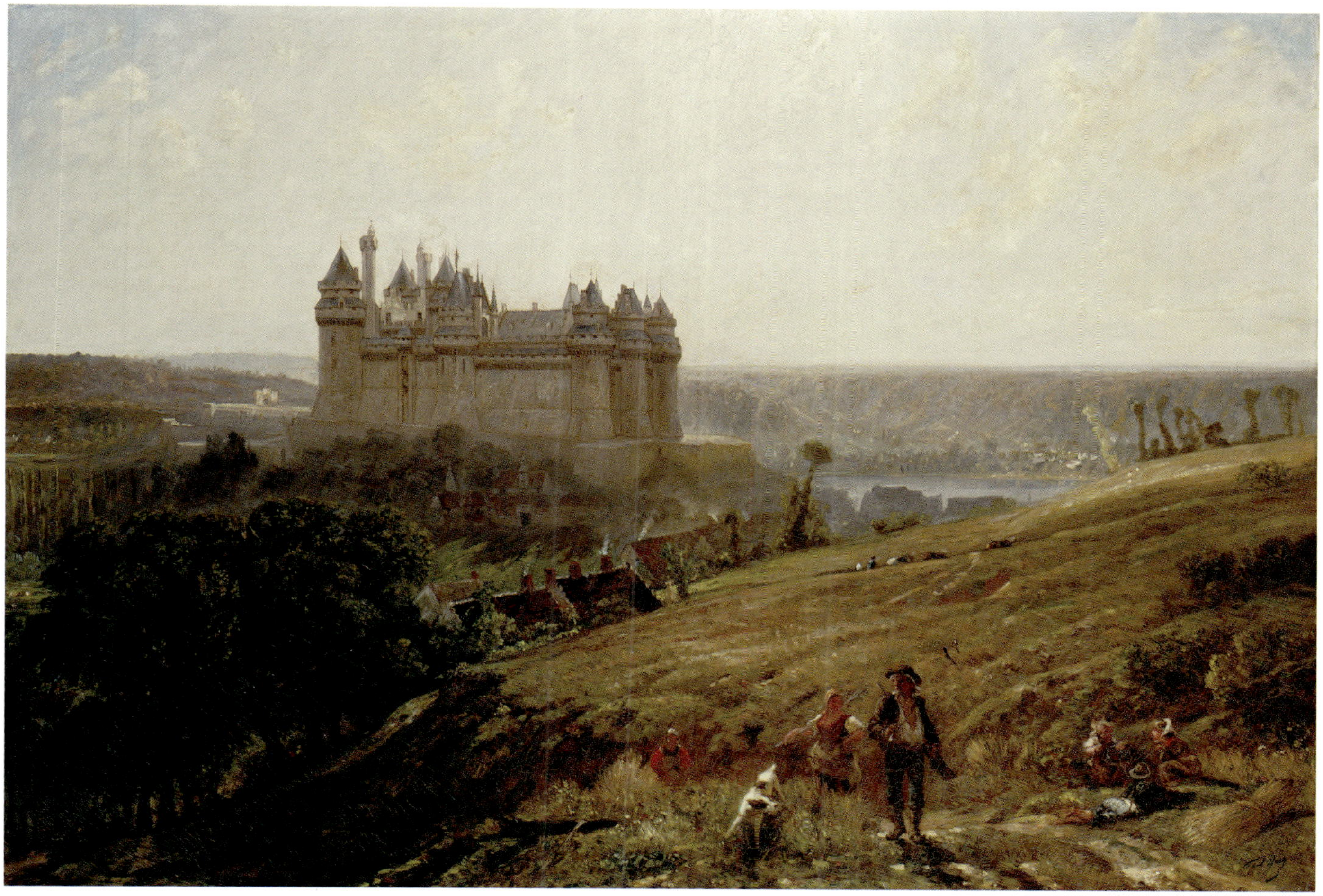

château in July 1865. He subsequently described the ambition of the project, comparing it to Queen Victoria's famed castle of Windsor just outside London:

> I have just arrived from Pierrefonds, where, in full sunlight, I made, in great heat, studies for a view of the restored château, which has been commissioned from me. This restoration will be admirably done by Viollet-le-Duc. The restoration has made great progress; this, alas, is the art of today! This trinket will certainly cost, I think, fifteen million francs; it will be beautiful and will make the fortune of the area. The emperor is making a Windsor out of it.[5]

Huet's plein air studies informed his painting, which represents the restored structure with meticulous architectural detail (fig. 59).[6] Huet carefully outlined the castle with a linearity that is rare in his output: the underdrawing is still clearly visible. The artist showed the château's eight towers

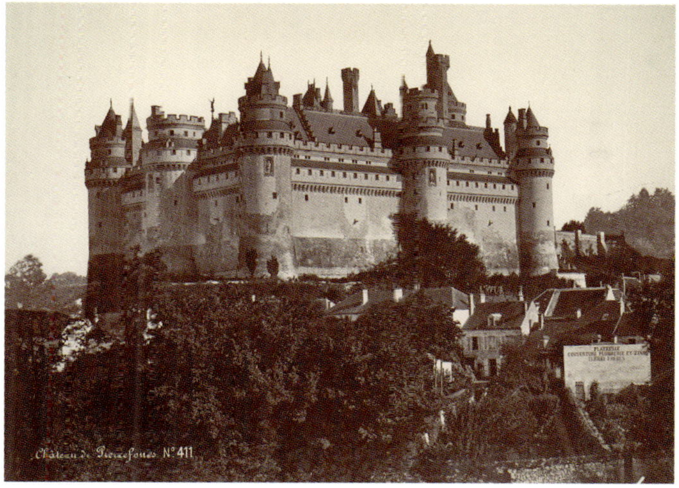

FIG. 55 Pierrefonds Château, general view, ca. 1874–90. Albumen print, 9⅞ × 14 in. (25.1 × 35.5 cm). A. D. White Architectural Photographs, Cornell University Library, Gift of Andrew Dickson White

PAUL HUET
FRENCH, 1803–1869

28

The Ruins of the Château of Pierrefonds

1867–68

Oil on canvas

$43\frac{11}{16} \times 63\frac{3}{16}$ in. (111 × 162 cm)

Musées nationaux du Palais de Compiègne,
Given by Miss Marie Dechaux in 1928, C.38.2634

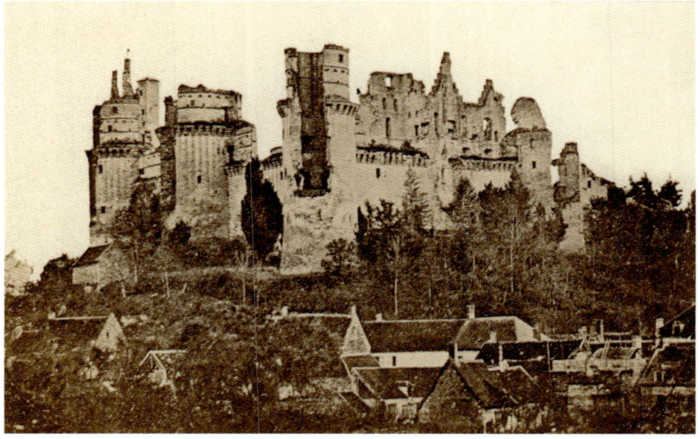

FIG. 60 Castle of Pierrefonds in Picardie, prerestoration, ca. 1857

with their recently added gray slate pointed roofs on an outcrop high above the landscape. In the distance is the river Oise, and the whole scene is suffused in a golden, luminous haze, probably of morning light. Huet also animated the foreground with a group of picturesque peasants. The artist's view can be contrasted with a photograph of the château in its ruined state, dating from the mid-1850s (fig. 60). The differences testify to the important, transformative changes made by Viollet-le-Duc. Huet's view certainly reinforced Napoléon III's vision of himself as inheritor of the prestige and military power of France's medieval tradition.

Huet showed the work at the Salon of 1867, where the emperor acquired it for four thousand francs. Soon after, he began a pendant showing the château in ruins. For the artist, this latter painting was an act of imaginative reconstruction, drawing on memory as well as on earlier studies that he made of the ruined château, dating back to the early 1830s.[7] Huet showed the castle from a different viewpoint and silhouetted against a stormy sky: a shaft of sunlight illuminates the monument from the right. His imaginative license is evident in the foreground, where the wind blows a woman's scarf and the nearby copse of trees in different directions.[8]

Huet exhibited *The Ruins of the Château of Pierrefonds* at the 1868 Salon, where it was acquired by the emperor for three thousand francs.[9] This was in fact Huet's last masterpiece, since he died in January 1869. Critical response at the Salon was enthusiastic. Huet was praised for the "poetry" of his work in contrast to the more dominant vogue for naturalism. Thoré for example, wrote, "Paul Huet . . . always brings a poetic sentiment into his painting. . . . His Ruins of the Château of Pierrefonds, exhibited in the central gallery, looks very impressive. It would do well in a museum, between a Troyon and Jules Dupré, to teach young landscapists not to seek too much detail in painting grass and foliage."[10] Huet's two works were subsequently shown together in his retrospective at the 1878 Exposition universelle but were split up in the early twentieth century and reunited in the Musée national du château de Compiègne only in 1987. —SK

1. See E. Viollet-le-Duc, *Description du château de Pierrefonds*, 2nd ed. (Paris: Bance, 1861), 31–32; quoted in French in Bruno Foucart, "Viollet-le-Duc et la restauration," in *Les lieux de mémoire*, ed. Pierre Nora (Paris: Quarto, 1997), 1:1635: "L'Empereur a reconnu l'importance des ruines de Pierrefonds au point de vue de l'histoire et de l'art. Le donjon et presque toutes les défenses extérieures reprennent leur aspect primitive; ainsi, nous pourrons voir bientôt le plus beau specimen de l'architecture féodale du XVe siècle en France renaître par la volonté auguste du souverain. Nous n'avons que trop de ruines dans notre pays et les ruines ne donnent guère l'idée de ce qu'étaient les habitations des grands seigneurs les plus éclairés du Moyen Âge, amis des arts et des lettres, possesseurs de richesses immenses. Le château de Pierrefonds, rétabli en totalité, fera connaître cet art à la fois civil et militaire qui, de Charles V à Louis XI, était supérieur à tout ce que l'on faisait alors en Europe. C'est dans l'art féodal du XVe siècle en France développé sous l'inspiration des Valois que l'on trouve en germe toutes les splendeurs de la Renaissance, bien plus que dans l'imitation des arts italiens."

2. Foucart, "Viollet-le-Duc," 1615: "un château de fées."

3. The interior restoration, by contrast, showed far more evidence of historical license.

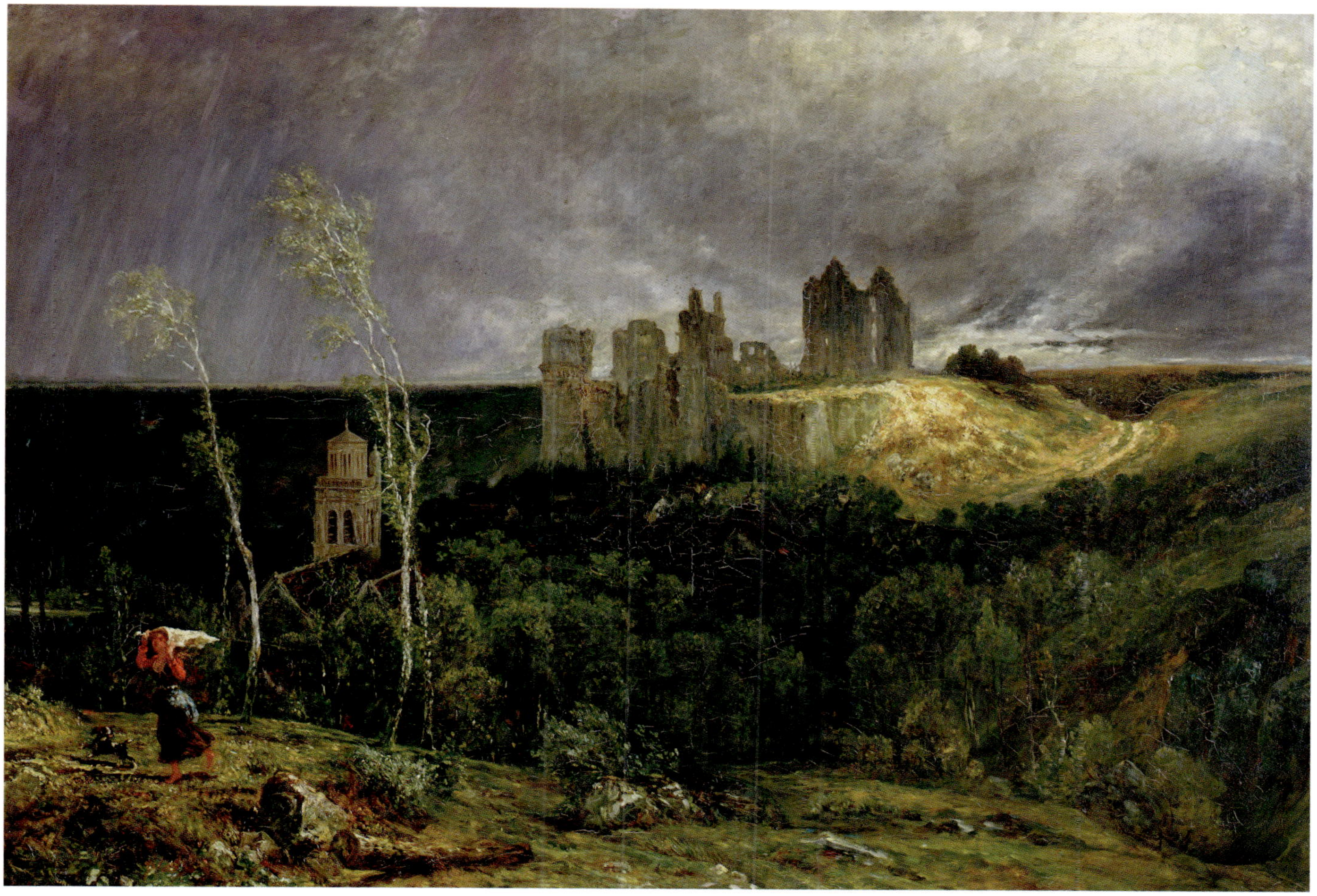

4. The circumstances of the commission are unclear. The artist notes the commission in his 1865 correspondence, but the painting was not officially acquired until June 21, 1867. See Catherine Granger, *L'empereur et les arts: La Liste Civile de Napoléon III* (Paris: École de Chartes, 2005), 548. See also Chiara O'Reilly, "L'histoire dans le paysage: Paul Huet et le château de Pierrefonds," *La Revue du Louvre et des Musées de France* 57, no. 1 (2007): 69–74.

5. Paul Huet to M. Sollier, in *Paul Huet (1803–1869), d'après ses notes, sa correspondance, ses contemporains*, ed. René Paul Huet (Paris: Librairie Renouard, 1911), 411: "J'arrive de Pierrefonds où, en plein soleil j'ai fait, pendant les grandes chaleurs, des études pour une vue du château restauré, qui m'est commandée. Cette restauration sera admirablement faite par Viollet-le-Duc. La restauration fait de grands progrès, c'est hélas! l'art d'aujourd'hui. Cette bagatelle coûtera bien, je pense, une quinzaine de millions; ce sera beau et fera la fortune du pays. L'Empereur en fait un Windsor." Later that year, on September 12, he wrote of his continued work on the painting (ibid., 412): "I've worked hard this summer and made progress, I think, without being sure on a painting [*The Château of Pierrefonds Restored*] which has been commissioned from me." (J'ai beaucoup travaillé cet été et avancé, je le crois du moins sans en être bien sûr, un tableau qui m'est commandé.)

6. Huet's vista is based largely on a black chalk and pen-and-ink drawing (private collection; see Christie's, Ashurst, Kent, December 15, 2000, lot 202), which shows the same view without the foreground staffage. This drawing suggests that the restoration was largely complete by the mid-1860s. See also the oil sketches *Pierrefonds during Restoration, through the Mist*, ca. 1865 (Musée de l'Île-de-France, Sceaux, P.60.26.3) and *Pierrefonds during Restoration*, ca. 1865 (private collection, reproduced in *Paintings by Paul Huet [1803–1869]*, exh. cat. [London: Heim Gallery, 1969], no. 99) and the watercolor *Château de Pierrefonds during Restoration*, ca. 1865 (private collection, reproduced in Pierre Miquel, *Paul Huet, de l'aube romantique à l'aube impressioniste, 1803–1869* [Paris: Somogy, 2011], 150).

7. See the oil sketches *The Ruins of Pierrefonds*, ca. 1834 (Musée de l'Île-de-France, Sceaux, P. 60.26.2) and *View of Pierrefonds* (Musée national du château de Compiègne C. 63.101). Huet's idea for this painting dated to the fall of 1865, when he wrote of his work on *The Château of Pierrefonds Restored* (Huet, *Paul Huet*, 412): "I want to pair it with a pendant, the ruins for which I have studies dating back thity-five years at least!" (Je veux y joindre le pendant, les ruines dont j'ai les études depuis trente-cinq ans au moins!)

8. See John House, *Landscapes of France: Impressionism and Its Rivals*, exh. cat. (London: South Bank Centre, 1995), 98.

9. See Granger, *L'empereur et les arts*, 548.

10. See T. Thoré, *Salons de W. Bürger, 1861–1870* (Paris: Vve Jules Renouard, 1870), 2:495: "Paul Huet . . . apporte toujours dans sa peinture un sentiment poétique . . . Ses Ruines du château de Pierrefonds, exposées dans la salle central, ont un très-grand air. Elles feraient bien dans un musée, entre un Troyon et un Jules Dupré, pour apprendre aux jeunes paysagistes à ne pas 'chercher la petite bête' sous les herbes et dans les feuillages."

29

JEAN-BAPTISTE-CAMILLE COROT

FRENCH, 1796–1875

Ruins of the Château of Pierrefonds

ca. 1840–45, reworked ca. 1866–67

Oil on canvas

29⁵⁄₁₆ × 41⅞ in. (74.5 × 106.4 cm)

Cincinnati Art Museum, Gift of Emilie L. Heine in memory of Mr. and Mrs. John Hauck, 1940.965

DURING HIS LONG CAREER, the prolific Jean-Baptiste-Camille Corot produced approximately three thousand paintings, including a wide range of landscapes, from plein air naturalistic views to historical subjects to late paintings of memory. As Charles Baudelaire noted as early as 1845, Corot was the leading figure—together with Théodore Rousseau—in the contemporary school of landscape painting.[1] While the majority of the other painters of the so-called Barbizon school—such as Rousseau, Narcisse-Virgile Diaz de la Peña, and Charles-François Daubigny[2]—concentrated on views of France's natural beauty, Corot showed a greater interest in his country's architectural history. He was particularly drawn to France's rich tradition of Gothic architecture and represented a variety of cathedrals and castles. His interest in medieval architectural design is evident not only in his paintings but also in his meticulous drawings.[3]

Corot showed particular interest in the fourteenth-century château of Pierrefonds, which had fallen into ruin by the early nineteenth century (see cat. 28). He first represented this château in the late 1820s and returned to it often as a subject, ultimately producing six views, of which *Ruins of the Château of Pierrefonds* is the largest.[4] Corot here represents the ruined turrets and keep of the château in the middle distance with the copse of trees to the left acting as a *repoussoir*, framing the scene. The castle ramparts are reflected in a still pool, while picturesque figures in a boat provide color accents.

According to Alfred Robaut, Corot's friend and early biographer, this work was originally painted directly after nature between 1840 and 1845, before being reworked shortly before its exhibition at the 1867 Exposition universelle.[5] Corot's changes to his painting are clearly evident from a surviving wood engraving of the work as it appeared

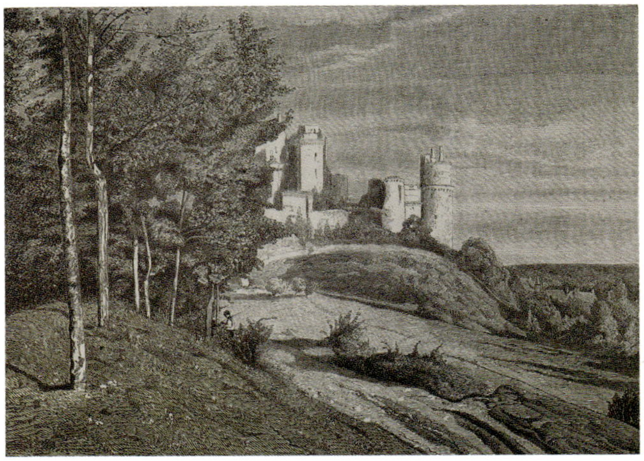

FIG. 61 Eugène Lavieille, after Jean-Baptiste-Camille Corot, *Château de Pierrefonds*. Wood engraving. From *Gazette des beaux-arts* 11, no. 5 (November 1, 1861): 421

in 1861 (fig. 61).[6] Initially, the foreground contained a grassy expanse and a single figure, carrying a stick and walking along a path. With his revisions, Corot replaced the grassy area with a pond and the moored boat. The château itself, however, remained unchanged, since the artist chose to ignore its recent restoration by Eugène-Emmanuel Viollet-le-Duc.

Corot's inclusion of this work in his 1867 Exposition universelle retrospective may have been motivated by a desire to win the emperor's patronage. After all, the emperor had financed the recent restoration of the château by Viollet-le-Duc and saw this campaign as a prime example of his aspirations for the renaissance of France. Although Napoléon III had recently patronized Corot's work—acquiring *Solitude: Souvenir of Vigen (Limousin)* (Thyssen-Bornemisza Collection) the previous year for the very large sum of eighteen thousand francs—he did not buy this painting. Corot's exhibition was, however, well received, securing his preeminent position within the French school. Théophile Thoré, for example, noted that "he has a certain charm that results from his almost mysterious impression."[7] In his final years,

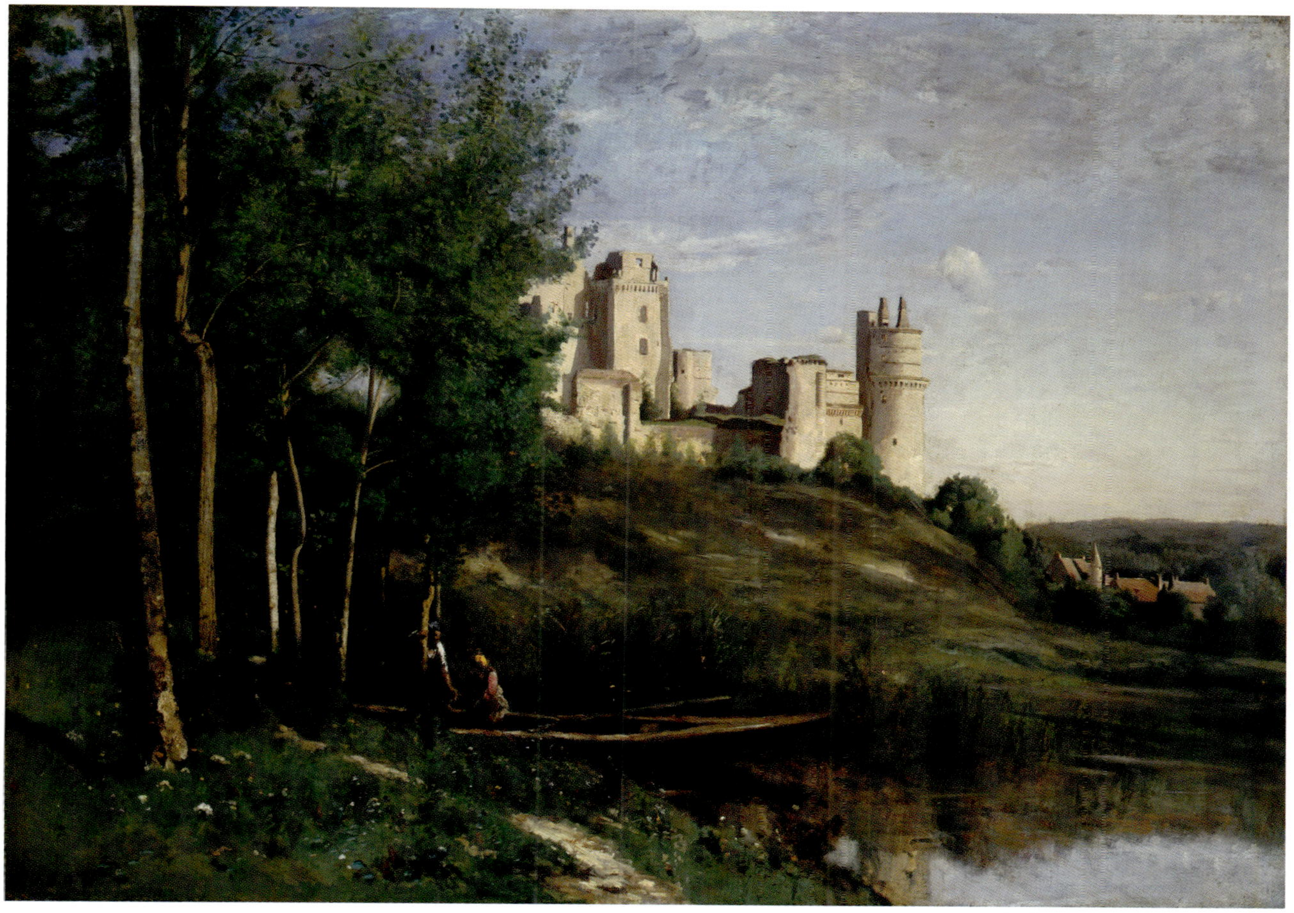

Corot felt out of step with the modern, industrial age and produced increasing numbers of views of France's architectural heritage—including a series of Mantes Cathedral as well as paintings of the belfry at Douai and Sens Cathedral.[8] In a disorienting and anxiety-inducing modern era, Corot found solace in his country's centuries-old architectural patrimony. —SK

1. Charles Baudelaire, "Salon de 1845," in *Charles Baudelaire, Art in Paris, 1845–1862: Salons and Other Exhibitions*, trans. and ed. Jonathan Mayne (Oxford: Phaidon, 1965), 24: "Corot stands at the head of the modern school of landscape."

2. Rousseau, on occasion, treated France's architecture, such as in his 1839 *Château of Chambord* (private collection), while Daubigny produced a series of views of the Château Gaillard, perched high above the Seine, in the 1870s; see, for example, *Château-Gaillard at Sunset*, ca. 1873 (Museum of Fine Arts, Boston). François-Louis Français also produced views of the château of Pierrefonds: see *Pierrefonds*, 1882 (Pierre Bergé et associés, Paris, March 26, 2004, lot 47), and the wash drawing *View of the Château of Pierrefonds*, ca. 1870 (Cleveland Museum of Art, 2008.30).

3. See, for example, the drawing of the western facade of Chartres Cathedral (1830) in the Musée du Louvre, Département des Arts graphiques, RF 23335.

4. See also *View of Pierrefonds* (private collection; Alfred Robaut, *L'oeuvre de Corot: Catalogue raisonné et illustré* [Paris: H. Floury, 1905], no. 212), *View of Pierrefonds* (Musée des Beaux-Arts, Quimper), *Souvenir of Pierrefonds* (Pushkin Museum of Fine Arts, Moscow), *View of Pierrefonds* (private collection; Robaut, no. 964), and *View of Pierrefonds* (private collection; Robaut, no. 965).

5. Ibid., no. 475: "reworked by its creator a little before 1867" (remanié par son auteur un peu avant 1867).

6. The initial stage was also photographed by Victor Laisné in 1853 and published in Théophile Silvestre, *Histoire des artistes vivants* (Paris: E. Blanchard, 1853). See Robaut, *L'oeuvre de Corot*, no. 475.

7. Théophile Thoré, "Exposition de 1867," in *Salons de W. Burger* (Paris: Vve Jules Renouard, 1870), 2:357: "il a un certain charme qui résulte de son impression presque mystérieuse."

8. *Mantes, View of the Cathedral and Town through Trees* (Musée des Beaux-Arts, Reims), *The Belfry of Douai* (Musée du Louvre, Paris), and *Interior of Sens Cathedral* (Musée du Louvre, Paris).

CHARLES NÈGRE
FRENCH, 1820–1880

30

Arles: Roman Ramparts

1852

Salt print from waxed paper negative

9 × 12¾ in. (22.9 × 32.4 cm)

Saint Louis Art Museum, Museum Shop Fund, 76:1989

31

Tarascon

ca. 1852

Albumen print from paper negative

9⁵⁄₁₆ × 11⅝ in. (23.6 × 29.5 cm)

The Metropolitan Museum of Art, New York, The Rubel Collection, Purchase, Lila Acheson Wallace Gift, 1997, 1997.382.63

IN THE SUMMER AND FALL OF 1852, Charles Nègre embarked on a photographic venture into the Midi, with the intention of producing photographs of the region's architectural marvels to sell to painters, sculptors, historians, and architects. Unlike the Mission héliographique photographers, who were tasked with following a specific itinerary and making informational records of assigned sites and structures, Nègre retained a more poetic sensibility when photographing his subjects, akin to the imagery of Eugène Isabey in his prints of architectural sites and ruins. Isabey's prints were included in Baron Isidore Taylor and Charles Nodier's monumental, multivolume *Voyages pittoresques et romantiques dans l'ancienne France* (1820–78), which explored the country's architectural patrimony in twenty-three volumes (plus an index volume), each one focusing on a different province. The publication, which collectively included approximately three thousand lithographs, was a direct precursor to the Mission héliographique, though less exclusively documentary and far more impressionistic in its descriptions.

Nègre sympathized with the notion of taking a more subjective approach, as conveyed in the *Voyages pittoresques*, when photographing monuments. This penchant is suggested in an unpublished introduction for his portfolio *Le Midi de la France*. As he wrote of his ultimate intentions for the project:

> In the reproduction of these monuments of the Middle Ages and ancient times that I am offering to the public, I have attempted to join the picturesque aspect to the serious study of details so sought after by artists, architects, sculptors and painters; each of these categories of artists will find in this collection subjects that will enter his own special frame of reference without losing their condition as art.[1]

Nègre identified which views he felt would appeal to each category of artist. For architects, he produced a "general view," trying to "avoid perspective distortions" and convey the "precision of a geometric elevation." For sculptors, he included larger, close-up views of architectural details; and for painters, with whom he shared the closest kinship, he "indulged in the picturesque," sacrificing details when necessary to achieve an overall "imposing effect." In conclusion, Nègre suggested that his intentions are aimed at "all those who dedicate themselves to the various studies of our national antiquities" and that his efforts would ultimately save viewers the cost and discomfort of traveling to these places themselves, as "the expense of journeys [is] sometimes costly and occasionally distressing."[2]

Nègre produced more than three hundred negatives for *Le Midi de la France*, but the portfolio was never published in its entirety.[3] The publisher Goupil et Vibert released

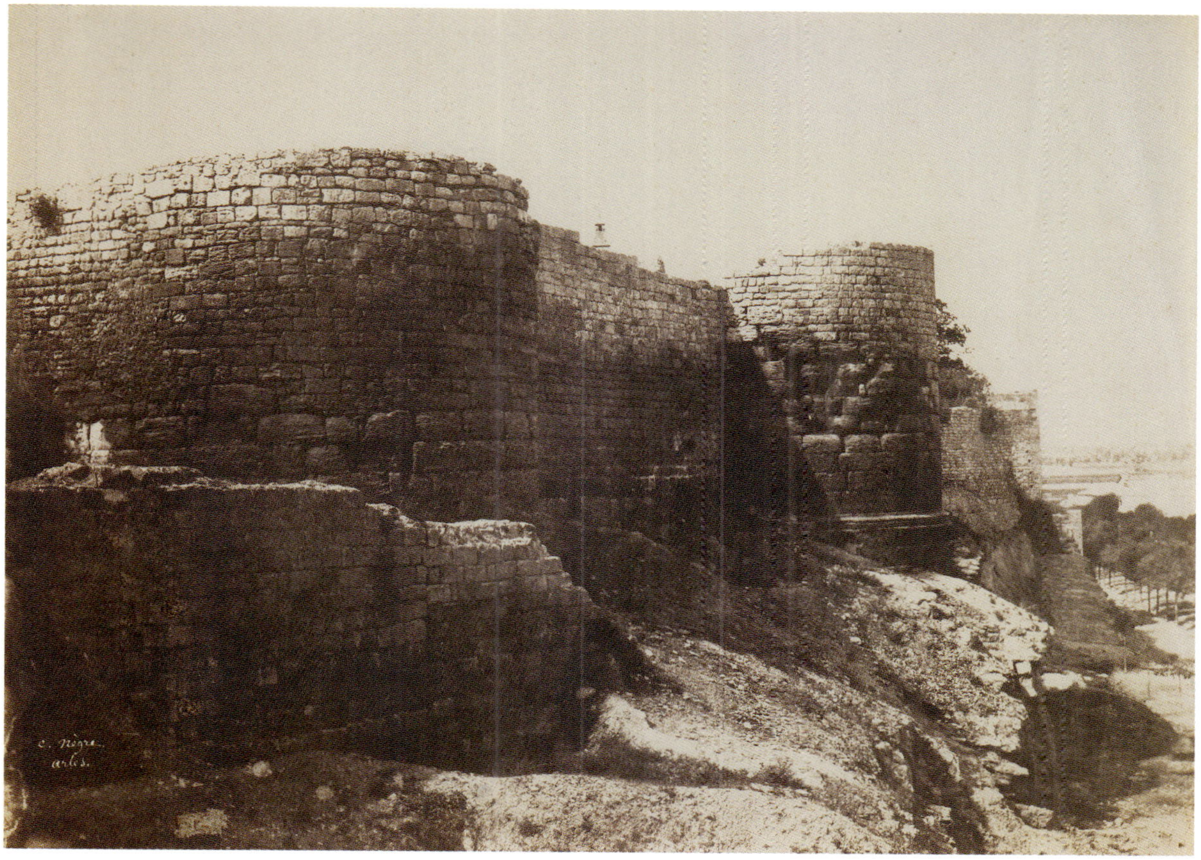
c. nègre.
arles.

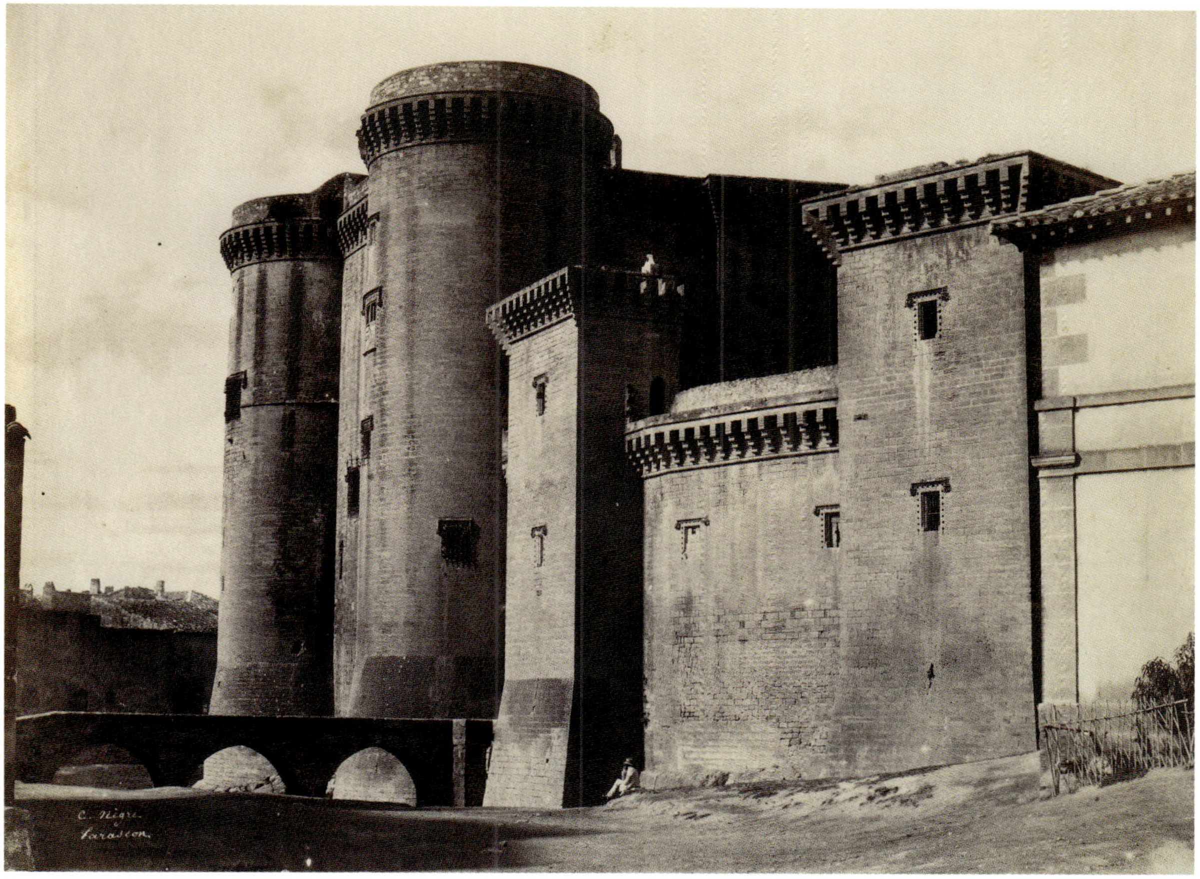
C. Nègre.
Tarascon.

a selection of five prints in 1854 (one of two such installments), but the portfolio did not receive wider circulation beyond this initial venture, despite the critic Henri de Lacretelle's enthusiastic and lengthy discussion of the work in *La lumière*. De Lacretelle's evocative descriptions reinforced the idea that Nègre's photographs did indeed serve as viable surrogates for the actual experience of traveling to the Midi. As he wrote: "M. Nègre, a pious son of the Midi, wanted to consecrate in his new art the first horizons that he saw. Warm Provence displays its folds of hills, its rolling waves, its swaying olive trees, in the beautiful portfolio he composed. He exhales in these acres blasts of sun, of sun condensed in the wind that breathes across the horns of the bulls of the Camargue."[4]

These "blasts of sun" are evident in his view of the Roman ramparts in Arles (cat. 30), which depicts the ancient remnants in raking sunlight that illuminates the top portion of the walls, while areas below remain steeped in heavy shadow. This view, as compared with Le Gray and Mestral's photograph of the ramparts of Carcassonne (cat. 25), emphasizes the overall rough-hewn qualities of the crumbling wall as it melds with the surrounding earth. Though architects may have found a view like this useful, its conception seems more Romantic in spirit, evoking as it does the reverie for ancient ruins as melancholic symbols of loss that permeates the travel writings of François-René de Chateaubriand and the poetry of Victor Hugo.

Nègre's view of Tarascon castle, by contrast, is a less poetic, more descriptive depiction of the imposing medieval citadel, situated on the left bank of the Rhone River (cat. 31). Here, the photographer worked with the bright Mediterranean sun to emphasize, through light and shadow, the monumental geometry of the fifteenth-century structure's immense, seemingly impenetrable walls, with their minimal fenestration and lack of ornamentation. Nègre also includes a seated figure at the base of the walls, at the edge of the moat that once surrounded the castle, which further imparts a sense of the building's enormous scale.[5] —AMW

1. This introduction exists in a handwritten document, discovered by M. Quentin in the Archives nationales, but has since been reprinted in full in various publications, including James Borcoman, *Charles Nègre, 1820–1880*, exh. cat. (Ottawa: National Gallery of Canada, 1976), 6–7, and André Jammes and Eugenia Parry Janis, *The Art of French Calotype with a Critical Dictionary of Photographers, 1845–1870* (Princeton: Princeton University Press, 1983), 262.

2. Borcoman, *Charles Nègre*, 6–7; and Jammes and Janis, *The Art of French Calotype*, 262.

3. This number derives from the latest research of Sylvie Aubenas and Paul-Louis Roubert, *Primitifs de la photographie: Le calotype en France, 1843–1860*, exh. cat. (Paris: Gallimard; Bibliothèque Nationale de France, 2010), 297. Borcoman notes (*Charles Nègre*, 32) that when Nègre first returned to Paris after his trip to the Midi, he had more than two hundred prints in his portfolio.

4. Henri de Lacretelle, "Albums photographiques, No. 1: M. Nègre," *La lumière*, February 12, 1853, 26: "M. Nègre, un pieux fils du Midi, a voulu consacrer par son art nouveau les premiers horizons qu'il a vus. La chaude Provence étale ses plis de collines, ses roulements de vagues, ses balancements d'oliviers, dans le beau portefeuille qu'il a composé. Il s'exhale de ces pages acres des bouffées de soleil, de ce soleil condensé dans le vent qui souffle à travers les cornes des taureaux de la Camargue."

5. Tarascon castle was the site of a Roman citadel consecrated to Jupiter. Over the centuries it became steeped in history and legend: during the first century AD it was believed that a dragonlike creature known as the Tarasque lived there. The structure Nègre photographed was built by King Louis II d'Anjou to police the Rhone, which formed the western border of Provence. This castle replaced the remnants of earlier medieval fortresses. His sons Louis III and René made further restorations, though René is credited with having made most of the interior renovations, making it hospitable for his court (the structure thus became known as King René's castle). Beginning in the seventeenth century and lasting through the early twentieth century, Tarascon was used as a military prison. In 1794 several of Robespierre's supporters were thrown to their deaths from the high terrace at the top of the castle. Prosper Mérimée included the castle on his inventory of historic monuments in 1840.

32

ÉDOUARD BALDUS
FRENCH, 1813–1889

Pope's Palace, Avignon

ca. 1854
Salt print from paper negative
13$\frac{13}{16}$ × 17$\frac{5}{16}$ in. (35.1 × 44 cm)
The Nelson-Atkins Museum of Art, Kansas City, Missouri, Gift of the Hall Family Foundation, 2011.21.2

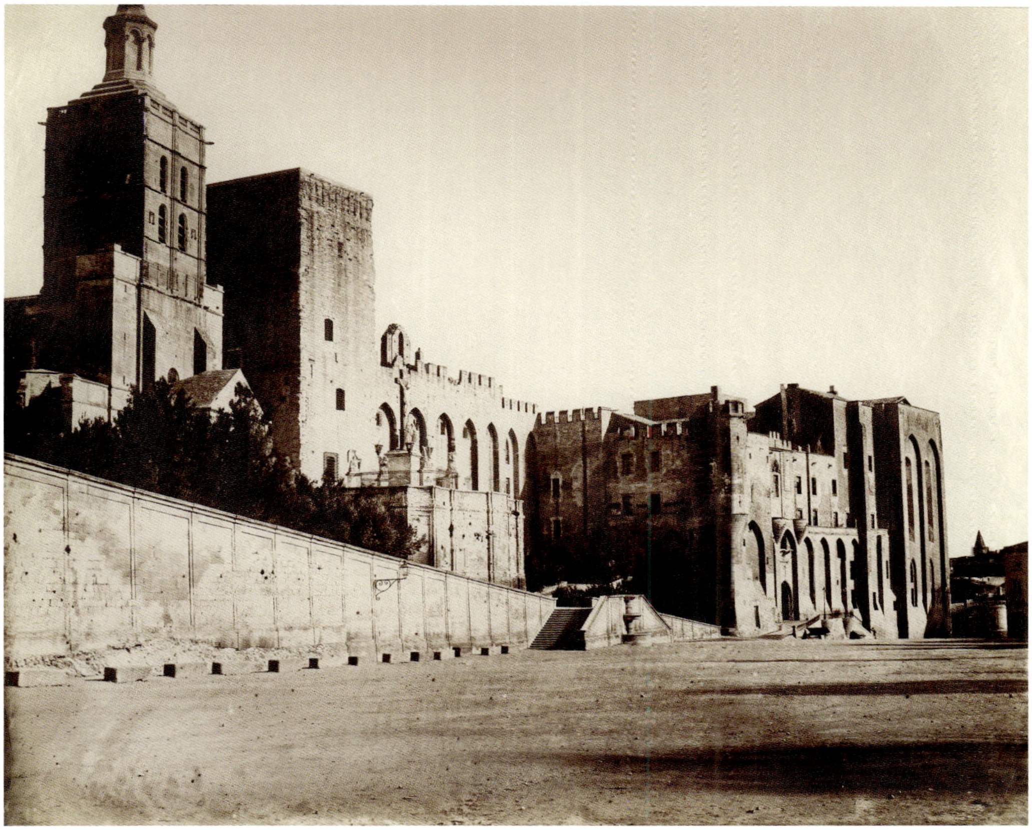

ÉDOUARD BALDUS TRAVELED to the South of France numerous times between 1851 and 1861 to photograph the medieval and Roman monuments of the Midi. His first extensive trip to the area took place during his time working for the Mission héliographique, for which he was given a list of fifty-one monuments. In April 1852, several months after having returned from the South, Baldus shared some of his views with a group that included Gustave Le Gray, Henri Le Secq, Charles Nègre, and Ernest Lacan, one of Baldus's greatest champions. Lacan wrote with enthusiasm in *La lumière* about the photographer's prints, singling out an early large-scale view of Avignon and noting: "He has enough talent and faith in his art to achieve even better than the beautiful."[1]

Baldus returned to the Midi in 1853 and 1854, in search of subjects to photograph that would both expand his existing stock and fulfill his four-year state-funded project, *Villes de France photographiées*. It was on this second journey that he produced this stunning, large-scale view of the pope's palace in Avignon. Here, Baldus found a vantage point that would allow him to record the greatest expanse of the palace fortress, including the high bell tower of Notre-Dame des Doms, the Palais Vieux of Benedict XII, who reigned from 1334 to 1342, and the Palais Neuf, built under Clement VI's reign (1342–52). Baldus worked with the bright sun at a time of day (likely either early morning or late afternoon) that ensured the light would fall on the exterior facets and create deep shadows, which helped clearly articulate the geometric

33

ÉDOUARD BALDUS
FRENCH, 1813–1889

Saint-Bénezet Bridge, Avignon

ca. 1860–61

Albumen print from collodion glass negative

8⁹⁄₁₆ × 10¹⁵⁄₁₆ in. (21.8 × 27.8 cm)

The Nelson-Atkins Museum of Art, Kansas City, Missouri, Gift of the Hall Family Foundation, 2010.35.1

forms of the immense palace. The overall lack of human figures—more likely the result of a long exposure rather than an actual dearth of human beings—further emphasizes the palace's colossal, dominating presence.

When Prosper Mérimée described the palace in his *Notes d'un voyage dans le Midi de la France* (1835), he observed: "In seeing the Palace of the Popes . . . one would say it was the citadel of an Asian tyrant rather than the residence of a vicar of a peaceful God."[2] Between 1309 and 1378 (a period known as the Babylonian Captivity), when Avignon was the papal seat of Western Christianity, many critics felt the papacy had strayed too far from its spiritual mission and fallen under the influence of the French king. Clement's extravagant (and reputedly dissolute) reign in particular disgusted the Italian humanist Petrarch, who lived for a time in Avignon. Petrarch wrote in a letter to a friend that he was living in France, the "Babylon of the West," a place where "the sun in its travels sees nothing more hideous than this place on the shores of the wild Rhone, which suggests the hellish streams of Cocytus and Acheron."[3]

Baldus returned to the South of France in about 1860 while making photographs on commission for the Paris–Lyon–Méditerranée rail line. At that time he made this view of the Pont Saint-Bénezet. In this image, Baldus included three of the four surviving arches, with the small chapel dedicated to St. Bénezet shown built atop the central pier. The bridge itself was constructed in the late twelfth century and was conceived, according to legend, by a twelve-year-old shepherd named Bénezet. The boy was said to have received the word of Christ in 1177 to build a bridge over the river at Avignon. His plea to the bishop of Avignon was angrily dismissed, but the boy insisted his mission was divinely ordained. Asked to prove the merit of his claim, Bénezet single-handedly carried a thirteen-by-seven-foot slab of stone through the town and down to the bank of the Rhone, where the first arch was to be built.[4] The bishop, duly convinced of Bénezet's miraculous vision, ordered construction of the bridge to begin immediately. The boy died in 1184, four years before the bridge was completed in 1188; a chapel to St. Bénezet was erected along one of the bridge's supporting piers.[5]

Over the centuries, however, owing to a combination of war damage and lack of repair, the bridge became increasingly fragile. Floods during the mid-seventeenth century swept away a large portion of the bridge, leaving only four arches, and the bridge was never fully restored. In 1820, because of increased demands for trade across the river, a second bridge was constructed just south of the old bridge. By the time Mérimée visited Avignon on his travels through the South of France in 1834, the old bridge had lain in partial ruin for two centuries. Mérimée listed the old bridge on his inventory of historic monuments in 1840, which saved the structure from complete destruction.

Baldus composed his scene with characteristic formal mastery. He included a triangular swath of the riverbank, to which an assembly of small wooden boats is moored, which creates a receding diagonal that complements the strong linear presence of the bridge itself. The slight curvature of the boats' sides further echoes the bridge's rounded arches. All of these pictorial elements bring the picture together with a sense of subtle dynamism. This photograph, as well as an albumen print of the pope's palace, appeared in the Paris–Lyon–Méditerranée railway album in a sequence of five images featuring Avignon (see cat. 76, pls. 24–28). —AMW

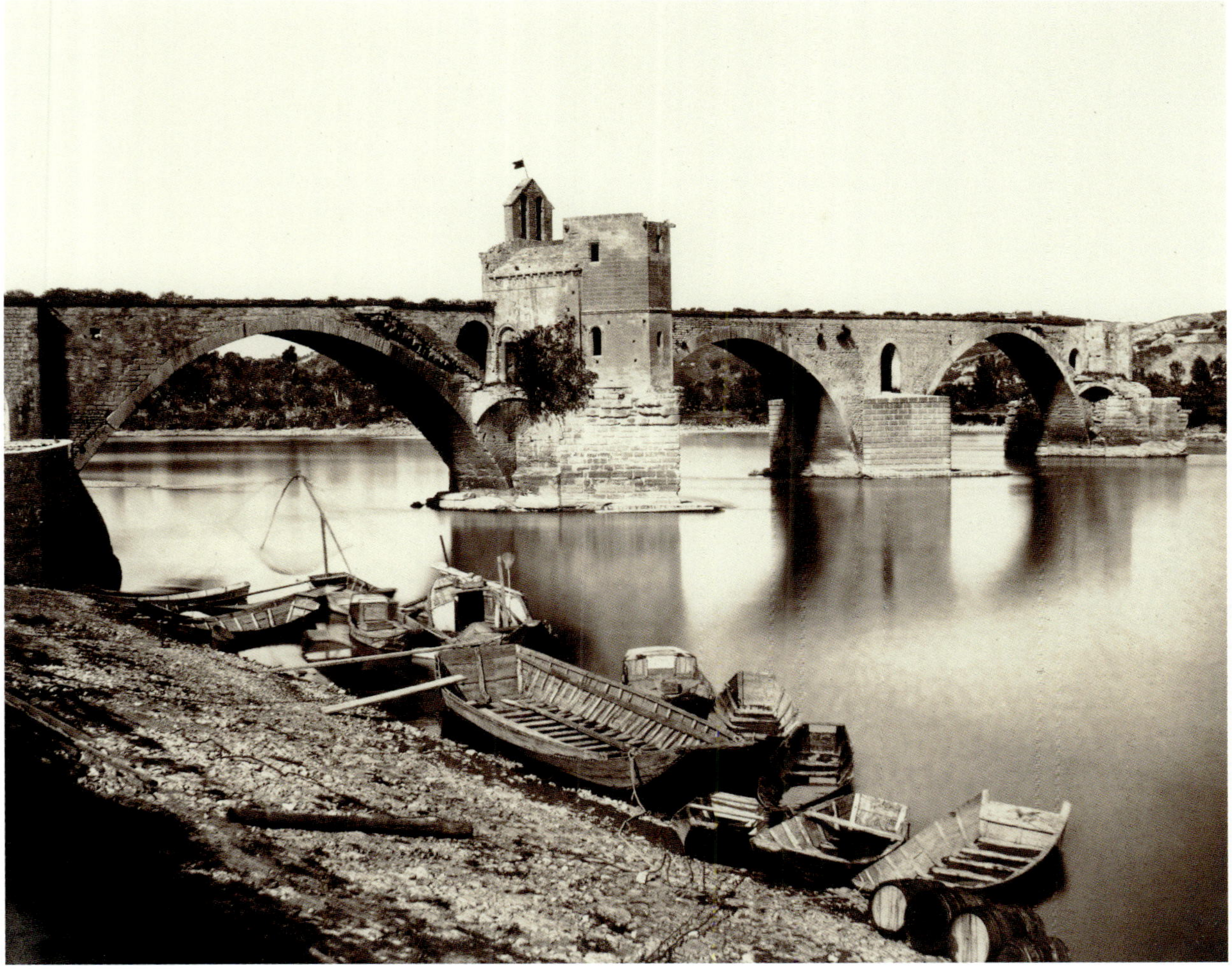

1. Ernest Lacan, "Réunion photographique," *La lumière*, April 24, 1852, 71–72. This text derives from the fuller passage: "Comment . . . rendre à nos lecteurs le sentiment que nous avons éprouvé, en voyant Avignon, la vieille cité chrétienne, avec son château des papes, grand comme une ville de guerre, son pont en ruines, ses deux fleuves jumeaux, sa ceinture crénelée, ses clochers, ses faubourgs, encadrés dans une épreuve de 50 cm par M Baldus? Il nous disait, en refermant son portefeuille, que tout ce qu'il venait de nous montrer n´était rien aupres de ce qu'il allait faire dans un prochain voyage; nous le croyons, malgré notre étonnement: il a assez de talent et de foi dans son art pour atteindre mieux encore que le beau."

2. Prosper Mérimée, *Notes d'un voyage dans le Midi de la France* (Paris: Librairie Fournier, 1835), 143: "A voir le château des papes . . . on dirait la citadelle d'un tyran asiatique plûtot que le demeure du vicaire d'un Dieu du paix."

3. James Harvey Robinson, *Readings in European History* (Boston: Ginn & Company, 1904), 502–3. In Greek mythology, Cocytus (the river of wailing) and Acheron (the river of woe) were two of the five rivers of the underworld.

4. This account derives from Theodore Andrea Cook, *Old Provence* (New York: Charles Scribner's Sons, 1905), 2:234–35.

5. In its finished state, the structure was 984 yards long and had twenty-two arches, spanning the entire river. It was an important passage for pilgrims traveling from Italy to Spain in the Middle Ages, and during the fourteenth century it was actively used when the papal court was in residence in Avignon. Often, while crossing the bridge from Avignon to Villeneuve, on the other side of the river where many of the cardinals lived, the popes stopped at the chapel to give a monetary offering to St. Bénezet, the founder of the guild of bridge builders.

ÉDOUARD BALDUS
FRENCH, 1813–1889

34

Pont du Gard

ca. 1861

Albumen print from collodion glass negative

10 11/16 × 17 1/8 in. (27.2 × 43.5 cm)

The Nelson-Atkins Museum of Art, Kansas City, Missouri, Gift of the Hall Family Foundation, 2008.41.5

35

Arles, Amphitheatre

ca. 1855–59

Albumen print from collodion glass negative

13 1/4 × 17 in. (33.7 × 43.2 cm)

The Nelson-Atkins Museum of Art, Kansas City, Missouri, Gift of the Hall Family Foundation, 2007.17.2

IN DECEMBER 1853, after Édouard Baldus had returned from his second major venture into the Midi to make pictures for the four-year project *Villes de France photographiées*, Ernest Lacan again gave readers of *La lumière* a lengthy, complimentary report of Baldus's accomplishments. In addition to lauding the "profound artistic sentiment that distinguished his prints, their gigantic dimensions, their perfection," Lacan promoted the work's historic significance in documenting France's diverse architectural styles for architects, painters, and archaeologists. "When his oeuvre is complete, [it will] offer . . . a collection of all types of construction, from the heavy edifices of the Roman colonies left in our ancient cities, to the hybrid constructions of the last century. All will have a place in this historic and artistic gallery."[1]

The monuments of greatest interest in the South of France were its Roman ruins and medieval structures: the architecture deemed important enough to preserve in the eyes of such prominent and influential figures as Prosper Mérimée, who placed many of these buildings on his official roster of historic monuments, as a result of his travels throughout the Midi in the 1830s and 1840s. Lacan's promotion of Baldus's photographs as having both artistic and historic merit for France is very much in line with the way Mérimée described the importance of his own cataloguing mission for the Commission des monuments historiques. Mérimée states as much in his introduction to his book *Notes d'un voyage dans le Midi de la France*: "However, today, as the study of our national antiquities begins to take favor, I think that the publication of these notes would be of several uses for the people who visit the places that I have traveled to. I believe I have rendered service to archaeology in provoking a new examination of the monuments I describe, drawing attention to the discussion of the questions I have touched upon." Significantly, Mérimée emphasizes the importance of personally traveling to these sites in order to give more truthful, firsthand accounts: "It is rare to arrive at the truth the first time it is revealed, even if we ourselves are convinced of the error."[2] It is within this tradition of firsthand, factual recording that Lacan situates the broader significance of Baldus's photographs as well.

Lacan's and Mérimée's enthusiasm for describing and documenting ruins and monuments was part of a much broader national effort to reconcile ancient virtues with those of modern civilization during a period in France's history when national unity was both desired and resisted. These efforts, however, depended on one's class, political affiliations, and degree of education. Whereas Revolutionaries called for a unified French nation and language, certain provinces—Provence in particular—fought to maintain a strong sense of individual identity, drawing on the region's rich Celtic, Greek, and Roman history. Many Provençals refused to relinquish the native Provençal language, Occitan, and actively celebrated its use in music and literature.[3]

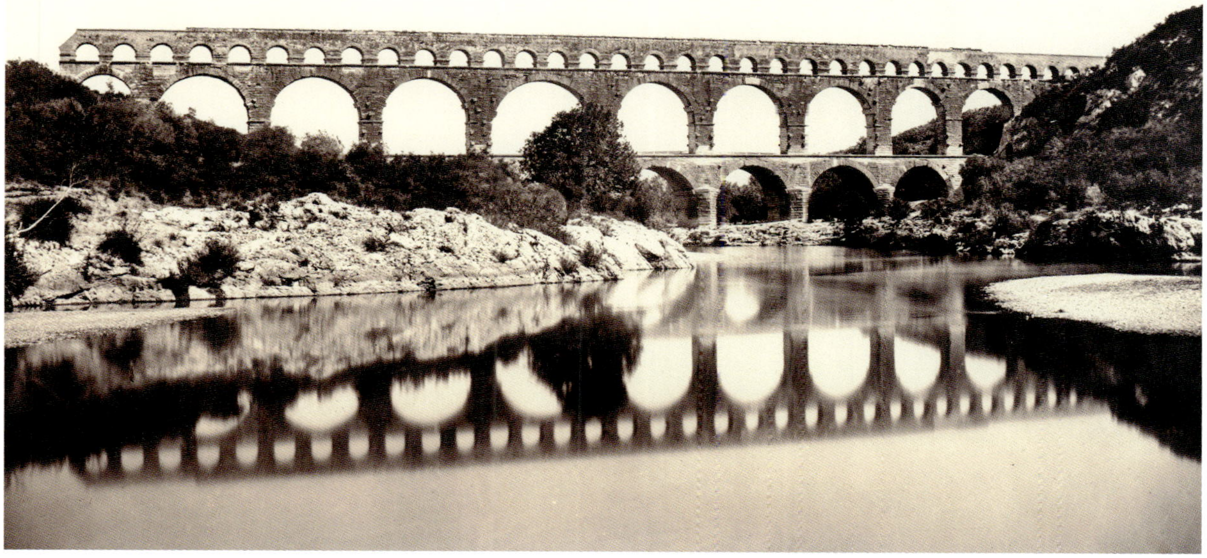

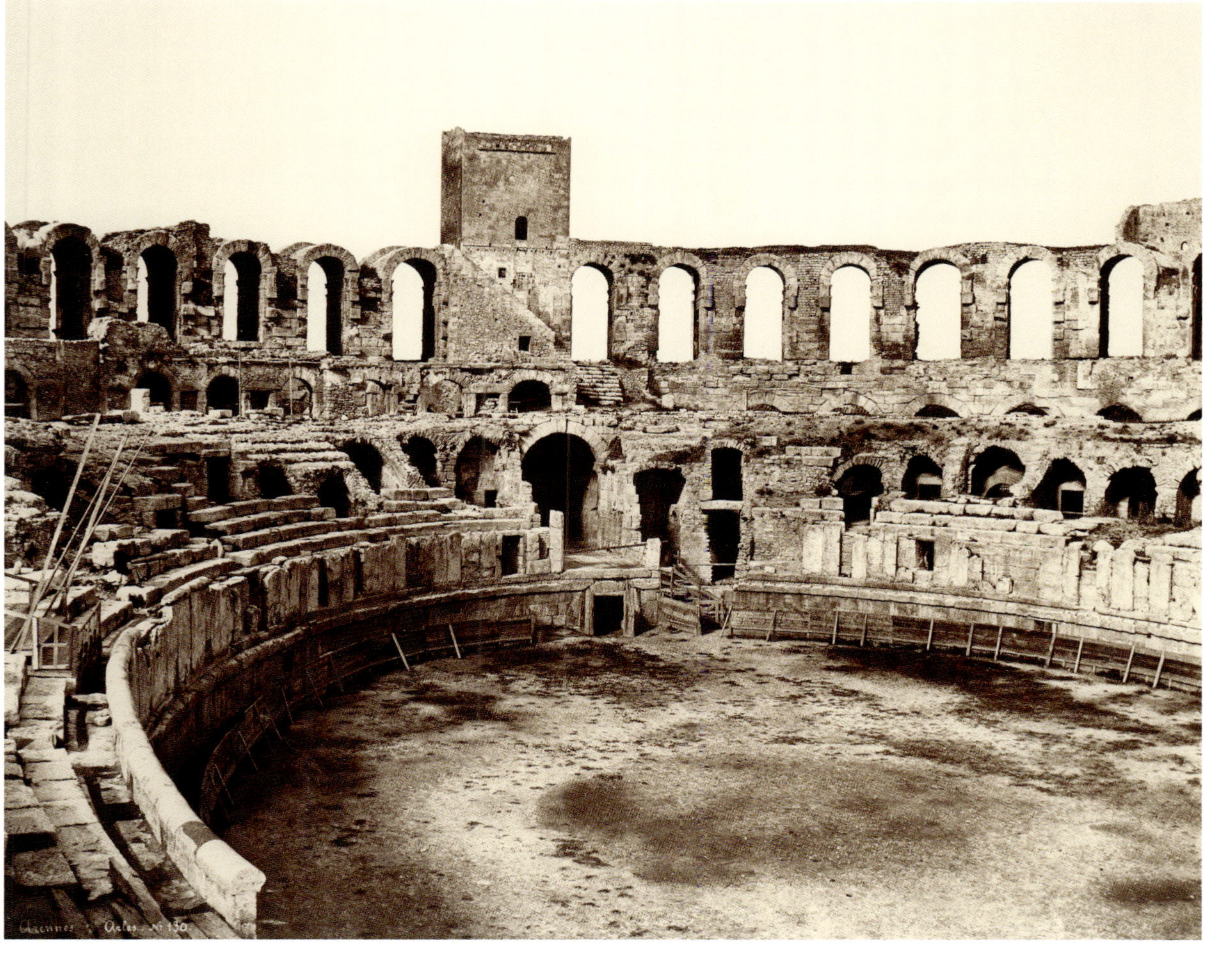
Arennes d'Arles. No 130.

36

ÉDOUARD BALDUS

FRENCH, 1813–1889

Tour Magne, Nîmes

1853; printed ca. 1860

Albumen print from collodion glass negative

17⅛ × 13⅛ in. (43.5 × 33.3 cm)

The Nelson-Atkins Museum of Art, Kansas City, Missouri, Gift of the Hall Family Foundation, 2009.27.8

Mérimée himself noted how few people spoke French in Provence, outside the cities of Marseille and Aix, where educated intellectuals had begun to embrace the fashions of Paris.[4] Baldus, as a Prussian-born, Parisian-based photographer, who was commissioned by both the state (for his *Villes de France photographiées*) and the Conseil d'Administration of the Southern Region (for the Paris–Lyon–Méditerranée railway album, for which many of his Midi photographs were also used), was necessarily indebted to the ideals of picturing a modern, French nation, unified by the architectural glories of its past, as well as the industrial and technological feats of its present.

The Roman ruins in and around Nîmes, Orange, and Arles were sites that had long been admired. Where once they would have been known largely to locals or to pilgrims traveling from Italy to Spain, by the late eighteenth and early nineteenth centuries, they had become destinations for litterateurs and Romantic travel writers who, like Mérimée, were often educated Parisians from the artistic and intellectual classes. With the expansion of road-, rail-, and waterways in the mid-nineteenth century, tourism vastly increased, making the role of the litterateur increasingly less significant. Amid this landscape in transition, Baldus took his camera and equipment to these well-known sites and made photographs.

Often, his photographs offered far less Romanticized accounts of these subjects than the written accounts that preceded him. When he first saw the Pont du Gard, en route from Arles to Avignon under storm-threatened skies, for example, Mérimée wrote this dramatic account: "The Gardon [river], swollen by prodigious rain, was overwhelmed and roiled with a terrible noise, its waters, the color of coffee, under the arches of the aqueduct; the sky was stormy, but a break of sunlight in the clouds gilded the monument, which seemed to sparkle with light; the savage site, the complete solitude of the place, the noise of the torrent, added a sublime poetry to the imposing architecture that offered itself to my eyes."[5] Baldus's photograph of the Pont du Gard is a far more placid conception of the Roman aqueduct (cat. 34).[6] In his image, the river's calm surface reflects with great fidelity the three-tiered, 160-foot-high structure. The Pont du Gard and its mirrored image are near-perfect reversals, creating a bold pattern of positive and negative shapes through the center of the composition. The photographic flattening of perspective further abstracts the light and dark forms of the architecture and its surrounding landscape, such that distinctions between the two are diminished as they appear to fuse into a single entity. Baldus included this photograph in the Paris–Lyon–Méditerranée album, preceded by an image of the ruins of a Roman mausoleum at Saint-Rémy and followed by a photograph of the more modern Durance Viaduct (see cat. 76, pls. 31, 33). These kinds of juxtapositions throughout the album reinforced the notion that the Second Empire's engineering feats—the new bridges and viaducts built to accommodate railway expansion—were of the same caliber and significance as the nation's venerable Roman remains.

Baldus also made a series of views in Nîmes, including a close-up view of the city's Tour Magne. The octagonal stone structure dates to pre-Roman times but was transformed during the reign of Augustus, when it was enlarged and incorporated into the city's defensive ramparts. Its location, on the top of Mont Cavalier, overlooking the city, was strategic: it likely served as both a watchtower and a communications site. In his spare, centralized image, Baldus isolated the huge stone mass from its immediate surroundings, likely

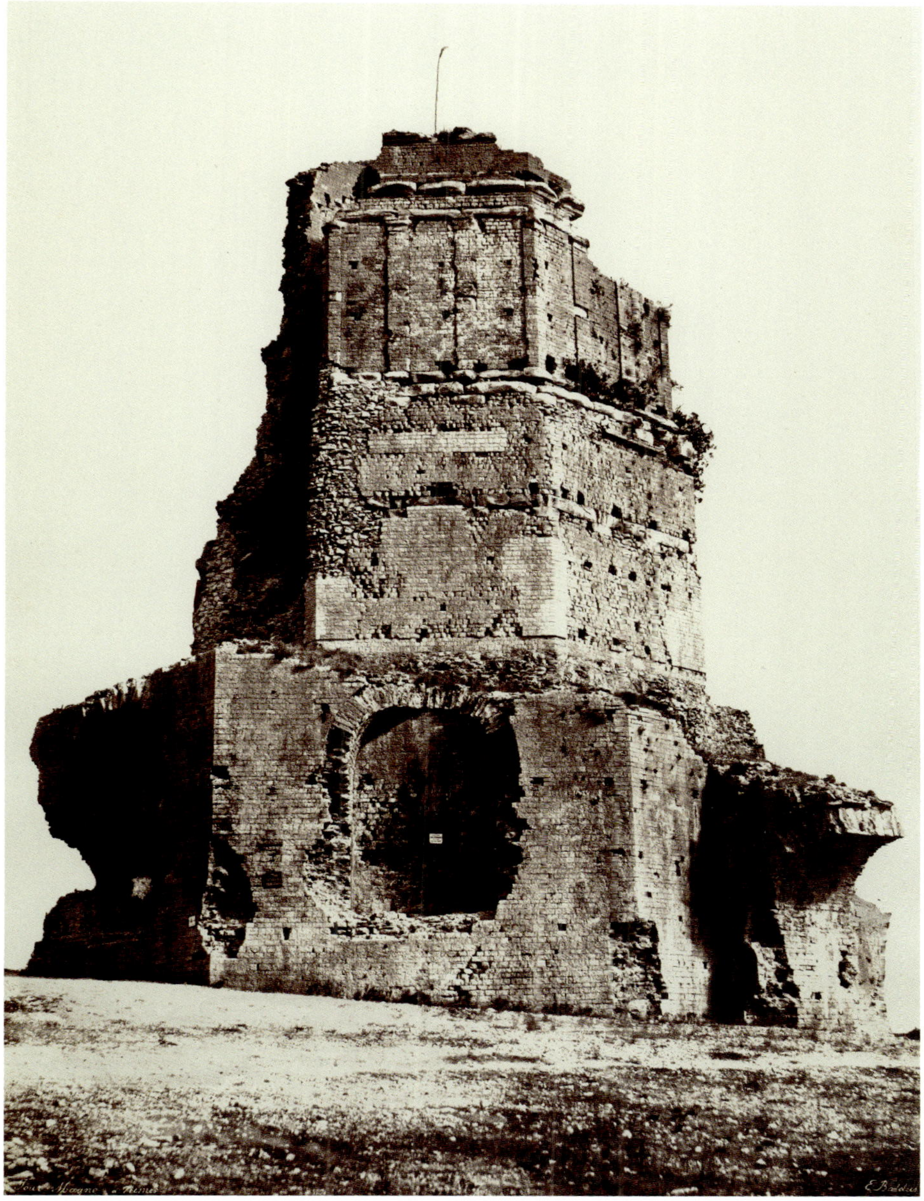

masking out the sky in the negative to ensure the proper exposure that would allow enough detailed visual information about the rough-hewn layers of masonry to be registered. Though the tower's exterior skin had eroded or been destroyed over the centuries, revealing its inner structure, the ruin remains a strong, majestic presence in Baldus's photograph, which conveys a sense of solidity and endurance, a means for picturing the nation's Roman past as a palpable part of the present.

In Arles, Baldus photographed all of the city's major monuments and ruins: the cloister of Saint-Trophime, the Roman theater, ruins of the Roman necropolis les Alyscamps, and the amphitheater (cat. 35). Mérimée described the amphitheater in 1835 as "the biggest that one knows in France. It is built on elevated vaults, and very solid, the nature of the terrain having probably required this precaution. It is impossible to see anything more imposing than the interior of this edifice, constructed of enormous blocks matched together with a completely Roman precision."[7] Built in the first century AD, the arena, which predates the much larger Roman Colosseum, was still an impressive structure in the nineteenth century. At the time Mérimée saw it, it had recently been cleared of the ramshackle housing that formerly occupied the interior elliptical space. The two-story arena held anywhere from twenty-five to twenty-six thousand spectators and contained 60 passages,

37

ÉDOUARD BALDUS

FRENCH, 1813–1889

Aigues-Mortes

1855–56

Albumen print from collodion glass negative

12³⁄₁₆ × 17³⁄₁₆ in. (31 × 43.7 cm)

Museum of Fine Arts, Houston, Gift of Manfred Heiting, The Manfred Heiting Collection, 2004.242

112 stairways, and 188 vomitories (entrances to the banks of seats).[8] The interior ellipse measured 149 by 117 yards. Though it had a wooden floor that was used for staging the kinds of blood sports between man and beast that entertained the Romans—during the reign of Diocletian, St. Genes was put to death by wild animals in this arena[9]—it was probably not flooded to allow for mock naval battles, as were the Colosseum and other larger venues. In his photograph, Baldus conveyed a sense of the scale and majesty of the Roman ruin by choosing a vantage point that allows the elegant curvature of the ellipse to lead the viewer's eye into and around the picture. Visible in the center of the composition is one of the towers that were added to the Roman structure during the Middle Ages, when the amphitheater was turned into a fortress.

Between Arles and the Mediterranean lay the vast, flat expanses of the Camargue, a marshy terrain characterized by briny lagoons (*étangs*) and reed marshes. This area, though known for its salt production and a particular breed of black, long-horned cattle that fed on the marsh grasses, was seen by many travelers as an unimpressive, disease-ridden, and melancholic place. At the mouth of the Rhone and to the west of the Camargue lay the aptly named Aigues-Mortes, "Dead Waters." The fortified, quadrangular city rose from the flat, surrounding marshland with a spare, imposing presence. Mérimée described Aigues-Mortes as giving "an exact idea of the art of fortifications of the thirteenth century."[10] The town itself was established by King Louis IX in 1240, as a Mediterranean port. His son, Philippe III, built the ramparts later in the century, to defend the isolated site from invaders. King Louis launched two crusades from the city: in 1248 the Seventh Crusade to Egypt and the Middle East; and in 1270 the Eighth Crusade to Tunisia, where he died early in the campaign. The city's history is also steeped in the religious conflicts of the sixteenth and seventeenth centuries. Between 1575 and 1622 Aigues-Mortes was considered a safe haven for Protestants. After the Edict of Nantes, which had protected the Protestants, was revoked in 1685, giving rise to severe repression, the city's Tour de Constance was used to imprison Protestants who refused to convert to Roman Catholicism. During the seventeenth and early eighteenth centuries, two hundred women were held captive there in unsanitary conditions, and many died during their incarceration.

Baldus's photograph of Aigues-Mortes readily conveys a sense of the site's starkness. Whereas the painter Frédéric Bazille focused on the more impressive entryway of the Porte de la Reine (cat. 39) or selected a distanced vantage point that included a large expanse of water in the foreground (cat. 38), Baldus chose to make his photograph from a middle distance, emphasizing one length of a rampart and a small area of barren ground outside the wall. The sky, which comprises approximately one-half of the composition, appears as a white, featureless void (a result of masking it out in the negative), which further emphasizes a sense of the city's isolation amid spare surroundings. —AMW

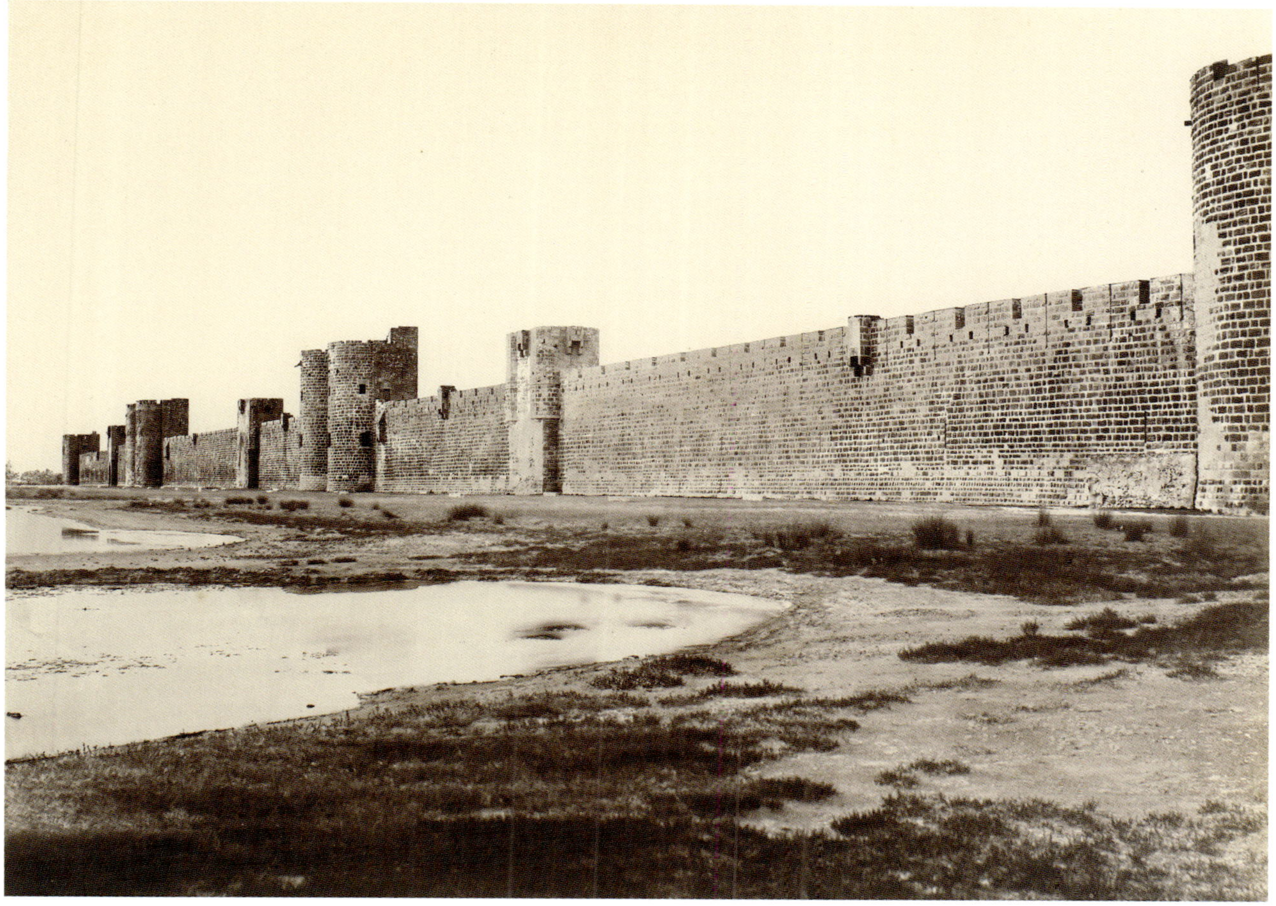

1. Ernest Lacan, "Revue photographique: M. Baldus," *La lumière*, December 17, 1853, 202: "Les perfectionnements qu'il a apportés aux procédés qu'il emploie, le sentiment profondément artistique qui distingue ses épreuves, leurs dimensions gigantesques, leur perfection, ont mis dès longtemps cet habile artiste au premier rang de nos photographes. . . . Il veut réunir dans ses cartons les vues des monuments qui représentent, en France, les divers styles d'architecture. Ainsi il pourra, quand son œuvre sera complète, offrir à l'architecte, au peintre, à l'archéologue, une collection de tous les types de construction, depuis les lourds édifices que les colonies romaines ont laissés dans nos villes anciennes, jusqu'aux constructions bâtardes du siècle dernier. Tout aura sa place dans cette galerie historique et artistique à la fois."

2. Prosper Mérimée, introduction to *Notes d'un voyage dans le Midi de la France* (Paris: Librairie Fournier, 1835), vi: "Toutefois, aujourd'hui que l'étude de nos antiquités nationales commence à prendre faveur, j'ai pensé que la publication de ces notes pourrait être de quelque utilité aux personnes qui visiteraient les lieux que j'ai parcourus. Je croirais avoir rendu service à l'archéologie en provoquant un nouvel examen des monumens que j'ai décrits, en attirant la discussion sur les questions que j'ai effleurées. Il est rare d'arriver du premier coup à la vérité se découvre, dût-on soi-même être convaincu d'erreur."

3. The poet Frédéric Mistral and a group of writers called the Félibrige were at the forefront of this movement in Provence. The writer Alphonse Daudet, a close friend of Mistral's, also set many of his stories in Provence.

4. Daniel Vitaglione, *The Literature of Provence: An Introduction* (Jefferson, N.C.: McFarland & Company, 2000), 13–14.

5. Mérimée, *Notes d'un voyage dans le Midi*, 316–17: "Le Gardon, grossi par des averses prodigieuses, était débordé et roulait, avec un bruit affreux, ses eaux, couleur de café, sous les arches d'aqueduc; le ciel etait a l'orage, mais une éclaircie dorait le monument qui paraissait étincellent de la lumière, le site sauvage, la solitude complète de lieu, le bruit du torrent, ajoutaient une poésie sublime à l'architecture imposante qui s'offrait à mes yeux."

6. The Pont du Gard was built in the first century AD and served as part of the thirty-one-mile aqueduct that ran from the source of the river, the Fontaine d'Eure near Uzès, north of Nîmes, to the castellum (a large water cistern fed by the aqueduct) in Nîmes. Its water channel, which ran through the top tier of small arches, was approximately 4½ feet wide by 5 to 6½ feet deep. It is estimated that the entire structure, which was made from the soft yellow limestone native to the area, known locally as *pierre de ver*, used 742 cubic feet of cut stone and weighs more than 50,000 tons.

7. Mérimée, *Notes d'un voyage dans le Midi*, 274: "C'est le plus grand que l'on connaisse en France. Il est bâti sur des voûtes élevees et très solide, la nature du terrain ayant probablement exigé cette précaution Il est impossible de voir rien de plus imposant que l'intérieur de cet édifice, construite d'énorme appareillés avec une précision toute romaine."

8. André Chagny, *Visions of France: Arles and La Camargue* (Lyon: G. L. Arlaud, 1929), 25.

9. Ibid., 7.

10. Mérimée, *Notes d'un voyage dans le Midi*, 346: "Les remparts de la ville, élevées par Philippe de Hardi, encore parfaitement conservé, peuvent donné une idée exacte de l'art de la fortification au XIIIème siècle."

38

FRÉDÉRIC BAZILLE

FRENCH, 1841–1870

The Ramparts at Aigues-Mortes

1867

Oil on canvas

23⅝ × 39⅜ in. (60 × 100 cm)

National Gallery of Art, Washington D.C., Collection of Mr. and Mrs. Paul Mellon, 1985.64.1

IN THE LATE SPRING OF 1867 the Impressionist painter Frédéric Bazille visited the fortified town of Aigues-Mortes on the Mediterranean coast of France. The town's impressive walls were described by the travel writer Adolphe Joanne as "perhaps the most complete and best-preserved example of medieval military architecture."[1] The name of this town derives from the Occitan, Aiguas Mortas, and translates literally as "Dead Waters." The city is indeed surrounded by stagnant lagoons as well as expansive salt marshes. Aigues-Mortes is particularly closely linked with the religious history of France. In the thirteenth century, the crusader king, St. Louis (Louis IX), established the town, making it the place of embarkation for the Seventh Crusade in 1248; it was further expanded by his eldest son, Philip the Bold. Subsequently, the town came to be associated with France's Protestant community and was one of eight safe havens granted to French Protestants in the late sixteenth century. Bazille's decision to visit the town may have been informed by this history, since he came from a prominent liberal Protestant family in nearby Montpellier. His father, a well-known senator, encouraged his son to paint a view of the town, noting: "I have never seen any painting representing Aigues-Mortes, and I am rather inclined to think that a landscape or marine (because Aigues-Mortes with its small port can provide either subject) of this unusual site in the Midi would have some interest."[2] Bazille was also a friend of the mayor of Montpellier, Jules Pagézy, who wrote an extensive two-volume history of Aigues-Mortes, focusing on its origins and early medieval history.[3]

Bazille produced three surviving landscapes of Aigues-Mortes during his 1867 visit, including the two here.[4] *The Ramparts at Aigues-Mortes* was painted from the west and shows a view across the shipping channel into the town: Louis IX had established a canal to the sea as early as the thirteenth century. At the far left is the Tour de Constance, the only tower surviving from Louis IX's time, while to the right is the Tour des Bourguignons, prominently reflected in the water.[5] The picture highlights Bazille's sensitivity to the intense light of the South. In contrast to this panoramic view, *Porte de la Reine at Aigues-Mortes* (cat. 39) is a close-up study, focusing on this impressive thirteenth-century gate into the city. Bazille emphasized the contrast between the shadowed foreground and the sunlit road (the rue Émile Jamais) into the city, which draws the eye into the composition. A horseman converses with a red-hatted man, while a woman sits on the ground knitting alongside two children and a wild white Camargue horse.[6]

Bazille seems to have envisaged these paintings as studies for a larger exhibition painting. He wrote to his mother in May 1867: "I have begun three or four landscapes of the area around Aigues-Mortes. In my large canvas, I am going to do the walls of the city reflected in a pond at sunset. This will be a very simple painting, which should not take long to do. Nevertheless, I would need at least eight beautiful days."[7] None of Bazille's surviving works represents a sunset, and this "large canvas" may have been lost or indeed never begun. Nonetheless, we may speculate that Bazille intended to create this larger painting for the Salon, where he had

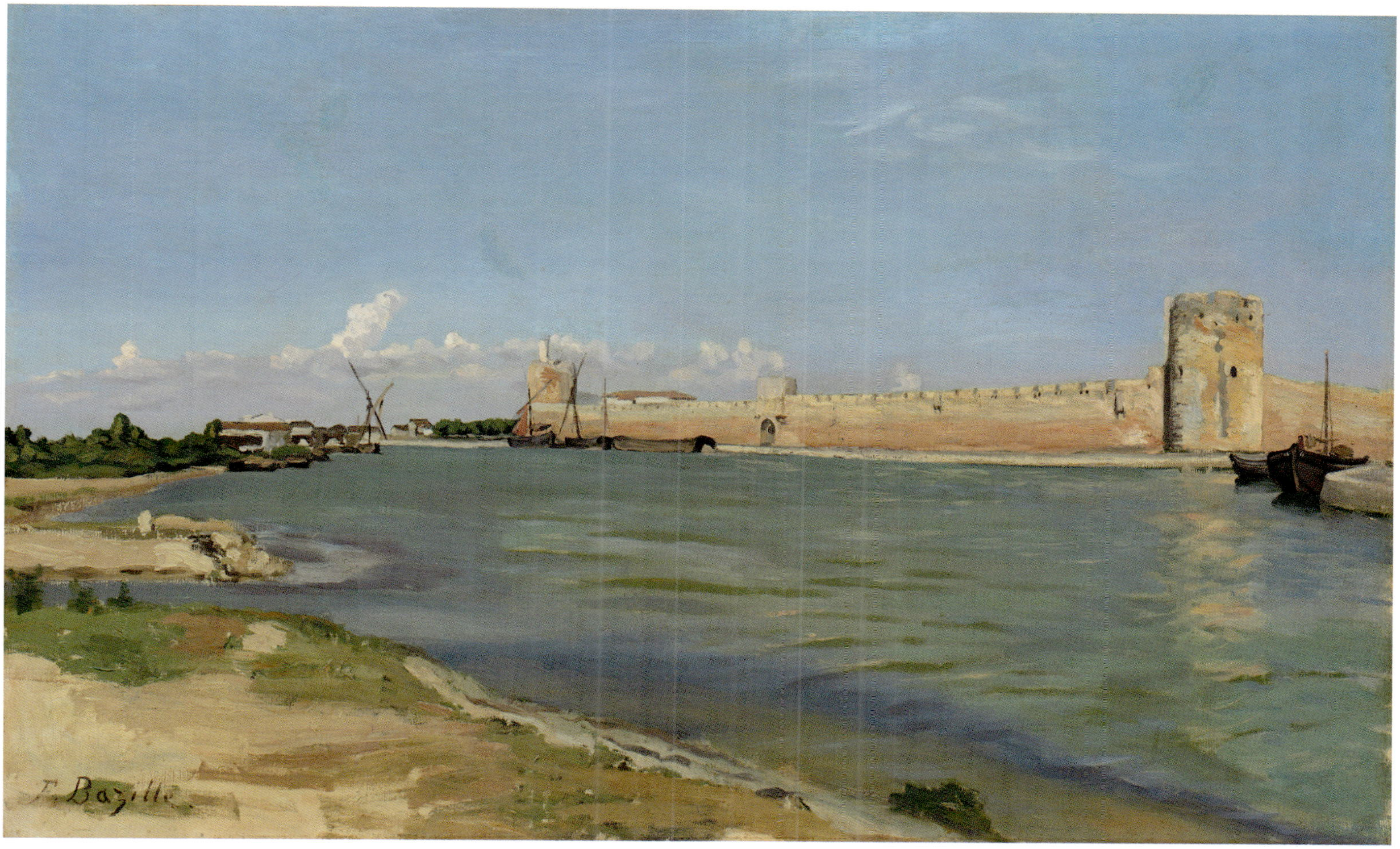
F. Bazille

39

FRÉDÉRIC BAZILLE
FRENCH, 1841–1870

Porte de la Reine at Aigues-Mortes

1867

Oil on canvas

31¾ × 39¼ in. (80.6 × 99.7cm)

The Metropolitan Museum of Art, New York, Purchase, Gift of Raymonde Paul, in memory of her brother, C. Michael Paul, by exchange, 1988. 1988.221

regularly exhibited in the 1860s. He would show a large landscape of nearby Lez (Minneapolis Institute of Arts) at the Salon of 1870.

Bazille had moved to Paris from his native Montpellier in 1862 and there became a central member of the Impressionist circle, establishing a particularly close friendship with Claude Monet. Nonetheless, he remained very attached to the landscape of the South; around half of his output represents scenes from his native Languedoc. Bazille had first planned to visit Aigues-Mortes in 1866 but was deterred by his father because of the risk of plague.[8]

Bazille's importance to the history of Impressionism is often overlooked because of his untimely death in the Franco-Prussian War in November 1870 at the age of twenty-eight. He had voluntarily enrolled with a Zouave unit and died attempting to storm a German position in eastern France after being shot twice in the stomach.[9] Only sixty-eight extant paintings by Bazille are known. His three views of Aigues-Mortes testify to his regional patriotism and indicate his important contribution toward representing the landscape of southern France. —SK

1. Adolphe Joanne, *Dictionnaire géographique de la France* (Paris: Hachette, 1869), 1:14: "peut-être le specimen le plus complet et le mieux conservé de l'architecture militaire au moyen age."

2. Gaston Bazille to Frédéric Bazille, July 14, 1866, in Michel Schulman, *Frédéric Bazille, 1841–1870: Catalogue raisonné; Peintures, dessins, pastels, aquarelles. Sa vie, son oeuvre, sa correspondance* (Paris: Éditions de l'Amateur–Éditions des Catalogues Raisonnés, 1995), 352: "Je n'ai jamais vu de peinture représentant Aigues-Mortes, et je suis assez porté à croire qu'un paysage ou qu'une marine (car Aigues-Mortes avec son petit port, peut fournir l'un ou l'autre sujet) de ce point peu commun du Midi, offrirait de l'intérêt."

3. Jules Pagézy, *Mémoires sur le port d'Aigues-Mortes*, 2 vols. (Paris: Hachette, 1879). The author's preface indicates that he had collected his documentary material by 1852.

4. The third painting is now in the Musée Fabre, Montpellier. See Schulman, *Frédéric Bazille*, cats. 32–34.

5. Bazille produced preparatory drawings of the ramparts and boats; see Musée du Louvre, Département des Arts graphiques, RF 5259, fols. 27 and 31.

6. For preparatory drawings for the horses in the foreground and the knitting woman, see ibid., fols. 21, 22, 23, and 43r.

7. Bazille to his mother, end of May 1867, in Schulman, *Frédéric Bazille*, 358: "J'ai commencé trois ou quatre paysages des environs d'Aigues-Mortes. Sur ma grande toile, je vais faire les murs de la ville se réfletant dans l'étang au coucher du soleil. Ce tableau sera fort simple et ne devrait pas être long à faire. Cependant il me faudrait au moins huit belles journées."

8. Gaston Bazille to Frédéric Bazille, July 14, 1866, in ibid., 352.

9. His patriotism and liberal devotion to the new republic are evident in a letter to his parents of September 6, 1870 (ibid., 383): "I am still stunned by the most recent news but, my God, well pleased with the Republic, provided that it lasts." (Je suis encore ahuri par les dernières nouvelles, mais ma foi bien content de la République, pourvu qu'elle dure.)

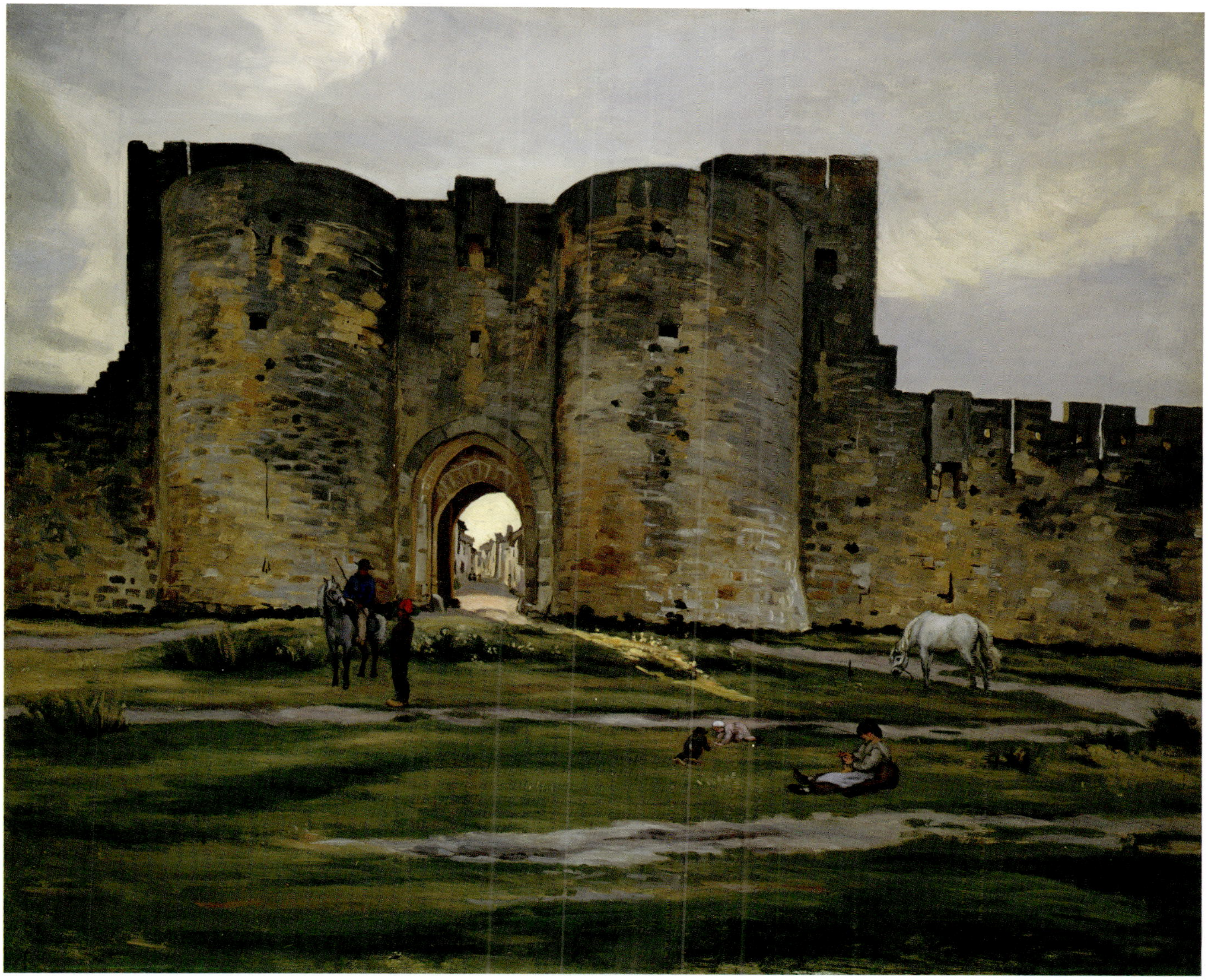

3

FORESTS AND RIVERS

IN THE MID-NINETEENTH CENTURY approximately one-seventh—or about 20 million acres—of France's entire surface was covered by forest.[1] The trees in these forests ranged from oak and beech in the center of France to pines in the East and the extensive olive groves in the South. Many of these forests dated to ancient Gallic times, when the majority of the country had been covered by woodland. As the writer Charles de Kirwan noted in 1869, "the forests that exist today in France, even the largest, represent only the insignificant remains of the imposing wooded masses that, a century before the Christian era, covered our country."[2] The prevalence of forests across France—as well as their historical importance—ensured that trees became symbols of national identity. The oak tree in particular was glossed with nationalistic resonances.

A particularly important wooded tract that had for centuries belonged to royalty was the Forest of Fontainebleau, just outside Paris. This became the center for the French school of landscape painting in the mid-nineteenth century. Painters such as Théodore Rousseau and Narcisse-Virgile Diaz de la Peña explored the varied iconography of the forest, as did photographers including Gustave Le Gray and Eugène Cuvelier. Naming great oaks after early French kings such as Clovis and Charlemagne gave the forest's trees nationalistic associations. Another highly important forested area was the Vosges and the Ardennes in eastern France, close to the German border. Gustave Doré pictured the pine forest tracts there as mysterious, secluded spots. As well as being sites resonant with history, forests became increasingly important as an economic resource because of their timber.

France's rivers also played a central role in the country's sense of emerging identity. The country's major rivers—particularly the Seine, Loire, and Rhone—served as potent symbols of nation. Particularly in times of historical change and turmoil, their tranquil passage embodied a sense of "deep France" (*la France profonde*). Charles-François Daubigny and Henri-Victor Regnault represented the Seine as a site of idyllic pastoral retreat in the face of rapid industrialization and growing tourism. Henri-Joseph Harpignies and Camille Silvy produced lush pastoral views of the tributaries of the Loire, the nation's longest river. Paul Guigou explored the more arid, sandy expanses of Provence in his views of the Rhone's tributary, the Durance.

Rivers embodied the idea, too, of France as a modern, industrial nation. They played a crucial economic role in transporting cargo around the country. In 1869 the waterways of France carried 2.5 million tons of cargo, only a little less than the railroad.[3] The Rhone was crucial to France's trade since it offered a direct route to the Mediterranean through the port of Marseille. Édouard Baldus recorded the river's transformation as a result of new bridges and viaducts built to accommodate the country's expanding railway. The Seine was also a particularly important trade artery as it ran through Paris to the port of Le Havre. Camille Pissarro represented the extensive barge traffic along this river as well as its tributary, the Oise.

Rivers also emerged as a major new site for leisure activity with the rise of boating as a pastime. Monet, in particular, focused on leisure boating scenes around Argenteuil, producing work that embodies the new middle-class confidence of the French Third Republic.

1. Charles de Kirwan, *La France forestière depuis les temps les plus reculés jusqu'à nos jours* (Paris: Charles Douniol, 1869), 37. Much of this land was owned by the state (around 7,413,161 acres), but the remaining 12,355,269 acres were privately owned and, as Kirwan complained, increasingly subject to deforestation.

2. Ibid., 6.

3. Much of this waterborne traffic also passed along France's canals, which expanded greatly in length during this period: in 1830 the French canal system had extended 1,126 miles; in 1876, it was 2,747 miles. The railroad carried 3.5 million tons of cargo at midcentury. James H. Rubin, *Impressionism and the Modern Landscape: Productivity, Technology, and Urbanization from Manet to Van Gogh* (Berkeley: University of California Press, 2008), 67–69.

THÉODORE ROUSSEAU
FRENCH, 1812–1867

40

The Rock Oak (Forest of Fontainebleau)

ca. 1860–67
Oil on panel
35 × 46 in. (88.9 × 116.8 cm)
Private Collection

THÉODORE ROUSSEAU represented the oaks of the Forest of Fontainebleau his entire life, first painting the forest in the late 1820s. Focusing on it for most of his career, he established himself as the leading landscape painter in the community of artists living at Barbizon in the mid-nineteenth century. Rousseau saw the forest's ancient oak trees as embodying the nation's long and storied history. In a letter of 1852 to Emperor Napoléon III, he argued strongly for the preservation of "these old trees, which for artists are the source from which they draw their inspiration, their joys, and their future, and which are for all visitors venerable souvenirs of past ages. I ask you to command that these reminders of Druidic times, of Charlemagne, St. Louis, Louis XII, and Napoleon be left to die tranquilly in peace."[1]

The Rock Oak depicts a gnarled, ancient oak, and, for the artist's biographer, Alfred Sensier, it was "one of the most beautiful creations of Rousseau."[2] The tree's branches in the upper part of the picture twist in contorted shapes; the sky in the distance is barely evident. Rousseau's color range is dominated by greens but offset by accents, such as the red berries of a holly bush, the coral-like pink branches of a shrub, and the touches of silver and Naples yellow on the bark of the tree. Rousseau created a closed, self-contained world into which light barely penetrates and in which there is no sign of human presence. The oak has pushed its way up through the surrounding moss-covered rocks, probably made of sandstone or limestone, the predominant rock forms in the forest.[3] Rousseau's work, indeed, references ancient geologic time, since both of these rocks had been formed thirty-five million years ago, when the Stampian Sea covered the center of France.

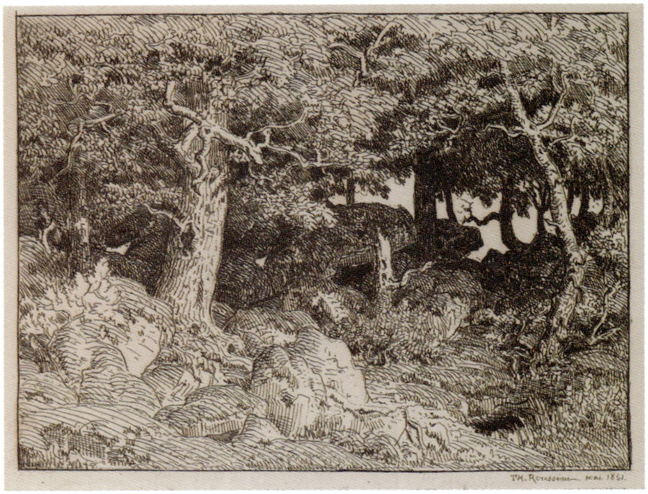

FIG. 62 Théodore Rousseau, *Oak Trees and Rocks*, 1861. Etching, $4^{15}/_{16} \times 6^{5}/_{8}$ in. (12.6 × 16.8 cm). Saint Louis Art Museum, Museum Purchase, 137:1914

The artist was painting this work at the time that the forest was emerging as a major tourist location. By midcentury, there were about ninety-three miles of paths through the forest laid out by the entrepreneur Claude-François Denecourt, and one hundred thousand tourists were said to visit the forest each year. Rousseau was very much aware of these changes. On May 23, 1860, he wrote to his old friend Théophile Thoré, who had recently returned to France from exile: "You will find the forest very changed, it is a park which is only lacking boxes of orange trees as replacements for its old oaks."[4] In this picture, however, he screened out all references to those recent transformations, emphasizing the primordial nature of the site.[5]

Rousseau showed the painting as his only exhibit at the 1861 Paris Salon. Thoré remarked on the work's majesty as well as its meticulous, pointillist paint surface. He noted that it was "very mysterious and very powerful, although too uniformly knitted, as they say in the studios."[6] Thoré

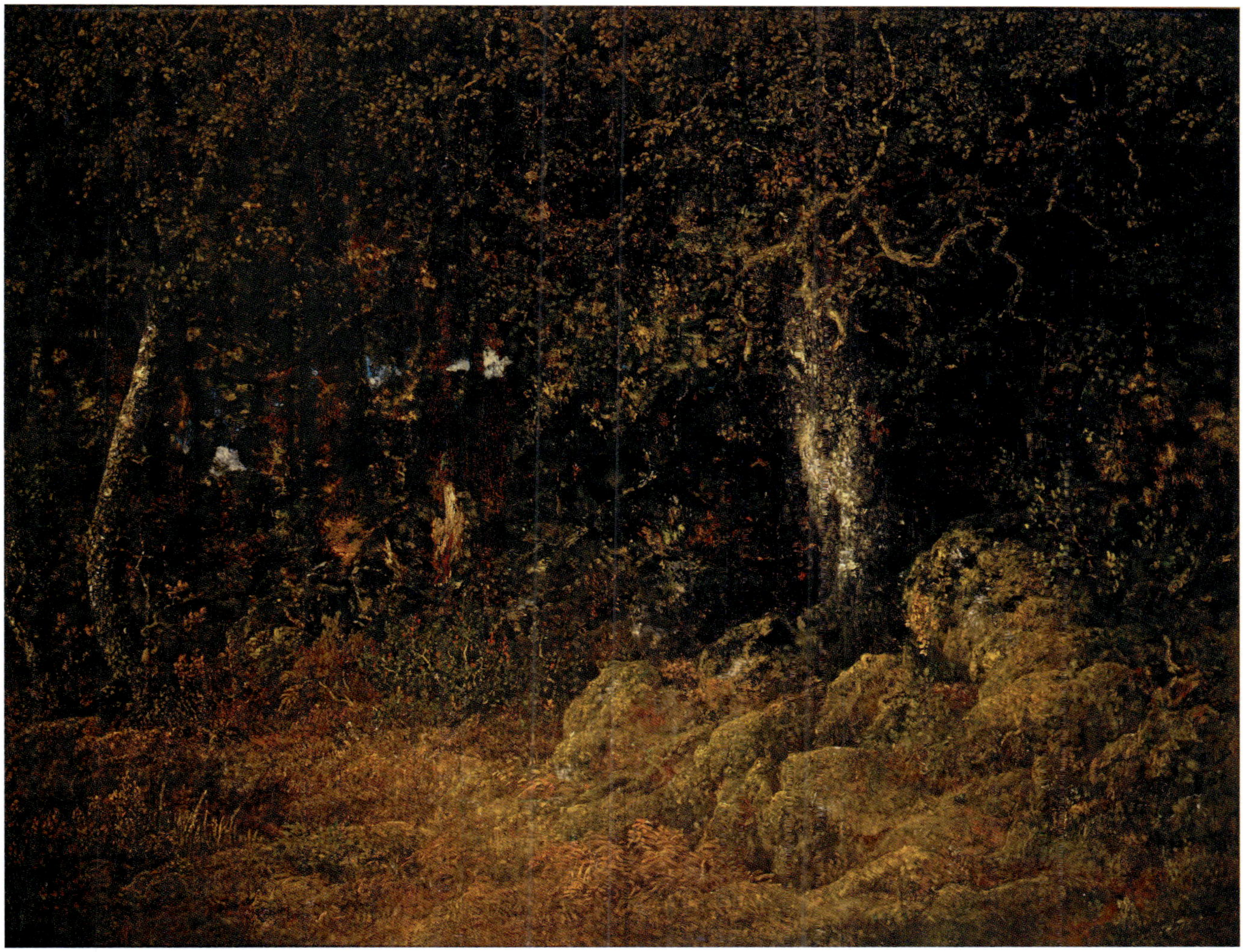

argued that the picture would benefit from being shown in a room on its own rather than in the melée of the Salon.[7] Most critics gave little attention to the subject of the painting and instead focused on its formal aspect, unable to comprehend Rousseau's flat, almost semiabstract work. Théophile Gautier referred to the picture's "strange aspect" as a result of "the bizarre tonality of its greens" and compared it to "a block of copper ore."[8] The most common critical response emphasized the uniformity of Rousseau's facture. Olivier Merson wrote that the picture was "uniformly detailed, the painter having proceeded with equal touches. It's like a needlepoint tapestry."[9] The caricaturist Galletti produced a cartoon of the picture as a "mosaic."[10]

In an attempt to promote the painting, Rousseau produced an etching, which was published in the *Gazette des beaux-arts* (fig. 62). The reversed composition provides a greater sense of spatial recession as well as a larger opening for the sky in the background: a foreground pool is also clearly evident in the right foreground. A relative novice in the practicalities of printmaking, Rousseau sought advice from the critic Philippe Burty and the young engraver Félix Bracquemond. Three states of the etching were produced.[11]

Rousseau sold *The Rock Oak* to the wealthy banker Ennemond Blanc in the summer of 1860, probably for a sum of 6,000 francs.[12] In the spring of 1862, Blanc put the work up for auction, where it was bought by Rousseau himself for the significant sum of 6,830 francs.[13] Rousseau continued to revise the picture in his final years, probably painting over the sky in the background, hence accounting for the difference from the etching in that area. He exhibited it again as a key work in his extensive retrospective at the 1867 Exposition universelle. Rousseau was awarded a Grand Medal of Honor, the only French landscape painter to receive such an award, signaling his growing international reputation. In the years to come, his prices would also escalate. The fortunes of *The Rock Oak* were symptomatic of this: the work sold at auction in May 1868 for 18,200 francs, three times its original price.[14] Rousseau's work, however, beyond its monetary value, speaks to the value of the ancient French history of the centuries-old oak and its millennia-old, prehistoric rocks. —SK

1. Translated and quoted in Greg Thomas, *Art and Ecology in Nineteenth-Century France: The Landscapes of Théodore Rousseau* (Princeton: Princeton University Press, 2000), 217.

2. Alfred Sensier, *Souvenirs sur Théodore Rousseau* (Paris: Techener, 1872), 258: "une des plus belles créations de Rousseau."

3. The site represented is unclear but may be in either the area of the Plâteau de Belle-Croix or Mont-Ussy, where oaks stand among rock formations.

4. Rousseau to Thoré, May 23, 1860, Bibliothèque nationale de France, Paris, MS n.a.f. 11955, no. 111: "Tu trouveras la forêt bien changée, c'est un parc qui n'attend plus que les caisses d'orangers en remplacement des vieux chênes."

5. Rousseau's painting is underpinned by at least three drawing studies, dating from 1858. The artist made two pencil studies (both private collection) and an ink study (27½ × 39⅜ in. [70 × 100 cm], location unknown). All three works appeared in his posthumous sale: *Vente Théodore Rousseau* (Paris: Hôtel Drouot, April 27–May 2, 1868), nos. 335–37.

6. W. Bürger, "Salon de 1861," in *Salons de W. Bürger, 1861 à 1868* (Paris: Ve Jules Renouard, 1870), 50: "très mystérieux et très fort, bien que trop uniformément tricoté comme on dit dans les ateliers."

7. Ibid., 50: "Cette peinture ne produit point au Salon tout son effet. Les belles choses gagnent à être isolées."

8. Théophile Gautier, *Abécédaire du Salon de 1861* (Paris: E. Dentu, 1861), 323: "un aspect étrange. Il ressemble, par la tonalité bizarre de ses verts, à un bloc de minerai de cuivre."

9. Olivier Merson, *La peinture en France: Exposition de 1861* (Paris: E. Dentu, 1861), 336: "uniformément détaillée, le peintre ayant procédé par touches égales. On dirait une tapisserie au petit point."

10. Reproduced in Simon Kelly, "'The Mystery of the Forest': Paintings of Fontainebleau at the Salon," in *In the Forest of Fontainebleau: Painters and Photographers from Corot to Monet*, ed. Kimberly Jones, exh. cat. (Washington, D.C.: National Gallery of Art, 2008), 148.

11. The first is very rare and without signature or date. In the second (fig. 62), the chiaroscuro contrast is more marked, and Rousseau added his signature and the date, May 1861. The third state appeared in the August 1861 issue of the *Gazette des beaux-arts* as part of Léon Lagrange's Salon review.

12. On July 21, 1860, Rousseau wrote a receipt (Cabinet de la Documentation, Musée du Louvre), "Reçu de M. Stevens la somme de deux mille francs en acompte sur six mille." The Belgian dealer Arthur Stevens collaborated closely with Ennemond Blanc. To promote his international profile, Rousseau planned to show the work at the Belgian Salon but did not because of misunderstandings with Stevens. Jean-François Millet lamented that Rousseau's work would not be seen in Brussels, since it was "a superb thing, which would have produced a great and good effect." See Millet to Théophile Thoré, [Barbizon], September 12, 1860, Institut Néerlandais, Paris. no. 6757: "C'est vraiment bien grand dommage que le tableau de Rousseau n'ait pu être envoyé à Bruxelles car c'est une chose superbe qui aurait produit un grand et bon effet."

13. See *Vente Ennemond Blanc* (Paris: Hôtel Drouot, April 7, 1862).

14. The picture was acquired from Rousseau by the dealers Paul Durand-Ruel and Hector Brame before being sold to the collector and composer Antoine Marmontel, in whose sale it appeared in 1868.

41

UNKNOWN PHOTOGRAPHER

Tree Study with a Horse-Drawn Carriage and a Portrait of a Photographer

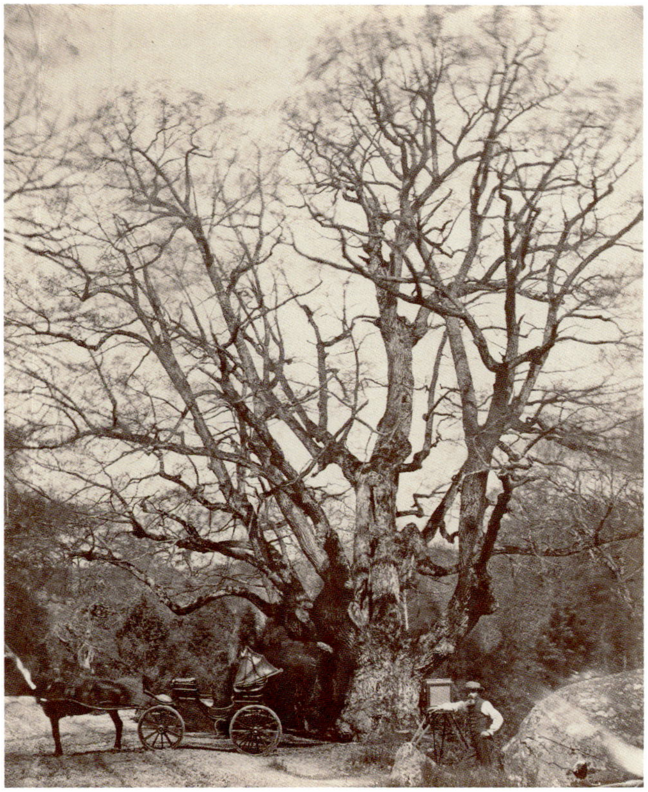

ca. 1860

Albumen print from collodion glass negative

12 × 9⅞ in. (30.5 × 25.1 cm)

The Nelson-Atkins Museum of Art, Kansas City, Missouri, Gift of the Hall Family Foundation, 2012.24.6

IN HIS 1840 *Guide du voyageur dans le palais et la forêt de Fontainebleau* (*Guide to the Palace and Forest of Fontainebleau*), Claude-François Denecourt outlined his purpose for guiding leisure-seeking visitors through the natural splendors of the Forest of Fontainebleau. As he wrote in the introduction to the section on the forest:

> But I am close to forgetting the picture of grandiose nature, as that must be the work of the painter or poet, for whom it inspires genius, and my mission is simply to direct the traveler who comes to admire the beauties. I myself am inspired by the sweet peace and happiness that reside at the bottom of these woods and wilderness that I have long traveled throughout, and, aided by the observations of the artists who frequent them daily, I have acquired knowledge of the locality which had enabled me to report all the picturesque parts, and to offer travelers the means to visit, with as much ease as leisure.[1]

Denecourt's impact on the way the Forest of Fontainebleau was experienced as nature—largely by bourgeois Parisians who could visit it via direct rail line from Paris beginning in 1849—was immense. He built on the public's knowledge of the forest grounded in literary and artistic precedents established during the 1820s and 1830s (his first guidebook appeared in 1839), as well as on the locally based literary perspectives of Etienne Jamin and Alexis Durand, who produced accounts of the forest in 1834 and 1836 respectively.[2] Denecourt's guides were meant less to inspire poetic meanderings through the forest in search of solitude and spiritual communion than to instruct urban travelers as to exactly where they should go and what they should see. Denecourt orchestrated an experience of the forest's savage beauties by aggrandizing existing features and vistas—the old-growth oak and beech trees of the Bas-Bréau, the unusual boulders of the Gorges d'Apremont, the sandstone plain of Macherin, and the marshy terrain of the Belle-Croix plateau. He also created an extensive system of pathways between them, often through his own brute force. Denecourt's vision of the forest, with its mixture of historic fact and fantastical invention aimed specifically at the newly leisured middle class, was ultimately an entrepreneurial business venture that both fed into and greatly expanded tourism to the area.

With developments in paper photography during the late 1840s and early 1850s, photographers began to frequent the forest, following the precedent of the Barbizon painters and graphic artists who sought subjects for the Parisian souvenir print markets. The bulk of a photographer's equipment was significant: these men (there were no known women practitioners in France at this time) had to bring not only their cameras, negatives, tripods, and dark cloths but all the chemical supplies necessary to develop and fix their

42

UNKNOWN PHOTOGRAPHER

Tree Study with a Photographer Lying Down, His Assistant, and a Horse-Drawn Carriage

ca. 1860

Albumen print from collodion glass negative

12 × 9⅞ in. (30.5 × 25.1 cm)

The Nelson-Atkins Museum of Art, Kansas City, Missouri, Gift of the Hall Family Foundation, 2012.24.7

negatives, which meant packing a darkroom tent for use in situ as well.

These two images convey a sense of what a typical excursion into the forest might have been like about 1860. Both photographs depict an unidentified, bearded photographer who has gone to the forest with an assistant. In catalogue 41, he stands in front of his large-format camera, which is situated to photograph a portion of the large oak tree that consumes most of the composition. He rests one arm on the apparatus, a hand on his hip, as he poses for his colleague. To the photographer's left is a horse and carriage with a top that unfolds over the passengers' seats. The same horse and carriage appear in catalogue 42, taken from a different vantage point. Here, the photographer is barely discernible against the background; he can be seen to the left of the tree's base, reclining with his eyes closed and his head resting on his elbow. Visible behind him is the white cloth exterior of his darkroom tent (fig. 63). The slightly blurred figure of his assistant stands in front of the oak tree.

Though these two photographs certainly serve as documents of the day's excursion, they also suggest, through the deliberateness of the photographer's pose and the inclusion of the camera and tent, a heightened degree of self-reflexivity on the part of the photographer and his assistant. Just as Jean-Baptiste-Camille Corot was often photographed outdoors, seated at his easel with a parasol at his back and his palette and brushes in his hand (see fig. 10), these men sought to affirm their artistic status as landscape photographers by depicting themselves in the act of discovering creative inspiration in the forest's unique and venerated arboreal specimens.

These images include both deciduous old-growth trees, such as the central oak, and a stand of pine trees, a species that was extensively planted in the 1830s and 1840s for

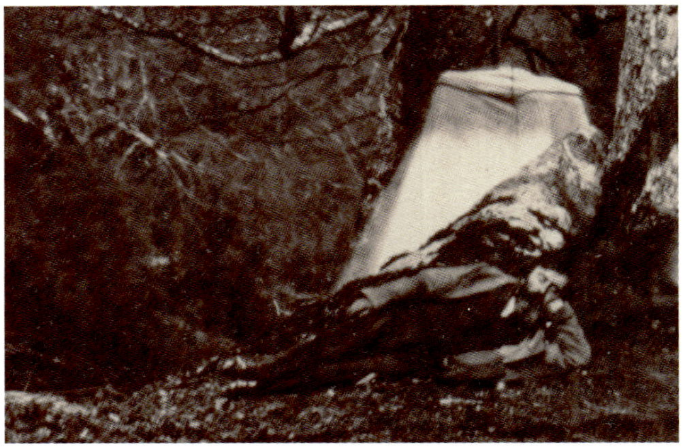

FIG. 63 Detail of cat. 42, showing photographer lying on ground next to tree

its commercial value to the lumber industry. The cutting down of Fontainebleau's oak trees for timber as well as the mass planting of pine trees were sources of great contention in the mid-nineteenth century. As Nicholas Green has noted, despite the fact that the state owned the forest, its maintenance and care were entrusted for many years to the Boisd'hyver family, who sanctioned the pine tree plantings to increase profits. Artists—Théodore Rousseau in particular—were among the most vocal opponents of this practice, decrying the loss of old-growth forest.[3] —AMW

1. Claude-François Denecourt, *Guide du voyageur dans le palais et la forêt de Fontainebleau* (Fontainebleau, 1840), 6: "Mais je suis près d'oublier que le tableau d'une nature aussi grandiose doit être l'oeuvre du peintre ou du poète, dont elle enflamme le génie, et que ma mission doit se borner à diriger le voyageur qui vient en admirer les beautés. Attiré moi-même par la douce paix et le bonheur qui résident au fond de ces bois et de ces déserts, je les ai longtemps parcourus, et, aidé par les observations des artistes qui les fréquentent journellement, j'ai acquis une connaissance de la localité qui m'a mis à même d'en signaler toutes les parties les plus pittoresques, et d'offrir au voyageur les moyens de les visiter; avec autant de facilité que d'agrément."

2. Nicholas Green, *The Spectacle of Nature: Landscape and Bourgeois Culture in Nineteenth-Century France* (Manchester: Manchester University Press, 1990), 162–63.

3. Ibid., 118.

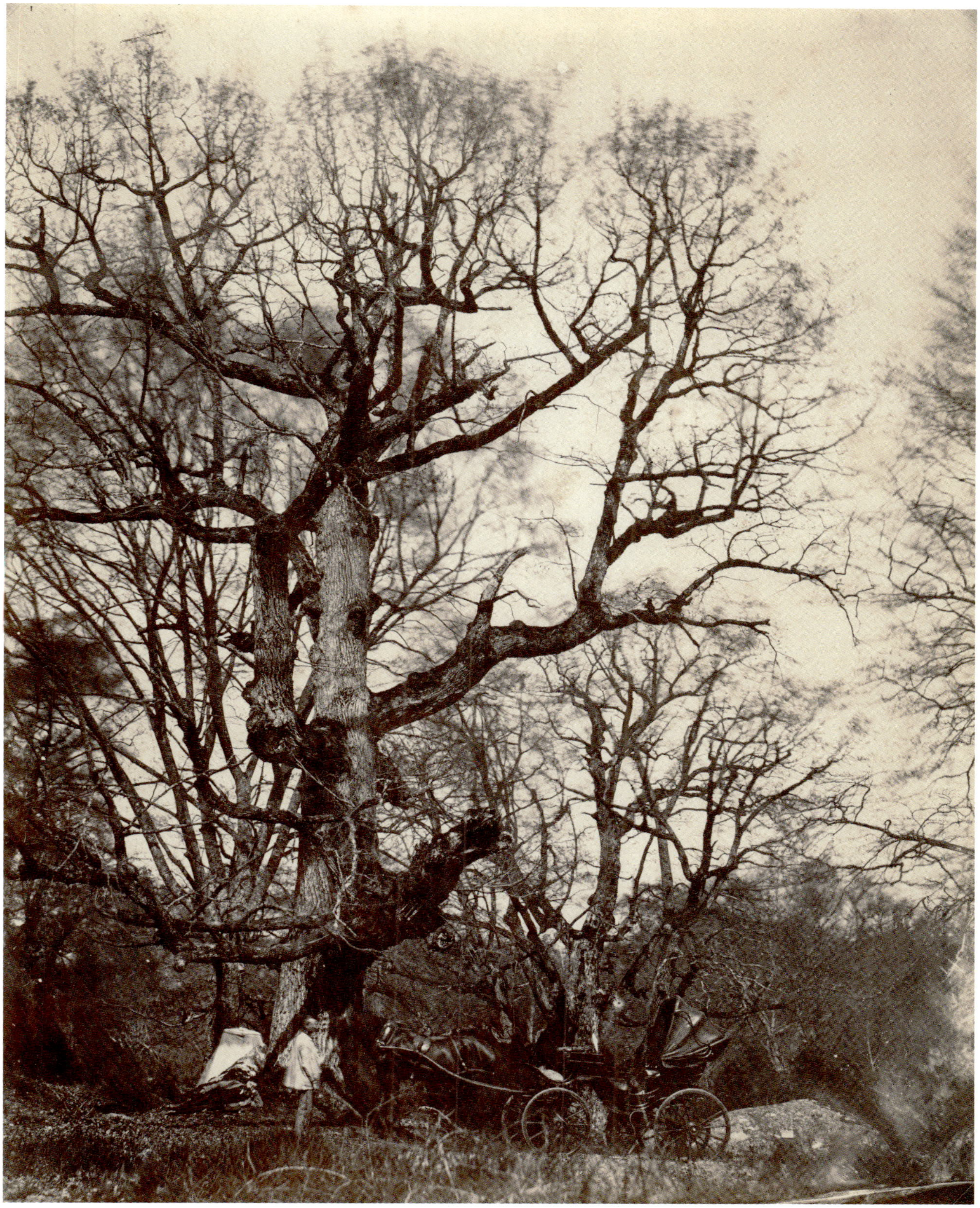

NARCISSE-VIRGILE DIAZ DE LA PEÑA
FRENCH, 1807–1876

43

The Approaching Storm

1872

Oil on wood panel

31⅛ × 41⅜ in. (79.1 × 105.1 cm)

The Nelson-Atkins Museum of Art, Kansas City, Missouri, Purchase: William Rockhill Nelson Trust, 31-60

THE FOREST OF FONTAINEBLEAU represented a site of seminal importance for the French landscape school. Narcisse-Virgile Diaz de la Peña painted there regularly from the late 1830s, moving to Barbizon at that time and emerging as a central figure in the colony of artists in the village. In the 1840s Diaz showed forest landscapes regularly at the Salon, winning praise for his rich color. For his principal critical apologist, Théophile Thoré, his paintings were like "a pile of precious stones."[1] In the years to come, Diaz enjoyed much market success with his landscapes, organizing at least eleven auctions of his paintings from 1849 until 1868.[2] He was particularly known for his atmospheric *sous-bois*, or forest interiors, but, in the final decade of his career, he produced several more expansive views of storms over open forest plains.[3]

The Approaching Storm is identified here for the first time as representing a group of oak trees on the ancient Gorges d'Apremont, a rocky plain in the center of the Forest of Fontainebleau. The stand of trees that appears in Diaz's work is the same as that represented in an earlier painting by Théodore Rousseau (fig. 64), dating from 1852. Diaz evoked the passage of the storm with rapid, gestural impasto. A pink ground, applied to the wood panel, is clearly visible in the sky, investing the work with a sense of warmth. The artist also animated his scene with the tiny figure of a peasant woman carrying a bundle of sticks.

The Gorges d'Apremont was a site of nationalistic controversy. In the early to mid-nineteenth century, it was extensively planted with pine trees of Russian origin for commercial reasons. The artists of the Barbizon colony strongly opposed this development, seeing these trees as despoiling indigenous French soil. Diaz's close friend Rousseau wrote to the emperor in 1852: "the forest administration

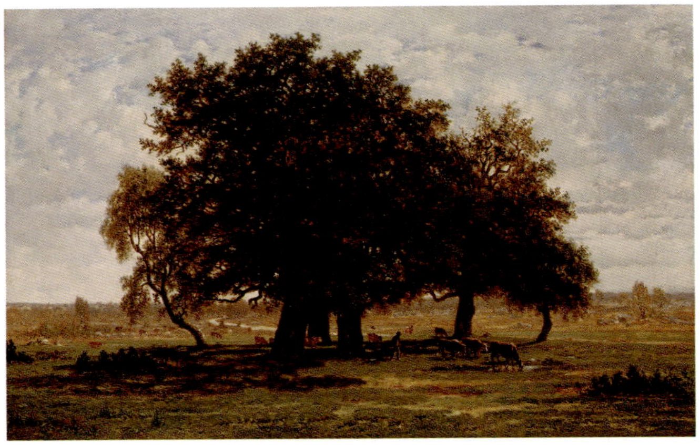

FIG. 64 Théodore Rousseau, *Group of Oaks in the Gorges d'Apremont*, 1852. Oil on canvas, 25 × 39¼ in. (63.5 × 99.7 cm). Musée du Louvre, Paris

. . . sow in profusion uncountable quantities of Northern Pines that are wiping out the forest's old Gaul character and will soon give us the severe and sad look of Russian forests."[4] This development was particularly evident on the Gorges d'Apremont, which "will soon disappear under a thick layer of green Pines whose first shoots are appearing already."[5] Diaz undoubtedly agreed with Rousseau's sentiments: his painting emphasizes the expansiveness of an area of the plain that had not yet been cultivated by pine trees. —SK

1. Théophile Thoré, *Salon de 1844* (Paris: Alliance des Arts, 1844), 34: "un monceau de pierreries."

2. See Simon Kelly, '"This Dangerous Game': Rousseau, Diaz and the Uses of the Auction in the Marketing of Landscapes," in *Soil and Stone: Impressionism, Urbanism and Environment*, ed. Richard Thomson and Frances Fowle (Aldershot: Ashgate, 2003), 33–48.

3. See, for example, *The Approaching Storm* (Norton Simon Museum of Art, Pasadena, Calif.), *The Storm* (The National Gallery, London), and *The Storm* (The Walters Art Museum, Baltimore).

4. Translated and quoted in Greg Thomas, *Art and Ecology in Nineteenth-Century France: The Landscapes of Théodore Rousseau* (Princeton: Princeton University Press, 2000), 215.

5. Ibid., 216.

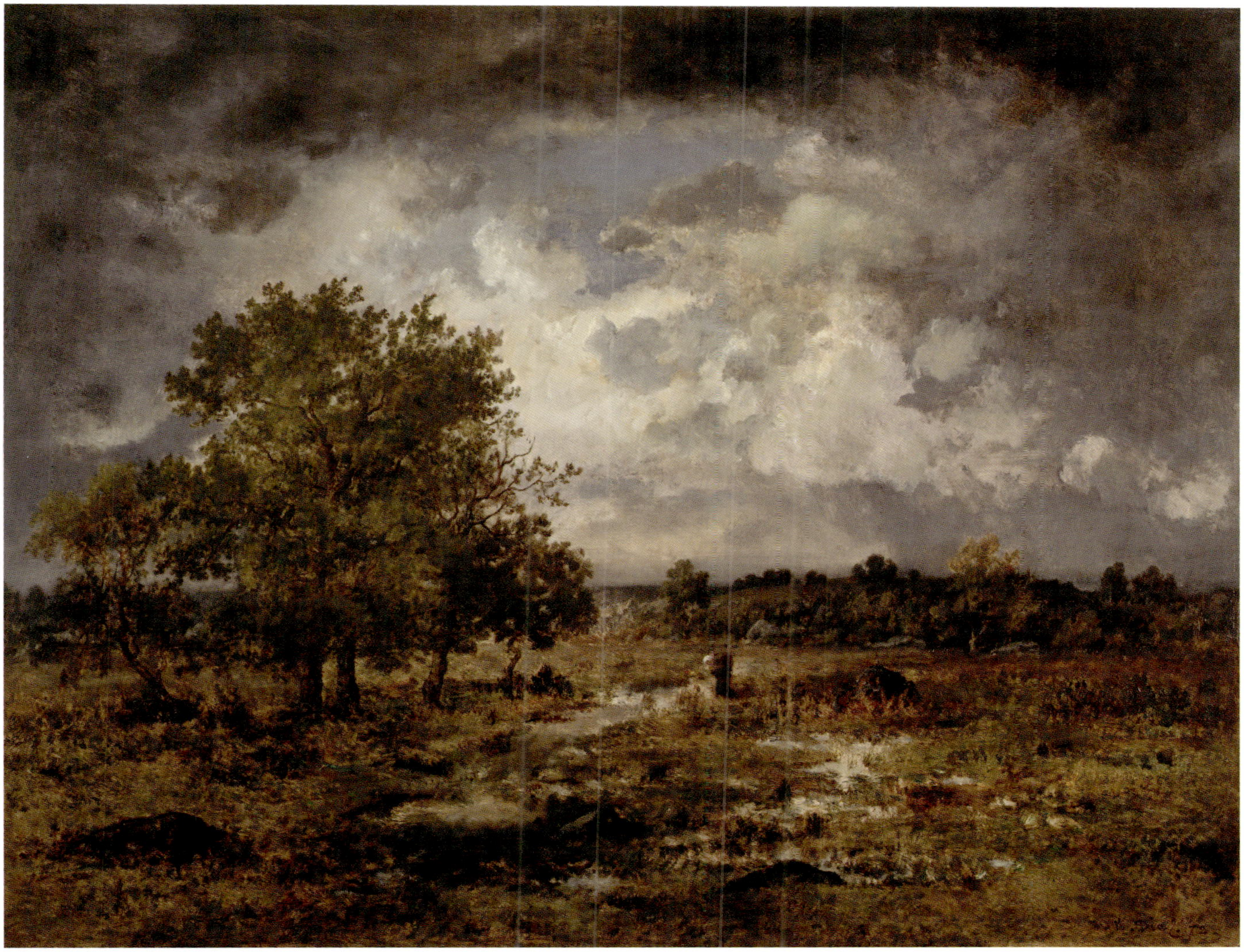

GUSTAVE LE GRAY

FRENCH, 1820–1884

44

Tree, Forest of Fontainebleau

ca. 1856

Albumenized salt print from collodion glass negative

12$\frac{9}{16}$ × 14$\frac{13}{16}$ in. (31.9 × 37.6 cm)

Museum of Fine Arts, Houston, Museum purchase with funds provided by the Brown Foundation Accessions Endowment Fund, The Manfred Heiting Collection, 2004.577

45

Beech Tree, Forest of Fontainebleau

ca. 1856

Albumen print from collodion glass negative

12½ × 16$\frac{5}{16}$ in. (31.8 × 41.4 cm)

National Gallery of Art, Washington, D.C., Patrons' Permanent Fund, 1995.36.93

GUSTAVE LE GRAY FIRST VENTURED into the Forest of Fontainebleau to make photographs in 1849. Those images, produced as salt prints from paper negatives, were his earliest attempts at artistic landscapes, produced at a time when he considered himself a painter as well as a photographer.[1] He submitted nine photographs to the Salon of 1850, including examples made in Fontainebleau, though the works were rejected once the selection committee realized that they were not lithographs.[2]

Le Gray's fervent desire to promote paper photography (as opposed to daguerreotypy) as an art form, rather than simply a tool of science, may have propelled him toward landscape, as it was a genre favored by several of photography's early critical voices, such as that of Paul Périer. In his review of the French photography shown at the 1855 Exposition universelle, Périer noted that of all the genres on display—picturesque views and landscapes, architecture, monuments and panoramic views, portraits, reproductions, genre, and science—landscapes were highly favored: "One must excuse us to decide the question of precedence after our predilections in favor of landscape. The contemplation of nature, the society of the woods, fields, large clouds, and vast horizons . . . have always seemed among the strongest among the quiet joys accorded to man."[3]

Francis Wey, also a critical voice in shaping early debates about photography, was a champion of Le Gray's photographic artistry. An art critic who lauded such painters as Paul Guigou, Paul Huet, and Jean-Baptiste-Camille Corot, Wey upheld the notion that "art should not be restrained to the servile imitation of nature."[4] To paint natural landscapes as experienced *en plein air* was to emphasize the artist's all-important individual interpretation of an actual subject, as opposed to re-creating a historical event from secondhand accounts in the form of history painting. Wey was also a strong proponent of realism (he championed Gustave Courbet's paintings and was a close friend of the painter), a term that first came into the discourse about 1851, at precisely the moment paper photography in France was gaining momentum among artistic amateurs and *peintres-photographes* like Le Gray. In carving out a critical niche for heliography, specifically, Wey believed that the calotype was eminently more suited to artistic transcription from nature than the daguerreotype. The calotype's ability to suppress a surfeit of details according to a "theory of sacrifices" allowed certain elements within a compositon to be rendered more sharply than others, which in turn permitted the artist better control over a scene's composition, based on a hierarchy of shape, form, and texture. The daguerreotype, in contrast, was far too harsh and direct in its transcriptions and thus incapable of achieving the same artistic status. Le Gray, in turn, upheld Wey's ideas in his own writings. In his 1852 technical treatise discussing the theory and practice

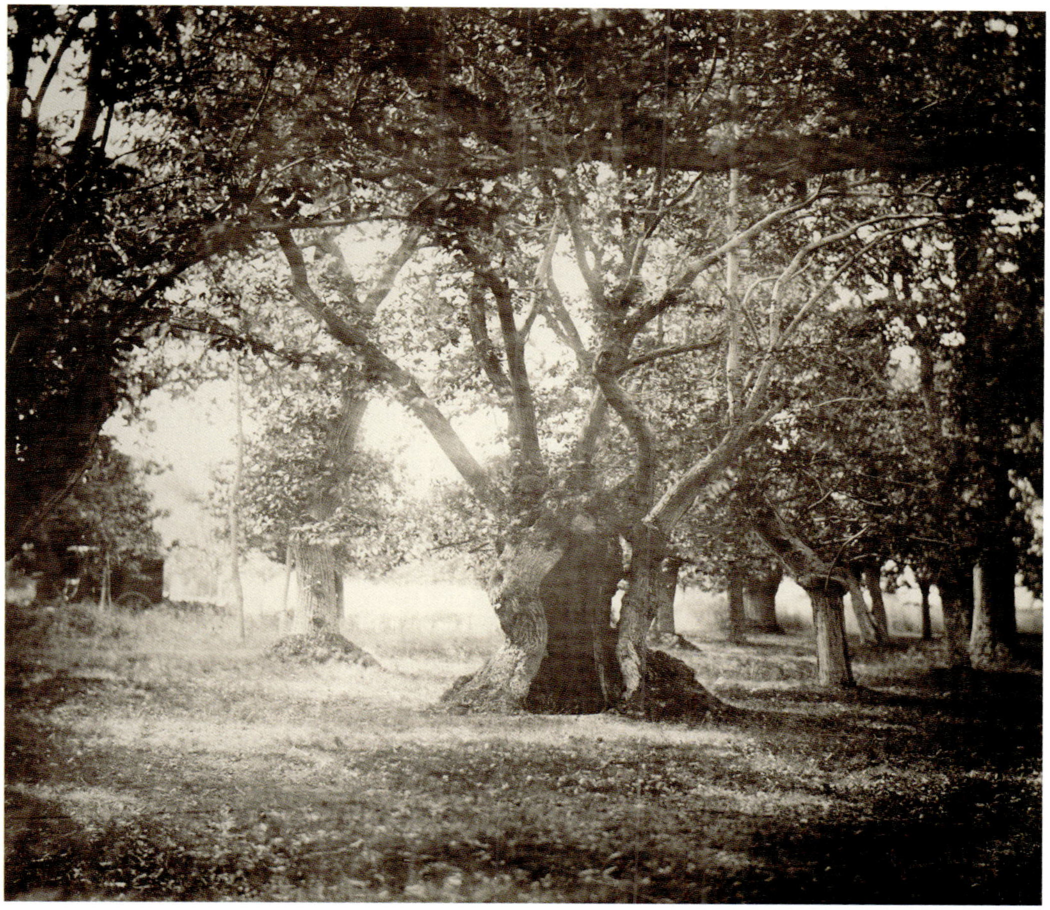

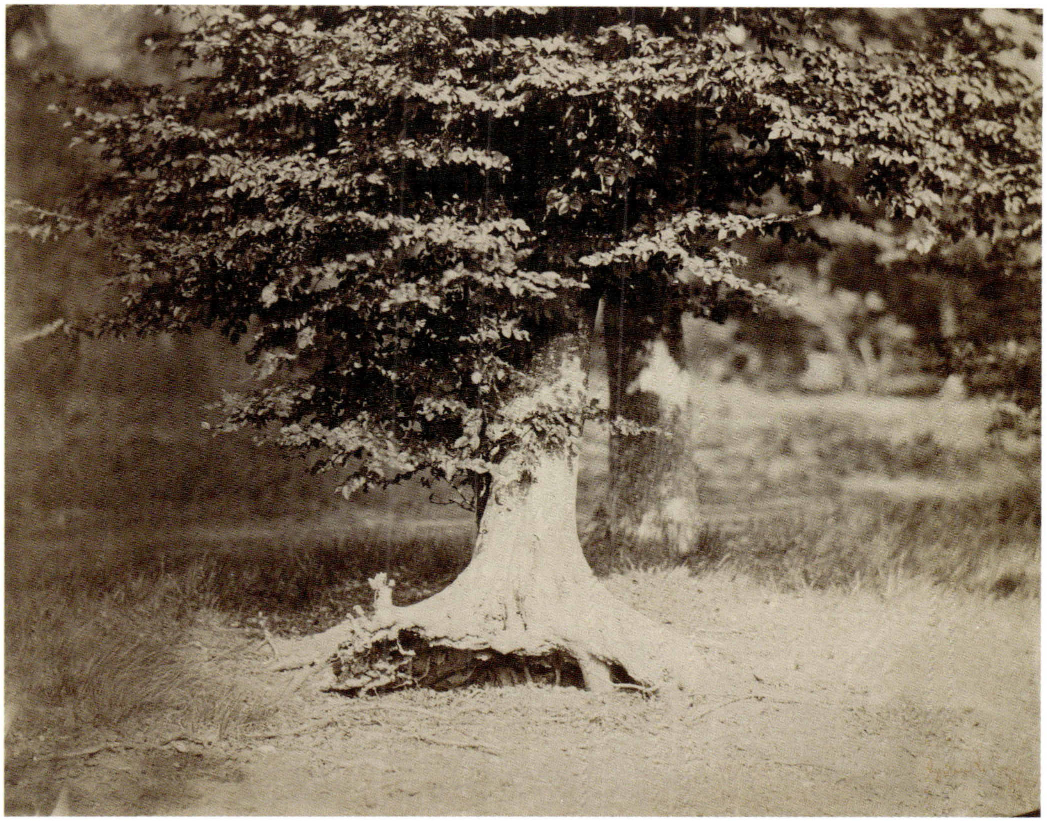

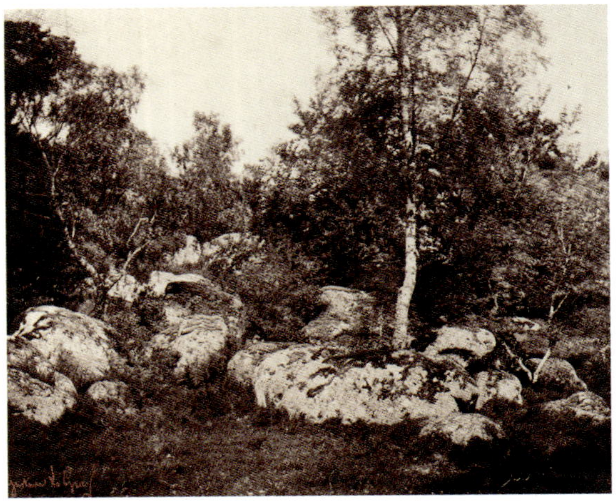

FIG. 65 Gustave Le Gray, *Forest Scene, Fontainebleau*, 1852. Albumenized or waxed salt print from waxed paper negative, 8⅛ × 10⅛ in. (20.6 × 25.7 cm). The Nelson-Atkins Museum of Art, Kansas City, Missouri, Gift of the Hall Family Foundation, 2006.44.12

of processing and manipulating paper and glass negatives, Le Gray specifically referenced the idea of the "theory of sacrifices": "In my opinion, the artistic beauty of a photographic print consists nearly always in the sacrifice of certain details, in a manner that produces a focus which sometimes approaches the sublime in art. . . . By varying the focus, the exposure time, the artist can make the most of one part or sacrifice another to produce powerful effects of light and shadow."[5] These aesthetic principles inform much of Le Gray's early Fontainebleau work.

By late 1850 or early 1851 Le Gray began to experiment with waxing his paper negatives, a technique he perfected and presented as his own invention to the Académie des sciences in February 1851. There were many advantages to this process: it allowed photographers to prepare negatives in advance; it helped to decrease development time; and it sharpened details by controlling (though not entirely eliminating) the diffusion of light as it passed through the fibrous paper substrate during printing. Because negatives could be prepared before going into the field, the process also lessened the physical load for photographers who traveled and thus facilitated a much greater degree of productivity: between twenty to thirty photographs per day were possible.[6] When Le Gray and Auguste Mestral collected images of the country's architectural patrimony for the state-sponsored Mission héliographique between June and September 1851, they worked exclusively with waxed paper negatives, having perfected the process's unique applications for architecture and landscape: its ability to render stone, foliage, and tree bark with rich tonal and textural subtlety.

By the time he ventured to Fontainebleau for a second major excursion into the forest in the spring or summer of 1852, Le Gray thus had extensive experience working outside the studio and better understood how the intricate forms of the natural world could be artistically transcribed in his photographs. This sensibility is evident in figure 65, in which he juxtaposed the rough-hewn textures of moss-covered rocks with the delicate lines of saplings. In general, Le Gray tended to photograph those sites that had fascinated the Barbizon painters Corot, Théodore Rousseau (e.g., cat. 40), and Narcisse-Virgile Diaz de la Peña, as well as the young Claude Monet, Pierre-Auguste Renoir, and Frédéric Bazille, among others. These subjects included the forest's venerated old-growth oaks in the Bas-Bréau, the lichen-covered boulders of the Gorges d'Apremont, and the tree-lined road to Chailly, which was the main coach route linking Paris and the forest.[7] As Eugenia Parry Janis suggested in her formative research on Le Gray, it is also likely that the photographer saw commercial viability in his choice of subject, particularly after tourism to the forest accelerated during the 1850s as a result of the direct rail line from Paris and the easy availability of Claude-François Denecourt's guidebooks.[8] Denecourt played up the historical and nationalistic resonances of the forest's great oak trees, whose hardy longevity made them a national symbol.

Le Gray's later Fontainebleau photographs of 1855–57 also show evidence of careful framing. In his image of a hollowed oak tree (cat. 44), Le Gray included a strong horizontal *repoussoir* in the form of a tree branch that extends over the entirety of the image's top portion. The effect is not unlike that of a curtain, raised to call attention to this unqiue arboreal specimen: with its dark internal cavity, splayed trunk, and twisted limbs, it takes center stage in Le Gray's composition. In another of his striking later photographs, Le Gray moved in even closer to his subject, focusing on a beech tree whose roots have begun to lift from the forest floor (cat. 45). Le Gray placed the bottom portion of the tree in the center of his photograph, orchestrating light and shadow such that the specimen seems intensely spotlit, emphasizing the venerable tree's plight as it appears to hover on the brink of toppling over. The bold simplicity of this composition, compared with his earlier views, demonstrates just how far Le Gray had progressed in his aesthetic conceptions of the forest, from quiet immersion and wonder to full, dramatic engagement with specific features.[9]

The significance of composition as a fundamental aspect of French painting—indeed, as a nationalistic trait—was noted by the art critic Théophile Thoré in his discussion of landscape paintings at the 1844 Salon: "the quality of composition is that which distinguishes our national artists, it is the principle of life."[10] Le Gray, whose training as a painter would have made him cognizant of this discourse, used the forms he found in the Forest of Fontainebleau to make unique compositions that could easily be considered as deriving from such a tradition. That the forest itself was deeply invested with French history makes Le Gray's Fontainebleau photographs rife with nationalistic resonances, in terms of both their subject matter and their style. Though many photographers—both artistocratic amateurs and those with commerical intent—traveled from Paris to Fontainebleau to try their hand at capturing the unique and savage beauty of the forest, Le Gray crafted a distinct vision. It would be left to his younger contemporary, Eugène Cuvelier, to produce a body of work as ambitious in its innovative artistry and evocation as Le Gray's. —AMW

1. As was common for many aspiring artists, Le Gray studied in Italy from 1843 to 1844. In 1848 he exhibited two paintings at the annual Salon in Paris. See annotated chronology in Eugenia Parry Janis, *The Photography of Gustave Le Gray*, exh. cat. (Chicago: Art Institute of Chicago; University of Chicago Press, 1987), 168–69.

2. The French art critic Francis Wey recounted Le Gray's experience at the 1850 Salon, noting: "Evidently, heliography proceeds from chemistry and physics; but from all evidence here, day by day, it is called to exert an immediate and profound influence on the domain of art." Wey, "De l'influence de l'héliographie sur les beaux-arts," *La lumière*, February 9, 1851, 2: "Evidemment, l'héliographie procède de la chimie et de la physique; mais, de toute evidence aussi, cette découverte perfectionnée de jour en jour, en appelée à exercer dans le domaine d'art une influence immédiate et profonde."

3. Paul Périer, "Exposition universelle 3ième article—Photographes français," *Bulletin de la Société française de la photographie*, July 20, 1855: "On nous excusera de trancher la question de préséance d'après nos prédilections déclarées en faveur du paysage. Le contemplation de la nature, la société des bois, des champs, des grands nuages et des vastes horizons . . . nous ont toujours semblé l'un des plus vifs, parmi les bonheurs tranquilles et partant durables accordés à l'homme ici-bas."

4. Quoted in Anne de Mondenard, "Entre romantisme et réalisme: Francis Wey (1812–1882), critique d'art," *Études photographiques*, no. 8 (November 2000): 24: "l'art ne doit pas être restraint à l'imitation servile de la nature."

5. Gustave Le Gray, *Photographie: Traité nouveau théorique et pratique des procédés et manipulations sur papier et sur verre* (Paris: Lerebours et Secrétan, 1852), 1–2; quoted in Sylvie Aubenas and Paul-Louis Roubert, *Primitifs de la photographie: Le calotype en France, 1843–1860*, exh. cat. (Paris: Gallimard; Bibliothèque Nationale de France, 2010), 92: "À mon point de vue, la beauté artistique d une épreuve photographique consiste au contraire preseque toujours dans le sacrifices des certains détails, de manière à produire une mise à l'effet qui va parfois jusqu'au sublime de l'art. . . . En variant la mise au point, le temps de pose, l'artiste peut faire valoir ou sacrifier telle ou telle partie, produire un effet puissant d'ombres et des clairs." Translated and quoted in André Jammes and Eugenia Parry Janis, *The Art of French Calotype with a Critical Dictionary of Photographers, 1845–1870* (Princeton: Princeton University Press, 1983), 202.

6. Sylvie Aubenas, *Gustave Le Gray, 1820–1884*, exh. cat. (Los Angeles: J. Paul Getty Museum, 2002), 260.

7. For a full exploration of the connections between painters and photographers in Fontainebleau, see Kimberly Jones et al., *In the Forest of Fontainebleau: Painters and Photographers from Corot to Monet*, exh. cat. (Washington, D.C.: National Gallery of Art, 2008).

8. Janis, *The Photography of Gustave Le Gray*, 47.

9. By about 1855 Le Gray began working with wet-collodion glass-plate negatives and albumen paper, a combination that rendered subjects in sharper detail than the waxed paper process. The enhanced contrast afforded by this process as compared with paper negatives also contributed to a bold, overall rendering.

10. T. Thoré, *Le Salon de 1844, précédé d'une lettre à Théodore Rousseau* (Paris: Alliance des Arts, 1844), 4: "La qualité de la composition est ce qui distingue nos artistes nationaux, et c'est là leur principe de vie."

EUGÈNE CUVELIER

FRENCH, 1837–1900

46

Untitled

ca. 1857–63

Albumen print from paper negative

7⅞ × 10¼ in. (20 × 26.1 cm)

The Nelson-Atkins Museum of Art, Kansas City, Missouri, Gift of the Hall Family Foundation, 2008.13.8

47

Sands of Macherin

ca. 1863

Salt print from paper negative

7¹³⁄₁₆ × 10¼ in. (19.8 × 26.1 cm)

The Nelson-Atkins Museum of Art, Kansas City, Missouri, Gift of the Hall Family Foundation, 2007.21.9

EUGÈNE CUVELIER PRODUCED perhaps the richest and most artistically varied body of photographs of the Forest of Fontainebleau, focusing almost exclusively on its diverse landscape for his life's work. Through the friendships of his father, Adalbert, with a group of artists in Cuvelier's hometown of Arras, Eugène came to know Jean-Baptiste-Camille Corot, who was a friend of the painter Constant Dutilleux. Dutilleux, the center of Arras's small artistic circle, made annual visits to Barbizon between 1851 and 1864. Corot visited Dutilleux in Arras in 1851 and the following year met Adalbert Cuvelier, who taught him the cliché-verre process. Eugène, who learned photography from his father and studied painting with Dutilleux, thus grew up in a fertile artistic milieu. Beginning in 1855 the adolescent Eugène accompanied Dutilleux on his teacher's regular sojourns to Barbizon. There, he met Louise Ganne, the daughter of the innkeeper, François, who operated the village's Auberge Ganne. This small inn served as the primary meeting place for artists such as Théodore Rousseau, Jean-François Millet, Charles-François Daubigny, and Paul Huet. When Eugène and Louise married in 1859, several painters were in attendance: Corot served as a witness, and both Millet and Rousseau were the men of honor.[1] From that point forward, with a few occasional views made in and around Arras, Cuvelier made Barbizon his home, and until his death in 1900, Eugène focused primarily on the landscape of Fontainebleau and the village environs.

Cuvelier rarely exhibited his work during his lifetime. Though he joined the Société française de la photographie in 1855, he does not seem to have been an active member, exhibiting his landscape views there only three times, in 1864, 1869, and 1870. He never operated a commercial studio or print-selling establishment, though he did sell some of his photographs to visiting artists, at times creating photographs of a specific point of view on request.[2] Unlike more commercially minded photographers like Gustave Le Gray, Cuvelier made only a few prints of each subject. Often, each print has a distinctive tonality, ranging from warm bisters to deep, rich purples, owing to variances in chemicals and development. Professionals tended to avoid this lack of standardization. Cuvelier's extensive and deliberate use of the paper negative, well past the time other photographers had turned exclusively to collodion on glass, suggests that he preferred the medium's capacities for rendering the transient effects of light and shadow with great tonal sensitivity and nuance, an aesthetic attesting to his painterly sensibilities.

Most of Cuvelier's subjects were easily accessible on foot from Barbizon: the Bas-Bréau, known for its old-growth trees (cat. 46); the spare, sandy expanses of the Macherin

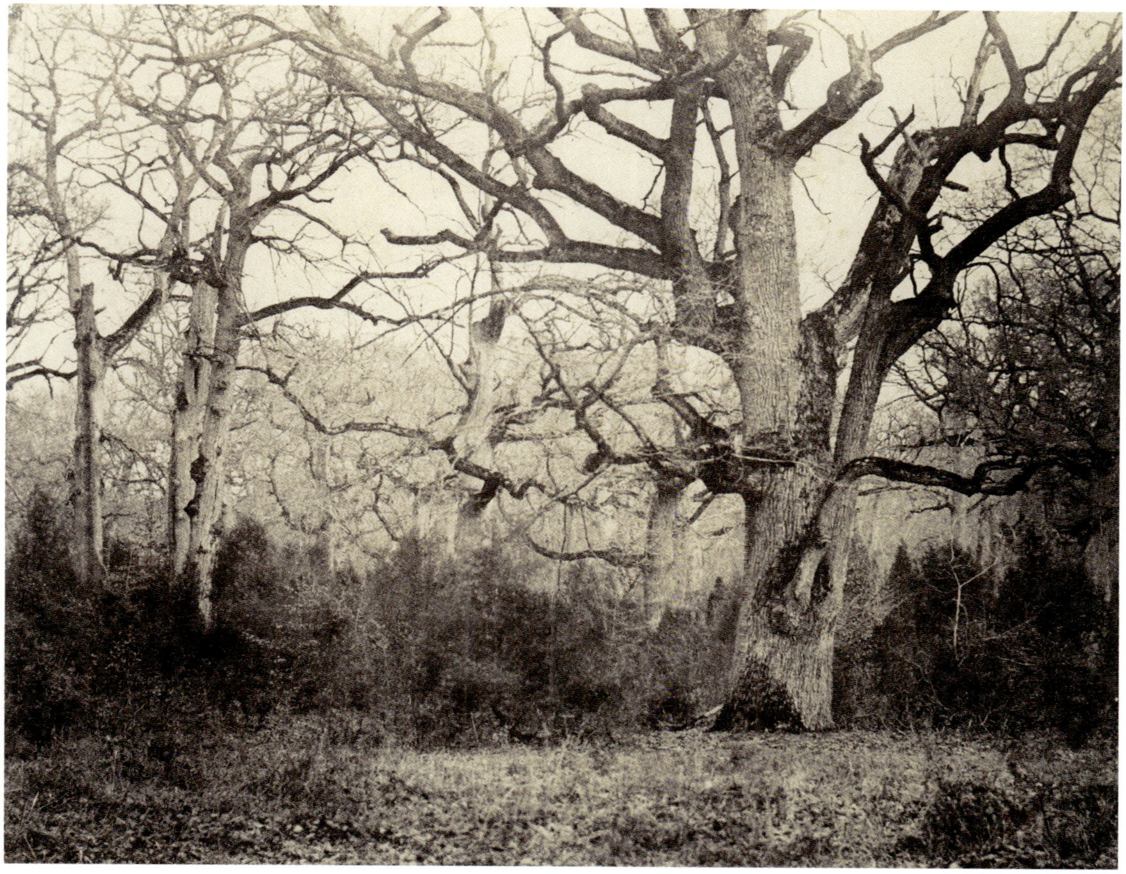

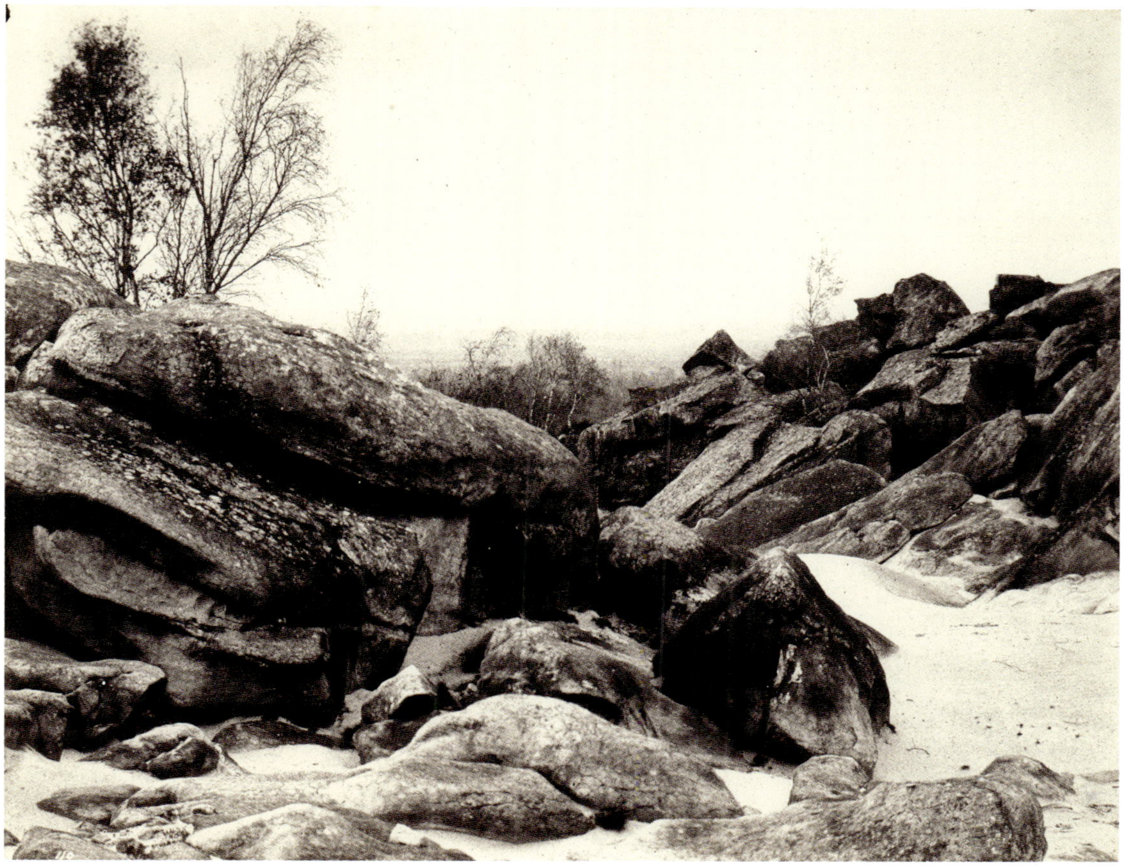

48

EUGÈNE CUVELIER
FRENCH, 1837–1900

The Clovis Oak

ca. 1860s

Salt print from paper negative

13⁵⁄₁₆ × 10 in. (33.8 × 25.4 cm)

The Nelson-Atkins Museum of Art, Kansas City, Missouri, Gift of the Hall Family Foundation in honor of the 75th anniversary of The Nelson-Atkins Museum of Art, 2007.21.7

(cat. 47); and the complex, marshy terrain of the Belle-Croix plateau. He also made many photographs in and around the village of Barbizon, focusing on the town's rustic dwellings, stone walls, and small, unpaved roadways. Though many of Cuvelier's photographs eschew the signs of tourism that were well in place by the 1860s, some images reference the forest's best-known features, which were outlined in Claude-François Denecourt's tourist guidebooks of the time. In one photograph, featuring the well-known Clovis Oak, Cuvelier depicted the tree in a state well past the age that it might have been harvested for timber (cat. 48). The dark recess of its hollowed trunk is given compositional strength through the contrast resulting from a salt print made from a paper negative. This tree, located in the Belle-Croix plateau, was named for the Frankish king Clovis (ca. 466–511), who ruled the kingdom of Gaul during the fifth century. Venerated as France's first Catholic ruler, Clovis united many Frankish tribes to drive the Romans from the area that now makes up parts of northern France and Belgium.

Oaks were considered France's national tree; their historical and symbolic associations extended back to the time of Gaul's Druidic culture. In the 1839 and 1840 editions of his *Guide du voyageur dans le palais et la forêt de Fontainebleau*, Denecourt featured the Clovis Oak as a site in the first of five suggested promenades, along with the "colossal and wildest" Charlemagne Oak, the Sully Oak (named for the duc de Sully, who was Henri IV's minister), and other trees named for the Frankish king Pharamond (ca. 370–437), the White Queen, and the more generic Bouquet of the King and Bouquet of the Queen.[3] By anthropomorphizing certain specimens and aligning them with France's historical rulers, Denecourt marked this "natural" landscape with nationalistic resonances, to appeal to the influx of urban tourists eager to escape the physical and psychic stresses of Parisian bourgeois life.

Taken collectively, however, Cuvelier's photographs were not meant as tourist souvenirs, despite the fact that his choice of subject matter may well have been guided by Denecourt's entrepreneurial vision. Unlike Le Gray, who lived in Paris and made trips to the forest to make photographs for both personal and professional reasons, or the photographers Achille Quinet and Alfred Briquet, who produced views purely for commercial purposes, Cuvelier was a sophisticated amateur, who paired his artistic training as a painter with his intimate knowledge of Fontainebleau to craft a complex vision of the forest, one that was neither the primeval vision of the Romantics nor the crowded, urban bourgeois retreat into "nature." —AMW

1. Malcolm Daniel, *Eugène Cuvelier: Photographer in the Circle of Corot*, exh. cat. (New York: Metropolitan Museum of Art, 1996), 4–5.

2. Sylvie Aubenas and Paul-Louis Roubert, *Primitifs de la photographie: Le calotype en France, 1843–1860*, exh. cat. (Paris: Gallimard; Bibliothèque nationale de France, 2010), 271.

3. Claude-François Denecourt, *Guide du voyageur dans le palais et la forêt de Fontainebleau* (Fontainebleau, 1840), 90. Nicholas Green notes that the 1839 and 1840 editions, which combined two separate brochures on the palace and the forest into one publication, were virtually identical. Green, *The Spectacle of Nature: Landscape and Bourgeois Culture in Nineteenth-Century France* (Manchester: Manchester University Press, 1990), 212n93.

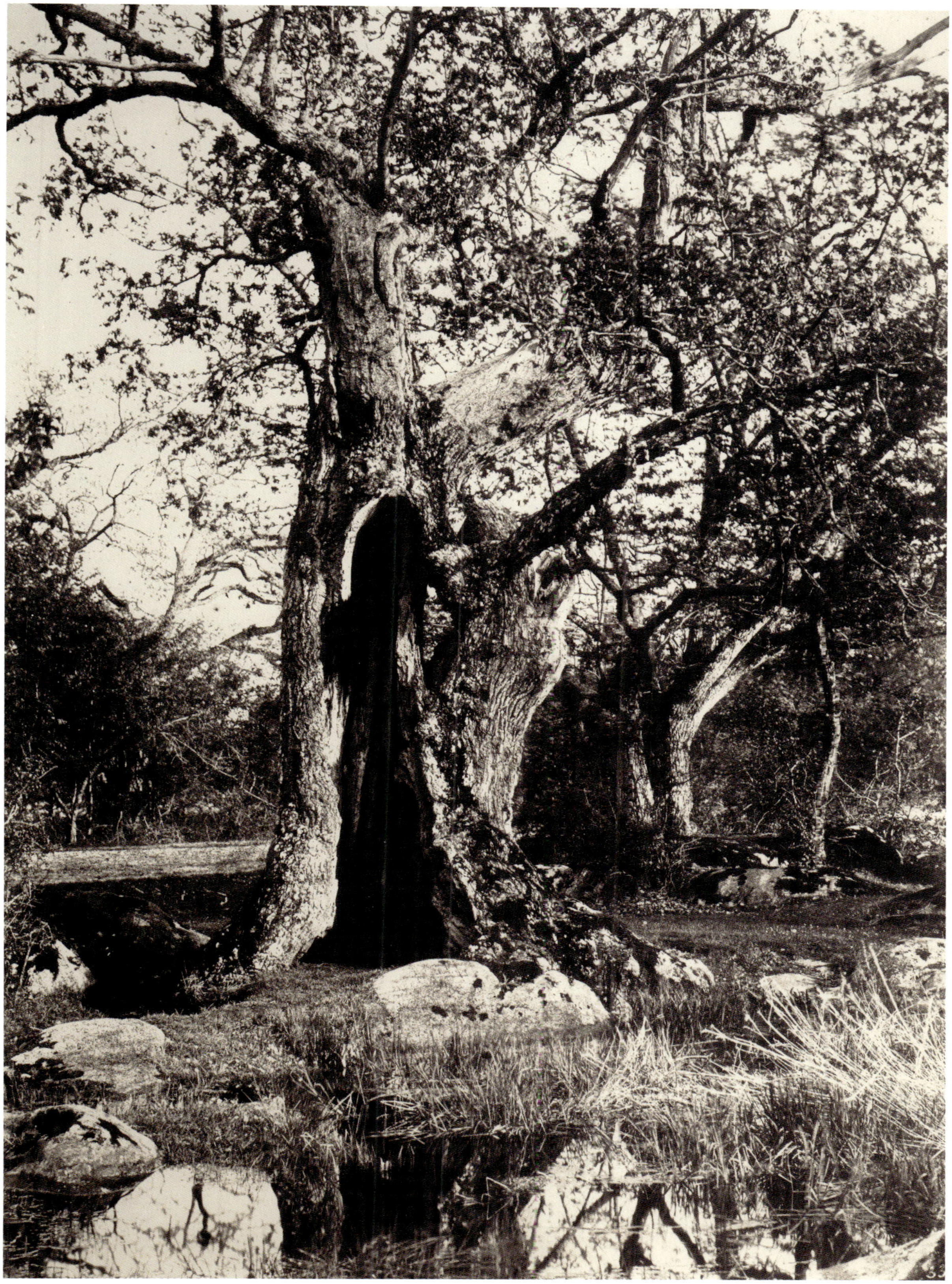

49

GUSTAVE DORÉ
FRENCH, 1832–1883

Deer in a Pine Forest (Vosges)

ca. 1865

Oil on canvas

76⅞ × 51⅜ in. (195 × 130 cm)

Carnegie Museum of Art, Pittsburgh, Gift of the family of Tillie S. Speyer in her memory, 80.9

GUSTAVE DORÉ'S PAINTING was previously titled *Forest at Twilight* but can be identified for the first time here as the picture that appeared in the artist's posthumous sale as *Deer in a Pine Forest (Vosges)*.[1] Doré represented a luminous, spotlit forest clearing in which a small stream trickles down the center foreground. The painting has a red studio stamp at bottom center, indicating it was included in the artist's studio sale after his death. As a young boy, Doré had explored the forests and mountains of the Vosges in eastern France, and he retained a lifelong love of this region, producing several pictures of the area.[2] Here, Doré depicted the forest in thick, impasted brushwork, giving it a sense of materiality, whereas the light falling into the clearing has an almost mystical, fairy-tale quality. Doré was well known as a book illustrator, and we can imagine this scene as a setting for his literary illustrations.[3] The presence of the deer may reflect the artist's interest in the work of Gustave Courbet.

The Vosges region stands on the western border of Alsace, a region of particular importance in defining the French nation in the nineteenth and early twentieth centuries. During this period, Alsace passed back and forth between France and Germany and became a symbol of wider nationalistic aspirations. Doré himself was Alsatian, having been born in the region's capital of Strasbourg, and was thus especially sensitive to the unstable history of the area. Doré felt the cession of Alsace to Germany in 1871 following the Franco-Prussian War as a national humiliation, and he made it the subject of several of his works, such as the allegorical *Wounded Alsace* (*L'Alsace meurtrie*) (fig. 66). In this painting, Alsace is represented as a woman in traditional Alsatian dress who holds the French flag tightly to her breast. The "wounded" woman mourns both the loss of her husband (an orphaned son is visible in the shadows behind her) and her French homeland. The Treaty of Frankfurt of May 10, 1871, had given Alsatians a stark choice: either leave the region and remain French or stay and become German.[4]

In painting *Deer in a Pine Forest (Vosges)*, Doré was therefore representing an important and contested location for France.[5] The scale and ambition of the work suggest that the artist intended it as an exhibition picture, but we have no evidence of this. The date, too, is unclear, although related works suggest that it may have been done in the mid-1860s. Despite these uncertainties, the work is emblematic of Doré's intense regional patriotism and his belief in the importance of the Vosges to the French nation. —SK

1. *Catalogue des tableaux, études et esquisses par feu Gustave Doré* (Paris: Hôtel Drouot, April 11–15, 1885), no. 50: "Biches dans une forêt de sapins (Vosges). Toile. Haut., 1m.95 cent; larg., 1m.30 cent."

2. In the Paris Salon of 1861, for example, he showed *A Small Valley in the Vosges: Morning* (private collection).

3. See particularly the forest illustrations for "Tom Thumb" ("Le Petit Poucet"), in *Les contes de Perrault, dessins par Gustave Doré* (Paris: J. Hetzel, 1867), http://gallica.bnf.fr/ark:/12148/bpt6k54186157, opp. 4.

4. See *Gustave Doré, un peintré né*, exh. cat. (Bourg-en-Bresse: Monastère Royal de Brou, 2012), 127. For the loss of Alsace, see Philippe Kaenel, "'L'Année terrible': Vue rapportée, caricaturée, reimaginée et allegorisée par Gustave Doré," in *Qu'est-ce que la guerre?*, dir. Yohan Ariffin and Anne Bielmann Sanchez (Lausanne: PPUR, Antipodes, 2012), 217–40.

5. Much of the Vosges region, including possibly the area in Doré's painting, remained with France after this treaty.

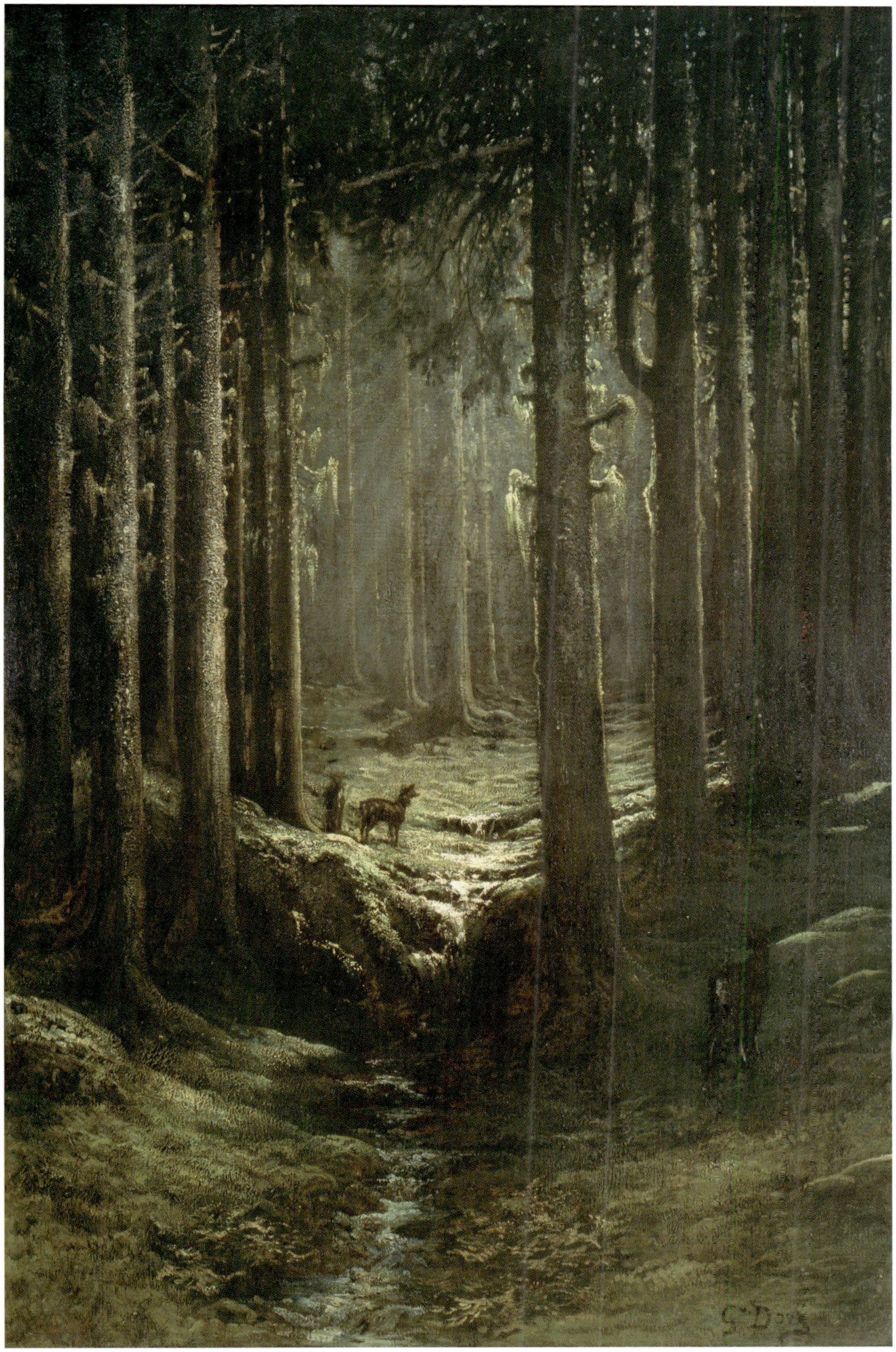

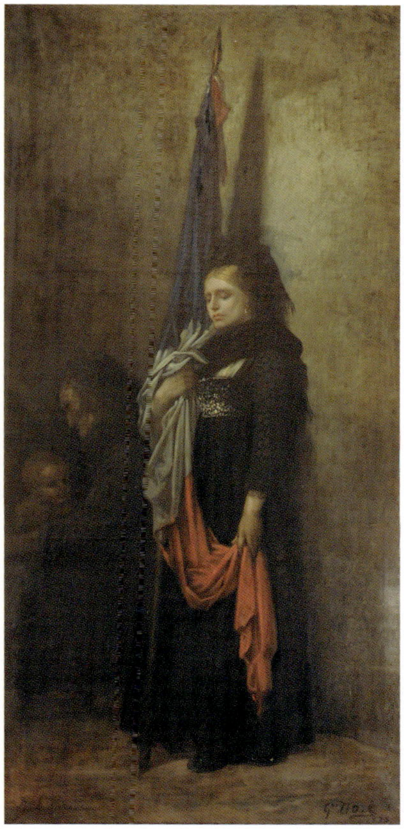

FIG. 66 Gustave Doré, *Wounded Alsace* (*L'Alsace meurtrie*), 1871. Oil on canvas, 138 × 70⅞ in. (350.5 × 180 cm). Département du Haut-Rhin, Colmar

50

CHARLES-FRANÇOIS DAUBIGNY

FRENCH, 1817–1878

Banks of the Oise at Auvers

1863

Oil on canvas

35 × 63½ in. (88.9 × 161.3 cm)

Saint Louis Art Museum, Friends Endowment, and gift of Justina G. Catlin in memory of her husband, Daniel Catlin, by exchange, 84:2007

CHARLES-FRANÇOIS DAUBIGNY was the best-known painter of rivers in mid-nineteenth-century France and enjoyed great commercial success with his tranquil riverine views. He focused particularly on representing the rivers around Paris, the Seine and its tributary, the Oise. Daubigny's river views were underpinned by diligent outdoor study, and in 1857 he constructed a studio boat, Le botin, to facilitate his study. This large-scale work shows a view of the Oise at Auvers, some twenty miles north of Paris, where Daubigny had built a house and studio in 1860. The picture is bathed in a soft, even light and highlights the artist's mastery of atmospheric effect. Daubigny animated the scene with a group of fishermen, but it is unclear if these are local peasants or tourists visiting from Paris (the woman to the left appears to be wearing a bourgeois yellow hat). Farther into the distance, a horse walks along a towpath. The Oise River was at this time becoming increasingly industrialized as factories sprang up along its banks (see cats. 82–84). Daubigny, however, screened out these modern elements, presenting an idyllic vision of the river.

Daubigny exhibited *Banks of the Oise at Auvers* at the 1863 Paris Salon. Critical response to the picture was positive and focused on the painting's atmospheric naturalism. The critic Émile Cantrel praised the artist as one "who seeks, surprises, and interprets in a quite personal manner the most fresh mysteries of nature, water and shadows."[1] Paul Mantz extolled the picture as an example of Daubigny's characteristic "restrained landscapes, full of tender greenery, bathed in an exquisite gray haze, such as one can see in the environs of Paris. M. Daubigny excels in his representations of a nature softened and without grandeur, although not without charm."[2] Alphonse Audéoud wrote of Daubigny's "gray and veiled painting."[3]

Daubigny kept careful account books of his sales, and this work appears in his record of 1863, where it was noted as having been sold for the substantial sum of four thousand francs to a M. Perrier, a wealthy businessman in the Champagne industry, based in Épernay in northeastern France.[4] Daubigny had initially requested five thousand francs but seems to have been happy with the sale and is known to have visited Perrier in August 1863 to assist in the hanging of the painting.[5] In the years to come, Daubigny would produce numerous variants of his Oise views, enjoying significant patronage not only in France but also with foreign collectors in the United States and Russia. Indeed, the artist produced a smaller variant of this painting, also in 1863 (private collection), although it is unclear if it is a sketch or a subsequent work.[6] *Banks of the Oise at Auvers* remained in the Perrier family until it was acquired by the Saint Louis Art Museum in 2007. —SK

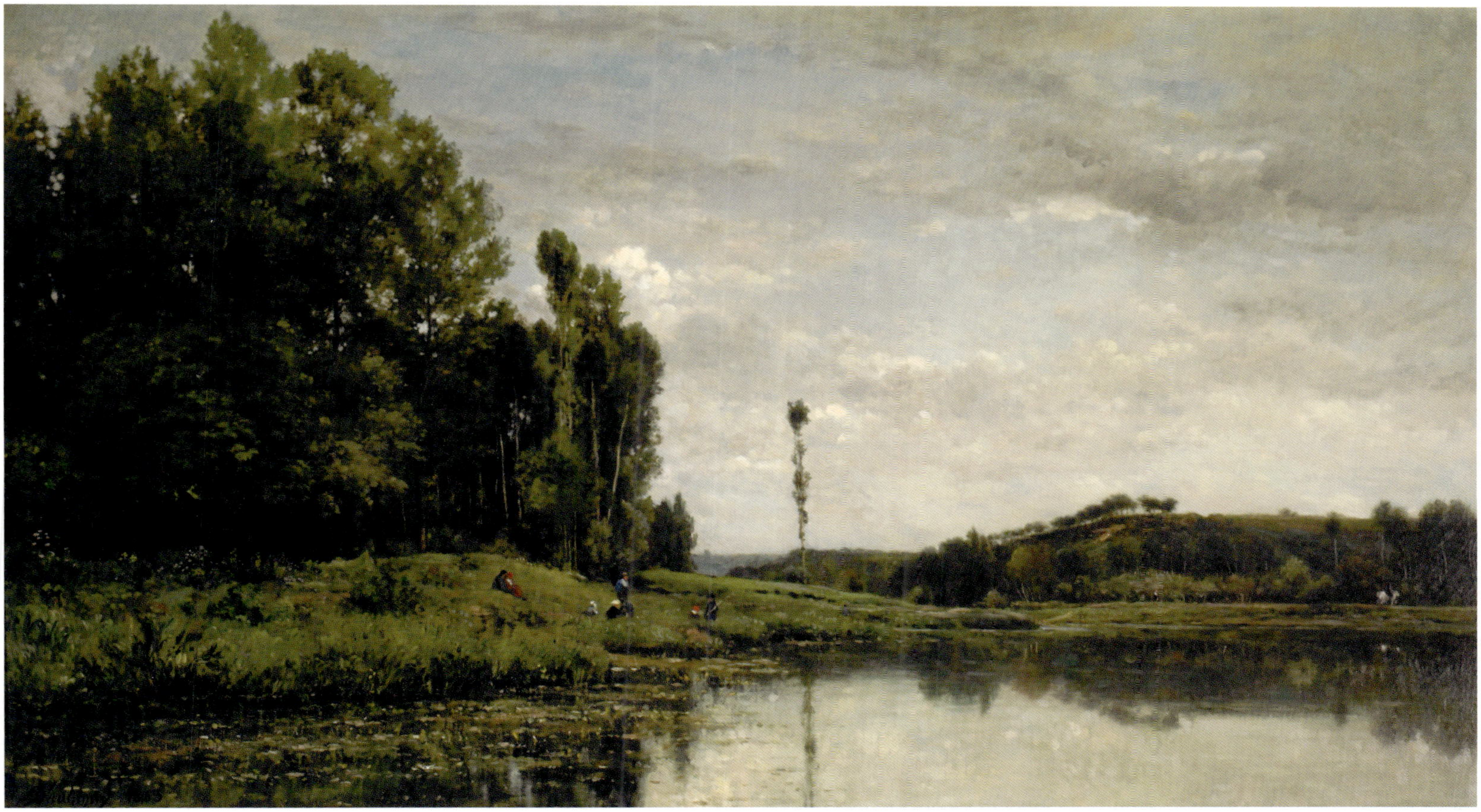

1. Émile Cantrel, "Salon de 1863: L'art," *L'artiste*, no. 9 (May 1, 1863): 199: "un paysagiste qui cherche, qui surprend, et qui interprète d'une façon toute personelle les plus frais mystères de la nature, des eaux et des ombrages."

2. Paul Mantz, "Salon de 1863," *Gazette des beaux-arts* 15 (1863): 39: "paysages modérés, pleins de tendres verdures, baignés de vapeurs d'un gris fin, tels que ceux qu'on peut voir dans les environs de Paris. M. Daubigny excelle dans ces représentations d'une nature adoucie et sans grandeur, sinon sans charme."

3. Alphonse Audéoud, "Exposition de 1863," *Revue indépendante*, September 1, 1863, 129: "sa peinture grise et voilée."

4. The record of the sale appears in one of Daubigny's extant stockbooks accompanied by a small pen-and-ink illustration of the picture, reproduced in Robert Hellebranth, *Charles-François Daubigny, 1817–1878* (Morges: Matute, 1976), 335. The drawing appears with the inscription "Les Pêcheurs à la Ligne, Exposition de 1863, 4,000 francs à M. Ch. Perrier."

5. Daubigny also intended to show *Banks of the Oise at Auvers* at the prestigious Parisian gallery of Louis Martinet in the summer of 1863, yet it is unclear if the work ever appeared there. In a note of July 2, 1863, to Martinet, Daubigny affirmed: "The price of painting . . . no. 513 [*Banks of the Oise at Auvers*] is 5,000" (Le prix de tableau . . . no. 513 [*Banks of the Oise at Auvers*], est de 5,000). See Étienne Moreau-Nélaton, *Daubigny raconté par lui-même* (Paris: H. Laurens, 1925), 83.

6. See *Fishermen on the Banks of the Oise* (*Pêcheurs au bord de l'Oise*), in Robert Hellebranth and Anne Hellebranth, *Charles-François Daubigny, 1817–1878 (Supplément)* (n.p., 1996), 18, no. 53.

51

CLAUDE MONET
FRENCH, 1840–1926

Autumn on the Seine, Argenteuil

1873

Oil on canvas

21⅜ × 28⅞ in. (54.3 × 73.3 cm)

The High Museum of Art, Atlanta, Purchase with funds from the Forward Arts Foundation, The Buisson Foundation, Eleanor McDonald Storza Estate, Frances Cheney Boggs Estate, Katherine John Murphy Foundation, and High Museum of Art Enhancement Fund, 2000.205

CLAUDE MONET represented France's rivers throughout his entire career, culminating in the Water Lilies paintings of his Giverny pond, which was irrigated by water from the nearby river Epte, a tributary of the Seine. Later, during the 1890s, he created his well-known images of poplar trees along that same river: these, a well-known Revolutionary symbol of liberty, probably reference his lifelong nationalism.[1] Within critical discourse, Monet was discussed above all as a painter of water and reflections. The critic Théodore Duret, for example, identified him as "par excellence the painter of water."[2] In portraying rivers, Monet concentrated chiefly on the Seine, which he first painted in the mid-1860s and regularly depicted during his time in Argenteuil, from 1871 until 1878.

Autumn on the Seine, Argenteuil is a pastoral view of the Petit Bras (Little Arm), a branch of the Seine that splits from the main stream to go around a small island, the Île Marante, which is about a mile and a half long. Monet depicted a group of unmanned sailing boats moored alongside the island to the left, a black-hulled skiff prominent among them. The colorful foliage frames a hazy, distant view of Argenteuil with, on the left, the Château Michelet, built in a Louis Treize style in 1871, and, on the right, the 132-foot steeple of the town church, constructed in 1866. Monet's painting is notable for the incandescent yellows and oranges of the autumnal leaves. He also painted two related pictures, showing the same viewpoint.[3]

By including several boats in this picture, Monet referenced the importance of boating to Argenteuil. He had already represented boating as a leisure activity in his work of the 1860s, especially his views at Sainte-Adresse in 1867 (cat. 109). His move to Argenteuil provided further opportunity for him to explore this iconography. By the mid-1850s the town was the principal boating center around Paris. As one commentator noted, "Nowhere in the immediate vicinity of Paris does the Seine present to amateur boaters a basin as favorable in length and breadth as well as current as at Argenteuil."[4] In 1858 the Société des régates parisiennes set up its sailing club, the Cercle de voile, at Argenteuil, and nine years later, the town was the location for the international sailing competitions held in conjunction with the Exposition universelle in Paris. Between 1872 and 1875 Monet produced large numbers of paintings of sailing here. His works tapped into an existing tradition of pastoral river views, particularly associated with his friend Charles-François Daubigny, but differed in the choice of modern leisure boats as well as a much brighter palette. Indeed, it has been argued that the modernity of Monet's subjects and style had political connotations, and that these riverscapes were "increasingly aligned with the new educated middle-class values of secular republicanism."[5]

Autumn on the Seine, Argenteuil probably appeared with the title *Effet d'automne* (*Autumn Effect*) at the second Impressionist exhibition, which opened in April 1876.[6] It had been acquired on February 5 of that year by the important patron of the Impressionists Victor Chocquet for one hundred francs and was listed in the catalogue as belonging to this collector.[7] Critics focused on the picture's intense color.[8] E. F., for example, noted that the work was "a firework awash with Bengal flames."[9] Another critic, Émile Blémont, wrote that Monet made "orgies of the rainbow."[10] The poet Stéphane Mallarmé remarked: "Claude Monet loves water, and it is his especial gift to portray its mobility and transparency, be it sea or river, gray and monotonous, or colored by the sky. I have never seen a boat poised more lightly on the water than in his pictures, or a veil more mobile and

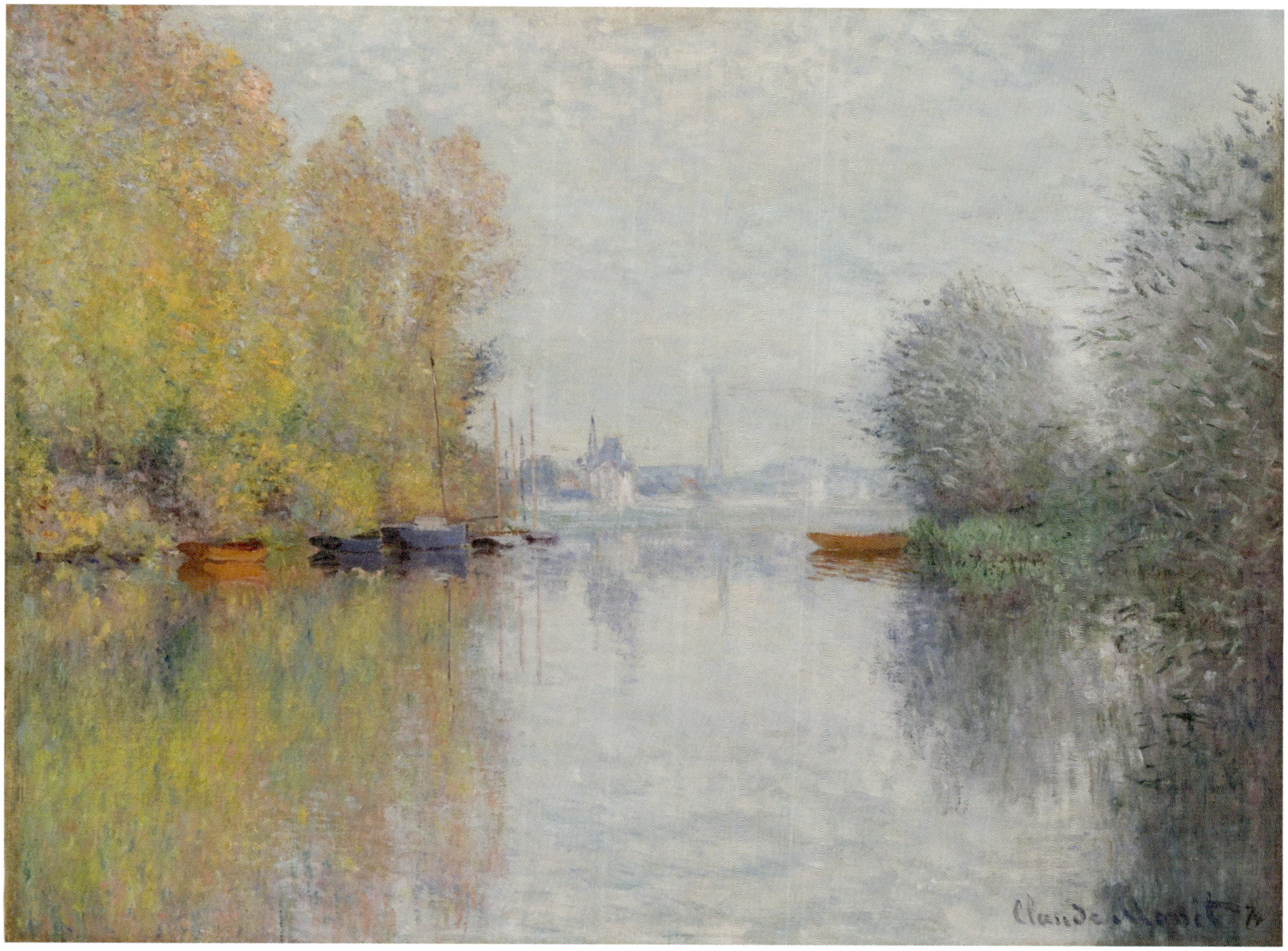

light than his moving atmosphere. It is in truth a marvel."[11] Considered alongside his images of modern bridges and factories, this work highlights the artist's engagement with Argenteuil's boating culture as another central aspect of the town's modernity. —SK

1. Paul Hayes Tucker, *Monet in the '90s: The Series Paintings*, exh. cat. (Boston: Museum of Fine Arts, 1990).

2. Théodore Duret, *Les peintres impressionistes* (Paris: H. Heymann & J. Perois, 1878), 19: "par excellence le peintre de l'eau."

3. *Argenteuil Seen from the Petit Bras of the Seine*, 1872 (Collection of Bob and Red Buisson, Atlanta; Daniel Wildenstein, *Monet*, vol. 2, *Catalogue raisonné* [Paris: Wildenstein Institute; Cologne: Taschen, 1996], no. 231), and *Autumn Effect at Argenteuil*, 1873 (Courtauld Institute of Art, London; Wildenstein, no. 290). See also *The Small Branch of the Seine at Argenteuil* (private collection, France; Wildenstein, no. 232), in which appears the same black-hulled boat as in the Atlanta picture.

4. Quoted in Paul Hayes Tucker, *Monet at Argenteuil* (New Haven: Yale University Press, 1982), 90.

5. Tricia Cusack, *Riverscapes and National Identities* (Syracuse, N.Y.: Syracuse University Press, 2010), 112.

6. The painting is inscribed 1874 at bottom right but is generally thought to have been painted in the fall of 1873. Monet often signed his works sometime later with inaccurate dates. In a note of 1889, he also remembered this painting as "Le Petit Bras, Argenteuil, automne 73." See Wildenstein, no. 291; and David A. Brenneman, *Monet: A View from the River*, exh. cat. (Atlanta: High Museum of Art, 2001), 47.

7. Ruth Berson, *The New Painting: Impressionism, 1874–1886; Documentation*, vol. 2, *Exhibited Works* (San Francisco: Fine Arts Museums of San Francisco, 1996), no. 158, *Effet d'Automne (appartient à M. Chocquet.)*. Monet titled the work "Esquisse (automne)" in his record of the sale in 1876 in his account book, Monet account book, 1872–76, Musée Marmottan Monet, Paris.

8. For a range of critical responses, see Brenneman, *Monet: A View from the River*, 35–39.

9. E. F., "Le groupe d'artistes de la rue Peletier," *Moniteur des arts*, April 21, 1867: "un feu d'artifice noyé dans les flammes de Bengale"; quoted in Berson, *The New Painting: Documentation*, vol. 1, *Reviews*, 83.

10. Émile Blémont, "Les impressionistes," *Le rappel*, April 9, 1876: "des orgies d'arc-en-ciel"; quoted in Berson, *Reviews*, 63.

11. Stéphane Mallarmé, "The Impressionists and Edouard Manet," *Art Monthly Review and Photographic Portfolio*, September 30, 1876; quoted in Berson, *Reviews*, 95.

HENRI-VICTOR REGNAULT
(PHOTOGRAPHER) FRENCH, 1810–1878

ALPHONSE-LOUIS POITEVIN
(PRINTER) FRENCH, 1819–1882

52

Sèvres, the Seine at Meudon

ca. 1853; printed 1855–60

Carbon print

12¼ × 16^{13}⁄16 in. (31.1 × 42.5 cm)

The J. Paul Getty Museum, Los Angeles, 92.XM.52

THE ART CRITIC THÉOPHILE THORÉ began his discussion of the 1844 Salon with a letter to his friend the painter Théodore Rousseau. In this missive, he expressed his desire for a more harmonious existence between nature and an increasingly industrialized and materialist socety. Though Thoré clearly felt that modernization threatened man's ability to immerse himself in nature (and thus renew his spirit), he was quick to acknowledge that one's Romantic yearnings for nature, art, and poetry were not incompatible with contemporary life. Rather, he asserted that men must reconcile their yearning for both pastoral escapes and social engagement to achieve a healthy, communal state of being. As he wrote: "It is not necessary, however, that love of nature, poetry, and art isolate us absolutely from men and society. On the contrary, this is the normal link between all men and all things."[1]

Photographers such as the chemist Henri-Victor Regnault, whose livelihood as director of the Manufacture impériale de Sèvres wholly depended on industrial progress, took up photography as an amateur pursuit, but he used it to create the kind of link between nature and industry that Thoré described. The majority of Regnault's photographs are landscapes or architectural views in and around Sèvres. At the same time he was making views of the factory grounds, he was creating artistic landscape studies that bore little or no trace of modern life. Indeed, Regnault seems to have taken an equal interest in both subjects, suggesting that he felt neither subject to be subservient to the other in aesthetic terms.

In this river scene, Regnault depicted an area along the Seine in nearby Meudon, one of the suburbs southwest of Paris. This region of Sèvres-Meudon attracted many landscape painters, including Jean-Baptiste-Camille Corot, Paul Huet, and Théodore Rousseau. Two of the Barbizon artists had direct ties to the neighborhood: Constant Troyon was born in Sèvres, and Narcisse-Virgile Diaz de la Peña grew up in Meudon.[2] Though the area was a thriving hub of commerce and industry—the river was one of the country's major waterways, and the docks at Sèvres housed most of the wine meant for Paris—Regnault's view includes none of that activity.[3] Instead, taking full advantage of the rectangle afforded by his large-format camera, he composed a thoroughly tranquil scene: the serene surface of the river recedes from foreground to middle ground, met by a tree-lined shore on the left and the more manicured riverbank fronting buildings to the right. The original, diffused tones of the salt print, which allowed for the diaphanous effects of light and mist that partially shroud the background, were effectively translated in Poitevin's carbon print from the negative (see cat. 53 for more on Alphonse-Louis Poitevin). This view, along with several others by Regnault, was included in Louis-Désiré Blanquart-Evrard's series *Études et paysages*, a portfolio that included works by Charles Marville as well as several works by unidentified photographers. It was printed and distributed between 1853 and 1854 and likely was intended as studies for painters.[4] —AMW

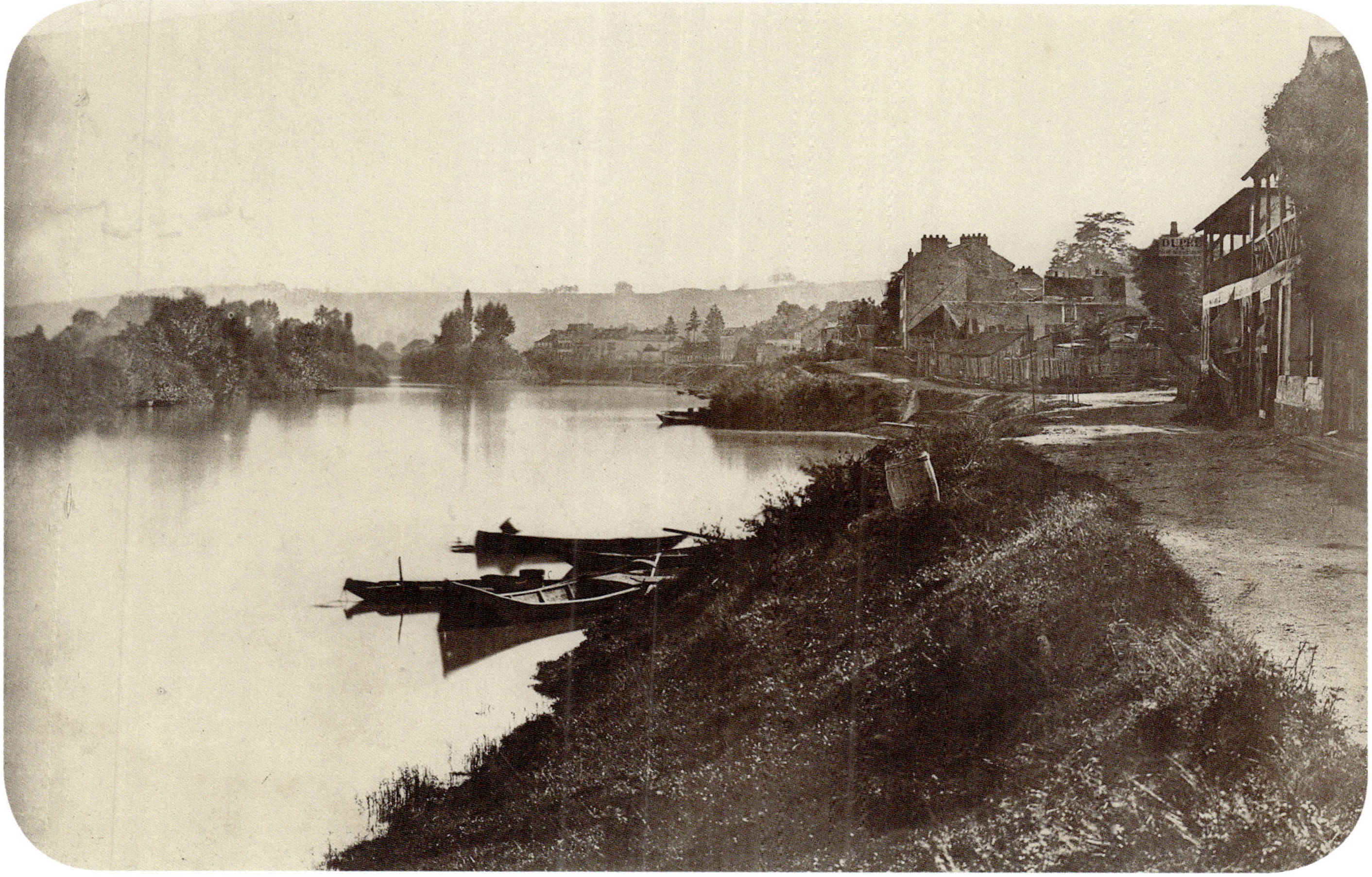

1. T. Thoré, *Le Salon de 1844, précédé d'une lettre à Théodore Rousseau* (Paris: Alliance des Arts, 1844), xxi: "Il ne faut pas cependant que l'amour de la nature, la poésie et l'art, nous isolent absolument des hommes et de la société. Bien au contraire, c'est là le lien normal de tous les hommes et de toutes les choses."

2. This history is outlined by Laurie Dahlberg in her formative study on Regnault, *Victor Regnault and the Advance of Photography: The Art of Avoiding Errors* (Princeton: Princeton University Press, 2005), 168.

3. Ibid., 169.

4. Reproduced in Isabelle Jammes, *Blanquart-Evrard et les origines de l'édition photographique français: Catalogue raisonné des albums photographiques éditiés, 1851–1855* (Geneva: Librairie Droz, 1981), 189.

ADALBERT CUVELIER
(PHOTOGRAPHER) FRENCH, 1812–1871

ALPHONSE-LOUIS POITEVIN
(PRINTER) FRENCH, 1819–1882

53

Effect of Fog

1852; printed 1855

Photolithograph

9⁹⁄₁₆ × 12¹³⁄₁₆ in. (24.3 × 32.5 cm)

The Nelson-Atkins Museum of Art, Kansas City, Missouri, Gift of the Hall Family Foundation, 2012.8.3

ADALBERT CUVELIER was a successful merchant and a refiner of vegetable oil and sugar in the city of Arras, in northern France on the Scarpe River. He began to experiment with photography in the early 1850s, and though there are few surviving prints, those that do exist attest to his high level of technical and artistic mastery. Cuvelier was also an amateur painter and became associated with the circle of artists surrounding Constant Dutilleux, through whom he met the artist Jean-Baptiste-Camille Corot in 1852. Cuvelier introduced Corot to the cliché-verre, a process by which a photographic print is printed from a hand-rendered negative—a curious hybrid of paper photography, etching, and drawing.[1] Both Adalbert and his son Eugène taught the process to several of the leading Barbizon artists, including Théodore Rousseau, Jean-François Millet, Charles-François Daubigny, and Paul Huet, often printing the artists' final negative drawings.[2] Adalbert seems to have photographed primarily in and around his hometown of Arras and made views of the town's architecture, as well as scenes along the Scarpe River. He also made several portraits of Corot.

At some point about 1855 the chemist and printmaker Alphonse-Louis Poitevin produced this simple yet atmospheric landscape by Cuvelier as a photolithograph. Poitevin, who was born in the Sarthe region of the Loire valley in northwestern France, was a central figure in the development of both photolithography and carbon printing. Poitevin became interested in photography while studying in Paris, soon after Louis-Jacques-Mandé Daguerre announced his invention of the medium in 1839. Frustrated by the daguerreotype's singular nature, Poitevin began working on a way to transfer daguerreotypes onto printing plates, experiments that led in 1854 to the invention of photographic engraving and, later, photolithography. In 1855 Poitevin resigned from his post at the Eastern Saltworks in Montmorot and moved to Paris to operate a printing establishment there. The business venture proved unprofitable, and two years later he sold his patent rights to the lithographer Joseph Lemercier.[3]

This particular image, meant to convey the suffused effects of fog in a landscape, was made from one of Cuvelier's paper negatives and later transferred to a plate to be inked and printed. Its tonal nuances demonstrate the degree of aesthetic control Poitevin was able to achieve with his process. Cuvelier's simply composed scene, a tree-lined body of water (possibly a section of the Scarpe River), achieves a heightened dimensionality between foreground, middle ground, and background through varying densities of ink. A stand of trees on the far right serves as a *repoussoir*, a dense contrast to the lighter gray tonalities of the trees farther in the distance. The ephemeral nature of fog is here beautifully rendered in a process that ensured far greater permanence than a silver-based photograph, as lithographic inks were inherently more stable than reduced compounds of silver. —AMW

1. To produce a cliché-verre, the artist draws with a stylus or etching needle on a glass plate that has been coated with either slightly fogged photographic emulsion or printer's ink. The matrix is then placed in direct contact with a chemically sensitized sheet of paper to produce a positive drawing. Its relative portability and ease made it popular among artists of the Barbizon school, who used it as a sketching tool.

2. Malcolm Daniel, *Eugène Cuvelier: Photographer in the Circle of Corot*, exh. cat. (New York: Metropolitan Museum of Art, 1996), 4–5.

3. Sylvie Aubenas and Paul-Louis Roubert, *Primitifs de la photographie: Le calotype en France, 1843–1860*, exh. cat. (Paris: Gallimard; Bibliothèque Nationale de France, 2010), 301.

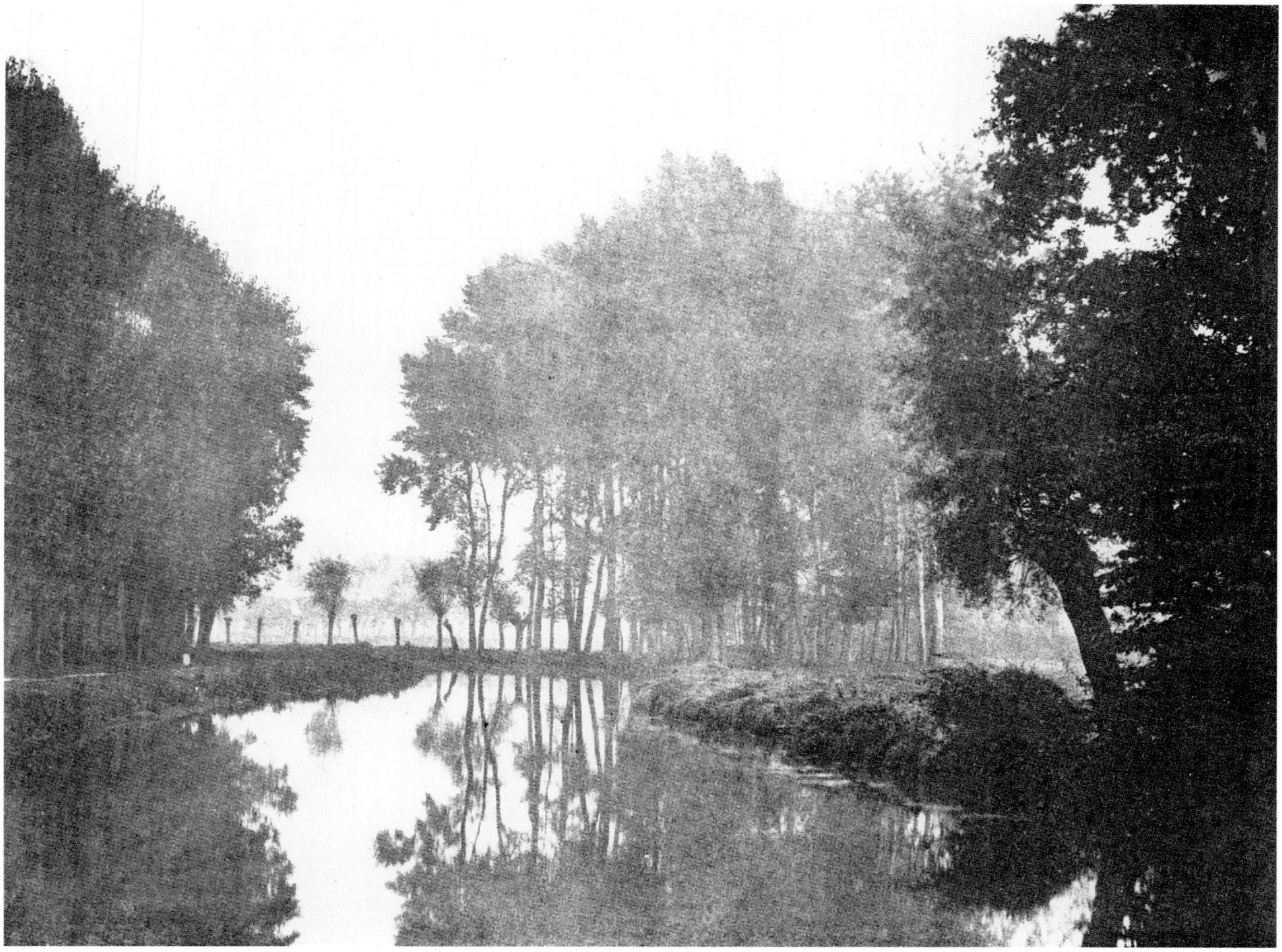

54

PAUL DELONDRE
FRENCH, 1834–1897

An Ancient Bridge

ca. 1865

Albumen print from paper negative

10⅝ × 15⅜ in. (27 × 39.1 cm)

The Nelson-Atkins Museum of Art, Kansas City, Missouri, Gift of the Hall Family Foundation, 2012.8.4

55

ANDRÉ GIROUX
FRENCH, 1801–1879

Peyreleau Bridge, Aveyron, Confluence of the Jonte and Tarn Rivers

ca. 1855

Albumen print from collodion glass negative

10¹¹⁄₁₆ × 14¹¹⁄₁₆ in. (27.1 × 37.3 cm)

The J. Paul Getty Museum, Los Angeles, 84.XP.776.14

ROCKY STREAMS, SUNLIT RIVERS, thatched cottages, and stone bridges were all motifs that repeatedly appeared in artistic photographs during the 1850s and 1860s. Paul Delondre specialized in such rustic landscapes, as exemplified in this image of a bridge spanning a small stream, possibly in the nearby region of Saint-Loup-de-Naud. Delondre exhibited his work in eight exhibitions of the Société française de la photographie, of which he was a member, between 1857 and 1870, as well as at the International Exhibition in London in 1862. There, the critic Ernest Lacan remarked on Delondre's "landscape studies," noting that "his negatives are excellent and his positive prints are remarkable for the beauty of their tones."[1]

André Giroux was best known as a landscape painter and regularly exhibited works in the annual painting Salons from 1819 through 1872.[2] He took up photography in the early 1850s, often heavily retouching his negatives with ink washes or scratching into the collodion emulsion in the manner of cliché-verre. In his review of Giroux's photographs at the Exposition universelle of 1855, Lacan praised the artist for his adept talent at retouching, noting that "an artist must be allowed to use all the means in his power to render nature's aspect with all possible truth and charm."[3]

Giroux's photographs served both as preparatory studies for his paintings and as photographic works of art in their own right. As one critic wrote: "M. Giroux's delightful landscapes display the technique of a genuine artist. They are small ready-made paintings: Nature seems to have posed for him, and taken it upon herself to compose these charming studies."[4] This landscape in Aveyron, located in the Midi-Pyrénées region of southern France, depicts a small bridge located at the confluence of the Jonte and Tarn Rivers. Giroux seems to have been drawn to such semimountainous, rustic landscapes as are found in Aveyron, Bouches-du-Rhone, Lozère, and Auvergne, since he made several photographs in these areas.[5] —AMW

1. Ernest Lacan, "La photographie à l'exposition internationale de Londres," *Le moniteur de la photographie*, September 15, 1862, 92: "M. Paul Delondre continue avec le même succès ses études de paysages. Ses clichés sont excellents, et ses épreuves positives sont remarquables par la beauté des tons."

2. Denis Canguilhem, "André Giroux, Painter-Photographer," in *André Giroux, 1801–1879*, exh. cat. (London: Wertheimer Foundation, 2004), 177.

3. Ernest Lacan, "Exposition universelle," *La lumière*, October 6, 1855, 158: "De nombreuses retouches rendent plus net et plus ferme le dessin souvent indécis des arbres dont les feuilles s'agitent au moindre vent. . . . Ces spécimens sont donc à la fois des dessins et des épreuves photographiques. . . . il doit être permis à l'artiste d'employer tous les moyens qui sont en son pouvoir pour rendre avec toute la vérité et tout le charme possibles l'aspect de la nature."

4. M. Fierlants, "Rapport sur la section de photographie à l'exposition des arts industriels de Bruxelles," *Bulletin de la Société française de la photographie* 4 (March 26, 1858): 107: "Les ravissants paysages de M. Giroux décèlent également le faire d'un véritable artiste. Ce sont de petits tableaux tout faits: la nature semble avoir posé devant lui, et s'être chargée elle-même du soin de composer ces charmantes études."

5. Many of these landscapes were featured in seven prints shown by Giroux in the annual exhibition of the Société française de la photographie in 1857.

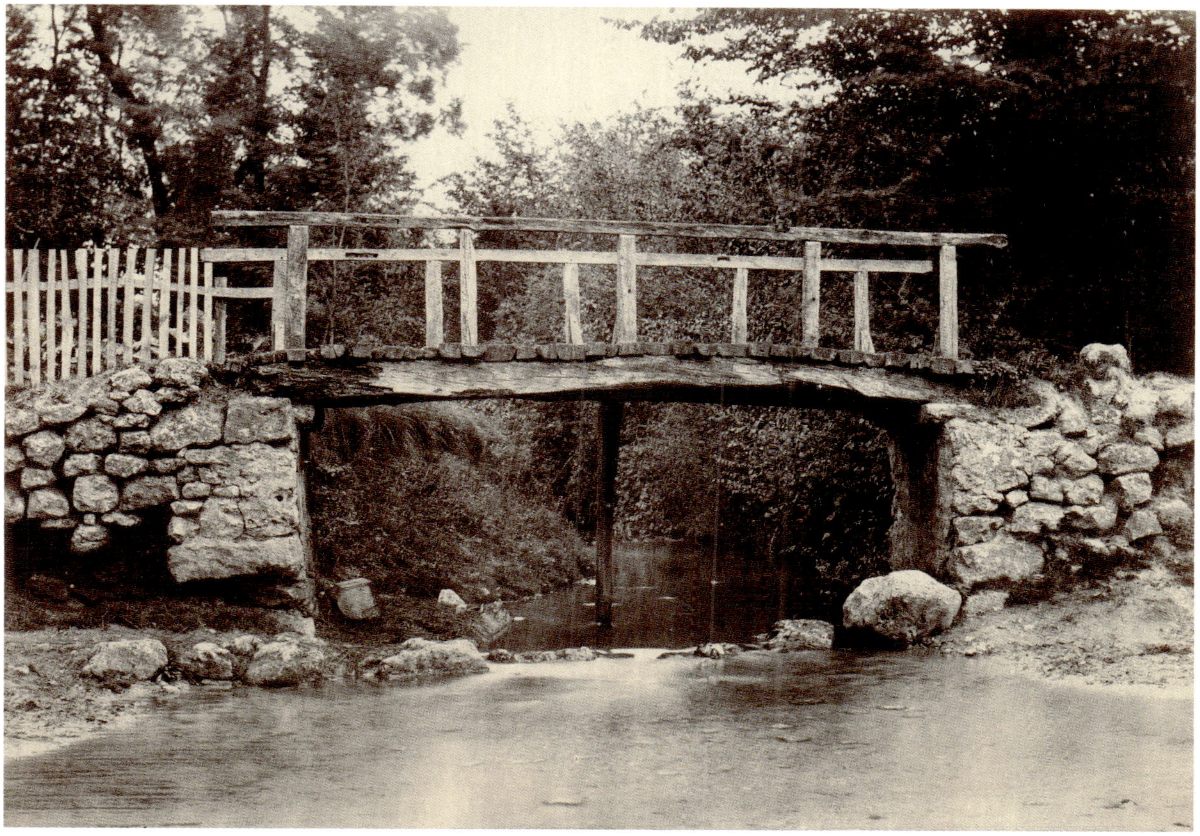

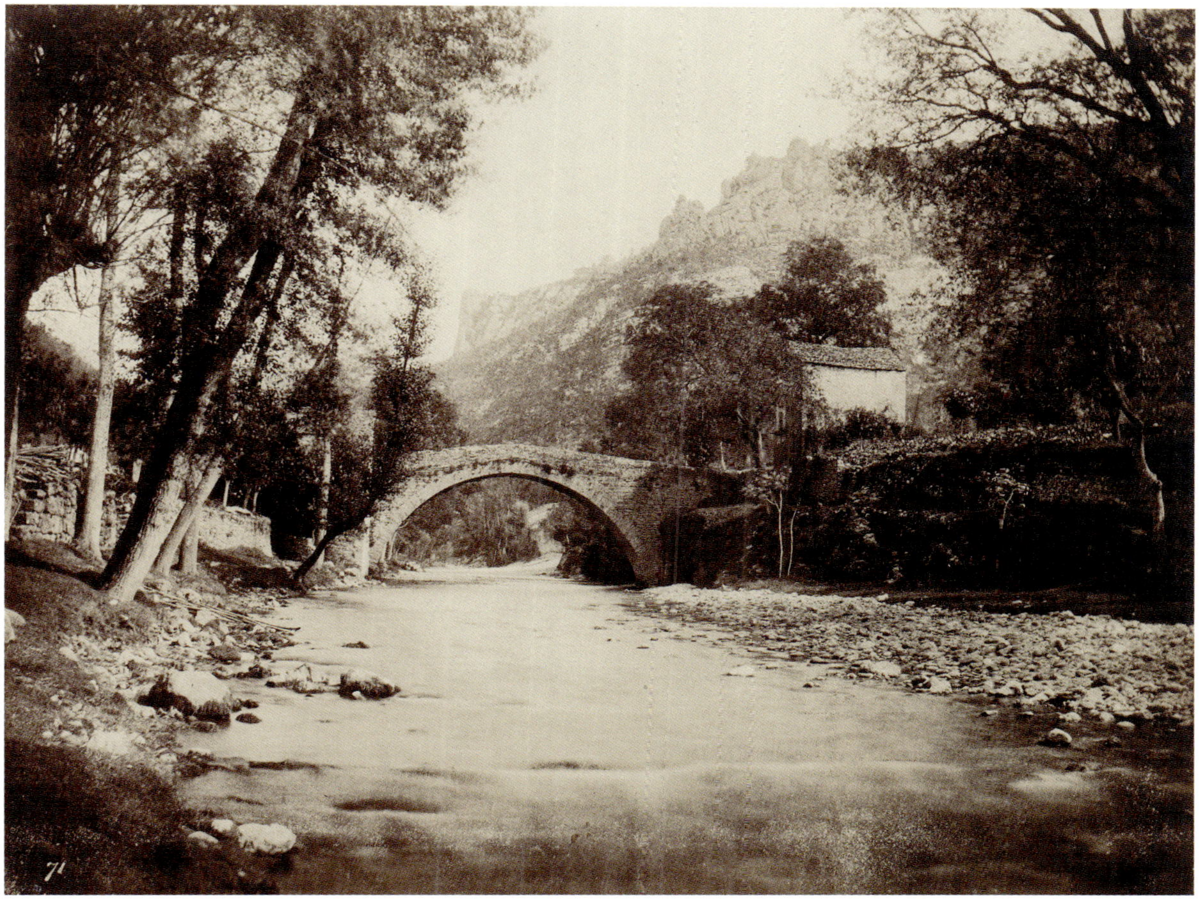
71

56

HENRI-JOSEPH HARPIGNIES

FRENCH, 1819–1916

A Meadow in the Bourbonnais, Morning

1876

Oil on canvas

44 × 66 in. (111.8 × 167.6 cm)

Brooklyn Museum, Gift of Mrs. Thomas F. Walsh, 55.18

IN HIS EARLY CAREER, Henri-Joseph Harpignies traveled to Italy and enjoyed some success at the Salon with views of that country. During the 1860s and 1870s, however, he turned to the painting of his native land and particularly the fertile Bourbonnais region in central France. He often represented the châteaux or churches of that historically significant area, which was the homeland of the great Bourbon dynasty of French kings. The Bourbonnais straddled the modern *départements* of the Allier and the Cher: Harpignies's choice of the more archaic name highlights the preindustrial aspect of the region. The artist's grand painting shows the area's rolling hills receding into the distance, while the strong horizontal of the river in the foreground anchors the composition.[1] Harpignies animated his scene with washerwomen as well as scattered cows, referencing the importance of livestock to the local agriculture. The artist's view embodies a conservative vision of *la France profonde*, suggesting the stabilizing effect of the rural world in the wake of the humiliation of the country's defeat in the Franco-Prussian War. At the same time, the picture is notable for the artist's emphasis on flat areas of color and strong outline, which creates a modern sense of abstract pattern.

Harpignies showed *A Meadow in the Bourbonnais, Morning* at the 1876 Salon as *Une prairie du Bourbonnais, par un effet de matin*, where it attracted praise, particularly for the artist's innovative approach to the massing of forms in his trees and fields. Charles Yriarte wrote that the artist had become "a determined modern painter. He has a new way of expressing masses, and shows them by way of a structure of distinct and precise outlines; from a few steps away, they are full of relief; from the normal viewing distance, these are patches of green one on top of the other."[2] Mario Proth noted,

> M. Harpignies has rarely sent a better submission than this year. The Prairie of the Bourbonnais, is, to speak casually, a daring coup. It strikes you immediately by the singular precision of the cast shadows. There is here an uncompromising effect, denoting one of those combinations of time and light that painters don't dare do willingly. I have never seen in any landscape more remarkable masses of trees. The horizon is vast, the perspective admirable. A powerful execution, particularly original, assures an exceptional distinction to this canvas in the work of the master.[3]

Harpignies subsequently exhibited the picture at the 1878 Exposition universelle as the centerpiece of his retrospective of five paintings, all of which represented the Allier and Bourbonnais regions, underscoring the artist's local patriotism.[4] The work stood out there, with critics again emphasizing its formal modernity. Gabriel Monod, for example, affirmed, "M. Harpignies only sees line and mass, he draws his trees and land with an almost black line."[5] Louis Enault described the painting as "a work very freely treated, with a loose handling, a thoughtful composition. In the foreground, one notices the transparency of the water, admirably rendered, and the beautiful lines disappearing toward the horizon."[6] Perhaps surprisingly, and possibly because of its formal modernity, the work was not acquired by the state, unlike other examples of the artist's views in the 1870s such as *The Oaks of Château-Renard (Allier)*, purchased at the 1875 Salon (see fig. 20). —SK

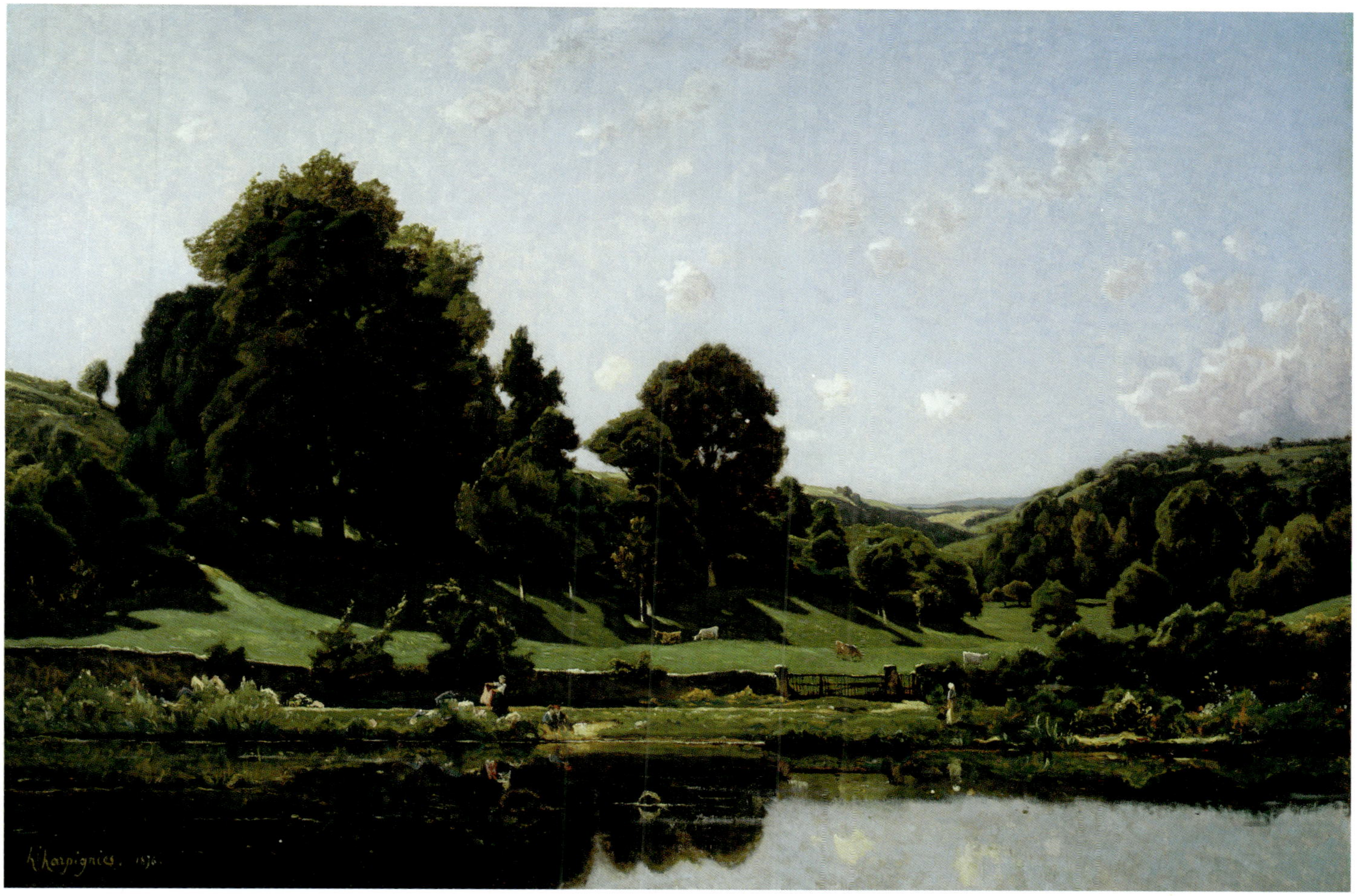

1. The river is unidentified but is probably the principal river of the region, the Allier, or one of its many tributaries.

2. Charles Yriarte, "Le Salon de 1876," *Gazette des beaux-arts* 14, no. 1 (July 1876): 32: "un paysagiste moderne determiné. Il a une façon nouvelle d'exprimer les masses, et les indique en leur donnant des silhouettes nettes et précises comme une architecture; à quelques pas, c'est plein de relief; au point de vue habituel, ce sont des taches vertes superposées."

3. Mario Proth, *Voyage au pays des peintres: Salon de 1876* (Paris: Henri Vaton, 1876), 62–63: "M. Harpignies a rarement fait un meilleur envoi que cette année. La Prairie du Bourbonnais est, pour parler familièrement, un coup de hardiesse. Elle vous frappe dès l'abord par la précision singulière des ombres portées. Il y a là un effet crû, dénotant une de ces combinaisons d'heure et de lumière où les peintres ne se hasardent pas volontiers. Je n'ai vu en aucun paysage de plus étonannts massifs d'arbres. L'horizon est vaste, la perspective admirable. Une exécution puissante, particulièrement originale, assure à cette toile une distinction exceptionnelle dans l'oeuvre du maître."

4. Harpignies also showed *Le Saut-du-Loup: View on the Allier* (Salon de 1873), *The Oaks of Château-Renard (Allier)* (Salon de 1875; see fig. 20), *Aumance Valley (Allier)* (Salon de 1875; Musée des beaux-arts, Valenciennes), and *The Small Village of Chasteloy (Allier)* (Salon de 1877).

5. Gabriel Monod, *Les beaux-arts à l'Exposition universelle* (Paris: Fischbacher, 1878): 34: "M. Harpignies ne voit que la ligne et la masse, il dessine d'un trait presque noir, ses arbres et ses terrains."

6. Louis Enault, *Les beaux-arts à l'Exposition universelle de 1878* (Paris: Gros, 1878), 77: "une oeuvre très-largement traitée, d'une libre facture, d'une composition savante On remarquera au premier plan la transparence de l'eau, admirablement rendue, et les belles lignes fuyant de l'horizon."

57

CAMILLE SILVY
FRENCH, 1834–1910

River Scene

1858

Gold-toned albumen print from two collodion glass negatives

9⅝ × 14⁷⁄₁₆ in. (24.5 × 37 cm)

Victoria and Albert Museum, London, Bequeathed by Chauncey Hare Townshend, 68:012

CAMILLE SILVY'S *River Scene* was celebrated in its day for its painterly composition and technical perfection. The subject of Silvy's photograph is the Huisne River, a tributary of the Sarthe in western France, which flows through the small market town of Nogent-le-Rotrou, Silvy's birthplace. As Mark Haworth-Booth has noted in his extensive research on this work, Silvy made his view looking from the Pont de Bois, employing the wet-collodion method, which ensured that such elements as the small figures on the riverbanks were rendered with sufficient clarity.[1] Silvy did not print *River Scene* in large quantities: today, only four full-scale prints are known, and each differs from the others in unique croppings, handwork, and tonal range.[2] This scarcity suggests the degree to which Silvy conceived of these photographs as distinct works of art. To produce this particular print, Silvy used at least two negatives, painting certain areas by hand, such as the clouds and foliage of the poplars, and burning in areas along the top edge of the sky. He likely used *sel d'or* (gold chloride) toning, which intensified the details and tonalities of the print, while also altering the coloration to cooler brownish-purple tones. All of these elements combined to create a masterwork, hailed in its day for its "exquisite and varied detail" and "calm, inviting beauty."[3]

River Scene was first shown in December 1858 at the third annual exhibition of the Photographic Society of Scotland. Here, it earned high praise: one critic wrote that it was "the most exquisite landscape we have seen in photography."[4] The following year, Silvy exhibited another print of the subject, titled *La vallée de l'Huisne* (*The Valley of the Huisne*), at the Photography Salon organized by the Société française de la photographie for the Salon des Beaux-Arts. This was the first year the official Salon admitted photography, albeit in a separate section accessible only by leaving the painting galleries, reentering the building through another door, and paying a separate admission charge.[5] *La Vallée de l'Huisne* was again singled out, this time by Louis Figuier, who noted: "It is impossible to compose with more art and taste than M. Silvy. *La Vallée de l'Huisne*, *Gué de la croix du Perche*, *Porte de l'église de Frangé*, are genuine tableaux in which one does not know whether to admire more the profound sentiment of the composition or the perfection of details. M. Silvy has an excellent system for the execution of these tableaux that we will want to see imitated."[6] Ernest Lacan called Silvy a "first-rank" landscape photographer, capable of producing "ravishing tableaux that have the merit of being as true as nature herself, while borrowing from art a glamour that gives poetry to the most ordinary places."[7]

Silvy's *River Scene* is thus considered, along with Gustave Le Gray's *Brig upon the Water* (cat. 103) and *The Breaking Wave—Mediterranean Sea* (cat. 108), among the earliest examples of ambitious landscape photographs conceived and critically received as high art, and not as simple recordings of natural phenomena. —AMW

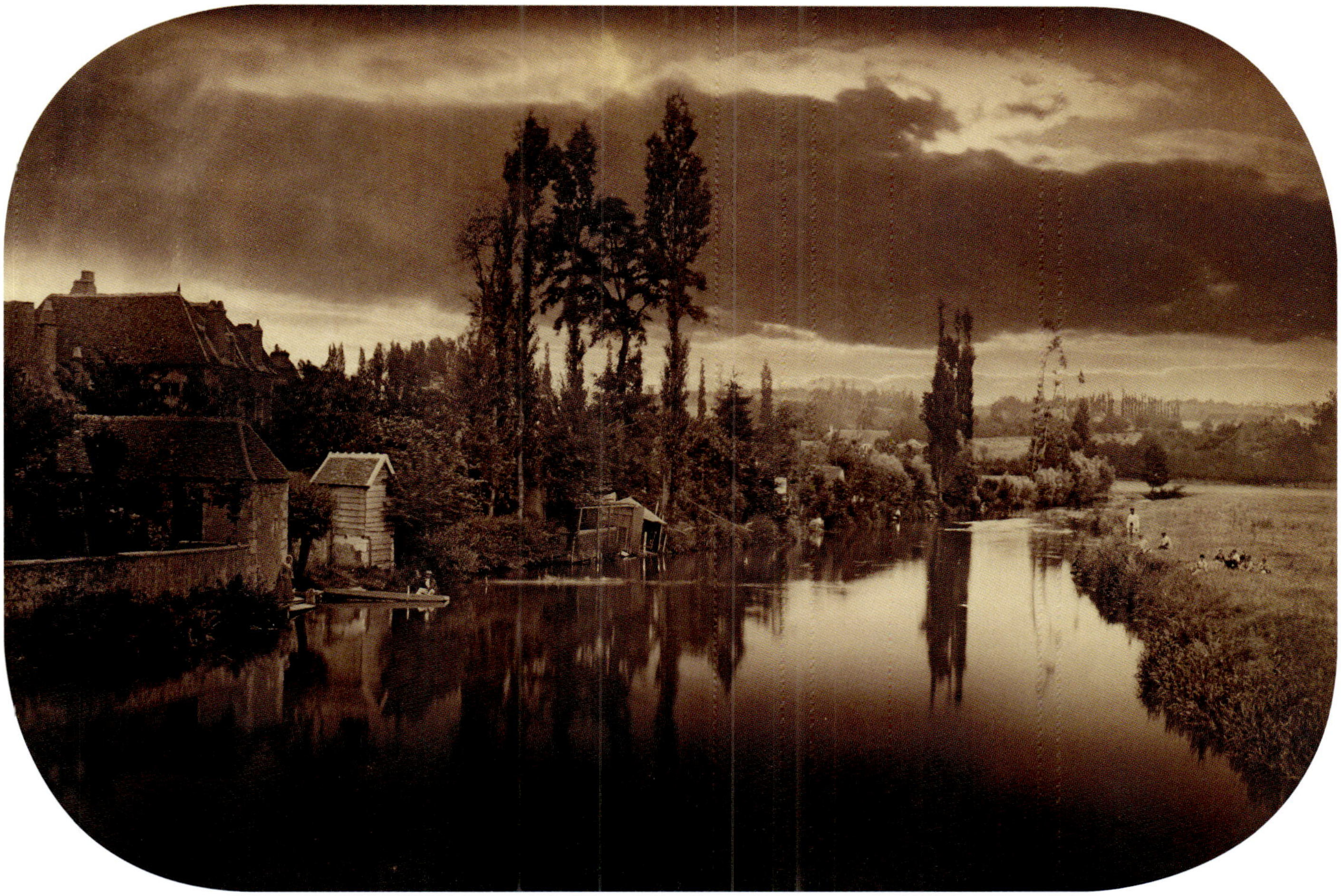

1. Mark Haworth-Booth, *Camille Silvy: River Scene, France* (Malibu, Calif.: J. Paul Getty Museum, 1992).

2. The two best prints are considered to be in the collections of The J. Paul Getty Museum, Los Angeles, and the Victoria and Albert Museum, London. The other two prints belong to the Société française de la photographie and the Musée municipal du château Saint-Jean in Nogent-le-Rotrou.

3. *Photographic Journal* 5 (1859): 179.

4. Quoted in Haworth-Booth, *Camille Silvy: River Scene, France*, 15.

5. Ibid., 32.

6. Louis Figuier, *La photographie au Salon de 1859* (Paris: Librairie de L. Hachette et Cie, 1860), 9; as cited in Haworth-Booth, *Camille Silvy: River Scene, France*, 37.

7. Ernest Lacan, *Photographic News*, July 9, 1859, 1.

PAUL-CAMILLE GUIGOU

FRENCH, 1834–1871

58

The Banks of the River Durance at Saint-Paul

1864

Oil on canvas

24½ × 58¼ in. (62 × 148 cm)

The Art Institute of Chicago, Searle Family Trust, 1986.137

"I CONSIDER PAUL GUIGOU the greatest painter of Provence. No one could paint better than he the luminosity of our beautiful land, the rugged poetry of its rocky and powdery soil. With great sincerity of vision, he made a truthful and faithful portrait of his little nation."[1] So wrote the Provençal poet Frédéric Mistral. Over the course of his relatively brief career, Guigou focused on depicting the expansive landscape of his native Provence. His work can be seen as a painterly counterpoint to Mistral's own literary evocations of the region. *The Banks of the River Durance at Saint-Paul* depicts the Durance River, a major tributary of the Rhone. The painting, organized in discrete planes, shows the river in the foreground with a rocky outcrop to the left and, to the right, the artist himself in conversation with his fellow Provençal painter Adolphe Monticelli. Guigou's work, which evokes the intense light of the South, is notable for its luminous color and minimalistic, stripped-down composition. Guigou's study of the local rock faces may reflect the growing interest in the geology and prehistoric history of the region, particularly evident in the work of the naturalist and geologist the marquis Gaston de Saporta.[2]

In 1854 Guigou moved to Marseille, where he studied with the painter Émile Loubon and formed part of a nascent Marseille school of painting. He subsequently lived in Paris in the 1860s and showed his Provençal views regularly at the Paris Salon. More than any other Provençal painter in his lifetime, he was able to promote his region on a national scale. The painting in Chicago has been identified as the canvas of that name shown at the 1864 Salon, which attracted critical praise.[3] The Provençal critic Marius Chaumelin wrote of the "daring of the composition," describing "a lightly undulating, sandy beach, which stretches as far as the eye can see and which is overlooked by large rocks, marked here and there with grass, on the left. The pale and limpid azure of the sky contrasts with the grayish color of the bank. This painting has a powerful and sober truth and is not lacking in poetry in its simplicity."[4] Théophile Gautier wrote of the "lively southern sentiment" of Guigou's work and went on: "The Banks of the Durance at Saint-Paul surprises and stimulates the eye by the brightness of the light, the intense blue of the waters, the very Provençal aridity of the sands, which could extend over the banks of the Nile and which only need flocks of ibis and flamingoes to have a completely Egyptian appearance."[5] Both critics, however, also referenced the presence of bathing children in the foreground, complicating the identification of the Chicago work as the 1864 Salon picture.[6] Guigou is known to have painted at least two variants on the present picture, and it is possible that the Salon painting was another, as yet unlocated, variant.[7]

Guigou died prematurely as a result of a cerebral hemorrhage in 1871. His paintings of Provence nonetheless formed an important precedent for his friend and fellow Provençal Paul Cézanne. —SK

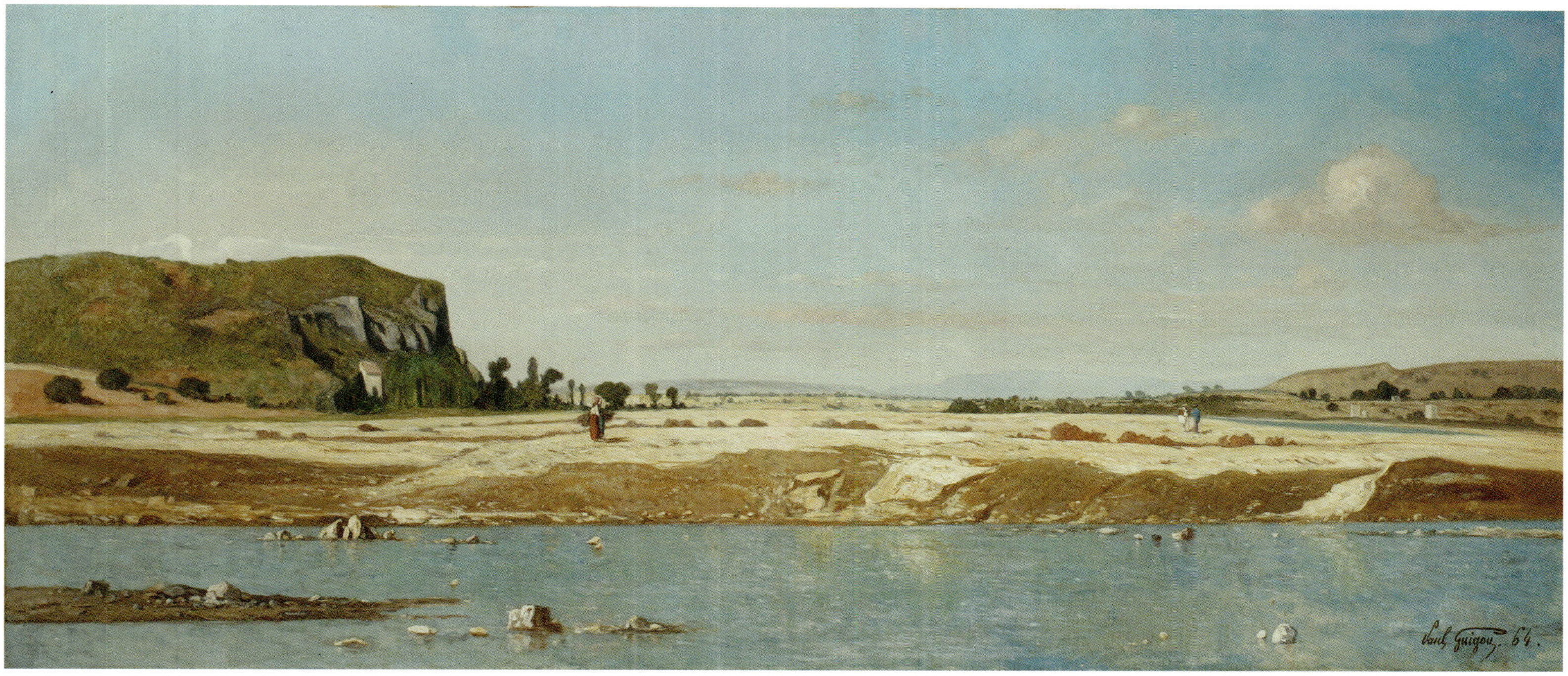

1. Quoted in Aaron Sheon, "Paul Guigou and Provence," in *Paul Guigou, 1834–1871*, exh. cat. (New York: William Beadleston, 1987), note 13.

2. See, for example, Gaston de Saporta, *Études sur la végétation du sud-est de la France à l'époque tertiaire* (Paris: V. Masson et Fils, 1863–67).

3. See, for example, Richard R. Brettell, "The Salon of 1864," in *French Salon Artists, 1800–1900* (Chicago: Art Institute of Chicago, 1986), 49.

4. Marius Chaumelin, "Lettre sur le Salon de 1864: Les artistes marseillais," *Tribune artistique et littéraire du Midi*, July 1864, 8; quoted in French in Claude-Jeanne Bonnici, *Paul Guigou* (Aix-en-Provence: Édisud, 1989), 10: "la hardiesse de la composition . . . une plage sablonneuse légèrement ondulée, qui s'étend à perte de vue et que dominent à gauche de grandes roches plaquées ça et là de gazon. L'azur pale et transparent du ciel contraste avec les teintes grisâtres de la grève. Ce tableau est d'une vérité sobre et forte et ne manque pas de poésie dans la simplicité."

5. Théophile Gautier, "Salon de 1864," *Le moniteur universel*, August 3, 1864, quoted in Bonnici, *Paul Guigou*, 10: "un vif sentiment méridional. Les Bords de la Durance à Saint-Paul (Bouches-du-Rhône) étonnent et réjouissent l'oeil par l'éclat de la lumière, le bleu intense des eaux, l'aridité toute Provençale des sables, qui pourraient s'étaler sur les berges du Nil et auxquels il ne manque, pour avoir l'air tout à fait égyptien, que ces bandes d'ibis et de flamants."

6. See, for example, Chaumelin, "Lettre sur le Salon de 1864: Les artistes marseillais," 8: "au premier plan une eau bleuâtre où quelques enfants prennent leur ébats." The configuration of the naked boys was probably very similar to that in an 1863 oil study (*Bords de la Durance à Saint-Paul*; in Bonnici, *Paul Guigou*, 149, no. 77). The Chicago picture is thinly painted, and the foreground shows little evidence of artistic changes: it would nonetheless be interesting to X-ray the picture for evidence of any pentimenti such as the group of boys.

7. See *Banks of the Durance* (Kimbell Art Museum, Fort Worth) and *Banks of the Durance at Saint Paul* (private collection; Bonnici, *Paul Guigou*, no. 77). Bonnici also lists another variant of exactly the same size and composition as the Chicago work (private collection; ibid., 152, no. 91).

4
RURAL AND AGRICULTURAL LIFE

IN THE NINETEENTH CENTURY, as it largely remains today, France was an agricultural nation. Though lagging behind its neighbors England and Germany in implementing factory-based industrialization, it was a major European force in terms of its agricultural output. Despite the growth of urbanization, the majority of the nation's population lived in the countryside. By 1900, 59 percent of the French people still lived in rural areas, and 42 percent of the workforce practiced farming and forestry. In the far more urbanized nation of England at that time, by contrast, 25 percent of the population lived in the countryside, and only 12 percent worked on farms.[1] Agriculture was the center of the French economy, as Napoléon had noted at the start of the nineteenth century.[2] The nation's self-definition was thus rooted in the land and what that land produced.

France's largest agricultural export was wine. Grapes were grown in seventy-two of the eight-six *départements*;[3] the principal wine-growing regions were Bordeaux, Burgundy, Champagne, the Loire valley, Alsace, the Côtes du Rhône, and the Midi. France had more vineyards (2,421 in 1875) and a far greater output of wine (2.2 million gallons in 1875) than any other European nation: it was by far the world's largest producer of wine.[4] Wine was thus especially important to the nation's identity. Painters represented the range of vineyards in the country, from Jules Breton's views of the high-end vineyards around Bordeaux to Claude Monet's view of the less prestigious sites around Argenteuil, just outside Paris.

France also had a massive livestock industry. In 1862 there were more than 10 million cattle and around 30 million sheep in France; in western Europe, only Germany had more livestock.[5] Diverse breeds of cows, such as the Friesian, Charolais, and Normande, were raised across the French nation and also now studied scientifically: the naturalist Émile Baudement, produced an extensive study of these breeds and their geographic distribution.[6] Cattle and sheep were valuable as sources not only of beef, veal, and lamb but also of butter and cheese, the latter being a particularly important farm product. Cheeses such as Camembert and Brie remain famed the world over to this day. Jean-François

Millet, Constant Troyon, and Adolphe Braun all explored the nation's rich cattle industry as artistic subjects, while Charles-François Daubigny depicted the seasonal collection of hay, a crucial farming practice for the livestock industry.

Farming was also widespread; France was the largest producer of wheat and sugar beets in western Europe, which were often grown on large-scale farms.[7] At the same time, traditional methods of peasant agriculture continued alongside these emergent capitalist farms. The French peasantry was slow to change its centuries-old customs. Many peasant families engaged in the agricultural practice of small-scale market gardening, whereby they worked their own plots of land and sold their produce at local markets. Camille Pissarro frequently recorded this activity, painting the market gardens around Pontoise.

Despite growing centralization, France's provinces displayed a wide range of rural traditions. Regions such as Brittany and Provence fiercely defended their local customs and costumes as well as their local languages and dialects. Breton explored the diversity of peasant life in Brittany, while Charles Nègre concentrated on the Midi region, and Henri Le Secq pictured age-old ways of life, as suggested by the rustic dwellings and troglodyte farms in central France.

1. Hugh Clout, *Agriculture in France on the Eve of the Railway Age* (London: Croom Helm, 1980), 3.

2. Ibid.

3. Robert Tombs, *France, 1814–1914* (Harlow: Longman, 1996), 297.

4. B. R. Mitchell, *International Historical Statistics: Europe, 1750–1988*, 3rd ed. (New York: Stockton Press, 1992), 312.

5. Ibid., 334. In 1862 France had 11.8 million cattle and more than 29 million sheep. There were 13.4 million cattle in Germany at this time, while Russia had 21 million cattle and 44.2 million sheep. Ibid., 336 and 357.

6. Émile Baudement, *Les races bovines au concours universet agricole de Paris en 1856: Études zootechniques* (Paris: Imprimerie Impériale, 1862)

7. Ibid., 213 and 249. France contained approximately 18.5 million acres of wheat-producing land in 1862. Great Britain, by contrast, contained around 3.5 million acres.

59

JEAN-FRANÇOIS MILLET
FRENCH, 1814–1875

Peasants Bringing Home a Calf Born in the Fields

1864

Oil on canvas

31 15/16 × 39 3/8 in. (81.1 × 100 cm)

The Art Institute of Chicago, Henry Field Memorial Collection, 1894.1063

JEAN-FRANÇOIS MILLET'S WORK focused on the peasantry of France, representing both the harshness and the inherent dignity that he found in their way of life. Millet himself grew up in a prosperous peasant family in the hamlet of Gruchy, near Gréville on the Normandy coast, and understood the rich traditions associated with the French rural world. *Peasants Bringing Home a Calf Born in the Fields* represents an important event for any rural community, namely, the birth of a calf, which is here being brought into the warmth of the home. The calf's mother tenderly licks her offspring, while the family's children wait expectantly at the doorway. Millet's painting was prompted by an event he witnessed when he returned to Gruchy in 1854. The artist understood the significance of the birth to peasant farmers—promising an important new source of income—and the literal closeness of farmers to their cattle, whose stalls were often alongside the family home. The brown Normande cows were valuable for their milk, from which butter and cheese (notably Camembert) were made, as well as for their beef.

Millet's scene was underpinned by a group of careful drawing studies, of both individual details and the overall composition.[1] The most developed compositional drawing (fig. 67) shows the calf as slightly larger, the men's legs slightly farther apart, and the children not yet included at the door of the house. Millet assigned a price of two thousand francs to the painting, which he intended for the banker Ennemond Blanc.[2]

Millet showed *Peasants Bringing Home a Calf Born in the Fields* at the 1864 Salon together with a second work, *Shepherdess with Her Flock* (Musée d'Orsay, Paris). The artist considered the former his more important submission.[3] The picture represents the culmination of a group of

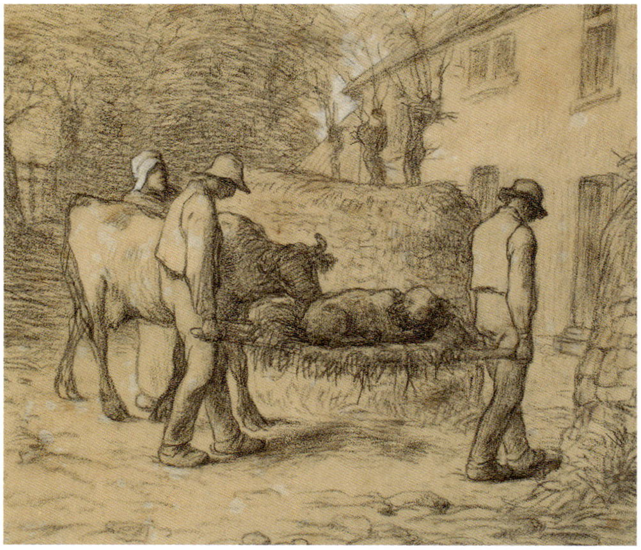

FIG. 67 Jean-François Millet, *Bringing Home the Newborn Calf*, ca. 1857. Charcoal with white heightening on cream wove paper, 10 5/8 × 12 11/16 in. (27 × 32.3 cm). Worcester Art Museum, Worcester, Massachusetts, Gift of Mrs. Howard W. Presto, 1974.329

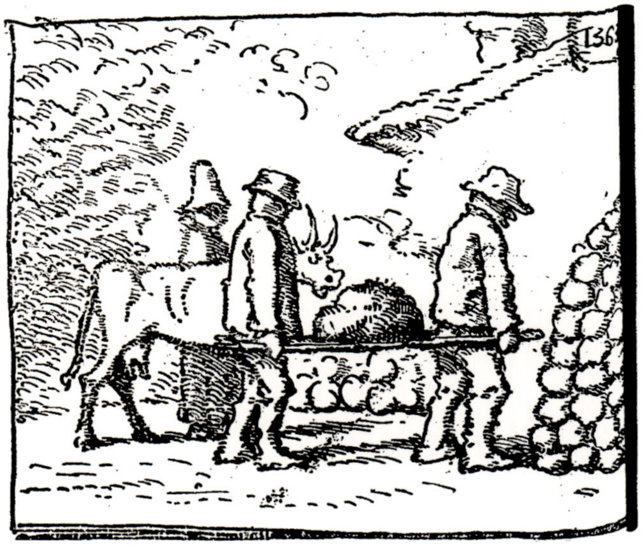

FIG. 68 Bertall, "Promenade au Salon de 1864," *Le journal amusant*, no. 438 (May 21, 1864), 2

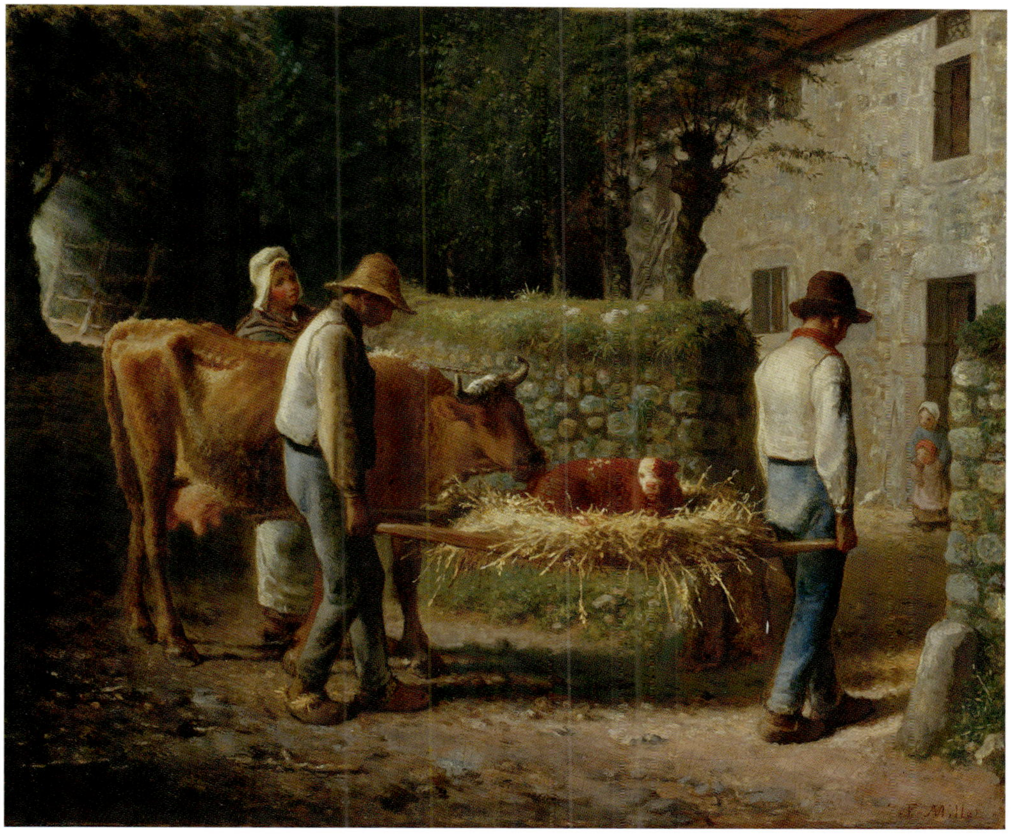

controversial peasant paintings that Millet showed at the Salon from 1857 until 1864, including *The Gleaners* (Musée d'Orsay, Paris) and *Man with a Hoe* (The J. Paul Getty Museum, Los Angeles). Critical response to his painting was generally negative. The artist was attacked for the lack of precise drawing in his figures and the absence of anatomical detail in his cows: a caricature by Bertall shows the calf as a large piece of larded and roasted veal (fig. 68).[4] The critical reception of the painting was carefully recorded by the artist's close friend Alfred Sensier in a series of little-known letters to the artist; they provide a remarkable record of the ongoing response to the picture.[5] On the day the exhibition opened, May 1, Sensier visited the show and wrote: "people find your Calf very beautiful. Your men are admired as well as the landscape. It's very strong, very powerful."[6] Not all agreed with this assessment. The painting attracted immediate hostile criticism from Jean Rousseau, the critic for the prominent daily newspaper *Le figaro*, who argued that Millet's figures were excessively ritualistic and mannered, as if in a religious procession. Sensier noted, "Jean Rousseau has already uttered three or four exaggerations in Figaro, in finding (the imbecile) that your peasants had the look of carrying the Holy Eucharist or that they would do well in the role of Egyptian priests carrying the bull of Apis."[7] Millet rebutted the criticism immediately, arguing for the essential naturalism of his painting and affirming that the posture of the calf bearers was simply based on the laws of gravity: "Apropos of what Jean Rousseau says . . . how does he expect them to carry it [the calf]? . . . The expression of two men carrying something on a litter depends upon the weight which hangs from their arms. So, if the weight were the same, whether they had the ark of the covenant or a calf, a lump of gold or a stone, the same expression would be the result."[8] Soon after, on May 12, Sensier had more positive news, noting that "your Calf is . . . very admired, and there are some artists who find it the most beautiful painting of the Salon."[9] In the weeks that followed, however, Sensier provided Millet with negative reviews from some of the most prominent critics of the day. On June 5, Sensier sent the review of Charles Clément in the widely circulated *Journal des débats*. This critic described the work as "an example of Millet's affectations of simplicity . . . giving a stupid appearance to the two peasants that nothing justifies . . . one can carry a calf on a support without creating the look of a burial."[10] On June 8, Sensier described the account of Millet's most hostile critic, Paul de Saint-Victor: the critic had "vented his spleen against the Calf," describing the painting's figures as mentally deranged, an "art of Bicêtre" [a notorious lunatic asylum in the south of Paris] and from the "Vale of Tempé [the celebrated site in Greek mythology of Apollo and the Muses] of idiots."[11] Subsequently, on July 27, Sensier noted Théophile Gautier's "condemnation for the Calf":[12] this critic had repeated the earlier comments of Jean Rousseau, attacking the excessive solemnity of the piece and again making the comparison between Millet's figures and Egyptian priests.[13] It seems that Millet reacted to this criticism, since in the later 1860s he submitted more of his landscape paintings to the Salon, and they proved less controversial. *Bringing Home a Calf Born in the Fields* enjoyed greater critical success when it was shown in Millet's extensive retrospective at the 1889 Exposition universelle. At that time, it was described by Vincent van Gogh as "so powerful that it makes you tremble."[14] —SK

1. These studies include examples in the Musée du Louvre, Département des Arts graphiques, RF 5737 and RF 5739; National Gallery of Art, Washington, D.C. (*The Newborn*, 1943.3.6258); and Albright-Knox Art Gallery, Buffalo (*Bringing Home the Newborn Calf*, 1954:1.3). See Robert L. Herbert, *Jean-François Millet*, exh. cat. (London: Arts Council of Great Britain, 1976), 143–45. There is also an oil sketch (private collection), which is reproduced in an engraving by Maxime Lalanne in Alexandre Piedagnel, *J.-F. Millet: Souvenirs de Barbizon* (Paris: Cadart, 1876), 60.

2. Millet to Sensier, April 4, 1864, Musée du Louvre, Depártement des Arts graphiques, Cote BS, b14, L336: "Je viens d'écrire à M. Blanc, d'abord pour lui dire que je lui destine mon Veau, qui est de mes deux tableaux la composition la plus importante . . . le prix de ce tableau est de 2,000 francs." (I have just written to M. Blanc, first of all to tell him that I am intending my Calf for him, that it is of my two paintings the more important composition . . . the price of this painting is 2,000 francs.)

3. Ibid.

4. Bertall, "Promenade au Salon de 1864," *Le journal amusant*, no. 438 (May 21, 1864): 2. The inscription reads: "Fricandeau Juice: Two kitchen helpers carry a fricandeau [a cut of veal larded and roasted in its own juices] into town, a poor passing cow recognizes the remains of its calf despite the sad way that Millet has prepared her. It's not a painting, it's an elegy." (Le Jus au Fricandeau: Deux gâte-sauce portent un fricandeau en ville, une pauvre vache qui passe reconnait les restes de son veau malgré la triste manière dont M. Millet l'a accomodé. Ce n'est pas un tableau, c'est une élégie.)

5. The letters are in the Musée du Louvre, Département des Arts graphiques. They are reproduced in Lucien Lepoittevin, *Une chronique de l'amitié: La correspondance intégrale du peintre Jean-François Millet* (Le Vast [France]: J. et L. Lepoittevin, 2005).

6. Sensier to Millet, May 1, 1864, Musée du Louvre, Département des Arts graphiques, Cote AR48, p. 102: "On trouve aussi le Veau très beau. Vos hommes sont admirés ainsi que le paysage. C'est très fort, très puissant."

7. Ibid.: "Jean Rousseau a déjà dit de vous trois ou quatre grands mots dans le Figaro, tout en trouvant (l'imbécile), que vos paysans avaient l'air de porter le Saint Sacrement, ou qu'ils feraient fort bien le rôle des prêtres égyptiens portant le boeuf Apis. Mais s'ils ont cet-air-là, mille fois tant mieux."

8. Quoted in Alfred Sensier, *Jean-François Millet: Peasant and Painter*, trans. Helena de Kay (New York: Houghton, Mifflin & Co., 1896), 171.

9. Sensier to Millet, May 12, 1864, Musée du Louvre, Département des Arts graphiques, Cote AR48, p. 105: "Votre Veau est . . . très admiré, et il est des artistes qui le trouvent le plus beau tableau du Salon."

10. Sensier to Millet, June 5, 1864, ibid., Cote AR48, pp. 109–11, quoting Clément, *Journal des débats*, June 2, 1864: "Je fais quelques réserves à l'égard d'un des tableaux de Millet, des paysans qui rapportent un veau né dans les champs. C'est par une de ces affectations de simplicité dont j'ai parlé que M. Millet donne à ces deux paysans une apparence niaise que rien ne motive. On peut porter un veau sur un brancard sans prendre pour cela un air d'enterrement."

11. Sensier to Millet, June 8, 1864, ibid., Cote AR48, p. 112: "Paul de Saint-Victor . . . a jeté son venin sur le Veau: 'art de Bicêtre, vallée de Tempé des idiots.'"

12. Sensier to Millet, July 27, ibid., Cote AR48, p. 119: "Gautier a, dit-on, parlé de vous dans le Moniteur: louange à la bergère, damnation sur le veau. Ils sont stupides et méchants."

13. Théophile Gautier, "Salon de 1864," 10e article, *Le moniteur universel*, July 25, 1864.

14. Vincent van Gogh to Émile Bernard, on or about Tuesday, November 26, 1889, in *Vincent van Gogh: The Letters; The Complete Illustrated and Annotated Edition*, ed. Leo Jansen, Hans Luijten, and Nienke Bakker, 6 vols. (London: Thames and Hudson in association with the Van Gogh Museum, 2009), no. 822: "I adore the true . . . so I bow before that study, so powerful that it makes you tremble, by *père* Millet, peasants carrying to the farmhouse a calf born in the fields."

60

JULES BRETON
FRENCH, 1827–1906

The Vintage at Château Lagrange

1864

Oil on canvas

36½ × 67 in. (92.7 × 170.2 cm)

Joslyn Art Museum, Omaha, Nebraska,
Gift of the Friends of Art Collection, 1932.3

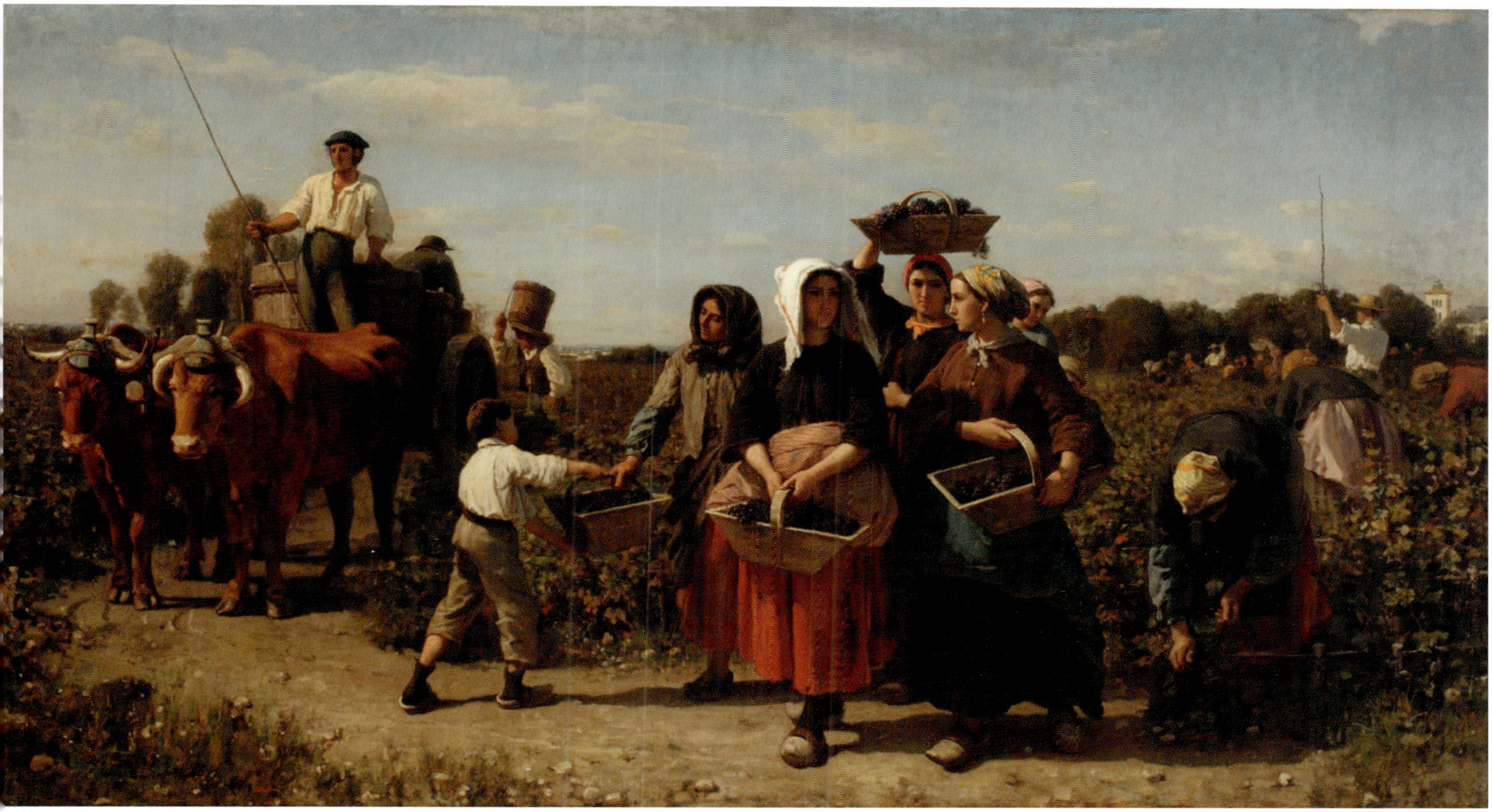

DURING HIS LONG CAREER, Jules Breton carefully documented the agricultural and rural customs of France, traveling extensively around his home country and representing regional traditions and costumes with ethnographic detail. Breton's patriotism is evident in his memoirs, in which he praised the civilizing role of France: "French art traverses the world like those broad rivers that flow on, free and peaceful, but irresistible in their course. . . . O France, who hast produced such artists, glory to thee!"[1] A fervent republican, Breton was deeply attached to France's peasantry while also recognizing that they provided a subject that brought him great commercial success and international fame. *The Vintage at Château Lagrange* represents the fall wine harvest in the famed vineyard of Château Lagrange just outside Bordeaux. The château still exists today and continues to produce wine, but its heyday was in the mid-nineteenth century, when it won prestigious international prizes for its wine. Its production was also increased by the installation of a pioneering drainage system with ceramic pipes laid beneath the soil throughout the vineyard.[2] Breton's colorful work provides considerable insight into the working practices of this large-scale commercial operation. The laborers, who lived on-site, are carefully represented: the composition focuses on a triangular group of three women

61

JULES BRETON

FRENCH, 1827–1906

The Washerwomen of the Breton Coast

1870

Oil on canvas

53¼ × 79¼ in. (135 × 201 cm)

The Grohmann Museum *Man at Work* Collection at Milwaukee School of Engineering

in conversation. In the fields behind them, stick-wielding, white-shirted supervisors oversee the workers. To the left is an ox-drawn cart with wooden vats, which are being filled with grapes.

The Vintage at Château Lagrange was commissioned in 1862 by the vineyard owner, comte Duchâtel, Minister of Finance under King Louis-Philippe, and was the artist's most important commission to date.[3] The count's château, with its impressive tower, is clearly visible at the far right of the painting. The picture thus fulfilled a propagandistic function in promoting the prestige of the count's vineyard.[4] Breton developed a good personal relationship with the count and his wife and spent the fall of both 1862 and 1863 at the château in order to research his paintings, producing several studies and using photographs of local peasants.

When Breton showed the painting at the 1864 Salon (with its ownership by Duchâtel identified in the catalogue), the critical reception of the painting was positive. The picture satisfied both left-wing and conservative critics who found common ground in Breton's naturalism. The radical critic Jules-Antoine Castagnary praised the work as "a spontaneous and voluntary return to a more truthful nature," in contrast to what he saw as an excessive sentimentality and refinement in the artist's earlier work.[5] The conservative Charles Clément, who knew the region well, described the picture as having "great local truth" and praised Breton's study of peasant dress as well as the landscape of the Médoc in the distance.[6] Following the Salon, Breton made some changes—particularly lightening the tones of his painting—before sending it to comte Duchâtel.

Breton subsequently turned his attention to Brittany and traveled to the far west of this region in 1865. He found an especial kinship with the area because of his own name. He later wrote: "I was profoundly struck by Finistère, under all its aspects, maritime, rural, and religious . . . I felt that I was indeed a descendant of the Bretons."[7] He returned to the region regularly until 1891, representing a range of local customs, including pardons (see fig. 49), as well as the landscape of the region. *The Washerwomen of the Breton Coast* shows the practice of washing laundry in tidal pools that the artist observed at the port of Douarnenez. Soon after first arriving at this port in 1865, he wrote on September 2:

> It would be difficult to imagine anything more beautiful than the Baie de Douarnenez, which is always thronged with fishing boats. The mountains surrounding it are charming and the water is as clear as the Mediterranean. Yesterday, we met some beautiful girls, really attractive, whose looks have never been recorded because this region has only ever been painted by superficial painters. There is one place which I am determined to visit frequently. It is a public washing place with laundresses coming and going all day, carrying their bundles of washing in beautiful attitudes. I do not think it will be difficult to persuade some of them to pose for me.[8]

Breton's painting, a complex, multifigure composition showing eleven women surrounding a pool, was indeed grounded in study of local models. The standing woman in the center rolling up her sleeves in preparation for doing the laundry is Breton's favored model, Jeanne Calvet, who worked as a sardine packer. At bottom right, the laundress who turns her head toward the spectator, providing a moment of spontaneous intimacy, is another Breton peasant, Marie Douaré.[9] Breton's painting is full of carefully observed regional details, whether the women's costumes, their scrubbing implements, or the distaff carried by the girl

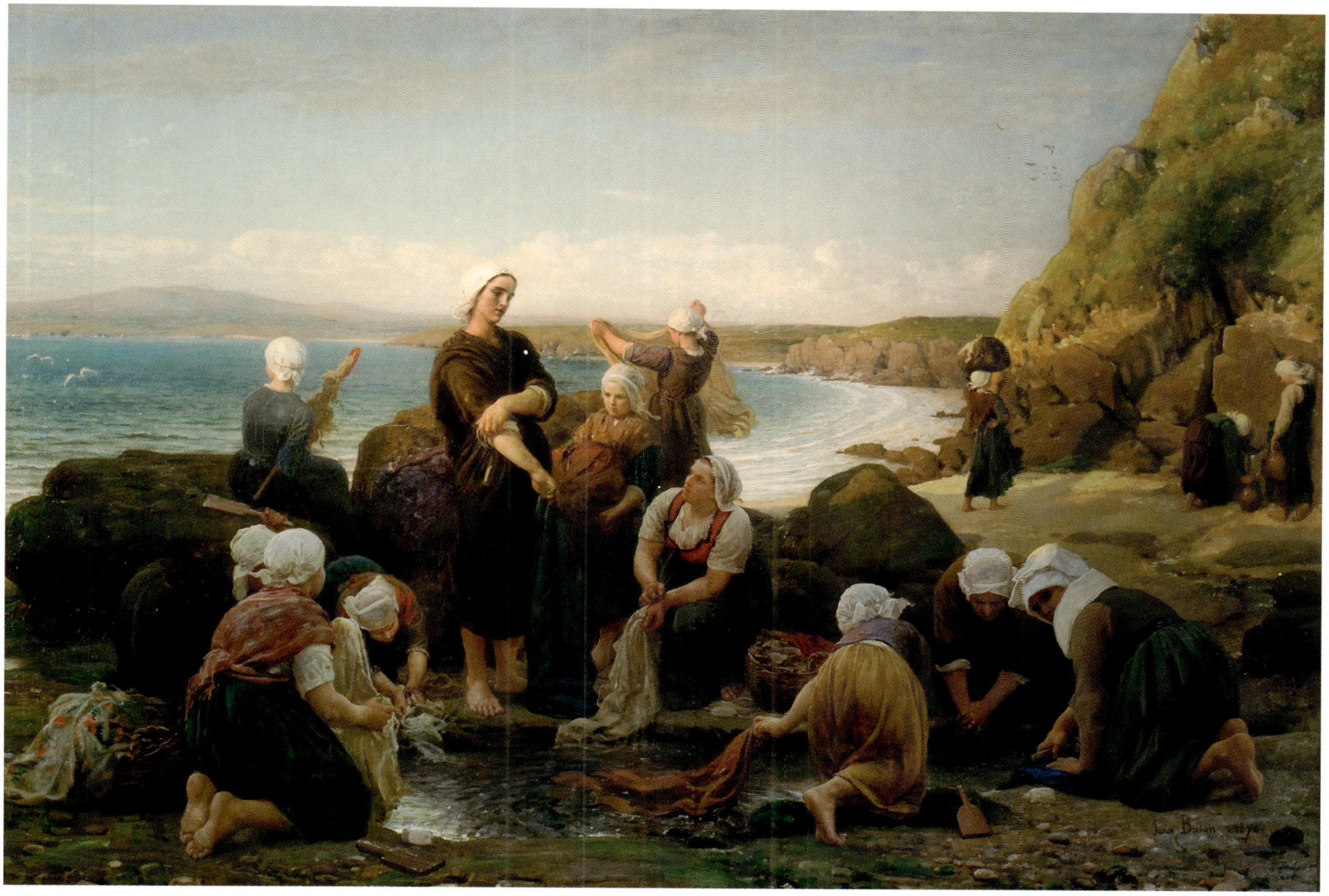

who sits on a rock at the left, spinning. To the back right, a woman carries laundry toward steps up the cliff side.

Breton later described his working process and highlighted the degree to which he focused on the distant landscape:

> The principal group was in the sun-flecked shadow, while sunshine flooded the background. Oh, the background! It was there that I had thought the chief beauty of my picture was to lie; and, leaving my figures in outline, I spent all my energies in working at the distances, not reflecting that their effect must depend on the firmness and the finish of the figures. But I put off touching these figures to the last, working desperately at the grottoes, the beach, and the villages rising one above the other on the shore, and which were to shimmer so poetically in the sunshine.[10]

He also noted his great struggles in completing the picture: "Finally, I was obliged to put aside this picture for another year. It had produced a buzzing in the ears which rendered me deaf, and other nervous disturbances which at times made work impossible for me."[11] Breton finally showed the work at the 1870 Salon, where it attracted criticism. Castagnary felt that the women were artificially posed and did not show evidence of carrying out work.[12] Clément was more complimentary, praising the artist's study of colorful regional dress: "without departing in any way from the truth, the painter has made the very most of the costumes."[13]

During the 1870s Breton returned regularly to Brittany in the summer months and produced several paintings of individual, heroically posed women. It is possible that the republican Breton may have been seeking to transform these peasants into symbols of national strength.[14] *The Wounded Seagull* (cat. 62) shows a woman in strongly outlined profile, wearing the typical Breton cap, or coiffe, whose twin ends the artist compared to "pointed wings."[15] Breton depicted Marguerite Moreau, his favorite peasant model in the 1870s,

62

JULES BRETON

FRENCH, 1827–1906

The Wounded Seagull

1878

Oil on canvas

36½ × 30⅜ in. (92.7 × 77.2 cm)

Saint Louis Art Museum, Gift of Justina G. Catlin, in memory of her husband, Daniel Catlin, 27:1917

who tenderly holds a seagull. The artist was intrigued by the sense of closeness with nature that he found in Breton women and described their "mystic wildness."[16] In the distance, healthy gulls fly over the sea, perhaps alluding to the future hope for this bird. Castagnary saw Breton's monumental peasant women as embodying the new rationalist ideals of the Third Republic, in contrast to retrograde Catholic superstition. In describing a similar painting in 1873, he wrote,

> There is no fear of returning to the past when one examines these high cheekbones and this energetic chin. Republican and rational, this strong woman will bring forth children that France deserves, republican and free-thinking children. . . . Isn't it already a strong sign of democratic progress to see a painter take a peasant woman for his model and by the force of style as well as elevation of feeling, make of her the characteristic representation of a whole race? There is in this idea the stamp of the Republic of 1870.[17]

The Wounded Seagull was acquired soon after its completion by the Saint Louis collector Daniel Catlin, indicating the early American interest in the work of Breton. The painting was shown in 1881 at the first special exhibition at the newly founded Saint Louis School and Museum of Fine Arts, the predecessor of the Saint Louis Art Museum. —SK

1. Quoted in Jules Breton, *The Life of an Artist*, trans. Mary J. Serrano (New York: D. Appleton and Company, 1891), 350.

2. See www.chateaulagrange.com; and Philippe Roudié, *150 ans d'évolution viticole en Médoc et au château Lagrange*, Cahier no. 2 (Château Lagrange, 2012). The château's wine had been prestigiously classified as a *troisième cru* (third growth) at the 1855 Exposition universelle in Paris and also won prizes at the London World Fair in 1862 and 1867 Paris Exposition universelle.

3. The comte Duchâtel had already acquired Breton's 1861 Salon painting *The Weeders* (Joslyn Art Museum, Omaha) and envisaged the painting of the wine harvest as a pendant to it.

4. See Linda Nochlin, *Realism* (Harmondsworth, U.K.: Penguin, 1981), 267.

5. Jules-Antoine Castagnary, "Salon de 1864," in *Salons, 1857–1870* (Paris: Bibliothèque Charpentier, 1892), 1:193: "un retour spontané et volontaire vers une nature plus véridique."

6. Charles Clément, "Exposition de 1864," 6e article, *Journal des débats*, June 2, 1864.

7. Quoted in Breton, *The Life of an Artist*, 308.

8. Quoted in Annette Bourrut Lacouture, *Jules Breton: Painter of Peasant Life*, exh. cat. (New Haven: Yale University Press in association with the National Gallery of Ireland, Dublin, 2002), 139.

9. The snapshot effect here may reflect Breton's interest in photography.

10. Breton, *The Life of an Artist*, 314.

11. Ibid., 315.

12. Castagnary, "Salon de 1870," in *Salons, 1857–1870*, 1:421: "M. Jules Breton has lost the grave and serious character which so struck us originally. His pretty women don't think enough about their work. . . . The Washerwomen are barely washing. Are they simply there to form pleasing groups which satisfy the gaze of the passer-by?" (M. Jules Breton a perdu le caractère grave et fort qui nous avait si frappé à l'origine. Ses jolies femmes ne songent pas assez à leur ouvrage. . . . Les Lavandières ne lavent guère. Sont-elles donc là uniquement pour s'arranger en groupes heureux et plaire à l'oeil du passant qui va venir?)

13. Charles Clément, "Exposition de 1870," *Journal des débats*, May 24, 1870: "sans s'éloigner en rien de la vérité, le peintre a tiré le plus heureux parti du costume."

14. Hollister Sturges, ed., *Jules Breton and the French Rural Tradition*, exh. cat. (Omaha, Nebr.: Joslyn Art Museum; New York: Arts Publisher, 1982), 19.

15. Breton, *The Life of an Artist*, 311.

16. Ibid., 308.

17. Castagnary, "Salon de 1873," in *Salons, 1857–1870*, 2:60–61: "Aucun retour au passé n'est à craindre, quand on examine ces pommettes saillantes et ce menton énergique. Républicaine et rationaliste, le forte femme nous fera les enfants que mérite la France, des enfants républicains et libres-penseurs. . . . N'est-ce pas déjà un grand signe du progrès démocratique, que de voir un peintre prendre une paysanne pour modèle et, par la force du style aussi bien que par l'élévation du sentiment, en faire la représentation typique de toute une race? Il y a dans cette idée le cachet de la République de 1870." Castagnary's words describe *La Bretonne*, a view of a Breton peasant woman carrying a candle, but they might equally apply to *The Wounded Seagull.*

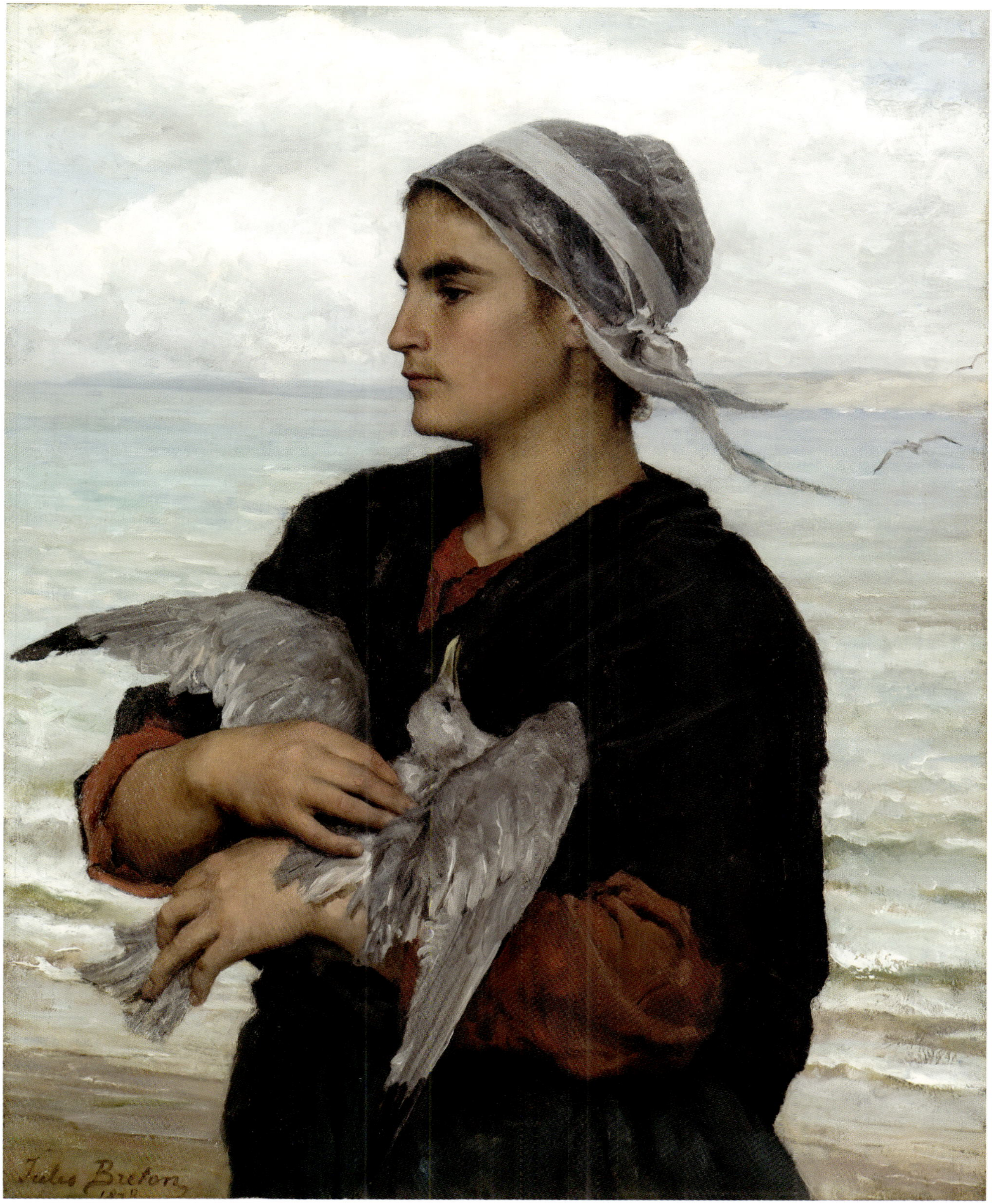
Jules Breton

GIRAUDON'S ARTIST

FRENCH, ACT. 1870s

63

Female Peasant in Profile, with Scythe

ca. late 1870s

Albumen print from collodion glass negative

$6\frac{5}{8} \times 4\frac{7}{16}$ in. (16.8 × 11.3 cm)

The Nelson-Atkins Museum of Art, Kansas City, Missouri, Gift of the Hall Family Foundation, 2009.6.71

"FOR MY PART, I WOULD RATHER live in a beautiful countryside, half thinker, half peasant, with a blouse and shoes, homemade bread, apples in my garden and a small, natural wine, than agitate myself with a life of artifice and turbulence in the midst of luxury and material enjoyment." Théophile Thoré wrote these words in his letter to Théodore Rousseau in 1844.[1] Thoré's conception of "half peasant," provincial life was not uncommon in post-Revolutionary France, particularly among the intellectual, literary, and artistic classes in Paris and other cities, who sought to articulate, in words and images, their concerns about the loss of *la France profonde* in the nation's provinces. The life of the peasantry was characterized as being not only closer to nature than life in the city but also as being more virtuous and authentic. Life in the city, in contrast, was often aligned with shallow materialism, anxiety, and turmoil.

In the first decades of the nineteenth century, and before the railways expanded after the 1840s, writers such as François-René de Chateaubriand, Stendhal, and Victor Hugo traveled extensively throughout France via coach to discover living history and/or what they perceived to be more authentic ways of life. They wrote of their encounters with provincial customs and traditions and their firsthand experiences of the nation's varied rural geography. Many of these accounts were Romantic in sentiment and included detailed, awe-inspired descriptions of the terrain and notable monuments, as well as dramatic personal reports of braving the elements and enduring such hardships of travel as bedbugs, interminable coach rides, gossiping locals, or "hideous old innkeepers who keep terrible inns."[2] Often, such writing reinforced the idea that rural life was stable, honorable, and, above all, timeless (if not a bit uncomfortable), and that France's inherent Frenchness resided in the provinces. This dichotomy—city/country, present/past, corruption/purity—became a common theme in literature and painting, particularly during the Second Empire, when Paris was radically transformed, the rail system grew, and France became an industrialized nation. As the pacing and social structure of modern life profoundly changed the country, so, too, did the desire by many to look back on a noble, preindustrial way of life, whether such a past truly existed or not.

Peasants, because they lived far removed from the modernity of the capital city, were thus seen as being untainted by its corruptive influences. As critics of the Second Empire's policies believed, a country that became increasingly centralized under the state was in danger of losing its grasp of regional histories and traditions. Peasants therefore appeared regularly in the canvases of such painters as Jean-François Millet. With a realist sympathy that many critics found distasteful, Millet endowed these men and women working the land with nobility (cat. 59). Rural subjects also figured prominently in Jules Breton's paintings of peasants engaging in rural agricultural customs, albeit seen in a more sanguine (and salable) light than Millet's unromanticized approach (cats. 60–62).

Recognizing the potential profitability of having a stock of peasant pictures as studies for artists, during the 1870s the Parisian publisher Adolphe Giraudon commissioned an unknown photographer to create a series of figure studies for painters. These images depict a variety of young female models, dressed in rural costumes, engaged in such activities as washing and hanging laundry, gathering sticks and hay, or acting as shepherdesses. The girls stand with appropriate props—scythes, baskets, or sheep—singly or in groups, as if to suggest they are actually pursuing these rustic activities.

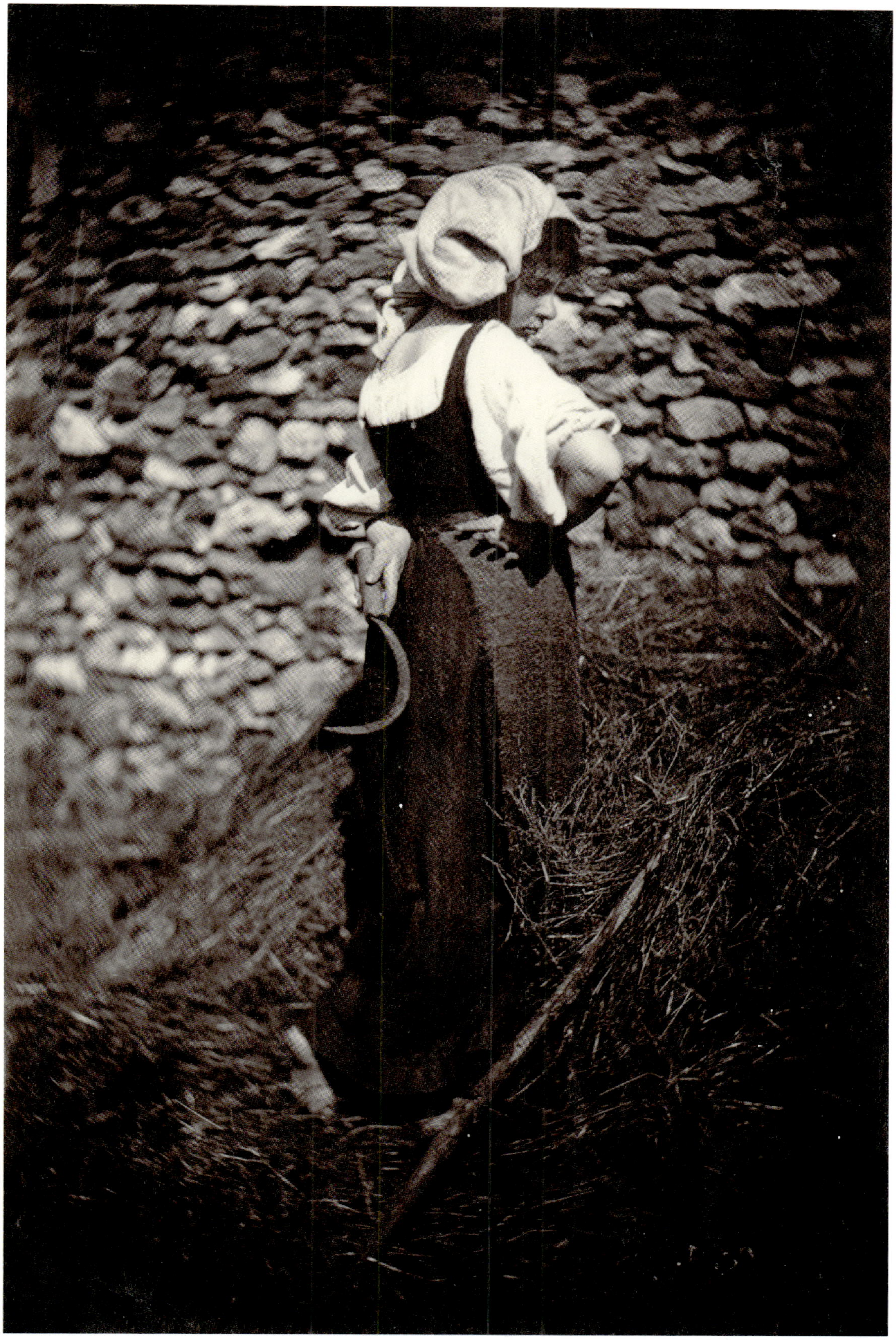

GIRAUDON'S ARTIST

FRENCH, ACT. 1870S

64

Two Female Peasants, One Standing, Doing Laundry

ca. late 1870s

Albumen print from collodion glass negative

4½ × 6½ in. (11.4 × 16.5 cm)

The Nelson-Atkins Museum of Art, Kansas City, Missouri, Gift of the Hall Family Foundation, 2009.6.72

65

Two Women Standing with Baskets

ca. late 1870s

Albumen print from collodion glass negative

4⅜ × 6¹¹⁄₁₆ in. (11.1 × 17 cm)

The Nelson-Atkins Museum of Art, Kansas City, Missouri, Gift of the Hall Family Foundation, 2009.6.73

In truth, these photographs documented not actual young peasant women but posed models. Though all peasants were seen, in mythologized terms, as embodying purity and simplicity, female subjects in particular engendered this response and thus figured prominently in rural scenes.[3]

Giraudon entered a highly competitive marketplace for commercial photographers in Paris in the mid-1870s: by 1877 there were more than 325 professional studios in the city, and approximately 20 of them were providing the types of artist studies that Giraudon was offering.[4] Thanks to an expansive network of clients and correspondents throughout Europe that he had established before 1877, Giraudon was able to build his stock of photographs of works of art and studies after nature to distinguish his wares from those of his rivals. The general themes of his collection include French architecture and reproductions of Italian, Flemish, Dutch, and German art. His rural peasant scenes were categorized as "studies after nature" and described in catalogues simply as "this collection, made by an artist in his hours of leisure, is remarkably beautiful; it offers precious resources to artist-landscapists."[5] Little else is known about these photographs, since the photographer's name was never mentioned, though it is thought the models were photographed in and around Fontainebleau. —AMW

1. T. Thoré, *Le Salon de 1844, précédé d'une lettre à Théodore Rousseau* (Paris: Alliance des Arts, 1844), xvii.

2. Hugo was speaking about the small town of Ernée, just east of Brittany. Victor Hugo, *En voyage France et Belgique* (Paris: J. Hetzel et Cie & Maison Quantin, 1892), 51. Though Hugo made the journey in 1834, many of his travel writings were published posthumously.

3. Robert L. Herbert notes this gender distinction, citing Breton's canvases in particular as being "far more acceptable" to the bourgeois Parisian public precisely because he painted peasant women with the kind of beauty that conformed to Salon standards. Herbert, *Peasants and "Primitivism": French Prints from Millet to Gauguin*, exh. cat. (South Hadley, Mass.: Mount Holyoke College Art Museum, 1995), 13.

4. Monique Le Pelley Fonteny, *Adolphe and Georges Giraudon: Une bibliothèque photographique* (Paris: Somogy Éditions d'Art; Bourges: Conseil Général du Cher, 2005), 22.

5. Ibid., 23.

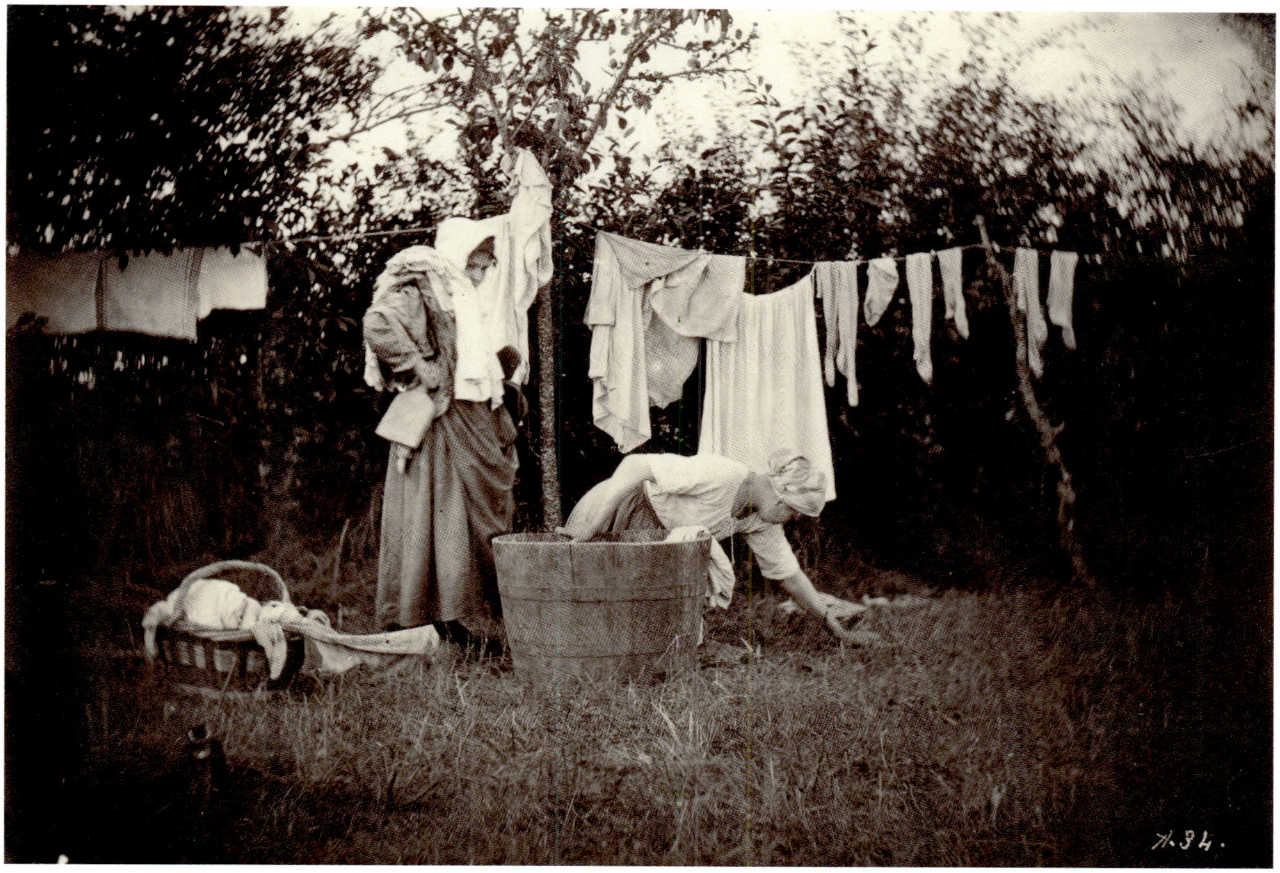

n.34.

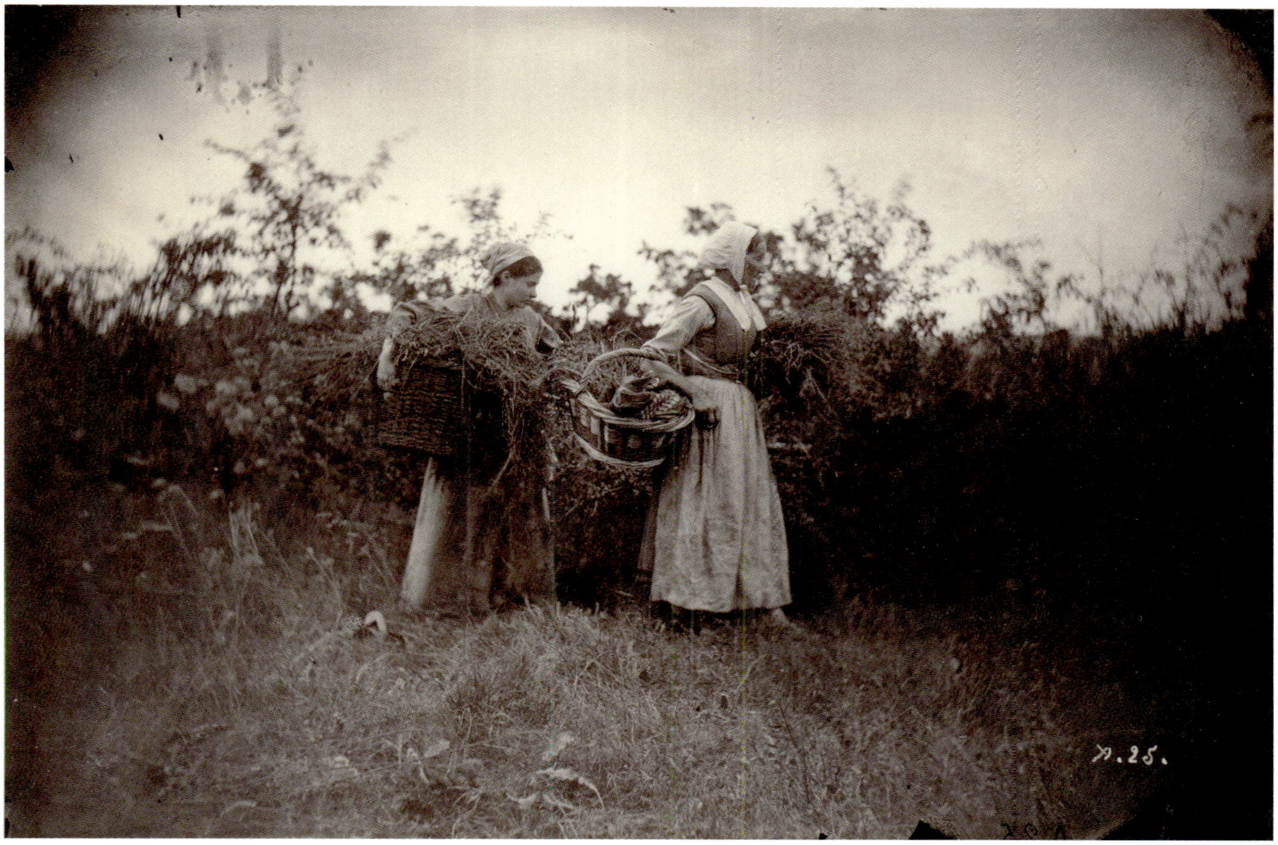

n.25.

66

CHARLES NÈGRE
FRENCH, 1820–1880

The Oil Presses at Grasse

1852

Waxed salt print from waxed paper negative

12$^{15}/_{16}$ × 9$^{1}/_{8}$ in. (32.7 × 23.2 cm)

Jay McDonald, courtesy of Hans P. Kraus Jr., New York

CHARLES NÈGRE WAS BORN in the southern town of Grasse, the son of a confectionary seller. Grasse was known for its perfume production, an industry that began during the Renaissance and proliferated during the nineteenth century, when industrial advances facilitated the extraction of natural scents from plants that grew in the surrounding countryside. Jasmine and lavender were especially sought and harvested in large quantities.

Though Nègre was "a pious son of the Midi," as Henri de Lacretelle described him, he spent many years in Paris, first as a painting student of Paul Delaroche beginning about 1839 and, later, as a drawing instructor at the École supérieure du commerce, a post he assumed in 1852. During this time, he exhibited award-winning paintings at the annual Salons (Napoléon III acquired works by him from the Salon of 1851).[1] Nègre took up photography about 1844, mastering the daguerreotype and, after 1848, the calotype. In August 1852 he left Paris for several weeks to photograph throughout his native Midi in hopes of publishing his images in several installments. Though *Le Midi de la France*, as the project was titled, did not come to full fruition, the venture resulted in hundreds of photographs that, at least among his colleagues, were greatly admired. In his lengthy appreciation of these works, de Lacretelle remarked specifically on Nègre's images of Grasse, noting that it seemed, when looking at them, one "drowns in its gardens and seems to swim in the vapor of a perfume boutique."[2]

In the image of a narrow, zigzagging street, Nègre composed a dynamic scene of tightly packed interlocking geometric planes. Situated throughout are figures: a woman stands at the bottom of the picture, washing clothes; and a man is seated at the end of a stone wall, which appears from Nègre's vantage point as a strong diagonal, one of many astute compositional devices the photographer employed to lead the viewer's eye throughout the scene. The flattening of perspective that occurs through photographic transcription further emphasizes the picture's jostling of forms. This kind of geometric spatial dissection would later be taken up by Paul Cézanne and eventually explored more fully in the Cubist landscapes of Georges Braque and Pablo Picasso. —AMW

1. James Borcoman, *Charles Nègre, 1820–1880*, exh. cat. (Ottawa: National Gallery of Canada, 1976), 52.

2. Henri de Lacretelle, "Albums Photographiques No. 1—M. Nègre," *La lumière*, February 12, 1853, 26: "noyée dans ses jardins, et qui semble nager dans une vapeur de boutique de parfumerie."

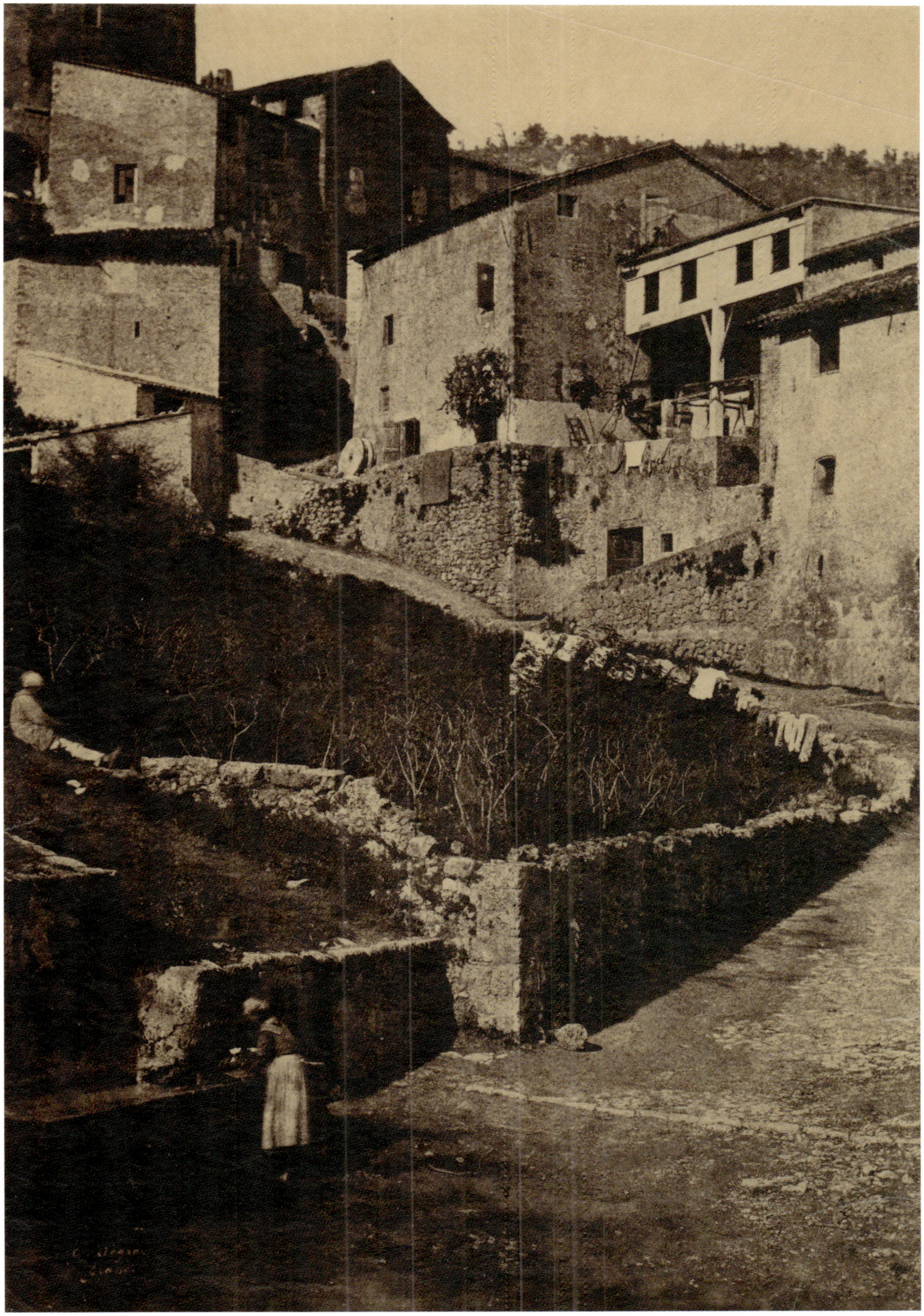

67

CHARLES NÈGRE
FRENCH, 1820–1880

A Young Girl from Arles

1852

Salt print from paper negative

7⅝ × 6⅞ in. (19.4 × 17.5 cm)

Philadelphia Museum of Art, Purchased with funds contributed by the American Museum of Photography, 1971-4-14

ON HIS 1852 VENTURE TO THE MIDI, Négre also traveled to Arles, where he made a few photographs of Arlésiennes: young women dressed in a traditional Provençal manner. He exhibited these works in 1856 at the L'association pour l'encouragement et le développement des arts industriels en Belgique, in Brussels, and at the second annual exhibition of the Société française de la photographie in Paris in 1857. In one image, Nègre depicted a young girl in Arlésienne costume, seated in front of a large basket, posed with her chin resting delicately on her hand. Unlike his earlier street scenes featuring young chimney sweeps walking along the streets of Paris, the young girl from Arles is shown seated and motionless, removed from any signs of modernity.

Indeed, the figure of the Arlésienne as a symbol of timeless, Provençal beauty features prominently in the poetry of Frédéric Mistral and the Félibrige writers of Provence. Mistral celebrated the comeliness, moral virtue, and chastity of this regional female stereotype. Anne Dymond notes that "types arlésiennes" were featured on postcards, particularly in the second half of the century, as tourism to the area increased. These women were often depicted as having dark hair and dark eyes, with hair parted down the middle. Their particular beauty was compared to that of the statues of classical antiquity, such as the Venus of Arles, a marble sculpture dating to the first century BC that was discovered in fragments in the Roman theater in Arles in the seventeenth century before being transferred to the Louvre.[1] Regional costume was also a defining characteristic. Though their actual garments varied throughout history, the version that came to be seen as typical was a dark dress covered by a pinafore-like piece of embroidered or lace-edged white cloth called a *modeste*. Often the type is seen wearing a choker with a cross around her neck.[2] The Arlésienne became popular in Paris in the later decades of the twentieth century after a short story written in 1866 by the Provençal writer Alphonse Daudet was recast several years later as a play, with accompanying music composed by Georges Bizet.[3] The Arlésienne type, as a chaste, traditionally costumed, non-Parisian female figure, came to be seen as a symbol for Provence itself. —AMW

1. As Anne Dymond notes, the beauty of the Arlésienne was not always aligned with chastity. In certain descriptions, these women were seen as courtesans. Dymond, "Displaying the Arlésienne: Museums, Folklife and Regional Identity in France," in *Folklore and Nationalism during the Long Nineteenth Century*, ed. Timothy Bacroft and David Hopkin (Leiden: Brill, 2012), 137–59.

2. Ibid., 151–52.

3. Ibid., 150.

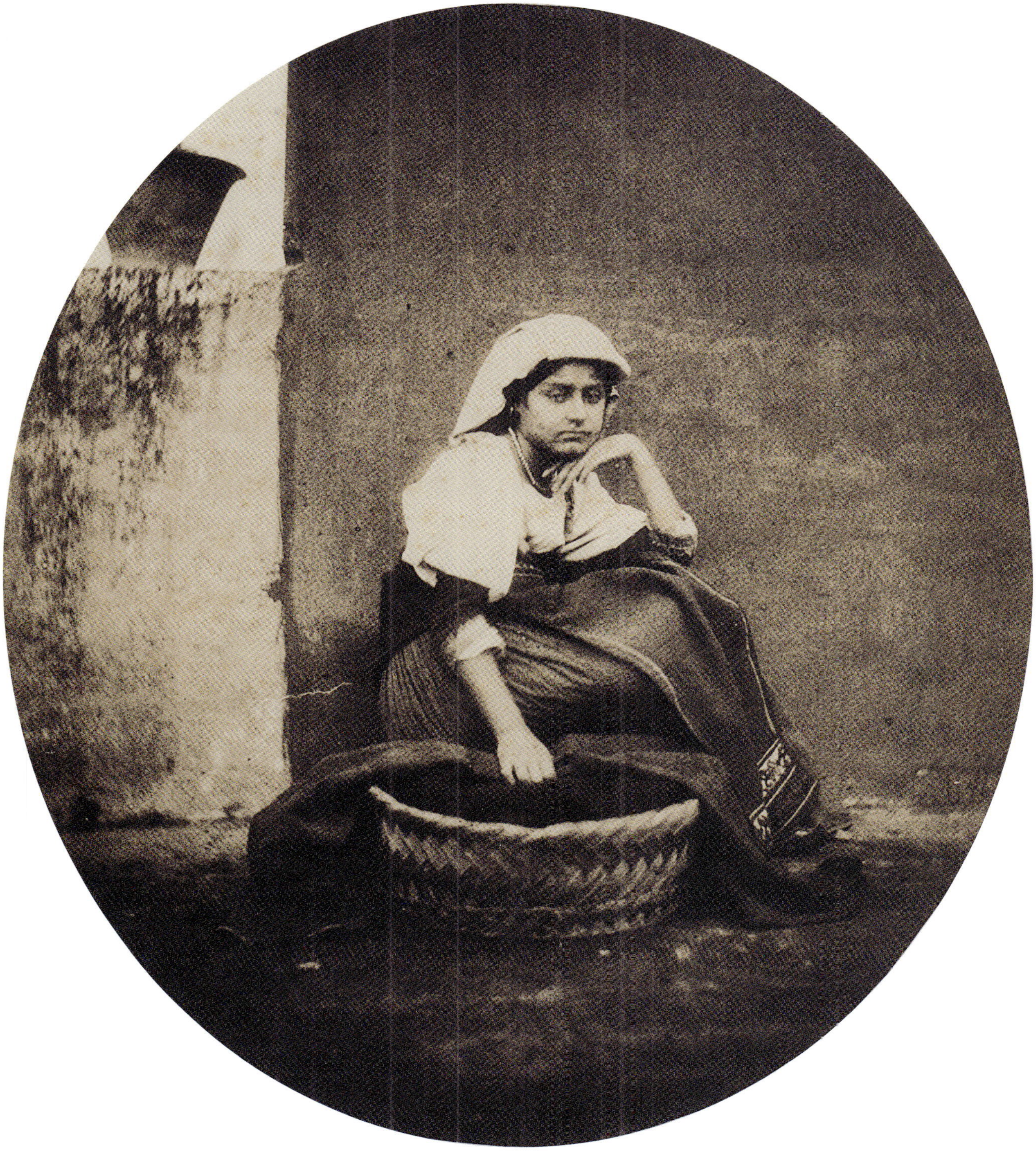

68

CONSTANT TROYON
FRENCH, 1810–1865

Cattle Pasture in the Touraine

1853

Oil on canvas

39⁵⁄₁₆ × 51⁵⁄₁₆ in. (99.9 × 130.3 cm)

The Nelson-Atkins Museum of Art, Kansas City, Missouri, Purchase: William Rockhill Nelson Trust, 31-47

CONSTANT TROYON'S WORKS carefully document the rural agriculture of France; he was particularly known as a painter of his country's many types of cattle and farm animals. His pictures reflect his study of animal anatomy as well as his debt to the seventeenth-century Dutch artists Aelbert Cuyp and Paulus Potter, whose works he had closely studied on a trip to the Netherlands in 1847. Troyon first came to prominence as a landscape painter in the 1840s and enjoyed great commercial success in his lifetime before suffering mental problems and entering an asylum in his final years. His pastoral visions of French agriculture, widely shown in England (which the artist visited in 1853), Belgium, and the Netherlands, helped to form international conceptions of the prosperity of French agriculture. Troyon's work also attracted considerable praise from the young Claude Monet, who saw several of the older artist's paintings at the 1859 Paris Salon; he responded particularly to Troyon's rendering of the changing moods of nature, describing the "marvelous" *Return to the Farm* (Musée d'Orsay, Paris) with "a wonderful sky . . . a lot of movement, wind in the clouds: the cows, the dogs are all magnificent."[1]

Cattle Pasture in the Touraine shows an area of rich farming land around the town of Tours, in the center of France. The cattle and bleating sheep evoke the very sounds of a rural scene;[2] the shepherd—or property manager—is on his horse to the right. This picture highlights Troyon's mastery of depicting changing cloud formations as well as his understanding of light, which here outlines the bodies of the cows. For the critic Paul Mantz, this work was one of the artist's masterpieces: "we have here a superb Troyon, ambitiously conceived, vigorously executed, and absolutely full of this luxuriant vitality that the master gave as much to his animals as to his blades of grass."[3]

The location has always been given generically as the Touraine, but when the picture appeared in an exhibition in 1883, the site was described as "near Château-le-Vallière."[4] The artist's early biographer, Henri Dumesnil, noted that Troyon spent the summer of 1853 at the château du Vivier-les-Landes, near the village of Château-Lavallière, on the south banks of the Loire River.[5] This château belonged to a patron yet to be identified, and the artist returned there regularly throughout the 1850s. —SK

1. Monet to Eugène Boudin, June 3, 1859, in Daniel Wildenstein, *Claude Monet: Vie et oeuvre* (Lausanne and Paris: La Bibliothèque des Arts, 1974), 1:419: "Le Retour à la Ferme est merveilleux, il y a un ciel magnifique . . . il y a beaucoup de mouvement, de vent dans les nuages: les vaches, les chiens sont de toute beauté."

2. The central standing cow is probably La Pie Rouge des Plaines breed and the recumbent brown cow is probably La Limousine.

3. Paul Mantz, "Troyon," *Gazette des beaux-arts* 18, no. 5 (May 1, 1865), 406: "c'est là un superbe Troyon, largement conçu, vigoureusement executé, et tout plein de cette vitalité luxuriante que le maître donnait à ses animaux comme à ses brins d'herbe."

4. See the major Parisian exhibition in 1883 of a hundred masterpieces from Parisian private collections, Albert Wolff, *Les cent chefs-d'oeuvre des collections parisiennes*, exh. cat. (Paris: Pillet et Dumoulin, 1883). Here it was titled *Pâturage de la Touraine, près Château-Lavallière*.

5. Henri Dumesnil, *Troyon: Souvenirs intimes* (Paris: H. Laurens, 1888), 67, 76–77: "After having gone to Normandy and Brie, Troyon went later to the château of Vivier-des-Landes, near Château-la-Vallière, the home of another fried, M. L., who painted and to whom he gave advice. He went there for seven or eight years." (Après être allé en Normandie et en Brie, Troyon se rendit plus tard en Touraine, au château du Vivier-des-Landes, auprès de Château-la-Vallière, chez un autre ami, M. L., qui faisait de la peinture et auquel il donna des conseils. Il vint là pendant sept ou huit ans.) Dumesnil noted that after Troyon went to England in May 1853, "he worked a lot on his return, during the summer that he spent almost entirely in Touraine, on the left bank of the Loire, not far from Sologne, at Vivier-les-Landes, in the property of his friend, M. L." (il travailla beaucoup à son retour, pendant l'été qu'il passa presque tout entier en Touraine, sur la rive gauche de la Loire, non loin de la Sologne, au Vivier-des-Landes, dans la propriété de son ami, M. L.)

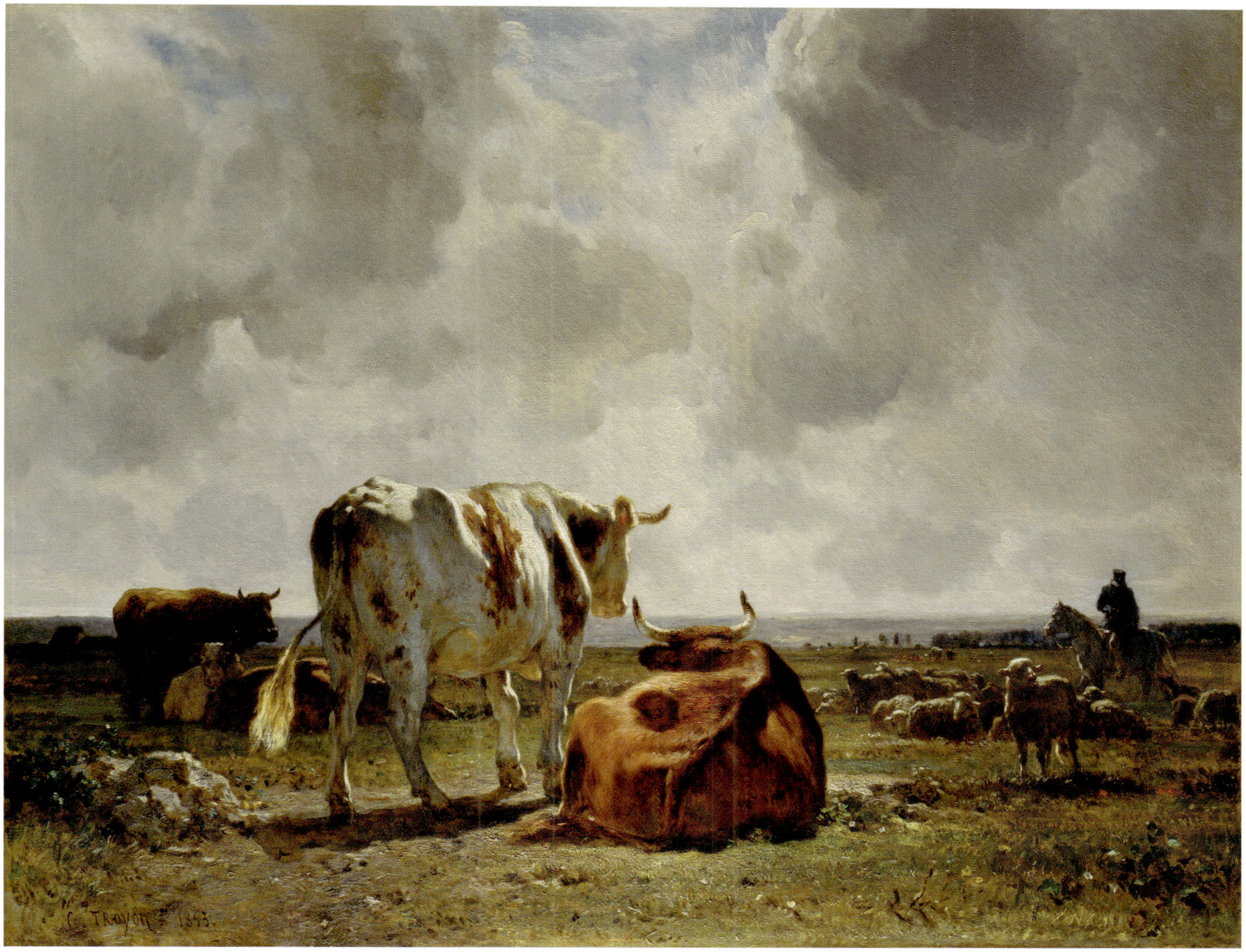
C. TROYON 1853.

69

HENRI LE SECQ
FRENCH, 1818–1882

Behind the Troglodyte Farm

ca. 1853

Salt print from waxed paper negative

20 × 12³⁄16 in. (50.9 × 31.1 cm)

The Cleveland Museum of Art, Norman O. Stone and Ella A. Stone Memorial Fund, 2004.32

DURING HIS BRIEF TIME AS A PHOTOGRAPHER, between about 1848 and 1856, Henri Le Secq produced some of photography's earliest and most accomplished architectural views, landscapes, and still lifes. A founding member of the Société héliographique, he was one of five photographers commissioned in 1851 to document the nation's architectural heritage, likely based on the merit of his photographs of Amiens. By 1852 he had already impressed critics and colleagues alike with his calotypes of Reims and Strasbourg Cathedrals. As Henri de Lacretelle opined in *La lumière*: "The entire cathedral has been reconstructed layer by layer with the marvelous effects of sun, shadow, and rain. M. Le Secq, too, has made his monument . . . M. Lesecq is one of the masters of photography."[1]

Le Secq came from a well-to-do family: his father was a clerk at the Prefecture of the Seine before Baron Georges-Eugène Haussmann was appointed prefect and in 1853 became mayor of what is today the fourth arrondissement. This background instilled in the young Le Secq a deep understanding of and appreciation for the city's historic architecture and neighborhoods.[2] He became, in essence, an antiquarian, and his fondness for the nation's past manifested itself in his choice of subject matter: Gothic cathedrals, medieval Parisian neighborhoods slated for demolition, and provincial landscapes and rustic scenes. Le Secq was also a painter of some talent. Like Gustave Le Gray and Charles Nègre, Le Secq trained in the studio of Paul Delaroche and regularly had his paintings accepted in the Salons, debuting in 1842, when he won a third-class medal. His use of photography was thus deeply informed by both his antiquarian sensibility and his artistic training. These two strains became particularly evident in his landscapes in and around the stone quarries, forests, and troglodyte dwellings of Montmirail, in the Loire valley, where he owned property and his wife's family resided.

Le Secq began to produce these landscapes about 1852, and many of them, such as this landscape view made near a troglodyte farm, were printed at an impressively large scale (up to 20½ × 15 in. [52 × 38 cm]). As Eugenia Parry Janis notes in her formative study on Le Secq's oeuvre, these landscapes are among the most striking and unusual of the period, owing to Le Secq's predilection for crafting unique compositions that foreground deep shadows and voids. In this scene, for example, Le Secq centers his image on the dark recess that is formed by the arched entrance to this cavernous structure, which is built into the earth itself. His use of paper negatives—a form he used exclusively—enhances the textural qualities of rough-hewn stone and shadow areas, adding to the image's rusticity. Troglodyte dwellings had a long history in France, particularly in the Loire valley region, where a soft white stone called tuffeau was prevalent and easily carved into underground dwellings. The term *troglodyte*, in reference to a person, dates back to the fifteenth century, when it described political activists who often lived underground to avoid paying taxes.

Ernest Lacan noted that the large scale of Le Secq's landscapes allowed the painter-photographer to achieve effects of light, shadow, and texture comparable to those of painters. Commenting on one rustic landscape, Lacan summarized: "It has the vigor, the intensity of light, the hardiness of a painting by [Alexandre] Descamps."[3] Le Secq, who had shown architectural views at the 1851 Great Exhibition in London, also displayed several photographs, including landscapes, at the Exposition universelle in 1855, winning a medal. Though it is not known why Le Secq abandoned photography at the height of such accomplishments, one

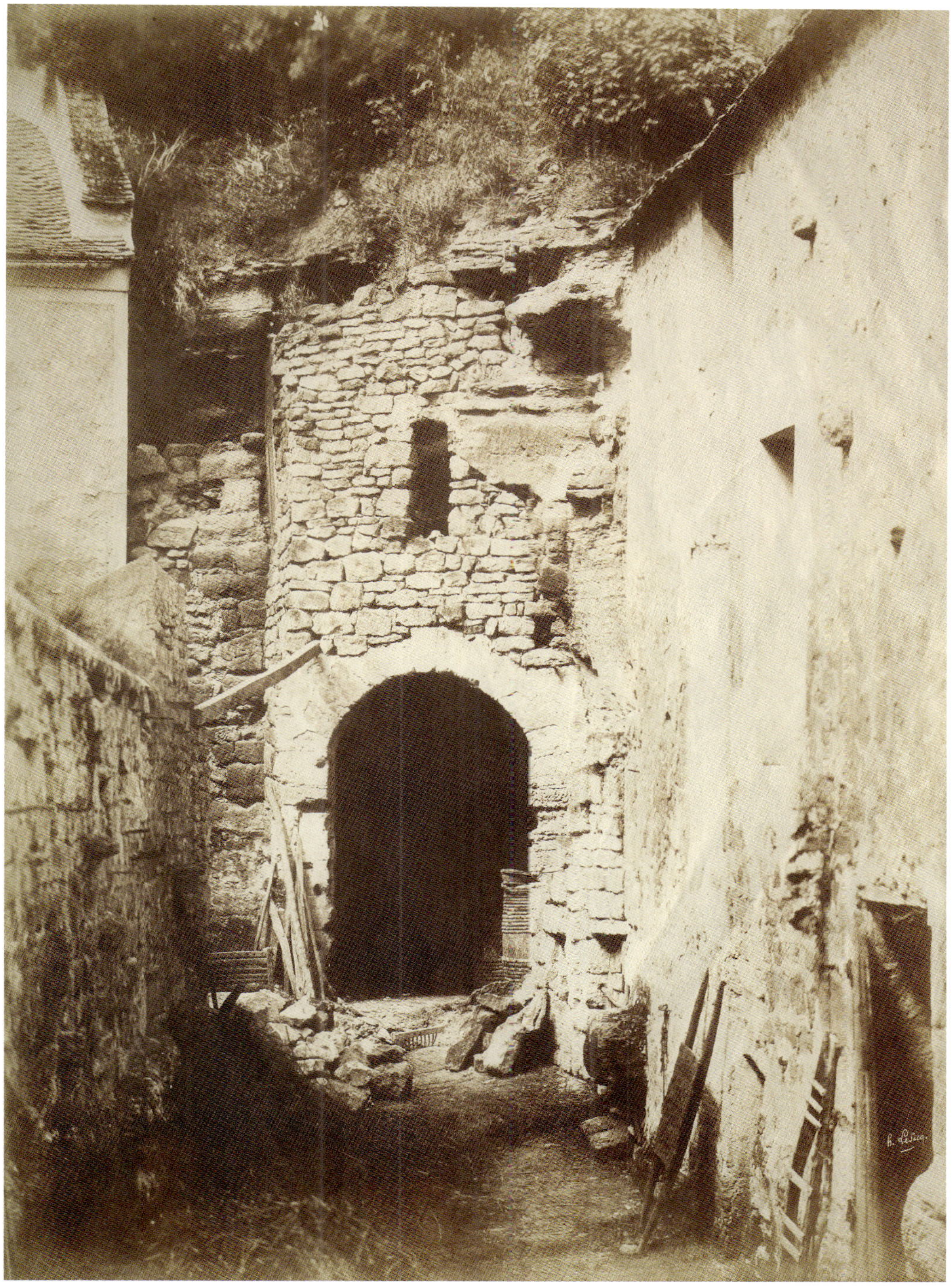

suspects it had to do with the increased commercialization of the medium by the 1860s, at the expense of serious artistic applications. Le Secq nonetheless continued to paint and exhibit in the annual Salons. He also collected prints by Jean-François Millet and Charles Meryon, as well as paintings by Johan-Barthold Jongkind and Charles-François Daubigny. Janis suggests that Le Secq may have even owned work by well-known Impressionist painters.[4] —AMW

1. Henri de Lacretelle, "Revue photographique," *La lumière*, March 20, 1852, 50: "La cathédrale entière est reconstruite, assise par assise, avec des effets merveilleux de soleil, d'ombre, et de pluie. M. Lesecq a fait aussi son monument . . . M. Lesecq [est] un des maîtres de la photographie."

2. André Jammes and Eugenia Parry Janis, *The Art of French Calotype with a Critical Dictionary of Photographers, 1845–1870* (Princeton: Princeton University Press, 1983), 207.

3. Ernest Lacan, "Revue photographique," *La lumière*, July 29, 1854, 118–19: "Elle a la vigueur l'intensité de lumière, la hardiesse d'une peinture de Decamps."

4. Jammes and Janis, *The Art of French Calotype*, 209.

70

CHARLES-FRANÇOIS DAUBIGNY
FRENCH, 1817–1878

Fields in the Month of June

1874

Oil on canvas

53 × 88 in. (135 × 224 cm)

Herbert F. Johnson Museum of Art, Cornell University, Ithaca, New York, Gift of Mr. and Mrs. Louis V. Keeler, Class of 1911, 59.087

ALTHOUGH BEST KNOWN as a painter of rivers, Charles-François Daubigny painted scenes of French agriculture throughout his career, including such major Salon submissions as *The Harvest* (1852; Musée d'Orsay, Paris) and *Wine Harvest in Burgundy* (1863; Musée d'Orsay, Paris), the latter a large-scale view that might be compared to Jules Breton's image of the wine harvest in the Bordeaux region (cat. 60). *Fields in the Month of June* can be seen as the culmination of the artist's study of French agricultural practices. The intensely colorful picture shows a summer scene of workers raking up grass to create haystacks; several have already been formed. This was a crucial part of annual farming activity, since it provided the hay for farm animals to eat during the winter months. A crescent moon is visible, and a line of crows crosses the sky. Daubigny probably observed the scene in the vicinity of Auvers, the town northeast of Paris where the artist had a studio from 1860. The composition is dominated by the field of wild red poppies (*Papaver rhoeas*) in the foreground, rendered in flickering touches of vermilion. Daubigny's interest in this subject may have been informed by the work of his younger friend Claude Monet, who had recently produced two smaller views of poppy fields, one of which appeared at the 1874 Impressionist exhibition (Musée d'Orsay, Paris). For Jean-Baptiste-Camille Corot, however, Daubigny's poppies were "blinding," and there were "too many" of them.[1]

Daubigny showed the painting at the 1874 Salon, where it attracted considerable interest.[2] Jules Claretie noted, "M. Daubigny is in complete possession of his virile talent. His *Fields in the Month of June*, highlighted with poppies, has an admirable breadth."[3] Louis Gonse praised the painting "with its splendid accent of poppies in flower . . . [it] count[s] among his strongest and most moving works."[4] The left-wing critic Jules-Antoine Castagnary wrote the most interesting commentary, in which he related the agricultural scene to the revival of France in the wake of the Franco-Prussian War:

> Messidor [the tenth month of the French Revolutionary calendar, June 19–July 18] has ripened the plain. The fields unfold, brightly colored from various crops. . . . In the foreground the red poppies bloom in long trails of crimson [*sic*]. Farther away, the laborers are at work. Grass has slid under the scythe; the rakes are at work, the haystacks stand and form a line. . . . Nothing resembles our country more than this productive plain and nothing offers a better idea of our resources than this apologia for agriculture. To promote the fertility of our French land after our five billion paid is an example of patriotism. Those to whom we address this can make of it what they will: for us, we will draw from it a thought of comfort and encouragement.[5]

Castagnary mentions the very large reparations of five billion gold francs that had been paid to Germany remarkably quickly by September 1873 and presents Daubigny's work as a symbol of the importance of agriculture to the French nation. The artist himself was becoming an increasingly significant figure in the French landscape school. Following the 1874 Salon, he received the prestigious award of officer of the Légion d'honneur. He exhibited *Fields in the Month of June* again in his noteworthy display of nine works at the 1878 Exposition universelle.[6] —SK

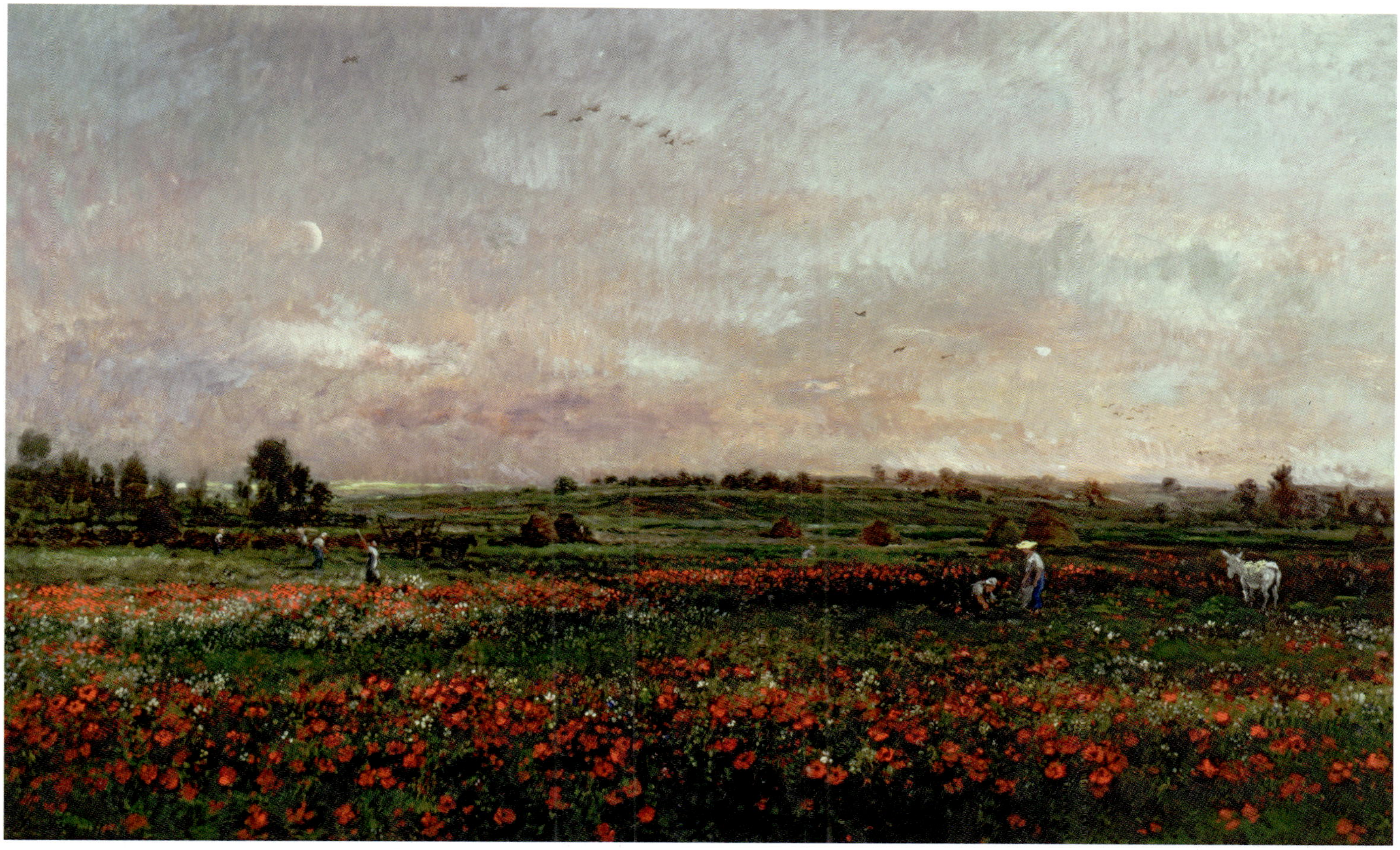

1. Étienne Moreau-Nélaton, *Histoire de Corot et de ses oeuvres* (Paris: H. Floury, 1905), 306: "Son champ de coquelicots est aveuglant. Il y en a trop."

2. The painting was reproduced in *L'illustration* on June 20, 1874 (drawn and engraved by M. Yon).

3. Jules Claretie, "Salon de 1874," in *L'art et les artistes français contemporains* (Paris: Charpentier, 1876), 266: "M. Daubigny . . . est en pleine possession de son mâle talent. Ses *Champs au mois de juin*, piqués de coquelicots, ont une largeur admirable."

4. See Louis Gonse, "Salon de 1874," *Gazette des beaux-arts* 10, no. 2 (August 1, 1874): 148: "*Les champs au mois de juin* avec leur note splendide de coquelicots en fleur et *La maison de la mere Bazot à Valmondois* [The Art Institute of Chicago] compteront parmi ses oeuvres les plus fortes et les plus émouvantes."

5. Jules-Antoine Castagnary, "Salon de 1874," in *Salons (1872–79)* (Paris: Bibliothèque Charpentier, 1892), 2:113: "Messidor a muri la plaine. Les champs se déroulent bariolés par les cultures diverses. . . . Aux premiers plans, les rouges coquelicots s'épanouisssent en longues trainées de pourpre. Plus loin, les travailleurs sont à l'ouvrage. L'herbe a glissé sous la faux; les rateaux fonctionnent, les meules de foin se dressent et s'alignent. . . . Rien ne ressemble plus à notre pays que cette plaine productive et rien ne donne plus l'idée de nos ressources que cette apologie de l'agriculture. Vanter la fécondité de la terre française apres nos cinq milliards payés, c'est un trait de patriotisme. Ceux à qui l'on s'adresse en prendront ce qu'ils voudront; nous, nous y puiserons une pensée de réconfort et d'encouragement."

6. The provenance of the Cornell painting is unclear. Daubigny's stock book indicates that the dealer Hector Brame commissioned a *Field of Poppies* in 1872 for one thousand francs. See Daubigny account book, Musée du Louvre, Département des Arts graphiques. This was probably a smaller painting than the Cornell work and possibly the related picture now in the Boijmans van Beuningen Museum, Rotterdam (see Robert Hellebranth, *Charles-François Daubigny, 1817–1878* [Morges: Éditions Matute, 1976], no. 144). For another work featuring poppies, see Hellebranth, no. 159.

71

CLAUDE MONET
FRENCH, 1840–1926

Vineyards in the Snow, Looking towards the Mill at Orgemont

1873

Oil on canvas

23 × 32 in. (58.4 × 81.3 cm)

Virginia Museum of Fine Arts, Richmond,
Adolph D. and Wilkins C. Williams Fund, 60.51

CLAUDE MONET'S VISION OF NATION was closely linked to his awareness of France as an agricultural land. During his long career, Monet periodically showed interest in the seasonal cycles of the rural calendar. Most famously, he produced his series of grain stacks in the 1890s. In the early 1870s, during his time at Argenteuil, he represented the vineyards that covered the slopes to the north, east, and west of the town. Argenteuil had been well known for its wine production since the Middle Ages, and it was still an important regional center for wine production in the nineteenth century. In earlier centuries, the quality of its wine had been noted—the abbé de Marolles praised it as the best in the Île-de-France in the early seventeenth century—but this was no longer the case by Monet's time, when the area's wine was known principally for its cheap price.[1] Adolphe Joanne noted that the Argenteuil vineyards produced "in good years up to 45,000 casks of mediocre wine."[2] With improved communications, the Argenteuil winegrowers were increasingly challenged by competition from other vintages from across the country. Growing suburban sprawl also threatened to replace their vineyards.

Vineyards in the Snow, Looking Towards the Mill at Orgemont depicts one of the area's vineyards, just to the north of Argenteuil, with its many bare stakes, as well as a furrowed field to the left. The artist rendered an effect of emptiness and bleakness, offset only by touches of color such as the line of grass still visible through the thin layer of snow. A contemporary print taken from a very similar angle (fig. 69) shows the change during harvest time, representing a scene of bustling vitality.[3] In the distance, Monet included a tiny windmill silhouetted against the expansive dove-gray sky, atop the slopes of Sannois. This was the mill at Orgemont that dated to medieval times but was no longer used for grinding grain. By the mid-nineteenth century, the mill had been converted to a restaurant (still in business today), largely because it offered impressive panoramic views south toward Paris.[4]

This painting appears in Monet's unpublished account book as *Moulin d'Orgemont, Neige* (*The Mill at Orgemont, Snow*). The account book indicates that the painting was sold to the dealer Paul Durand-Ruel on February 24, 1873, for six hundred francs as part of a substantial batch of works.[5] The price of the painting was twice as much as Monet charged for other Argenteuil pictures of similar scale around this time, suggesting the importance that he ascribed to it. —SK

1. See Paul Hayes Tucker, *Monet at Argenteuil* (New Haven: Yale University Press, 1982), 23.

2. Adolphe Joanne, *Dictionnaire géographique de la France* (Paris: Hachette, 1869), 1:167: "Argenteuil . . . Vignoble produisent dans les bonnes années jusqu'à 45,000 pièces de vin médiocre."

3. Monet also painted a more summery view of the vineyards, seen from the opposite direction, looking south from the Sannois hills toward the town of Argenteuil (private collection; Daniel Wildenstein, *Claude Monet: Biographie et catalogue raisonné* [Lausanne and Paris: La Bibliothèque des Arts, 1985], 1: no. 219).

4. See Paul Hayes Tucker, *The Impressionists at Argenteuil*, exh. cat. (Washington, D.C.: National Gallery of Art, 2000), 18–19.

5. Monet account book, 1872–76, Musée Marmottan Monet, Paris.

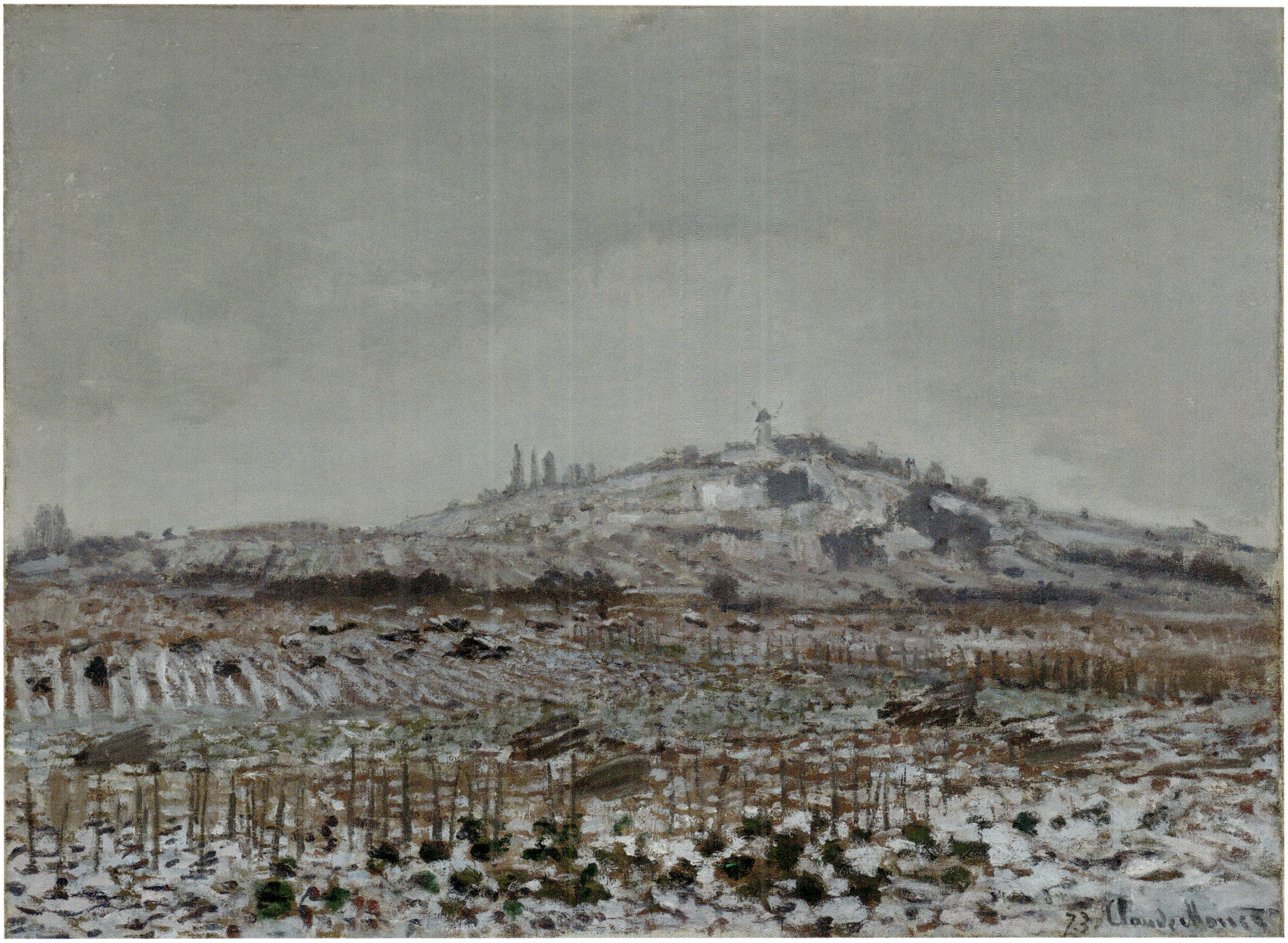

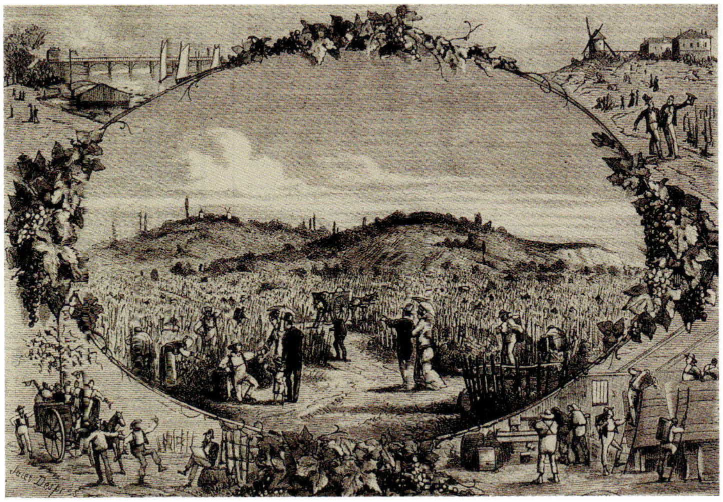

FIG. 69 Jules Despres, *The Wine Harvest at Argenteuil*, 1877. Cabinet des Estampes, Bibliothèque nationale de France, Paris

72

CAMILLE PISSARRO

FRENCH, 1830–1903

The Cabbage Harvest, L'Hermitage, Pontoise

1875

Oil on canvas

24¼ × 25½ in. (50 × 64.8 cm)

Cincinnati Art Museum, Gift of Albert P. Strietmann, 1952.240

73

The Artist's Palette with a Landscape

ca. 1878–80

Oil on panel

9½ × 13⅝ in. (24.1 × 34.6 cm)

The Sterling and Francine Clark Art Institute, Williamstown, Massachusetts, 1955.827

OF ALL THE IMPRESSIONISTS, Camille Pissarro had an unusually complex relationship with his adopted country of France. Pissarro was born in the Danish colony of Saint Thomas in the West Indies, where he lived until the age of twenty-five, with the exception of two and a half years in Venezuela, from 1852 to 1855. He moved to France permanently in 1855. Retaining his Danish citizenship until the end of his life, he nonetheless developed a strong sense of patriotism for France, even seeking to enlist in the French army at the time of the Franco-Prussian War. Unsuccessful, he took his family to England for their safety. From here, he looked fondly to France, noting: "it's only abroad that one feels the extent to which France is beautiful, great, hospitable, what a difference here, one discovers only suspicion, indifference and even greed among brothers."[1] Pissarro felt a particular attachment to the French peasantry, developing a rural ideal of small, self-contained, and self-sufficient communities—rather than large-scale mechanized farms—that embodied his aspirations for social equality.

From 1872 until 1882 Pissarro lived in the hamlet of L'Hermitage on the edge of the larger town of Pontoise, some twenty miles northwest of Paris. During this time, he painted about three hundred works of this area, focusing particularly on the rural economy of L'Hermitage. He found here a dense patchwork of market gardens (*jardins potagers*), with each peasant family owning a block of land: this small-scale, decentralized agriculture fitted well with Pissarro's ideals. *The Cabbage Harvest, L'Hermitage, Pontoise* shows one such garden with a peasant man and woman collecting cabbages in large sacks. These cabbages—the key product of the community—would be sold in local markets or fairs. Pissarro painted several views of cabbage gardens in the 1870s and was often caricatured in the press for focusing on such ostensibly lowly subject matter. Even the radical critic Jules-Antoine Castagnary noted in 1874, "he has a regrettable predilection for market-gardens and does not hesitate to paint cabbage or any other domestic vegetables."[2] Undeterred, Pissarro exhibited views of cabbage gardens at the Impressionist exhibitions not only in 1874 but also in 1877 and 1879.

The Cabbage Harvest, L'Hermitage, Pontoise represents a key event in the rural calendar and is comparable to the artist's other harvesting views, such as those of grain on the nearby Vexin plain or of apples in the 1880s. Pissarro framed the present scene with a representation of the houses of L'Hermitage in a dense pattern of verticals, diagonals, and horizontals. The tall building with red chimney at the top center is the château des Mathurins, a former convent dating to the early seventeenth century and, by the 1870s, the house of the radical feminist Maria Deraismes. Pissarro represented this house in about ten paintings. One such view (fig. 70) highlights the extent to which the garden of the "château" was actually developed and cultivated with a wide range of plants and flowers. Seen here from a distance, though, the building appears within a broader and more rustic context. Deraismes was a committed republican

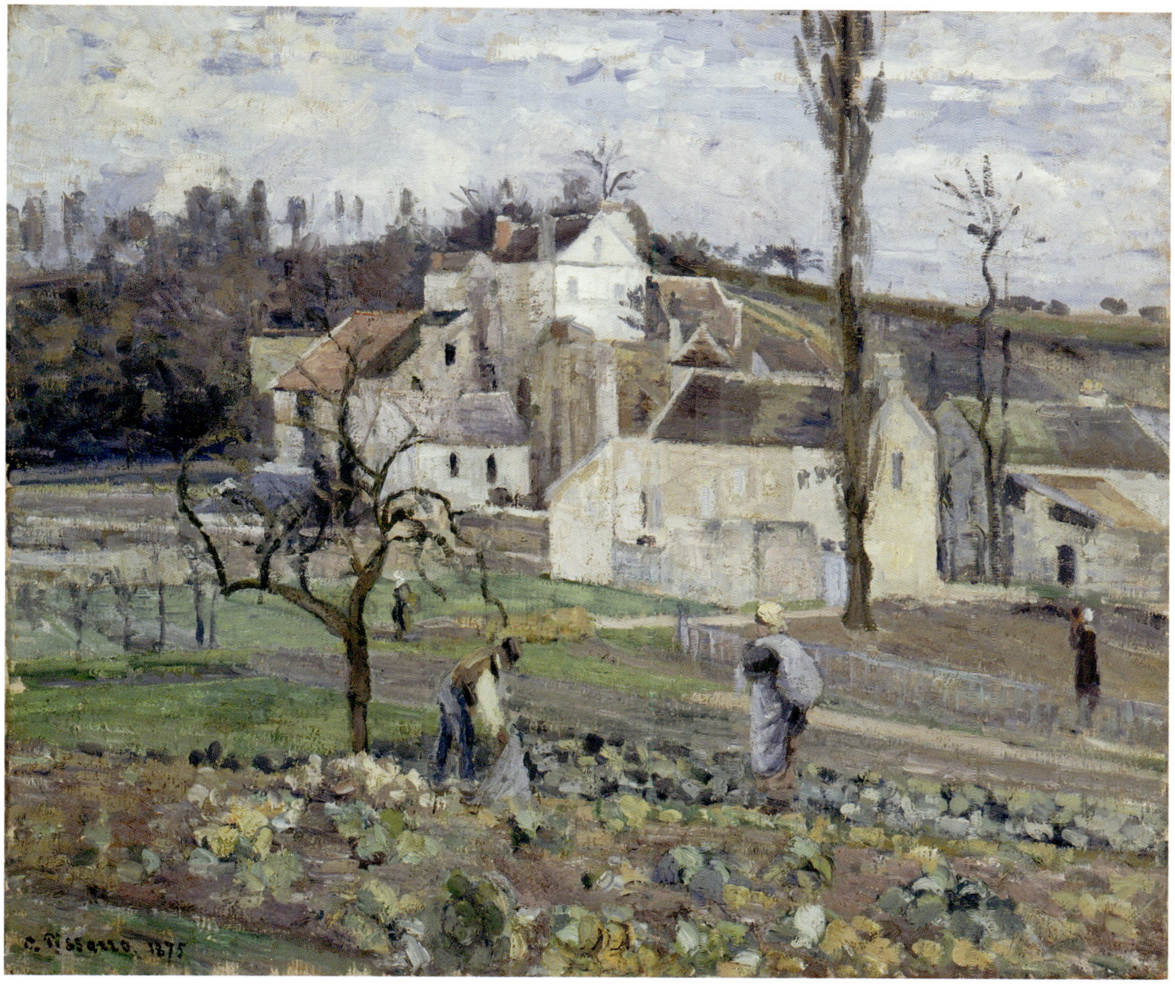
C. Pissarro. 1875

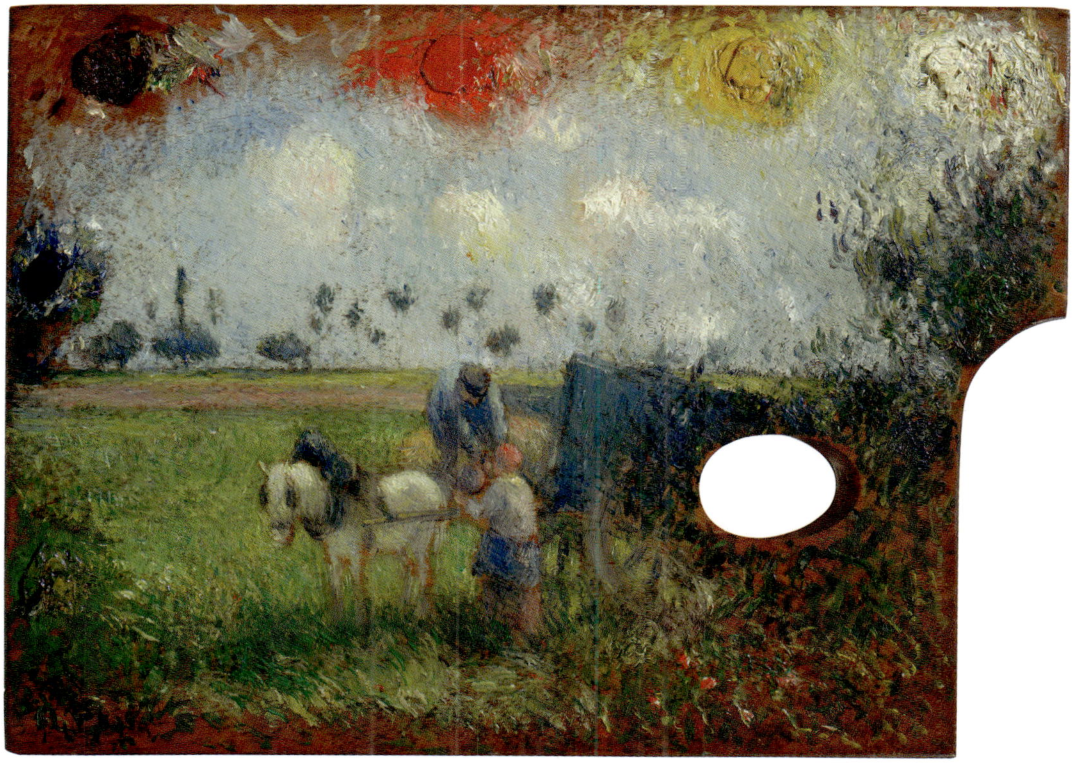

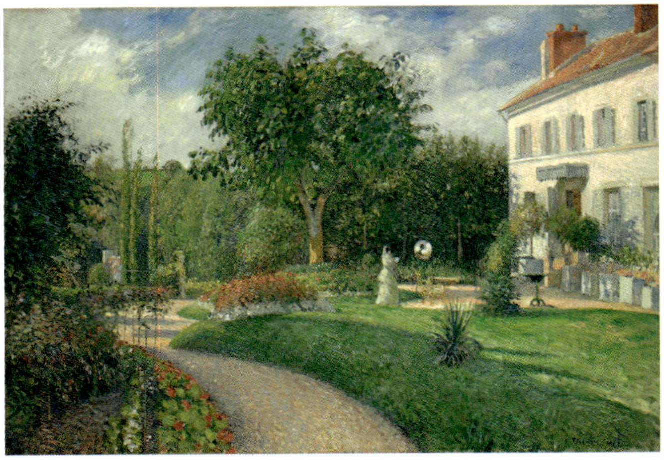

FIG. 70 Camille Pissarro, *The Garden of Les Mathurins at Pontoise*, 1876. Oil on canvas, 44⅝ × 65⅛ in. (113.4 × 165.4 cm). The Nelson-Atkins Museum of Art, Kansas City, Missouri, Purchase: William Rockhill Nelson Trust, 60-38

and a prominent figure in campaigning for women's rights in the late nineteenth century. Her radical ideals undoubtedly made her sympathetic to Pissarro, whose own anarchist philosophy made him the most politicized of all the Impressionists. For Pissarro, anarchism represented a political philosophy promoting decentralized rural communities, rather than referencing the modern meaning of the term, a lack of order.

The Artist's Palette with a Landscape further highlights Pissarro's commitment to rural labor. The artist shows a man and woman loading a cart in the fields around Pontoise. As has been noted, Pissarro identified on a visceral level with the workers he depicted, seeing the work of building up the paint surface on a panel or canvas as analogous to the peasant activity of plowing or harvesting the land.[3] Pissarro produced this image as a "decorated palette" for a local collector, a M. La Place, owner of La Grande Pinte brasserie on the place des Martyrs in Paris.[4] At this point, Pissarro's prices were still low, and he charged the modest sum of only fifty francs. The artist included the six basic colors—white, yellow, orange-red, violet-red, blue, and green—around the edges of the palette, using these colors to build up his composition. The work highlights his experiments with color, which would become even more apparent in the 1880s following his association with the Neo-Impressionist group around Georges Seurat.

Pissarro's identification with France became more complex as he aged. In March 1886 he noted, "From all sides I hear . . . that France is lost, that it's in decadence, that Germany gains ground, that artistic France is beaten by mathematics, that the future belongs to mechanics, engineers, big financiers, Germans and Americans—as if we could foresee the future's surprises. Indeed, yes, France is sick, but from what? . . . That's the question. It's sick from transformation, it can do without it, that's for certain."[5] Pissarro's words are elliptical but probably suggest that, by this time, France's future lay not in modern engineering and technology but in a celebration of its established rural and agricultural traditions. —SK

1. Pissarro to Théodore Duret, June 5, 1871, in Janine Bailly-Herzberg, ed., *Correspondance de Camille Pissarro*, (Paris: Presses Universitaires de France, 1980), 1:64: "ce n'est qu'à l'étranger que l'on sent combien la France est belle, grande, hospitalière, quelle différence ici, on ne recueille que le mépris, l'indifférence, et meme la grossièreté, parmi les confrères, la jalousie et la défiance la plus égoïste—ici, il n'y a point d'art, tout est affaire de commerce."

2. Jules-Antoine Castagnary, *Le siècle*, April 29, 1874: "Il a un penchant déplorable pour les terres maraîchères, et ne recule devant aucune representation de choux ni de légumes domestiques."

3. See Richard R. Brettell, *Pissarro's People*, exh. cat. (San Francisco: Fine Arts Museums of San Francisco, 2011), 165–69.

4. La Place had built up a collection of palettes (including one by Édouard Manet). In an undated letter to Claude Monet, Pissarro recommended that his artist-friend produce a palette for the collector. See Pissarro to Monet, in Janine Bailly-Herzberg, ed., *Correspondance de Pissarro* (Paris: Valhermeil, 1991), 5:399: "une palette ornée." See also entry by Richard Kendall, in *Nineteenth-Century European Paintings at the Sterling and Francine Clark Art Institute*, ed. Sarah Lees (Williamstown, Mass.: Sterling and Francine Clark Art Institute, 2012), 2:593–94.

5. Pissarro to Lucien Pissarro, March 1886, in Janine Bailly-Herzberg, ed., *Correspondance de Pissarro* (Paris: Valhermeil, 1986), 2:30: "De tous côtés j'entends dire . . . que la France est perdue, qu'elle est en décadence, que l'Allemagne gagne du terrain, que la France artiste est battue par les mathématiques, que l'avenir est aux mécaniciens, aux ingénieurs, aux gros financiers, allemands et américains. Comme si nous pouvions prévoir les surprises de l'avenir. Parbleu, oui, la France est malade, mais de quoi? . . . Voilà la question. Elle est malade de transformation, elle peut y passer, c'est certain."

74

ADOLPHE BRAUN

FRENCH, 1812–1877

Study of Cows

ca. 1860s; printed ca. 1880s

Toned carbon print

11¹¹⁄₁₆ × 14¾ in. (29.7 × 37.5 cm)

The Nelson-Atkins Museum of Art, Kansas City, Missouri, Gift of the Hall Family Foundation, 2006.44.1

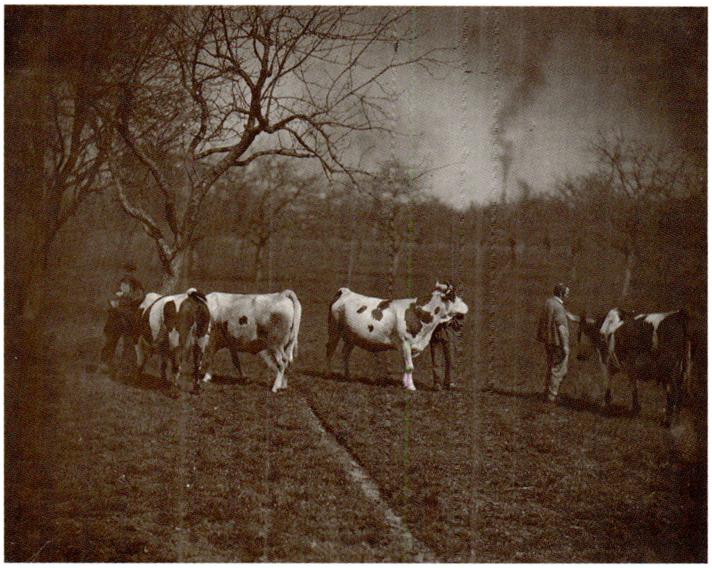

ADOLPHE BRAUN WAS AN ALSATIAN-BORN commercial photographer who began his career as a fabric designer in Mulhouse. By the early 1850s Braun had become interested in the possibilities of photography. He first gained recognition for his photographs of floral specimens, which were intended to improve patterns for textile designs. When he showed a series of flower studies at the Exposition universelle in 1855, he earned a first-class medal and received wide praise from critics and fellow photographers, as well as from Empress Eugénie, who awarded him a gold medal.[1]

By 1857 Braun had formed the company Braun et Cie with the help of his two sons, Henri and Gaston. He published an album of Alsatian imagery, *L'album de l'Alsace,* in 1857 and in 1859 began to produce hundreds of stereographs, specializing in German, Swiss, and French Alpine landscapes popular with tourists (cat. 91). During the 1860s Braun et Cie became a booming commercial studio, which at its height was capable of producing several hundred prints per day.[2] The studio expanded its photographic offerings beyond landscapes. Its commercial catalogues list a series titled *Animaux de ferme,* simply composed images of cows, horses, sheep, and other farm animals. This image depicts a group of cows and their keepers, standing in an open area. Visible in the background are sparsely planted trees and a smokestack from which a dark, billowing stream of smoke emanates. The resulting image, produced in a commercial studio, with its juxtaposition of farm animals and signs of modern industry, is a perfect nexus of the city/country, industry/agriculture dichotomies that informed artistic landscape production during the 1850s and 1860s. This real-life confrontation of cows and smokestacks, given a credibility that photography was believed to impart, was precisely the kind of complexity that Impressionists like Camille Pissarro and Claude Monet readily observed and included in their modern French landscapes (see cats. 82–84, 87). —AMW

1. Christian Kempf, "Adolphe Braun's Photographic Enterprise," in *Image and Enterprise: The Photographs of Adolphe Braun,* ed. Maureen C. O'Brien and Mary Bergstein, exh. cat. (New York: Thames & Hudson in association with Museum of Art, Rhode Island School of Design, Providence, 2000), 29n3.

2. Kempf, "Adolphe Braun's Photographic Enterprise," 27.

5

RAILROADS AND FACTORIES

THE INDUSTRIAL REVOLUTION came later to France than to Great Britain. Nonetheless, France emerged in the nineteenth century as a powerful manufacturing nation. France's industrial growth, closely related to an emerging sense of nationhood, was linked to the railroad. The Second Empire saw the massive expansion of the nation's rail network. In 1851 there were only 2,018 miles of rail track in France, whereas Germany could boast twice as much rail track and Great Britain, three times as much. The size of France's rail network, however, increased fivefold to 9,658 miles by 1870. By then, the country's rail system was only a little behind those of Germany and Great Britain in total length.[1] Six regional companies serviced the nation's network: the Northern, Eastern, Western, Orléans, Paris–Lyon–Méditerranée, and Midi Railways. These companies maintained considerable autonomy; a nationalized railway system would come into operation in France only in the first half of the twentieth century.[2]

The railroad system was represented initially in prints and photographs, most notably Édouard Baldus's two remarkable albums for the Northern Railway and Paris–Lyon–Méditerannée Railway: these highlight the new bridges, viaducts, and rail stations built by the railroad. Painters were slower to represent the new form of transport. In 1861 the prominent critic Champfleury affirmed: "What could be more fantastic than a large machine, its fire-breathing belly and large red eyes flying like the wind through the countryside at night, driven by gnome-like creatures all black with coal and coke? Is not the engine and the role it plays in the countryside sufficient material for a fine picture?"[3] The Impressionists took up the challenge. Claude Monet, in particular, focused on the Western Rail line running through the suburb of Argenteuil, where he lived, producing several views of the trains and new railroad bridge there.

In the early part of the nineteenth century, France's industry also lagged behind that of other European nations. Its coal production in 1851, for example, only 4,960,400 tons, was surpassed by Belgium, Germany, and, above all, Great Britain, which far exceeded all other European nations.[4] France's coal production had, however, quadrupled to 18,739,292 tons by 1878, when it had overtaken Belgium. Several publications now celebrated France's industrial prowess, most notably Julien Turgan's nineteen-volume *Les grandes usines: Tableau de l'industrie française au XIXe siècle*, published from 1860 to 1885. Industry was concentrated around Paris and also Clermont-Ferrand in the center of France. The Le Creusot ironworks in this area was France's largest factory complex, employing approximately thirty thousand workers in the mid-nineteenth century.[5]

Photographers—such as Gustave Le Gray and especially Henri-Victor Regnault—and printmakers depicted factories beginning in the 1850s. Painters again were slower to embrace industry in their iconography. As with the train system, the Impressionist painters were among the first to adopt the subject, focusing on the factories around Paris. Camille Pissarro produced a detailed series of factory views around Pontoise. Armand Guillaumin painted the large factories at Ivry, southeast of Paris. Edgar Degas and Claude Monet were less systematic in their representation of factories but nonetheless produced important views of the subject.

1. B. R. Mitchell, *International Historical Statistics: Europe, 1750–1988*, 3rd ed. (New York: Stockton Press, 1992), 655.

2. The rail companies in France were nationalized in 1937 as the Société nationale des Chemins de fer (SNCF).

3. Champfleury, *Grandes figures d'hier et d'aujourd'hui* (Paris: Poulet-Malassis et de Broise, 1861), 261.

4. Mitchell, *International Historical Statistics*, 416–17. In 1851 England produced 71,650,235 tons of coal. In 1878 France produced 18,739,292 tons; Belgium, 16,424,439 tons; Germany, 43,651,528 tons; and Great Britain, 148,812,027 tons.

5. It was described by G. Bruno in 1877 as "one of the largest factories in Europe." See G. Bruno, *Le tour de la france par deux enfants* (Paris: Belin, 1877), 110.

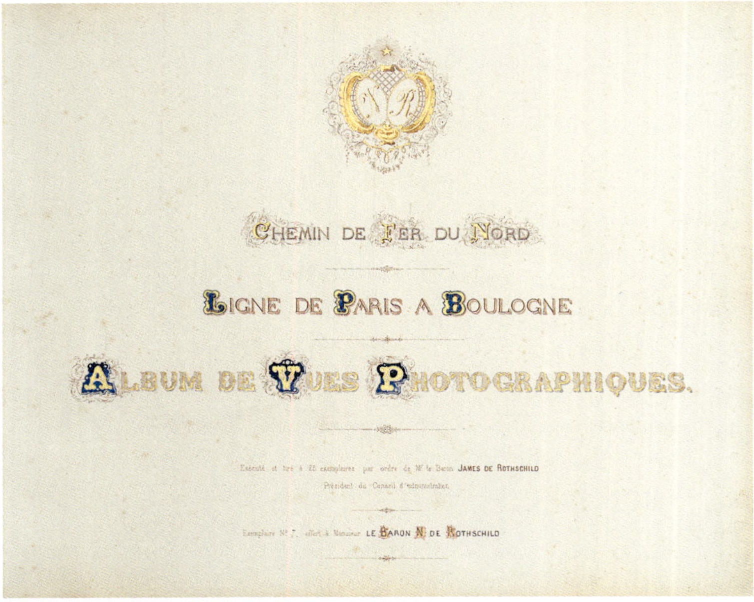

75

Northern Railway: Line from Paris to Boulogne

1855

Album containing 50 albumen prints from collodion glass or paper negatives: 1 illustrated map of 24 small prints by Furne fils et H. Tournier (act. Paris, France); 36 prints by Édouard Baldus (French, 1813–1889); 7 prints by Hippolyte-Auguste Collard (French, 1811–1887); 6 prints by unknown photographers

25 copies printed. Copy no. 7, offered to Monsieur le Baron N. de Rothschild

15¾ × 20½ × 2 in. (40.0 × 51.5 × 4.5 cm)

Canadian Centre for Architecture, Montréal, PH1981:1025:001–050

ON THE OCCASION OF QUEEN VICTORIA'S visit to France in August 1855, Édouard Baldus was commissioned by the wealthy industrialist baron James de Rothschild to produce an album of photographs along the route of the Northern Railway (Chemin de fer du Nord) that would include "the most noteworthy monuments and views between Paris and Boulogne-sur-Mer."[1] As president and chief stockholder in the Northern Railway, Rothschild had a vested interest in celebrating the company's achievement in building what was at the time the fastest rail line in France and to align himself with the Second Empire's most progressive accomplishments. Similarly, by visually associating past architectural and engineering feats with those of the present, the queen's album served a nationalistic purpose, asserting France's status as a leading industrial force, on par with Great Britain, whose railroads were far more established by the mid-1850s. The British, in fact, were deeply interested in the establishment of a rail line from Boulogne to Paris, since it promised to benefit their own trade with Continental Europe. The queen's album was clearly conceived as a tool to foster diplomatic relations between the two countries. Titled *Visite de Sa Majesté la Reine Victoria et de Son Altesse Royale le Prince Albert 18–27 août 1855: Itinéraire et vues du Chemin de fer du Nord*, this lavishly designed object was bound in gilded red leather and featured an ornate, inscribed title page. Also included were two maps depicting the route from Paris to Boulogne, with decorative borders and inset photographs of the two rail stations that bookended the rail journey.

The album reproduced here is not the queen's album but, rather, one of the twenty-five albums that were produced later as an edition. Unlike the queen's album on which they were based, these albums were not aimed at fostering diplomatic relations between England and France. Instead, as Malcolm Daniel's formative research has shown, these albums were likely made—at Rothschild's request—to be given to the board of directors of the Compagnie du Chemin de fer du Nord, as documentation of the company's achievements under Rothschild's direction. Though inspired by the queen's album, the Northern Railway albums differ significantly. Approximately one-third of their fifty photographs do not appear in the queen's album, largely views of newly constructed rail stations, bridges, and viaducts along a branch of the rail line between Saint-Denis and Creil (via Chantilly) that was not open when the queen made her journey in 1855 but that was functional by May 1859.[2] Many of these newer views differ stylistically from the Baldus images that were included in the queen's album, leading to the conclusion that Baldus was not their sole author. Rothschild seems to have drawn on the stock of other photographers, such as that of Hippolyte-Auguste Collard, who had also been hired to make photographs of the Northern Rail line's engineering endeavors before 1859.[3]

The Northern Railway albums, therefore, focus less on the historical architecture and monuments that appeared along the queen's 1855 route and highlight instead the engineering feats of the rail company. They begin with an

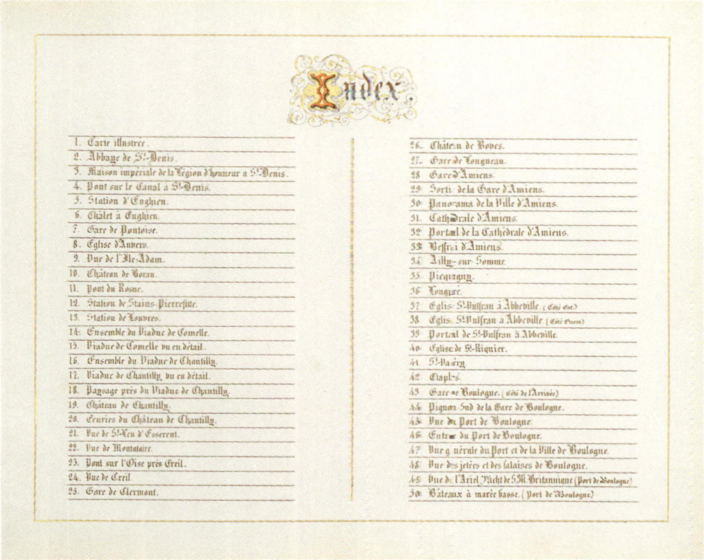

Index.

1. Carte illustrée.
2. Abbaye de S.t-Denis.
3. Maison impériale de la Légion d'honneur à S.t-Denis.
4. Pont sur le Canal à S.t-Denis.
5. Station d'Enghien.
6. Châlet à Enghien.
7. Gare de Pontoise.
8. Eglise d'Auvers.
9. Vue de l'Ile-Adam.
10. Château de Boran.
11. Pont du Rosne.
12. Station de Stains-Pierrefitte.
13. Station de Louvres.
14. Ensemble du Viaduc de Comelle.
15. Viaduc de Comelle vu en détail.
16. Ensemble du Viaduc de Chantilly.
17. Viaduc de Chantilly, vu en détail.
18. Paysage près du Viaduc de Chantilly.
19. Château de Chantilly.
20. Ecuries du Château de Chantilly.
21. Vue de S.t-Leu d'Esserent.
22. Vue de Montataire.
23. Pont sur l'Oise près Creil.
24. Vue de Creil.
25. Gare de Clermont.
26. Château de Boves.
27. Gare de Longueau.
28. Gare d'Amiens.
29. Sortie de la Gare d'Amiens.
30. Panorama de la Ville d'Amiens.
31. Cathédrale d'Amiens.
32. Portail de la Cathédrale d'Amiens.
33. Beffroi d'Amiens.
34. Ailly-sur-Somme.
35. Picquigny.
36. Longpré.
37. Eglise S.t-Vulfran à Abbeville. (Côté Est)
38. Eglise S.t-Vulfran à Abbeville. (Côté Ouest)
39. Portail de S.t-Vulfran à Abbeville.
40. Eglise de S.t-Riquier.
41. S.t-Valéry.
42. Etaples.
43. Gare de Boulogne. (Côté de l'Arrivée)
44. Pignon Sud de la Gare de Boulogne.
45. Vue du Port de Boulogne.
46. Entrée du Port de Boulogne.
47. Vue générale du Port et de la Ville de Boulogne.
48. Vue des jetées et des falaises de Boulogne.
49. Vue de l'Ariel Yacht de S.M. Britannique (Port de Boulogne)
50. Bateaux à marée basse. (Port de Boulogne)

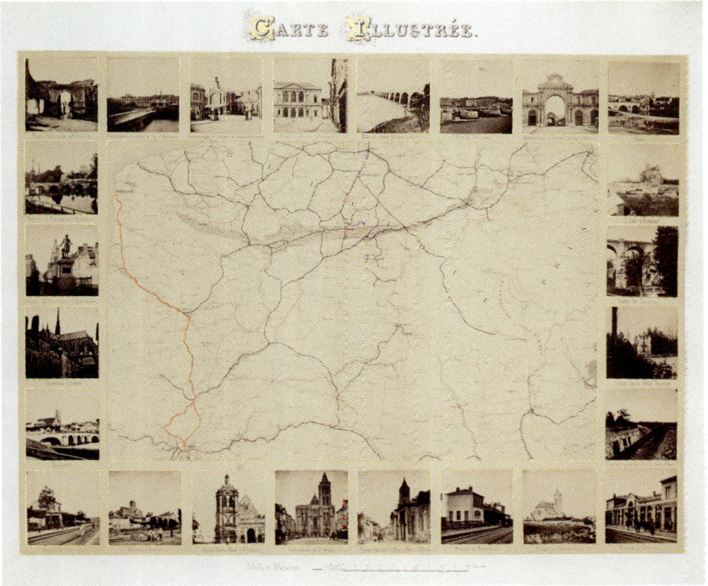

1

inscribed title page, an index of all the plates (illustrated here), and an illustrated map of the route (pl. 1), which is framed by twenty-four inset albumen prints of the monuments, viaducts, and rail stations visible along the way. The larger plates are sequenced to reflect what one would see traveling from Paris to Boulogne, beginning with Baldus's view of the abbey at Saint-Denis and ending with his photograph of the port of Boulogne. Within the sequence are depictions of both sacred and secular architecture, including several Gothic structures: the thirteenth-century church at Auvers (pl. 8), Amiens Cathedral (pls. 30–33), and the church of Saint-Riquier (pl. 40). Two photographs of Enghien show the train station and a small chalet (pls. 5, 6). Enghien, just north of Paris, was a commune developed in 1850 around the area's lake and natural thermal baths. Its proximity to the capital city made it a popular, though exclusive, retreat for the aristocracy and members of the imperial family. The album also includes one of Baldus's most striking photographs of the skeletal remains of the ninth-century château of Boves (pl. 26), a medieval castle that fell into ruin during the late sixteenth century and was written about by Victor Hugo, who visited the site in 1835. The majority of the album's photographs, however, focus not on architecture and ruins of the past but on the viaducts, bridges, and rail stations associated with the Northern Railway in particular and Second Empire progress more broadly.

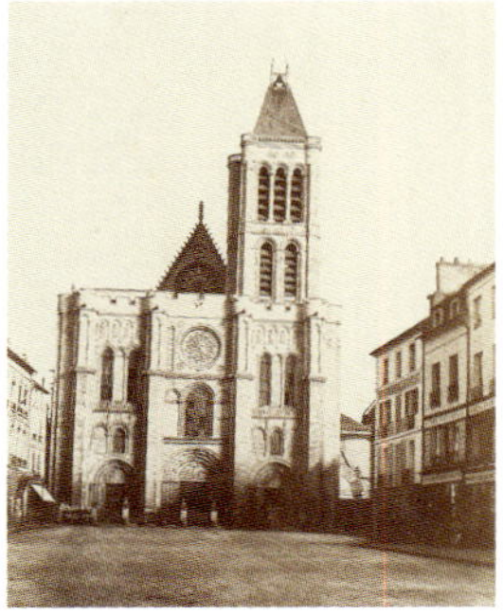
2

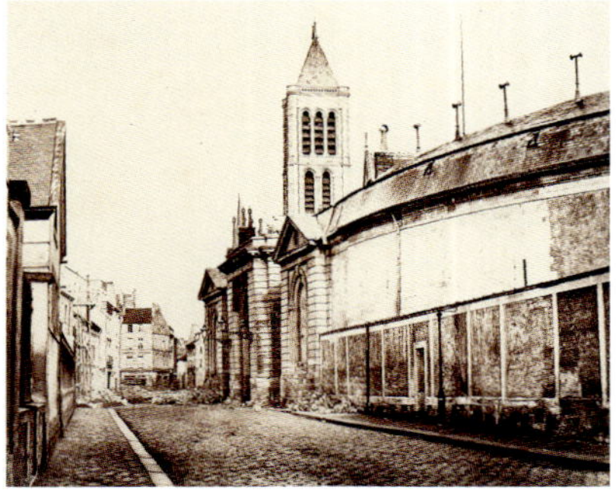
3

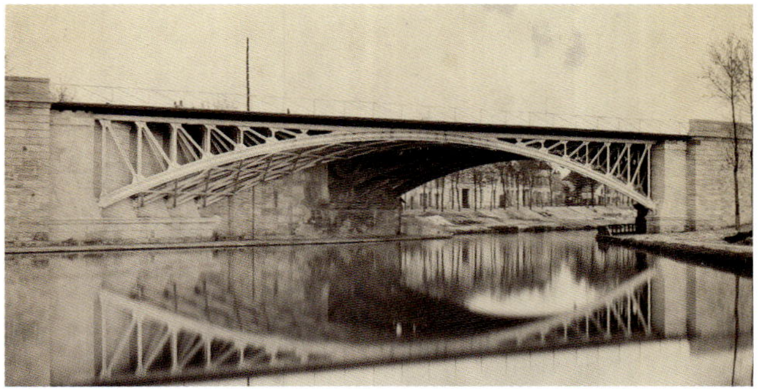
4

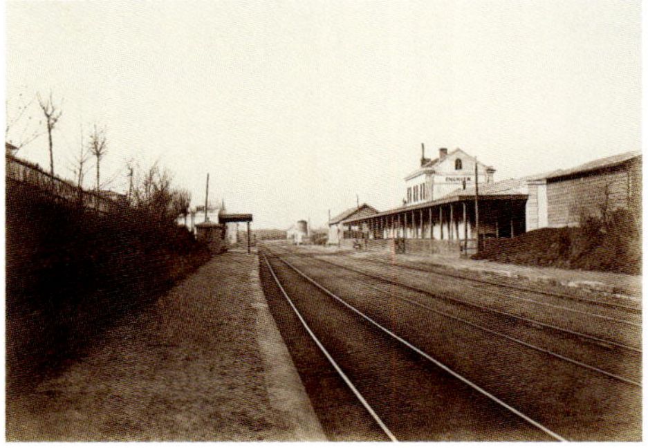
5

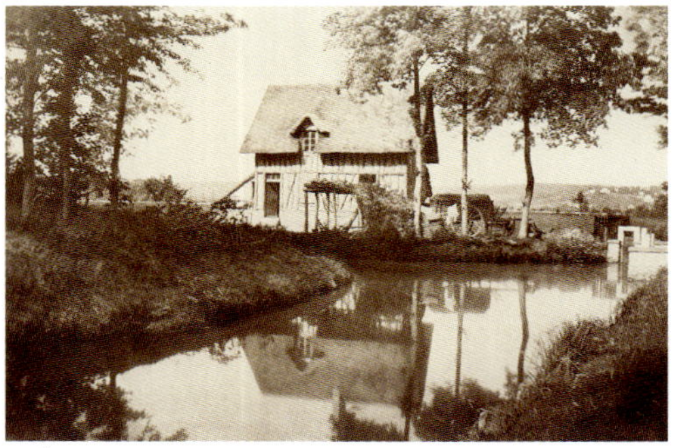
6

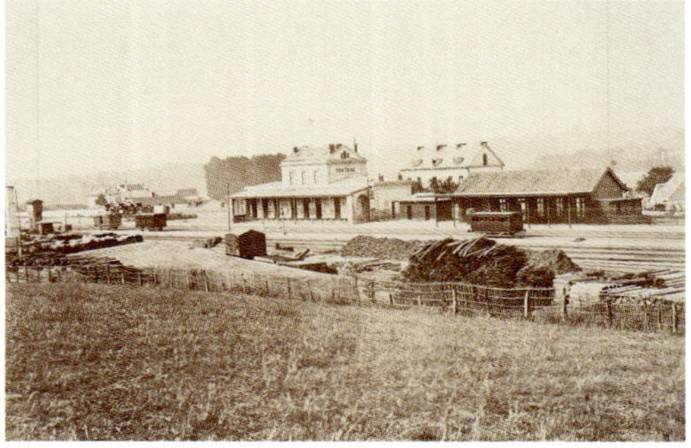
7

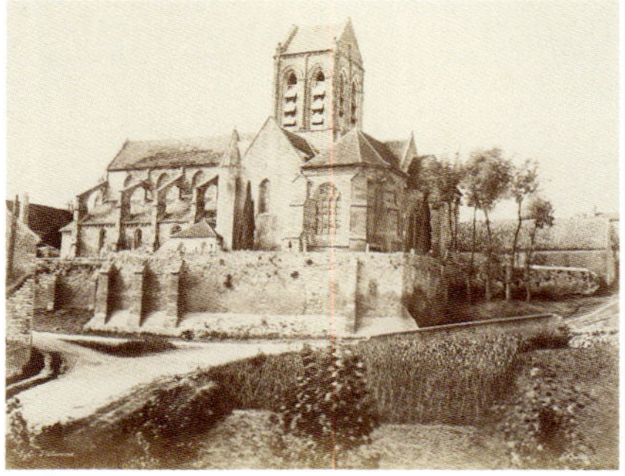
8

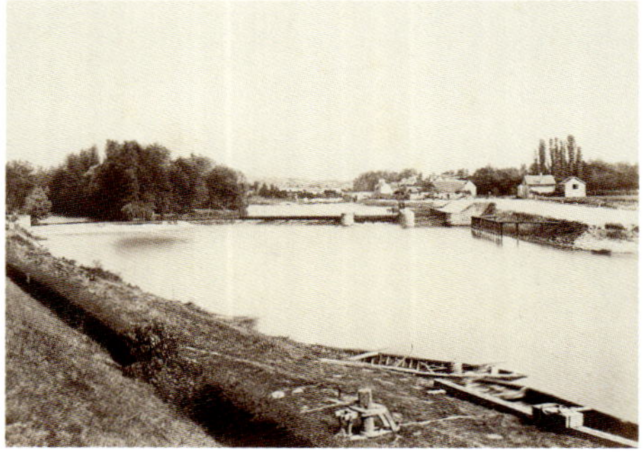
9

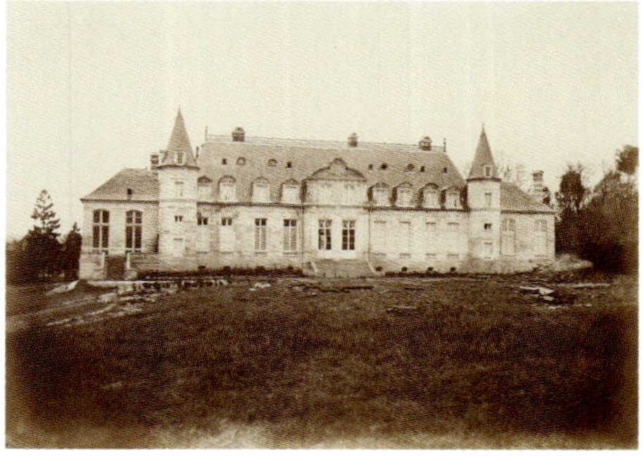
10

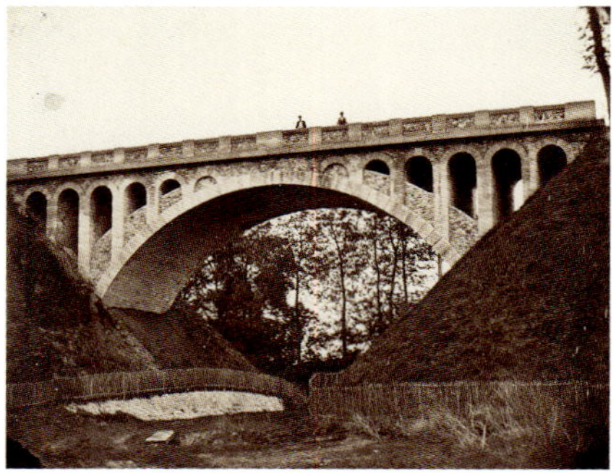
11

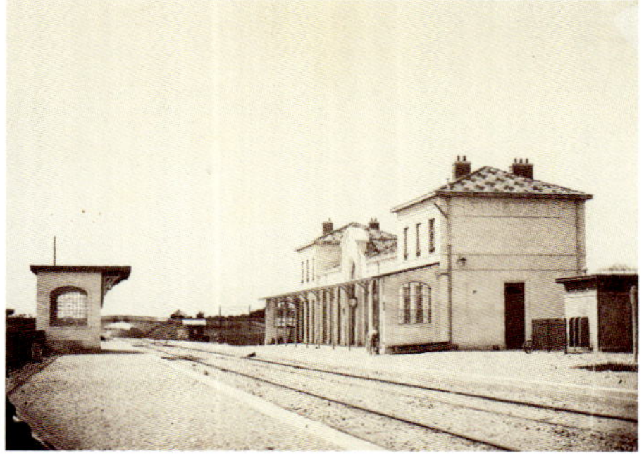
12

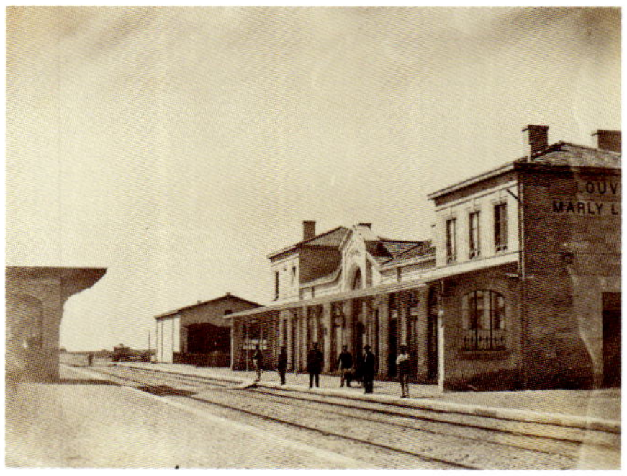
13

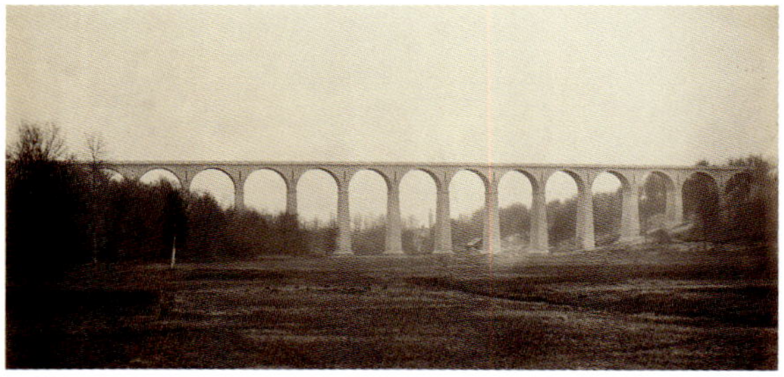
14

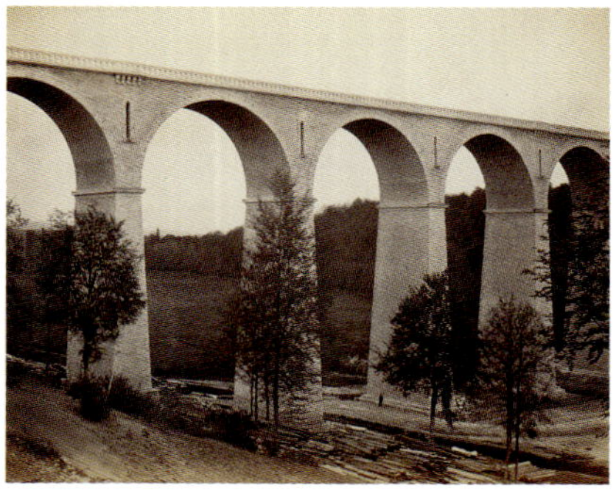
15

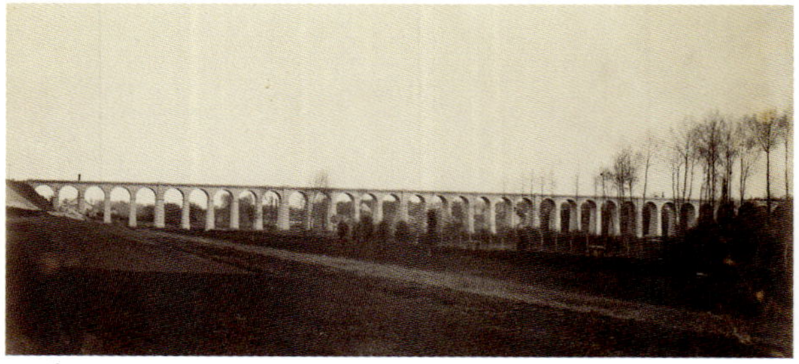
16

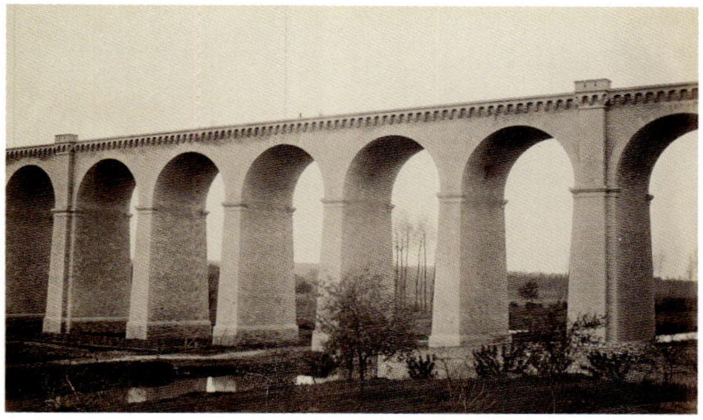

17

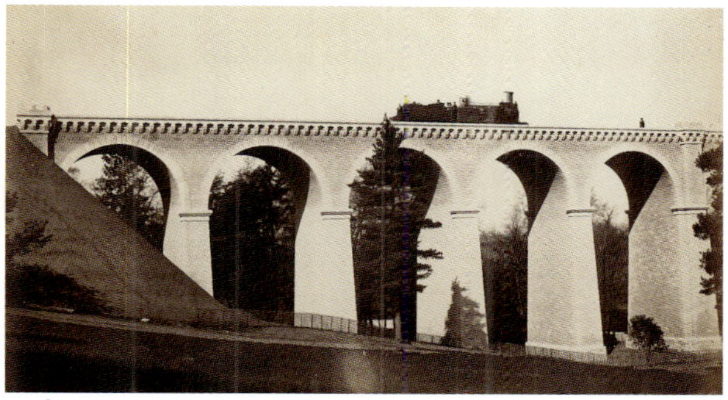

18

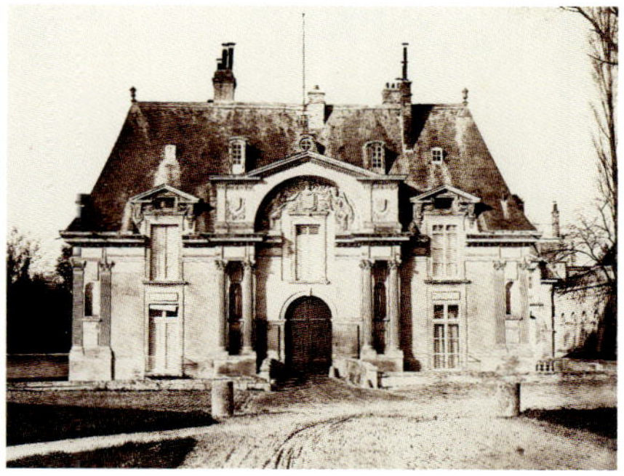

19

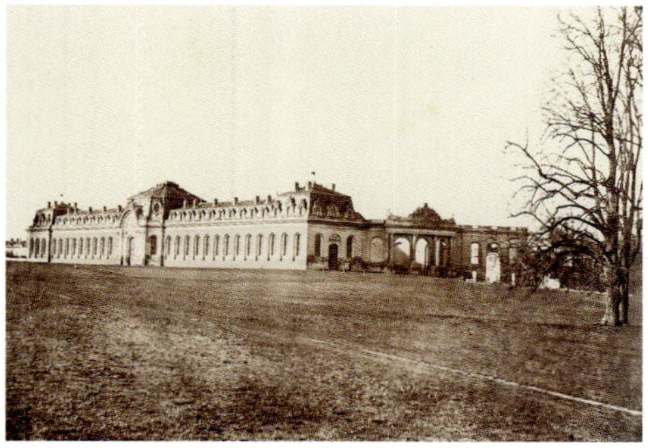

20

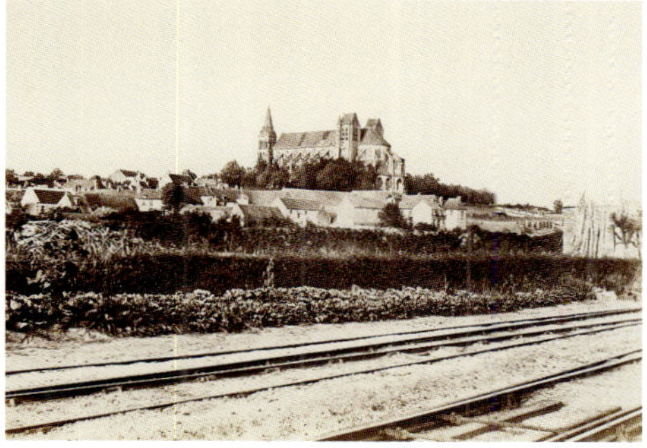

21

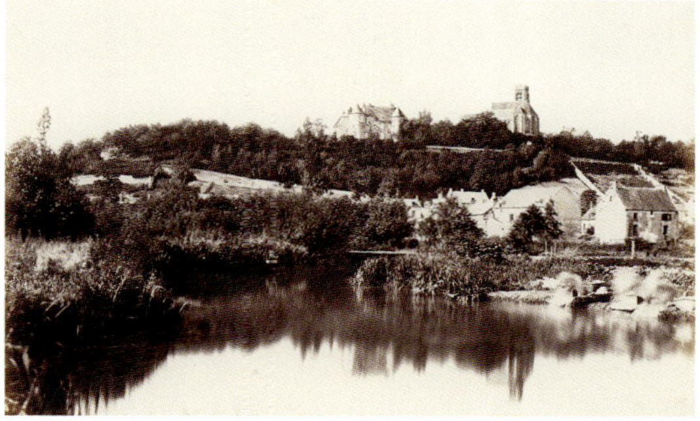

22

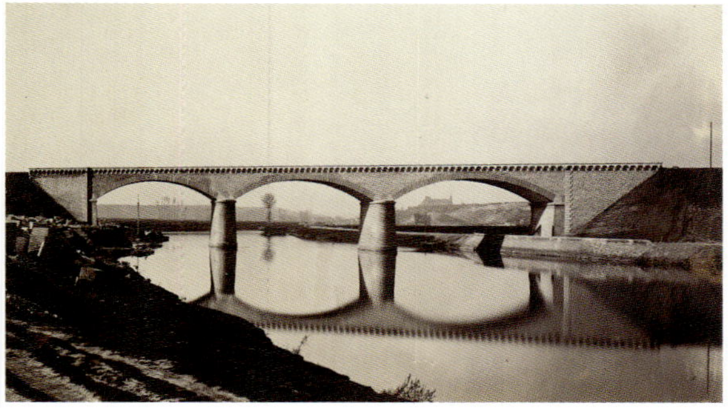

23

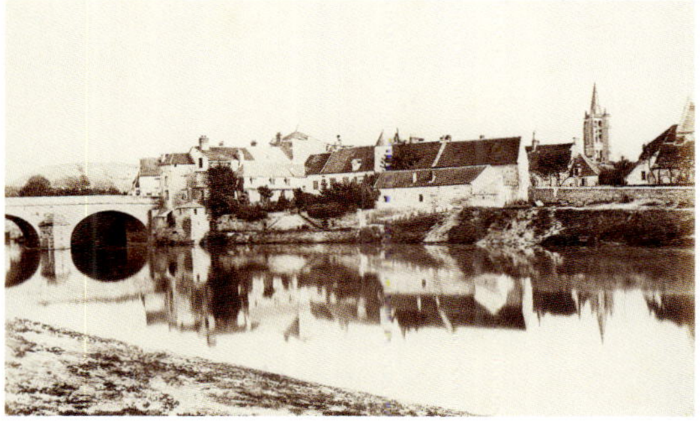

24

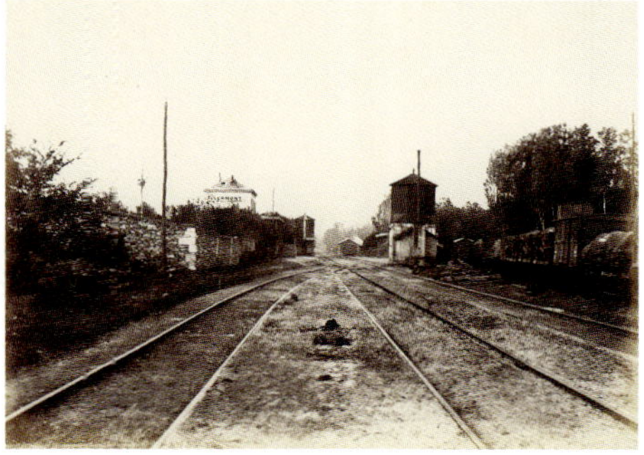

25

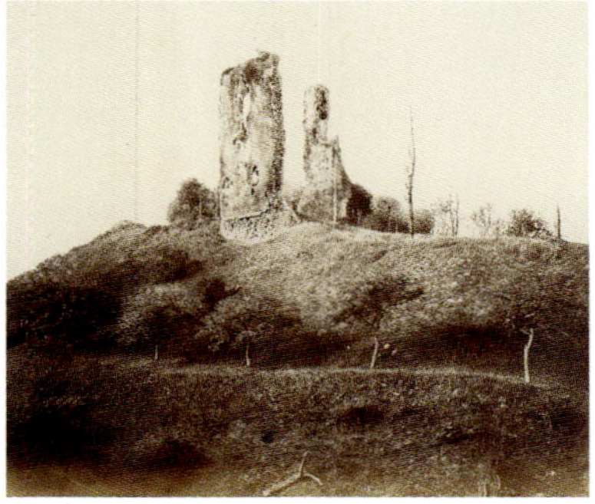

26

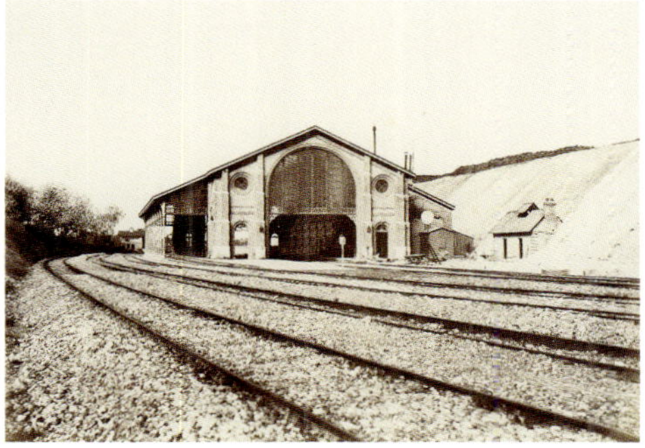

27

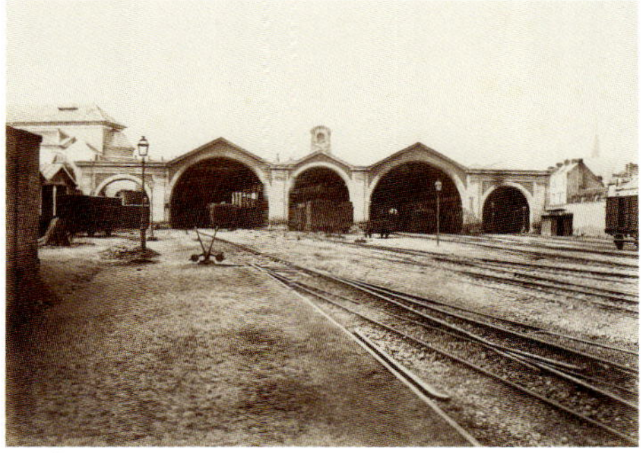

28

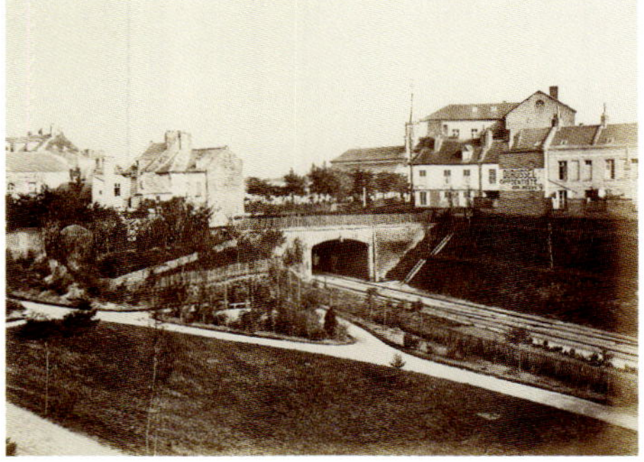

29

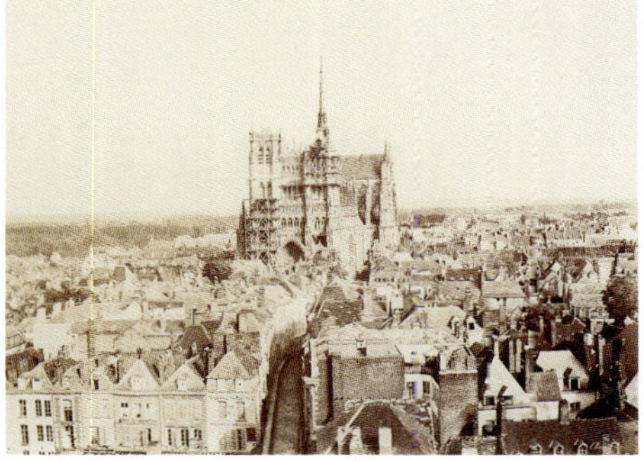

30

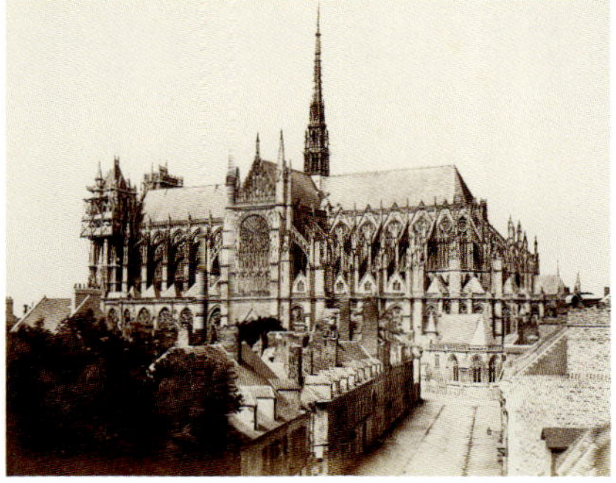

31

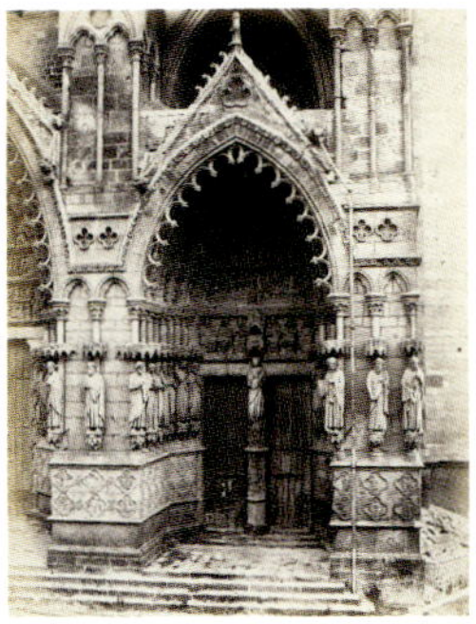

32

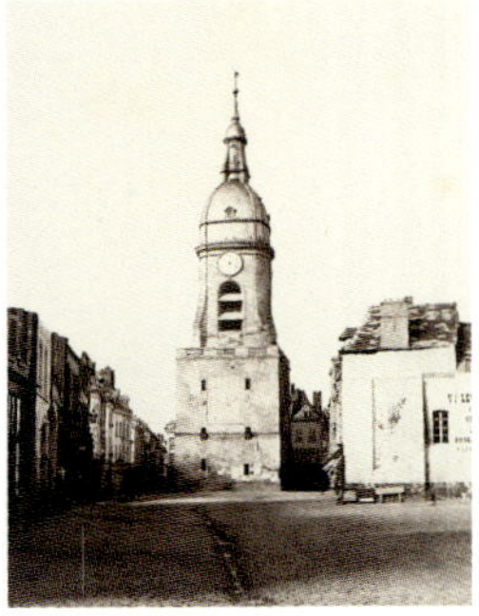

33

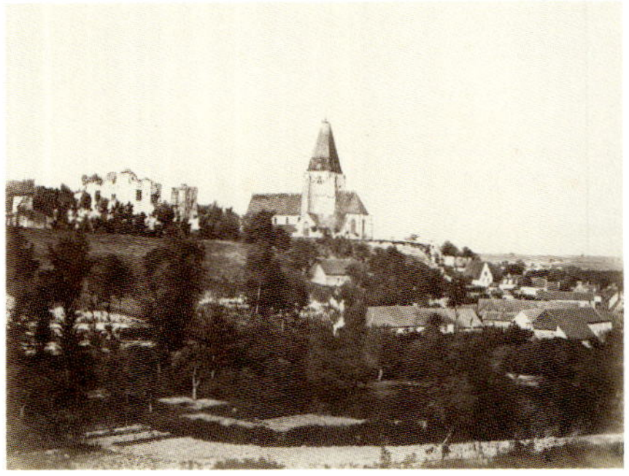

34

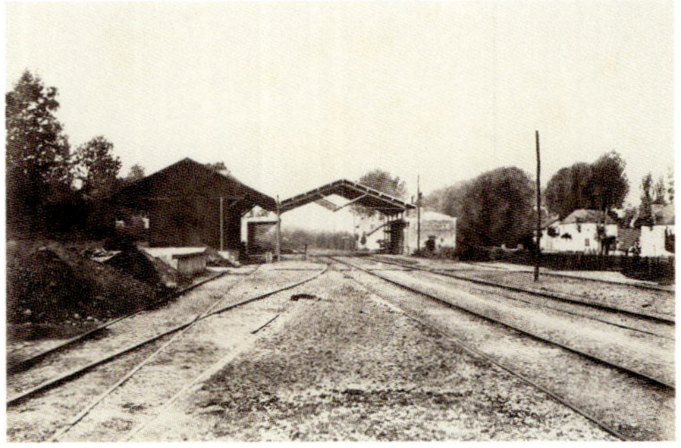

35

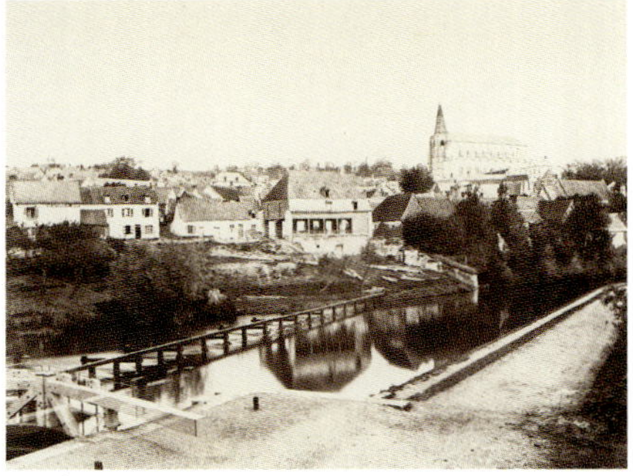

36

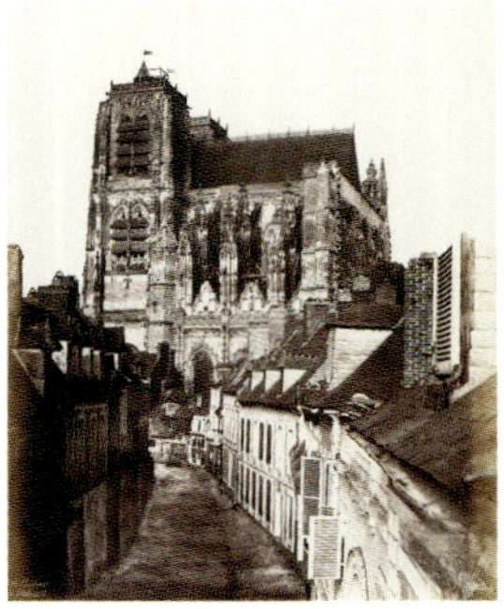

37

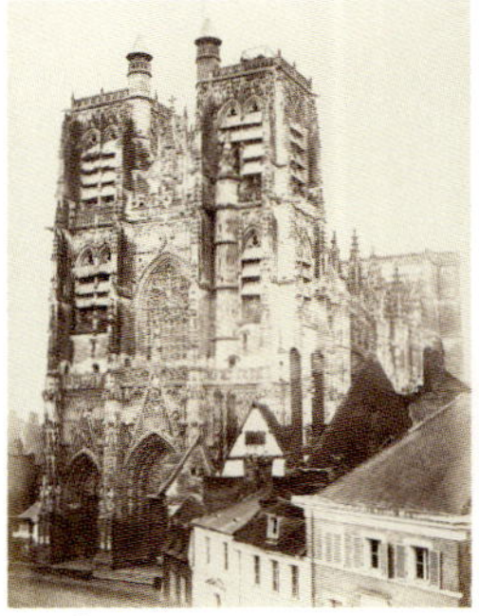

38

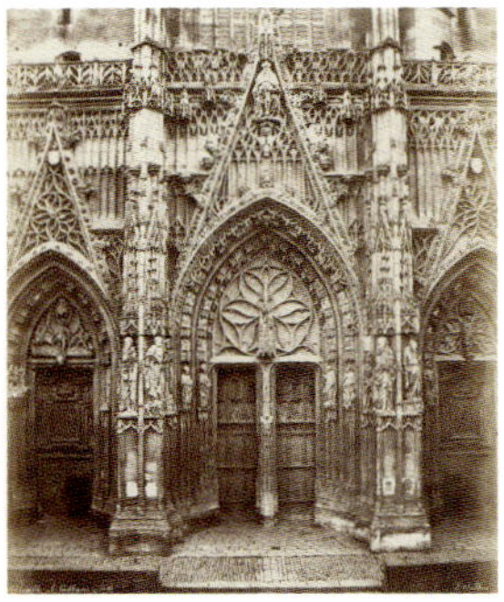

39

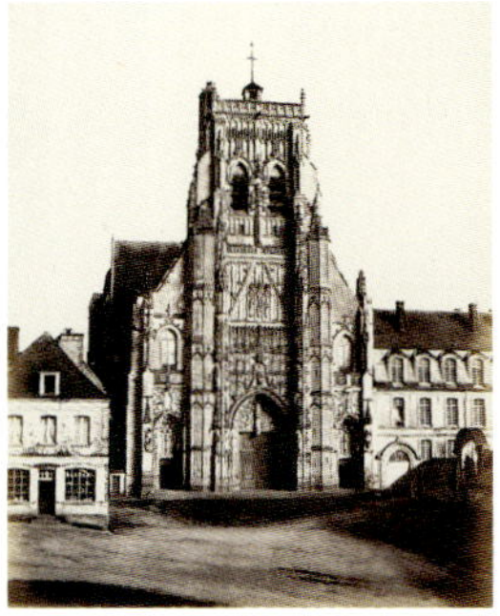

40

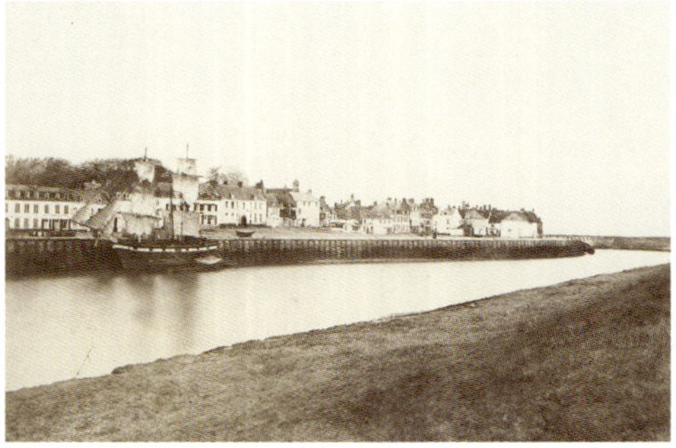

41

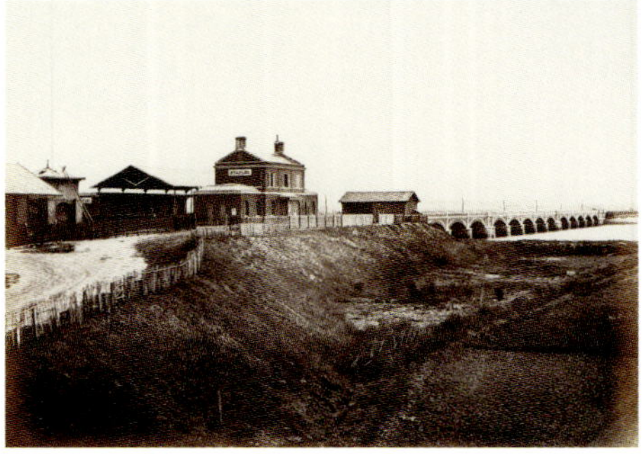

42

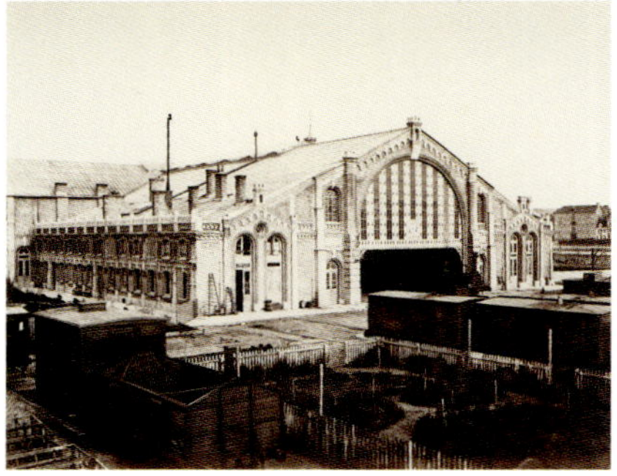

43

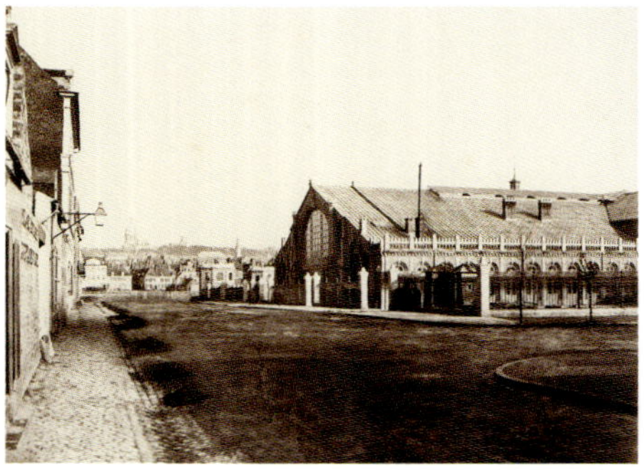

44

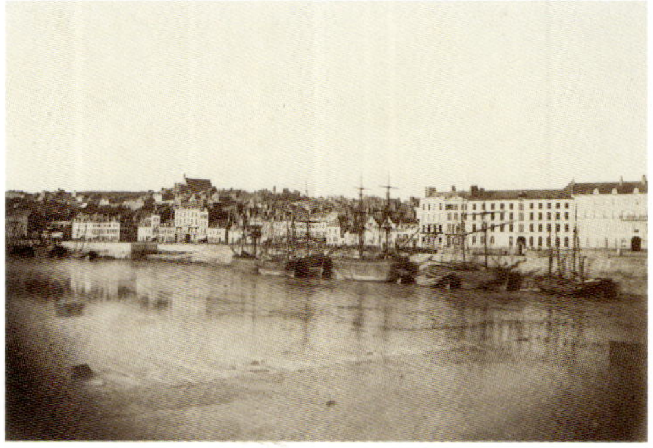

45

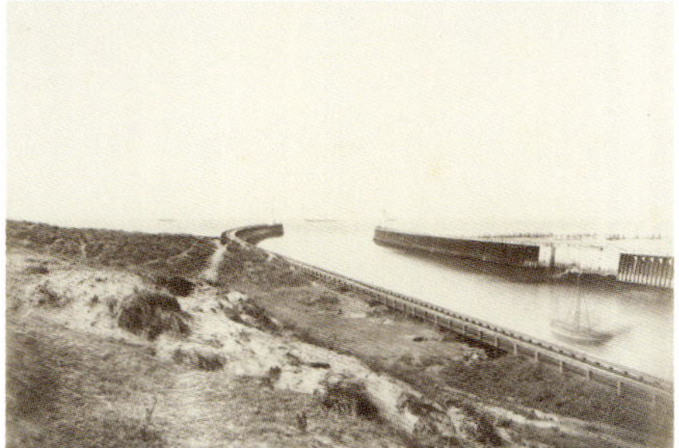

46

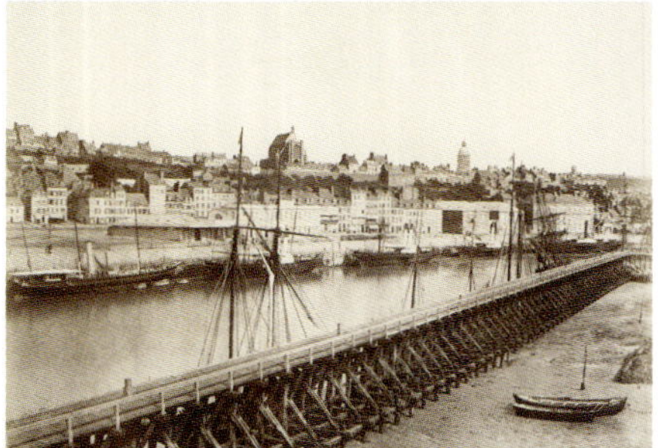

47

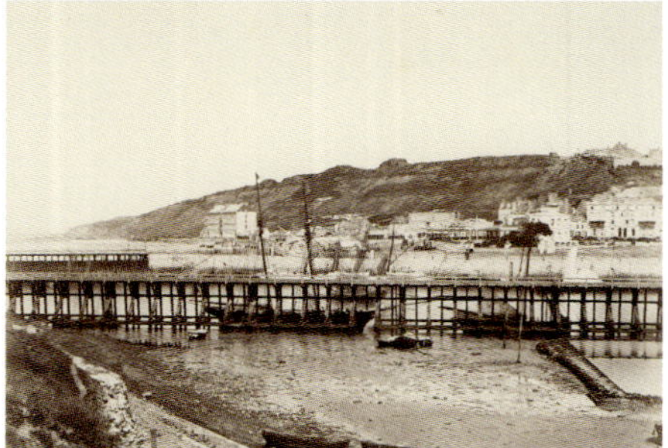

48

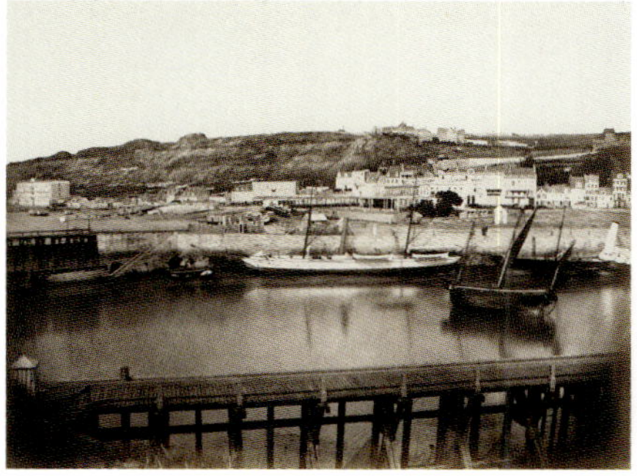

49

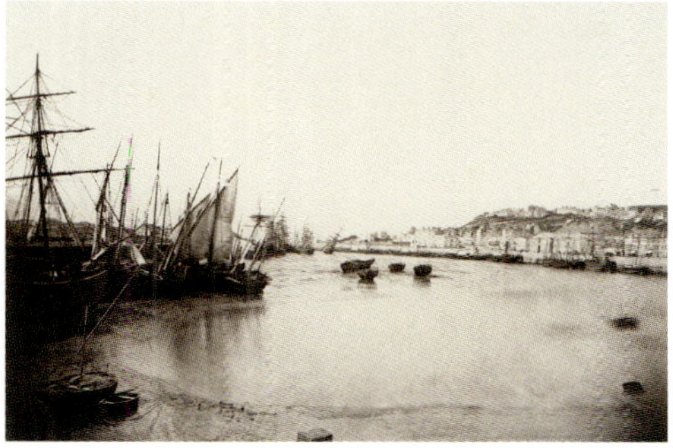

50

1 Furne fils and H. Tournier, Illustrated map
2 Édouard Baldus, *Abbey of Saint-Denis*
3 Unknown photographer, *Imperial House of the Legion of Honor at Saint-Denis*
4 Hippolyte-Auguste Collard, *Bridge on the Canal at Saint-Denis*
5 Édouard Baldus, *Railway Station, Enghien*
6 Édouard Baldus, *Chalet, Enghien*
7 Édouard Baldus, *Railway Station, Pontoise*
8 Édouard Baldus, *Church at Auvers*
9 Édouard Baldus, *View of l'Île-Adam*
10 Édouard Baldus, *Château of Boran*
11 Unknown photographer, *Bridge across the Rhone*
12 Unknown photographer, *Stains-Pierrefitte Station*
13 Unknown photographer, *Louvres Station*
14 Hippolyte-Auguste Collard, *General View of the Comelle Viaduct*
15 Hippolyte-Auguste Collard, *Detail View of the Comelle Viaduct*
16 Hippolyte-Auguste Collard, *General View of the Chantilly Viaduct*
17 Hippolyte-Auguste Collard, *Detail View of the Chantilly Viaduct*
18 Hippolyte-Auguste Collard, *Landscape near the Chantilly Viaduct*
19 Unknown photographer, *Château of Chantilly*
20 Unknown photographer, *Stables of the Château of Chantilly*
21 Édouard Baldus, *View of Saint-Leu d'Esserent*
22 Édouard Baldus, *View of Montataire*
23 Hippolyte-Auguste Collard, *Bridge across the Oise near Creil*
24 Édouard Baldus, *View of Creil*
25 Édouard Baldus, *Clermont Railway Station*
26 Édouard Baldus, *Château of Boves*
27 Édouard Baldus, *Longueau Railway Station*
28 Édouard Baldus, *Amiens Railway Station*
29 Édouard Baldus, *Amiens Railway Station Exit*
30 Édouard Baldus, *Panorama of City of Amiens*
31 Édouard Baldus, *Cathedral of Amiens*
32 Édouard Baldus, *Portal of the Cathedral of Amiens*
33 Édouard Baldus, *Belfry of Amiens*
34 Édouard Baldus, *Ailly-sur-Somme*
35 Édouard Baldus, *Picquigny*
36 Édouard Baldus, *Longpré*
37 Édouard Baldus, *Church of Saint-Vulfran at Abbeville, East Side*
38 Édouard Baldus, *Church of Saint-Vulfran at Abbeville, West Side*
39 Édouard Baldus, *Portal of Saint-Vulfran at Abbeville*
40 Édouard Baldus, *Church of Saint-Riquier*
41 Édouard Baldus, *Saint-Valéry*
42 Édouard Baldus, *Etaples*
43 Édouard Baldus, *Boulogne Railway Station, Arrivals*
44 Édouard Baldus, *South Gable of the Boulogne Railway Station*
45 Édouard Baldus, *View of the Port of Boulogne*
46 Édouard Baldus, *Entrance of the Port of Boulogne*
47 Édouard Baldus, *General View of the Port and City of Boulogne*
48 Édouard Baldus, *View of the Piers and Cliffs of Boulogne*
49 Édouard Baldus, *View of the yacht HMS "Ariel," Port of Boulogne*
50 Édouard Baldus, *Boats at Low Tide, Port of Boulogne*

76

ÉDOUARD BALDUS
FRENCH, 1813–1889

Railway from Paris to Lyon and the Mediterranean

1861

Album containing 69 albumen prints, including 2-part panoramas, from collodion glass or paper negatives

18⅜ × 24$\frac{5}{16}$ × 2½ in. (47 × 62.8 × 6 cm)

Canadian Centre for Architecture, Montréal, PH1981:0816:001–069

In July 1861 Baldus received his second major railway commission, from the Conseil d'administration of the Southern Region of rail networks, to produce an album of photographic views along the rail line from Lyon to Marseille and Toulon. The route of the Paris–Lyon–Méditérranée (PLM) line was established in 1842, soon after the state established its plan for the development of six major rail lines (*grands réseaux*). The PLM album comprises sixty-nine photographs. Though some were made specifically for the project, many were drawn from stock photographs Baldus had produced during the previous decade on his various ventures to the South of France.[4] To a greater degree than the editioned album for the Northern Line, the selection and sequencing of photographs in the PLM album suggest a more thoughtful, deliberate attempt to align past and present as a continuous lineage. For example, Baldus included a view of the Pont Saint-Bénezet (also known as the Pont d'Avignon and the subject of the popular children's song "Sur le Pont d'Avignon") (cat. 33), a bridge constructed in the twelfth century. He also featured the Pont de la Mulatière (pls. 4, 5), a structure built during the Revolutionary era but that had been reinforced during the 1850s to accommodate the new rail line. In a sequence toward the end of the album, Baldus included a photograph of the Roman-era Pont du Gard (cats. 34 and 76, pl. 32), originally built to allow the aqueduct of Nîmes to cross the Gardon River. Close to this image are photographs of more recently constructed bridges and viaducts, such as those at Durance and Tarascon (pls. 33–35). United by Baldus's characteristically bold, un-Romanticized style, subjects steeped in Roman history are visually linked to those inspired by Second Empire ideals. These monuments and structures, brought together in a photographic album, were also joined geographically by the railroad, which was perhaps the single greatest influence on connecting France's past traditions and cultures, as found most prevalently in the provinces, with their rapidly modernizing landscape, which had its nexuses in Paris, Lyon, and Marseille.

Finally, Baldus's photographs in the PLM album emphasize the significant relation between man-made structures and the natural landscape to a greater degree than his earlier railway album commission. One of the most majestic views depicts the approach to the mountain pass at Donzère, between Lyon and Nîmes (pl. 20). Here, Baldus composed the landscape in such a way that the gently curving railroad tracks lead the viewer into the scene from the foreground to the middle ground, where they disappear behind the hillside. The cloudless sky consumes half the image, thus functioning as a key compositional component, albeit as negative space. Nowhere in the image does the viewer get the sense of the railway as being an incursion in the landscape. Rather, the thin tracks appear to harmonize visually with the natural terrain's curves and swells. —AMW

1. [Ernest Lacan], "Album offert à S. M. la reine Victoria," *La lumière* 5, no. 35 (September 1, 1855): 134.

2. Malcolm Daniel, "Édouard-Denis Baldus and the Chemin de Fer du Nord Albums," *Image* 35, nos. 3–4 (Fall–Winter 1992): 5.

3. Ibid., 17.

4. Malcolm Daniel, *The Photographs of Édouard Baldus*, exh. cat. (New York: Metropolitan Museum of Art; Montreal: Canadian Centre for Architecture, 1994), 82.

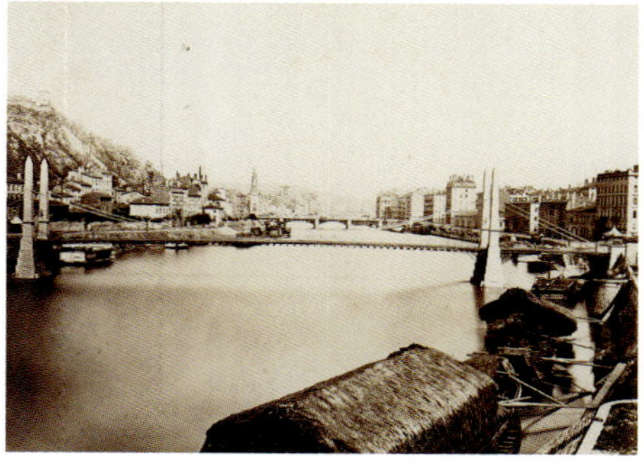
1

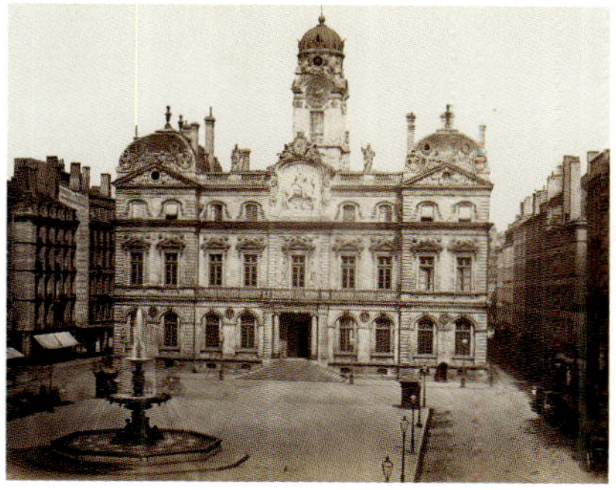
2

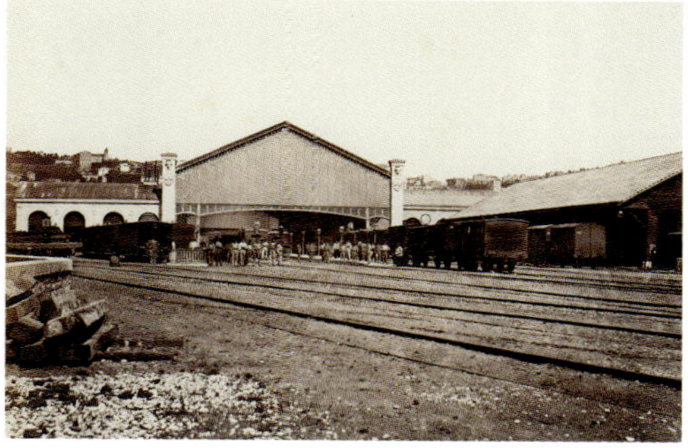
3

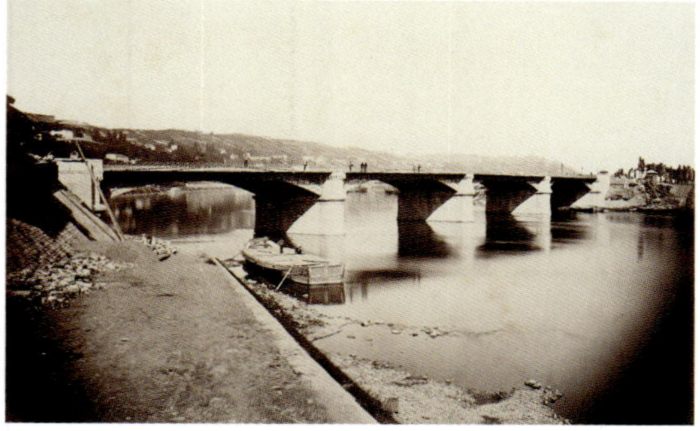
4

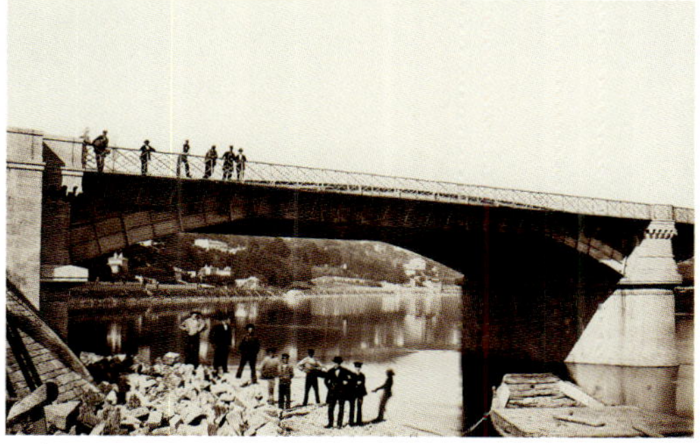
5

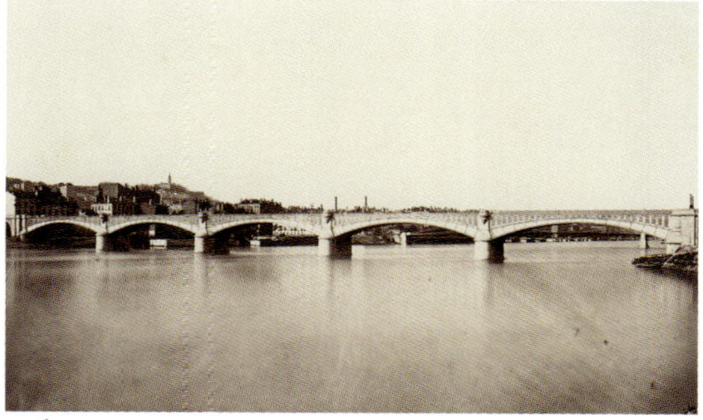
6

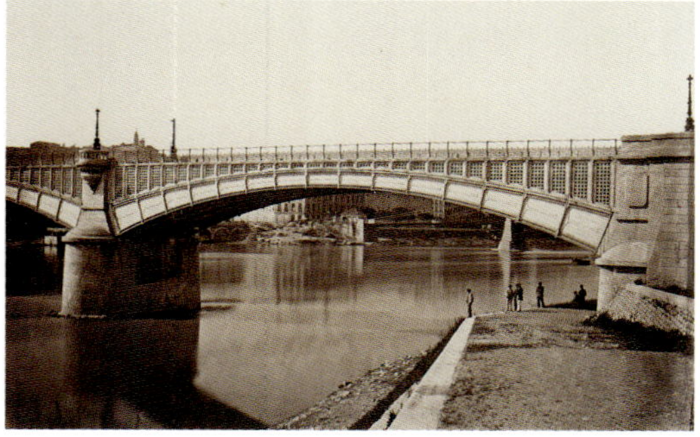
7

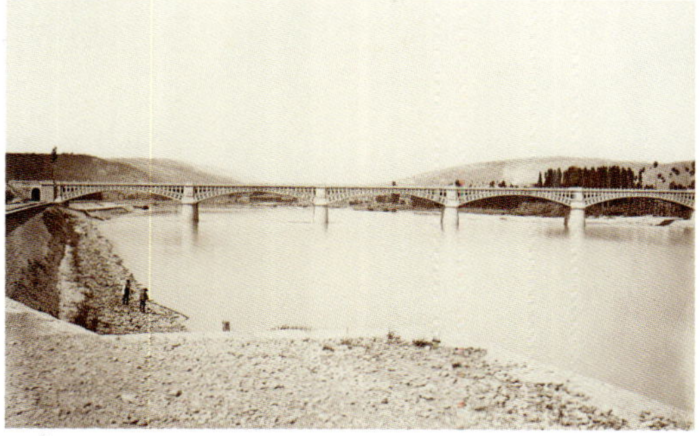
8

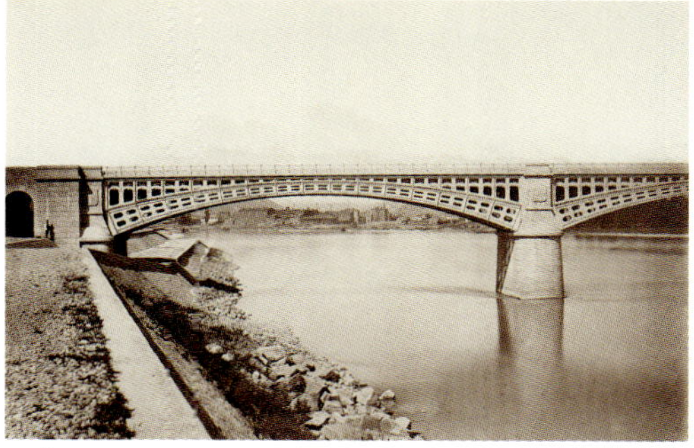
9

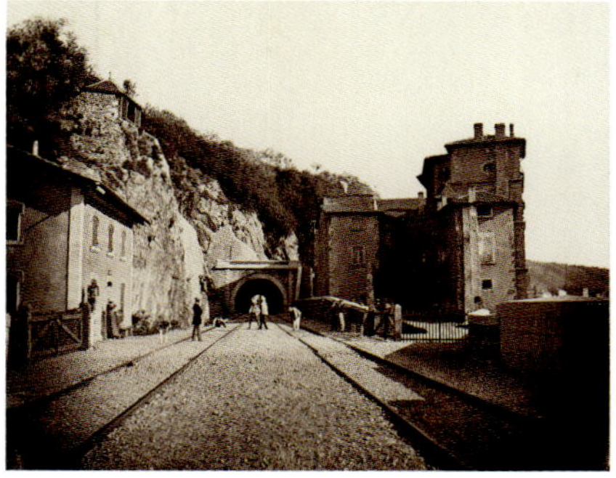
10

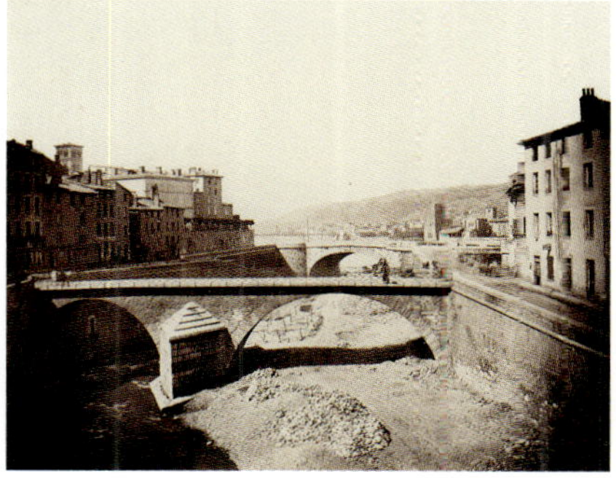
11

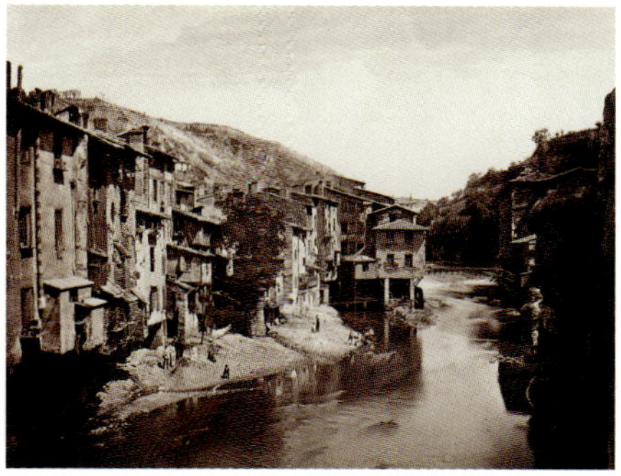
12

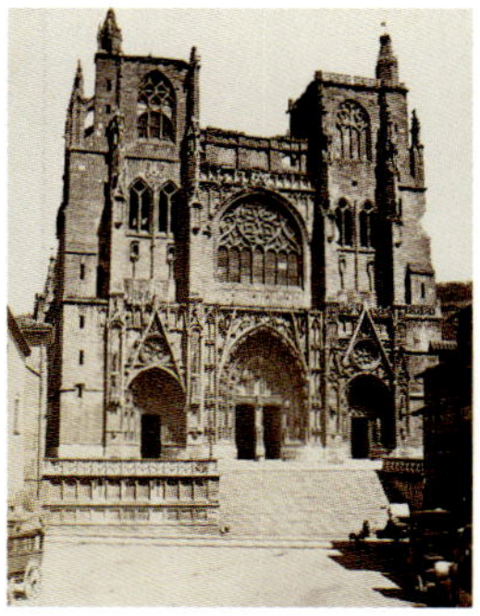
13

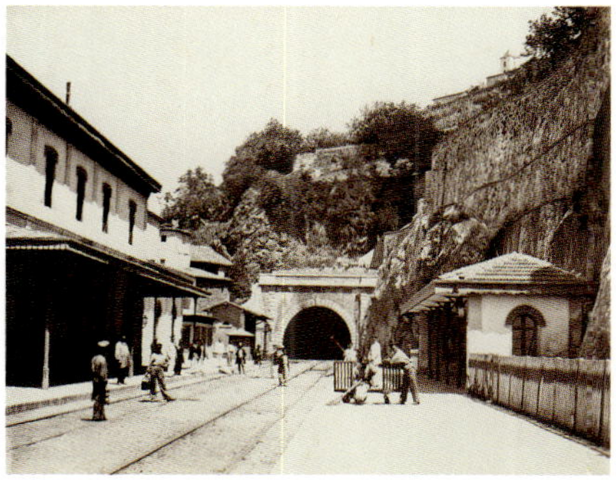
14

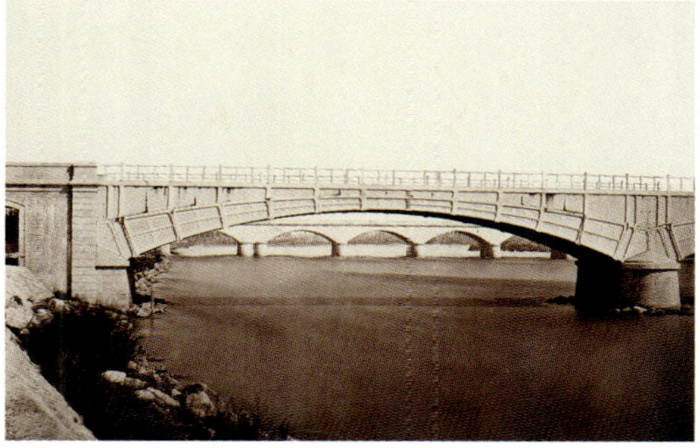
15

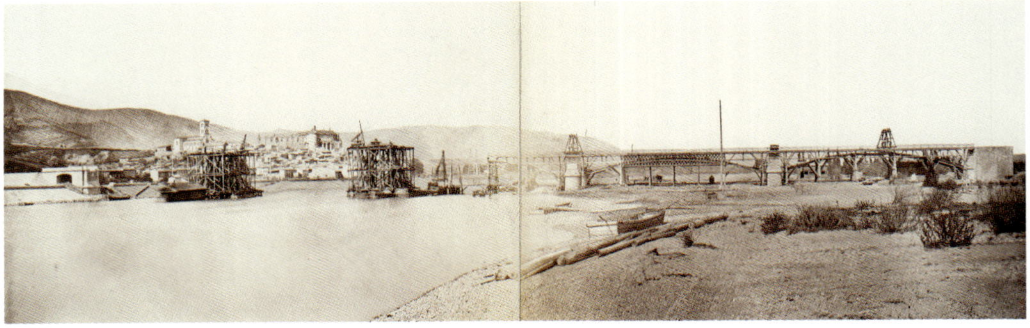
16

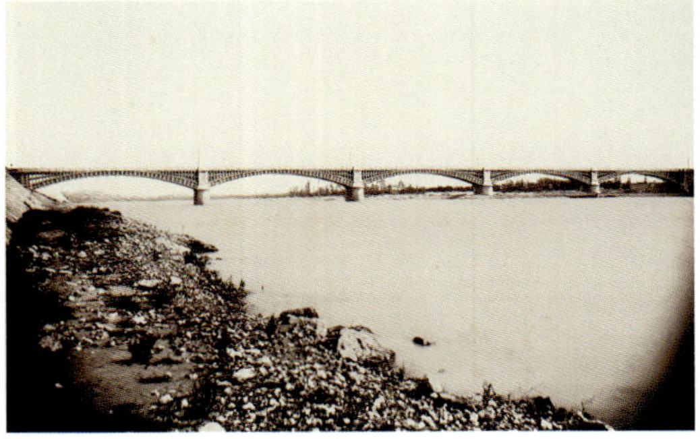
17

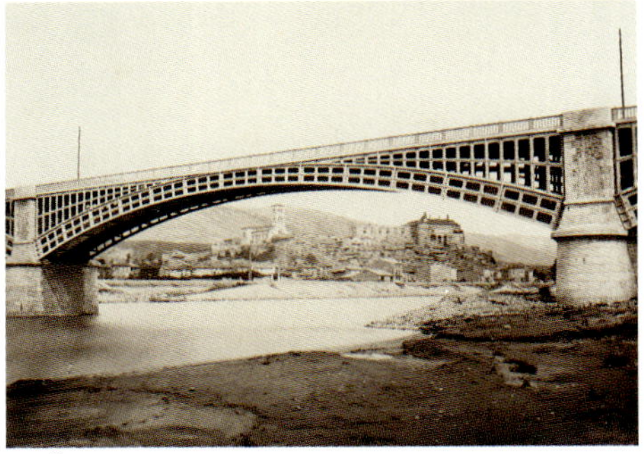
18

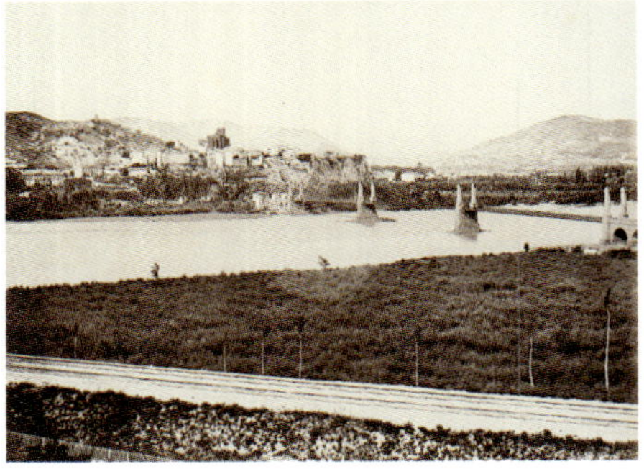
19

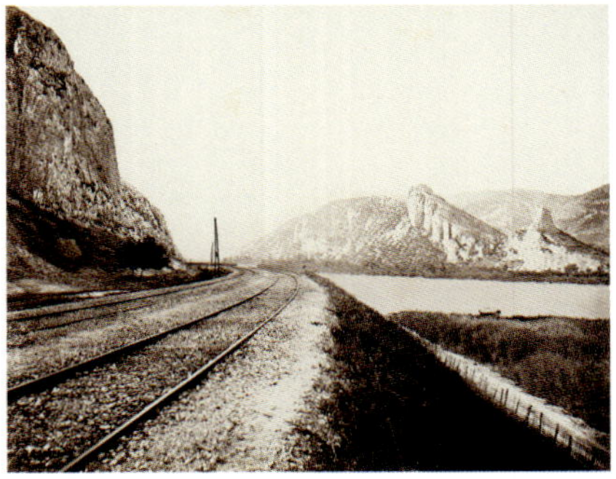
20

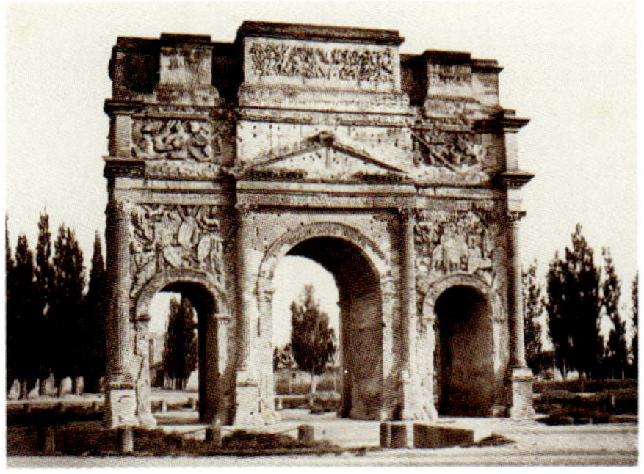
21

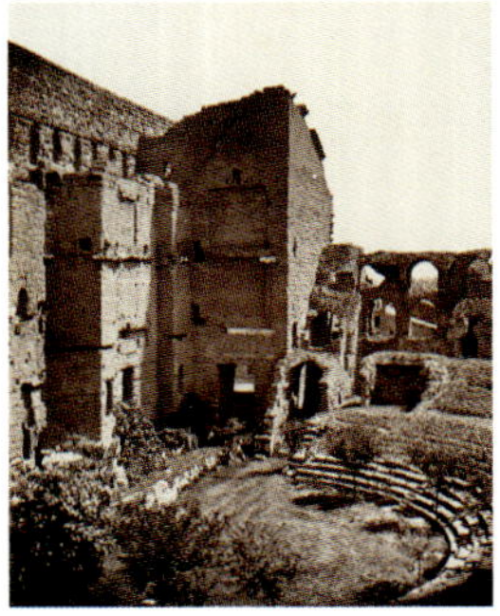
22

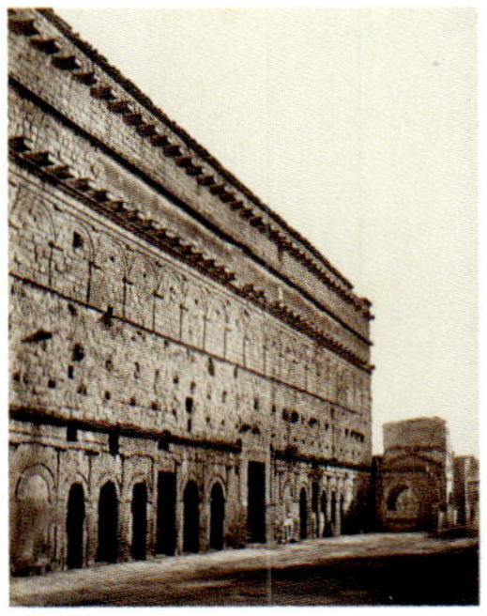
23

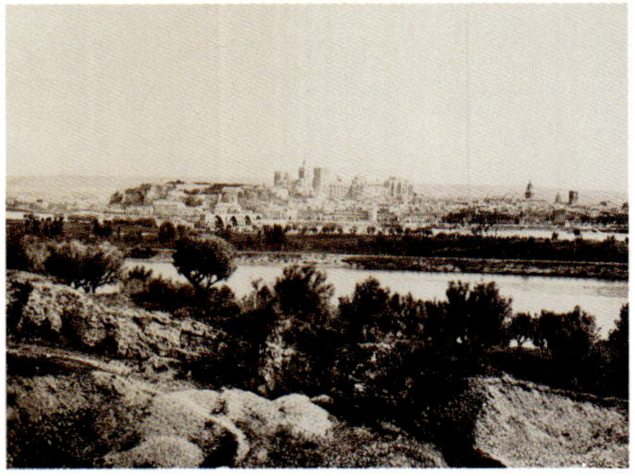
24

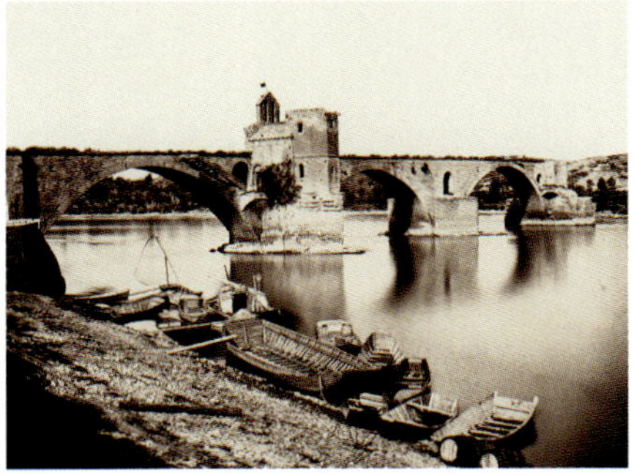
25

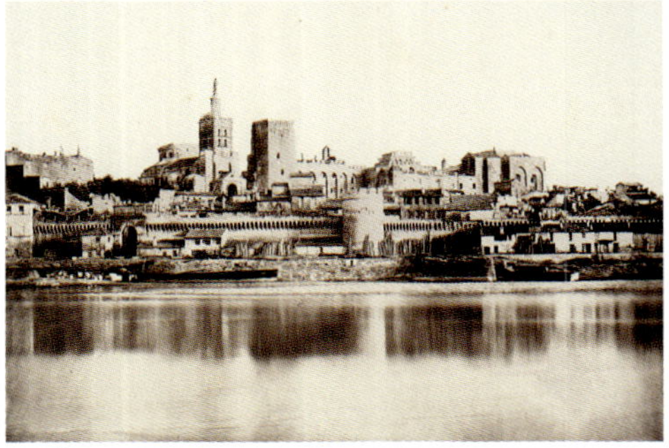
26

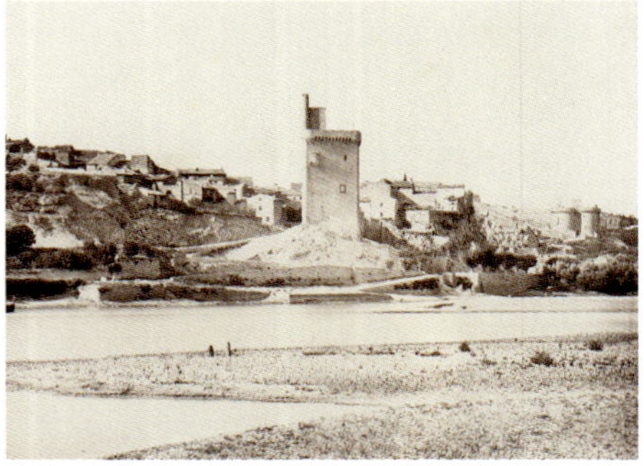
27

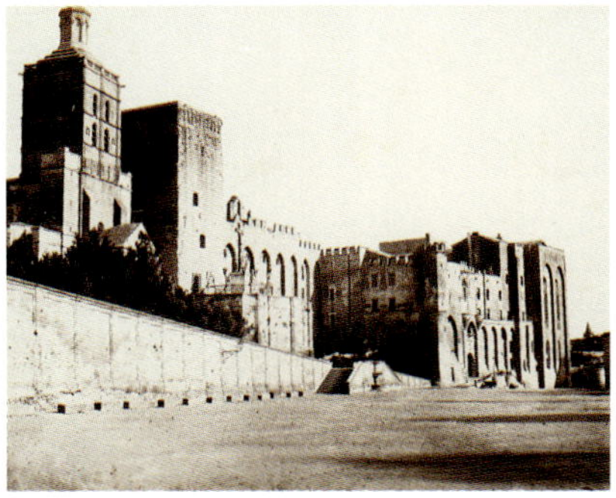
28

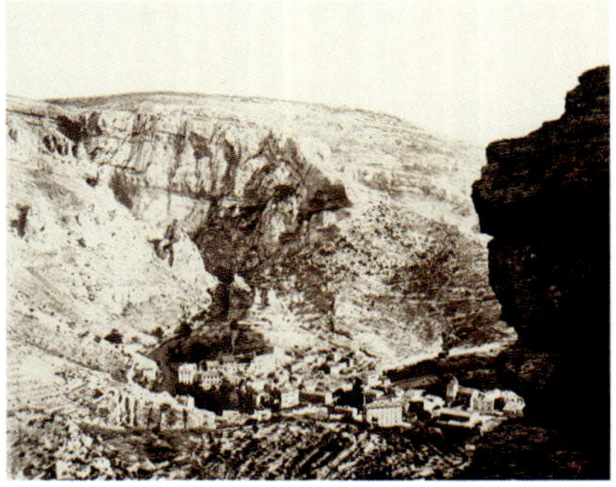
29

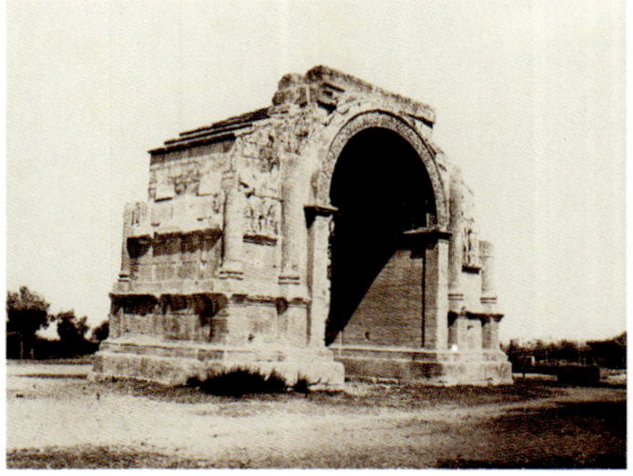
30

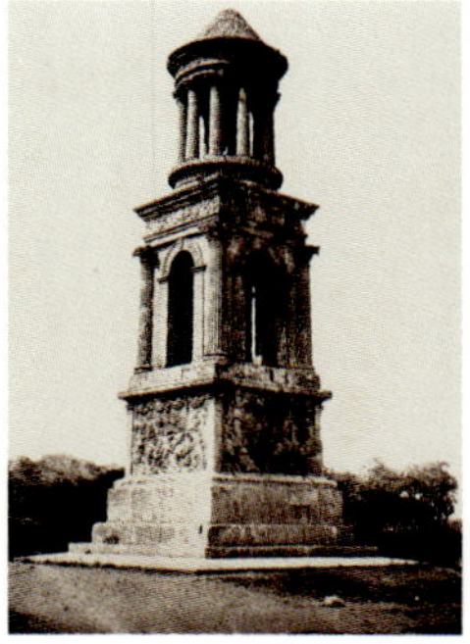
31

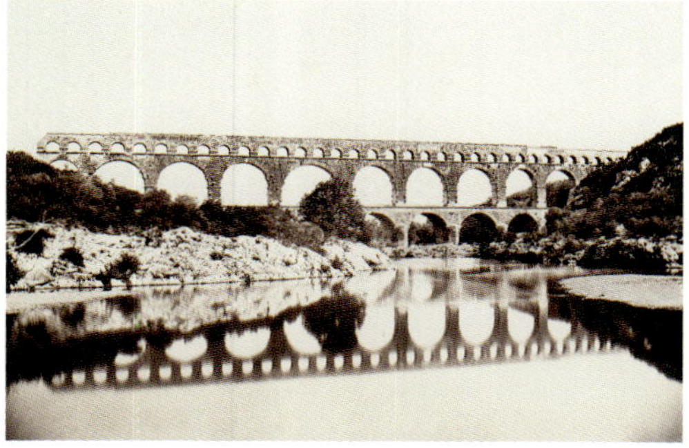
32

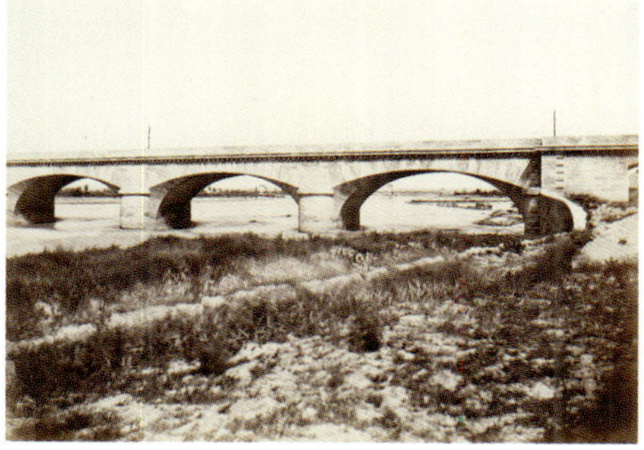
33

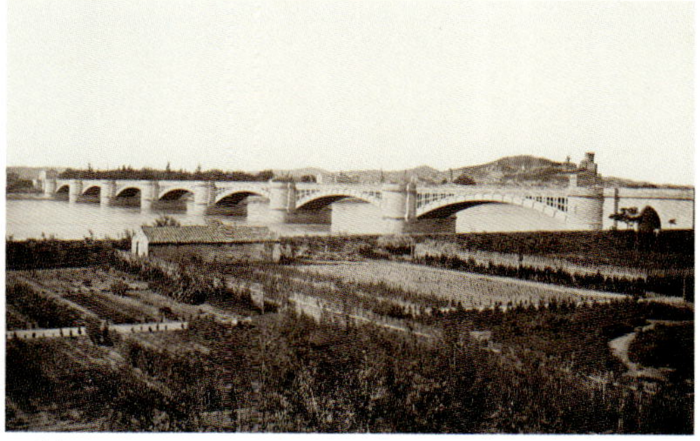
34

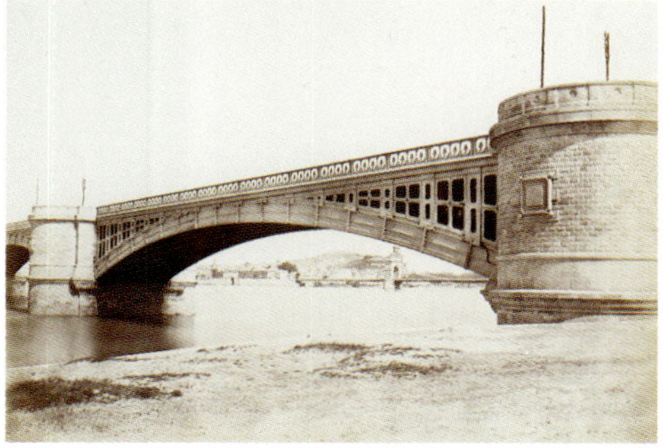
35

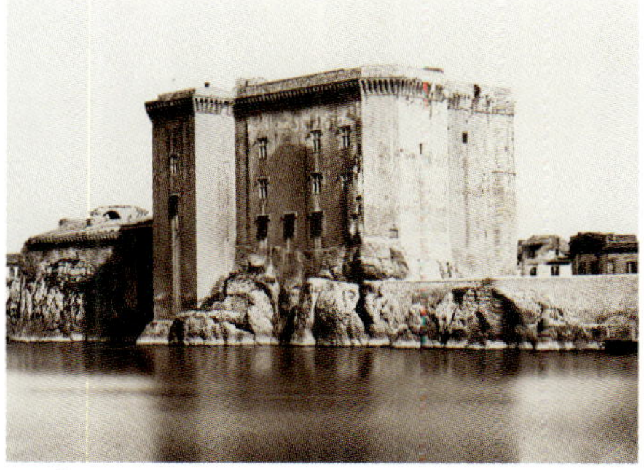
36

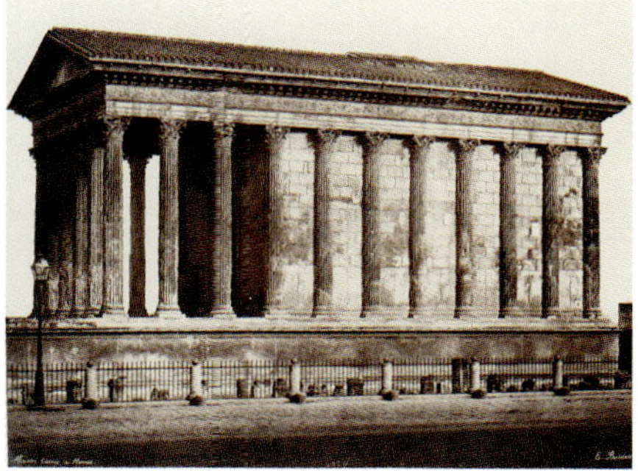
37

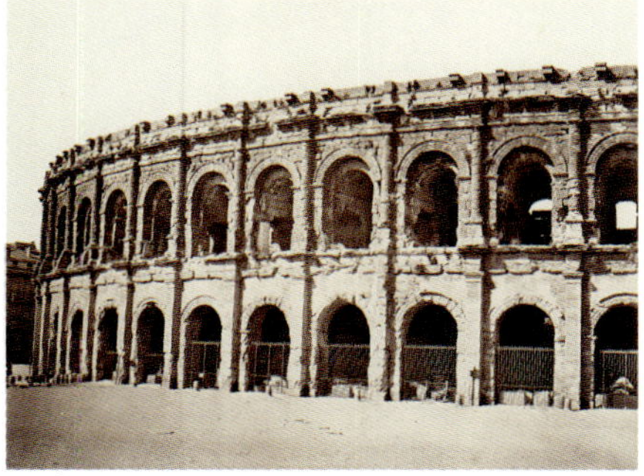
38

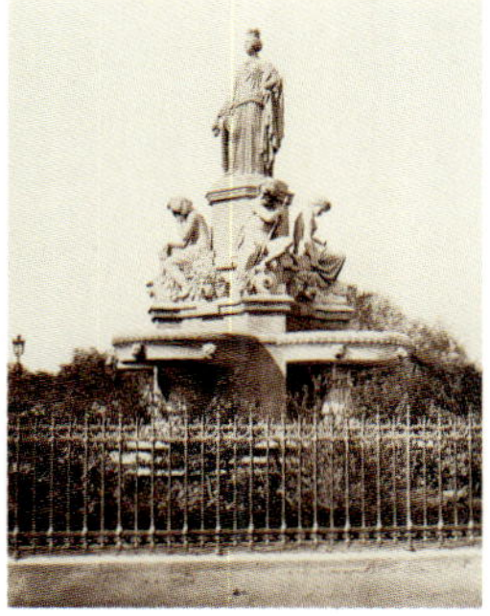
39

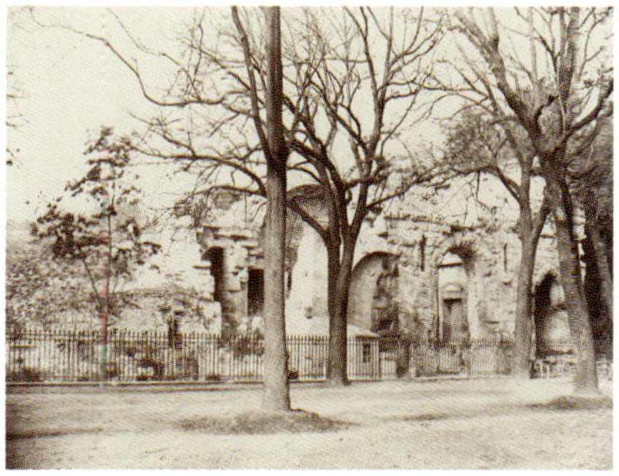
40

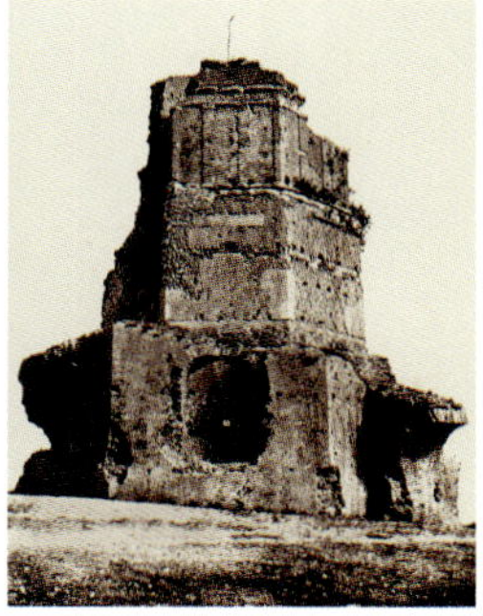
41

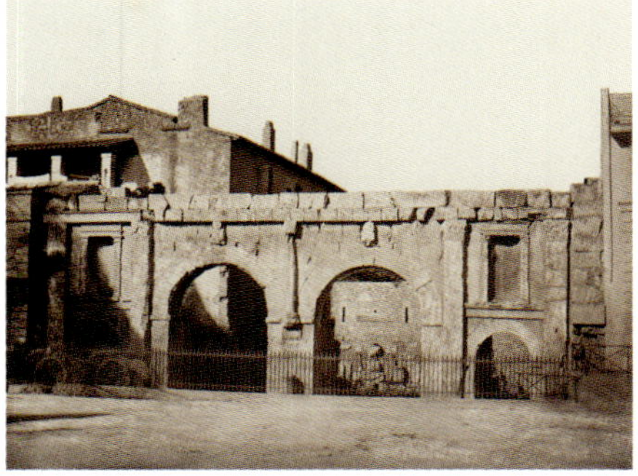
42

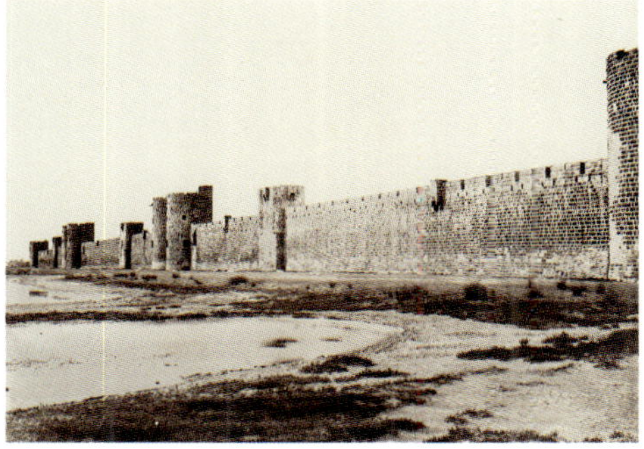
43

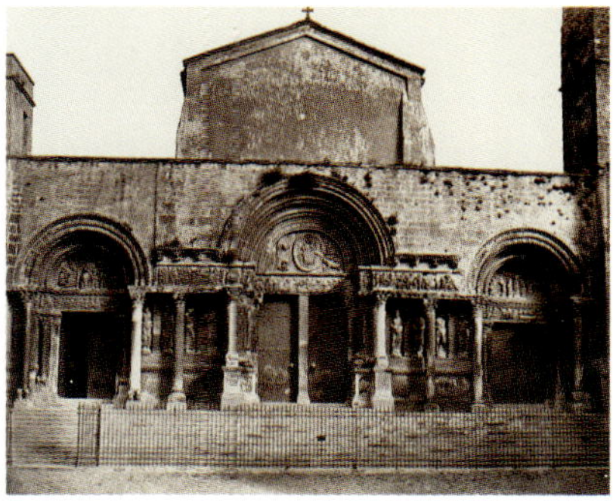
44

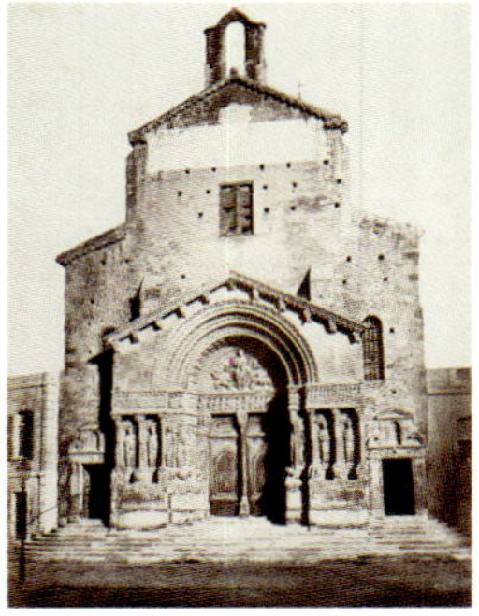
45

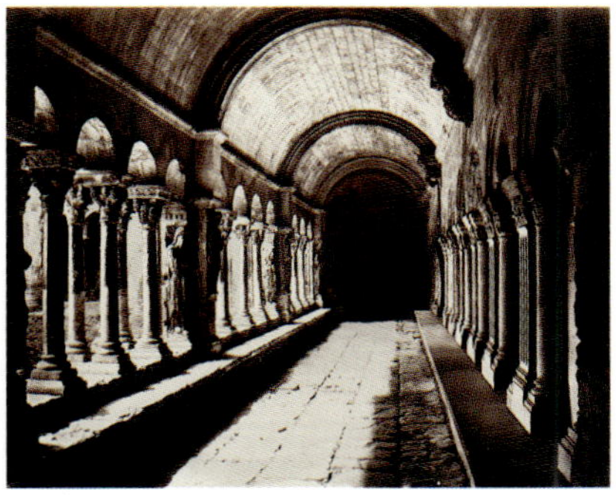
46

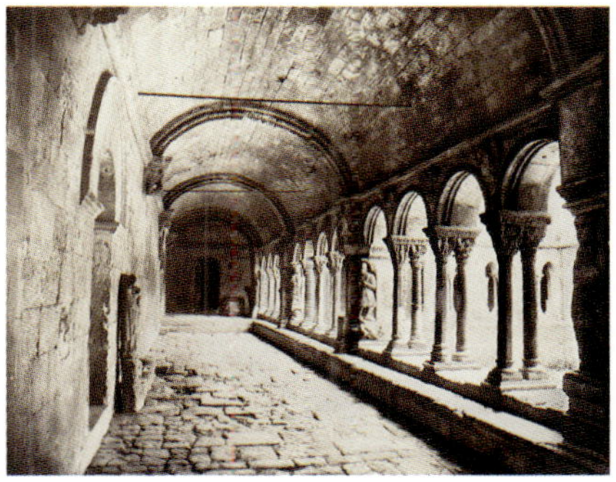
47

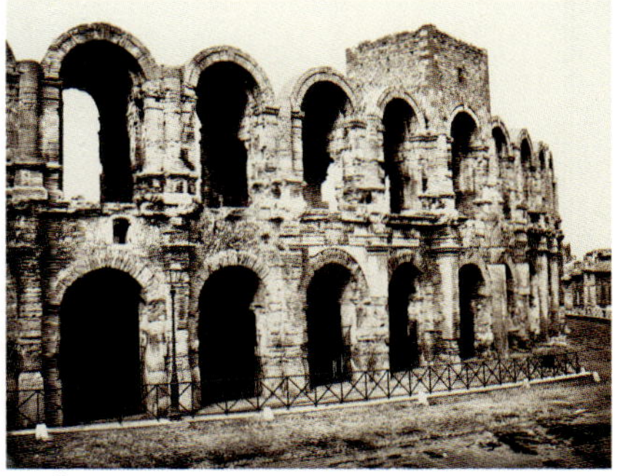
48

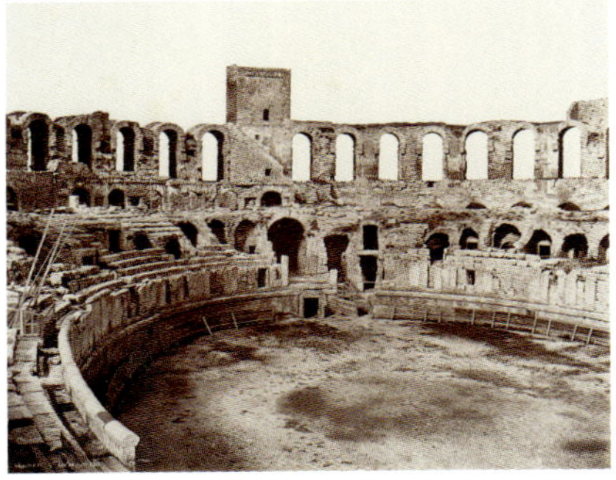
49
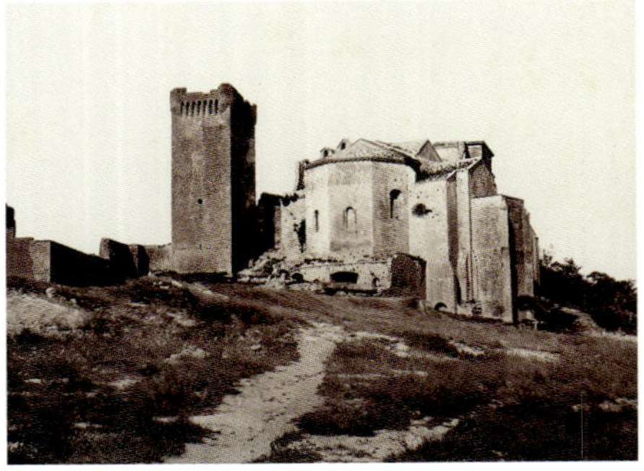
50
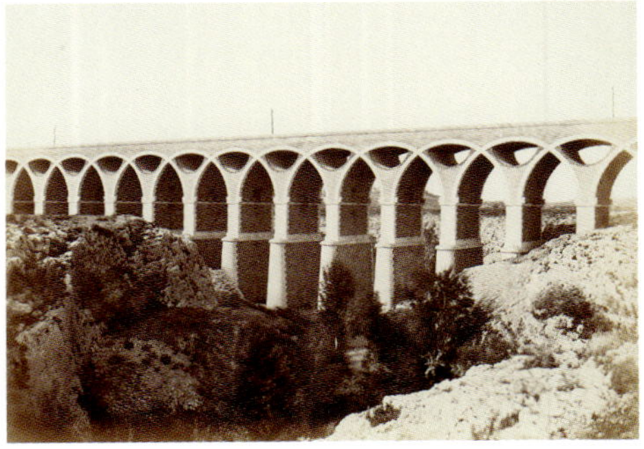
51
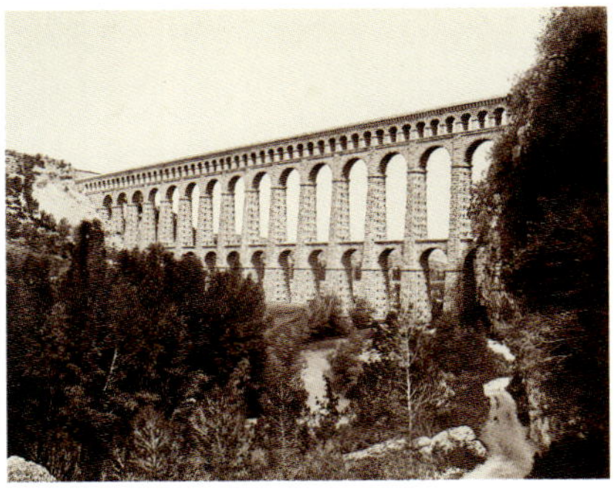
52
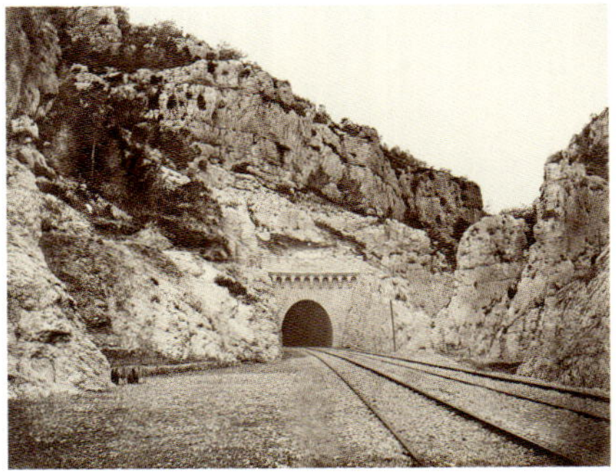
53
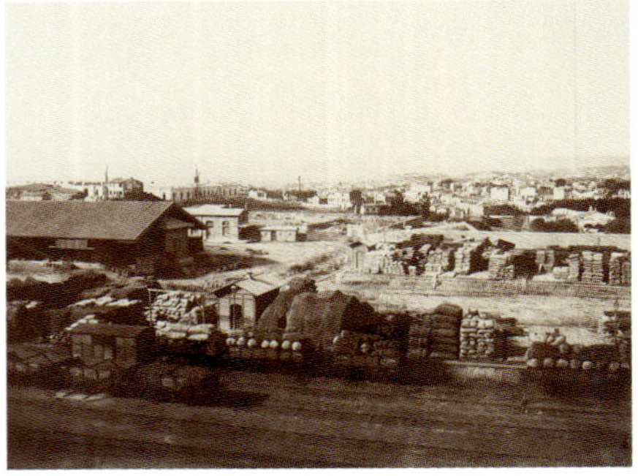
54
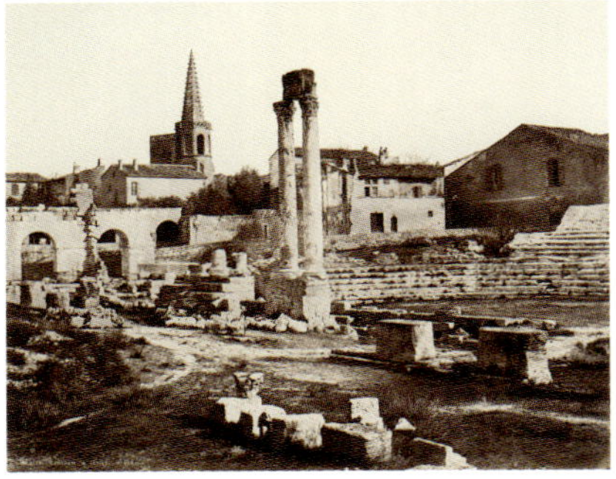
55
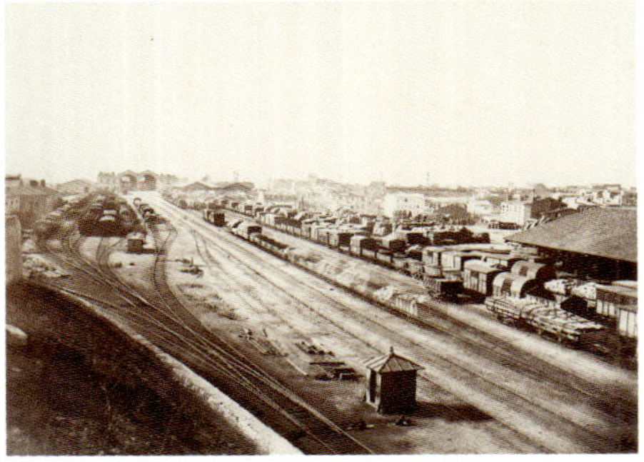
56
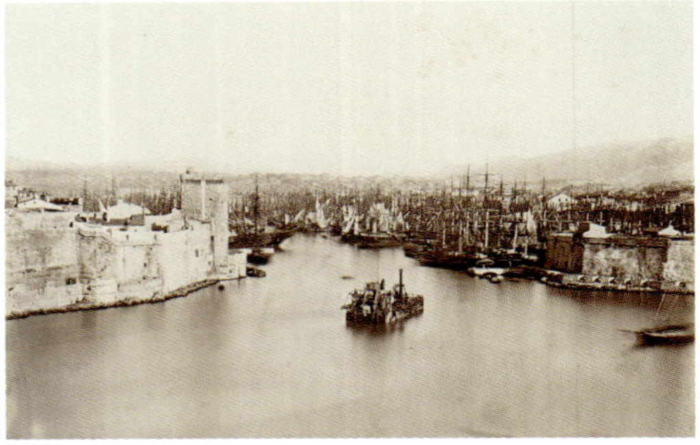
57
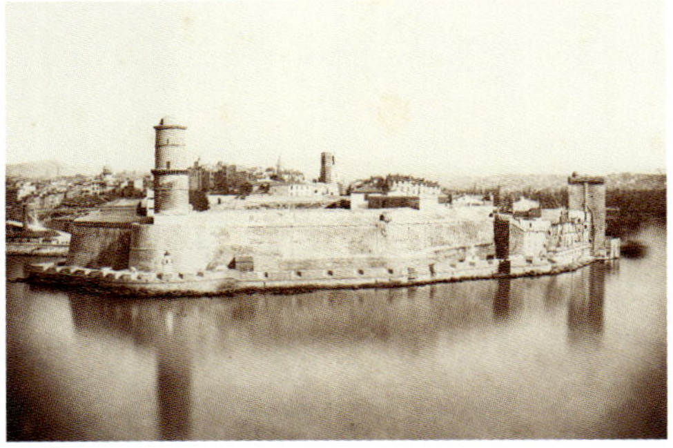
58
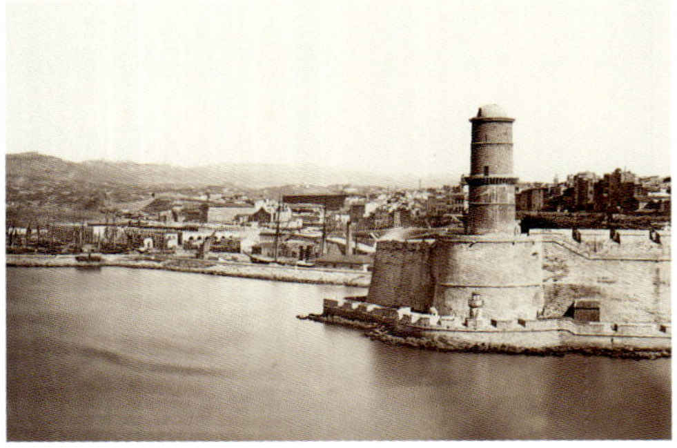
59
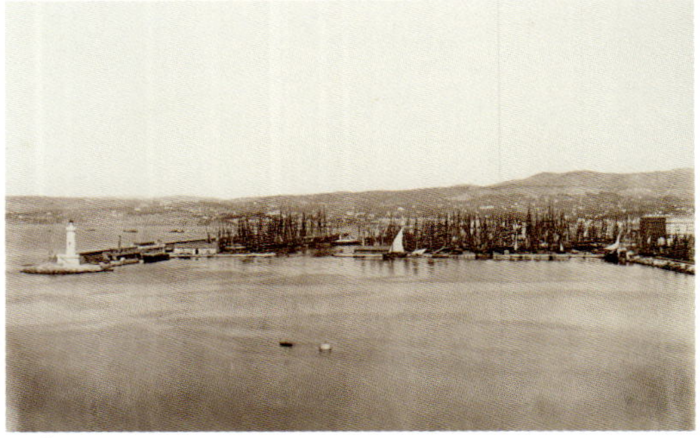
60
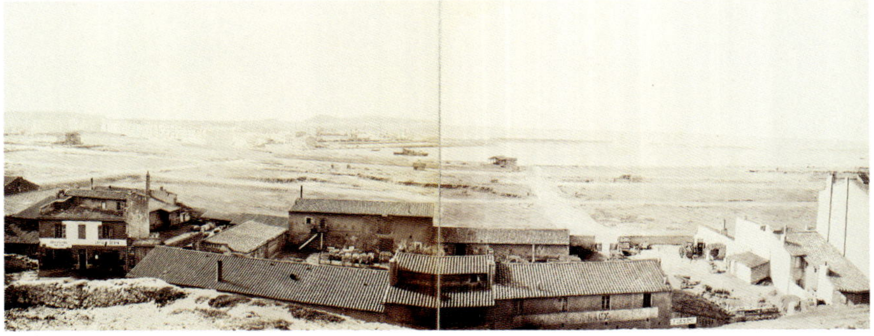
61
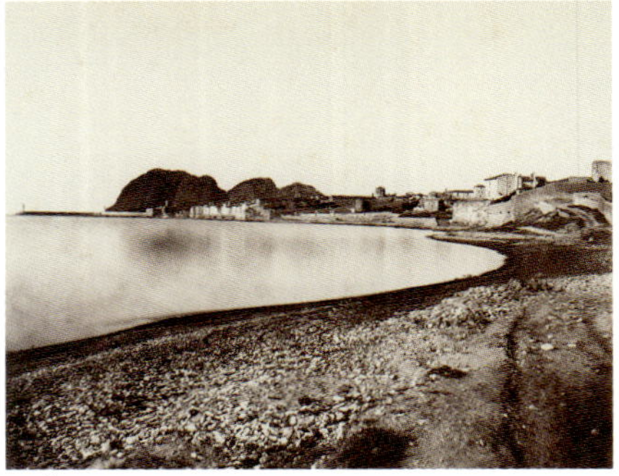
62

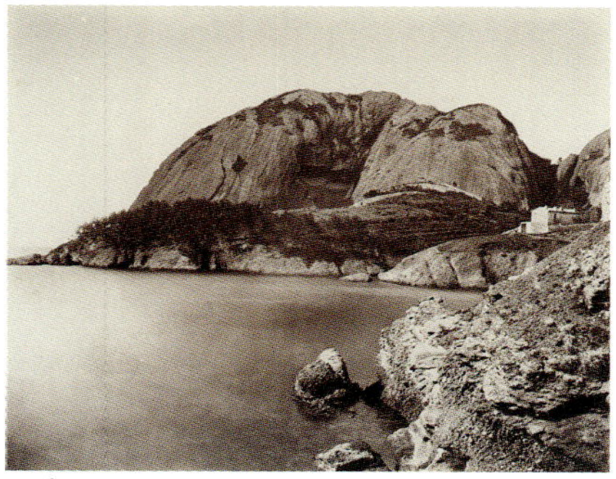
63

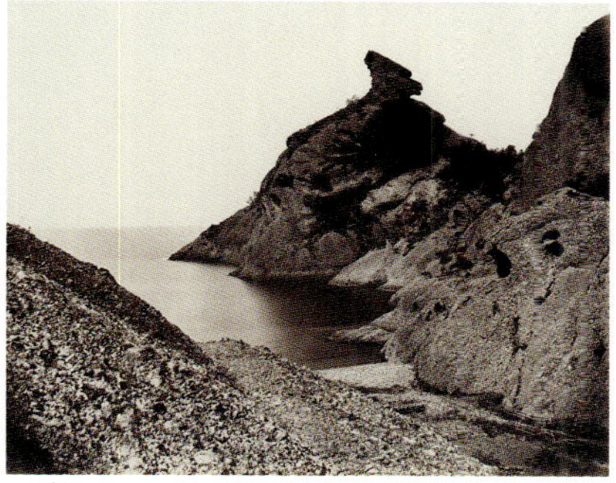
64

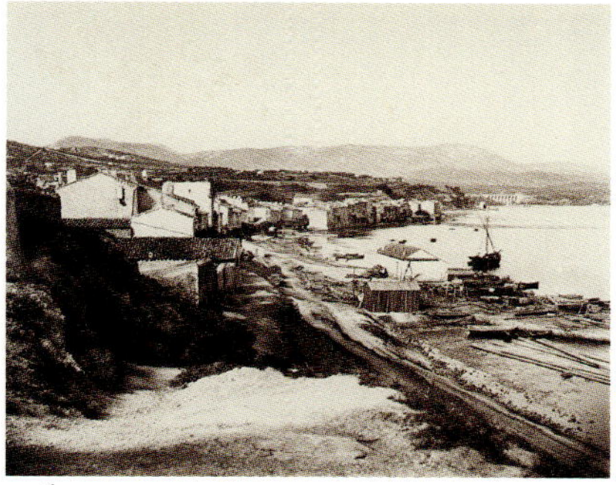
65

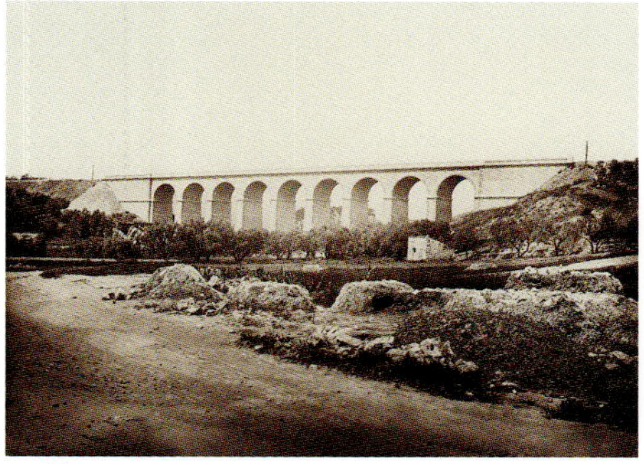
66

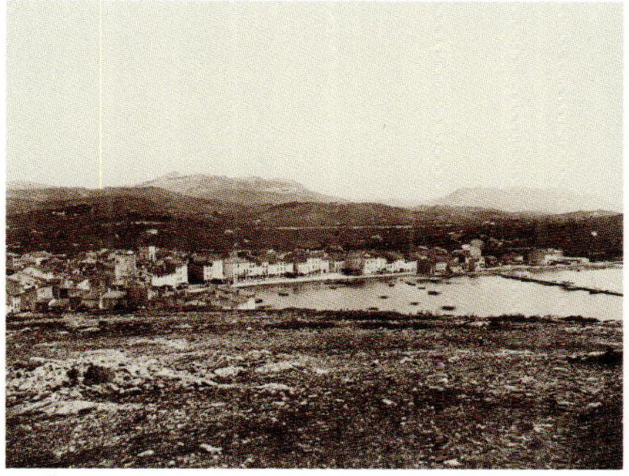
67

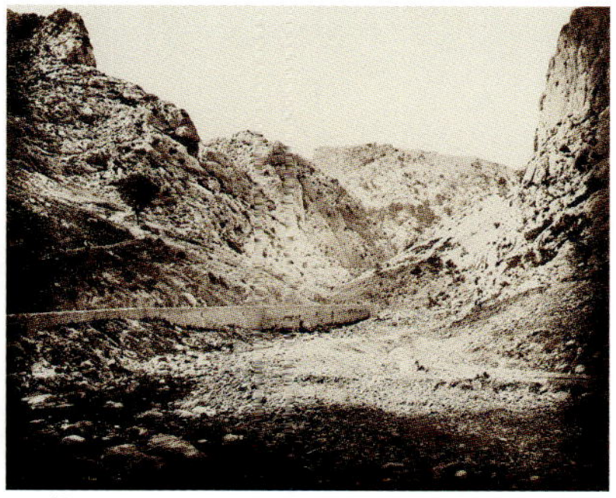
68

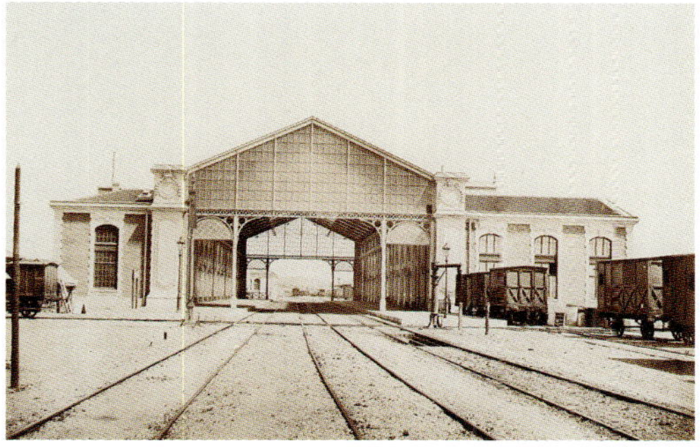
69

1 *Lyon*
2 *City Hall, Lyon*
3 *Perrache Railway Station, Lyon*
4 *La Mulatière Bridge*
5 *La Mulatière Bridge*
6 *Viaduct across the Rhone, Lyon*
7 *Viaduct across the Rhone, Lyon*
8 *Viaduct at Givors*
9 *Viaduct at Givors*
10 *Tunnel, Vienne*
11 *Saint-Colombe, Vienne*
12 *Saint-Jean, Vienne*
13 *Saint-Maurice, Vienne*
14 *Tunnel, Vienne*
15 *Viaduct across the Isère*
16 *La Voulte*
17 *Viaduct at La Voulte*
18 *Viaduct at La Voulte*
19 *Viviers*
20 *Entrance to the Donzère Pass*
21 *Antique Arch, Orange*
22 *Antique Theater, Orange*
23 *Antique Theater, Orange*
24 *Avignon*
25 *Saint-Bénezet Bridge, Avignon*
26 *Avignon*
27 *Villeneuve-lès-Avignon*
28 *The Popes' Palace, Avignon*
29 *Vaucluse*
30 *Saint-Rémy*
31 *Saint-Rémy*
32 *Pont du Gard*
33 *Viaduct across the Durance*
34 *Viaduct at Tarascon*
35 *Viaduct at Tarascon*
36 *Château, Tarascon*
37 *Maison Carrée, Nîmes*
38 *Amphitheater, Nîmes*
39 *Fountain, Nîmes*
40 *Temple of Diana, Nîmes*
41 *Tour Magne, Nîmes*
42 *Gate of Augustus, Nîmes*
43 *Aigues-Mortes*
44 *Saint-Gilles*
45 *Saint-Trophime, Arles*
46 *Cloister of Saint-Trophime, Arles*
47 *Cloister of Saint-Trophime, Arles*
48 *Amphitheater, Arles*
49 *Amphitheater, Arles*
50 *Montmajour*
51 *Viaduct at Saint-Chamas*
52 *Roquefavour*
53 *La Nerthe Tunnel*
54 *Marseille*
55 *Roman Theater, Arles*
56 *Marseille*
57 *Marseille*
58 *Marseille*
59 *Marseille*
60 *Marseille*
61 *Marseille*
62 *La Ciotat*
63 *The "Eagle's Beak," La Ciotat*
64 *"The Monk," La Ciotat*
65 *Bandol*
66 *Viaduct at Bandol*
67 *Saint-Nazaire*
68 *Gorges d'Ollioules*
69 *Toulon*

77

CLAUDE MONET

FRENCH, 1840–1926

Railroad Bridge, Argenteuil

1874

Oil on canvas

21⅜ × 28⅞ in. (54.3 × 73.3 cm)

Philadelphia Museum of Art, John G. Johnson Collection, 1917, Cat. 1050

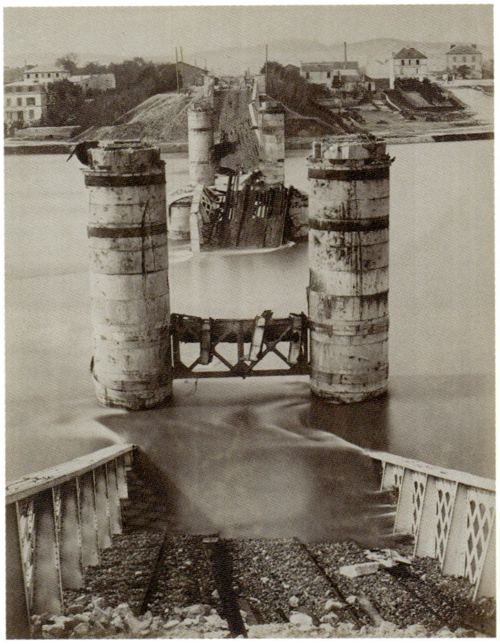

FIG. 71 Jules Andrieu, *Disasters of the War: Pont d'Argenteuil*, autumn 1870 or 1871. Albumen print, 14¾ × 11½ in. (37.7 × 29.4 cm). National Gallery of Canada, Ottawa

CLAUDE MONET'S ENGAGEMENT with the representation of railroads is concentrated in the decade of the 1870s. He spent much of this time in the suburb of Argenteuil, some seven miles northwest of the center of Paris, where the artist lived with his wife and young son from 1871 until 1878. Argenteuil was a suburb that had expanded rapidly since the opening of a railway line to the capital in 1851 that formed part of the Western Railway (Chemin de fer de l'Ouest). At the time of Monet's arrival, the town had recently been occupied by Prussian soldiers and forced to pay a significant indemnity of fifteen thousand francs. Monet painted several views of Argenteuil's railroad and bridges, and they spoke to the regeneration of the town in the wake of the Franco-Prussian War. These works exist alongside his better-known views of modern leisure during the same period and represent a central element in the Impressionist imaging of industry and the railroad.

Monet painted five views of the railroad bridge at Argenteuil that had been rebuilt in 1872, following its destruction by retreating French soldiers in 1870.[1] The destroyed bridge was later recorded in a series of impressive photographs by Jules Andrieu: one shows the bridge's twisted shape, lying in the river (fig. 71). Originally built in 1863, the bridge consisted of a single, machine-made iron trestle, weighing 881 tons and supported by four slim concrete piers 46 feet high.[2] The bridge was a source of local pride, since it had been constructed by the Joly ironworks factory at Argenteuil. It arguably had national importance because of its radical, simplified design. According to the local journalist Jules Beaujanot, it had no equal in France in terms of its modern design, with the exception of the bridges recently built at Bordeaux and Strasbourg.[3] The structure was also, however, a source of controversy. As Paul Hayes Tucker has shown, local opinion was divided. For many, its minimalist design and absence of decoration were offensive; as M. Lebeuf, the editor of the local Argenteuil newspaper, noted in 1863, the bridge was a "heavy and primitive work . . . a wall of iron that is impenetrable to the eye."[4] *Railroad Bridge, Argenteuil* shows the bridge's four sets of concrete piers and iron trestle from an oblique angle; a bank of vegetation in the foreground allows the bridge to appear integrated into the natural scenery. A puffing locomotive moves away from the near bank, while the three orange cars to the right represent the rear of another train, approaching Argenteuil. The scene is lit by warm sunlight, which strikes the right side of the piers, while the sailboat references the importance of boating to the riverside town.

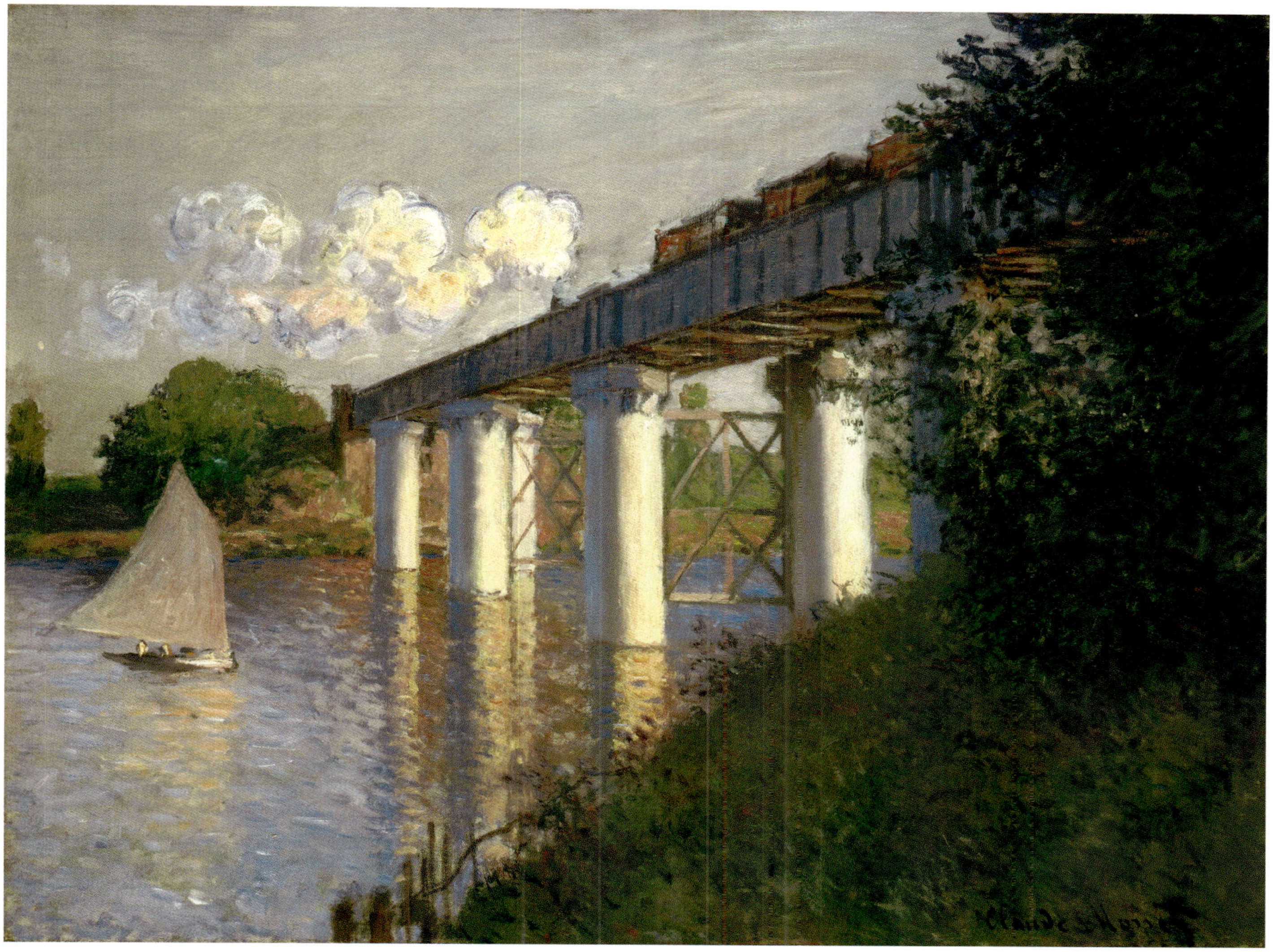

In a much sketchier view, *The Promenade with the Railroad Bridge, Argenteuil* (cat. 78), Monet represented the bridge much farther in the distance. The structure is rendered in thin, rapidly applied, long brushstrokes with little attention given to the trestle and piers. Instead, Monet emphasized the breadth of the bridge, which extended 219 yards across the river; here, it runs in a horizontal line across the full width of the canvas. It also dissects the steeple of the Saint-Denis Basilica in Argenteuil, built recently in 1866. Monet's viewpoint is from the south Gennevilliers bank one-third mile upriver, looking west. In the foreground, he painted his wife Camille, fashionably attired in a white dress trimmed with black, a blue hat, and carrying a yellow parasol. To the left is the artist's young son, Jean, in a yellow straw hat, gray suit, and black tie. In this idyllic scene, Monet underscored the rich green bank of vegetation and cropped out the industrial docks and factories, which were just out of sight to the right. Nonetheless, a train with several cars can be seen crossing the bridge. Monet has here fused the twin modern elements of leisure and industry. His brushwork is extremely sketchy, with much of the light gray ground showing through, particularly in the sky and river.

Monet also depicted the highway bridge in Argenteuil that had been built in 1831 from traditional materials of wood and stone but had been destroyed in the Franco-Prussian War (cat. 79). The bridge was swiftly reconstructed in 1871–72; it measured forty-nine feet high, and its seven arches spanned the 219 yards between the two banks. Monet produced about ten views of this new structure from a variety of angles.[5] The bridge had been rebuilt with iron,

78

CLAUDE MONET

FRENCH, 1840–1926

The Promenade with the Railroad Bridge, Argenteuil

1874

Oil on canvas

21⅛ × 28⅜ in. (53.7 × 72.1 cm)

Saint Louis Art Museum, Gift of Sydney M. Shoenberg Sr. 45:1973

79

The Highway Bridge at Argenteuil

1873

Oil on canvas

17¾ × 27½ in. (45.1 × 69.9 cm)

Virginia Museum of Fine Arts, Richmond,
Gift of Anna L. and Fleetwood Garner, 2006.29

rather than wood, arches, thus creating a far more modern effect.[6] In *The Highway Bridge at Argenteuil*, Monet looked at the structure close up, focusing on the arch to the far right: the perforated arch extends between stone piers, with five short ribs and two diagonal braces on either side and about twenty short beams supporting the roadbed. Monet's detailed rendering highlights the engineering prowess of the structure, but he offset the resolute modernity of the scene by including pedestrians and a horse-drawn carriage to the left. The bridge was owned and run by the town of Argenteuil, and a red brick tollhouse is to the right, providing a rich color accent against the surrounding greens. Beneath the bridge are the rental boathouses of Petit-Gennevilliers. Monet painted his scene from a grassy, open vantage point, although directly behind him was the industrial loading dock for the port of Argenteuil.

These three works thus document Monet's interest in the railroad and infrastructure of bridges around Argenteuil.[7] By the late 1870s, he had turned away from such subject matter to more pastoral views, following his move to the rural town of Vétheuil in 1878. —SK

1. In addition to the works in the present exhibition, see Daniel Wildenstein, *Monet*, vol. 2, *Catalogue raisonné* (Paris: Wildenstein Institute; Cologne: Taschen, 1996), nos. 279 (private collection), 319 (Musée d'Orsay, Paris), and 320 (Musée Marmottan, Paris). The latter two are variants on *The Railroad Bridge at Argenteuil*, showing the bridge from the same angle with different light effects and levels of finish. For Monet's views of trains at Argenteuil, see *The Railway Station at Argenteuil* (Musée de Luzarches, Conseil général du Val d'Oise, Cergy-Pontoise; Wildenstein, no. 242), *The Train Engine in the Snow* (Musée Marmottan Monet, Paris; Wildenstein, no. 356) and *Train in the Snow at Argenteuil* (private collection; Wildenstein, no. 360).

2. An engraving of the bridge appeared in *Le monde illustré* on August 29, 1863; see Paul Hayes Tucker, *Monet at Argenteuil* (New Haven: Yale University Press, 1982), 74.

3. Cited in ibid., 72.

4. Quoted in ibid., 73.

5. For two views of the bridge under repair, see Wildenstein, nos. 194–95 and, for a range of other views, nos. 311–17.

6. Tucker, *Monet at Argenteuil*, 196, argues that the new bridge, in contrast to the railroad bridge, remained wedded to the past: "Besides being fabricated to fit the dimensions of the openings between the stone pylons, the arches were designed to imitate the form and appearance of the older wooden ones; they were even perforated, giving them a decorative hand-crafted appeal which like the wooden arches stood in marked contrast to the stripped-down, impersonal appearance of the railroad structure."

7. Monet showed a view of the railway bridge (probably Wildenstein, no. 279) and one of the highway bridge (probably Wildenstein, no. 311) at the 1876 Impressionist exhibition (both works belonging to the opera singer Jean-Baptiste Faure), but neither attracted much critical attention. *Railroad Bridge, Argenteuil* was sold to the dealer Paul Durand-Ruel in 1876. *The Promenade with the Railroad Bridge, Argenteuil* was sold to the painter Jacques-Émile Blanche.

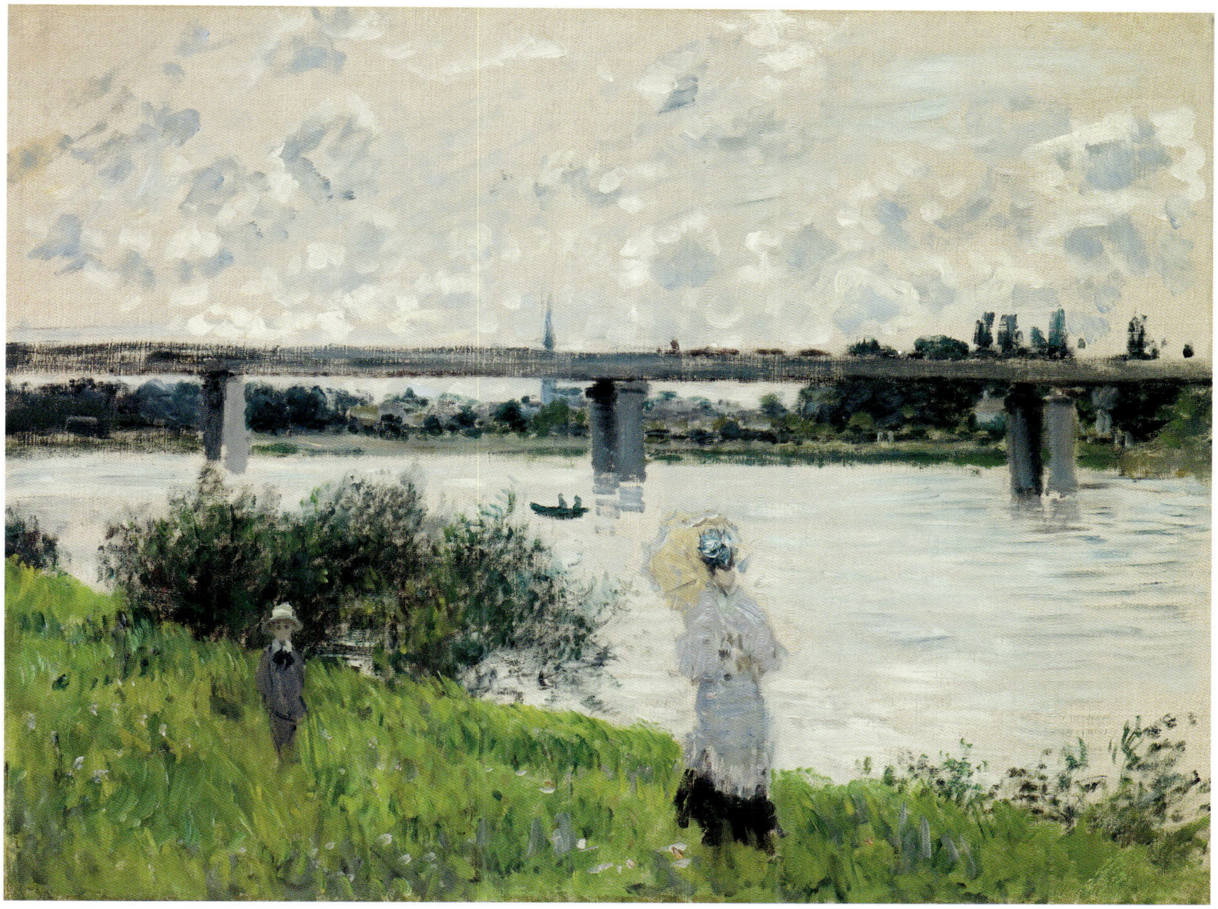

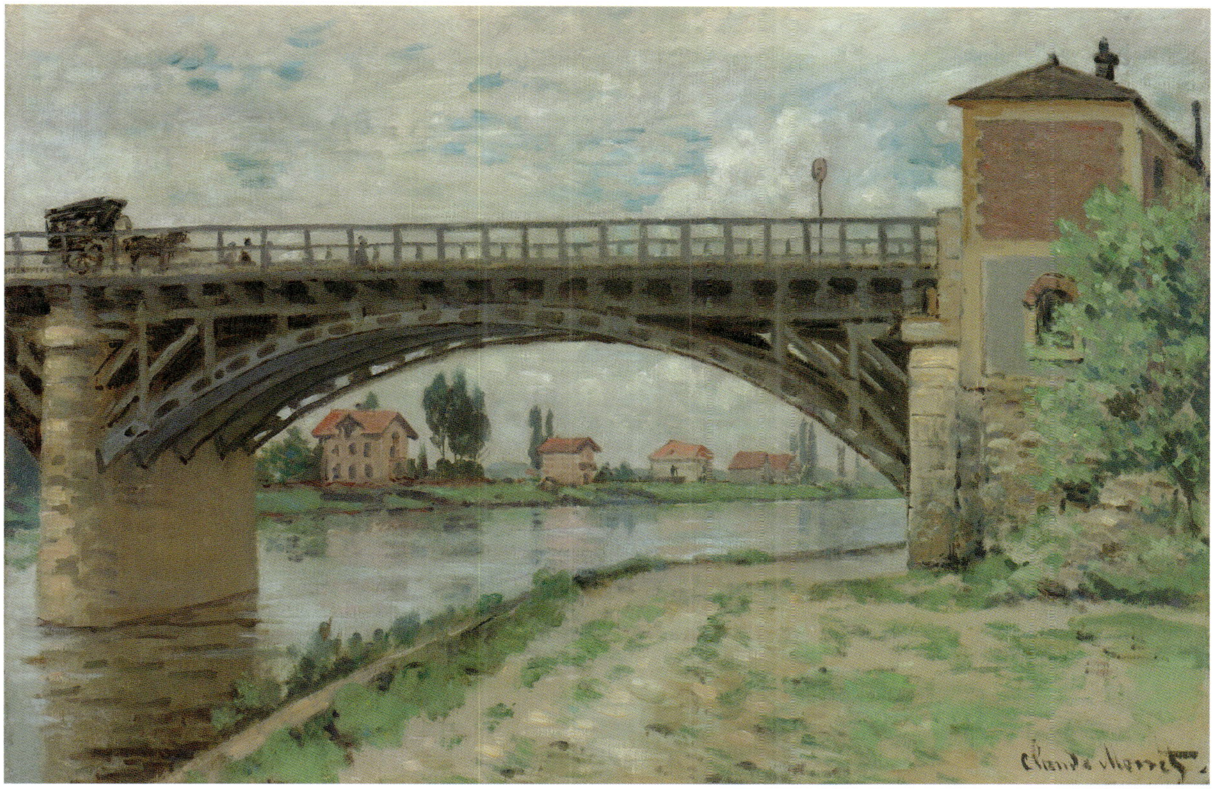
Claude Monet

80

GUSTAVE LE GRAY
FRENCH, 1820–1884

Factory, Terre-Noire

1851–55
Salt print from waxed paper negative
9 11/16 × 12 7/8 in. (24.6 × 32.7 cm)
The J. Paul Getty Museum, Los Angeles, 2002.13

81

HENRI-VICTOR REGNAULT
FRENCH, 1810–1878

Sèvres Factory, Paris

1851
Salt print from paper negative
13 5/16 × 17 15/16 in. (33.8 × 45.6 cm)
The Nelson-Atkins Museum of Art, Kansas City, Missouri,
Gift of the Hall Family Foundation, 2011.12.33

DEPICTIONS OF FACTORIES were exceedingly rare in French artistic amateur photography of the 1850s and 1860s. Gustave Le Gray made two known negatives of an unidentified factory in central France, an area known for its rich deposits of iron ore and coal, which were raw materials used in the production of steel and iron. This one is an extraordinary picture: the fibrous nature of Le Gray's paper negative diffuses the dark tonalities of the blackened earth in the foreground and imparts an overall grainy, somewhat murky quality to the photograph. The smoke billowing from the structure, against a backdrop of spare, unforested terrain, adds to this effect.

Henri-Victor Regnault, who was instrumental in fostering photography's early technical development in France, was one of the few photographers who made several views of a factory and its grounds.[1] The Manufacture impériale de Sèvres, the national porcelain works, was located at the southwestern edge of Paris. Beginning in 1852, Regnault served there as director. The manufactory was directly associated with the changing politics of the state: as regimes changed, so did the official decorative patterns and procedures of porcelain manufacture. During the Second Empire, critics of Napoléon III's modernization policies felt that the Manufacture impériale de Sèvres had strayed too far from traditional craft in the campaign to employ new industrial techniques.[2] Regnault, a chemist, was assigned to his post just a few months after Napoléon III came to power and was accused of favoring science and industrial progress at the expense of aesthetic nuance and artistic expertise. Amid this political turmoil, Regnault took up photography, through a community at Sèvres that had begun to flourish as a result of the efforts of Louis-Rémy Robert, who ran the works' painting studio and had been experimenting with the medium before Regnault's arrival. Both men made portraits, landscapes, and views of the factory's buildings and grounds.

The large-format photograph by Regnault featured here depicts the site as seen from the entrance of the Parc de Saint-Cloud. Considered alongside his more artistically conceived river scenes (cat. 52) and landscapes, Regnault's views of Sèvres present a more complicated notion of the mid-nineteenth-century landscape, one that was shaped by both modern industry and natural forces. Such subjects were taken up by Camille Pissarro and Claude Monet in their later Impressionist canvases (see cats. 82–84, 87). —AMW

1. Regnault worked closely with colleagues Jean-Baptiste Biot and Louis-Désiré Blanquart-Evrard to test Blanquart-Evrard's modifications to William Henry Fox Talbot's calotype process during the 1840s and early 1850s. Regnault was a founding member of the Société héliographique and president of the Société française de la photographie from 1855 to 1868.

2. This synopsis is indebted to the formative research of Laurie Dahlberg, *Victor Regnault and the Advance of Photography: The Art of Avoiding Errors* (Princeton: Princeton University Press, 2005), esp. 55–60 for a discussion of how the changing politics of the state affected activities at Sèvres.

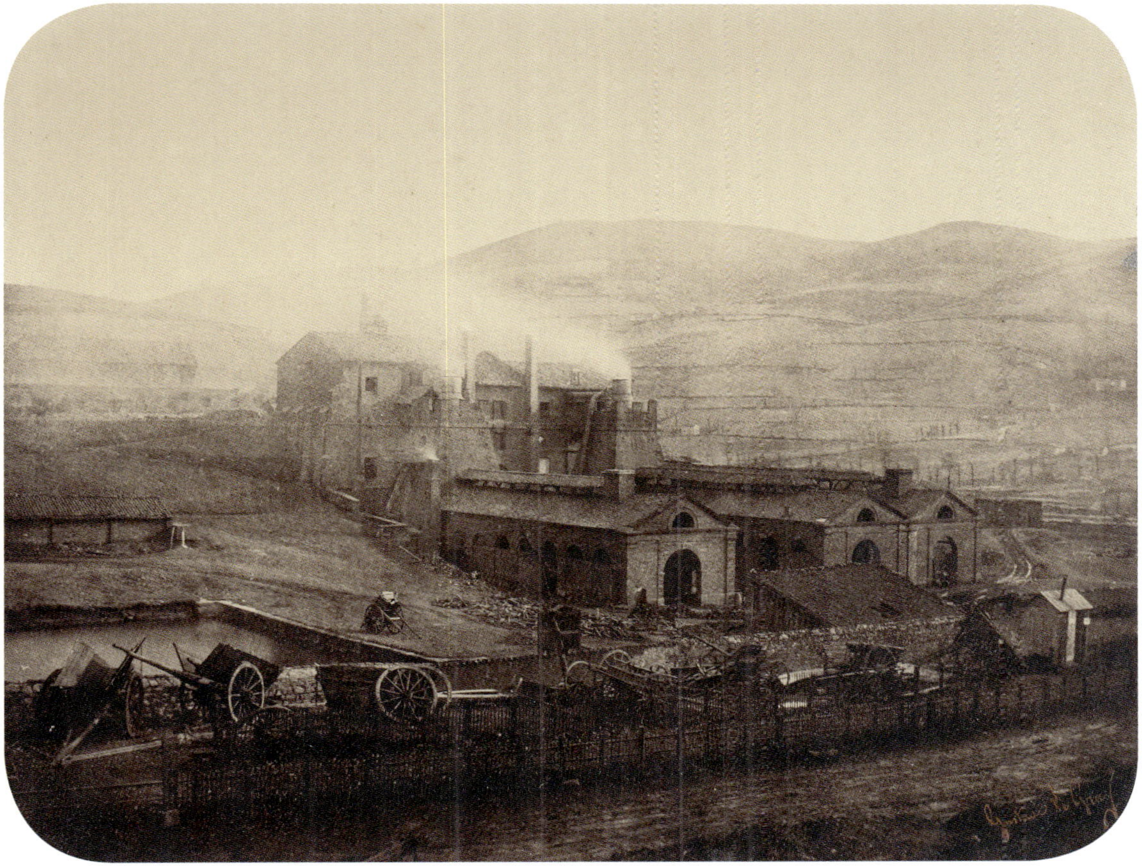

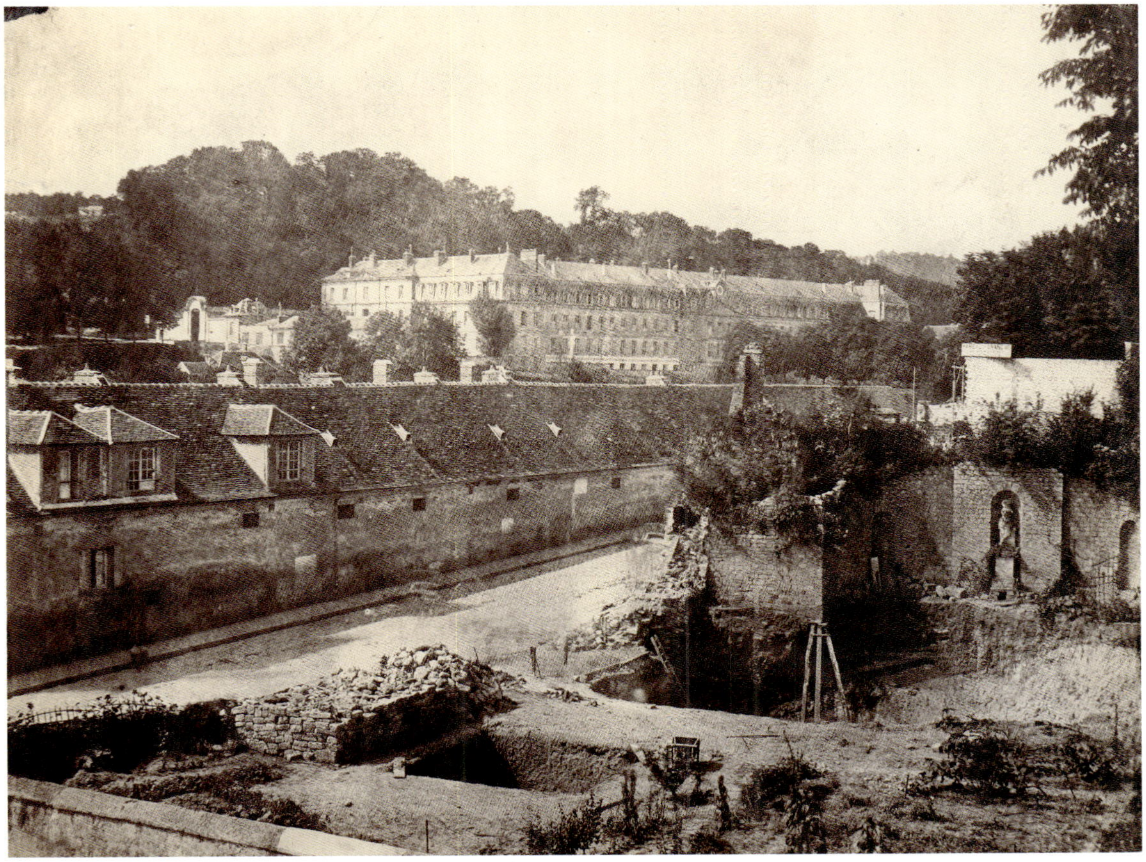

CAMILLE PISSARRO
FRENCH, 1830–1903

82

Banks of the Oise at Pontoise

1867

Oil on canvas

18 × 28⅛ in. (45.7 × 71.5 cm)

Denver Art Museum, Gift of the Barnett and Annalee Newman Foundation in honor of Annalee G. Newman, 2001.310

83

Factory near Pontoise

1873

Oil on canvas

18⅜ × 22 in. (46.7 × 55.9 cm)

Michele and Donald D'Amour Museum of Fine Arts, Springfield, Massachusetts, The James Philip Gray Collection, 37.03

FOR MOST OF HIS CAREER, Camille Pissarro was known principally as a painter of agricultural scenes, but he also produced a significant body of factory pictures. During his time in Pontoise, from 1866 until 1869 and again from 1872 until 1882, he painted twenty-eight factory views, including the three works here.[1] These paintings represent an important record of the industrial changes in the town and a vital contribution to the wider Impressionist interest in representing modern industry.

In 1867 Pissarro painted *Banks of the Oise at Pontoise*, an expansive view of Pontoise looking across the Oise River from the towpath by the village of Saint-Ouen-l'Aumône.[2] Pissarro's scene is topographically accurate and depicts a town that had been recently transformed by the arrival of the Industrial Revolution. Although Pissarro included at left the bell tower of the medieval church of Saint-Maclou, the scene is dominated by the billowing smokestack of the gasworks (the Usine de gaz), which had opened only in October 1867.[3] The smaller factory stack of an older distillery is visible to the left by the riverbank. To the right, Pissarro rendered the starkly horizontal line of the railroad bridge, recently constructed in 1863, which had extended the rail track from Paris across the Oise.[4] Heralded for its modern design, this iron trestle structure rested on concrete piers; it would be destroyed by the Prussians in 1870.[5] Pissarro also included several barges, alluding to the significance of Pontoise as the most important barge port on the Oise. The painting shows the new industrial center of Pontoise, recording the transformations to the town brought by factories and the railroad, although the artist framed these elements within a natural setting, particularly the line of poplar trees, which provides a *repoussoir* in the right foreground. Pissarro's composition is rendered in a pattern of verticals and horizontals and in a palette-knife technique, suggesting a debt to Gustave Courbet.

Pissarro left Pontoise in 1869 but returned in 1872 to find a town that had been occupied by the Prussians. He soon showed an interest in representing two new factories built close to the town; these scenes may speak to his nationalistic pride in the area's rapid regeneration. In 1873 he painted *Factory near Pontoise*, a view of a factory that had been constructed in 1872, was owned by J. Chalon et Cie, and specialized in the manufacture and sale of industrial and commercial alcohol distilled from sugar beets.[6] Pissarro represented the factory with its eighty-foot-high smokestack alongside two smaller stacks. This is an exceptional image within the artist's oeuvre of factory paintings because of its close-up, resolutely frontal view. As Richard Brettell has shown, the houses to the left did not exist and were probably added to emphasize further the scale of the smokestack.[7] The roofs of the factories also seem to have been elongated vertically. White draft horses are in the foreground, while the three poplars to the right echo the lines of the factory smokestacks. Pissarro painted three other paintings of this

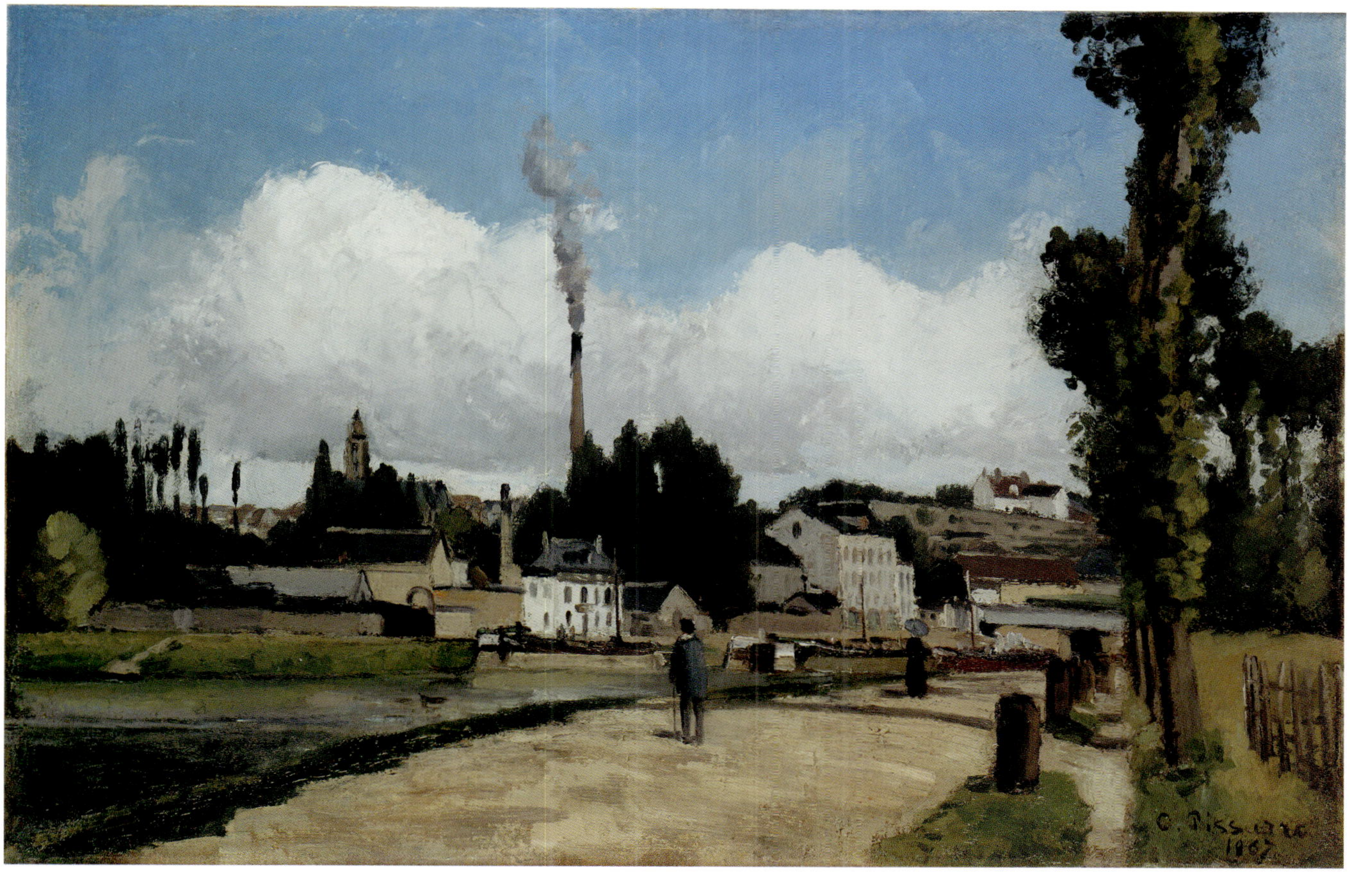

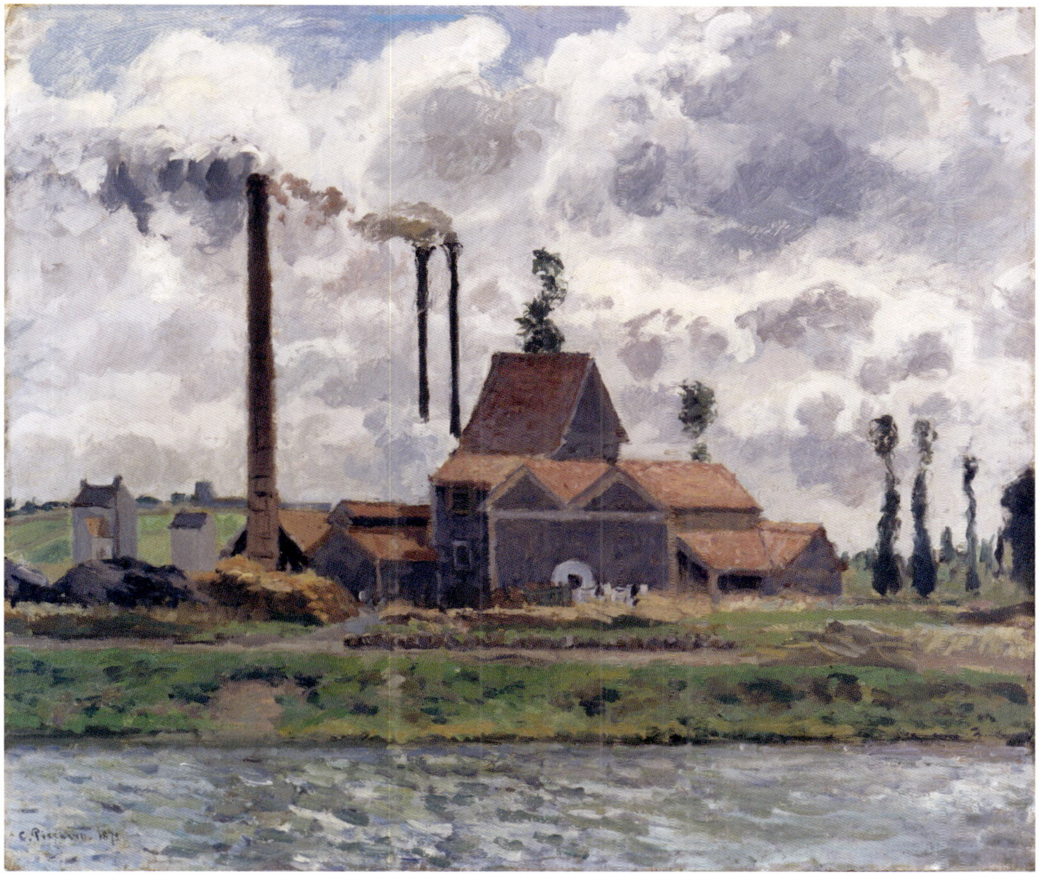

84

CAMILLE PISSARRO
FRENCH, 1830–1903

The Banks of the Oise near Pontoise

1873
Oil on canvas
15 × 21¾ in. (38.1 × 55.2 cm)
Indianapolis Museum of Art, James E. Roberts Fund, 40.252

factory in 1873, although they situate the structure within a more panoramic context.[8]

In *The Banks of the Oise near Pontoise*, also from 1873, Pissarro painted a very different factory view. Here, the artist represented another factory also built in 1872. Owned by a M. Camille Arneuil, it specialized in the manufacture of commercial wall paints.[9] This was smaller than the Chalon structure, and Pissarro placed its sheds and single smokestack within a panoramic landscape, with the sky taking up about two-thirds of the composition. Pissarro's work includes other modern elements. To the right is a puffing train moving along the Paris–Lille line, a track that had opened in 1846 and belonged to the Compagnie du Chemin de fer du Nord. On the river is a barge, perhaps transporting grain from the surrounding wheat fields, here visible to the right. The scene is animated by a carriage and a peasant woman (wearing a bright orange head scarf) on the road to the nearby town of Auvers. Pissarro's painting is vigorously worked in highly gestural impasto, particularly in the sky and the trees to the left.

Pissarro's three views highlight his interest in industry; he found inspiration in the Chalon factory throughout the 1870s. The artist never discussed industry in his letters of the 1860s and 1870s, so it is difficult to ascertain the attitude conveyed in these paintings. An ecological reading might suggest his opposition to factories as despoiling the landscape. The Chalon factory, in fact, soon developed a notorious reputation in the 1870s for its stench and pollution of the river. Pissarro, moreover, never exhibited his early factory views at the Impressionist shows—perhaps suggesting a reluctance to present himself publicly as a painter of industry. Later in his career, his opposition to capitalism, in the form of large, metropolitan factories, would become increasingly evident. Yet, these earlier paintings of essentially small-scale factories, inserted into the broader natural and agricultural landscape, can be seen as generally affirmative. They embody a vision of an "agro-industrial paradise," central to the anarchist thinking with which Pissarro closely aligned himself.[10] Industry and agriculture here worked hand in hand to assist in the growth of the French nation. —SK

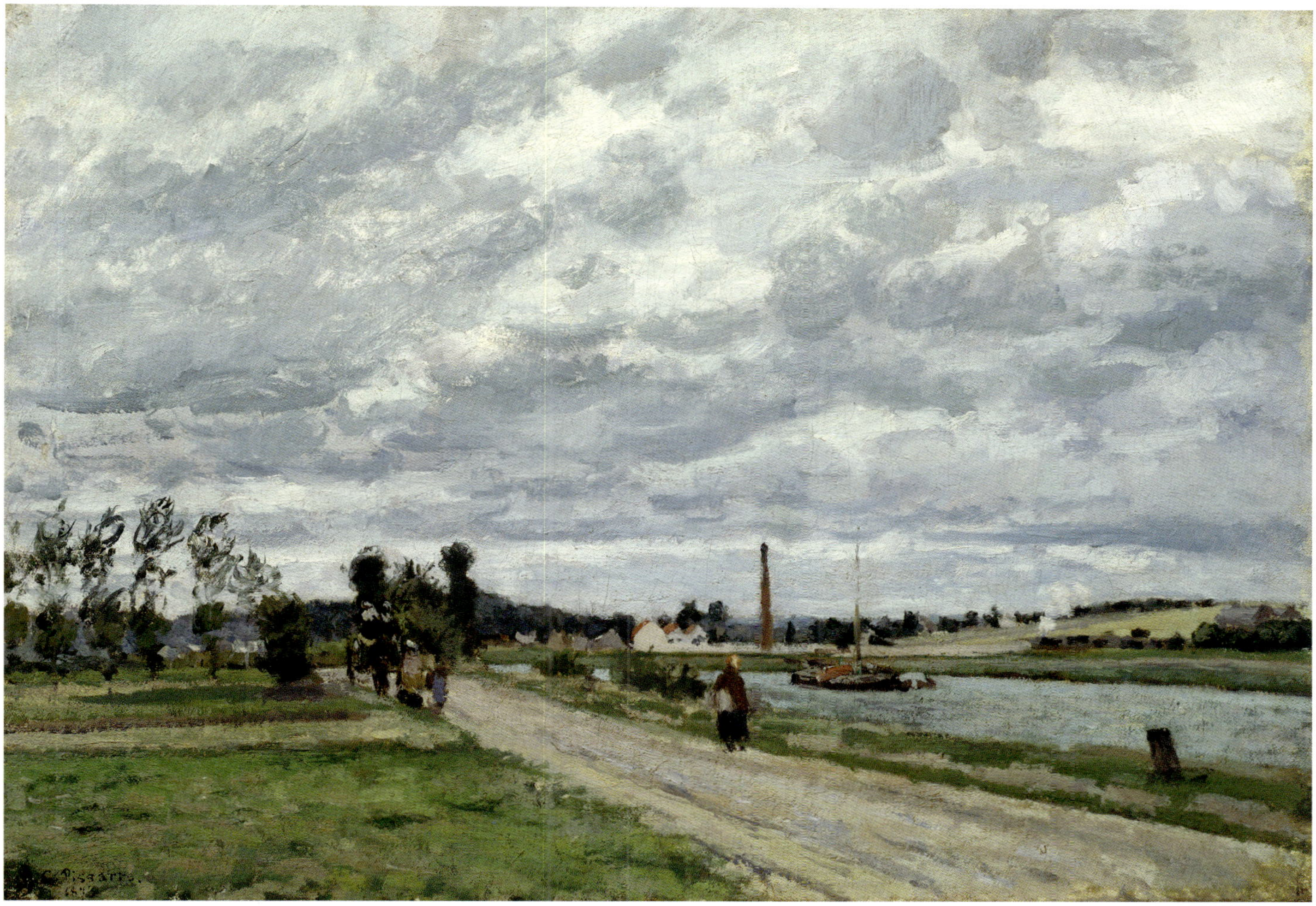

1. See Joachim Pissarro and Claire Durand-Ruel Snollaerts, *Pissarro: Critical Catalogue of Paintings* (Paris: Wildenstein Institute; Milan: Skira, 2005), 2: nos. 130, 229, 249, 250, 274, 275, 297–300, 302, 303, 441, 453–59, 491, 495, 511–13, 542, 551, 586.

2. Pissarro also produced a more detailed pencil study of this view (*View of Pontoise*, 1867, pencil on paper, 11 × 17¾ in. [28 × 45 cm]; private collection), reproduced in Richard R. Brettell, *Pissarro and Pontoise: The Painter in a Landscape* (New Haven: Yale University Press, 1990), 79.

3. See ibid., 80. The painting must date to the early fall of 1867, given Pissarro's dated signature and the greenery still on the trees.

4. In 1846 the rail track had been constructed only as far as Saint-Ouen-l'Aumône on the southern bank of the Oise.

5. For an engraving of the Pontoise bridge, published in *L'illustration* in December 1863, see Terence Maloon, ed., *Camille Pissarro*, exh. cat. (Sydney: Art Gallery of New South Wales, 2005), 16.

6. See Brettell, *Pissarro and Pontoise*, 25. Pissarro and Durand-Ruel Snollaerts, *Pissarro: Critical Catalogue*, 2:236, describe the structure as a "treacle distillery and potash factory" and note that the Chalon firm had applied in 1871 for permission to build the factory, receiving a prefectural permit on April 13, 1872.

7. Brettell, *Pissarro and Pontoise*, 84.

8. Pissarro and Durand-Ruel Snollaerts, *Pissarro: Critical Catalogue*, 2: nos. 297, *Factory at St-Ouen-l'Aumône* (private collection, U.K.), 299, *Factory on the Banks of the Oise, Saint-Ouen-l'Aumône* (The Israel Museum, Jerusalem), and 300, *Factory on the Banks of the Oise, Saint-Ouen-l'Aumône* (Sterling and Francine Clark Art Institute, Williamstown, Mass.). He also produced a watercolor of the factory, *Flood of the River Oise at Pontoise* (private collection), and an etching, *Factory at Pontoise* (see Loys Delteil, *Camille Pissarro: L'oeuvre gravé et lithographié; Catalogue raisonné* [1923; San Francisco: Alan Wofsy Fine Arts, 1999], no. 10).

9. Brettell, *Pissarro and Pontoise*, 25.

10. See Joachim Pissarro in Richard R. Brettell and Joachim Pissarro, *Manet to Matisse. Impressionist Masters from the Marion and Henry Bloch Collection*, exh. cat. (Kansas City, Mo.: Nelson-Atkins Museum of Art, 2007), 77.

85

ARMAND GUILLAUMIN

FRENCH, 1841-1927

Landscape, Île de France

ca. 1872–75

Oil on canvas

19⅜ × 25¾ in. (49.2 × 65.4 cm)

Promised gift of Robert L. and Barbara Bloch in honor of his parents, Henry and Marion Bloch, and the 75th anniversary of The Nelson-Atkins Museum of Art

ARMAND GUILLAUMIN was an important, if often overlooked, member of the Impressionist circle. He exhibited at six of the eight Impressionist shows and was particularly close to Camille Pissarro and Paul Cézanne in the 1870s. He worked *en plein air* with both of these artists, and Cézanne even made a painted copy (Kunsthalle, Hamburg) of Guillaumin's *The Seine at Bercy* (Kunsthalle, Hamburg).[1] In the late 1860s and early 1870s Guillaumin focused on industrial views of Paris and its environs. James Rubin has noted that "Guillaumin deserves credit as the first [Impressionist] to center attention on them [factories] in the context of economic power and development."[2]

In *Landscape, Île de France*, smoke belches from the smokestacks, mingling with the gray, cloudy sky. The site can be identified for the first time here as the expansive factory complex at Ivry, southeast of Paris. The painting is related to an 1865 drawing by Guillaumin, *Landscape at Ivry*.[3] There were two main factories at Ivry: the Guibal rubber factory, founded in 1851; and the larger steel forges, established by the Coutant family. The latter extended over some 8.6 acres and specialized in the melting down and recasting of scrap metal in a range of forms such as bolts and rivets. Both factories were described in some detail by Julien Turgan in his great encyclopedia of French factories, *Les grandes usines de France*.[4] Guillaumin's painting is part of a larger group of at least six views of the Ivry factories, painted between about 1869 and about 1875.[5] The artist generally showed them alongside the Seine with the river clearly visible. This picture is exceptional in depicting the factories from an inland viewpoint, and we may imagine the Seine River lying on the other side of the factory before the distant hills. The painting has previously been dated to about 1876–77, but the new identification (and relationship to the drawing) suggests an earlier dating, to about 1872–75.[6]

Guillamin's painting is arranged in a series of horizontal planes, offset by the diagonal of the enclosed garden in the foreground. The diagonal red roof also provides a strong color accent within the dominant green palette. Guillaumin included elements of rural agriculture, a plowman and two white horses in the foreground, which are echoed by a similar pairing of plowman and horses at the back left. In the mid-nineteenth century, as Ivry became increasingly industrialized, older agricultural traditions collided head-on with the transforming presence of factories. Nonetheless, the two elements were not necessarily incompatible, and Guillaumin's work can be related to the idea of the integration of field and factory labor promoted in contemporary journals such as Gustave Tissandier's *La nature*, first published in 1873.[7] This idea would be further developed later in the century in the anarchist thinking espoused by his friend Pissarro.[8]

In addition to his factory views, Guillaumin produced images of the railroad around Paris, including bridges and stations, a number of which were shown at the Impressionist exhibitions.[9] He had direct experience of the railroad, having worked as a clerk on the Paris–Orléans line from 1860. He also painted several views of the Seine as an industrial waterway, highlighting the importance of its barge traffic.[10] Guillaumin's work, as a whole, represents a significant contribution to the wider Impressionist project of representing modern industry. —SK

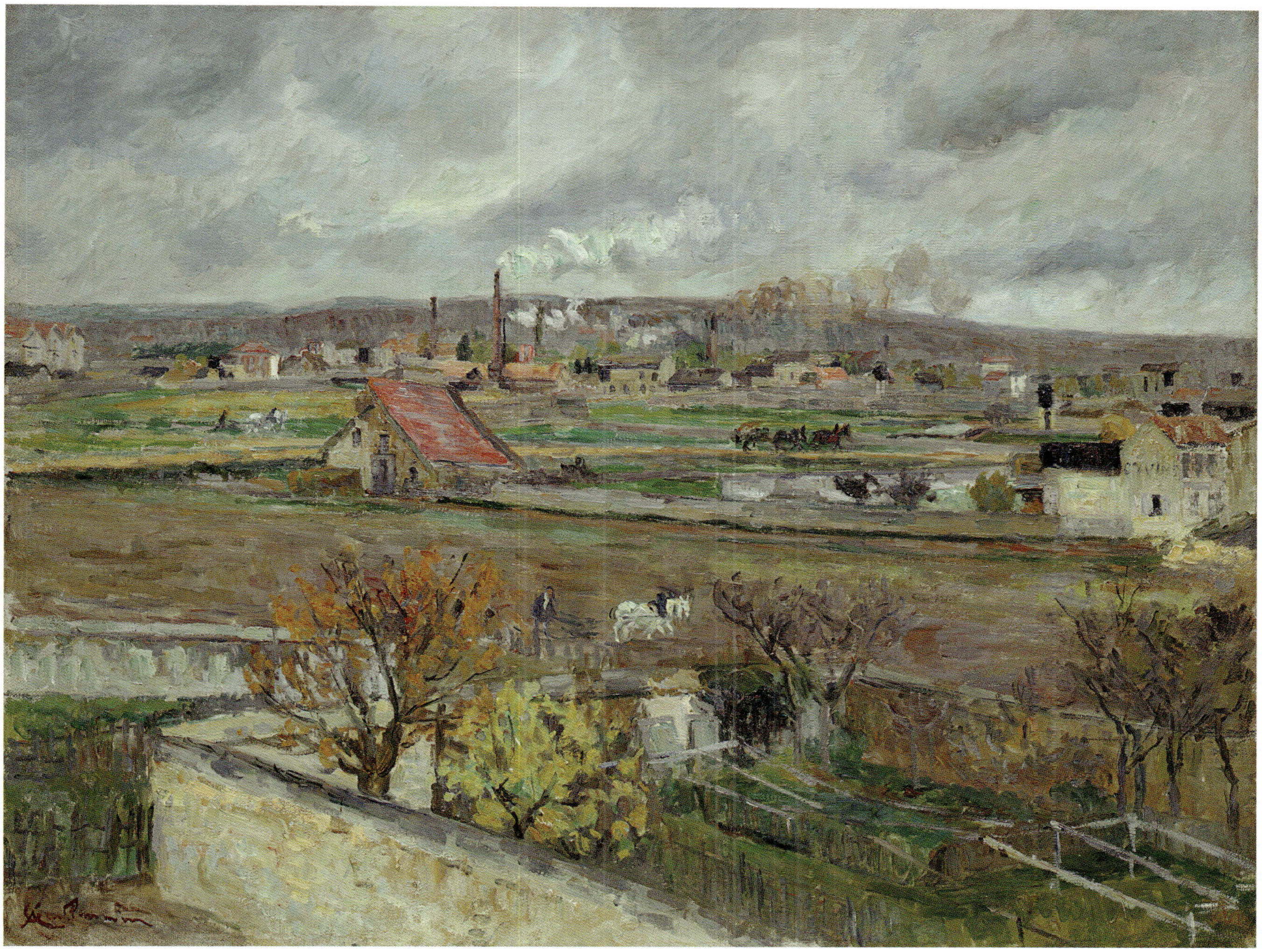

1. John Rewald, in collaboration with Walter Feilchenfeldt and Jayne Warman, *The Paintings of Paul Cézanne: A Catalogue Raisonné* (New York: Harry N. Abrams, 1996), 1:199–201, no. 293.

2. James Rubin, *Impressionism and the Modern Landscape: Productivity, Technology, and Urbanization from Manet to Van Gogh* (Berkeley: University of California Press, 2008), 132, and also 70–72, 105–7, and 134–36.

3. The pencil drawing (location unknown)—Guillaumin's earliest known drawing—is reproduced in Christopher Gray, *Armand Guillaumin*, 2nd ed. (Chester, Conn.: Pequot Press, 1972), 3: "a scene along the Seine, probably showing the forges at Ivry." Gray, 219, no. G1, gives the size of the drawing as approximately 12⅝ × 18⅞ in. (32 × 48 cm) and a provenance of formerly Mme Marguerite Guillaumin.

4. See Julien Turgan, *Les grandes usines, études industrielles en France et à l'étranger* (Paris: Michel Levy Frères, 1868), 8:177ff., for a nonillustrated overview of the rubber factory. See Turgan, *Les grandes usines, études industrielles en France et à l'étranger* (Paris: Calman-Levy, 1882), 14:1–32, for a lengthy description of the forges with an engraving of the factory exterior and six engravings of its interior.

5. Georges Serret and Dominique Fabiani, *Armand Guillaumin, 1841–1927: Catalogue raisonné de l'oeuvre peint* (Paris: Mayer, 1971), nos. 17–20, 25, 28. Perhaps Guillaumin's best-known factory view is *Setting Sun at Ivry* (Musée d'Orsay, Paris), which was shown at the first Impressionist exhibition. See also *The Seine at Ivry* (Musée du Petit Palais, Geneva), which is not included in Serret and Fabiani. There are two other drawings of Ivry (see Gray, *Guillaumin*, nos. 12 and 13).

6. This new dating has been provided by Stephanie Chardeau-Botteri of the Comité Guillaumin, e-mail to author, February 26, 2013. Mme Chardeau-Botteri also agrees with the new Ivry identification.

7. Richard R. Brettell, "Landscape, Nature and 'La Nature,'" in *From Corot to Monet: The Ecology of Impressionism*, ed. Stephen F. Eisenman (Milan: Skira, 2010), 59–70.

8. For an analysis of the juxtaposition of new and old in this painting, see Joachim Pissarro, in Richard R. Brettell and Joachim Pissarro, *Manet to Matisse: Impressionist Masters from the Marion and Henry Bloch Collection*, exh. cat. (Kansas City: Nelson-Atkins Museum of Art, 2008), 74–77.

9. *Bridge over the Marne at Nogent* (The Metropolitan Museum of Art, New York) and *Aqueduct at Arcueil, Sceaux Railroad Line* (The Art Institute of Chicago).

10. *The Seine in Paris, Rainy Weather* (Museum of Fine Arts, Houston).

86

EDGAR DEGAS

FRENCH, 1834–1917

Henri Rouart in Front of His Factory

ca. 1875

Oil on canvas

25¾ × 19⅞ in. (65.6 × 50.5 cm)

Carnegie Museum of Art, Pittsburgh, Acquired through the generosity of the Sarah Mellon Scaife Family, 69.44

EDGAR DEGAS FULLY EMBRACED the idea of the imaging of modern life, focusing particularly on Parisian scenes of ballet dancers, nightlife and cafés, and prostitutes. He came from a wealthy banking family and projected an aura of upper-class detachment throughout his career, despite changing his name from the more aristocratic De Gas. His landscapes form an important, although often overlooked, genre within his overall output, and his fascination with industrial themes is clear from a passage in one of his notebooks in which he planned a series of works around the idea of smoke and steam: "On smoke—people's smoke, from pipes, cigarettes, cigars; smoke of locomotives, tall chimneys, steamboats, etc.; smoke confined in the space under bridges; steam."[1] The project was never realized, but Degas did paint several factories in the backgrounds of his landscapes, often in racehorse scenes.[2]

Henri Rouart in Front of His Factory is Degas's most ambitious view of a factory complex. Rouart (1833–1912) was an old friend of Degas from their school days together and is depicted here in detached profile in top hat and velvet-collared coat.[3] Degas and Rouart attended the Lycée Louis-le-Grand in Paris between 1845 and 1853. Their contact diminished until both fought together in Paris during the Franco-Prussian War, when Degas was a lieutenant under Rouart's command. He subsequently dined at least once a week at Rouart's house, maintaining this practice for much of the rest of his life. Rouart was a talented artist in his own right (who showed at seven of the eight Impressionist exhibitions), a major collector, and an accomplished entrepreneur who owned two large factories in France and helped to found another in New Orleans in America. Rouart's factory in Paris was on 137, boulevard Voltaire, in the 11th arrondissement and specialized in the construction of ice-making machines, both for households and on a much larger industrial scale.[4] A successful engineer, Rouart was a pioneer in the technology of refrigeration in the nineteenth century in the days before the refrigerator.[5] He refined and patented the technology for the artificial production of ice and was even hired by the city of Paris to produce ice for the preservation of corpses in the city's principal morgue. His ice-making machines "for the congelation of meat and corpses"[6] won numerous prizes in the industrial fairs and Expositions universelles of the mid- to late nineteenth century. Degas himself is known to have visited the factory on the boulevard Voltaire.[7] Rouart also owned a second factory at Montluçon in the industrial heartland of France, close to Clermont-Ferrand—a factory dedicated to the production of iron tubing.[8] A third factory in New Orleans, the Louisiana Ice Works, was a pioneering ice-making plant, which had opened in 1868 as the first and largest of its kind in the world, using technology developed by Rouart. Degas visited New Orleans from November 1872 until March 1873 and in all likelihood went to see this factory.[9] The low buildings and smokestacks in the background of Degas's painting are very similar to those in a contemporary print of the ice works (fig. 72).[10]

It is difficult to identify with certainty which of Rouart's three factories is represented in Degas's painting, and the artist himself may not have intended topographic exactitude, perhaps including the factory elements as generalized examples of his friend's industrial accomplishments—following his strategy in his portraits of including accompanying motifs to illuminate a sitter's personality. When this painting was first exhibited at the 1877 Impressionist show, no explicit reference was made to a particular factory and the picture was described simply as *Portrait of*

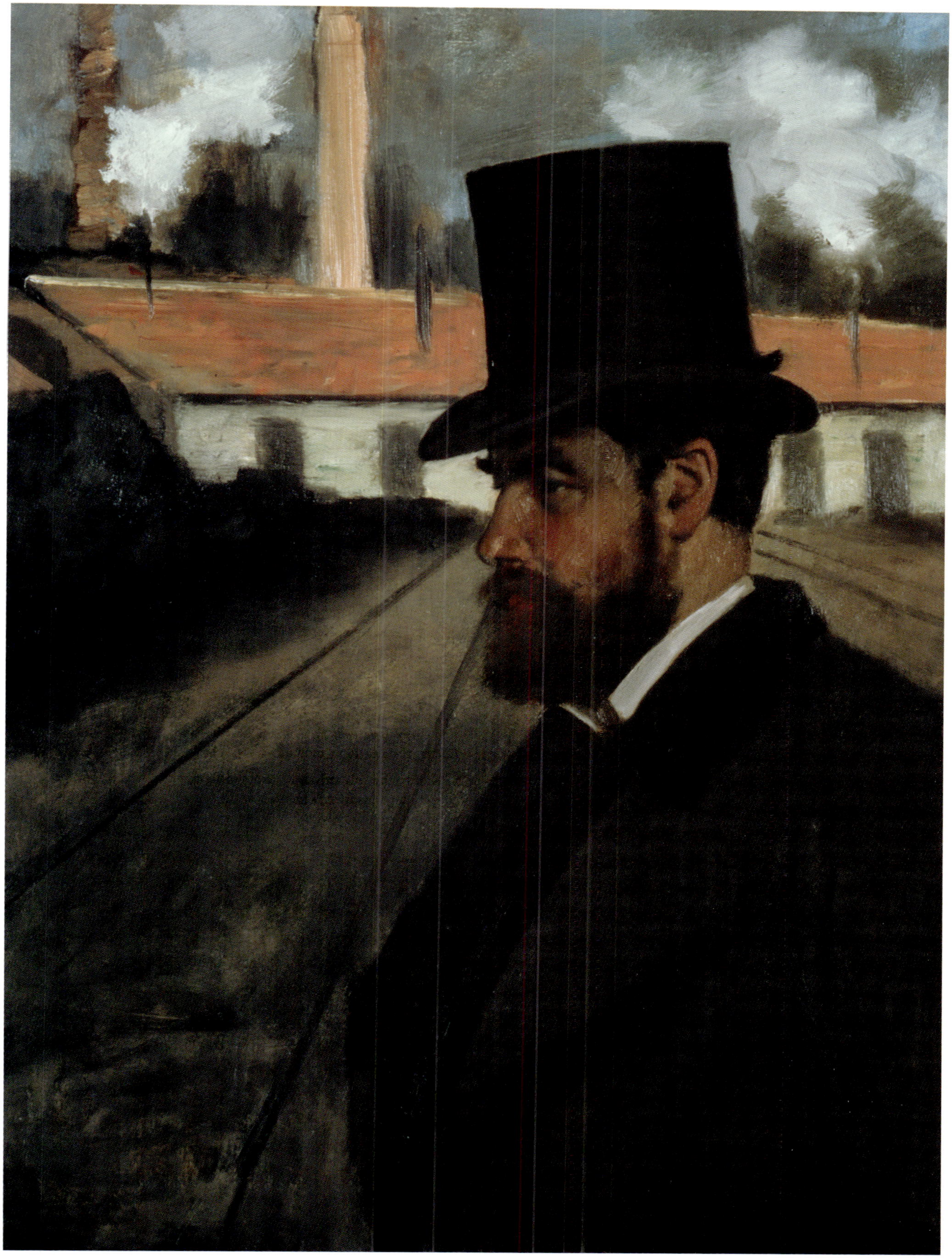

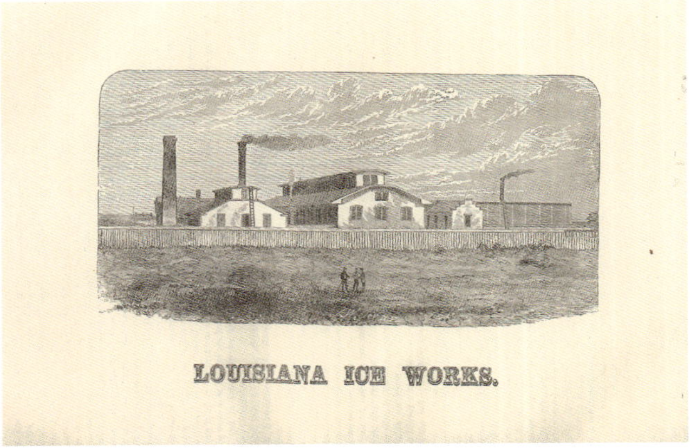

FIG. 72 *Louisiana Ice Works*. From Edwin Lewis Jewell, *Jewell's Crescent City, Illustrated* (New Orleans, 1974), 101

Monsieur H. R. . . .[11] Degas certainly used the industrial elements to expertly situate his sitter. The prominent smokestack echoes the line of Rouart's top hat, while the vertiginous lines of the railroad frame his head. The swirling white smoke picks up the white of his collar, and the reds of the roof echo his ruddy complexion. The blacks of the coal heap to the right mimic the grays and blacks of Rouart's coat. Degas's painting is an important commentary on his respect for his friend as an engineer and entrepreneur. The artist's letters from America in 1872–73 highlight his admiration for American technological prowess; he wrote of the sleeper rail cars that he took from New York to New Orleans as a "marvelous invention."[12] *Henri Rouart in Front of His Factory* is a testament to his pride in French technology. —SK

1. Theodore Reff, *The Notebooks of Edgar Degas* (Oxford: Clarendon Press, 1976), 1:134: "Sur la fumée / fumée des fumeurs, pipes cigarettes, / cigares / fumée des locomotives, des hautes cheminées / des fabriques, des bateaux à vapeur, etc. / écrasement des fumées sous les ponts // la vapeur."

2. For example, *The Gentleman's Race before the Start*, ca. 1860–62 (Musée d'Orsay, Paris), *Racehorses before the Stands*, 1866–68 (Musée d'Orsay, Paris), and *Horses in a Meadow*, 1871 (National Gallery of Art, Washington, D.C.). Paul-André Lemoisne, *Degas et son oeuvre*, 4 vols. (Paris: Arts et Métiers Graphiques, 1946–49; repr. in 5 vols., New York: Garland, 1984), 5: nos. 101, 289. Degas also produced a remarkable, abstracted view of factory smoke in a monotype etching, *Factory Smoke*, ca. 1876–79.

3. Degas's closeness to Rouart is evident in a letter to his friend of August 8, 1873; Marcel Guérin, ed., *Lettres de Degas* (Paris: Éditions Bernard Grasset, 1945), 31: "Le coeur est comme bien des instruments, il faut le frotter et s'en server beaucoup pour qu'il reluise et aille bien. Le mien, c'est encore vous qui le frottez, plutôt que son propriétaire." (The heart is like many an instrument, it must be rubbed up and used a lot so that it keeps bright and well. For my own it is rather you who rubs it than its owner.) Degas painted Rouart several times and also painted his wife and family.

4. See David Haziot, *Le roman des Rouart (1850–2000)* (Paris: Fayard, 2012), 18–24. See also Jean-Dominique Rey, *Henri Rouart, l'oeuvre peinte*, exh. cat. (Paris: Musée Marmottan Monet; Éditions Hazan, 2012), 131, which identifies the background of Degas's portrait as the boulevard Voltaire factory: "Troisième exposition impressionante. Degas y expose son portrait d'Henri Rouart devant la cheminée de son usine du boulevard Voltaire."

5. Rouart had founded his business, Mignon et Rouart (Ancienne Maison Mignon et Rouart, which later became Rouart frères et Cie), with Java Mignon in 1860. On September 26, 1865, Mignon and Rouart received a patent for their invention of an improved apparatus for freezing liquids, a refinement of the process originally discovered by Ferdinand Carré. The two men developed an aqua-ammonia absorption system; this involved the compression of liquefied ammonia gas in water.

6. *International Health Exhibition, Official Guide* (London: William Clowes and Sons, 1884), 189.

7. In an undated letter, probably from the mid-1870s, Degas wrote to Henri Rouart, "I'm leaving for the boulevard Voltaire to dine with your brother [Alexis Rouart]." (Je pars pour le boulevard Voltaire diner chez votre frère); Guérin, *Lettres de Degas*, 61.

8. An early postcard of this factory indicates that its architecture of low roofs and factory stacks was very close to that in Degas's painting. See *L'usine des Fers Creux et le Pont des Îles*, postcard no. 346560, http://www.habitants.fr/cartes_postales_1900_montlucon_03185.html.

9. Shortly after his arrival, he wrote to Rouart of his dinner with Mathieu-Joseph Bujac, his friend's manager at the factory, and noted, "One day I shall go to the ice factory with him." Degas to Henri Rouart, December 5, 1872, in Guérin, *Lettres de Degas*, 27: "J'irai un jour à la fabrique de glace avec lui [M. Bujac]." Bujac had also written a book on Rouart's invention; Mathieu-Joseph Bujac, *Artificial Refrigeration, Carré's and Mignon and Rouart's Continuous Freezing Process* (Philadelphia, 1870).

10. The rail tracks that ran along Tchoupitoulas Street to the factory in New Orleans may also have informed the strong receding diagonals of the tracks in Degas's painting. Rebecca Demuth, Marilyn Brown, and Paul Hayes Tucker have argued that the painting can be identified as a view of the Louisiana Ice Works (fig. 72). See Rebecca R. Demuth, "Edgar Degas, Henri Rouart: Art and Industry" (MA thesis, University of Pittsburgh, 1982). See also Marilyn R. Brown, *Degas and the Business of Art: A Cotton Office in New Orleans* (University Park: Pennsylvania State University Press, 1994), 122–26; and Paul Hayes Tucker, *Museum of Art, Carnegie Institute Collection Handbook* (Pittsburgh, Pa.: Museum of Art, 1985), 92.

11. See Ruth Berson, *The New Painting: Impressionism, 1874–1886; Documentation*, vol. 2, *Exhibited Works* (San Francisco: Fine Arts Museums of San Francisco, 1996), 73.

12. Guérin, *Lettres de Degas*, 16: "You cannot imagine what this marvelous invention is like." (Vous ne pouvez donc vous rendre compte de cette merveilleuse invention.)

87

CLAUDE MONET
FRENCH, 1840–1926

View of Argenteuil—Snow

1874–75

Oil on canvas

21½ × 25⅝ in. (54.6 × 65.1 cm)

The Nelson-Atkins Museum of Art, Kansas City, Missouri, Gift of the Laura Nelson Kirkwood Residuary Trust, 44-41/3

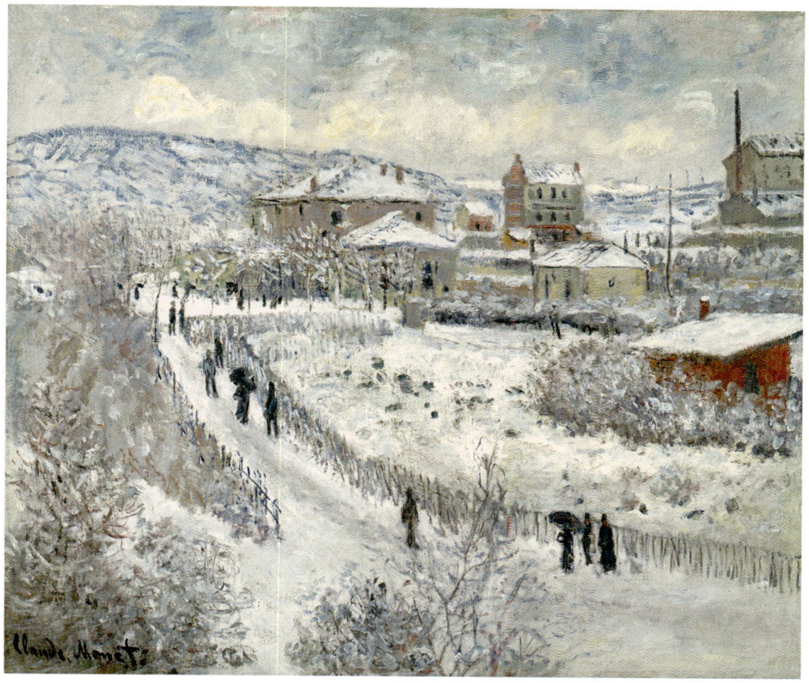

CLAUDE MONET'S IMAGING OF INDUSTRY is focused on the 1870s: the artist produced several views of Argenteuil that testify to the town's industrial expansion. Monet's embrace of the industrial landscape is most evident in his detailed representations of factories at Rouen in 1872, particularly in *The Cargo Convoy* (see fig. 19) and *The Robec Stream* (Musée d'Orsay, Paris), the latter showing a close-up view of the weaving factories for which that city was well known. At Argenteuil, his engagement with industry was more distanced; factories were generally placed in the background or on the margins of his compositions.[1] The town was, however, an important industrial center, particularly known for the Joly ironworks, which employed 350 workers in three factories and was known not only for constructing Argenteuil's bridge but also for providing the iron for the grand pavilions of Paris's market, Les Halles.[2] The town also had several industries such as tanneries and chemical plants. *View of Argenteuil—Snow* was painted from Monet's studio window and depicts the pink railroad station and an unidentified factory and smokestack to the far right. The artist showed the boulevard Saint-Denis leading toward the station, with several figures moving along the road through the rain and snow. A red shack is on the railway embankment, and the rail track is just out of the picture to the right.[3] Monet's view is very sketchily painted, with the gray ground clearly visible. The artist's representations of factories ceased after his move to the more pastoral setting of Vétheuil in 1878. —SK

1. Daniel Wildenstein, *Monet*, vol. 2, *Catalogue raisonné* (Paris: Wildenstein Institute; Cologne: Taschen, 1996), nos. 219, 222–24, 354, 362.

2. James H. Rubin, *Impressionism and the Modern Landscape: Productivity, Technology, and Urbanization from Manet to Van Gogh* (Berkeley: University of California Press, 2008), 142.

3. See the view of the boulevard Saint-Denis from the opposite direction (Museum of Fine Arts, Boston), in which the figures are moving uphill and the red shack is on the left rather than the right.

6

MOUNTAINS

THE TRAVEL WRITER ADOLPHE JOANNE noted in 1869: "The mountain chains [of France] border . . . the territory and separate it from all the surrounding countries, in a manner to give it all around . . . a series of natural frontiers."[1] France's mountains were grouped largely along its eastern and southern boundaries and established its geographic frontier: the Alps created a natural border with Italy, while the Pyrenees separated the nation from Spain. Mountains, therefore, reinforced the country's sense of difference from other European nations.

The Alps are the highest mountains in Europe and were particularly important to French national pride after much of the range was annexed from the Kingdom of Sardinia in 1860. This territory included Mont Blanc, Europe's highest mountain at 15,781 feet. This acquisition was a major foreign policy success for Napoléon III and the Second Empire and played a prominent role in the imperial vision of France as a prosperous and expansionist nation. In the decade that followed, the Alps—and Mont Blanc, in particular—were represented first by the Bisson frères in an album with a clear nationalistic agenda. The painters Théodore Rousseau and François-Louis Français also explored the peaks in panoramic views, as did Eugène-Emmanuel Viollet-le-Duc. The Alps took on literary associations as well. The historian Jules Michelet saw Mont Blanc in anthropomorphic terms as "the great hermit, the dumb giant."[2]

The Pyrenees are also a very tall range—the second highest in Europe—and the tallest peak, Pic de Vignemale, measures 10,820 feet. The region was celebrated in midcentury travel literature such as Hippolyte Taine's *Voyage aux eaux des Pyrénées* (1855). The geographer Elisée Reclus also waxed lyrical over the mountains, focusing especially on the region's Cirque de Gavarni: "No spectacle is more grandiose and more overwhelming . . . than that of these vast and deserted cirques . . . where the only voice is that of avalanches and waterfalls."[3] The Pyrenees were also associated with the battle of Roncevaux Pass in 778, in which the Frankish leader Roland was killed; the battle is the subject of the eleventh-century poem *The Song of Roland*. A small international group of photographers operated in the Pyreneees in the early 1850s, and the region was visited by the aristocratic amateur photographer Joseph Vigier. Brother and sister painters, Auguste-François and Rosa Bonheur, also explored these peaks on several visits. If France's highest mountains were grouped along its borders, the Massif Central region in the center of the country is also a very significant range. The Auvergne region—part of this massif—rises as high as six thousand feet and is particularly known for its distinctive landscape of craters and dormant volcanoes, or *puys*.

In the mid-nineteenth century France's mountains were increasingly investigated from a scientific point of view. Viollet-le-Duc closely examined the Alps, arguing that the essential structure of its mountain forms could be reduced to fundamental geometric shapes, as with enormous buildings. The volcanic history of the Auvergne region attracted the attention of an international range of geologists including the Englishmen Charles Lyell and George Poulett Scrope.[4] Both these writers found an argument in the region's mountains for the earth's regular evolution by natural processes over the course of millennia, in contrast to the claims of the creationists who argued that the world was made as described in the biblical narrative. Painters such as Jean-François Millet explored the geographic particularities of the region. Elsewhere, Gustave Courbet represented the lower mountain ranges of the Franche-Comté, which ran close to the German border in eastern France, also paying close attention to geology.

1. Adolphe Joanne, *Dictionnaire géographique, administratif et postal de la France* (Paris: Hachette, 1869), 1:VI.

2. Jules Michelet, *La montagne* (Paris: Librairie Internationale, 1868), 4.

3. Quoted in Joanne, *Dictionnaire géographique, administratif et postal de la France*, s.v. "Pyrénées," 2:1868.

4. Charles Lyell, *A Manual of Elementary Geology* (New York: D. Appleton & Co., 1853), 178–90; and George Poulett Scrope, *The Geology and Extinct Volcanoes of Central France* (London: John Murray, 1858).

THÉODORE ROUSSEAU

FRENCH, 1812–1867

88

View of Mont Blanc, Seen from La Faucille

1863–67

Oil on canvas

$35\frac{1}{2} \times 46\frac{1}{2}$ in. (90 × 118 cm)

The Minneapolis Institute of Arts, The Putnam Dana McMillan Fund, 2010.62

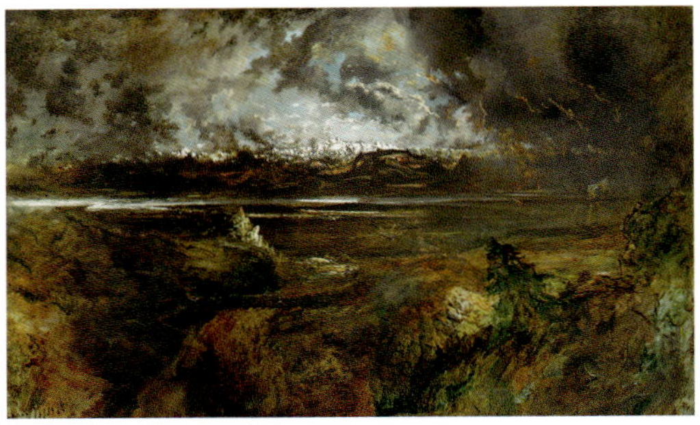

FIG. 73 Théodore Rousseau, *Mont Blanc, Seen from La Faucille, Thunderstorm*, 1834. Oil on canvas, $56\frac{3}{4} \times 94\frac{1}{2}$ in. (143 × 240 cm). Ny Carlsberg Glyptotek, Copenhagen, Denmark

THÉODORE ROUSSEAU is best known for his paintings of the Forest of Fontainebleau, but over the course of his career he also represented all the major mountain ranges of France: the Alps, Pyrenees, Auvergne, and Jura. He visited the Alps for protracted stays in 1834 and 1863 and was presented by his apologist, Théophile Thoré, as an Alpine mountaineer, who "descended the Saint-Bernard pass in winter, feet in the snow, bag on his back, for forty-five miles without stopping."[1] Rousseau produced a broad range of paintings, drawings, and watercolors in an attempt to understand both the geological configuration of the Mont Blanc mountain range as well as its accompanying dramatic weather effects. Early in his career, he painted an enormous storm view of the Mont Blanc massif (fig. 73), which he continued to refine until his death. On his first visit in 1834, he described his pantheistic sensation of finding the divine presence within Alpine peaks.[2] In this late painting, *View of Mont Blanc, Seen from La Faucille*, Rousseau produced a contrasting work with a sense of Olympian calm.[3] The distant mountains are laid out before the spectator, seen from the pass of La Faucille in the Jura, with Lake Geneva in the middle ground. Rousseau's representation of the mountains is highly accurate (each of the peaks can be identified) and reflects his diligent study of the range, of which he produced eight surviving drawings on his 1863 trip.[4] Rousseau also showed the changes to the landscape brought by modernity by including telegraph poles on the mountain pass to the right, indicating that this pass was a major communications route between France and Switzerland.

View of Mont Blanc, Seen from La Faucille was commissioned in 1862 for the very large sum of twenty-four thousand francs by the Alsatian businessman Alfred Hartmann.[5] Rousseau worked on the picture intermittently between 1863 and 1867, meticulously building up his picture surface to create an unusual proto-pointillist effect and revising the lighting structure of the composition, ultimately darkening the foreground in an attempt to underscore the luminosity of the distances. The artist's mountain peaks have an inner light, reminiscent of watercolor, while the sky is rendered in an intense ultramarine blue. In his late correspondence, Rousseau placed his attitude to light in a metaphysical framework, emphasizing his search for a "luminous expression" reflecting a universal truth behind appearances.[6]

Rousseau showed *View of Mont Blanc, Seen from La Faucille* at the 1867 Salon, where its facture attracted considerable criticism; his rounded paint marks were caricatured as "Brussels sprouts."[7] His earlier supporter, Thoré, noted that the painting had a "knitted" effect, as if it were "a tapestry fragment, with uniform stitches."[8] The artist's chiaroscuro was also unfairly criticized as mannered and lacking in naturalism.[9] Nonetheless, Rousseau's supporters recognized the importance of the work in his oeuvre: the artist's biographer, Alfred Sensier, described it as "one of the most beautiful pages of modern art."[10] Théophile Silvestre noted that it was the "artist's first emotion [a reference to Rousseau's early visit to the Alps] and his last painting."[11] The picture was shown at a time when the artist was enjoying considerable recognition. A retrospective of his work could

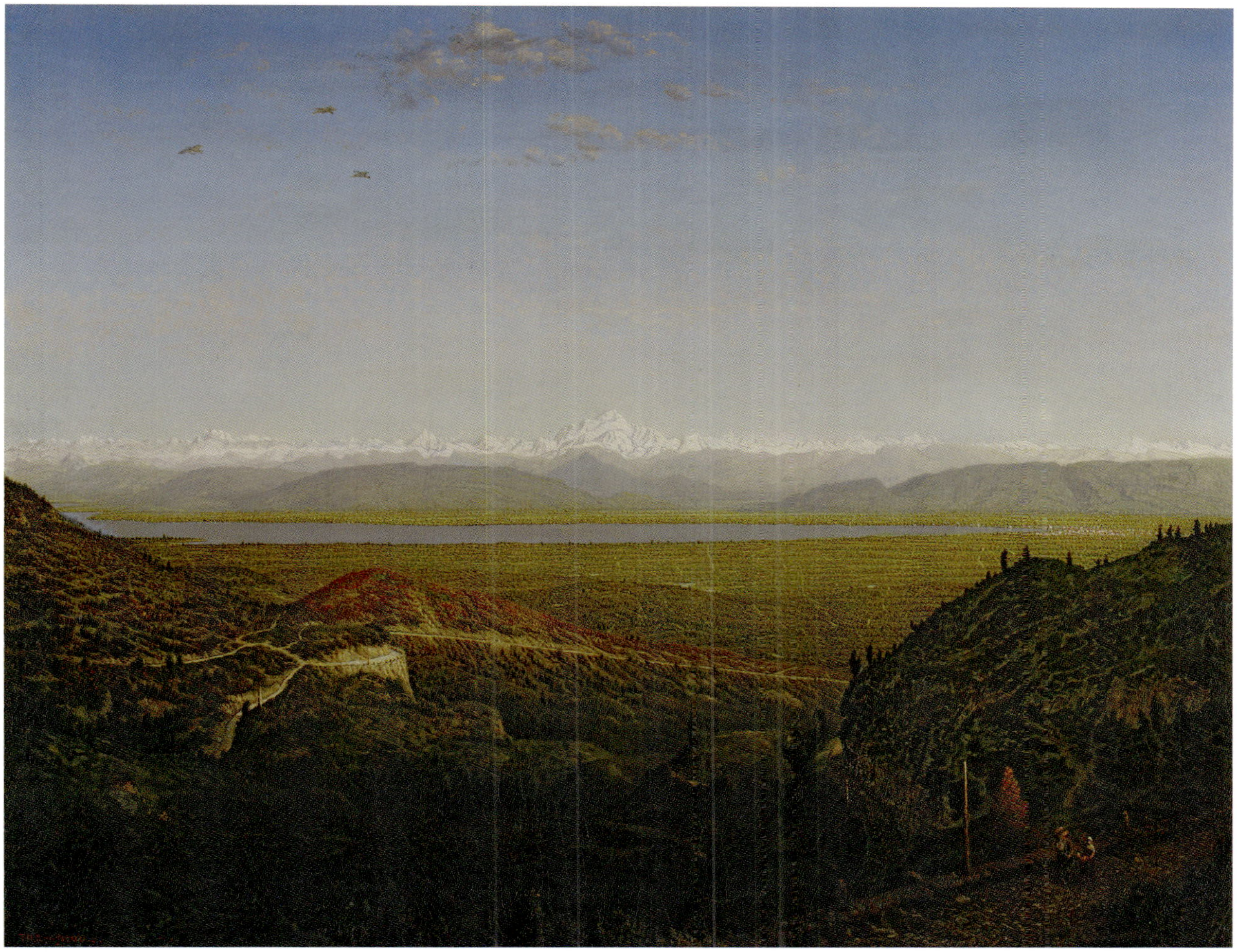

be seen at the 1867 Exposition universelle, where he was the only French landscape painter to receive a first-class medal, and that same year the dealer Paul Durand-Ruel organized an extensive retrospective of 109 sketches and paintings. In August 1867 Rousseau suffered a stroke from which he never recovered. —SK

1. Théophile Thoré, "Par monts et par bois: La forêt de Fontainebleau," *Le constitutionnel*, November 27, 1847: "Rousseau a descendu [*sic*] le Saint Bernard, en hiver, les pieds dans la neige, le sac sur le dos, dix-huit lieues sans s'arrêter."

2. Quoted in Alfred Sensier, *Souvenirs sur Théodore Rousseau* (Paris: Techener, 1872), 66: "I'm adopting a tone of the Supreme Being . . . what proud idea can resist the idea of a demigod . . . who breathes in all the winds." (Je me donne un ton de l'Être supreme . . . quelle idée orgueilleuse peut résister la nature d'un demi-dieu . . . qui respire à tous les vents.)

3. See Simon Kelly, "New Discoveries: View of Mont Blanc, Seen from La Faucille," *Nineteenth-Century Art Worldwide* 8, no. 1 (Spring 2009), http://www.19thc-artworldwide.org/index.php/spring09/64-new-discoveries-theodore-rousseaus-view-of-mont-blanc-seen-from-la-faucille.

4. To the left of Mont Blanc, Rousseau rendered (from right to left) Mont Maudit, Mont Blanc du Tacul, and the Aiguille du Midi. For the artist's drawings, see Michel Schulman, with the collaboration of Marie Bataillès and Virginie Sérafino, *Théodore Rousseau (1812–1867): Catalogue raisonné de l'oeuvre graphique* (Paris: Éditions de l'Amateur–Éditions des Catalogues Raisonnés, 1997), nos. 709–16.

5. Hartmann ultimately rejected the work and sold it to Paul Durand-Ruel and Hector Brame for 14,300 francs in February 1867.

6. Quoted in Sensier, *Souvenirs sur Théodore Rousseau*, 280: "une expression lumineuse."

7. Bertall [Charles-Albert d'Arnoux], "Le Salon depeint par Bertall," *Le journal amusant*, June 1, 1867: "Les Choux de Bruxelles . . . par M. Rousseau."

8. Théophile Thoré, "Exposition universelle de 1867," in W. Bürger, *Salons de W. Bürger, 1861 à 1868* (Paris: Ve Jules Renouard, 1870), 2:355: "C'est tricoté comme un morceau de tapisserie, à point égal."

9. See Maxime du Camp, *Les beaux-arts à l'Exposition universelle et aux Salons de 1863, 1864, 1865, 1866 & 1867* (Paris: Ve Jules Renouard, 1867), 286–87.

10. Sensier, *Souvenirs sur Théodore Rousseau*, 296: "une des plus belles pages de l'art moderne."

11. Théophile Silvestre, "L'oeuvre posthume de Théodore Rousseau," in *Catalogue de la vente qui aura lieu par suite du décès de Théodore Rousseau* (Paris: Hôtel Drouot, April 27–May 2, 1868), 26: "sa premiere emotion et son dernier tableau."

89

FRANÇOIS-LOUIS FRANÇAIS
FRENCH, 1814–1897

Mont Blanc, Seen from Saint-Cergues (Jura)

1869

Oil on canvas

$51^{13}/_{16} \times 64^{13}/_{16}$ in. (131.5 × 164.7 cm)

Musée d'Orsay, on deposit at the Musée des beaux-arts, Chambéry, Gift of the Société des Amis du Musée d'Orsay, RF 1990.12

THE WORK OF THE SUCCESSFUL academic landscape painter François-Louis Français was often caricatured as archetypally French because of the artist's very name. In his early career, Français had worked closely with such avant-garde artists as Théodore Rousseau and Narcisse-Virgile Diaz de la Peña, but during the Second Empire, he increasingly moved in official circles, receiving awards and academic approval, largely because of his meticulous, linear approach. His Salon submissions oscillated between literary, mythological scenes and views of France, with a particular focus in the 1860s and 1870s on the country's mountain ranges, especially the Franche-Comté and the Alps. Français traveled to the Alps in the summers of 1868 and 1877, and this painting dates from his first visit. Français represented a panoramic view from Saint-Cergues in the Jura region, showing the Mont Blanc range in late afternoon, the moon already visible. Lake Geneva can be seen in the middle distance, while the foreground is animated by autumnal foliage, goats, and mountain flowers, rendered in touches of red and yellow. The viewpoint is very similar to Rousseau's earlier *View of Mont Blanc, Seen from La Faucille* (cat. 88) and may have been intended as a response to his friend's work.[1] Français's painting highlights his diligent study of the mountain range and is underpinned by a meticulous drawing, which was probably made *en plein air* in 1868.[2]

Français showed this painting at the 1869 Salon with the title *Le Mont-Blanc, vu de Saint-Cergues (Jura)*, and it attracted praise from conservative critics. Charles Clément, for example, described the picture as "created with an infinite amount of spirit and taste" and praised the artist's foreground, where "we see rocks, bushes, flowers, executed with the delicacy and style of which the artist has given so many examples."[3] Clément contrasted the merits of Français's naturalistic precision with Rousseau's surfaces and light effects, which he disliked and saw as too mannered. Français showed this view of Mont Blanc again in his exhibition of three paintings at the 1878 Exposition universelle. His display there enjoyed considerable success, securing his prominent place in the French school, and he received a gold medal. For Gabriel Monod, Français's Mont Blanc view was "one of the most beautiful pictures of mountains that has ever been painted."[4] For Louis Enault, Francais's submission justified his medal of honor as "the painter always faithful to the purest and highest traditions of art."[5] —SK

1. Français's picture was acquired by the Alsatian patron Alfred Hartmann, who had commissioned Rousseau's mountain painting before ultimately rejecting it. Hartmann, however, retained Français's work until his death.

2. *View of Mont Blanc, Seen from Saint-Cergues*, 1868, pencil on paper (private collection). There is also a related oil study (private collection); see Tajan, Paris, *Tableaux anciens et du XIXe siècle*, March 26, 2008, lot 164.

3. Charles Clément, "Exposition de 1869," *Le journal des débats*, June 16, 1869: "tourné avec infiniment d'esprit et de goût . . . on voit se détacher des roches, des buissons, des fleurs exécutés avec la delicatesse et le goût dont l'artiste nous a donné tant d'exemples."

4. Gabriel Monod, *Les beaux-arts à l'Exposition universelle* (Paris: Fischbacher, 1878), 34: "un des plus beaux tableaux de montagnes qui aient jamais été peints."

5. Louis Enault, *Les beaux-arts à l'Exposition universelle de 1878* (Paris: Gros, 1878), 54: "le peintre toujours fidèle aux plus purs comme aux plus hautes traditions de l'art."

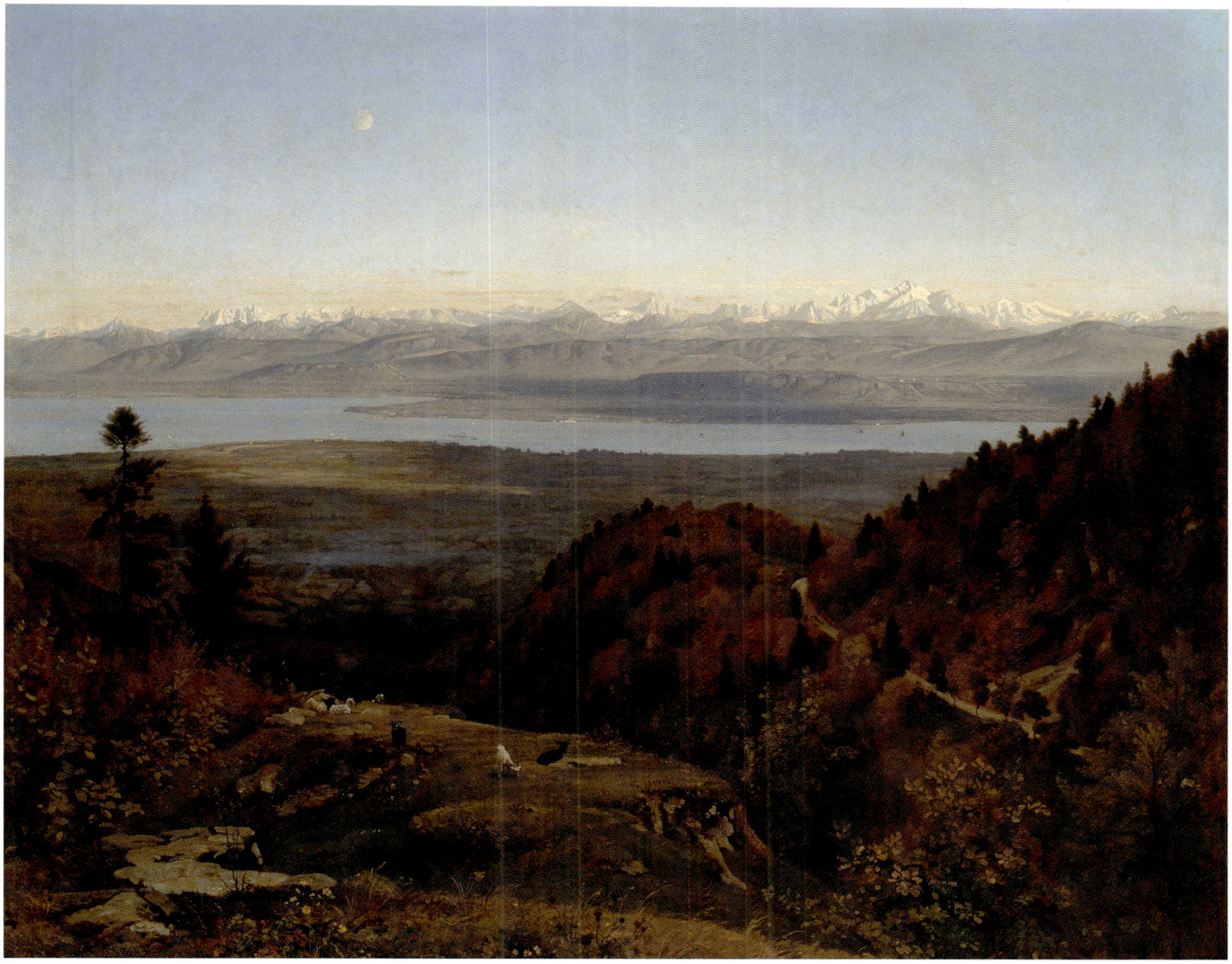

90

EUGÈNE-EMMANUEL VIOLLET-LE-DUC

FRENCH, 1814–1879

Mont Blanc Seen from the Massif, Les Aiguilles Rouges

1874

Watercolor heightened with gouache over traces of graphite on two sheets of blue-gray wove paper

11 7/16 × 26 1/8 in. (29 × 66.4 cm)

The Metropolitan Museum of Art, New York, Purchase, Isaacson-Draper Foundation Gift, 2005, 2005.78

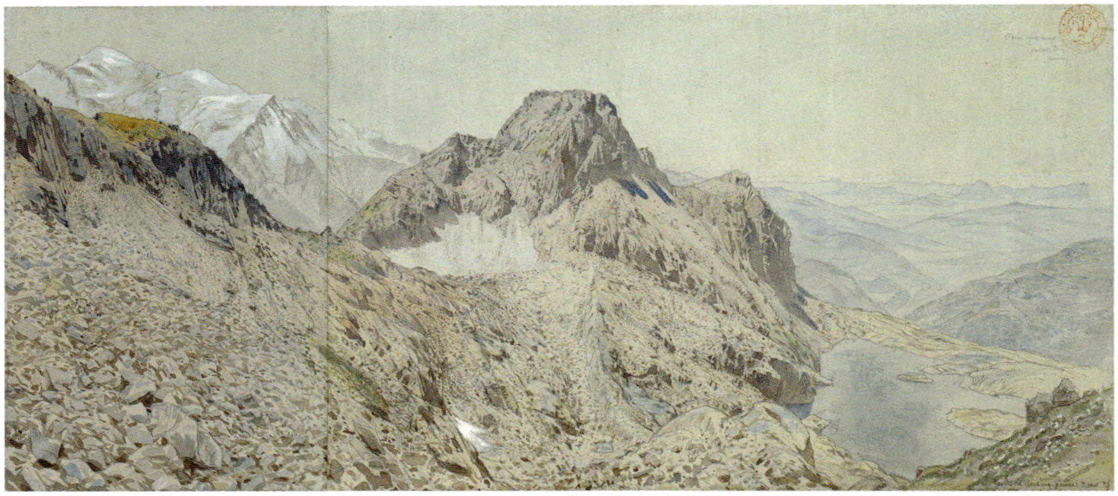

EUGÈNE-EMMANUEL VIOLLET-LE-DUC is best known as an architect at the forefront of the restoration of France's medieval monuments in the mid-nineteenth century. In his later career, however, he studied mountains and particularly the Alps, returning there every year from 1868 until 1875 for prolonged periods of summer sketching and study.[1] In the mountains, he found satisfaction and affirmed, "More than ever I find myself content and in control of my ideas in these solitudes."[2]

Mont Blanc Seen from the Massif, Les Aiguilles Rouges is a detailed panoramic view, showing the snowcapped peak of Mont Blanc to the left. The work is inscribed "lac au col de l'aigue pourrie, août 7, 1874" (lake at the pass of the Aigue pourrie, August 7, 1874), referencing the expanse of water at bottom right, which can be identified as Lake Cornu. The viewpoint is from the Aiguilles Rouges, a great range of peaks running parallel to the Mont Blanc massif. The specificity of the date indicates that this work was painted directly outdoors on two separate sheets of paper, which were subsequently attached to each other.

Viollet-le-Duc's watercolor is a private study undertaken as part of his long-term project to produce a detailed geological study of the Mont Blanc mountain range. His efforts resulted in the publication of the important scientific work *Le massif du Mont-Blanc, étude sur sa construction géodésique et géologique, sur ses transformations et sur l'état ancien et moderne de ses glaciers* (Paris, 1876). The text of this book highlighted his profound understanding of the geology of the area and was illustrated with 112 views and diagrams as well as a detailed map. An overview of these illustrations reveals that Viollet-le-Duc's background in architecture encouraged him to think about the underlying geometric structure of the mountains in the region. Viollet-le-Duc was also a founding member of the Club alpin français in 1874. His nationalistic interest in both architecture and mountain scenery might be compared with that of his English counterpart, John Ruskin.[3] —SK

1. For a detailed chronology of these trips, see Pierre A. Frey, "Eugène Viollet-le-Duc, itinéraires d'un architecte-géologue," in Pierre A. Frey and Lise Grenier, *Viollet-le-Duc et la montagne* (Grenoble: Éditions Glénat, 1993), 54–70.

2. Viollet-le-Duc to his wife, Chamonix, July 21, 1871, quoted in Cynthia Gamble, "John Ruskin, Eugène Viollet-le-Duc and the Alps," *Alpine Journal* 104 (1999): 195: "Plus que jamais je me trouve heureux et possesseur de mes idées dans ces solitudes."

3. Gamble, "John Ruskin, Eugène Viollet-le-Duc and the Alps," 185–96.

91

ADOLPHE BRAUN
FRENCH, 1812–1877

Mont Chamounix: Mont Blanc Chain

ca. 1865

Stereograph; albumen prints from collodion glass negatives

Each image, 3 × 2 ¹³⁄₁₆ in. (7.5 × 7.2 cm) on 3⅜ × 6¹⁵⁄₁₆ in. (8.6 × 17.4 cm) mount

George Eastman House, Rochester, New York, Purchased from Mrs. Richmond W. Strong; ex-collection of Richmond W. Strong, 1981:6557:0001

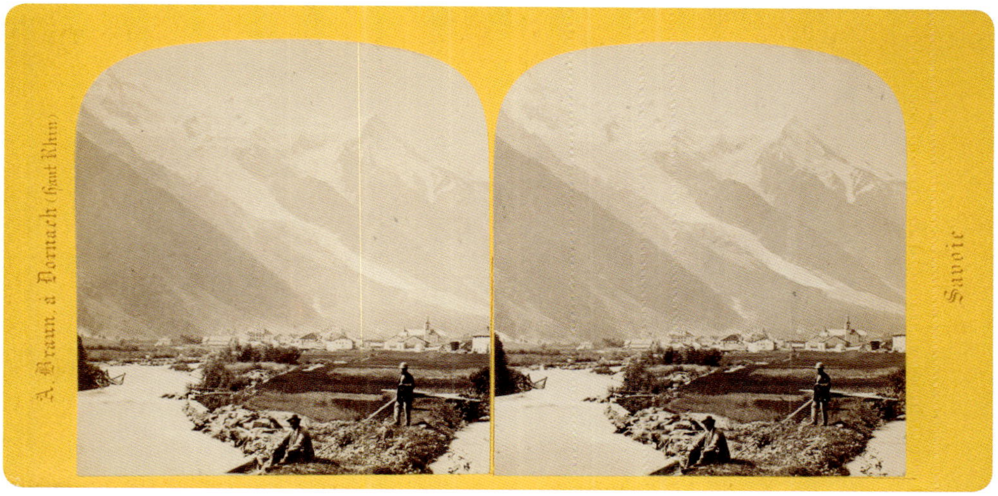

STEREOGRAPHS (also known as stereoscopic or simply stereo views) were invented and perfected during the 1850s, after the invention of the wet-collodion-on-glass method and their popular introduction at the 1851 Great Exhibition at the Crystal Palace, in London. Stereographs were sold as rectangular cards on which two nearly identical photographs of a subject were mounted such that when seen through a stereo viewer, they merged into a three-dimensional image. As popular interest in Alpine imagery grew during the 1850s and 1860s, demand for these views increased. The leisured classes bought stereo views both to experience these landscapes vicariously and to collect them at an affordable cost.

The commercial photographer Adolphe Braun capitalized on this growing market. After producing *L'album de l'Alsace* (1859)—a compilation of large-scale landscape views and imagery of his native region, financially backed by the emperor himself—Braun concentrated on landscape stereoscopy. His primary intention was to produce stereo collections of geographic regions, focusing at first on popular tourist destinations in Switzerland and Germany. After France's annexation of Savoy in 1860, he made several stereo views of the Mont Blanc massif and Chamonix valley, often composing his scenes to amplify a three-dimensional effect. In this stereo view, for example, he included figures in the foreground and printed them with greater contrast than the more diffusely rendered mountain backdrop. These compositional devices and atmospheric effects draw the viewer into the scene. Typically, Braun priced his stereo views at fourteen francs per dozen, or the equivalent of a factory worker's weekly wages. He sold his views through the most respected distributors in Paris, including Alexis Gaudin, the publisher of *La lumière*, and Goupil & Co., the city's top dealers in fine art reproductions, to ensure as broad a market as possible.[1] —AMW

1. Deborah Bright, "Souvenirs of Progress," in *Image and Enterprise: The Photographs of Adolphe Braun*, ed. Maureen C. O'Brien and Mary Bergstein, exh. cat. (New York: Thames & Hudson in association with Museum of Art, Rhode Island School of Design, Providence, 2000), 98.

92

AUGUSTE-ROSALIE BISSON

FRENCH, 1826–1900

The Ascent of Mont Blanc

1861

Albumen print from collodion glass negative

15⁹⁄₁₆ × 9⁵⁄₁₆ in. (39.6 × 23.7 cm)

The Metropolitan Museum of Art, New York, Gilman Collection, Purchase, Alfred Stieglitz Society Gifts, 2005, 2005.100.54

AFTER THE FIRST SUCCESSFUL summiting of Mont Blanc by the Frenchmen Michel-Gabriel Paccard and Jacques Balmat in 1786, the Alps became a destination for climbers eager to test their mettle against the forces of nature. Scientists in the nascent fields of geology, geodesy (the science of determining the earth's size, shape, and gravitational field by locating fixed points on its surface), geography, botany, and glaciology also took an increased interest in the region. Maps and written travel accounts began to appear, and the sense of fear and danger that had long been associated with the Alps began to dissipate, supplanted by fascination, awe, and wonder. Romantic writers in the late eighteenth and early nineteenth centuries further fueled such sentiments. Jean-Jacques Rousseau's novel *La nouvelle Héloïse*, 1761, the travel accounts of François-René de Chateaubriand (*Voyage au Mont Blanc, et réflexion sur les paysages de montagne*, 1805), the poetry of Percy Bysshe Shelly (*Mont Blanc*, 1817), and Victor Hugo's *Voyages aux Alpes*, 1829, among others, prominently feature the region. Tourism began to increase, particularly after the establishment of nearby rail lines in the 1850s. A nationalistic fascination with Mont Blanc in particular greatly intensified after June 1860, when the Savoy region was ceded to France by the Kingdom of Sardinia (part of modern-day Italy). Maps of the Mont Blanc massif were soon redrawn to indicate border changes that definitively included the Mont Blanc summit as French territory: one of the first to appear was produced by an army cartographer, Captain Jean-Joseph Mieulet, in 1865 (fig. 74).

Thus, by the time Auguste-Rosalie Bisson made his first photographic study in the Alps in June 1854, the fervor for all things Alpine was well established in the French imagination. Before Auguste-Rosalie (and possibly his older brother Louis-Auguste) joined the imperial entourage on its voyage to the Savoy in September 1860, he had already made at least three photographic trips to the region, in 1855, 1858, and 1859. By this date, the Bissons had succeeded in producing large-scale panoramic views with great success. This was no easy task, given the technical challenges of carrying up the mountain the camera, equipment, glass plates, the apparatus for the darkroom tent, and all the associated chemicals. The writer, editor, and critic Ernest Lacan gave a brief summation of this achievement in one review of April 1859, noting that while tourists could easily climb to sites carrying little more than a telescope, a raincoat, and a sketchbook, the photographer's requirements were far more cumbersome. "When it is necessary to transport all the camera apparatus and delicate bottles that the slightest shock can break, the chemical products quick to taint, with a tent for operations, it is indispensable to appoint numerous staff, and the difficulties are colossal if not insurmountable."[1] Auguste-Rosalie's successful summiting of Mont Blanc in July 1861 was thus both a physical and a technical feat. Animated written accounts in the extensive press coverage of his ascent detailed the photographer's heroic travails in battling high winds and heavy snowfall. Subzero temperatures caused water to freeze and chemicals to crystallize as he attempted to coat and develop his glass negatives on-site. When Auguste-Rosalie arrived in Chamonix after his successful ascent, he was greeted with fireworks and fanfare. "Everyone is joyous," noted one report, "and M. Bisson himself more than anyone."[2] Auguste-Rosalie made another trip to the Alps in 1862 and again reached the summit.

After the 1860 imperial trek to the Savoy, the Bissons produced seven nearly identical souvenir albums of

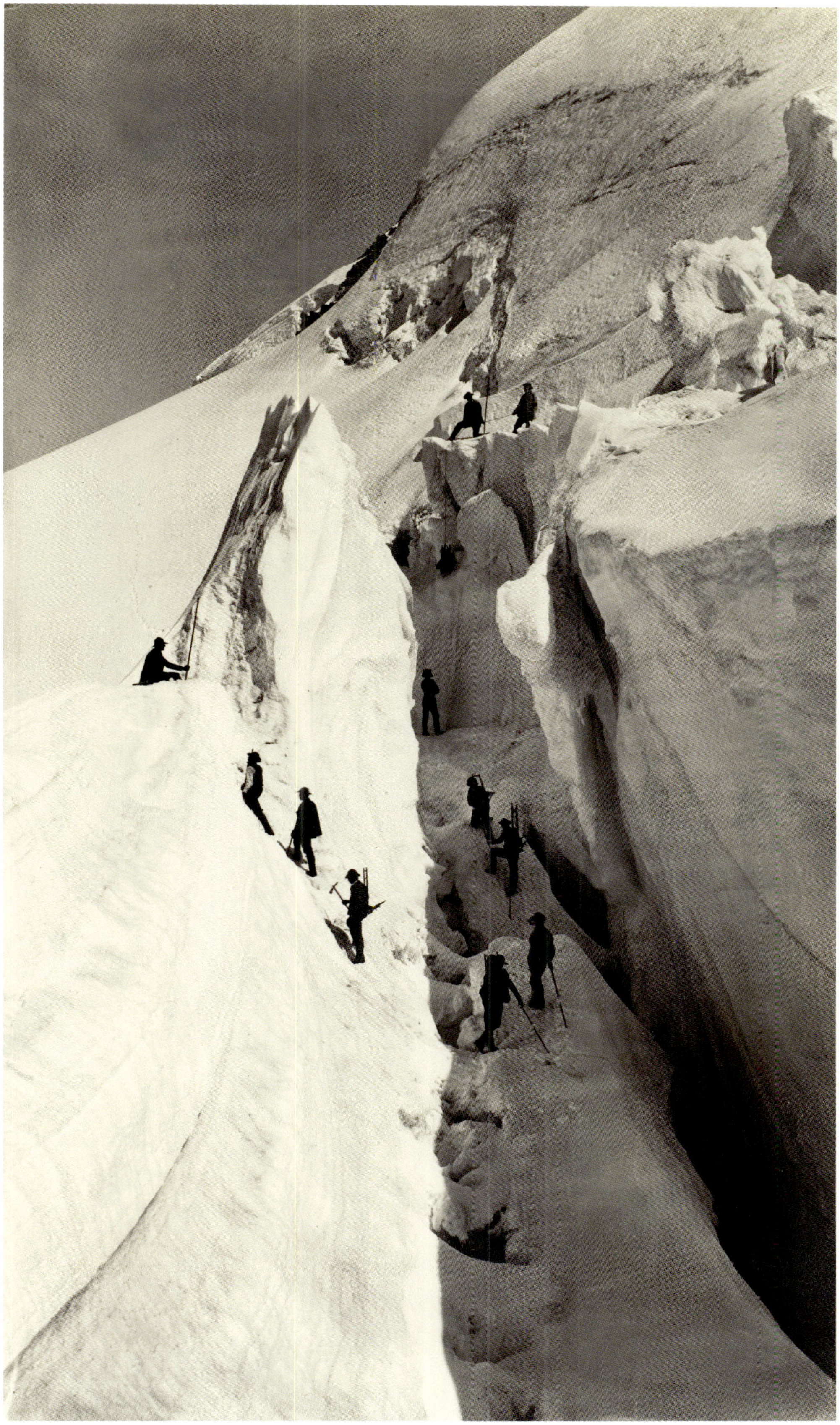

twenty-four albumen prints titled *Haute-Savoie, le Mont Blanc et ses glaciers: Souvenir du voyage de LL. MM. l'Empereur et l'Impératrice*. In addition to Napoléon III, owners of the album included Victor Emmanuel II (king of Sardinia until March 17, 1861, when he assumed the title king of Italy) and the architect Eugène-Emmanuel Viollet-le-Duc, who was also an avid Alpinist (see cat. 90). The two albums currently housed in the collections of the George Eastman House and the Bibiothèque nationale de France contain the same photographs, arranged in such a way that the viewer is meant to experience a sort of virtual ascent (though the sequencing is not completely faithful to what one might directly encounter during the actual experience). The first five photographs depict distant views of the mountain range, as seen from the Chamonix valley, including such well-known features as the Glacier des Bossons and the Glacier des Bois, as well as Mont Blanc itself (pls. 1–5). Included in the next sequence of photographs are notable geological formations along the ascent: the jagged needlelike peaks of the Aiguilles du Midi, de Greppond, de Blaitières, de Plan, d'Argentière, and the Aiguille Verte (pls. 8–10), and stunning views of the Mer de Glace (pls. 11, 15), the longest glacier in France. One of these views depicts the French flag, planted in the glacier's ice (pl. 15). Two-thirds of the way through the album appears the one plate to include human figures, who are shown as small, seemingly insignificant presences making their way through the icy terrain. From there, the photographs include an image depicting the meeting of the Bossons and Taconnay glaciers (pl. 17) and two views looking back down at Chamonix from a scenic vista known as the Chapeau (pls. 18, 19). The final five photographs include another view of Mont Blanc, as seen from a point known as "the garden" (pl. 21), areas around the peak known as Géant (pls. 22, 23), and the final view of the Chamonix valley, as seen on the Montanvers route's descent (pl. 24). Several of these same photographs were mentioned by Lacan in his review of April 2, 1859, in *La lumière*, suggesting that these albums were compiled from prints taken on different trips, not exclusively on the 1860 venture. —AMW

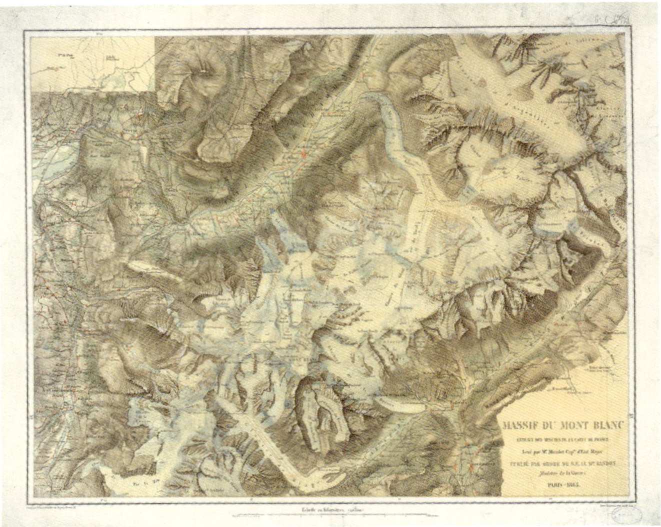

FIG. 74 Jean-Joseph Mieulet. *Massif du Mont Blanc extrait des minutes de la carte de France [Document cartographique] levé par M. Mieulet, capitaine d'État major*, 1865. Bibliothèque nationale de France, Paris

1. Ernest Lacan, "Revue photographique," *La lumière*, April 2, 1859, 55: "Mais quand il faut transporter avec soi toute une cargaison d'appareils délicats de flacons, de bassines que le moindre choc peut briser, de produits chimiques prompts à s'altérer, avec une tente pour les opérations, il est indispensable de s'adjoindre un personnel nombreux, et les difficultés prennent alors des proportions colossales quand elles ne deviennent pas tout à fait insurmontables."

2. "Ascension du Mont-Blanc par un photographe," *Revue photographique* 6 (1861): 252: "Le soir Chamonix est illuminé de feux de Bengale, un feu d'artifice est tiré, tout le monde est joyeux, et M. Bisson à lui seul autant que tout le monde!"

AUGUSTE-ROSALIE BISSON
(FRENCH, 1826–1900)

LOUIS-AUGUSTE BISSON
(FRENCH, 1814–1876)

93

Mont Blanc and Its Glaciers

1860

Album containing 24 albumen prints from collodion glass negatives

17⁵⁄16 × 25 × 1 in. (44 × 63.5 × 2.5 cm)

George Eastman House, Rochester, New York, Gift of Eastman Kodak Company; ex-collection of Gabriel Cromer, 81:1014:00001–0024

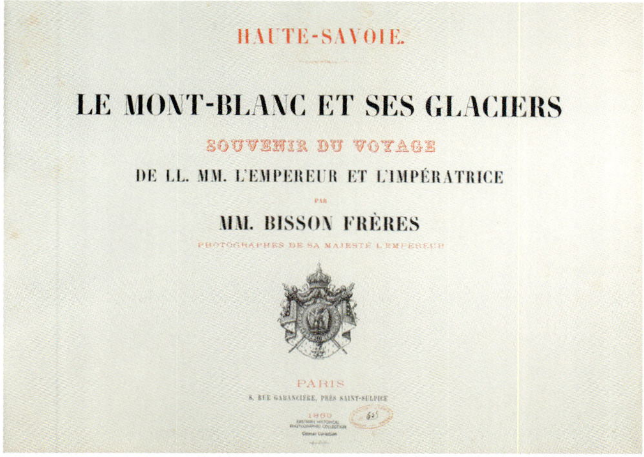

HAUTE-SAVOIE.

LE MONT-BLANC ET SES GLACIERS

SOUVENIR DU VOYAGE

DE LL. MM. L'EMPEREUR ET L'IMPÉRATRICE

PAR

MM. BISSON FRÈRES

PHOTOGRAPHES DE SA MAJESTÉ L'EMPEREUR

PARIS

8, RUE GARANCIÈRE, PRÈS SAINT-SULPICE

1860

TITLE PAGE

1 *Les Montées, près Servoz*
2 *Entrée de la vallée de Chamonix, aux Ouches*
3 *Glacier des Bossons*
4 *Glacier des Bois*
5 *Mont-Blanc, vu de Chamonix*
6 *Bourrasque au Mont-Blanc, vue de Planpraz*
7 *Mont-Blanc, vu de Planpraz*
8 *Aiguille du Midi*
9 *Aiguilles du Greppond, de Blaitières et de Plan*
10 *Aiguille d'Argentière et Aiguille Verte*
11 *Mer de Glace, vue de la Flégère*
12 *Source de l'Arveiron*
13 *Aiguille du Dru et Aiguille Verte*
14 *Les Grandes Jorasses et le Tacul, vus du Montanvers*
15 *Pyramide de l'Impératrice (Mer de Glace)*
16 *Ascension au Mont-Blanc par MM. Bissons frères*
17 *Séracs, Rencontre des Bossons et du Taconnay*
18 *Vallée de Chamonix, vue du Chapeau*
19 *Aiguille des Charmoz, vue du Chapeau*
20 *Séracs du Géant (chaine du Mont-Blanc)*
21 *Mont-Blanc, vu du Jardin*
22 *Col de Géant*
23 *Le Jardin, vu du Glacier du Géant*
24 *Vallée de Chamonix (Descente du Montanvers)*

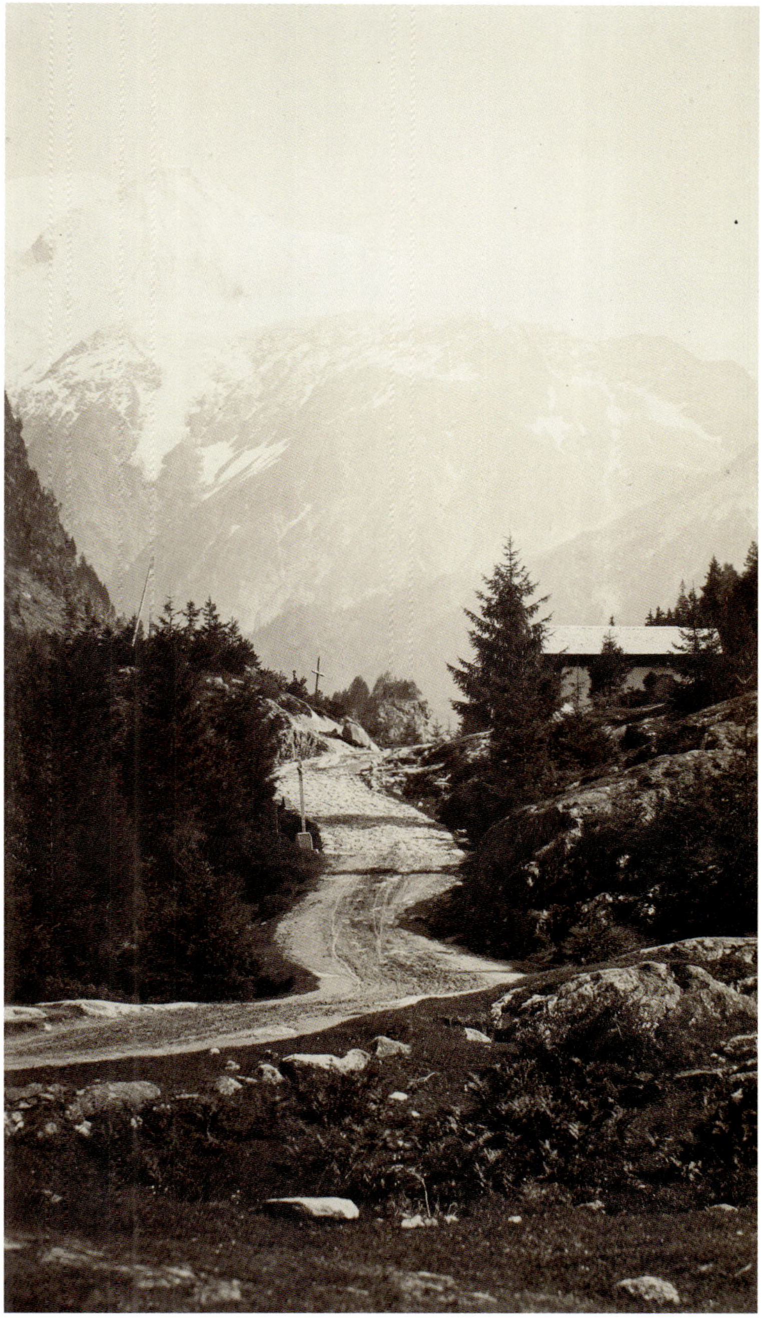

1

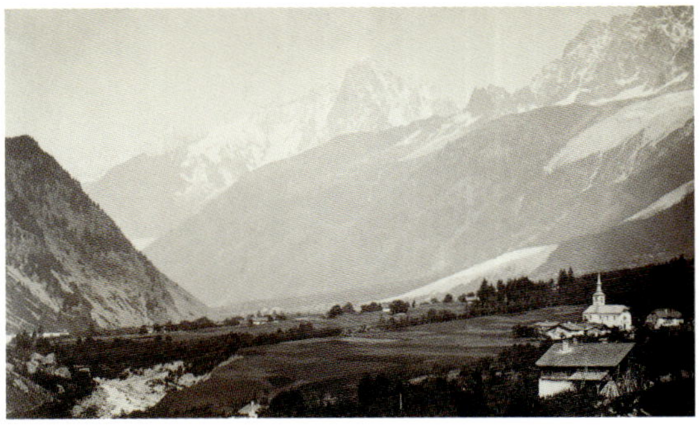
2

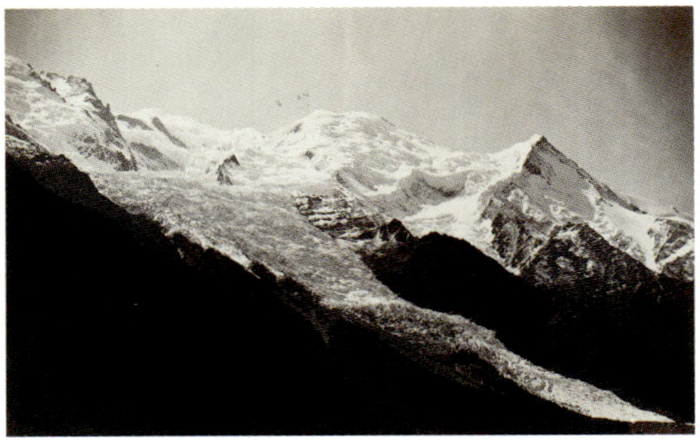
3

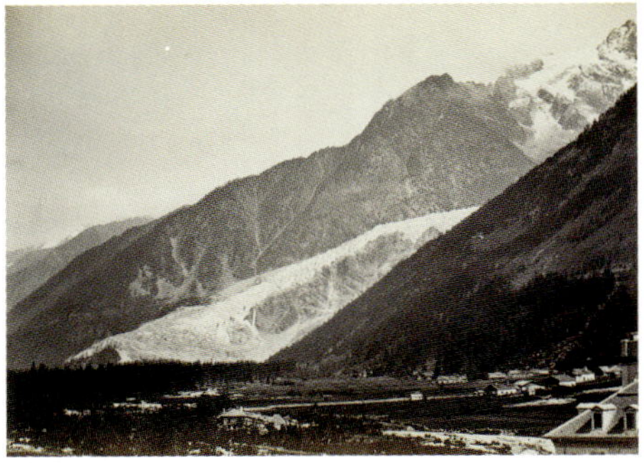
4

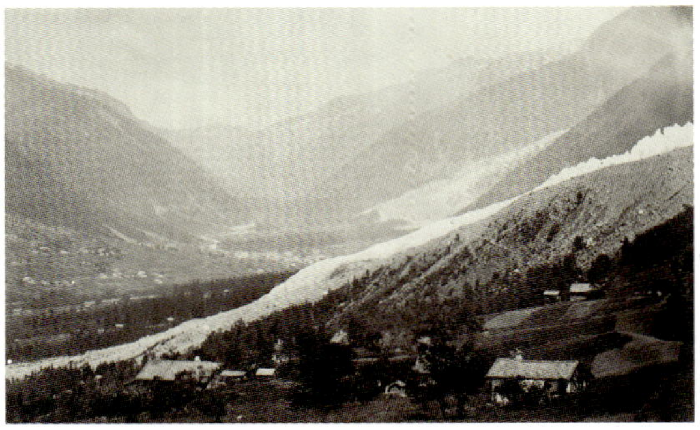
5

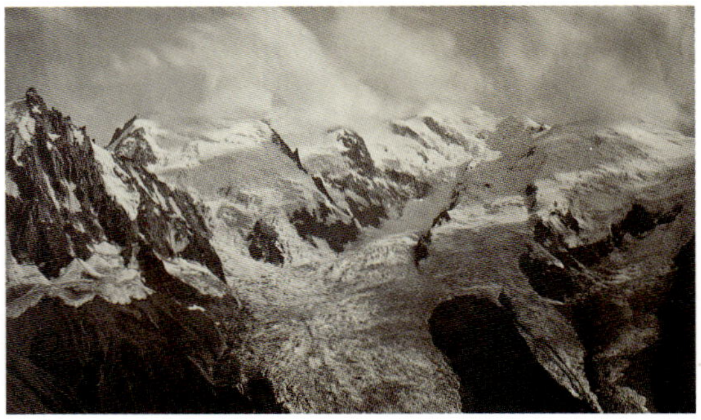
6

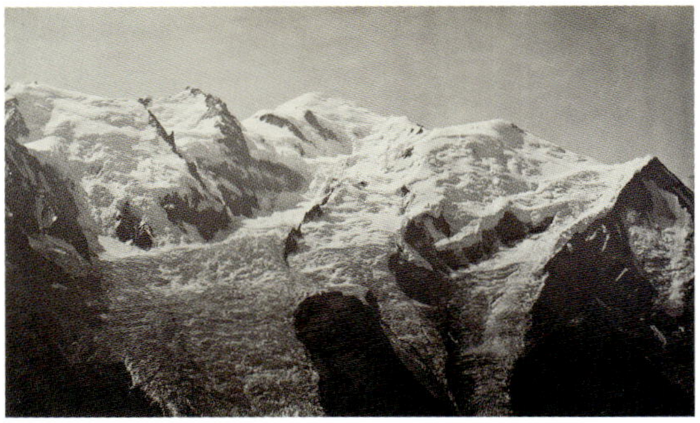
7

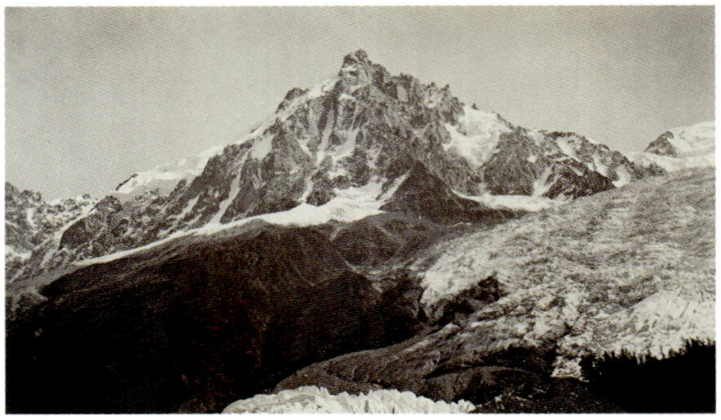
8

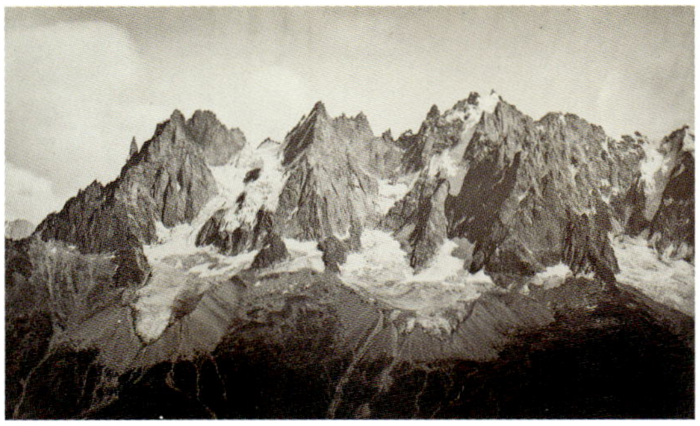
9

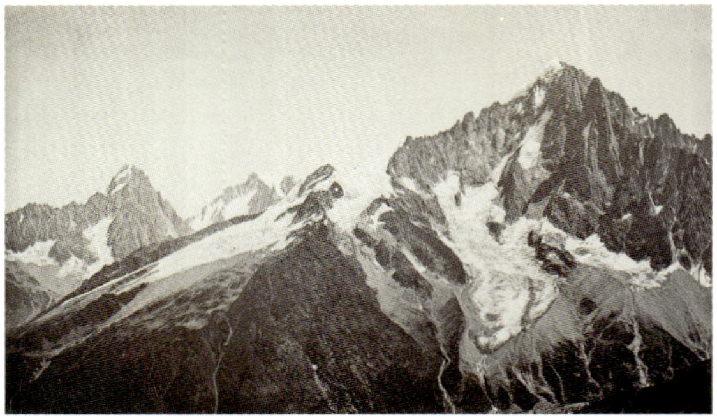
10

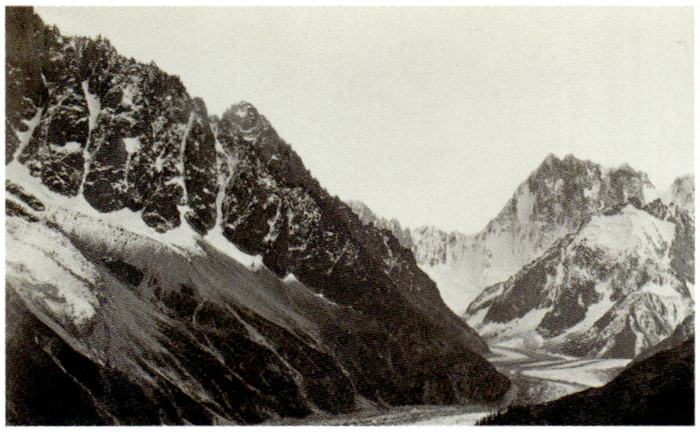
11

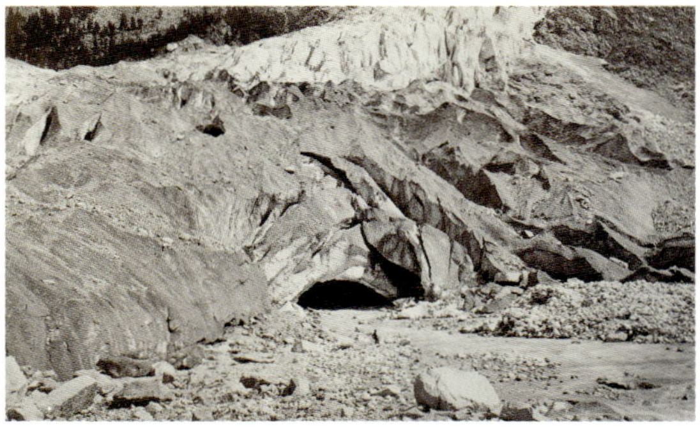
12

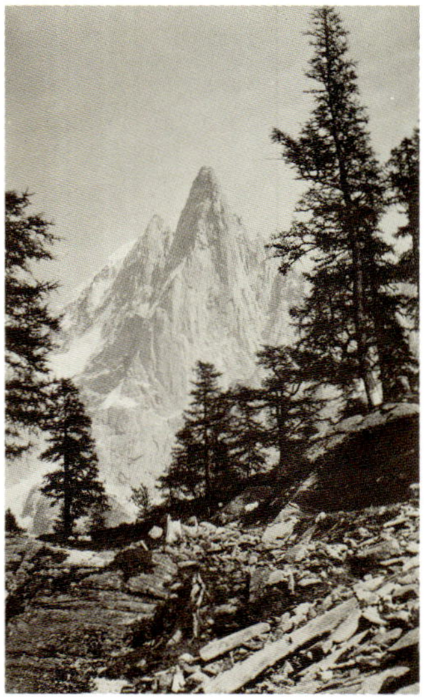
13

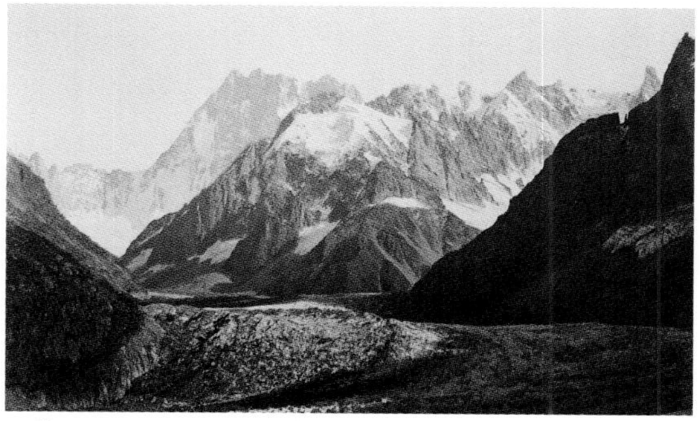
14

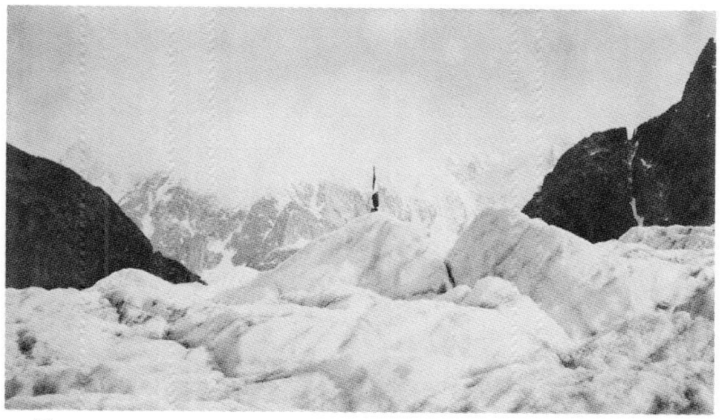
15

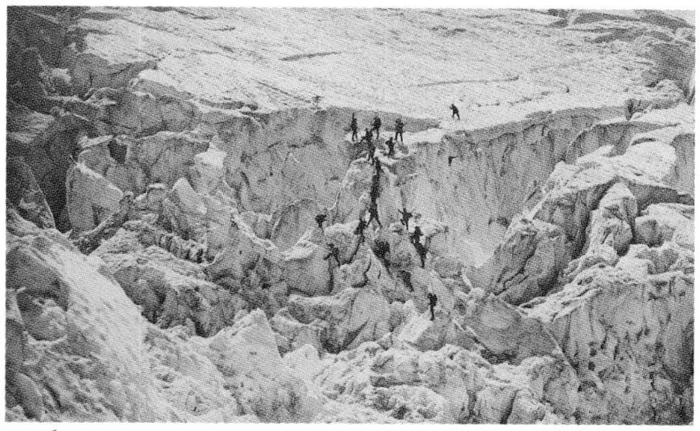
16

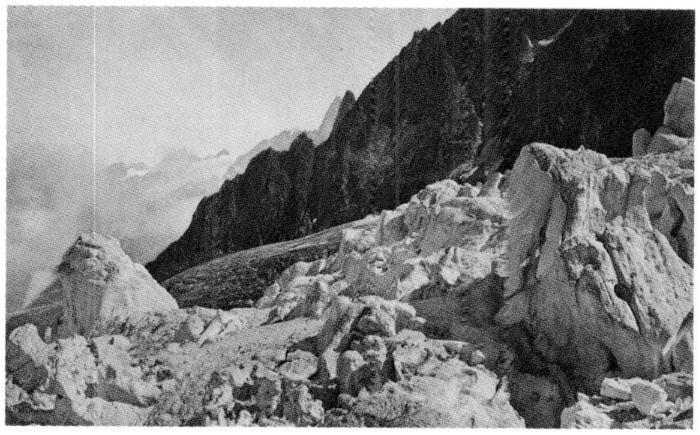
17

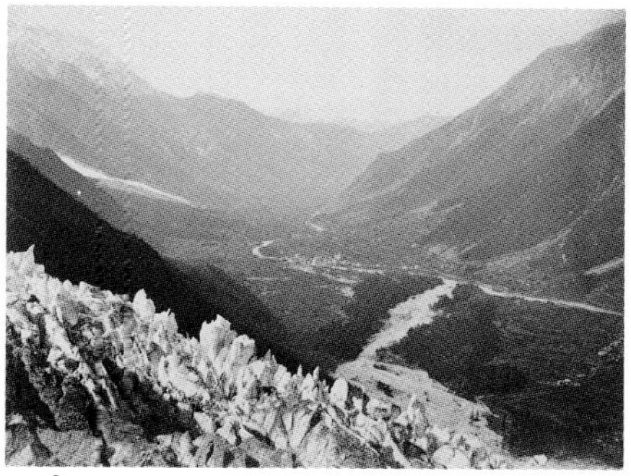
18

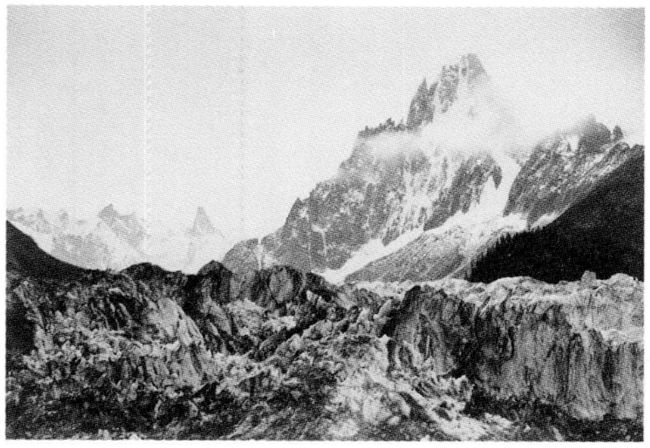
19

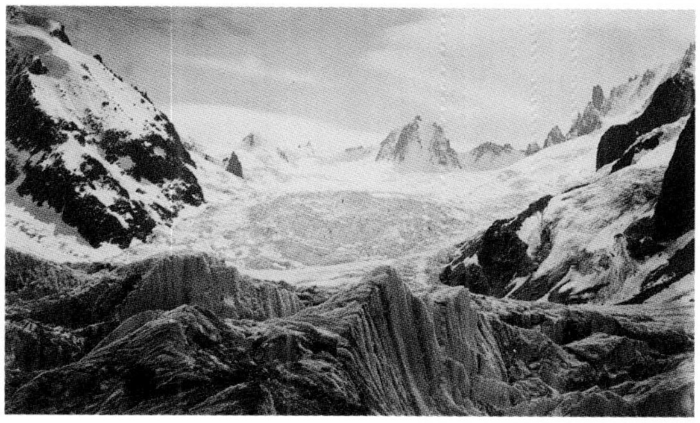
20

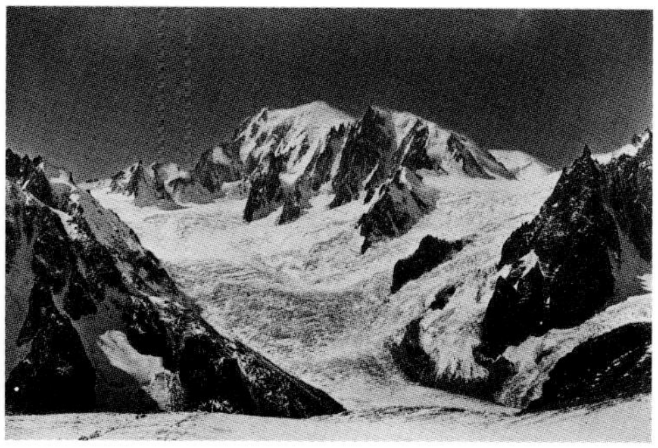
21

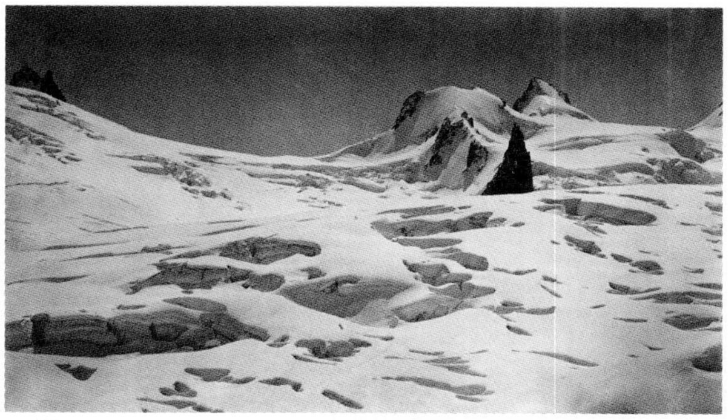
22

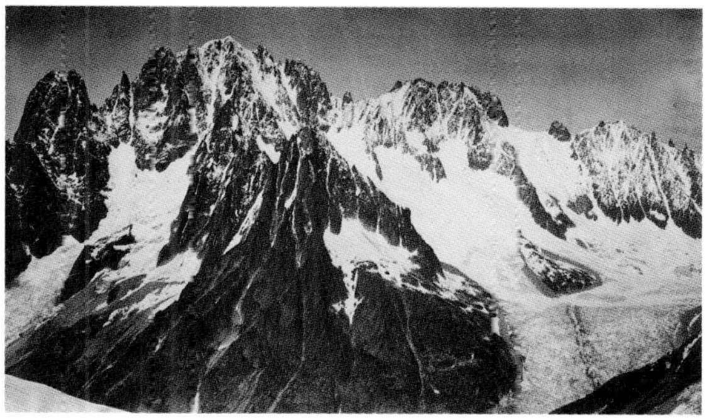
23

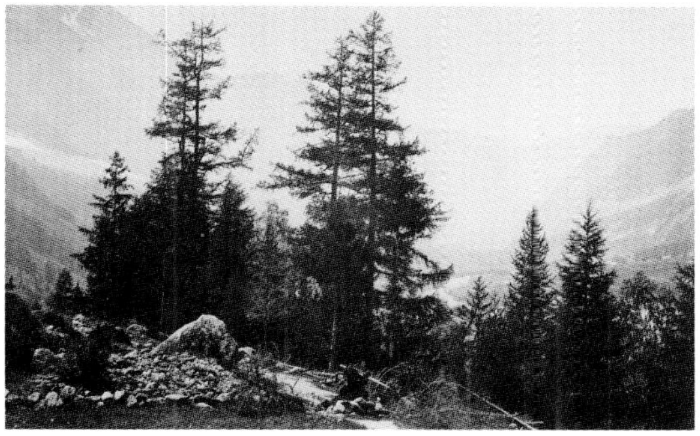
24

AIMÉ CIVIALE
FRENCH, 1821–1893

Ventilators Constructed to Aid the Tunneling of the Alps (Côté de Modane)

ca. 1858

Salt print from paper negative

10⅝ × 14⅛ in. (27 × 35.9 cm)

The Nelson-Atkins Museum of Art, Kansas City, Missouri, Gift of the Hall Family Foundation, 2010.18.9

AIMÉ CIVIALE'S PHOTOGRAPHS of the Pyrenees and the Alps were produced and discussed as aids for the study of geography, geology, and geodesy. Civiale, the son of a member of the Académie des sciences and a graduate of the École polytechnique, took great interest in these subjects and was a strong advocate of photography's scientific, fact-gathering potential. In an 1860 report to the Académie des sciences, Civiale spoke of these applications for photography, noting that although mountain landscapes offered photographers picturesque and artistic subject matter, they might also be seen as informational resources for geology and geography. Civiale's working methods were meticulous and systematic, as suggested in his directions for picture making in the mountains: "to form views on a single sheet of paper, it suffices to indicate the direction of the optical axis of the instrument that the camera makes to the horizon, if the slope of the terrain and the proximity of the view do not permit the maintenance of a horizontal position."[1] Civiale was devoted to the dry waxed paper process, which was more portable and less fragile than the chemicals and glass negatives required for the wet-collodion process preferred by such contemporaries as the Bisson frères.[2] Civiale, in fact, was making accomplished mountain views, in both the Pyrenees and the Alps, at about the same time as the Bissons: he traveled through the Pyrenees in the summers of 1857 and 1858 and throughout the Alps from 1859 to 1868. He exhibited his views regularly in exhibitions of the Société française de la photographie in 1859, 1861, 1863, 1865, and 1869, as well as at the Exposition universelle of 1867 in Paris.

Civiale's ultimate goal was to produce a comprehensive photographic and scientific survey of the great mountain ranges of France, Switzerland, and Austria. In his publication *Les Alpes au point de vue de la géographie physique et de la géologie: Voyages photographiques dans le Dauphiné, la Savoie, le Nord d'Italie, la Suisse et le Tyrol* (1882), Civiale gave some indication of his working methods and accomplishments to date, with a systematic recording of the location and direction of view for each of his photographs, as well as texts describing elevations and distances between topographic formations. This particular view, which depicts large ventilators constructed in the course of drilling a tunnel through the Alps, was listed by Civiale as one of approximately eleven photographs taken in this area in the Modane region of Savoy, known for its sandstone mixtures of quartz and quartzites.[3] —AMW

1. M. A. Civiale, "Note sur l'application de la photographie à la géographie physique et à la géologie," *La lumière*, May 12, 1860, 74: "Pour les vues formées d'une seule feuille, il suffit d'indiquer la direction de l'axe optique de l'instrument et l'angle vertical que la chambre noire fait avec l'horison, si la pente du terrain et la proximité la vue à prendre ne permettent pas de la maintenir dans une position horizontale."

2. Civiale discusses his preference for the waxed paper process over collodion on glass in his book *Les Alpes au point de vue de la géographie physique et de la géologie: Voyages photographiques dans le Dauphiné, la Savoie, le Nord d'Italie, la Suisse et le Tyrol* (Paris: J. Rothschild, 1882), 3: "The process on glass gives without doubt more finesse; but the process on paper gives a sufficient sharpness for the reproduction of landscapes and even for faraway horizons; I have photographed mountain chains at a distance surpassing 100 kilometers. The finesse given by glass [negatives] is not a big enough advantage to compensate for its fragility. . . . Another grave inconvenience is the weight and addition of considerable baggage." (Le procédé sur glace donne sans doute plus de finesse; mais le procéde sur papier donne une netteté suffisante pour les reproductions de paysages et même pour les horizons les plus lointains; j'ai photographié des chaînes de montagnes à une distance dépassant 100 kilomètres. La finesse donnée par la glace n'est pas un avantage assez grand pour compenser sa fragilité. . . . Un autre inconvénient très grave est le poids et l'augmentation considérables des bagages.)

3. Ibid., 134.

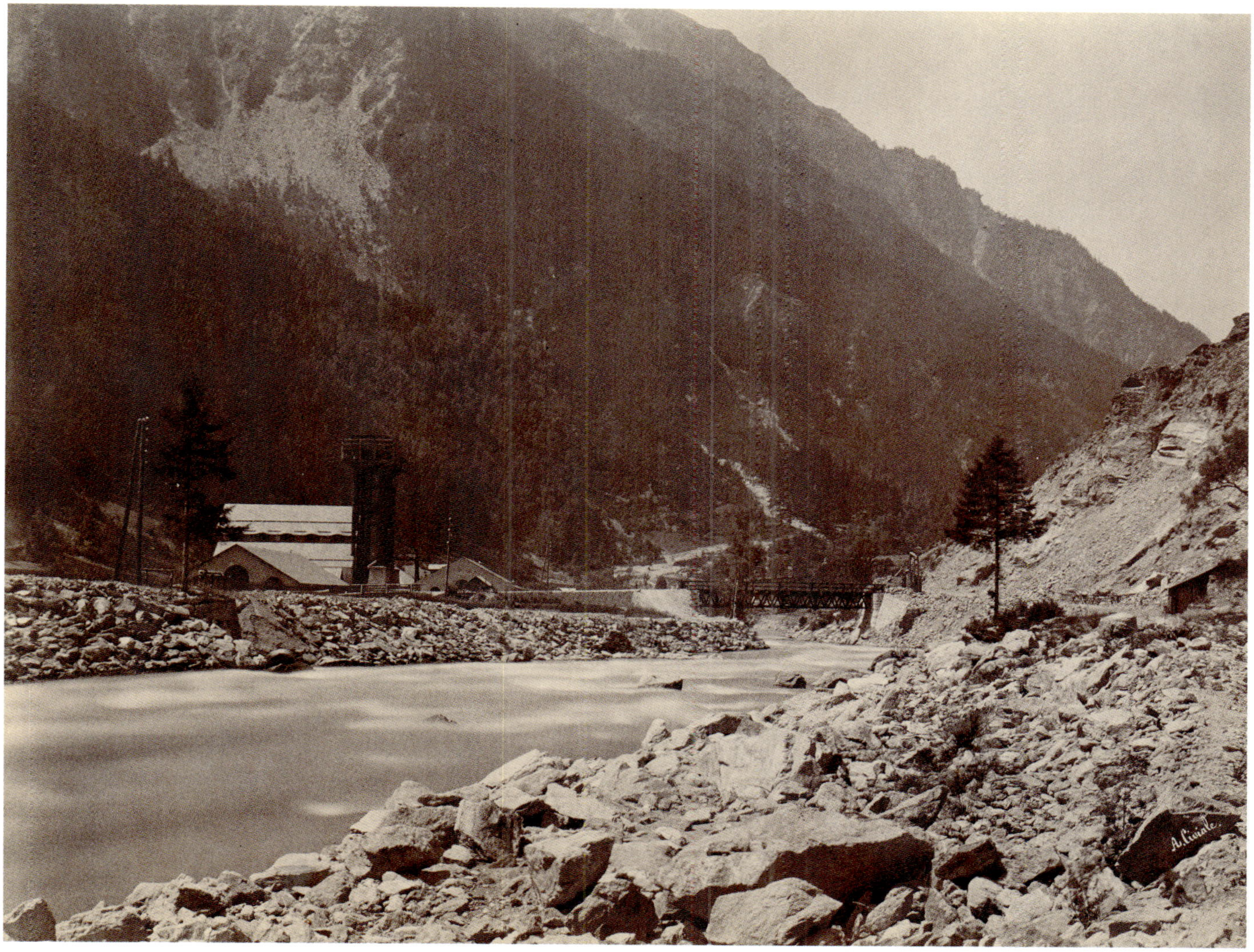
A. Civiale.

NARCISSE-VIRGILE DIAZ DE LA PEÑA

FRENCH, 1807–1876

95

The Pyrenees, the Peak of the Midi de Bigorre

1871–72

Oil on wood panel

8⁵⁄₁₆ × 10⅝ in. (21.2 × 27 cm)

The Cleveland Museum of Art, Severance and Greta Millikin Collection, 1964.293

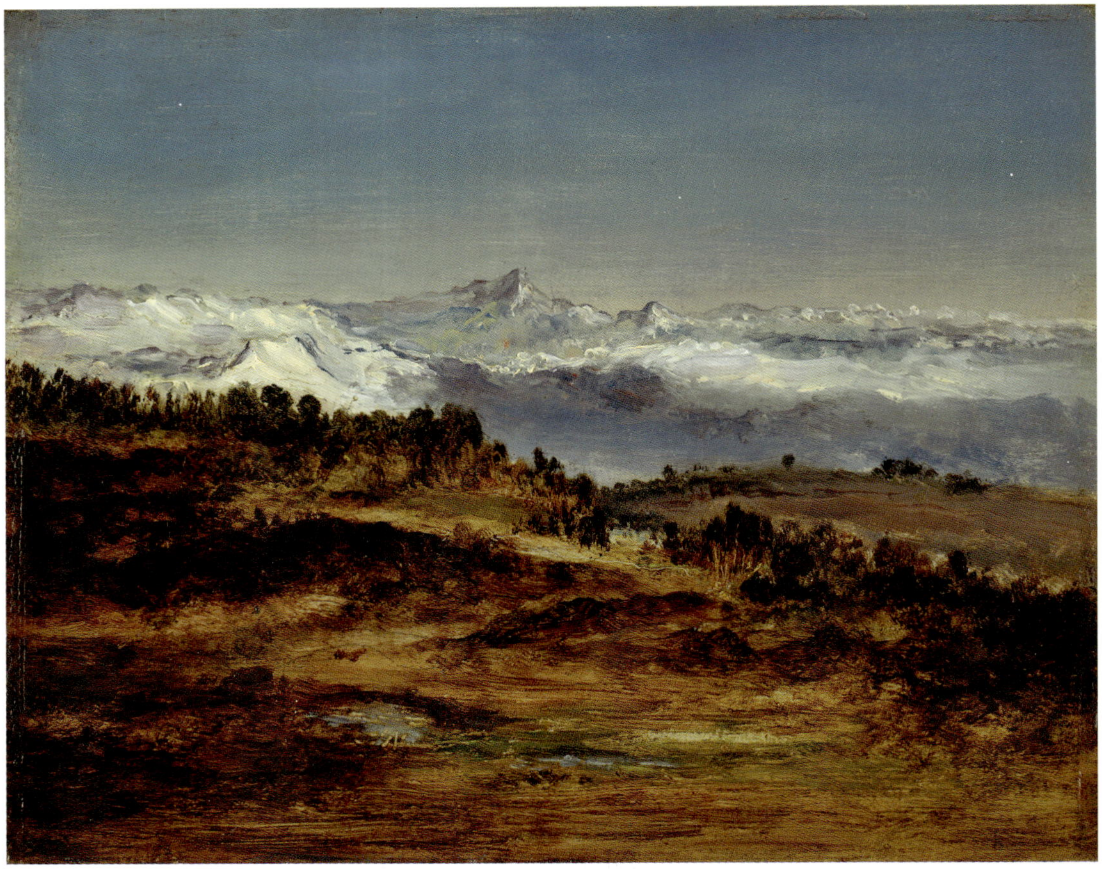

IN HIS EXTENSIVE LANDSCAPE OUTPUT, Narcisse-Virgile Diaz de la Peña concentrated on paintings of the Forest of Fontainebleau, but late in his career, he also produced a small group of pictures of the Pyrenees. In the fall of 1871 he traveled to the Pyrenees on doctor's orders in the hope that the warmer climes of the South would aid his failing health. The location of these mountains may have appealed to Diaz because of his Spanish heritage, his parents having moved from Spain to Bordeaux, where he was raised. This painting represents the grand Pic du Midi de Bigorre (9,439 ft.), in the center of the Pyrenees chain.[1] Diaz rapidly brushed in the mountain range as well as the foreground hills and contrasted the foreground in shadow with the luminous distances. Diaz painted several views of the Pyrenees, returning in the fall of 1872.[2] His interest in the region was probably also encouraged by the experience of his artist friends Théodore Rousseau and Jules Dupré, who had visited the Pyrenees in 1844. —SK

1. An inscription on the reverse of the panel reads "Les Pyrénées / le pas du Loup." This represents the site of Diaz's viewpoint and is in the district of Hèches, some 12½ miles north of Arreau. See Louise d'Argencourt, *The Cleveland Museum of Art: European Paintings of the 19th Century* (Cleveland: Cleveland Museum of Art, 1999), 1:246–47.

2. See, for example, *Les Pyrénées*, ca. 1870 (Musée du Louvre, Paris), and *View of the Pyrénées* (Museum Mesdag, The Hague).

96

ROSA BONHEUR
FRENCH, 1822–1899

Grazing Sheep in the Pyrenees

ca. 1868

Oil on canvas

12⅝ × 17¹⁵⁄₁₆ in. (32 × 45.5 cm)

Dahesh Museum of Art, New York, 1997.46

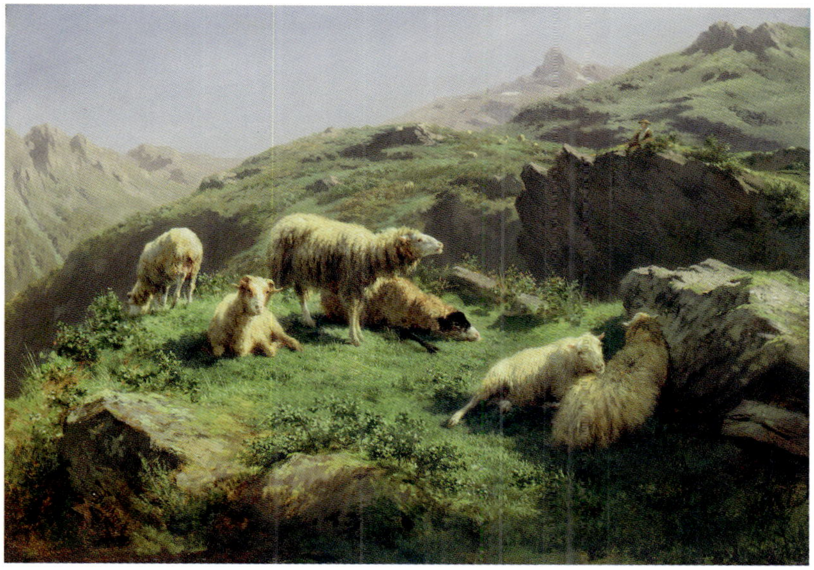

ROSA BONHEUR, who enjoyed great international fame in mid-nineteenth-century France, was undoubtedly the best-known French female artist at this time. Her work was especially appreciated in England. Known for her detailed study of animals, the artist kept a stable of cows, horses, and sheep in her Parisian studio to aid her studies. Over the course of her career, Bonheur traveled extensively around France, focusing on the mountain ranges of Auvergne and the Pyrenees. She first visited the Pyrenees in 1846 and returned in 1850, when she traveled incognito as a man, even receiving a cross-dressing permit to facilitate her studies.[1] At that time, she wrote of the "grandiose wildness" of the Pyrenees.[2] She noted that she was "expecting that these mountains, higher and more picturesque than the ones in Auvergne, would open up new horizons for my painting. I wasn't wrong. These mountains—which Louis XIV had declared abolished—so enthralled me that I've often gone back."[3]

Grazing Sheep in the Pyrenees shows a flock grazing on the upland pastures in the summer, having been moved from their winter ground in the lowlands. On an 1853 visit to the Pyrenees, Bonheur had even considered bringing back one of these sheep to her Paris stable, noting, "I love so much these small sheep."[4] Bonheur often represented Pyrenean shepherds, showing an interest in the peasant culture of the region: the shepherd is here visible behind the rock to the right. The luminous distance also highlights the artist's careful study of the peaks and geological features in the region such as the Cirque de Gavarnie and the Montagne Perdue. Bonheur also produced a related watercolor, *Herd of Sheep in the Pyrenees* (Dahesh Museum of Art, New York), signed and dated 1868; this painting may date from around the same time. —SK

1. Gretchen van Slyke, trans., *Rosa Bonheur by Anna Klumpke: The Artist's [Auto] Biography* (Ann Arbor: University of Michigan Press, 1997), 137: "Before setting out . . . I requested permission to wear men's clothing. So we didn't ride sidesaddle . . . but sat aside our steeds like real horsemen." A police order of 1800 had attempted to restrict the practice of women wearing men's clothing. Any woman wishing to do so subsequently required permission from the prefecture of police. Women risked arrest without this permission.

2. Quoted in Marie Borin, *Rosa Bonheur: Une artiste à l'aube du feminisme* (Paris: Pygmalion, 2011), 125: "sauvagerie grandiose."

3. Van Slyke, *Rosa Bonheur by Anna Klumpke*, 137. Bonheur's words reference Louis XIV's 1659 Treaty of the Pyrenees between France and Spain and his quip that the new closeness between the two countries ensured that "there are no more Pyrenees!" Quoted in S. A. Bent, ed., *Familiar Short Sayings of Great Men* (1887), s.v. "There are no more Pyrenees," http://www.bartleby.com/344/254.html.

4. Quoted in Theodore Stanton, *Reminiscences of Rosa Bonheur* (New York: Appleton, 1910), 16–17.

97

JOSEPH VIGIER
FRENCH, 1821–1894

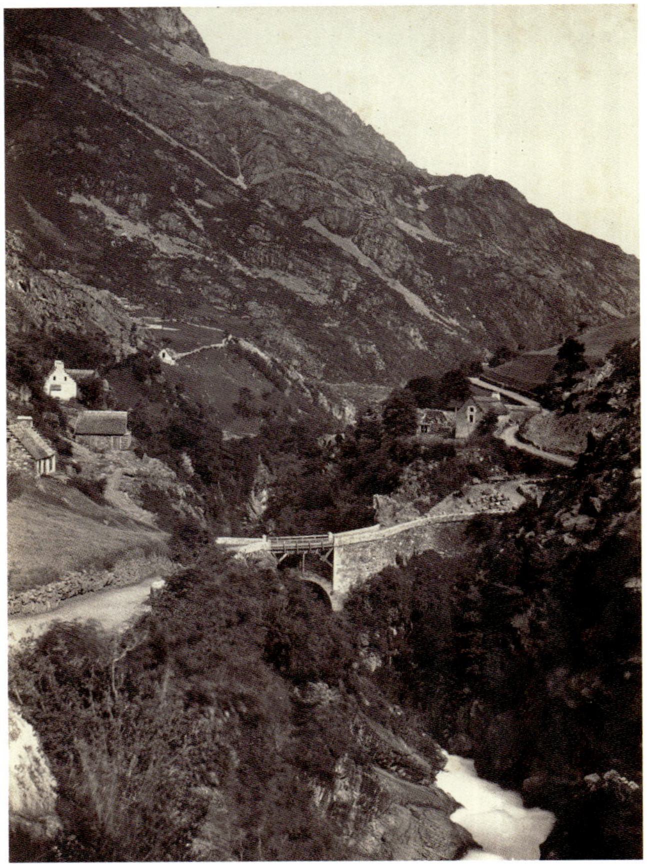

Saint-Sauveur, Pont de Sia (Gavarnie Route)

1853

Salt print from paper negative

14 × 10½ in. (35.6 × 26.7 cm)

The Nelson-Atkins Museum of Art, Kansas City, Missouri, Gift of the Hall Family Foundation in honor of the 75th anniversary of The Nelson-Atkins Museum of Art, 2008.25.26

JOSEPH VIGIER came from a wealthy family that had amassed its fortune through the establishment of six bathing establishments, Bains Vigier, located along the Seine in Paris. A student of Gustave Le Gray, Vigier became an accomplished amateur photographer and was a founding member of the Société héliographique (1851) and the Société française de la photographie (1854). During the summer of 1853, he traveled to the Pyrenees and made a series of views that resulted in an album of thirty prints. While it is not known for certain if his view of Saint-Sauveur was included in that particular album, it appeared in another album of thirty-eight salt prints titled *Voyage dans les Pyrénées*, which Vigier produced that same year.[1]

The critic Ernest Lacan described Vigier's acomplishment as a "masterpiece of the genre," suggesting that while ordinarily one travels to the Pyrenees for health reasons, to take the "waters of Bagneres, de Cauterets or Saint-Sauveur," or for a respite from "the noise and agitations of the big city," Vigier "has returned with the Pyrenees themselves."[2] Praised for their artistic virtuosity—the use of aerial perspective, linear compositional devices, and moody evocations—Vigier's views were, for Lacan, more than simply a record of this mountainous terrain. They evoked legends of France's past—in particular, the story of Roland, the storied military leader and nephew of Charlemagne, whose defeat in the battle of Ronceveaux by Basque forces became the source for the heroic eleventh-century poem *The Song of Roland*. In his discussion of Vigier's album, Lacan quoted the writer Paul Nibelle, whose *Légendes de la vallée* describe the landscape of the Pyrenees in mythic terms: "The arid and barren soil is strewn with broken, blackened rocks, accumulated or dispersed across the plain, like the debris from a battle of giants."[3] Lacan also spoke poetically of the landscape's Romantic and historic resonances: "This convulsive nature, desolate, is full of a virile and savage poetry, it has a sadness full of grandeur, it speaks to the hearts that have suffered, with all the eloquence of despair."[4] —AMW

1. For a fuller account of the contents of the album from which this photograph derives, see Larry J. Schaaf and Russell Lord, "Joseph, Vicomte Vigier Voyage dans les Pyrénées," *Sun Pictures* 16, exh. cat. (New York: Hans P. Kraus Jr., 2007).

2. Ernest Lacan, "Les Pyrénéés par M. Le Vicomte Vigier," *La lumière*, February 11, 1854, 21: "chef-d'oeuvre du genre"; "les eaux bien-faisantes de Bagnères, de Cauterets ou de Saint-Sauveur"; "des bruits et des agitations de la grande ville"; "a rapporté les Pyrénées elles-même."

3. Quoted in ibid.: "Le sol aride et nu est jonché de rochers brisés, noircis, accumulés ou dispersés dans la plaine, comme les débris d'un combat de géants." According to legend, the mountain pass that is today located on the Franco-Spanish border—known as La brèche de Roland (The Breach of Roland)—was carved by Roland's sword in the battle of Roncevaux.

4. Ibid.

98

AUGUSTE-FRANÇOIS BONHEUR
FRENCH, 1824–1884

Landscape in Auvergne (Puy)

ca. 1850

Oil on paper mounted on canvas

7½ × 16⅞ in. (19.1 × 42.9 cm)

Brooklyn Museum. Healy Purchase Fund B, 1993.36

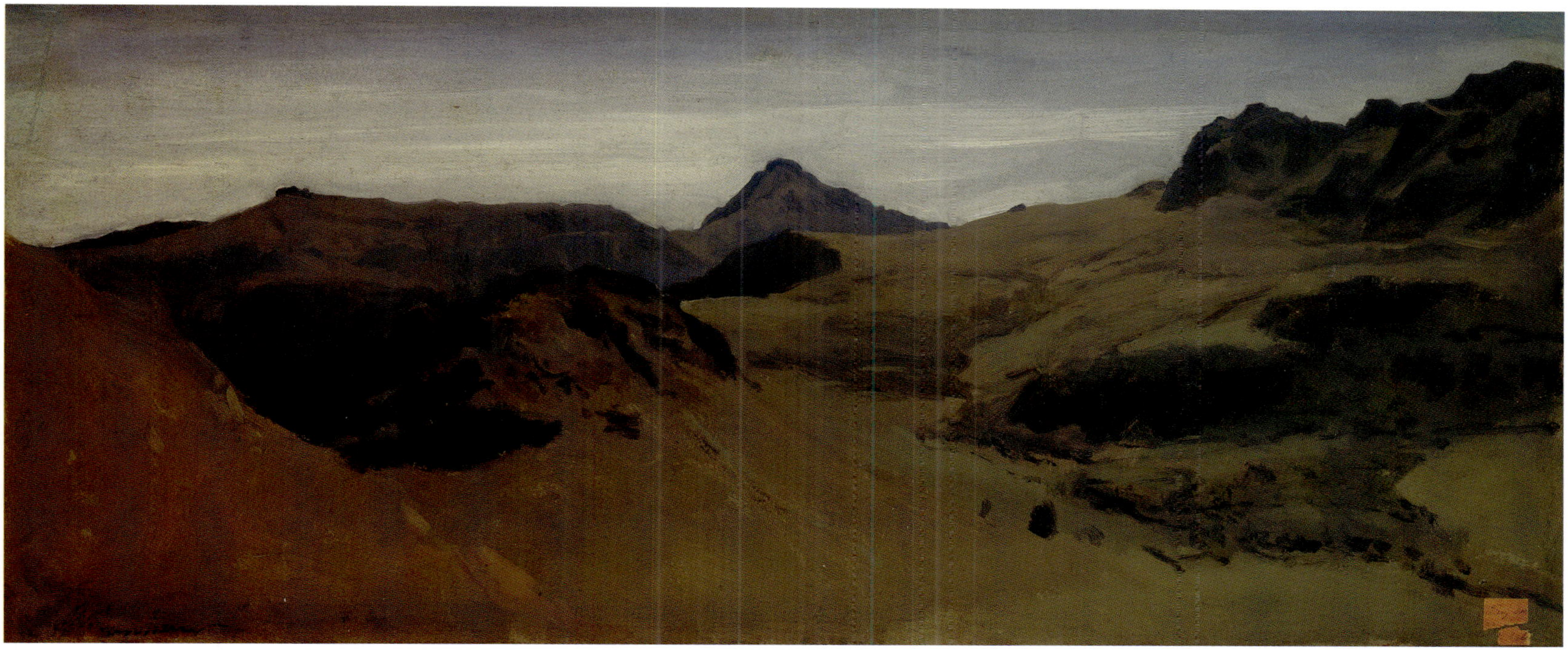

AUGUSTE-FRANÇOIS BONHEUR has been overshadowed in death by his more famous elder sister, Rosa, but in his lifetime, he enjoyed considerable fame and international success, particularly with English collectors. Auguste was best known for his representations of animals (as both a painter and a sculptor), but he was also a talented landscape painter. Over the course of his career, Bonheur showed a particular interest in mountain scenery, focusing on the mountain ranges of Auvergne and the Pyrenees and often showing representations of these regions at the Paris Salon. These two oil sketches were outdoor studies—both have pin holes still visible in their corners where they were affixed to boards.

Landscape in Auvergne (Puy) shows a panoramic expanse of grasslands and mountains in this ancient volcanic region in central France. The paper label, "puy," affixed by the artist at bottom right, references the dormant volcanoes (*puys*) for which the region was renowned: one of these is visible in the middle distance. Bonheur first traveled to Auvergne in

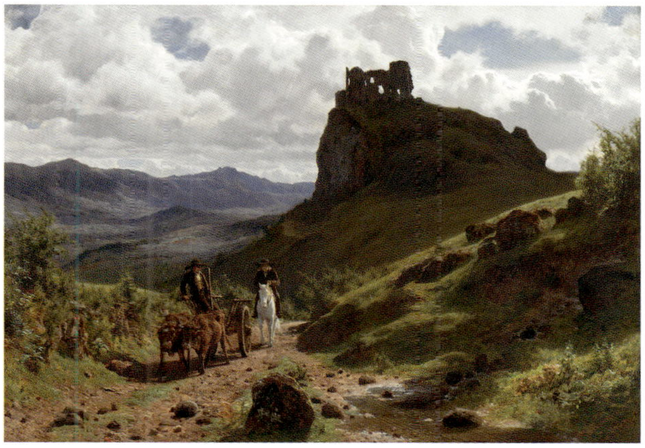

FIG. 75 Auguste-François Bonheur, *The Ruins of the Château d'Apchon*, 1852. Oil on canvas. National Museums Liverpool, Sudley House

99

AUGUSTE-FRANÇOIS BONHEUR
FRENCH, 1824–1884

Mountains with Mist (Aspes, Pyrenees)

ca. 1858

Oil on paper mounted on canvas

10½ × 16⁹⁄₁₆ in. (26.7 × 42.1 cm)

Brooklyn Museum, Healy Purchase Fund B, 1993.123.1

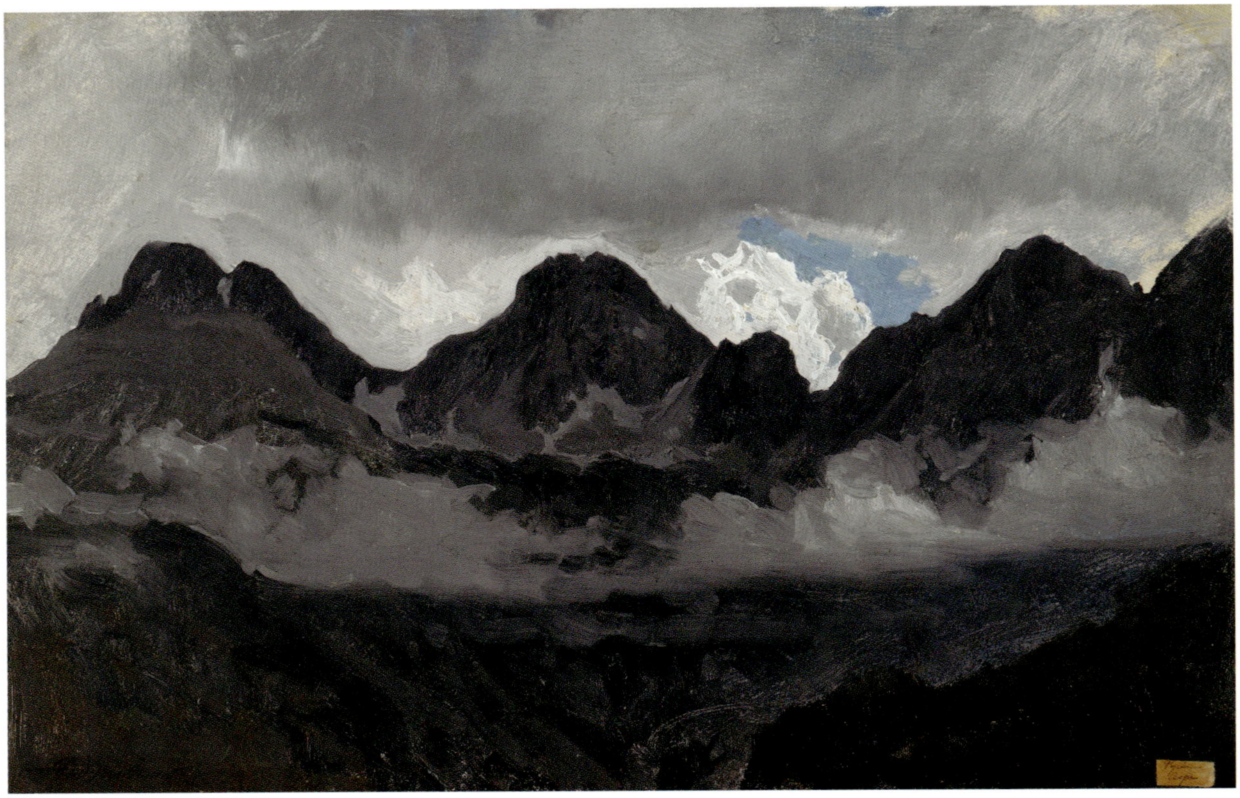

1850 and returned regularly thereafter. Studies like this one underpinned his more finished exhibition paintings such as *The Ruins of the Château d'Apchon* (fig. 75), a view of a ruined castle shown at the 1853 Paris Salon, in which the distant mountain range is also carefully represented.

Mountains with Mist (Aspes, Pyrenees) shows a line of peaks in the Pyrenees framed by clouds above and below. A label at the lower right indicates that the mountains are the Aspes range in the western Pyrenees, with the prominent Aspe peak (8,678 ft.) in the center framed by smaller peaks. Bonheur was exploring still relatively uncharted territory; the Aspe mountain would not be climbed until much later.[1] Bonheur first traveled to the Pyrenees in 1846 and returned in 1858. This study probably dates from the latter trip. Such studies aided the major views of the Pyrenees that he showed at the Salons of 1859, 1861, and 1863 and that attracted critical praise for their careful renderings of the region's mountainous scenery.[2] —SK

1. The Aspe peak was climbed for the first time by a certain E. Wallon in about 1880.

2. In 1861, for example, Bonheur showed the *Encounter of Two Herds in the Pyrenees* (private collection). See John Sillevis, "New Discoveries: Auguste Bonheur's *La Sortie du pâturage*," *Nineteenth-Century Art Worldwide* 6, no. 1 (Spring 2007), http://www.19thc-artworldwide.org/index.php/spring07/139-new-discoveries-auguste-bonheurs-la-sortie-du-paturage.

100

GUSTAVE COURBET
FRENCH, 1819–1877

The Valley of Ornans

1858
Oil on canvas
23½ × 33⅜ in. (59.7 × 85.4 cm)
Saint Louis Art Museum, Museum Purchase, 74:1937

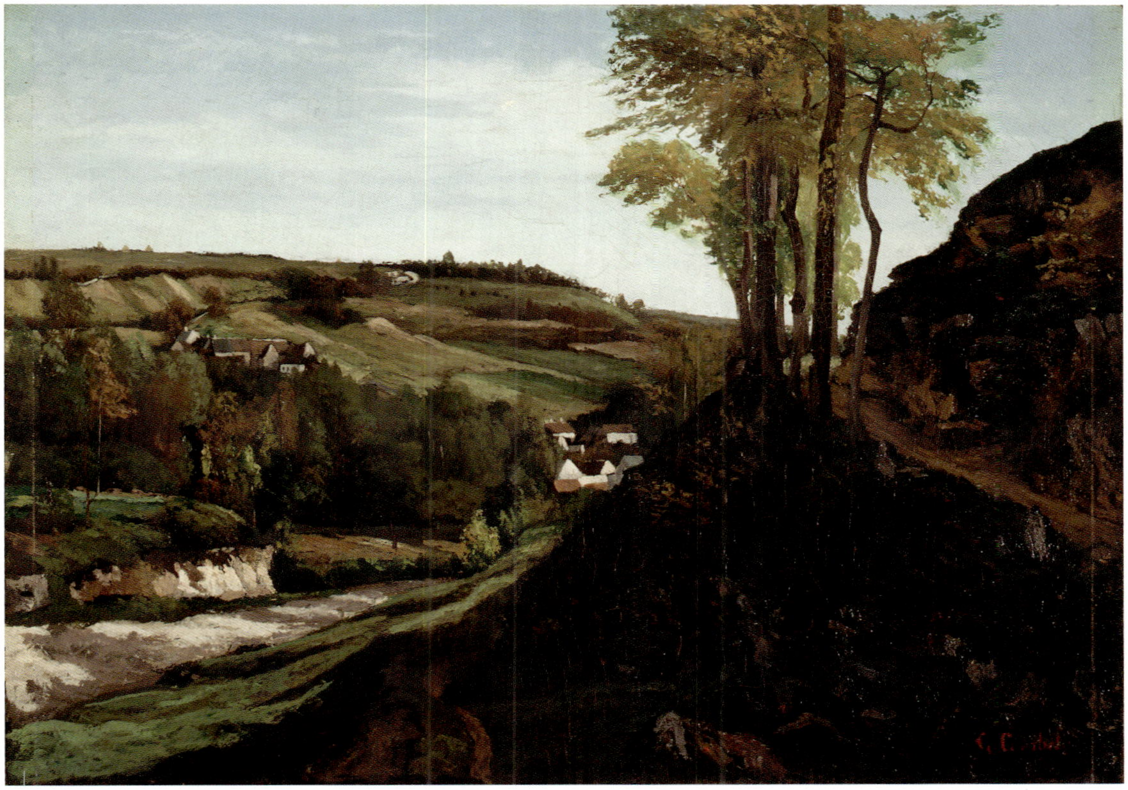

AROUND TWO-THIRDS of Gustave Courbet's output of paintings consists of landscapes. Although best known as a chronicler of French provincial life, Courbet placed landscape painting at the absolute center of his production. He focused particularly on the representation of his native Franche-Comté region, painting large numbers of views of the area's mountainous landscape. These two paintings show the river Loue, a tributary of the larger river Doubs, at different places along its passage through the Franche-Comté landscape. Courbet was fascinated by this river. He represented it often, and he frequently followed its course, riding on his faithful donkey, Gérôme. As the artist famously remarked, "To paint a landscape, you have to know it."[1]

The Valley of Ornans represents the rugged terrain of Courbet's birthplace of Ornans. Although he moved to Paris in the 1840s, the artist returned to his hometown regularly. While in Paris, he maintained his regional accent and insisted on his independence and difference from what he perceived as the excessive refinements and pretentiousness of the capital. In this highly structured composition, he contrasted the shadowed hill at right with the sunlit view to the left, where the muddy river Loue cuts diagonally across the composition. The flattened surfaces in the painting are evidence of Courbet's characteristic use of the palette knife. His unusual, antiacademic palette-knife technique provided a formal realization in paint of his nonconformist temperament. Despite his individualistic approach, by the late 1850s Courbet had established himself as a major landscape painter. In 1860 the avant-garde critic Zacharie Astruc visited the artist's studio, where he probably saw this work, and noted, "As a landscape painter, he dominates the contemporary school with Corot."[2]

101

GUSTAVE COURBET
FRENCH, 1819–1877

Landscape near Ornans

1864

Oil on canvas

35 × 50⅛ in. (88.8 × 127.2 cm)

Toledo Museum of Art, Purchased with funds from the Libbey Endowment, Gift of Edward Drummond Libbey, 1964.59

Landscape near Ornans shows the river Loue as it cuts its way between limestone cliffs.[3] A path follows along the riverbank. As has been noted, this is probably a composite image, bringing together sites from different locations in the Franche-Comté. The cliff face at top left is, for example, the Roche du Mont, the signature limestone cliff that rises above Ornans and which served as the backdrop for Courbet's famed *Burial at Ornans* (Musée d'Orsay, Paris).[4] The picture dates from 1864, when the artist spent virtually the whole year in the Franche-Comté, painting the range of the area's landscape. Courbet has signed and dated this work prominently in red at bottom left. This was surely a marketing ploy—indeed, his landscapes enjoyed considerable commercial success with both Parisian and Franc-Comtois patrons—but, as Michael Fried has suggested, Courbet may also have been alluding to his own blood and the visceral insertion of his own body into his native landscape.[5]

Courbet's use of the palette knife here mimics the very surface of the rocks; the artist once affirmed, "Try a brush to do rocks like that, rocks that have been eroded by the weather and the rain, which have formed long seams from top to bottom."[6] Such words reflect his interest in the geology of the region, and he was in fact a member of the local geological society. He even produced a work titled *The Crumbling Rock, Geological Study* in 1864, for the local geologist, Jules Marcou.

Courbet took pride in the history of regional independence of the Franche-Comté and saw the region's democratic history as offering a model for the whole of France.[7] In the same year that he painted *Landscape near Ornans*, he wrote a remarkable letter to Victor Hugo, the great radical poet and novelist, who was then in exile in Guernsey. Courbet emphasized the value of his region for France during a period of political oppression:

> I have the fierce independence of the mountain dweller. . . . You, poet, know better than anyone else that our part of the world is fortunately in France, the reservoir of those men who at times are as disruptive as the land to which they belong but who are also often hewn from granite. . . . in spite of the oppression that weighs on our generation, in spite of the fact that my friends are in exile, hunted down . . . there are still four or five of us left. We are strong enough, despite the renegades, despite the France of today with its demented sheep. We will save art, the life of the mind, and integrity in our country. . . . The viewpoints of our mountains . . . offer us the limitless spectacle of immensity. . . . I love terra firma and the orchestration of the countless herds that inhabit our mountains.[8]

The letter highlights Courbet's democratic vision for his nation, and especially the importance of art—and specifically views of the Franche-Comté mountains—to this vision. The artist, however, perhaps overemphasized his outsider position: his Franche-Comté view *Le puits noir* (Musée d'Orsay, Paris) was acquired the following year by the emperor. Nonetheless, Courbet's radicalism remained. He would play a prominent role in the failed Paris Commune in 1871 and subsequently be sent into exile, dying outside his beloved homeland. —SK

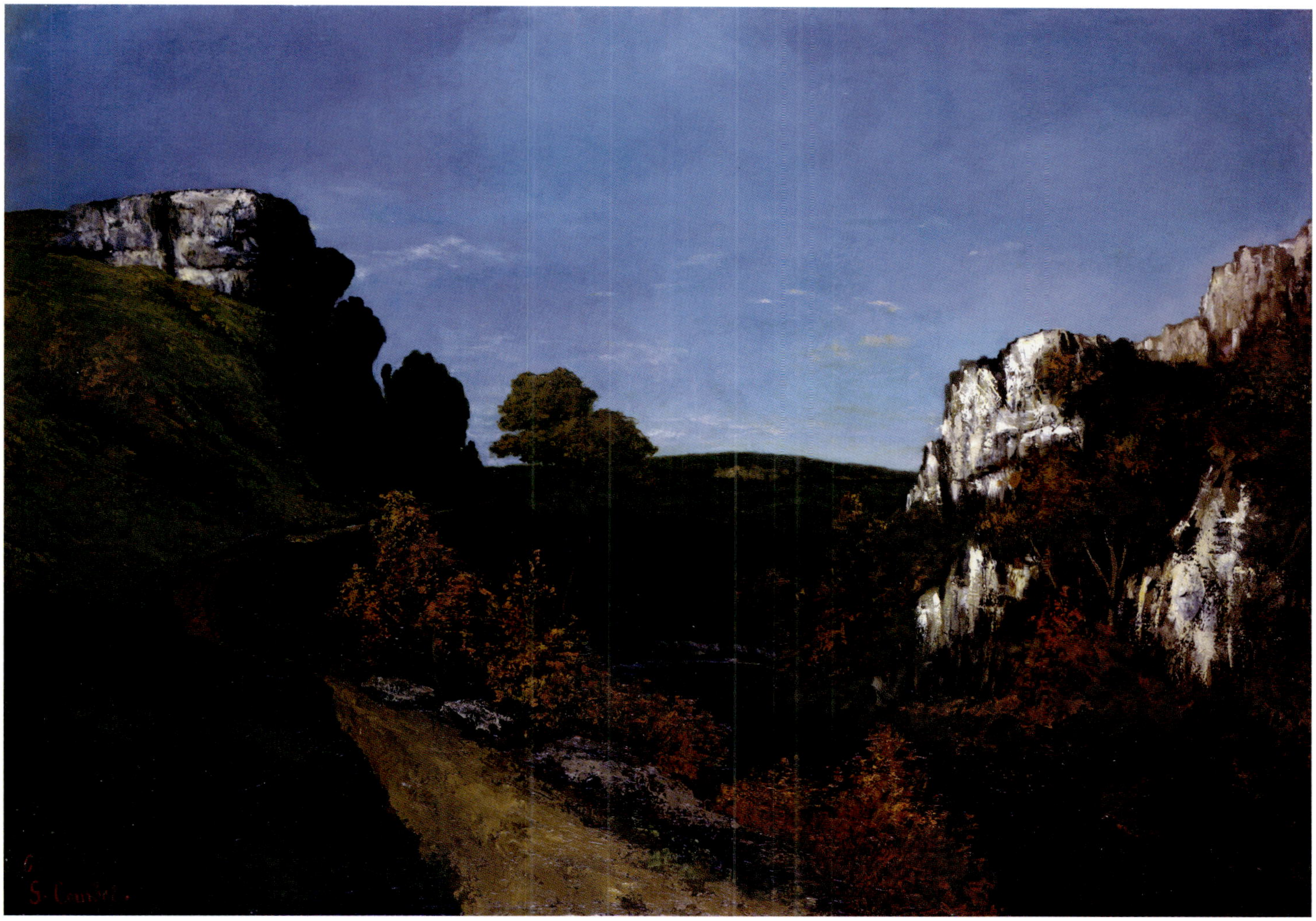

1. Quoted in *Gustave Courbet*, exh. cat. (New York: Metropolitan Museum of Art; Ostfildern: Hatje Cantz, 2008), 228.

2. Zacharie Astruc, *Les Quatorze Stations du Salon* (Paris, 1859), 394; quoted in ibid., 237.

3. Courbet produced a similarly scaled variant of this work (Des Moines Art Center, Des Moines, Iowa) and a smaller variant (Neue Pinakothek, Munich).

4. See Mary Morton and Charlotte Eyerman, *Courbet's Landscapes*, exh. cat. (Los Angeles: J. Paul Getty Museum, 2006), 55.

5. Michael Fried, *Courbet's Realism* (Chicago: University of Chicago Press, 1990).

6. Quoted in Petra ten-Doesschate Chu, *The Most Arrogant Man in France: Gustave Courbet and the Nineteenth-Century Media Culture* (Princeton: Princeton University Press, 2007), 149.

7. See Klaus Herding, *Courbet: To Venture Independence* (New Haven: Yale University Press, 1991).

8. Gustave Courbet to Victor Hugo, November 28, 1864, in *Letters of Gustave Courbet*, ed. and trans. Petra ten-Doesschate Chu (Chicago: University of Chicago Press, 1992), 248–49.

102

JEAN-FRANÇOIS MILLET

FRENCH, 1814–1875

Le Puy de Dôme

ca. 1866

Black conté crayon and pastel on gray paper

18½ × 22⅛ in. (47 × 56.2 cm)

Frick Art & Historical Center, Pittsburgh

IN THE SUMMER OF 1866 Jean-François Millet traveled to the mountainous volcanic region of Auvergne in the center of France. The pretext of the journey was a visit to the spa at Vichy for his wife's health. Soon, though, Millet became intoxicated by the landscape of the area, whose drama was new to him, since his previous experience of nature had been the flatter topographies of Normandy and the Forest of Fontainebleau. After he returned from his first visit, Millet wrote excitedly,

> My head is full of all that we saw together in Auvergne. Everything is jumbled together in my brain. Volcanic mounds, pointed rocks, chasms, barren wastes, and green slopes! The glory of God dwelling on the heights, the topmost peaks wrapt in storm and cloud! I hope that all these confused impressions will settle down in the course of time.[1]

This pastel shows in the distance the extinct volcanic peak of Le Puy de Dôme—an enormous lava plug and the most distinctive mountain of the Auvergne region, rising to a height of 4,800 feet. Millet visited the peak in July 1866 and was particularly impressed by the way in which clouds enshrouded its top. He wrote at this time:

> The clouds very often stay stuck to the summits of the mountains. Sometimes also, the sun comes to crown them through a glory of clouds. The summit of the mountain is often as if melted. The rays come toward us and also pass through the different planes. These effects here are indescribable and have never been represented in painting, to my knowledge at least. It's the greatest fantasy that one can imagine.[2]

Le Puy de Dôme was produced on his return to Barbizon and shows dark clouds surrounding the peak while the sky is lighter to the left and right. In a related pastel (fig. 76), Millet showed a different light effect, with the sun dramatically illuminating the clouds around the mountain.

Millet was fascinated not only by the volcanic landscape of the region but also by the peasants who made their living there. Auvergne was (and is) one of the poorer regions of France but was well known for its agriculture and particularly its cheeses (including Bleu d'Auvergne and Roquefort). Although there is little arable land in the region, thousands of acres of upland pasture are grazed by cows, goats, and sheep. In *Le Puy de Dôme*, Millet shows a goatherd wearing the traditional peasant costume of the region: the distinctive straw hat, a woolen cloak, and wooden clogs (sabots). She sits knitting, feet splayed outward, while her goats graze around her.

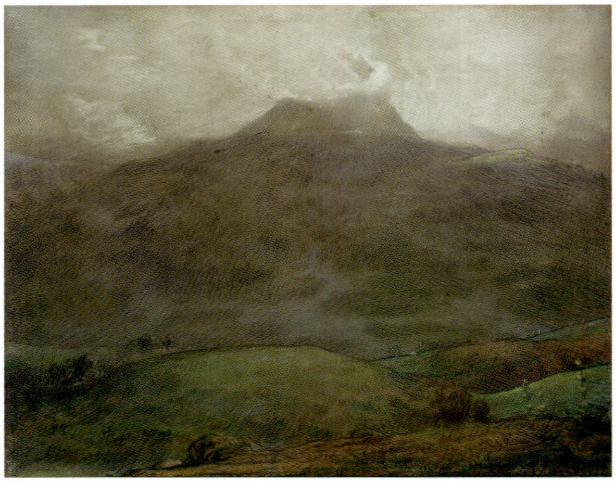

FIG. 76 Jean-François Millet, *View of Puy-de-Dôme*, 1866. Pastel on paper, 21⅝ × 26⅞ in. (55 × 68.2 cm). Museum of Fine Arts, Budapest

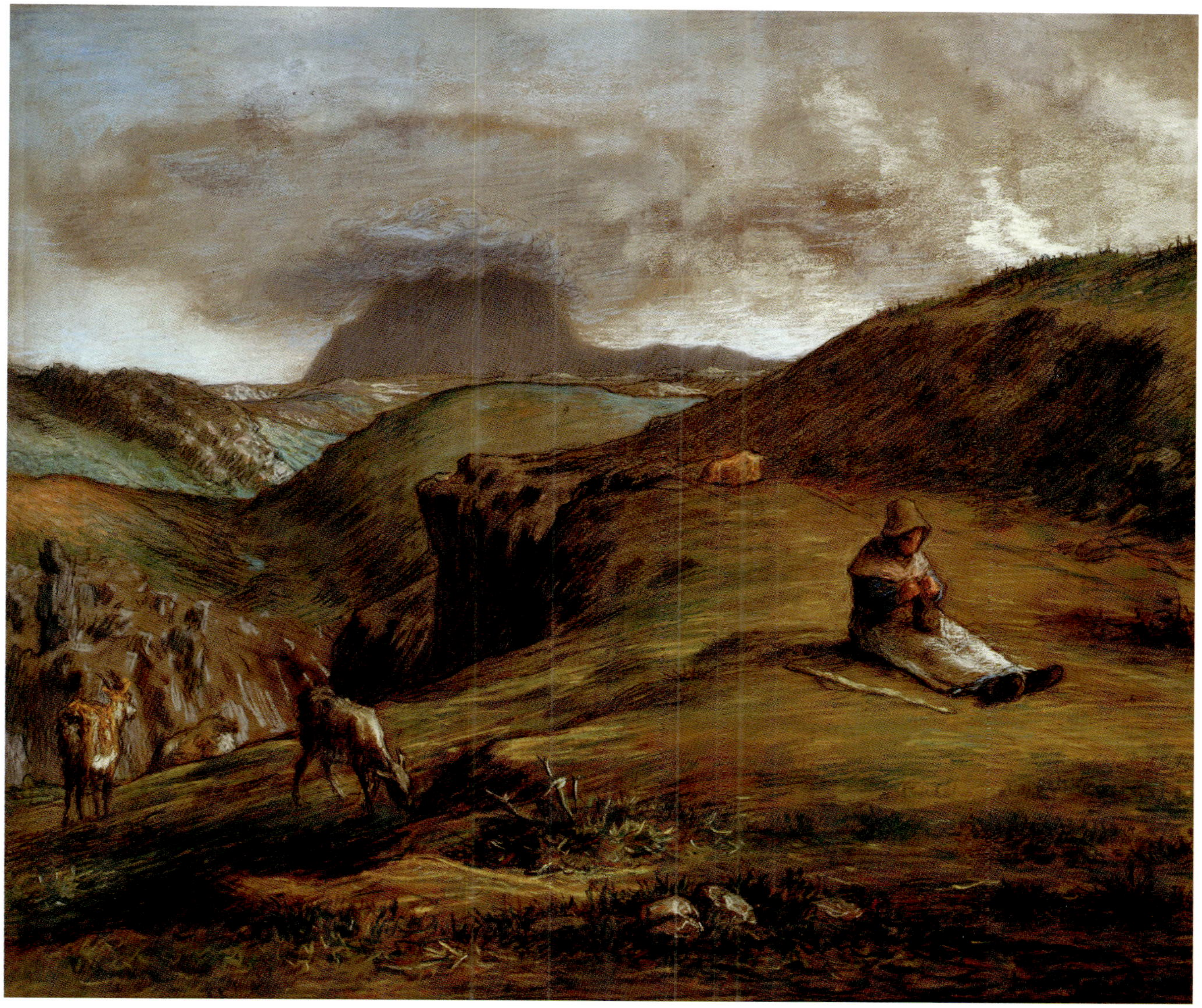

Le Puy de Dôme was produced for the Parisian architect Émile Gavet (who probably paid 350 francs for it), who commissioned a large number of pastels from Millet in the mid- to late 1860s. The work highlights the artist's mastery of pastel. Millet used black conté crayon, to outline the mountainous landscape, and rich tones of green, yellow, and blue pastel. Much of the gray color of the paper is allowed to show through, as in the sky. Millet returned to Auvergne in 1867 and 1868, and produced a large number of paintings and pastels of the region, which form an important and distinctive group in his output. —SKW

1. Millet to Chassaing, July 19, 1866, in Julia Cartwright, *Jean-François Millet: His Life and Letters* (London: Swan Sonnenschein & Co., 1896), 295.

2. Nathalie Roux and Françoise Gibert, eds., *Jean-François Millet: Voyages en Auvergne et Bourbonnais, 1866–1868*, exh. cat. (Milan: Skira, 2002), 66 and 118–19: "Les nuages restent très souvent accrochés aux sommets des montagnes. Quelquefois aussi le soleil dans une gloire de nuages vient leur faire un couronnement. Le sommet de la montagne en est comme fondu. Les rayons arrivent vers nous & passent aussi entre des différents plans. Ces aspects là sont indescriptibles & n'ont jamais été représentés en peinture, à ma connaissance du moins. C'est le plus haut fantastique qu'on puisse imaginer." Millet's commentary was accompanied by a summary sketch of *Le Puy de Dôme*: Bibliothèque nationale de France, Département des Estampes, SNR Millet Boîte 6.

7

MARINE VIEWS: PORTS AND TOURISM

AS THE HISTORIAN JULES MICHELET NOTED in *La mer*, France "has the admirable advantage of having two seas,"[1] the Atlantic to the west and north and the Mediterranean to the south. The mid-nineteenth century saw increasing exploration of these two coasts. The fact that France encompassed these two very different coastlines and climates—northern and temperate, southern and Mediterranean—became central to the country's sense of identity. In 1878 the writer Louis Simonin even described France as the "isthmus of Western Europe,"[2] emphasizing the country's fortuitous geographic position, with its Atlantic coast looking toward Britain and America and its Mediterranean coast looking to Africa and the East following the opening of the Suez Canal in 1869. Painters and photographers explored the range of the nation's coastlines and marine climates.

In the early nineteenth century, perceptions of the sea changed: it was no longer viewed as something frightening and dangerous—as had largely been the case in the eighteenth century—but was increasingly seen as a site of popular entertainment.[3] In the North, the Normandy coast was notable for its shingle beaches, rugged cliffs, and temperate climate marked by scudding, dramatic clouds. A tourist industry in France grew up in the 1850s and 1860s on this coast, driven by the expansion of the railroad network from Paris. A thriving industry of guidebooks, such as those of Adolphe Joanne, developed. The period saw the emergence of such popular tourist resorts as Sainte-Adresse and Trouville, which were recorded in atmospheric photographs by Gustave Le Gray as well as richly colorful paintings by Claude Monet and Eugène Boudin. Farther to the north, Boulogne also developed as a resort, and its hordes of new visitors were represented in the work of Édouard Manet. In the West, Brittany also had a distinctive coastline, which attracted increasing tourism, and was painted by Berthe Morisot and Jules Breton. The Mediterranean coast was notable for its sunny climate, intense light, and attractive sandy beaches and rocky cliffs. Because it is farther from Paris than the Normandy coast and because the railroad spread more slowly there, tourism did not come into its own there until the 1880s. Nonetheless, coastal locations such as

Tamaris and La Ciotat became increasingly attractive and were explored in the writings of George Sand, the paintings of Auguste Aiguier, and the photographs of Édouard Baldus. The rise of tourism thus encouraged the idea of the regional difference of France's coasts as an important part of the geographic diversity of the nation.

France was also a powerful maritime force, with major international ports such as Marseille, Le Havre, Bordeaux, and Nantes. Its commercial fleet increased significantly in the mid-nineteenth century, although it was still considerably smaller than that of the maritime nation of Great Britain. In 1878 France's fleet totaled 14,939 sailboats and 588 steamboats as opposed to Britain's 21,058 sailboats and 4,826 steamboats.[4] Manet represented examples of France's sail and steam power off the coast of Boulogne, while Morisot painted the naval port of Lorient in the West. Le Gray produced impressive photography of boats in Le Havre, France's second-biggest port. In the South, the Mediterranean was crucial to France's trade, and Marseille was the country's largest port. On the eve of the opening of the Suez Canal, one writer patriotically affirmed that Marseille would now become "the premier commercial emporium for the world."[5] Baldus represented this city as a thriving port, while Pierre Puvis de Chavannes focused on it as a welcoming commercial center for immigrants to France.

1. Jules Michelet, *La mer* (Paris: Hachette, 1861), 361.

2. Louis Simonin, *Les grands ports de commerce de la France* (Paris: Hachette, 1878), 49.

3. See Alain Corbin, *The Lure of the Sea: Discovery of the Seaside in the Western World, 1750–1840* (Harmondsworth, U.K.: Penguin, 1995).

4. See B. R. Mitchell, *International Historical Statistics: Europe, 1750–1988*, 3rd ed. (New York: Stockton Press, 1992), 690–92.

5. Sebastien Bertaut, "Marseille d'hier, d'aujourd'hui, de demain" (June 2, 1867); quoted in Aimée Brown Price, *Pierre Puvis de Chavannes*, vol. 2, *A Catalogue Raisonné of the Painted Work* (New Haven: Yale University Press, 2010), 138.

103

GUSTAVE LE GRAY
FRENCH, 1820–1884

Brig upon the Water

1856

Albumen print from collodion glass negative

12⅝ × 16 in. (32.1 × 40.6 cm)

The Nelson-Atkins Museum of Art, Kansas City, Missouri, Gift of the Hall Family Foundation in honor of the 75th anniversary of The Nelson-Atkins Museum of Art, 2007.17.22

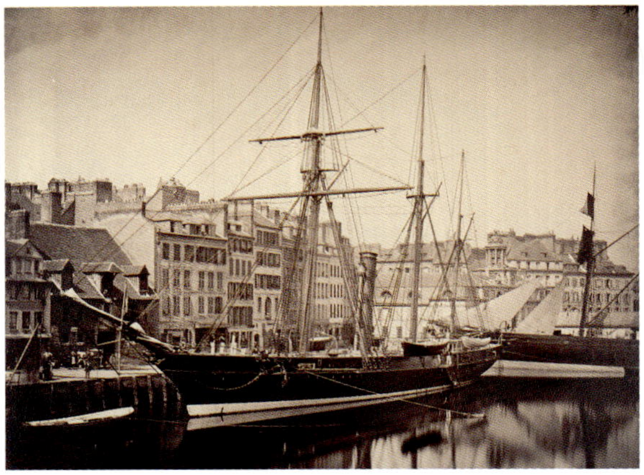

FIG. 77 Gustave Le Gray, *The Imperial Yacht, "La Reine Hortense," Le Havre*, 1856. Albumen print from collodion glass negative, 12½ × 16¼ in. (31.8 × 41.3 cm). The Metropolitan Museum of Art, Gilman Collection, Purchase, Jennifer and Joseph Duke Gift, 2005 (2005.100.273)

GUSTAVE LE GRAY produced three categories of seascapes between 1856 and 1858. These differ in intention and geographic location, though they share similar aesthetic sensibilities. The earliest views were made in the summers of 1856 and possibly 1857, in Normandy. Several negatives were made at Le Havre, an industrial port established in the early sixteenth century and enlarged in 1852, when the city's ramparts were pushed back during the early years of Napoléon III's rule. One majestic view features a group of ships leaving the port of Le Havre (cat. 104). The bold, graceful silhouettes of these vessels, sailing into the seemingly infinite sea in waning light, owes a clear debt to Romantic conceptions of the sea voyage as akin to mortal passage.[1] At Le Havre, Le Gray also made a photograph of the imperial yacht—*La Reine Hortense*—which was docked at the port, just before Prince Napoléon's expedition to Greenland in July 1856 (fig. 77). Also included in this early Normandy group were several views of the beach Sainte-Adresse that bear a remarkable compositional similarity to Claude Monet's later canvases of 1867 (cats. 106, 107, 109, fig. 78). The Sainte-Adresse pictures speak to the transformation of this former fishing village into a leisure resort town: in one view, a sign for the Dumont Baths is visible in the foreground.

Brig upon the Water, Le Gray's best-known marine view, was also included in this group (cat. 103), and it firmly established the photographer's artistic credentials. Le Gray used the wet-collodion method, working with large-format glass negatives, which allowed him to achieve a degree of detail and luminosity that was difficult, if not impossible, to obtain using paper negatives. The photograph was widely exhibited, garnering enormous critical praise and enjoying immediate popular appeal in both England, where it was first shown in London on November 6, 1856, at a meeting of the Photographic Society of London. Soon after it was shown in Paris, where it was included in the second exhibition of the Société française de la photographie in February 1857. By that date, Le Gray had received more than fifty thousand francs' worth of orders for the photograph.[2] One advertisement of December 22, 1856, suggested no fewer than eight hundred prints of "Legray's famous picture of sea and clouds" were available for purchase through the London dealers Murray & Heath.[3] The success of *Brig upon the Water*, as well as two related views made at the same site (*The Sun at Its Zenith* and *The Haloed Sun*) derived in large part from the works' dramatic light and atmospheric effects. One reviewer in 1857 noted that Le Gray's photographs were "delicious marines, which made a startling sensation in London."[4] Another writer compared the seascapes to a biblical scene, remarking: "It is as when Jacob's ladder of angels was but just withdrawn, and the radiance above and below, where it rested on earth and sky, had not yet melted out."[5]

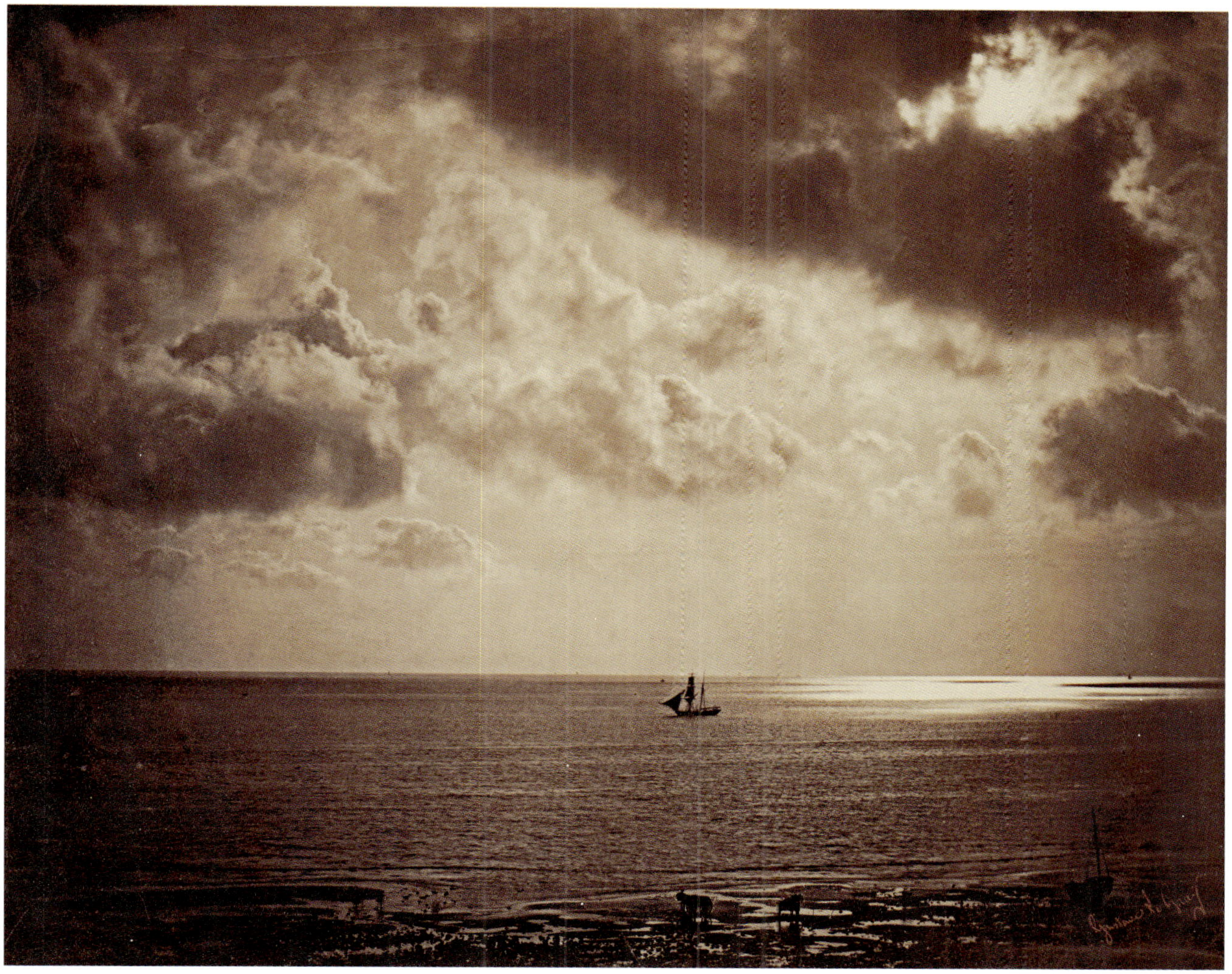

For *Brig upon the Water*, Le Gray was also lauded for his technical mastery in being able to render, in a single negative, both sea and clouds with an equal degree of detail and tonal nuance.[6] Such a feat was rare with outdoor landscapes of the period, as the time necessary to expose details on the ground often overexposed the sky, with the result that many photographers painted the sky area in their negatives black, or perhaps painted in a few clouds. One way to circumvent the problem was to combine elements of two or more negatives, such that in the final printing both the sky and ground (or sea) areas retained the necessary detail and tone. Le Gray mastered this skill, and though *Brig upon the Water* was made using one negative, many of his later seascapes were, indeed, made from multiple negatives. Between 1857 and 1859 he also toned many of them using gold chloride, which produced exceptionally rich tonalities when used with albumen paper. Le Gray himself kept relatively quiet on the particulars of his craft, perhaps to guard against potential competitors, some of whom accused him outright of deliberately misinforming or misleading the public about his techniques and chemical formulas to drum up business.[7]

After the resounding success of the 1856 seascapes, in the spring of the following year, Le Gray traveled to the South of France, where he produced two Mediterranean seascapes near Sète that were also considered technical and artistic triumphs. Both *The Great Wave, Sète* and *The Breaking Wave—Mediterranean Sea* (see fig. 29 and cat. 108) were hailed for the "instantaneous effect" of showing waves crashing against rocks: one writer reviewing the former reported that the exposure lasted a mere one-twentieth of a second, a feat that had not been accomplished previously.[8]

Le Gray's third group of marine views feature a festooned French fleet at Cherbourg in August 1858, on the occasion of a series of fêtes there inaugurating, among other events, the filling of a basin named after Napoléon III at the newly expanded port. This event was part of the imperial family's

GUSTAVE LE GRAY
FRENCH, 1820–1884

104

Group of Ships Departing Le Havre

ca. 1856

Albumen print from collodion glass negative

12⅛ × 16 in. (30.8 × 40.6 cm)

The Nelson-Atkins Museum of Art, Kansas City, Missouri, Gift of the Hall Family Foundation, 2007.21.18

105

The French Fleet at Cherbourg

1858

Albumen print from collodion glass negative

11¾ × 16 in. (29.8 × 40.6 cm)

The Nelson-Atkins Museum of Art, Kansas City, Missouri, Gift of the Hall Family Foundation, 2007.21.17

visit to Brittany and Normandy, which was reported widely in the press. Ernest Lacan described the event in *La lumière*, commenting on "the multitude of visitors, foreigners, tourists, artists, and writers" who had gone to Cherbourg. Lacan noted that there were at least sixty photographers in attendance who strove to create "a souvenir of one of the greatest events of the epoch, and to trace one of the most beautiful pages in our history."[9] In these images, Le Gray strove less to create a timeless, Romantically inspired artistic photograph than to document a contemporary event that celebrated Second Empire achievements. He nonetheless crafted his compositions with characteristic sensitivity to light, sea, and sky, capturing such momentary elements as the clouds of smoke billowing from a gun salute welcoming the English monarchs to Cherbourg.[10] —AMW

1. Le Gray's stunning print *Departing Ships Leaving Le Havre* of 1856 was—despite its technical perfection and painterly affinities—produced in far fewer numbers, for reasons that remain unclear. See Sylvie Aubenas, *Gustave Le Gray, 1820–1884*, exh. cat. (Los Angeles: J. Paul Getty Museum, 2002), 107.

2. As reported in *Revue photographique* 16 (February 1857): 213.

3. See Ken Jacobson, *The Lovely Sea-View: A Study of the Marine Photographs Published by Gustave Le Gray, 1856–1858* (Petches Bridge, Essex: Ken and Jenny Jacobson, 2001), 12–13. Jacobson raises the important question of whether the concurrent emergence of specialist photographic print sellers at the time Le Gray produced commercially viable seascapes helped the sale of *Brig upon the Water* considerably.

4. Ernest Lacan, "La photographie en Angleterre," *La lumière*, December 27, 1856, 201: "C'est ainsi que les merveilles de la photographie française ont pu être admirées, 'depuis les gigantesques reproductions d'architecture de Baldus (dont l'entrée du Louvre est un si splendide spécimen) jusqu'aux délicieuses marines de Le Gray, qui font à Londres une si vive sensation.'"

5. *Journal of the Photographic Society of London* 3, no. 51 (February 21, 1857): 214.

6. This, at least, was the claim he made when he exhibited a print at the second annual exhibition of the Société française de la photographie in 1857, by titling it *Le brick, marine avec nuages obtenus simultanément* (*The Brig, Marine with Clouds Obtained Simultaneously*).

7. For a summation of the debates, see André Jammes and Eugenia Parry Janis, *The Art of French Calotype with a Critical Dictionary of Photographers, 1845–1870* (Princeton: Princeton University Press, 1983), 38–39.

8. These two Mediterranean views and one other photograph made at the military Camp de Châlons were the only three photographs for which Le Gray filed for copyright protection. See Aubenas, *Gustave Le Gray*, 148 and 367.

9. Ernest Lacan, "Revue photographique," *La lumière*, October 16, 1858, 166: "Comme on devait s'y attendre au milieu de la multitude de visiteurs, d'étrangers, de touristes, d'artistes, d'écrivains qui se pressaient à Cherbourg pendant les fêtes, il se trouvait bon nombre de photographes armés de toutes pièces. . . . On en a compté, dit-on, plus de soixante . . . alors, qu'il s'agissait de reproduire le magnifique spectacle de deux flottes réunies sous les regards d'une foule enthousiaste, accourue de tous les coins de l'Europe, de perpétuer le souvenir d'un des plus grands événements de l'époque et de tracer une des plus belles pages de notre histoire."

10. Jacobson, *Lovely Sea-View*, 26–30, has postulated that Le Gray may not have been the only "author" of these seascapes, citing the possibility that he might have worked with the negatives of Cyrus Macaire, a photographer who, in partnership with his brothers Hippolyte and Jean-Victor, was known for his marine subjects and for a time kept a commercial studio in Le Havre as well as Paris.

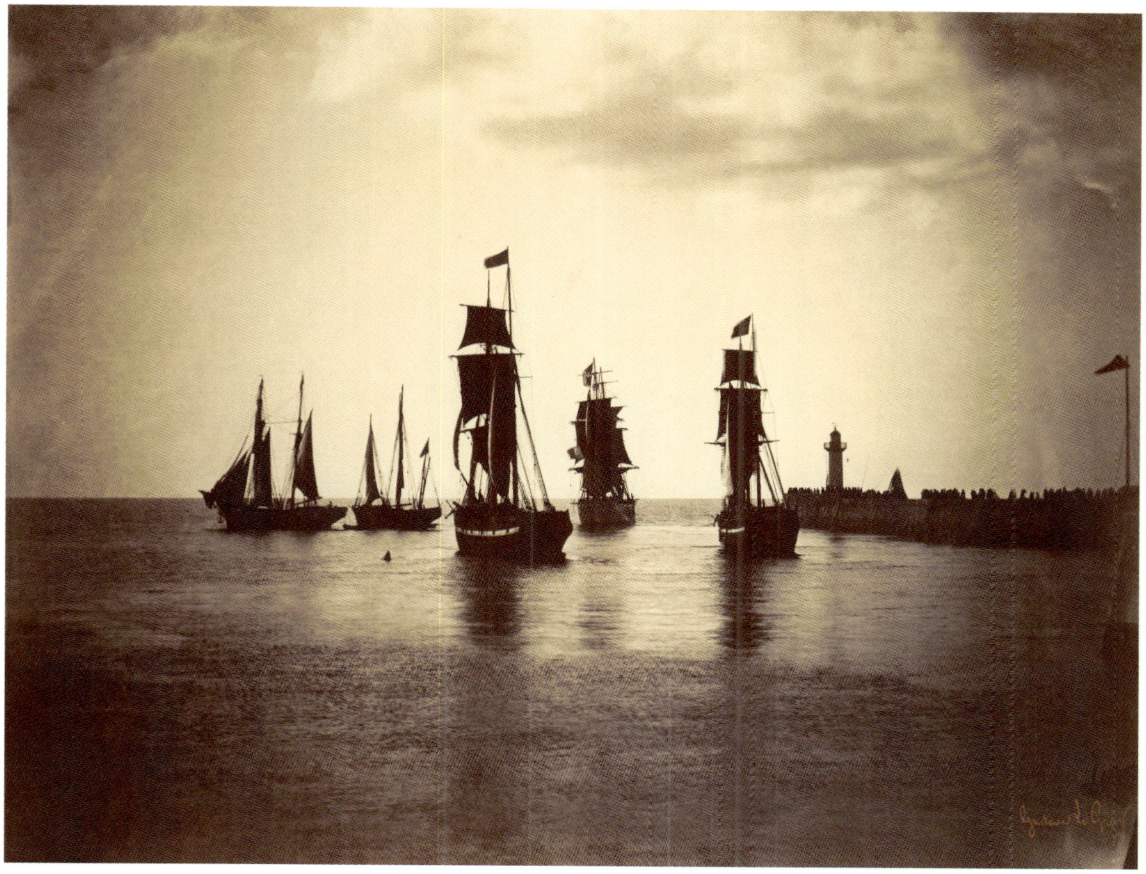

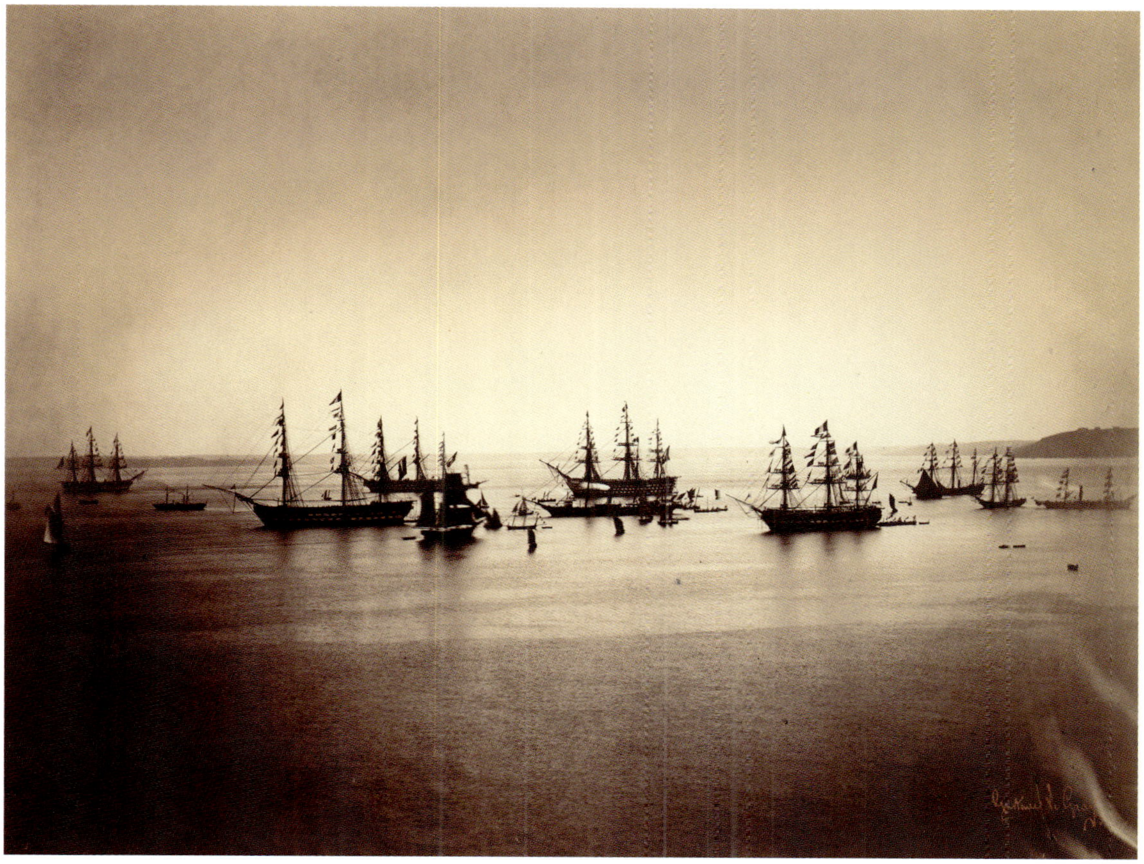

GUSTAVE LE GRAY
FRENCH, 1820–1884

106

The Beach at Sainte-Adresse, with the Dumont Baths

1856–57

Albumen print from collodion glass negative

12½ × 16 in. (31.7 × 41 cm)

The Art Institute of Chicago, Hugh Edwards Fund, 1971.577.8

107

The Beach at Sainte-Adresse

1856–57

Albumen print from collodion glass negative

12¼ × 15¼ in. (31.3 × 38.5 cm)

The Art Institute of Chicago, Hugh Edwards Fund, 1971.577.15

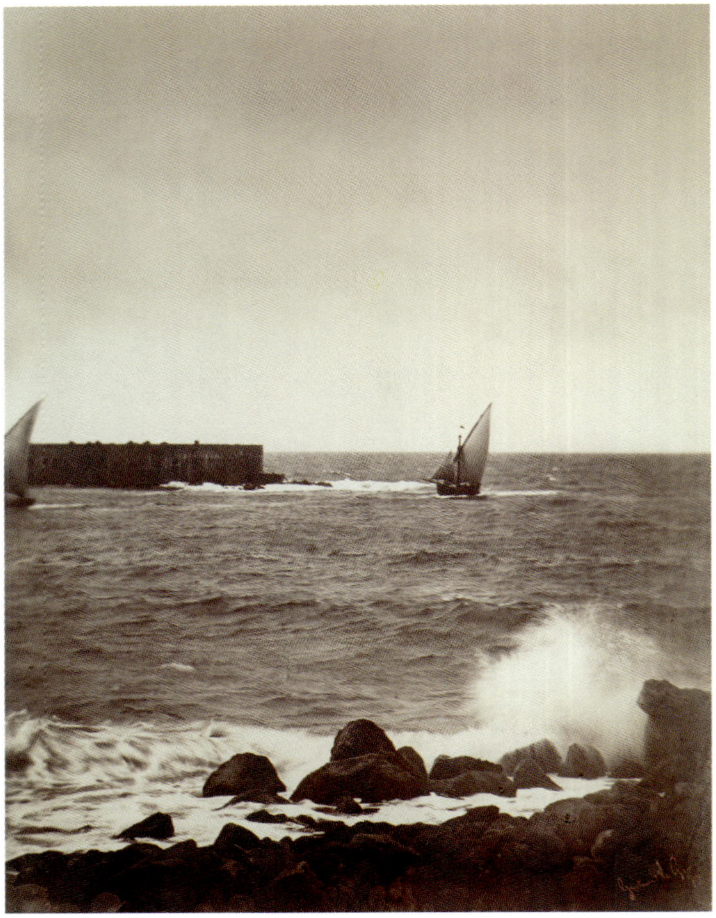

108

108

The Breaking Wave—Mediterranean Sea

1857

Albumen print from collodion glass negative

16⅜ × 12¹³⁄₁₆ in. (41.7 × 32.5 cm)

The Victoria and Albert Museum, London, Bequeathed by Chauncey Hare Townshend, 68.003

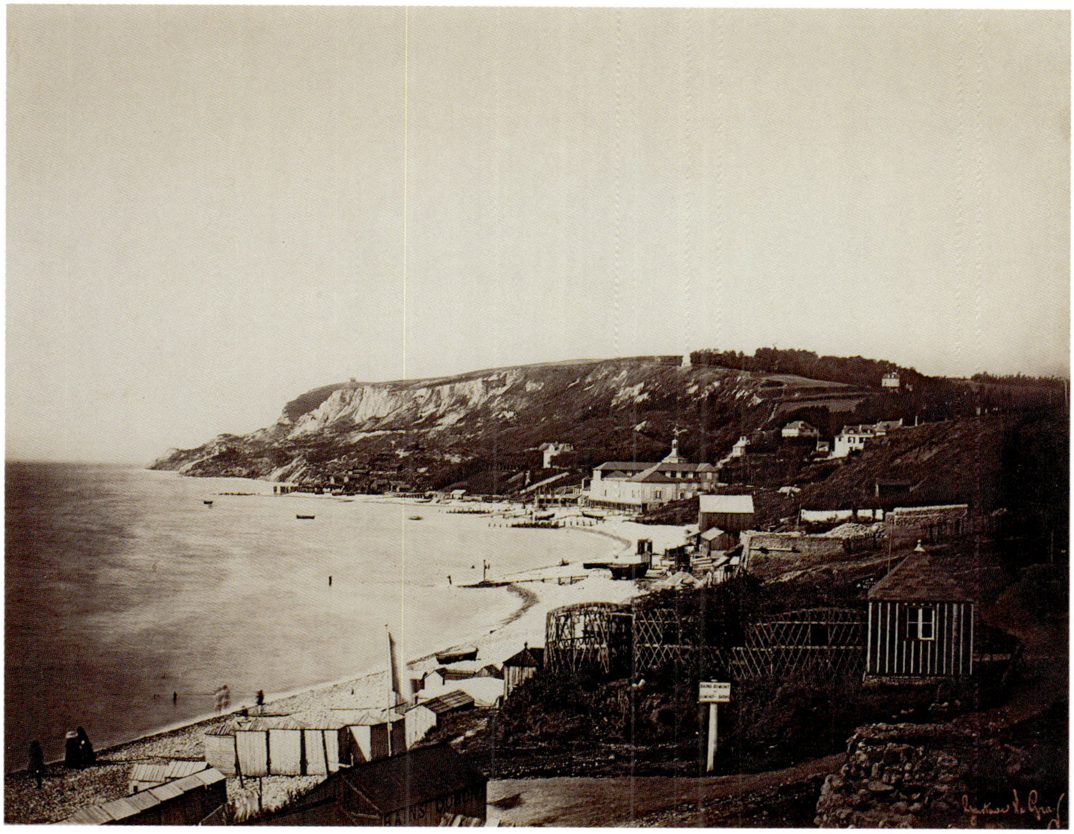

106

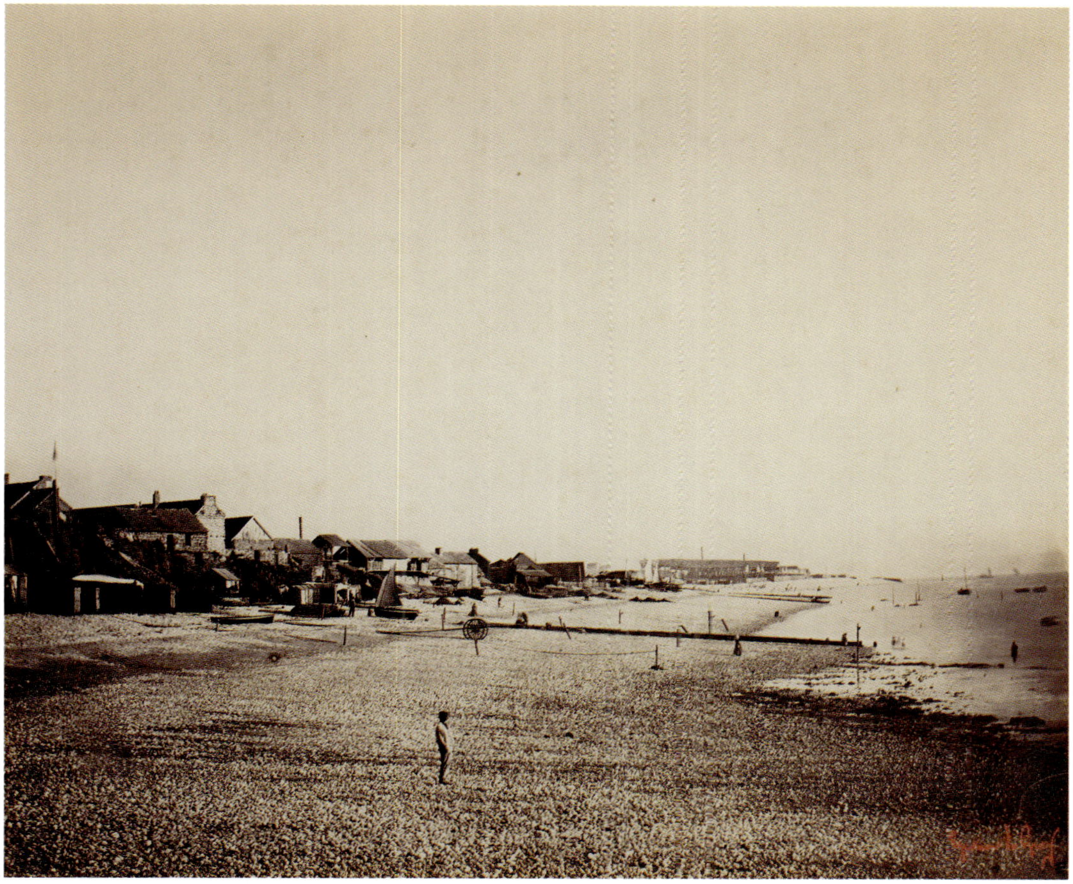

107

109

CLAUDE MONET
FRENCH, 1840–1926

Regatta at Sainte-Adresse

1867

Oil on canvas

29⅝ × 40 in. (75.2 × 101.6 cm)

The Metropolitan Museum of Art, New York, Bequest of William Church Osborn, 1951, 51.30.4

CLAUDE MONET WAS BROUGHT UP by the sea and always felt a close affinity with the varied shorelines of France. Over the course of his career, he painted the Normandy and Brittany coasts as well as the shores of the Mediterranean. In the 1860s and 1870s he focused particularly on Normandy, representing such tourist resorts as Sainte-Adresse, Étretat, and Trouville as well as Le Havre, where he grew up. Monet's earliest views emphasize local fishing communities, but, in 1867, he concentrated for the first time on an iconography of tourism during a visit to Sainte-Adresse, a suburb of Le Havre, which expanded considerably in the 1850s and 1860s.[1] The writer Eugène Chapus noted in 1855: "Sainte-Adresse, which will soon be a much frequented part of the town of Le Havre, is a pretty village; there are still present there all the seductions of solitude, silence, and oceanic contemplation, although, for several years, little houses, refreshment stands, kiosks, and pavilions multiply in its delicious valley, preparing, in some ways, by way of bricks and stones, for its coming transformation."[2] As Chapus also remarked, the attractions of Sainte-Adresse had first been discovered by the British in the early nineteenth century, before the resort had been further popularized in the writings of Alphonse Karr, especially his novel *Les soirées de Sainte-Adresse* (1853).[3] By 1866 Adolphe Joanne pointed out that "for several years, kiosks, pavilions and villas multiply there."[4] The resort's importance for British visitors is evident in Gustave Le Gray's photograph of the resort in 1856 (cat. 106), in which the signs for the baths are clearly visible in both French and English.

Regatta at Sainte-Adresse shows several yachts just off the coast, their distinctive white sails contrasting with the brown sails of a single fishing boat. Saint-Adresse was at that time particularly well known as a yachting center. The first yacht club in France—the Société des Regates du Havre—had been founded there in 1838, and it enjoyed the patronage of prominent aristocrats, including the prince de Joinville, son of Louis-Philippe, and, during the Second Empire, Jérome Bonaparte and Prince Napoléon.[5] The club regularly organized regattas—generally on the weekend—as a way of attracting visitors. These were inspired by British models, again highlighting the significance of British influence.[6]

During his 1867 visit, Monet stayed with his aunt Sophie Lecadre, who owned a villa at Sainte-Adresse. In the foreground of his painting, Monet represented his aunt and her family seated on the beach, while his father, Adolphe Monet, was the model for the man in light gray standing just behind. The artist also referenced the impact of tourism through the inclusion of a recently constructed villa on the promontory at the top left. Monet mentioned this picture in a letter to Frédéric Bazille on June 25, 1867: "I have been among my family for a fortnight . . . I have around twenty canvases well under way, some stunning marines . . . among my marines, I am doing the regattas at Le Havre with many people on the beach and the harbor covered with small sails."[7] The artist painted a pendant view during his summer visit (fig. 78), in which he showed the same viewpoint but at low rather than high tide. In the latter painting, Monet depicted a group of fishermen in the foreground, highlighting the continuing importance of the local fishing community. At the same time, he pointed to the presence of tourism through the figures of a fashionably dressed couple seated on the beach, with the man looking into the distance through a telescope.

Monet continued to paint the Normandy coast in the late 1860s, representing the resorts of Étretat in 1869 and

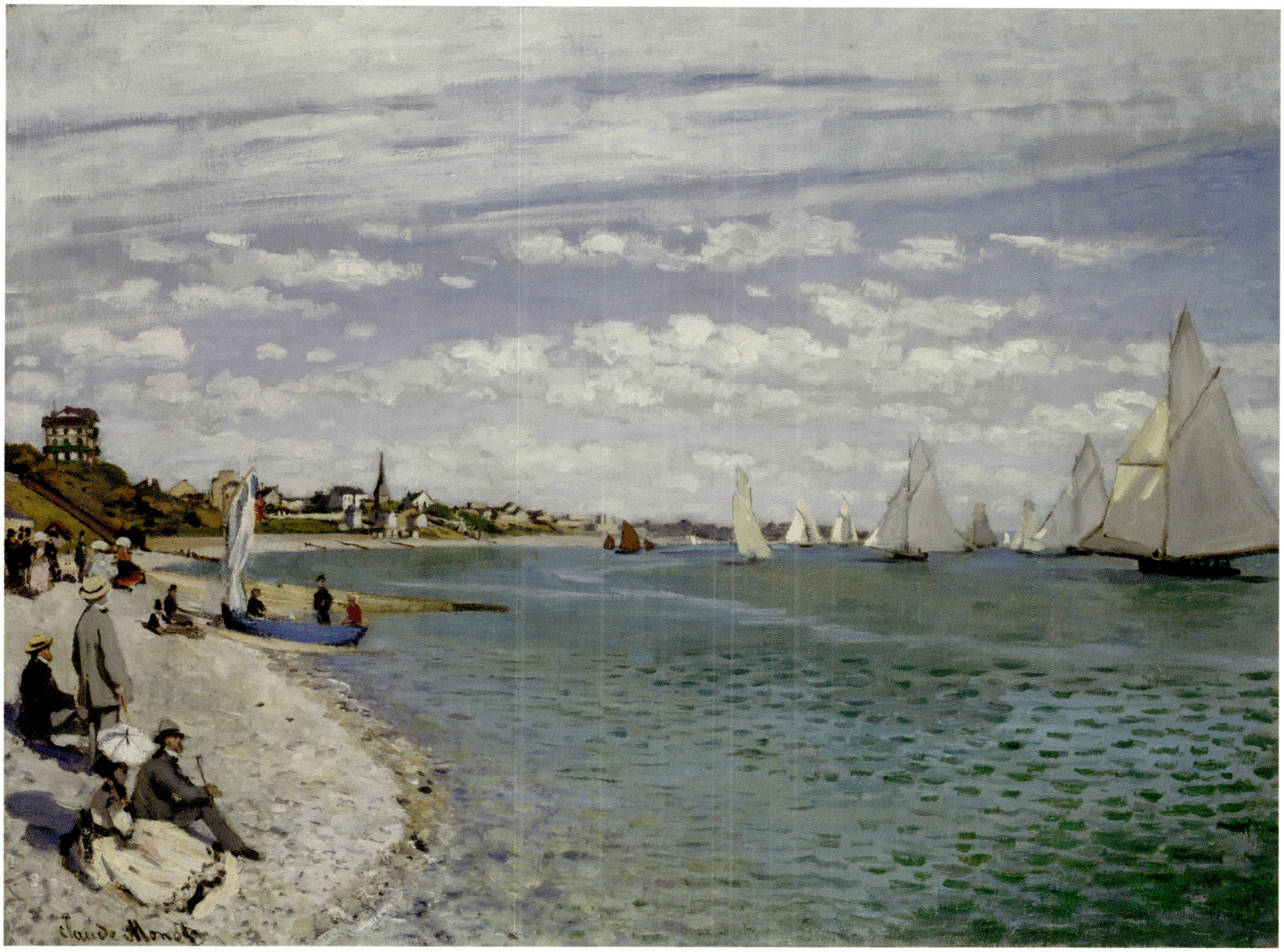

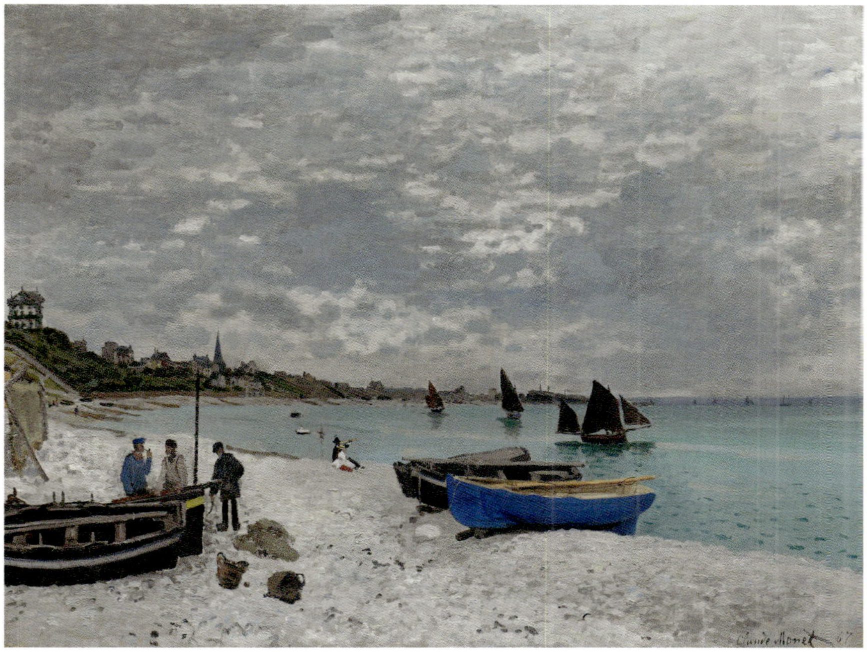

FIG. 78 Claude Monet, *The Beach at Sainte-Adresse*, 1867. Oil on canvas, 29⅞ × 40⅜ in. (75.8 × 102.5 cm). The Art Institute of Chicago, Mr. and Mrs. Lewis Larned Coburn Memorial Collection, 1933.439

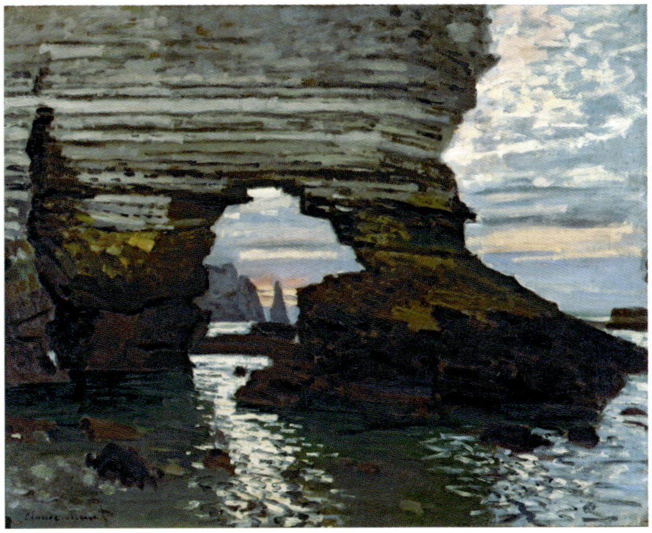

FIG. 79 Claude Monet, *The Porte d'Amont, Étretat*, ca. 1868–69. Oil on canvas, 31⅛ × 38¾ in. (79.1 × 98.4 cm). Fogg Museum, Harvard Art Museums, Cambridge, Massachusetts, Gift of Mr. and Mrs. Joseph Pulitzer, Jr., 1957.163

Trouville in 1870, depicting not only the tourists but also the picturesque motifs that attracted them to the coast. At Étretat, for example, he focused on the site's distinctive chalk cliff formations. These attracted increasing interest from geologists in the mid-nineteenth century at a time when science was looking to natural phenomena as a means of challenging the biblical narrative of the world's Creation and affirming the idea of the gradual evolution of the earth's surface over millennia. In 1869 the abbé Cochet noted that the arches and needle of Étretat—"these pyramids of chalk, these arches that the waves had formed"—were a "unique phenomenon in Europe," where "the geologist will find evidence of how many changes that this earth has seen; he will count, if he can, the innumerable deposits which have formed the beds of sand, clay and flint which today compose the ground of Étretat. . . . The cross section of our majestic cliffs, our beautiful needles, our large arches will provide him with useful observations and valuable research."[8] In painting *The Porte d'Amont, Étretat* (fig. 79), Monet meticulously delineated the rock strata of one of these cliffs and, in so doing, acknowledged ancient geologic time. Étretat's famed needle is also visible in the distance beneath the arch. In his paintings of Sainte-Adresse, however, Monet stressed this location as a modern, fashionable tourist destination. —SK

1. See Robert L. Herbert, *Monet on the Normandy Coast: Tourism and Painting, 1867–1886* (New Haven: Yale University Press, 1994), 11–14.

2. Eugène Chapus, *De Paris au Havre* (Paris: Hachette, 1855), 228–30: "Sainte-Adresse, qui ne sera plus bientôt qu'un quartier très-fréquenté de la ville du Havre, est un joli village; il y règne encore toutes les séductions de la solitude, du silence et de la contemplation océanique, quoique depuis plusieurs années les petites maisons, les vides-bouteilles, les kiosques, les pavillons se multiplient dans sa vallée délicieuse, en préparent en quelque sorte, à force de briques et pierres, l'heure de sa prochaine transformation."

3. Alphonse Karr, *Les soirées de Sainte-Adresse* (Paris: Michel Lévy Frères, 1853).

4. Adolphe Joanne, *Dictionnaire géographique, administratif et postal de la France* (Paris: Hachette, 1869), 2:1021: "Depuis plusieurs années, les kiosques, les pavillons, les villas s'y multiplient."

5. For the history of regattas at Sainte-Adresse, see www.lesregates.com.

6. As Herbert notes, *Monet on the Normandy Coast*, 137, in 1848 there were already sixty-six thousand British residents in France, particularly in the North (and especially Le Havre), while Anglican church services were available in twenty-five French towns.

7. Monet to Bazille, June 25, 1867, in Daniel Wildenstein, *Claude Monet: Biographie et catalogue raisonné*, vol. 1, *1840–1881* (Paris and Lausanne: La Bibliothèque des Arts, 1974), 423–24: "Je suis au sein de la famille depuis quinze jours . . . j'ai une vingtaine de toiles en bon train, des marines étourdissantes . . . parmi mes marines, je fais les régates du Havre avec beaucoup de personnages sur la plage et la rade couverte de petites voiles."

8. Abbé Cochet, *Étretat: Son passé, son present, son avenir* (Dieppe: Imprimerie d'Émile Delvoye, 1869), 11: "géologue, il dira combien de revolutions cette terre a été le théâtre; il comptera, s'il le peut, les innombrables alluvions qui ont formé les lits de sable, d'argile et de silex qui composent aujourd'hui le sol d'Étretat. . . . La coupe de nos majestueuses falaises, de nos belles aiguilles, de nos grandes arches lui fournira d'utiles observations et de savantes recherches. . . . ces pyramides de craie, ces arches que les flots ont formées, phénomène unique en Europe, si l'île de Wight n'existait pas." The French geologist who showed the greatest interest in the Étretat cliffs was Antoine Passy. His *Description géologique du département de la Seine Inférieure* (Rouen: Nicétas Periaux, 1832) includes three prints of the cliffs (pls. V, VI, VII). The English geologist Charles Lyell also referenced the needle and arch at Étretat as a comparison with chalk needles on the Isle of Wight in England and an example of regular geological processes over time. See *A Manual of Elementary Geology* (New York: D. Appleton & Company, 1853), 241.

110

LOUIS-ALPHONSE DAVANNE

FRENCH, 1824–1912

Ships in Harbor at Le Tréport in Normandy

1870

Albumen print from collodion glass negative

9⅜ × 12⁵⁄₁₆ in. (23.8 × 31.3 cm)

The Nelson-Atkins Museum of Art, Kansas City, Missouri, Gift of the Hall Family Foundation, 2006.44.6

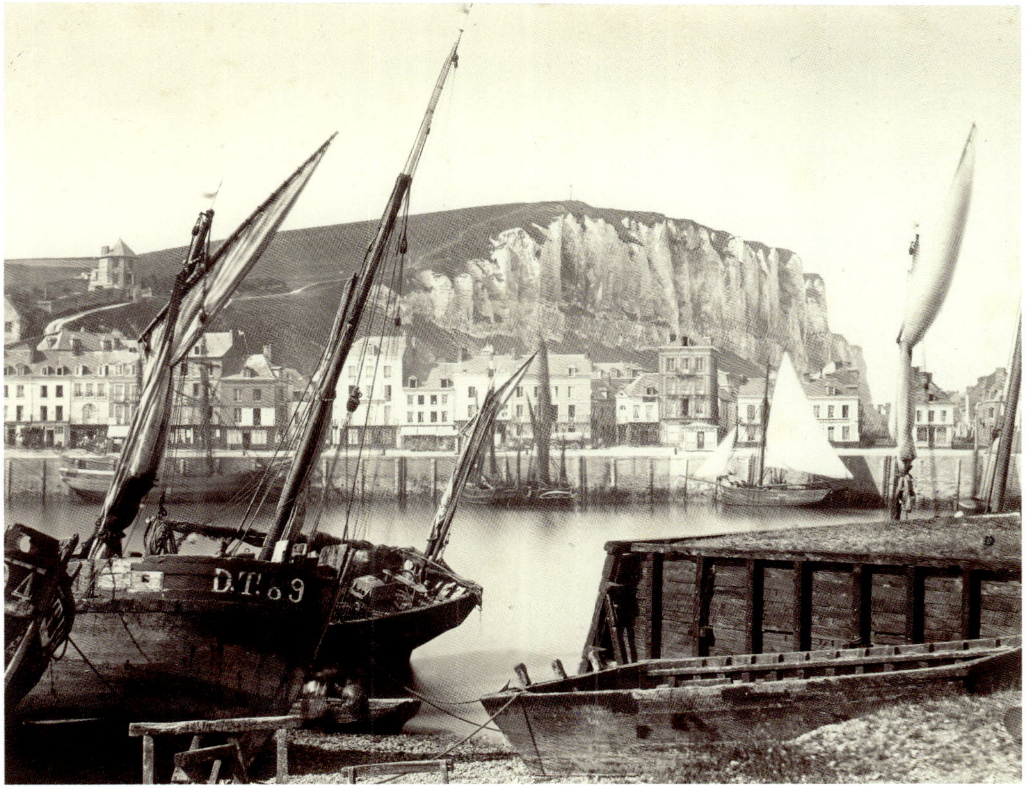

THE SON OF A WEALTHY BOURGEOIS FAMILY, Louis-Alphonse Davanne was one of several amateurs who pursued photography without having to make a living from print sales. Educated as a chemist, Davanne put this scientific knowledge to use in his extensive research on improving the tonal consistency and permanence of photographic negatives and prints. Introduced to photography by the optician Noël-Marie-Paymal Lerebours, he was a founding member of the Sociéte française de la photographie and stayed actively involved in the group throughout his life, becoming vice president in 1867 and serving as president from 1876 to 1901. In the course of his research, he collaborated with Lerebours, the chemist Charles-Louis Barreswill, and the lithographic printer Joseph Lemercier to develop a system called *lithophotographie*, which produced more uniform, stable prints than those that relied exclusively on silver-based materials, which were light sensitive.

Davanne produced a number of prints during his vacations to various parts of France and abroad, including a series made on the Normandy coast during the 1860s. Unlike Le Gray's marine views, which are characterized by dramatic light effects, ships at sea, and the meeting of ocean and sky, Davanne's photographs of the Normandy coast tend toward the picturesque. In this image, he composed his scene to feature the distinctive white limestone cliffs of Étretat in the background and a dynamic array of small, moored fishing boats in the foreground. —AMW

111

EUGÈNE BOUDIN
FRENCH, 1824–1898

The Beach at Trouville

1869

Oil on panel

8⅞ × 14⅜ in. (22.5 × 36.5 cm)

Saint Louis Art Museum, Museum Purchase, 5:1934

THE MARINE PAINTER EUGÈNE BOUDIN explored the varied coastlines of France, representing the Southwest but concentrating on Brittany (see fig. 48) and, above all, the Normandy coast. His devotion to his homeland is evident in a letter written during a visit to Antwerp in 1871. He noted: "People make a great fuss about these towns in the Low Countries; I find them interesting, undoubtedly, but I'm not mad about them and the beautiful views in our France, not to mention Brittany, mean just as much and even more to me."[1] In the 1860s Boudin emerged as the most diligent chronicler of the new tourist classes who traveled to the Normandy coast. He focused particularly on the resort of Trouville, which had been popularized by the visits of Empress Eugénie and Emperor Napoléon in 1863. Adolphe Joanne remarked that Trouville, after being little known at the start of the century, was now "à la mode," welcoming more than twenty thousand visitors every summer, many of whom came on the train from Paris. The guide continued: "it's Paris transported during two or three months to the side of the Ocean with its qualities, its ridiculous ways and its vices."[2] From 1864 until 1867 Boudin regularly exhibited views of Trouville at the Paris Salon.

The Beach at Trouville shows groups of elegant women dressed in gowns of various hues of red, yellow, green, and pink. A few men can also be seen: one is next to his companion at the center, one is seated to the far left, and another is slightly apart from the leftmost group of women. A bathing cabin is visible at far right at the edge of the ocean, as are several swimmers. Boudin's feelings about the leisured classes that he represented were ambivalent. In 1867, shortly after visiting a pardon in Brittany, he contrasted the rustic honesty of Breton peasants with the "idle laziness" of Trouville vacationers, describing the beach, with the emphasis there on fashionable appearance, as a "ghastly masquerade."[3] A year later, his attitude was more favorable: "don't the bourgeois, who stroll on the jetty toward the sunset, have the right to be fixed on canvas, to be brought to the light? Between ourselves, they are often resting from hard toil, these men who emerge from their offices and their studies."[4] Boudin's pictures provided a model for his young friend Claude Monet, who painted a series of views of Trouville in 1870. —SK

1. Boudin to Ferdinand Martin, July 1871, in G. Jean-Aubry, *Eugène Boudin d'après des documents inédits* (Paris: Les Éditions Bernheim-Jeune, 1922), 79: "On fait grand bruit de ces villes des Pays-Bas; je trouve cela intéressant, sans doute, mais je n'en suis pas fou et les beaux horizons de notre France, sans parler du pays Breton, m'en dissent tout autant et même plus."

2. Adolphe Joanne, *Itinéraire général de la France: Normandie* (Paris: Hachette, 1866), 391: "c'est Paris transporté pendant deux ou trois mois aux bords de l'Océan avec ses qualities, ses ridicules et ses vices."

3. Boudin to Ferdinand Martin, August 25, 1867, in Aubry, *Boudin*, 65: "une affreuse mascarade . . . la paresse désoeuvrée."

4. Boudin to Ferdinand Martin, September 3, 1868, in ibid., 70: "ces bourgeois qui se promènent sur la jetée vers le coucher du soleil, n'ont-ils aucun droit d'être fixés sur la toile, d'être amenés à la lumière. Entre nous, ils se reposent souvent d'un rude labeur, ces gens qui sortent de leurs bureaux et de leurs cabinets."

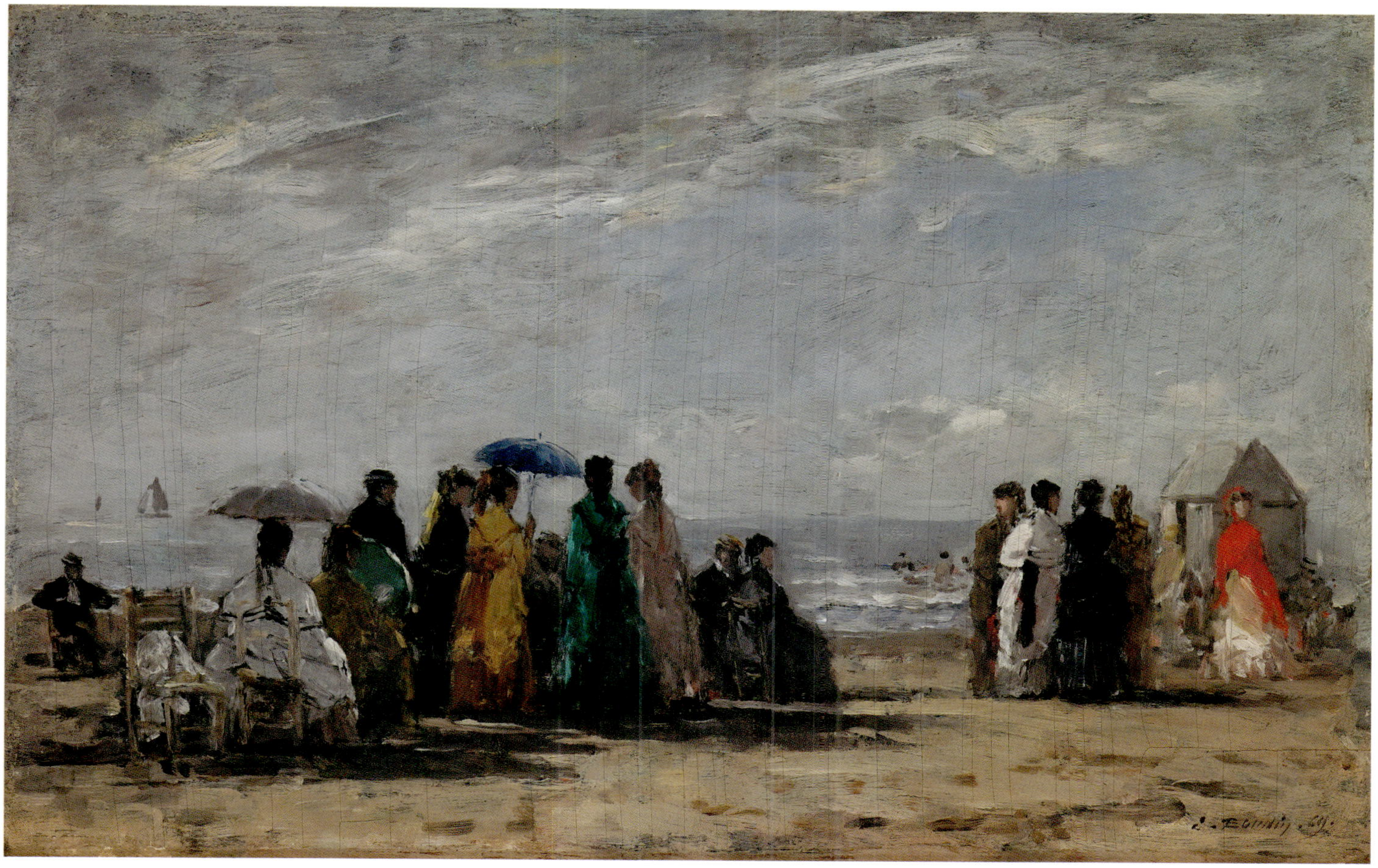

JEAN-BAPTISTE-CAMILLE COROT

FRENCH, 1796–1875

112

The Beach, Étretat

1872

Oil on canvas

14 × 22³⁄₁₆ in. (35.6 × 56.4 cm)

Saint Louis Art Museum: Museum purchase, 63:1932

DURING HIS LONG CAREER, Jean-Baptiste-Camille Corot represented many sites along the coastline of France, such as the ports of La Rochelle in the West and Dunkirk and Boulogne in the North. He first painted on the Normandy coast in 1820s and returned there intermittently.[1] In the summer and fall of 1872, he made an extensive six-month tour around the country, which included a two-week stay at the port of Étretat, from September 8 to 21, during which time he stayed with his patrons the Stumpf family. On this trip, he produced at least seven oil sketches, *The Beach, Étretat* among them.[2] Despite his many travels in Normandy, this was probably his first time at Étretat, and he may have been encouraged to visit not only by the invitation of his patrons but also by the recent Étretat views by Gustave Courbet, including *The Étretat Cliffs after the Storm* (Musée d'Orsay, Paris), which was shown at the 1870 Salon.[3]

The Beach, Étretat represents a line of three fishing boats on the beach with their masts lowered.[4] Étretat was a fishing village whose considerable prosperity in the mid-nineteenth century was based on the fishing of herring, mackerel, and whiting in the English Channel. Étretat lacked a natural harbor or a pier, meaning that fishing boats had to be hauled up the steep shingle beach.[5] The object in the right foreground is a wooden winch used to pull up boats, a task that habitually fell to the women of the village. These winches are clearly visible in a panoramic photograph of the beach by Louis-Alphonse Davanne from 1864 (fig. 80). In Corot's painting, a handful of figures—presumably fishermen, some repairing nets and boats—are next to the boat farthest in the distance. Two small figures in the foreground walk along the shingle, moving away from the viewer. The unusual cropping of the winch may reflect the artist's interest in photography.[6]

In the distance, Corot shows the white chalk cliff of the Porte d'Amont, its arch just visible beneath the mast of the right-hand boat. The tiny chapel of Notre-Dame-de-la-Garde, built as recently as 1856 in a thirteenth-century style and dedicated to the protection of sailors, is visible at top right on the crest of the promontory. Étretat attracted increasing numbers of tourists in the mid-nineteenth century, principally on account of its highly distinctive chalk cliffs, not only the Porte d'Amont but also the more dramatic Porte d'Aval with its needle to the west. Guidebooks detailed the history and folklore of these sites, and a casino opened in 1852, encouraged by the building of a road from Le Havre that very year.[7]

Corot's six-month trip around France, which must have been tiring for a man of seventy-six who was suffering from gout, has been read convincingly as referencing the artist's nationalistic sentiment as part of a "healing process" in the wake of the trauma of the Franco-Prussian War.[8] Corot had stayed in Paris in 1870–71, when the Prussians invaded. He had even painted a nightmarish vision of the city in flames, *The Dream* (Musée Carnavalet, Paris), in September 1870. His view of Étretat is one of a series in which he rediscovered the energy and vitality of traditional French ways of life, including the long fishing tradition of Étretat. —SK

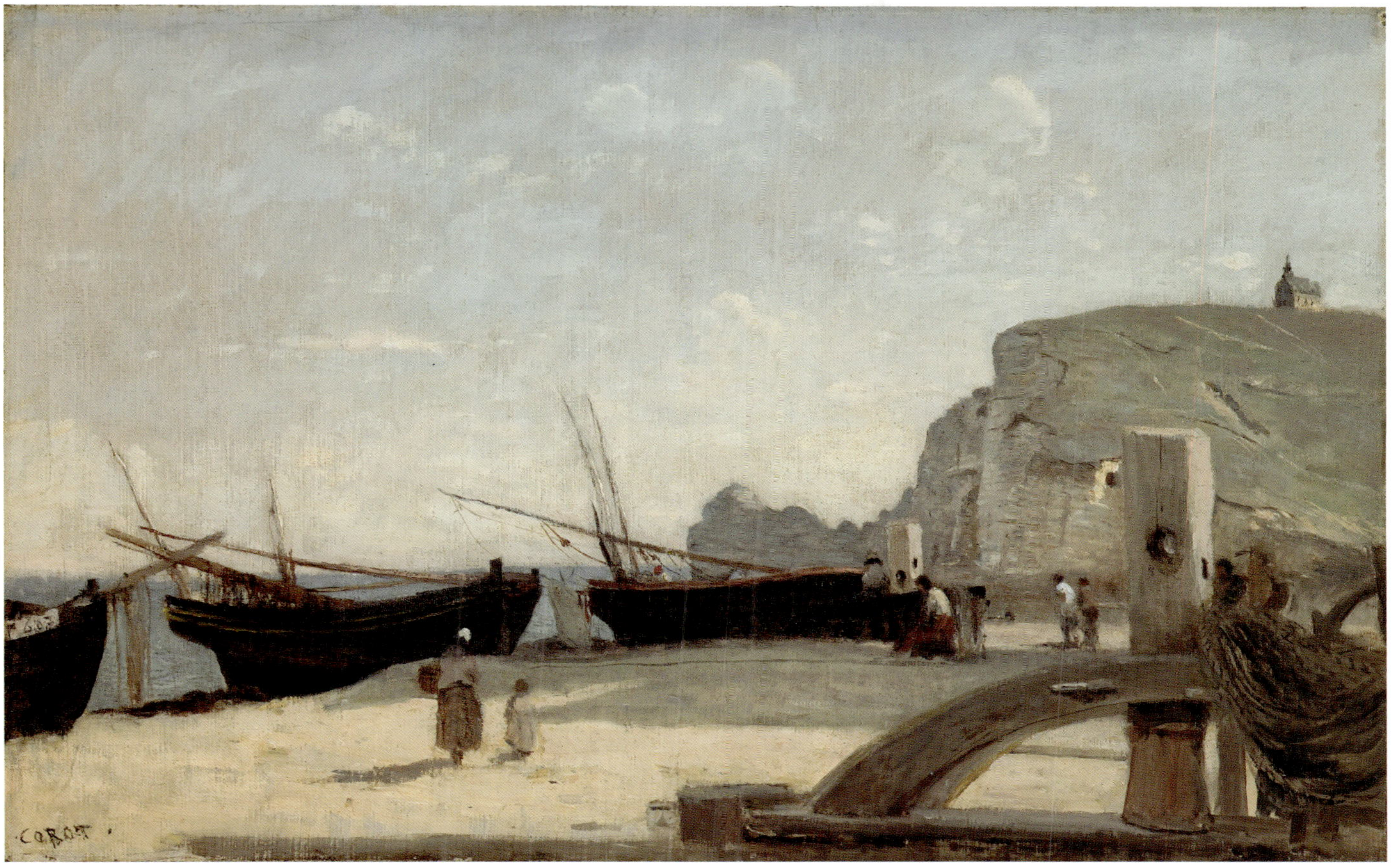

1. Corot visited Normandy in 1846, 1851, 1853, 1855, 1856, 1858, 1863, and 1865.

2. See Alfred Robaut, *L'oeuvre de Corot: Catalogue raisonné et illustré* (Paris: H. Floury, 1905), nos. 2054, 2055, 2056, 2057, 2059, 2060, 2073. See also *A Windmill at Étretat* (Musée du Louvre, Paris), *Beach near Étretat* (National Gallery of Art, Washington, D.C.), and Bruno Delarue, *Les peintres à Étretat, 1786–1940* (Yport: Madoluce, 2005), 102–7.

3. It is possible that Corot visited Étretat in 1865, but this remains unclear.

4. Corot's composition is also based on a pencil sketch of the site in the Musée du Louvre, Département des Arts graphiques, reproduced in Delarue, *Les peintres à Étretat*, 104–5.

5. See David Hopkin, "Fishermen, Tourists and Artists in the Nineteenth Century: The View from the Beach," in *Impressionists by the Sea*, ed. John House, exh. cat. (London: Royal Academy of Arts, 2007), 30–37. See also Frances Fowle, "The Lure of Étretat," in *The Draw of the Normandy Coast, 1860–1960*, ed. Margaret Burgess, exh. cat. (Portland, Maine: Portland Museum of Art, 2012), 40–63.

6. Three hundred photographs were found in his studio at his death.

7. Eugène Chapus, *De Paris au Havre* (Paris: Hachette, 1855), includes a detailed description of Étretat as well as a line engraving of the Porte d'Aval and its needle. For accounts of the history and folklore around Étretat, see particularly Abbé Cochet, *Étretat, son passé, son présent, son avenir* (Dieppe: Émile Delevoye, 1869), 145–46.

8. Richard R. Brettell and Stephen F. Eisenman, *Nineteenth-Century Art in the Norton Simon Museum* (New Haven: Yale University Press for the Norton Simon Art Foundation, 2006), 1:112–14.

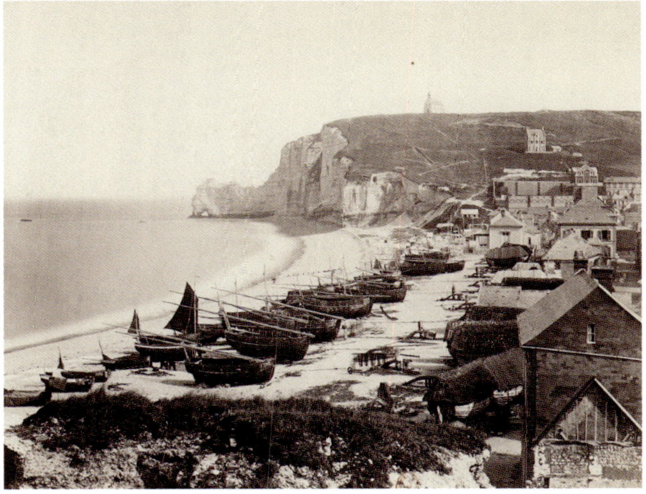

FIG. 80 Louis-Alphonse Davanne, *No. 1. Étretat, the Chapel*, 1864. Albumen print, 8½ × 11¼ in. (21.7 × 28.5 cm). Department of Prints and Photographs, Bibliothèque nationale de France, Paris

113

ÉDOUARD MANET
FRENCH, 1832–1883

The Steamboat, Seascape with Porpoises

1868

Oil on canvas

32$\frac{1}{16}$ × 39½ in. (81.4 × 100.3 cm)

Philadelphia Museum of Art, Bequest of Anne Thomson in memory of her father, Frank Thomson, and her mother, Mary Elizabeth Clarke Thomson, 1954, 1954-66-3

OVER THE COURSE OF HIS CAREER, Édouard Manet painted the coasts of France on a number of occasions, producing about forty seascapes within a total oeuvre of approximately four hundred works.[1] More of Manet's seascapes are connected with the northern port of Boulogne than any other place.[2] Boulogne was a site of major importance to the French economy. As Adolphe Joanne noted in 1869, "it's the third port in France [after Le Havre and Marseille] in terms of the importance of its transactions and, after Calais, the most frequently chosen by travelers going from France to England and England to France."[3] Boulogne's trade and tourism had expanded considerably following the opening of the rail line from Paris in 1848, a link documented in the photographs of Édouard Baldus (cat. 75). Many travelers also used the popular Folkestone–Boulogne route to go between England and France.[4] Manet is known to have visited Boulogne on at least two occasions, in 1864 and 1868. These two works date from the latter trip, made with his wife, Suzanne, and son, Léon Leenhoff, which lasted about two months, from July to September.[5]

The Steamboat, Seascape with Porpoises shows a brig, a commercial transport ship, flying the French flag. A sailor wearing a yellow hat is visible at the stern, observing porpoises at play in the water below. Farther in the distance is a steamboat—possibly an English Channel packet steamer going between Folkestone and Boulogne—puffing out a dense cloud of steam and leaving a dark trail in the water.[6] Smaller fishing boats can be seen to right and left. Manet's painting reflects his careful study of the structure of ships themselves—particularly evident in the rigging of the boat to the left; this interest can be traced to his youth, when he sailed from Le Havre to Rio de Janeiro and back in 1848–49. This experience at sea gave Manet a deep understanding of ships and their workings. The porpoises—rarely, if ever, seen in the channel—add a fictive element to the painting and are probably a memory of the artist's early travels as a teenager. On his trip to South America, he had recorded seeing porpoises: "They are huge creatures, schools of 10 or 12 swim around the ship, especially the bows; they swim like lightning and are a very difficult target."[7]

The second painting by Manet, *On the Beach at Boulogne*, is a strange, almost surreal work with many figures arranged in a deliberately naive and detached fashion. Manet's picture explores the new tourist culture that developed at Boulogne in the mid-nineteenth century, especially following the 1863 opening of an impressive new bathing establishment, covering sixteen thousand square feet. Manet's picture depicts members of the beach club at Boulogne, who had special access to particular parts of the beach, as well as this new bathhouse. The artist himself had taken out a subscription to it on his first visit to Boulogne in 1864 and probably did the same in 1868.[8] Within a composition organized into three distinct bands of sand, sea, and sky, Manet represented several fashionably dressed groups, including a woman in pink with two children, a young girl with a pink parasol in the center, and a man in gray with a parasol to the right, the tails of his jacket caught by a gust of wind. The cropped form of a donkey, available for hire to transport visitors along the beach, is also visible. Closer to the sea, a woman appears to be looking into the distance through binoculars, while near her is a ginger-haired boy wearing a cassock, perhaps a priest in training. To the back left is a horse-drawn bathing machine, essentially a wooden cabin on wheels. These had been invented in Boulogne in order to transport swimmers in their bathing costumes into the water in privacy.

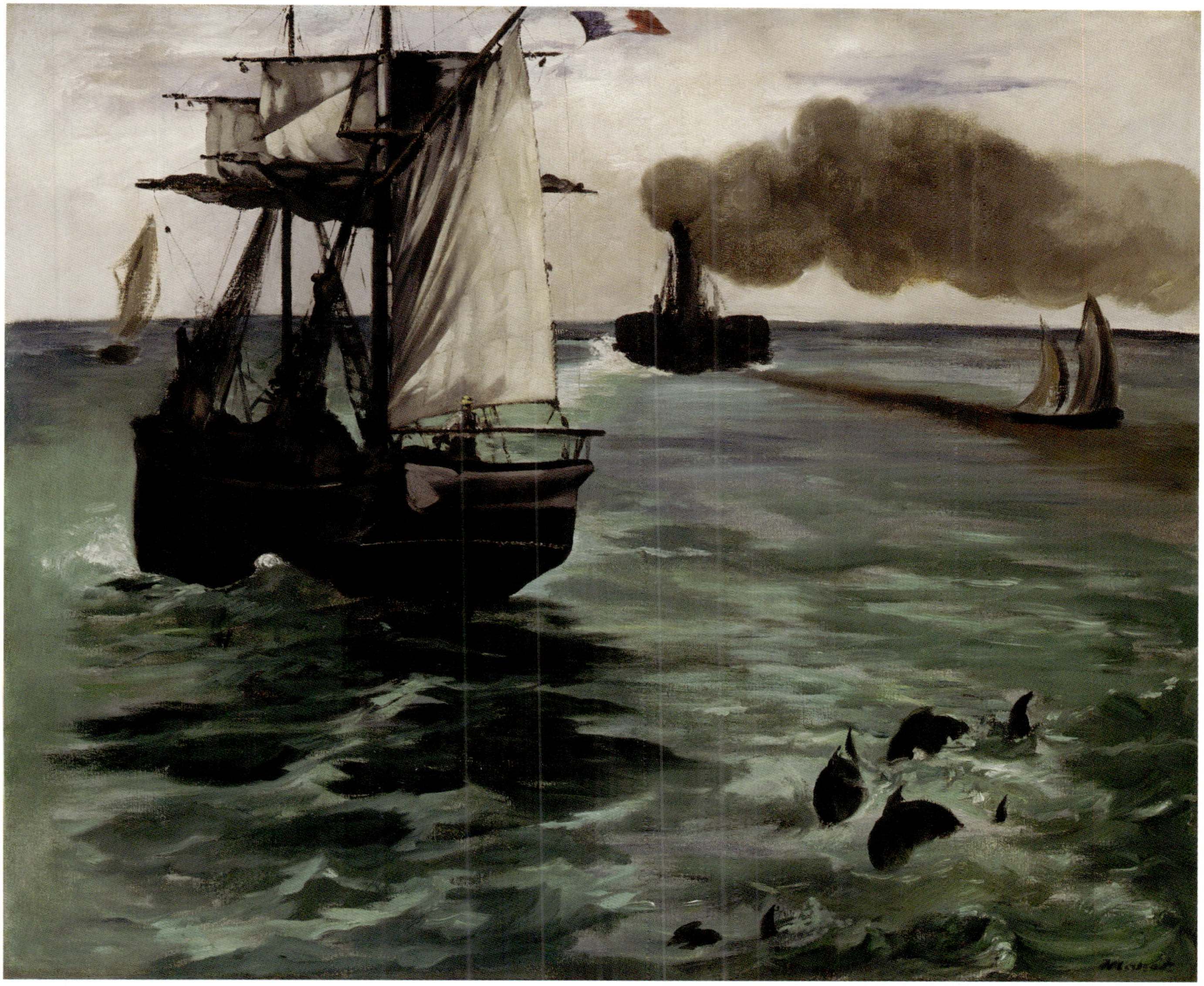

Manet's seemingly random arrangement of figures in *On the Beach at Boulogne* was in fact based on careful study. The artist produced at least eighteen pencil sketches of individuals and groups—probably made *en plein air*—which he then assembled in his final painting in the studio.[9] He also made extensive changes to his composition.[10]

In addition to the new tourist culture, Manet's work references the range of maritime trade at Boulogne, showing a variety of vessels in the distance, including, from left to right, a two-masted pilot boat, a steamer belching smoke on the horizon, a commercial clipper, and a brown-sailed fishing boat. These two paintings by Manet thus highlight the national and international importance of Boulogne as both a trading and a tourist destination.[11] —SK

114

ÉDOUARD MANET
FRENCH, 1832–1883

On the Beach at Boulogne

1868

Oil on canvas

12¾ × 26 in. (32.4 × 66 cm)

Virginia Museum of Fine Arts, Richmond,
Collection of Mr. and Mrs. Paul Mellon, 85.498

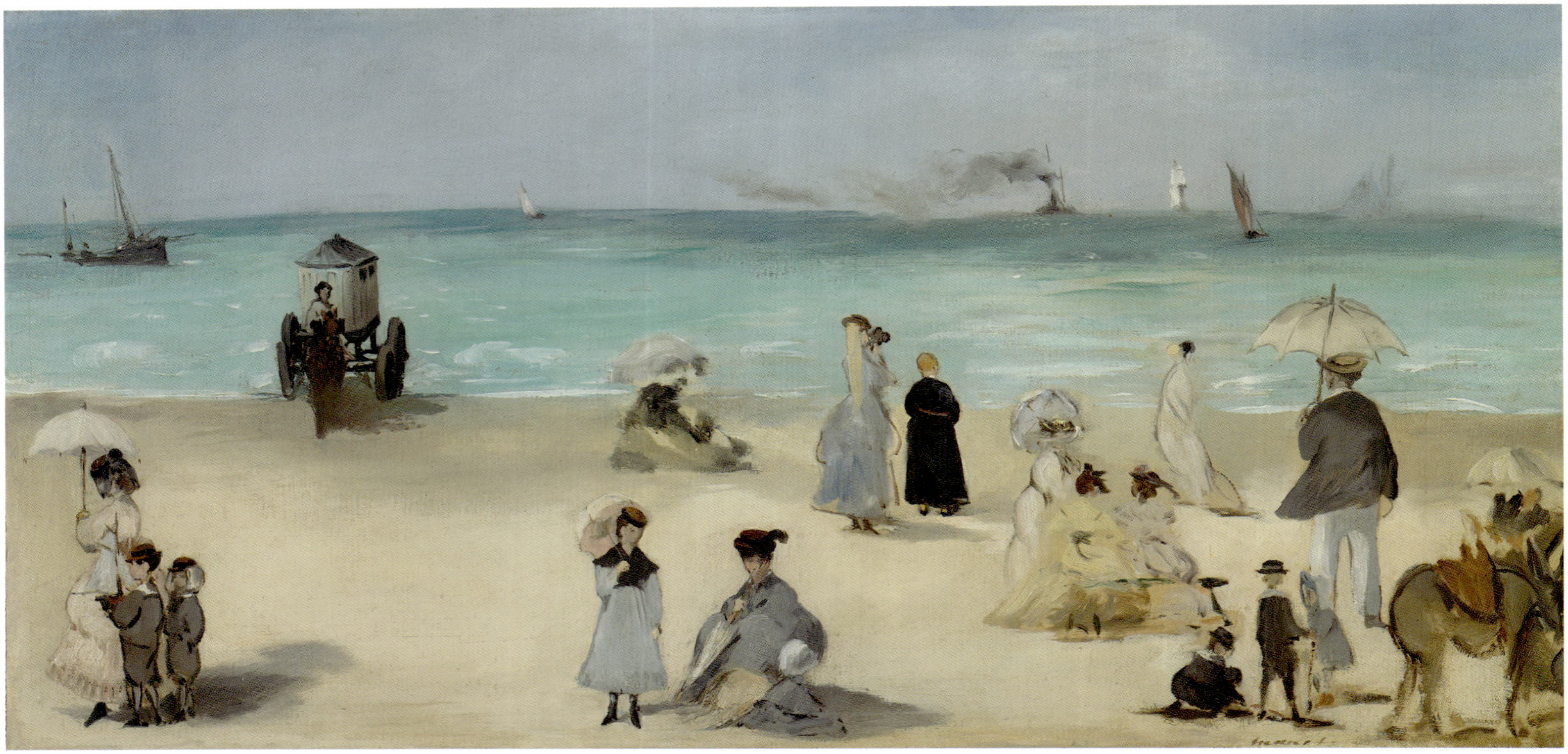

1. Manet also painted at Arcachon in the Southwest in 1871 and Berck on the north coast of France in 1873.

2. For the most detailed study of Manet's time at Boulogne, see Juliet Wilson-Bareau and David Degener, "Manet and the Sea," in *Manet and the Sea*, ed. Juliet Wilson-Bareau and David Degener, exh. cat. (Philadelphia: Philadelphia Museum of Art, 2003), 55–101.

3. Adolphe Joanne, *Dictionnaire géographique, administratif et postal de la France* (Paris: Hachette, 1869), 1:324: "C'est le 3e port de la France pour l'importance de ses transactions et, après Calais, le plus fréquemment choisi par les voyageurs allant de France en Angleterre ou d'Angleterre en France."

4. By 1866 one-tenth of the population of Boulogne was of English origin. Adolphe Joanne, *De Paris à Boulogne* (Paris: Hachette, 1866), 224.

5. Manet rented an apartment in Boulogne on rue Napoléon from July 15 to August 17, and at 156, rue de Boston from August 18 onward.

6. See Wilson-Bareau and Degener, *Manet and the Sea*, 108, for a watercolor study of the steamboat. This double-page study comes from a Boulogne 1868 (Whatman) sketchbook (private collection, London).

7. Manet to his mother, December 28, 1848; translated and quoted in Juliet Wilson-Bareau, ed., *Manet by Himself* (London: Macmillan, 1991), 20.

8. The beach club records for 1864 indicate Manet's one-month subscription, but the records for 1868 have been lost. See Wilson-Bareau and Degener, *Manet and the Sea*, 63.

9. See a second Boulogne 1868 (Whatman) sketchbook, Musée d'Orsay, held at Musée du Louvre, Département des Arts graphiques, RF 11.169.

10. These changes are evident in an X-radiograph.

11. *On the Beach at Boulogne* remained in Manet's studio until his death and was in his studio sale. *The Steamboat* was sold in 1880 to a person named Weiz for the substantial sum of five thousand francs.

115

ÉDOUARD BALDUS

FRENCH, 1813–1889

Marseille

ca. 1861

Albumen print from collodion glass negative

10 1/16 × 17 1/4 in. (25.6 × 43.8 cm)

The Nelson-Atkins Museum of Art, Kansas City, Missouri, Gift of the Hall Family Foundation, 2008.41.4

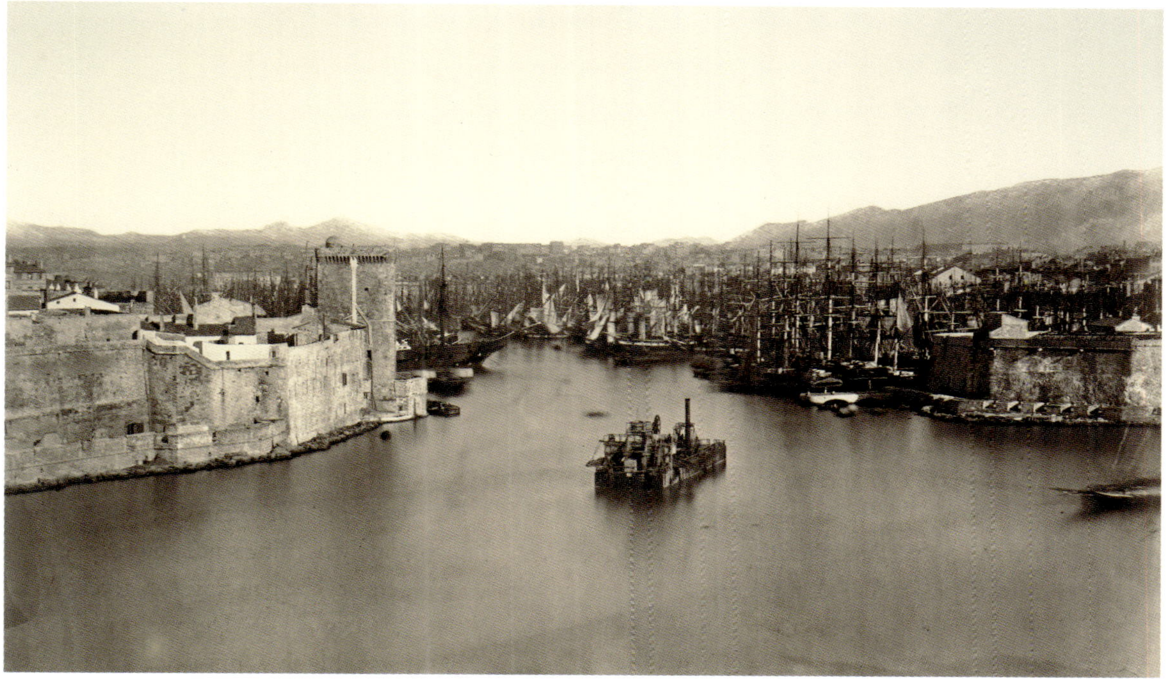

MARSEILLE, FRANCE'S OLDEST PORT CITY, was founded by Greek mariners in 600 BC, who established the site as a trading post. In the first century BC, it was conquered by Julius Caesar and became a part of France in the 1480s. During the Revolution, hundreds of enthusiastic volunteers from the city headed north to Paris, singing an anthem known as the "War Song of the Army of the Rhine," which had recently been composed by a captain of engineers stationed in Strasbourg. The song soon became known as "La Marseillaise" and was voted the country's national anthem on July 14, 1792. The song was banned during the Napoleonic era and during the Second Empire as well but reinstated in 1879.

By the mid-nineteenth century, Marseille had become an important industrial port, particularly after France colonized Algeria in 1830, thus increasing trade with North Africa. Commercial activity accelerated even further after 1869, with the opening of the Suez Canal. Napoléon III recognized the strategic and economic significance of Marseille, and, at his directive, the city underwent rapid and radical transformations during the 1850s, much like those of Paris (see cats. 22, 23). Édouard Baldus's photographs depict the city's old port as a thriving industrial hub. This photograph was included in the album *Chemin de fer de Paris à Lyon et à la Méditerranée* in a sequence of seven photographs of Marseille (cat. 76, pl. 57). It depicts the old port, dense with dozens of ships that appear as a thicket of masts. This view, and its inclusion in the album, conveys the city's commercial and industrial significance, as well as the rail line's importance in connecting the Mediterranean port with the Parisian capital. —AMW

116

BERTHE MORISOT

FRENCH, 1841–1895

The Harbor at Lorient

1869

Oil on canvas

17⅛ × 28¾ in. (43.5 × 73 cm)

National Gallery of Art, Washington D.C., Ailsa Mellon Bruce Collection, 1970.17.48

BERTHE MORISOT WAS A CENTRAL FIGURE within the Impressionist group, exhibiting at seven of their eight group shows. Her work in the 1870s sold for higher prices than that of other Impressionists such as Claude Monet, Pierre-Auguste Renoir, and Alfred Sisley.[1] Much writing on Morisot has focused on the extent to which her subject matter was circumscribed by her femininity, affecting her ability to travel easily around Paris as a flaneur and accounting for her concentration on scenes of domestic life. Yet, Morisot's work—particularly early in her career—explored themes of industry and commercial trade. She also produced several marines, in which she represented a range of modern boats and shipyards.[2] Morisot explored the coast of Brittany in the 1860s and focused on the Normandy coast and the Isle of Wight, in the English Channel, in the 1870s.

The Harbor at Lorient depicts Berthe's older sister, Edma, sitting on the harbor wall in the important port of Lorient in southern Brittany. Lorient had been a key base for French colonialism since the mid-seventeenth century, when it was established by the Compagnie des Indes, the equivalent of the Dutch and English East India Companies.[3] The town was in fact named L'Orient in reference to the eastern countries with which it traded. The loss of colonies in the East led to the decline of Lorient as a trading base and the end of the Compagnie des Indes in 1794. In the nineteenth century, Lorient's prosperity depended above all on its role as a military arsenal, with prominent shipyards constructing military vessels and particularly iron frigates in the 1860s and 1870s. Adolphe Joanne noted in 1869, "Lorient holds the leading position in France in terms of naval construction."[4]

Morisot painted *The Harbor at Lorient* during the summer of 1869 when she visited Edma, who had recently married Adolphe Pontillon, a naval officer stationed in Lorient. The artist paid careful attention to her sister's fringed dress, touched with purple, and her parasol. She also carefully represented the surrounding harbor. To the left is the Tour de la Découverte (a signaling tower built in 1737), visible above a group of houses on the quai des Indes. Several boats line the quays, including a large three-masted ship to the right on the quai de Rohan; a single boat is sailing into the harbor.

Morisot's work was painted after a period of self-doubt. On May 11, 1869, she wrote to her sister, "I am absolutely counting on my visit to Lorient to do something passable. I have done absolutely nothing since your departure and I'm beginning to despair. My painting has never felt as bad to me as in the past few days."[5] Despite her misgivings, *The Harbor at Lorient* is highly sophisticated in its palette. The delicate, pearly tones suggest Morisot's continuing interest in the blond *peinture claire* of Jean-Baptiste-Camille Corot. The black of Edma's hat is echoed in the hulls of the boats, and the white of her dress, in the houses and tower to the left. Morisot's picture is also a testament to her closeness to her sister, her favored model in the late 1860s and early 1870s. The two women had studied with Corot and his pupil Achille Oudinot, and both showed work at the Paris Salon from 1864 until 1868. Edma, however, gave up painting after her marriage. Separation was difficult for the two sisters, following Edma's move to Lorient. Shortly after her arrival in Brittany, Edma wrote: "I am often with you in my thoughts, my dear Berthe. I follow you everywhere in your studio and wish that I could escape, if only for a quarter of an hour, to breathe again that air in which we lived."[6] Berthe replied, "You have not chosen the worst option . . . remember it is sad to be alone."[7]

Morisot received high accolades for *The Harbor at Lorient* on her return to Paris. Her mother wrote to Edma,"I think the two paintings she [Berthe] has brought back are pretty; they look very well in the studio."[8] Pierre

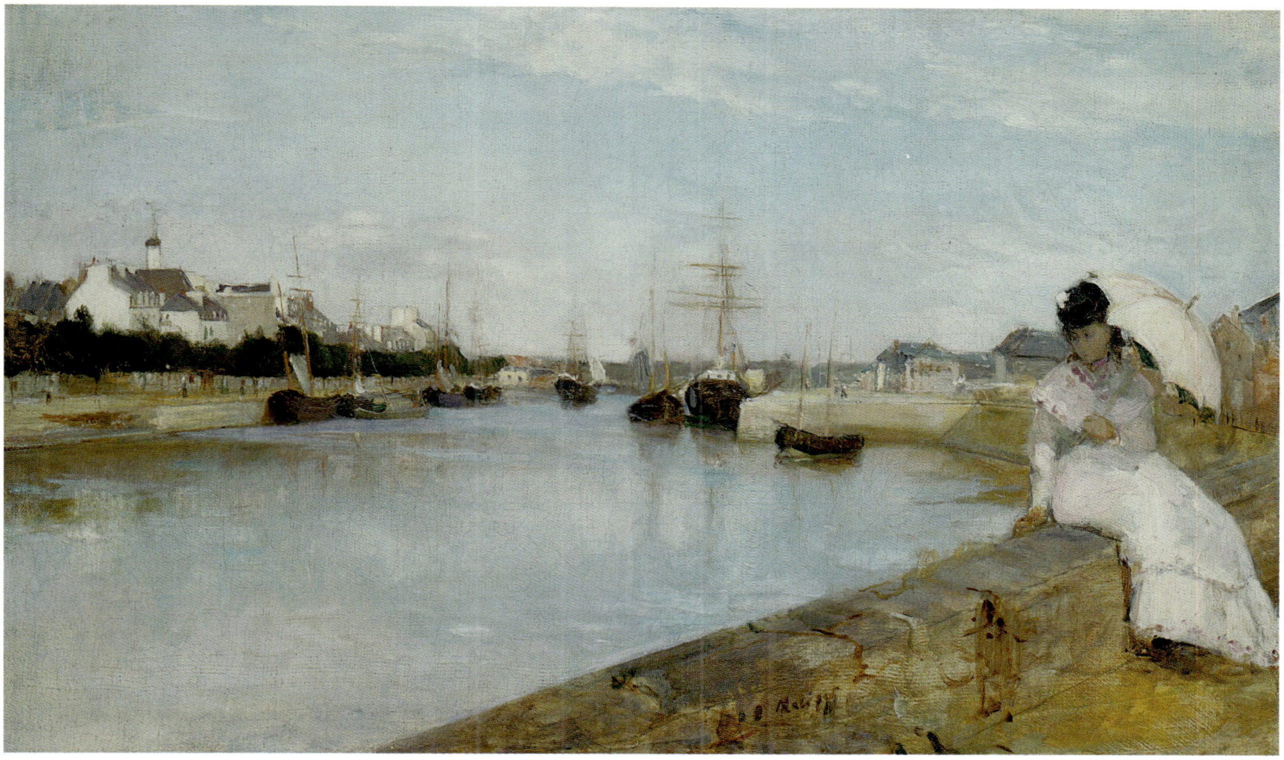

Puvis de Chavannes, who had recently completed his own seascape of Marseille (cat. 119), praised the work when he saw it in Morisot's studio, particularly the treatment of receding perspective. On September 28, 1869, Morisot wrote,"I received a visit from Puvis de Chavannes. He saw what I had done at Lorient and seemed to find it not too bad; tell Adolphe that in examining the jetty, he praised my knowledge of perspective and that naturally I gave full credit where it was due."[9] Édouard Manet, also a seasoned marine painter (cats. 113, 114), likewise approved of it. Morisot noted, "The Manets came to see us Tuesday evening, they visited the studio; to my great surprise and satisfaction, I received the highest praises. . . . Ever since I was told that without knowing it I produced masterpieces at Lorient, I stand dumbfounded before them and no longer feel capable of anything."[10] Morisot gave *The Harbor at Lorient* to Manet as an indication of her admiration for her fellow artist. It is possible that the work was subsequently exhibited at the first Impressionist exhibition in 1874.[11] —SK

1. In an auction of work by Monet, Renoir, Sisley, and Morisot organized by the artists themselves in 1875, Morisot's *Interior* achieved the highest price of 480 francs. *Catalogue des tableaux et aquarelles par Claude Monet, Berthe Morisot, A. Renoir, A. Sisley, 24 Mars, 1875* (Paris: Hôtel Drouot, 1875).

2. See, for example, *The Boatyard*, shown at the 1876 Impressionist exhibition; Ruth Berson, *The New Painting: Impressionism, 1874–1886; Documentation*, vol. 2, *Exhibited Works* (San Francisco: Fine Arts Museums of San Francisco, 1996), 60, no. II-174.

3. Claude Nières, *Histoire de Lorient* (Toulouse: Éditions Privat, 1988); and Yann Lukas, *Lorient, histoire d'une ville* (Quimper: Éditions Palatines, 1997).

4. Adolphe Joanne, *Dictionnaire géographique, administrative et postal de la France* (Paris: Hachette, 1869), 1:1245: "Lorient tient le 1er rang en France pour les constructions navales." In 1861, for example, the port launched the iron frigate *La Couronne*.

5. Quoted in Alain Clairet, Delphine Montalant, and Yves Rouart, *Berthe Morisot, 1841–1895: Catalogue raisonné de l'oeuvre peint* (Montolivet: CÉRA-NRS Éditions, 1997), 44: "Je compte absolument sur mon séjour à Lorient pour faire quelque chose de passable. Je n'ai absolument rien fait depuis ton départ et je commence à m'en désoler. Jamais ma peinture ne m'a paru aussi mauvaise que depuis quelques jours."

6. Ibid., 42.

7. Ibid.: "tu n'as pas pris le plus mauvais lot . . . songe que la solitude est bien triste."

8. Madame Morisot to Edma, August 7, 1869, ibid., 46: "J'ai trouvé très jolies les deux peintures qu'elle a rapportées: elles font très bien dans l'atelier." The other work painted in Lorient is a seated portrait of Edma (National Gallery of Art, Washington, D.C.).

9. Ibid., 46.

10. Ibid., 46–47: "Les Manet sont venus nous voir mardi soir, on a visité l'atelier; à mon grand étonnement et contentement, j'ai recueilli les plus grands éloges. . . . Depuis qu'on m'a annoncé que, sans m'en douter, j'avais fait des chefs-d'oeuvre à Lorient, je reste ébahie devant et ne me sens plus capable de rien."

11. Ibid., 120, no. 17, for the identification of *The Harbor at Lorient* as the *Marine* shown at the 1874 Impressionist show. This is disputed by Bill Scott in "Berthe Morisot," in *Manet and the Sea*, ed. Juliet Wilson-Bareau and David Degener, exh. cat. (Philadelphia: Philadelphia Museum of Art, 2003), 232. Scott identifies the marine exhibited in 1874 as *Harbor at Cherbourg* (Virginia Museum of Fine Arts, Richmond).

117

JULES BRETON

FRENCH, 1827–1906

Élodie with a Sunshade: Bay of Douarnenez (Woman with Parasol)

1870–71

Oil on canvas

25⅝ × 35⅝ in. (65 × 91 cm)

Grohmann Collection, Milwaukee

JULES BRETON'S VIEWS OF BRITTANY generally focused on the indigenous peasant culture, but in this work he represented his wife, Élodie, as a tourist, seated high above the Bay of Douarnenez. The town of Douarnenez at the western tip of Brittany had considerable importance as a fishing port; its sardine fishing fleet comprised eight hundred ships and employed four thousand men.[1] With the arrival of the railroad in 1862, its natural beauty also began to attract tourists. Adolphe Joanne noted of the bay: "its expanse, the beauty of its coves and the promontories that the Black Mountain projects over the waves, the 1,200 fishermen's huts in the recesses of the shore, make this one of the most remarkable gulfs of Brittany."[2] The appearance in 1867 of Joanne's guidebook to Brittany, the seventh in a series of eight provincial guides, encouraged touristic exploration of the region as a whole.[3]

Breton married Élodie, the daughter of his former art teacher, Félix de Vigne, in 1858. In this painting, Breton shows the face of his wife in shadow and her parasol and yellow dress brightly lit by the sun. On June 11, 1870, Breton wrote to his brother, Louis, of painting this picture of Élodie "in a yellow dress in the shade of her parasol, sitting on a grassy bank with a red shawl on her knee. There are some pine branches behind her, and some gorse around her. The sea in the background is the brightest emerald blue possible . . . by means of a large plank that I have had made I shall go and finish it on the same spot."[4] The work was completed the following year, either in the artist's Paris studio or, as the final sentence of the letter quoted above suggests, on a return visit to the location. Breton's painting is notable for its use of luminous primary colors—the yellow of the dress complemented by the red of the shawl and the blue of the distant sea.[5] We may imagine that she is holding a guidebook to the region. Breton also paid careful attention to the rendering of the far-off mountain of Le Ménez-Hom, rising to 1,083 feet, a site of important Celtic history in the region. The artist later described the "heath-clad hills of the menez c'hom, pink like the peach-blossom, rose in the limpid atmosphere."[6]

Decades before the better-known arrival of Paul Gauguin and the school of Pont-Aven, Breton's work highlights the early emergence of Brittany as a tourist destination. Breton himself, who had first visited Douarnenez in 1865, returned there regularly with Élodie until 1891. —SK

1. Adolphe Joanne, *Dictionnaire géographique, administratif et postal de la France* (Paris: Hachette, 1869), 1:733.

2. Ibid. 1:840: "Son étendue, la beauté de ses indentations et des promontoires que la Montagne Noire projette sur ses flots, les 1200 hameaux de pêcheurs dans les replis du rivage, en font l'un des golfes les plus remarquables de la Bretagne."

3. Patrick Young, *Enacting Brittany: Tourism and Culture in Provincial France, 1871–1939* (Farnham, U.K.: Ashgate, 2012), 55. Adolphe Joanne, *Itinéraire général de la France: Bretagne* (Paris: Hachette, 1867).

4. Jules Breton to Louis Breton, June 11, 1870; translated and quoted in Annette Bourrut Lacouture, *Jules Breton, Painter of Peasant Life*, exh. cat. (New Haven: Yale University Press in association with the National Gallery of Ireland, 2002), 140. The original French appears in the French edition of this catalogue by the same author, *Jules Breton: La chanson des blés* (Paris: Somogy Éditions d'Art in association with the Musée des Beaux-Arts d'Arras, Musée des Beaux-Arts de Quimper, and National Gallery of Ireland, 2002), 140: "en robe jaune à l'ombre de son parasol, tenant sur ses genoux un tour de lac rouge, est assise dans la lande: quelques branches de pin se mêlent légèrement à sa silhouette qu'accompagnent des ajoncs. Au fond, une tranche de mer aussi bleu émeraude que possible . . . au moyen d'une grande planche, que je me suis fait faire, j'irai le terminer sur place."

5. Breton also produced an oil sketch for the painting in which Élodie appears slightly smaller within the landscape context; *Study for Woman with Parasol*, 1870, 21 × 33 cm (Musée du Petit Palais, Paris).

6. Jules Breton, *The Life of an Artist*, trans. Mary J. Serrano (New York: D. Appleton and Company, 1891), 310.

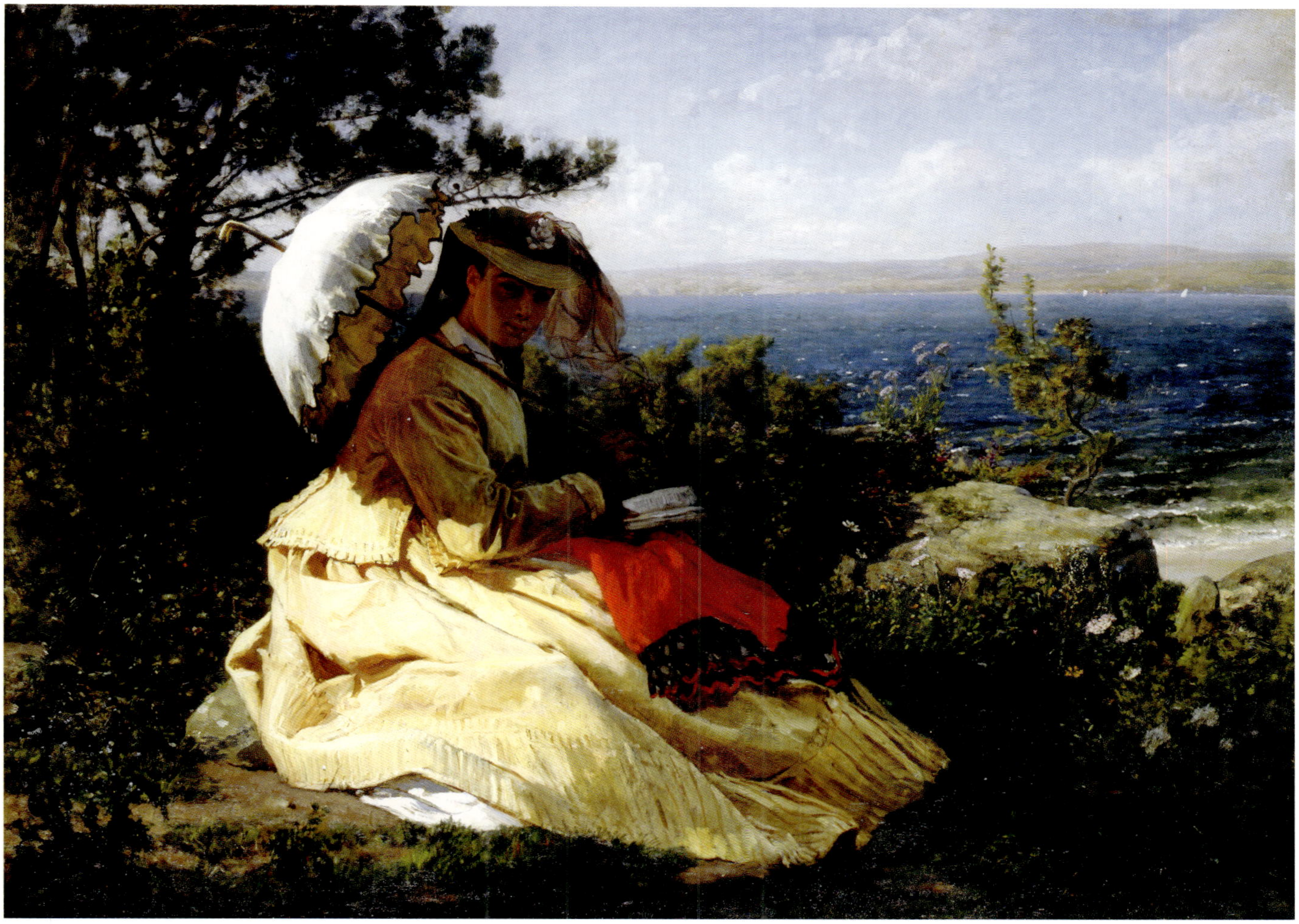

118

LOUIS-AUGUSTE AIGUIER

FRENCH, 1814–1865

Tamaris, Toulon Harbor

1865

Oil on canvas

39 × 62¼ in. (99 × 158 cm)

Musée d'art de Toulon

IN 1861 THE PROVENÇAL CRITIC Marius Chaumelin wrote: "Our Provence has, like the North, its mild and mysterious aspects. M. Aiguier dedicates himself to fixing the delicate and fugitive impressions of these on the canvas."[1] As this writer noted, Louis-Auguste Aiguier concentrated on making views of Provence, and particularly the Mediterranean coast. A native of Toulon, Aiguier exhibited regularly at the Paris Salon from 1855 until 1865, emerging as a significant member of the school of Marseille, which promoted the southern landscape to a national audience.[2] He was the only painter to represent this school in the display of French paintings at the International Exhibition in London in 1862. Despite critical success, Aiguier was a part-time painter who also worked as a milliner. The critic Louis Enault described him as "painter the morning, hatmaker the evening, but always inventive, whether he is crumpling the ribbons of a bonnet or sketching the landscape of a Provençal idyll."[3] Aiguier's output was relatively small. His posthumous sale included 40 paintings and 193 studies, and he sold only about 20 works in his lifetime.[4]

Tamaris, Toulon Harbor, Aiguier's last major work, is his masterpiece. Three boats are attached to mooring posts by the shore, while a single figure in red collects fishing nets. The pentimenti of two more boats, as well as other figures, are visible to the left. Aiguier's tranquil view showing the jetty of the village of Tamaris provides little suggestion of the nearby presence of the military port of Toulon, France's second-largest naval base (after Brest in Brittany), where the French Mediterranean fleet was stationed.[5] Tamaris had also recently attracted attention as the setting for George Sand's novel of the same name, published in 1862, in which the author evoked the "beautiful summer nights" and harmonies of the sea breeze" of the Mediterranean coast.[6] In the distance of Aiguier's work is the silhouetted headland of Cap Sicié with the rectangular houses of the hamlet of Les Sablettes at its base. The composition is characterized by its abstract quality, reduced to a series of flat, minimalistic bands. The sea is rendered in blue green, and the sunset is painted in golden yellow, rising to blue. The work is also notable for its quality of light, reflecting the artist's study of the seventeenth-century painter Claude Lorrain as well as the southern atmosphere itself.[7]

Aiguier showed *Tamaris, Toulon Harbor* at the 1865 Salon, where it was seen with several other views by the school of Marseille. Critical response was positive. Chaumelin affirmed, "This painting has something grave and mysterious, which renders well the impression of twilight."[8] Ernest Chesneau, in lamenting the artist's untimely death, picked out this view "of that sea whose particular beauties he understood and translated admirably," noting that "he had often exhibited evening views of a profound serenity in the blue immensity."[9] Aiguier was, however, criticized for a lack of detail and modeling in his forms, precisely the aspect that lends his work a particular modernity today.[10]

Tamaris, Toulon Harbor was bought by the town of Toulon in 1866. In the decades before the Provençal work of Vincent van Gogh and the mature Paul Cézanne, Aiguier's painting highlights the importance of the school of Marseille in representing the light and landscape of the Mediterranean coast. —SK

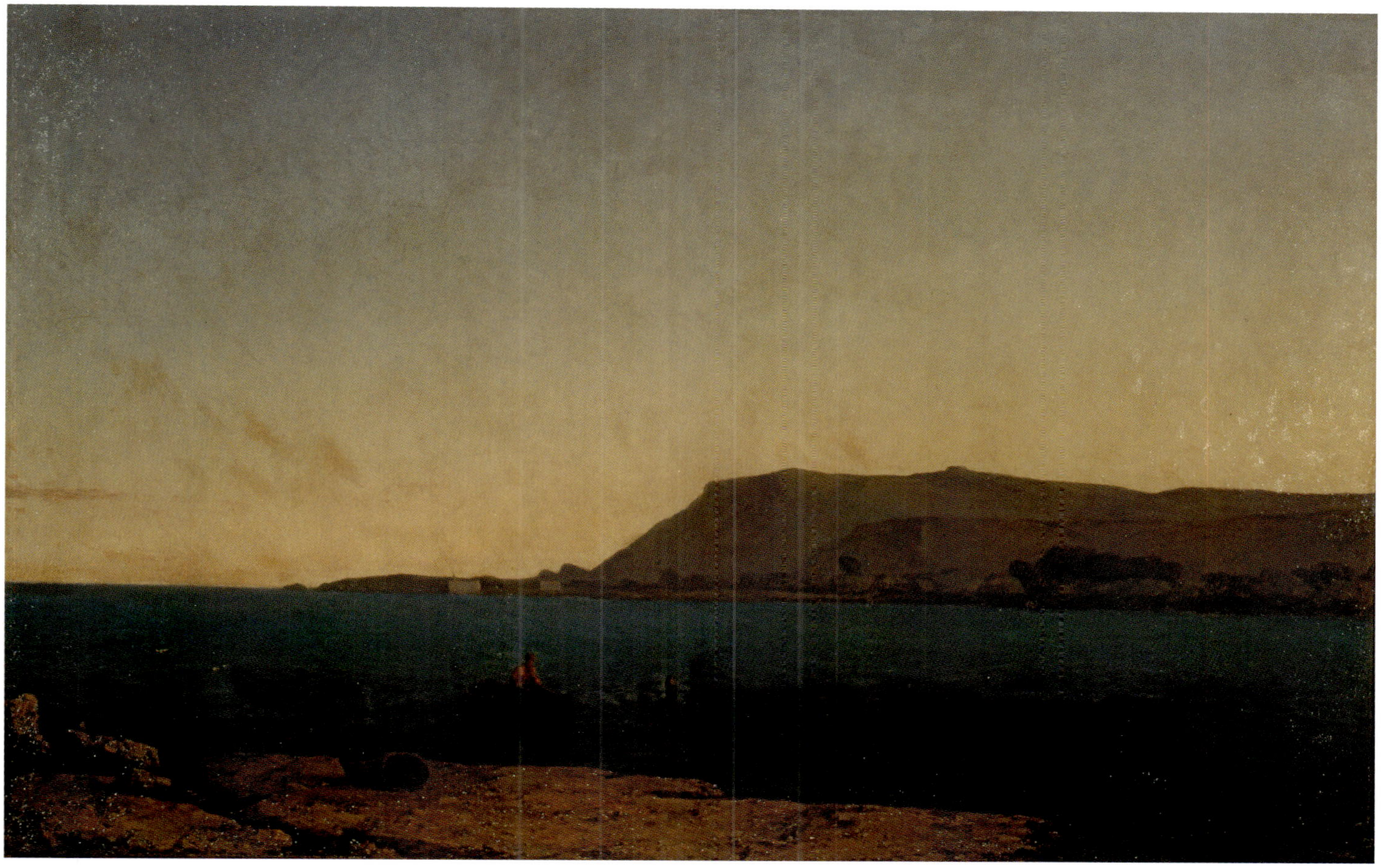

1. Marius Chaumelin, “Société artistique des Bouches-du-Rhône—Exposition de 1861,” 2nd article, *Tribune artistique et littéraire du Midi*, 179: “Notre Provence a, comme le Nord, ses aspects doux et mystérieux; M. Aiguier s'attache à en fixer sur la toile les délicates et fugitives impressions. Il peint la nature aux heures de calme et de recueillement.” Quoted in Jean-Roger Soubiran, *Le paysage provençal et l'école de Marseille avant l'impressionisme, 1845–1874*, exh. cat. (Paris: Réunion des Musées Nationaux; Toulon: Musée de Toulon, 1992), 426.

2. For Aiguier's career, see Soubiran, *Le paysage provençal et l'école de Marseille avant l'impressionisme*, 412–26.

3. Louis Enault, “Exposition des beaux-arts à Marseille,” *Le monde illustré* 5, no. 139 (December 10, 1859): 384: “peintre le matin, modiste le soir, mais toujours inventeur, soit qu'il chiffonne les rubans d'un bonnet ou qu'il esquisse le paysage d'une idylle Provençale.”

4. Soubiran, *Le paysage provençal et l'école de Marseille avant l'impressionisme*, 556–57.

5. For an overview of the painting, see John House, *Landscapes of France: Impressionism and Its Rivals*, exh. cat. (London: South Bank Centre, 1995), 82.

6. George Sand, *Tamaris* (Paris: Michel Lévy Frères, 1862), 119: “délices des belles nuits d'été . . . harmonies de la brise marine.”

7. As Brigitte Gaillard has noted, in discussion with the author, Aiguier's treatment of light is in fact rather different from the actual more limpid and rosy light around Toulon. Aiguier's work was transformed by his experience of seeing the work of Claude Lorrain at the Musée du Louvre in 1853.

8. Marius Chaumelin, “Les artistes provençaux au Salon de 1865,” *Tribune artistique et littéraire du Midi*, 26; quoted in Soubiran, *Le paysage provençal et l'école de Marseille avant l'impressionisme*, 418: “Ce tableau a quelque chose de grave, de mystérieux qui rend bien l'impression du crepuscule.”

9. Ernest Chesneau, “Salon de 1865: Animaux, omissions, conclusions,” *Le constitutionnel*, no. 181 (June 30, 1865): 1: “Nous avons appris tout récemment la mort de M. Aiguier, qui avait au Salon de 1865 une Vue de la Méditerranée, de cette mer dont il comprenait et traduisait admirablement les beautés particulières. Il avait souvent exposé des Soirs d'une sérénité profonde dans l'immensité bleue.”

10. Léon Lagrange, “Salon de 1864,” *Gazette des beaux-arts* 17, no. 1 (July 1, 1864), 18: “M. Aiguier . . . too ready to sacrifice the modeling of trees, land, factories.” (M. Aiguier . . . trop prompt à sacrifier le modelé des arbres, des terrains, des fabriques.)

119

PIERRE PUVIS DE CHAVANNES

FRENCH, 1824–1898

Marseille, Gateway to the Orient

ca. 1868–69

Oil on canvas

38¾ × 57⅝ in. (98.4 × 146.4 cm)

The Phillips Collection, Washington, D.C., Acquired 1923, 1617

PIERRE PUVIS DE CHAVANNES was praised in his own time as the archetypal national painter; he produced patriotic murals around the country for many of the state's regional museums, including those in Amiens, Rouen, Lyon, and Marseille.[1] These murals represented images of specific regions as well as allegorical renderings of history, evoking a vision of French nationhood. The critic Alphonse Germain maintained, "What Rembrandt is to Holland, Puvis de Chavannes will be to France—he is ours. Thanks to his 'thusness,' our art will become national again."[2]

Marseille, Gateway to the Orient is a study for one of these patriotic murals (fig. 81), which was commissioned by the city of Marseille in June 1867, together with a pendant representing the city's ancient Greek history (fig. 82).[3] The two murals were to be placed on either side of the grand stairway in the Marseille arts museum, the Palais Longchamp, itself built in 1862 as an important part of the urban reconstruction of the city, which was recorded in the photographs of Adolphe Terris (cats. 22, 23). The details of the commission stipulated that Puvis's murals represent pagan and Christian Marseille, "treated in a severe and monumental manner."[4] To render the Christian aspect of the city, Puvis chose to represent it in the modern era as a busy and welcoming metropolis. His painting emphasizes Marseille as an international trading hub and crucial site of entry into France for immigrants. The writer Louis Simonin noted in 1878 that "the whole world" could be found here: "walk along the quays and you will find there at times the Chinese man with long hair falling in a tress down his back, the Parsee with pointed hat, the Hindu with white caftan, the black man with swaying walk who sings the refrain of his native country, the English or American sailor with cap and clothed in oilskin."[5] Marseille, indeed, experienced considerable growth at midcentury; its population increased from 198,000 in 1851 to 300,000 in 1866, making it second only to Paris in terms of population in France.[6]

Puvis's painting shows travelers on the prow of a ship arriving in the port of Marseille.[7] The artist depicted a cosmopolitan range of passengers, including, to the left, a seated Greek Orthodox priest, a figure wearing a yellow robe and caftan, and a woman on a carpet with her child and attendant. The fainter forms of the ship's sailors are visible in the right foreground. In the distance can be seen the port and lighthouse of Marseille as well as several ships, including the cropped prow of a vessel. The red, yellow, and green color accents of the passengers' costumes are offset by the intense blue of the ocean. Puvis's study is faintly squared up for transfer to the larger mural. The artist made several compositional changes in the final painting (fig. 81). He added, for example, the seated figure of a Jew with a red beard to the right. A Turkish flag is also about to be raised, making clear the nationality of the ship. Puvis described the composition of his painting thus:

> The city, seen from the sea, is spread out on the horizon. Its piers open out to the vessels that sail toward her before the wind. One of them, cut in half by the frame, comprises the foreground. On the craft's deck, representatives of all the various races of the Levant. An Armenian, a Jew, a Greek, an Arab take their places naturally and, mixing with sailors busy with maneuvers, and seated or leaning on the rail, they contemplate the sea of the Gauls. This is Marseille, "Gateway to the Orient."[8]

Puvis's words highlight the variety of immigrants in the painting as well as the nationalistic idea of the Mediterranean as a Gallic sea. Napoléon III had indeed proudly—and

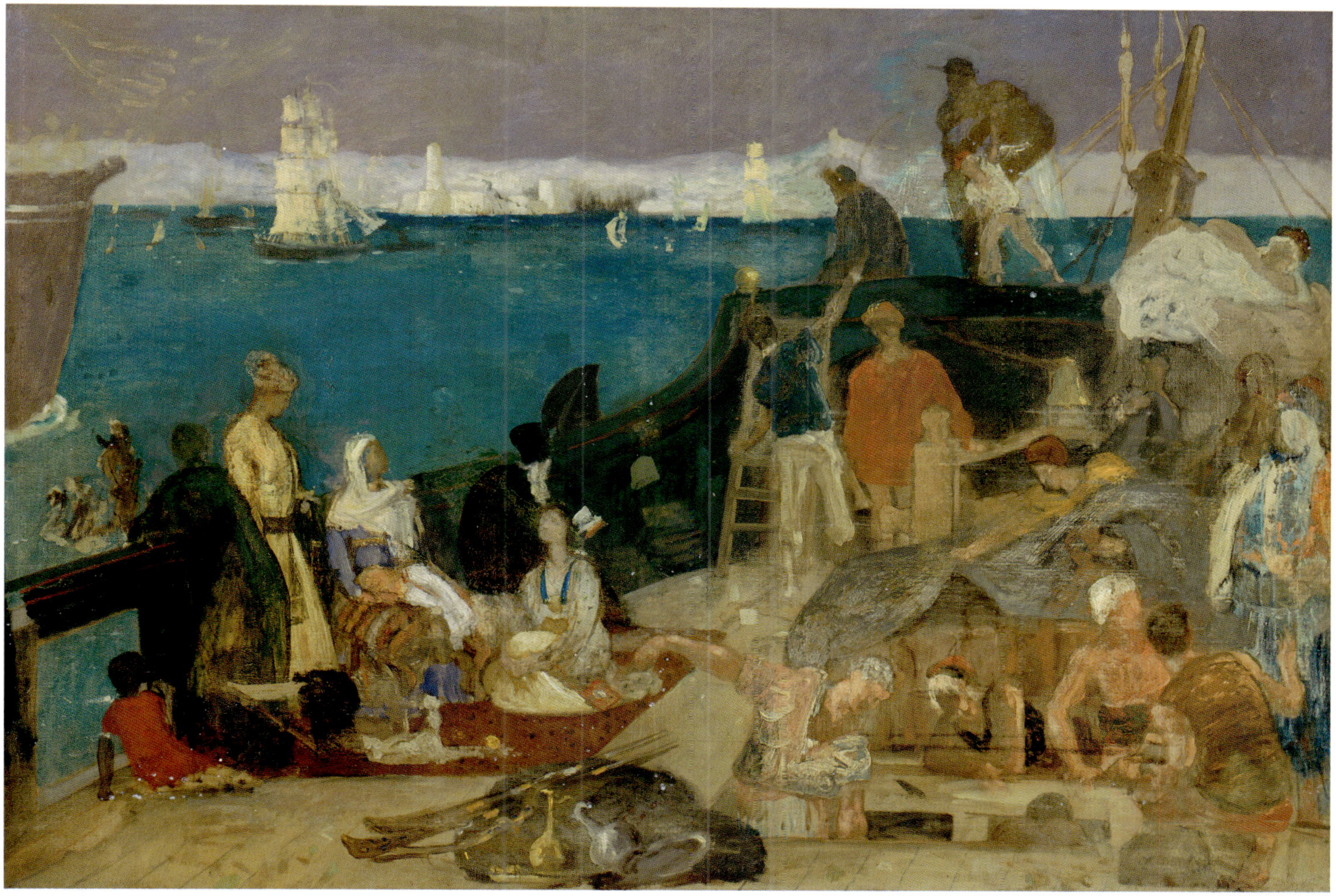

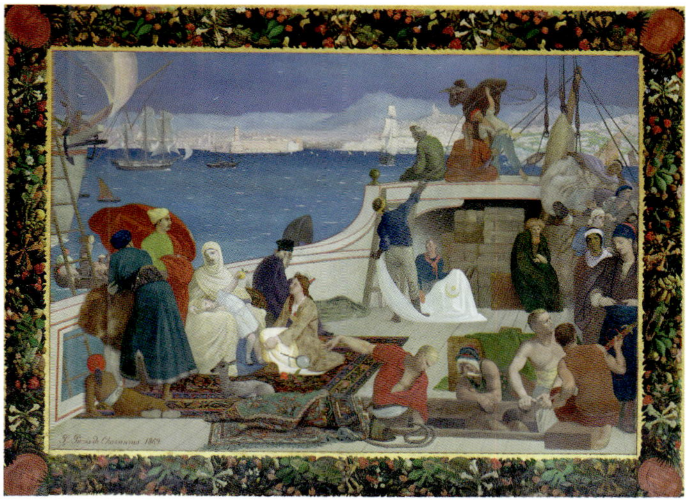

FIG. 81 Pierre Puvis de Chavannes, *Marseille, Gateway to the Orient*, 1869. Oil on canvas, 13 ft. 10½ in. × 18 ft. 6½ in. (4.2 × 5.7 m). Musée des beaux-arts, Marseille, France

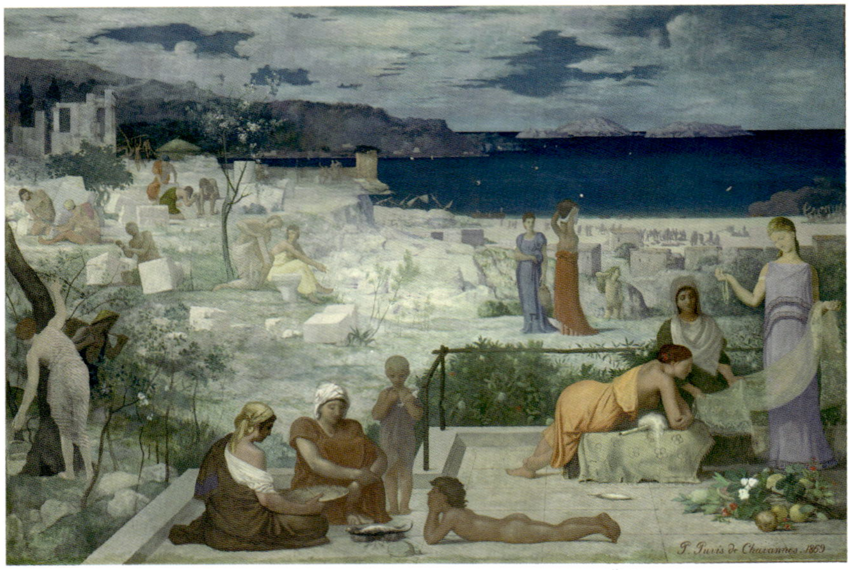

FIG. 82 Pierre Puvis de Chavannes, *View of Massilia (The Greek Colony, Marseille)*, 1869. Oil on canvas, 14 ft. × 18 ft. 6½ in. (4.2 × 5.7 m). Musée des beaux-arts, Marseille, France

hubristically—proclaimed that the Mediterranean was a "French lake."[9] Marseille's expansion in the Second Empire made it the leading European port after Liverpool and London, as well as the largest port in France.[10] The importance of the city was further advanced by the opening of the Suez Canal in November 1869, which created a direct trading link to the Far East; Puvis's murals were unveiled to coincide with the opening of the canal. Despite the ambitions of the city, Marseille's international significance would diminish by the end of the nineteenth century, when northern European ports such as Rotterdam and Hamburg grew in importance.

Puvis's pendant mural, *View of Massilia (The Greek Colony, Marseille)* (fig. 82), evoked the ancient world and referenced the history of Marseille as France's oldest city, having been founded as a Greek colony in 600 BC by the Phocaeans (Ionian Greeks). The two murals, *Marseille, Gateway to the Orient* and *View of Massilia (The Greek Colony, Marseille)*, thus summed up the importance of Marseille to France in terms of the nation's origins and ancient history and also its modernity and future commercial aspirations. —SK

1. Jennifer L. Shaw, *Dream States: Puvis de Chavannes, Modernism, and the Fantasy of France* (New Haven: Yale University Press, 2002), 1.

2. Quoted in ibid.

3. For a detailed overview of the studies and murals, see Aimée Brown Price, *Pierre Puvis de Chavannes*, vol. 2, *A Catalogue Raisonné of the Painted Work* (New Haven: Yale University Press, 2010), 138–47. See also Geneviève Drocourt, "Puvis de Chavannes et le décor de l'Escalier d'honneur du Palais Longchamp," in *Puvis de Chavannes et le musée des beaux-arts de Marseille*, exh. cat. (Marseille: Musée des Beaux-Arts, 1984).

4. The two works were commissioned for the modest sum of ten thousand francs on July 25, 1867. Puvis was originally asked to represent antique and modern art in Provence, including an episode from the life of the Marseillais sculptor Pierre Puget. The mandate was altered in an amended contract of October 18, 1867, although it is unclear whether this was at the request of Puvis or the municipal council.

5. Louis Simonin, *Les grands ports de commerce* (Paris: Hachette, 1878), 6–7: "Marseille, c'est le monde entier. Promenez-vous le long des quais, et vous y rencontrez par instants le Chinois à la longue queue tombant en tresse sur le dos, le Parsis au bonnet pointu, l'Hindou au cafetan blanc, le nègre à la demarche déhanchée, qui s'en va chantonnant un refrain du pays natal, le matelot anglais ou américain à la casquette, aux vêtements de toile cirée."

6. See Price, *A Catalogue Raisonné*, 139.

7. Puvis's title was based on lines from an 1839 poem by Victor Hugo: "There is in the night of Avignon a breath of the sky of Greece and Italy. One senses in this charming breeze that the door to the Orient is there, quite near, ajar." Quoted in ibid., 146.

8. Translated and quoted in ibid.: "La ville, vue de la mer, se déploie à l'horizon. Ses moles s'ouvrent aux navires qui cinglent vers elle. Un d'eux, coupé à moitié par le cadre, forme un premier plan. Sur le pont du vaisseau, tous les types figurant les diverses races du Levant. Un Arménien, un Juif, un Grec, un Arabe, viennent naturellement se placer et, mêlés aux matelots actifs à la manoeuvre, assis ou accoudés aux bastingages, ils contemplent la mer des Gaules. C'est 'Marseille Porte de l'Orient.'"

9. Quoted in Nina Athanassoglou-Kallmyer, "Excavating Greece: Classicism between Empire and Nation in Nineteenth-Century Europe," *Nineteenth-Century Art Worldwide* 7, no. 2 (Autumn 2008), http://www.19thc-artworldwide.org/index.php/autumn08/94-excavating-greece-classicism-between-empire-and-nation-in-nineteenth-century-europe.

10. Marseille had by far the nation's largest number of steamboats in port, 201 in 1869, contrasting with only 56 in Le Havre, its closest competitor. By 1880 Marseille was home to more than half of the national steamboat fleet. Elaine Richard and Roland Caty, "Le port et le négoce," in *Marseille au XIXème: Rêves et triomphes*, exh. cat. (Marseille: Musée de Marseille; Paris: Réunion des Musées Nationaux, 1991), 74.

Chronology, 1850–1880

SYDNEY NORTON

1850

HISTORY & CULTURE

A recently completed railroad line facilitates travel between Paris and Auvers-sur-Oise.

PAINTING

Théodore Rousseau is a member of the Salon jury and exhibits 7 paintings, principally of the Forest of Fontainebleau. Pierre Puvis de Chavannes and Gustave Doré show at the Salon for the first time.

Auguste-François Bonheur travels to Auvergne, which he will visit for the rest of his life. He often exhibits paintings of this region at the Salon.

Rosa Bonheur visits the Pyrenees, traveling incognito as a man, and painting peasant culture of the region.

François-Louis Français begins to frequent Honfleur and, with Jean-Baptiste-Camille Corot, Gustave Courbet, Eugène Boudin, and Johan-Barthold Jongkind, paints the harbor town and its environs. Over the next two decades, Français will visit Alsace, Belgium, Switzerland, and the Alps.

PHOTOGRAPHY

Gustave Le Gray publishes the first edition of his *Traité pratique de photographie sur papier et sur verre*. Throughout the 1850s he attempts to make a living as a portrait photographer, establishing a studio, laboratory, and training school in Paris.

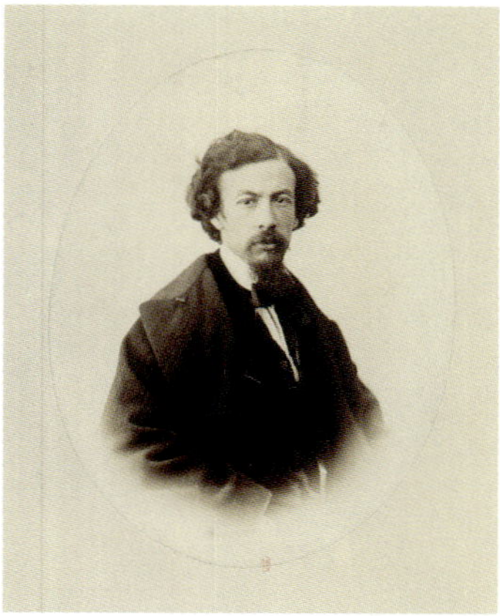

Gustave Le Gray, *Self-Portrait*, 1857–60. Bibliothèque nationale de France, Paris

Charles Marville begins making photographs as paper negatives.

1851

HISTORY & CULTURE

May 1–October 15: the first world's fair, the Great Exhibition of the Works of Industry of All Nations, takes place in London in the Crystal Palace in Hyde Park.

December 2: Louis-Napoléon III seizes power in a military coup d'état that results in the fall of the Second Republic.

A railway line opens between Paris and Argenteuil.

Victor Hugo goes into exile.

PAINTING

June: Jongkind and Eugène Isabey make marine sketches together in Étretat.

Boudin receives a stipend to study for 2 years in Paris.

Corot paints a series of works at the port of La Rochelle.

Jules Breton resides in Paris for 3 years under extreme financial constraints. He stays briefly in Ghent and Brussels.

PHOTOGRAPHY

January: founding of the Société heliographique in Paris. In February the society publishes the first issue of its weekly, *La lumière*, the organization's main organ.

April: Le Gray reveals his waxed paper negative process to members of the Société héliographique.

May: exhibitors at the London Great Exhibition include Louis-Désiré Blanquart-Evrard, Le Gray, and Henri Le Secq.

September: Blanquart-Evrard opens the first large-scale photographic printing establishment, the Imprimerie photographique, in Lille.

The Commission des monuments historiques, an agency established and supported by the French government, commissions five members of the Société héliographique—Édouard Baldus, Le Gray, Le Secq, Hippolyte Bayard, and Auguste Mestral—to travel around France and document historic structures (the Mission héliographique).

1852

HISTORY & CULTURE

February 17: press censorship is introduced by decree.

March 25: right of public assembly restricted.

September 14–October 16: Napoléon III's first of 2 visits to Provence.

December 2: Napoléon III is proclaimed emperor of the Second Empire (1852–70), a regime characterized by prosperity, building, and liberal expansion.

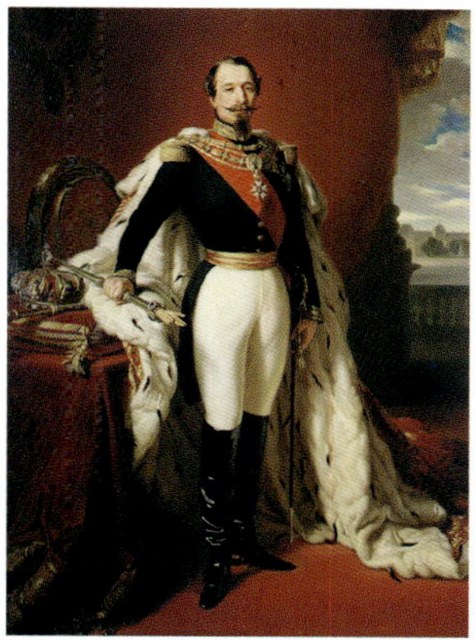

Franz Xavier Winterhalter, *Portrait of Napoléon III*, 1855. Oil on canvas. Museo Napoleonico, Rome, Italy

PAINTING

March: Henri-Joseph Harpignies returns home from Italy and settles in Paris. He is inspired by the landscapes of Corot.

July 15: Puvis de Chavannes moves to 11, place Pigalle, where he will remain until 1897.

Breton resides in Paris but makes landscape studies in the neighboring towns of Clamart, Meudon, and Saint-Nom-La Bretèche.

Corot, Charles-François Daubigny, Français, and Auguste Ravier paint at Crémieu, 25 miles east of Lyon.

PHOTOGRAPHY

During the spring and summer, Le Gray photographs in the Forest of Fontainebleau, at times accompanied by the photographer John Beasley Greene.

Le Secq and Charles Nègre photograph Notre-Dame in Paris. Le Secq also photographs landscapes and travels to Montmirail, where he owns property, to photograph stone quarries and woods.

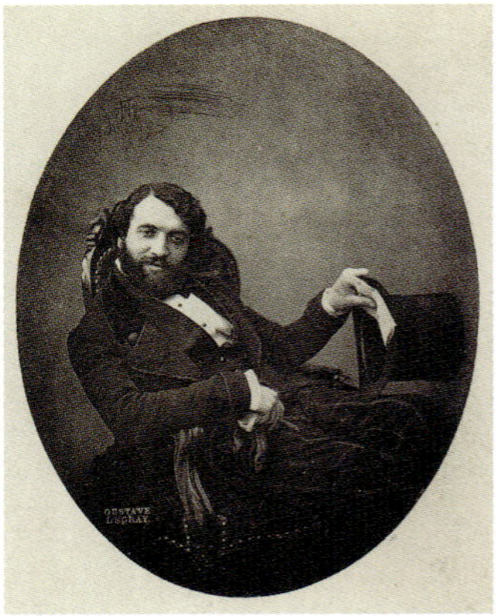

Gustave Le Gray, *Portrait of Henri Le Secq*, 1848. Musée Le Secq des Tournelles, Rouen

Baldus secures state funding for *Villes de France photographiées*, an extended series of architectural views of monuments and buildings in Paris and the provinces.

Nègre photographs landscapes and monuments in the Midi, with the intention of publishing an extensive album, *Le Midi de la France*.

1853

HISTORY & CULTURE

January 29–30: Napoléon III marries Eugénie de Montijo, countess of Teba.

June 22: Baron Georges-Eugène Haussmann, whose revolutionary urban design will transform Paris into a city of expansive boulevards, is appointed prefect of the Seine.

October: an outbreak of cholera occurs in Paris, with episodes continuing through 1855; 143,478 people die.

French railway company Chemin de fer du Midi is established.

PAINTING

Summer: Boudin's first trip to Finistère in Brittany, which he will visit regularly between 1865 and 1876.

October: Édouard Manet takes a walking tour of the Normandy coast and makes studies from nature at Sainte-Adresse.

Louis-Auguste Aiguier moves to Paris and studies the landscape paintings of Claude Lorrain.

Rosa Bonheur and her companion Nathalie Micas visit the Pyrenees. When they return to Paris, they move into a spacious new studio at 32, rue d'Assas, which contains stables and pens for their growing menagerie of animals.

Land in the Forest of Fontainebleau is set aside for a preserve, thanks to the efforts of Rousseau and others. The plan for the preserve is instituted by imperial decree in 1861.

Constant Troyon visits England, where his pastoral visions of French agriculture are widely shown. During the summer he paints near the village of Château-Lavallière on the southern banks of the Loire River.

PHOTOGRAPHY

April: Adalbert Cuvelier teaches Corot the cliché-verre process.

May: the art dealer Adolphe Goupil sells landscape and architectural views by Le Gray and Le Secq in Paris.

Fall: Baldus travels and photographs in the Midi.

1854

HISTORY & CULTURE

March 27: France and England declare war against Russia in support of Turkey, beginning the Crimean War. Their troops land in Crimea on September 14 and are victorious over the Russians 6 days later.

The Provençal poet Frédéric Mistral, an advocate for political and cultural decentralization, establishes the Félibrige, a poetic society intended to restore luster to the language and culture of the *pays d'oc* (Occitania).

PAINTING

Breton moves back to Courrières (Pas-de-Calais), his birthplace.

Paul Guigou moves to Marseille, where he helps form a nascent Marseille school of painting.

Jean-François Millet visits his birthplace, Gruchy, with his family.

Courbet spends time in Montpellier with his friend the art collector Alfred Bruyas.

PHOTOGRAPHY

Summer: Baldus travels through Auvergne.

Société héliographique dissolves; in November, the Société française de la photographie (SFP), an organization dedicated to the artistic aspects of photography, is formed.

1855

HISTORY & CULTURE

May 15–November 15: Exposition universelle takes place for the first time in Paris, with 24,000 exhibitors and 5,162,330 visitors. The exhibition's principal building is the enormous Palais de l'Industrie.

Inauguration of the Paris–Lyon–Méditerranée Railway.

Chemin de fer de l'Ouest is established.

PAINTING

At the Exposition universelle Rousseau exhibits 13 paintings and receives a first-class medal. Works by Aiguier, Breton, Auguste and Rosa Bonheur, Corot, Courbet, Daubigny, Narcisse-Virgile Diaz de la Peña, Doré, Français, Harpignies, Paul Huet, and Millet are also shown.

In addition to showing 11 works at the Exposition universelle, Courbet arranges a solo exhibition, "Pavilion of Realism," in a tent opposite the Palais des Beaux-Arts. Among the 40 works featured are landscapes of the Franche-Comté and the Forest of Fontainebleau.

Camille Pissarro moves to Paris from Saint Thomas (West Indies). He visits the Exposition universelle, where he admires works by Eugène Delacroix, Corot, and Courbet.

PHOTOGRAPHY

October: Gustave Le Gray et Cie is established with Barnabé-Louis-Gabriel-Charles Malbec de Montjoc, the marquis de Briges, as a silent partner.

Late December or early January 1856: the Bisson frères open a large studio at 35, boulevard des Capucines, with the financial backing of Daniel Dollfus-Ausset.

Baldus receives 2 important commissions, the first from Baron James de Rothschild to produce an album of views along the Northern Rail line from Paris to Boulogne for Queen Victoria and Prince Albert, and the second from the state to photograph the construction of the new Louvre.

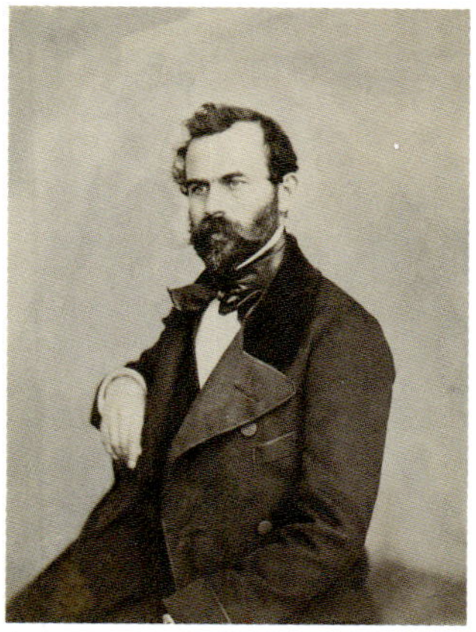

Édouard-Denis Baldus, *Self-Portrait*, 1853. Bibliothèque nationale de France, Paris

At the Exposition universelle in Paris, Baldus, the Bisson frères, Nègre, Le Gray, and Le Secq win medals. Photographs by André Giroux, Vigier, Regnault, and Adolphe Braun are also shown.

1856

HISTORY & CULTURE

March 16: Prince Imperial is born.

March 30: the Treaty of Paris, signed by the allies (France and England) and Russia, ends the Crimean War. France gains a leading position on the Continent over Russia.

PAINTING

Claude Monet meets Boudin, who introduces him to plein air painting in Normandy.

Guigou is inspired by Courbet's work during a brief visit to Paris; when he returns to Provence, he begins to paint in the most desolate and barren parts of the countryside.

Armand Guillaumin moves to Paris from Moulins to learn drawing at the École municipale.

PHOTOGRAPHY

June: Baldus photographs the flooding of the Rhone valley, as well as Lyon, Tarascon, and Avignon.

Summer: Le Gray makes his first series of marine views along the Normandy coast, including several photographs around the port of Le Havre. Among these is *Brig upon the Water* (cat. 103).

September: Eugène Cuvelier visits Fontainebleau and stays at the Auberge Ganne.

Le Gray moves into his studio at 35, boulevard des Capucines, below that of the Bisson frères.

1857

HISTORY & CULTURE

January 1: law stipulates subsidies for 3 transatlantic maritime services: Le Havre to North America; Saint-Nazaire to Antilles; and Bordeaux to South America.

August 6–10: Emperor Napoléon III and Empress Eugénie visit England.

August: inauguration of the new Louvre.

Gustave Flaubert publishes the novel *Madame Bovary* serially in *La revue Paris*. He is prosecuted for "violation of morality."

Charles Baudelaire publishes the poetry collection *Les fleurs du mal* (*The Flowers of Evil*), for which he is fined for breach of public morality.

Eugène-Emmanuel Viollet-le-Duc begins restoration of the château of Pierrefonds, 60 miles northeast of Paris.

PAINTING

June: at the Salon, Breton's *The Blessing of the Wheat in Artois* wins a second-class medal and is purchased by the state (see fig. 38).

Summer: Corot travels extensively through Brittany, Normandy, and Auvergne. In September he spends 2 weeks in Boulogne.

Summer: at Montmorency, Pissarro follows Corot's advice to paint from nature.

PHOTOGRAPHY

April: Le Gray makes a second series of marine views in Sète, most notably *The Great Wave, Sète* (see fig. 29) and *The Breaking Wave—Mediterranean Sea* (cat. 108).

July: the Bisson frères are given the title *photographes de l'Empereur*.

1858

HISTORY & CULTURE

January: Anglo-French expeditionary forces land in China and occupy Canton.

August: Napoléon III and Empress Eugénie visit Normandy, with guests Queen Victoria and Prince Albert. The event includes inaugurating the Bassin Napoléon with a series of joint naval maneuvers by the French and British fleets.

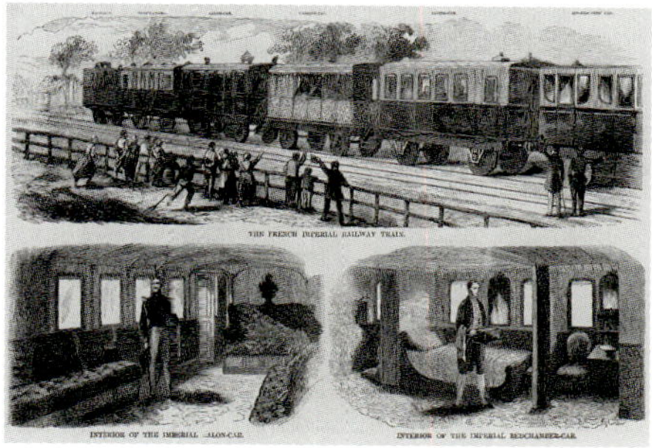

Napoléon III's Imperial Railway Train, 1850s

An unsuccessful attempt to assassinate Napoléon III spurs new security laws allowing for arbitrary arrest and deportation.

PAINTING

April 28: Breton marries Élodie de Vigne, the daughter of his painting teacher in Ghent.

Summer: in Honfleur, Boudin paints *Festival in the Harbor of Honfleur*, his first rendering of a regatta.

Emperor Napoleon commissions *The French Fleet Traveling from Cherbourg to Brest* (see fig. 9) and other large-scale propagandistic works of France's marine strength from Théodore Gudin.

PHOTOGRAPHY

July: Auguste-Rosalie Bisson takes photographs in the Mont Blanc massif.

Marville photographs recently renovated parks for the city of Paris, including the Bois de Bologne and the Bois de Vincennes.

Braun publishes an album of Alsatian landscapes and for the next 4 years photographs landscapes throughout Switzerland, Germany, and France.

1859

HISTORY & CULTURE

May 3: France declares war against Austria after Austria invades Piedmontese territory. France is victorious in battles at Montebello, Magenta, and Solferino.

November: Charles Darwin publishes *On the Origin of Species*.

Paris city limits are expanded, doubling the city's area and increasing the number of inhabitants by 200,000.

PAINTING

April: Baudelaire meets Boudin in Honfleur and pays tribute to his pastel sky studies in the "Salon de 1859."

Mid-May: Monet visits Paris.

Courbet visits Ornans and the Normandy coast, where he meets Boudin and Baudelaire.

PHOTOGRAPHY

March 7: Eugène Cuvelier marries Louise Ganne, daughter of the proprietor of the Auberge Ganne, where the artist stays in Fontainebleau.

August: Auguste-Rosalie Bisson makes photographs during a failed attempt to reach the summit of Mont Blanc.

1860

HISTORY & CULTURE

August–September: Emperor Napoléon III, Empress Eugénie, and their imperial entourage travel to Savoy, Nice, Corsica, and Algeria.

As part of the treaty with Piedmont, France annexes the Alps and the Alpes-Maritimes, including Nice and Savoy.

Anglo-French expeditionary forces land in China, capturing Peking (Beijing). They sack and burn the Summer Palace.

PAINTING

Monet enrolls at the Académie Suisse, where he meets Troyon and Pissarro.

Berthe Morisot and her sister Edma study with Corot, who introduces them to plein air painting. They stay with him until 1862.

Boudin paints his first scenes of vacationers on the beach at Trouville.

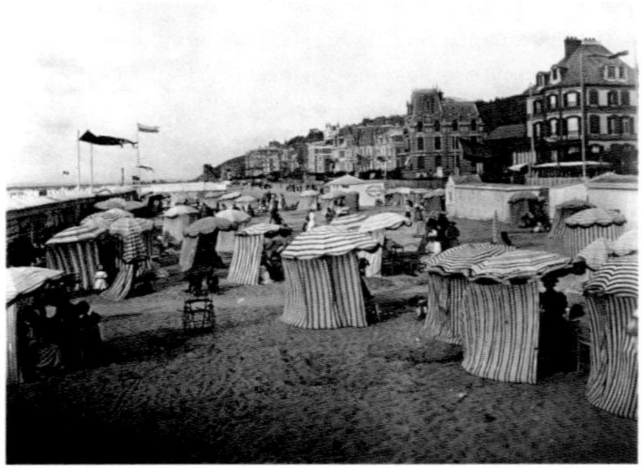

Trouville, ca. 1860s

Rousseau and Millet spend time in the Franche-Comté and Switzerland.

Guillaumin moves to Montmartre and begins working as a clerk for the Paris–Orléans railway. He begins study at the Académie Suisse, where he meets Pissarro and Paul Cézanne.

Daubigny moves to a studio near Auvers-sur-Oise, about 20 miles northwest of Paris.

PHOTOGRAPHY

February: the firm Gustave Le Gray et Cie is dissolved; Le Gray moves to 15, rue Saint-Lazare. In May he leaves France with writer Alexandre Dumas.

One or both of the Bisson frères accompany the imperial entourage on their journey to Mont Blanc. Auguste-Rosalie succeeds in exposing several glass negatives during the climb.

Baldus travels to the Dauphiné, Savoy, and Nice to photograph the landscape and towns.

1861

HISTORY & CULTURE

June: France declares neutrality in the United States Civil War.

October 31: France, Britain, and Spain launch a military expedition to Mexico in response to the country's suspended payment of its international loans.

Opening of Strasbourg–Kehl railway and bridge across the Rhine River.

Construction begins on the Paris Opéra, designed by Charles Garnier and conceived by Baron Haussmann as the converging point of several major boulevards.

PAINTING

April: Cézanne moves to Paris from Aix and studies at the Académie Suisse.

April: Monet's studies are interrupted by military service in Algeria.

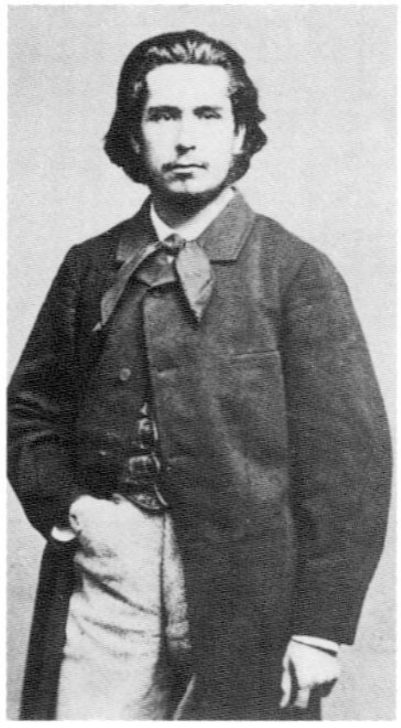

Etienne Carjat, *Claude Monet*, ca. 1864. Collection Toulgouat

November: Pierre-Auguste Renoir attends the independent studio of the academic painter Charles Gleyre, where he meets Frédéric Bazille, Monet, and Alfred Sisley.

Fall: Edgar Degas stays with his friend Paul Valpinçon in Normandy, where he makes his first studies of horses.

Pissarro registers to copy in the Louvre. At the Académie Suisse, he meets Guillaumin and Cézanne.

PHOTOGRAPHY

July 25: Auguste-Rosalie Bisson reaches the summit of Mont Blanc and makes 3 exposures.

July: the Conseil d'administration of the Southern Region commissions Baldus to create a photographic album, *Chemins de fer de Paris à Lyon et à la Méditerranée*, with views of the landscape, monuments, and railway structures along the southern line.

1862

HISTORY & CULTURE

May 1–November 1: the International Exhibition of Industry and Art takes place in London.

Spanish and British withdraw from Mexican expedition, while the French military resumes hostilities and is defeated at Puebla.

Treaty of Saigon between France and Annam (present-day Vietnam); 3 provinces go to France.

Arrival of the railroad in Brittany.

Emperor Napoléon receives Otto von Bismarck, minister president of Prussia, and proposes an alliance between the 2 nations.

Victor Hugo publishes *Les misérables*.

PAINTING

Autumn: Breton makes 2 visits (a second time in autumn 1863) to the Bordelais, where he conducts research for his painting *The Vintage at Château Lagrange* (cat. 60) at the request of his patron, comte Duchâtel.

Bazille moves to Paris from Montpellier and studies at Gleyre's studio, where he meets Monet, Sisley, and Renoir.

At the International Exhibition in London, Rosa Bonheur, Breton, Daubigny, Diaz, Français, Harpignies, Millet, Rousseau, Troyon, and Viollet-le-Duc exhibit works. Aiguier is the only painter to represent the Marseille school with *Fishermen at Saint-Mandrier* and *Gulf of Val Bonête*.

Renoir is admitted to the École des beaux-arts.

Guigou returns to Paris from Provence, exhibiting at the Salon the following year and showing his work regularly until 1870.

Degas meets Manet while copying at the Louvre and through him makes contact with the young Impressionists.

PHOTOGRAPHY

August: Auguste-Rosalie Bisson makes views of Mont Blanc.

Winter: Le Gray establishes himself in Egypt.

At the International Exhibition of Industry and Art, London, Baldus shows 2 albums that include views of the Dauphiné and Savoy and photographs of the new Louvre.

1863

HISTORY & CULTURE

August: Cambodia becomes a French protectorate.

Opposition to government policies makes headway in the cities. Authorities tolerate workers' associations, grant amnesties, and relax censorship.

A railway station in Trouville opens, giving rise to an increase in tourism at the beaches in Normandy.

Empress Eugénie and Emperor Napoléon III visit Trouville.

PAINTING

Early spring: Monet and Bazille leave Gleyre's studio and paint in Chailly-en-Bière, a small village near Barbizon visited often by Rousseau and Millet. Renoir and Sisley join them in April.

May: state-organized Salon des Refusés shows paintings excluded by the Salon jury in an annex of the Palais de l'Industrie on the Champs-Élysées. Works by Jean-Charles Cazin, Guillaumin, Jongkind, Manet (*Le déjeuner sur l'herbe*; Musée d'Orsay, Paris), Pissarro, and Cézanne are included.

The Salon becomes an annual event; artists are restricted to submitting 2 works per year.

Rousseau makes an extended visit to the Alps, where he produces paintings, drawings, and watercolors of the Mont Blanc range.

Publication of Baudelaire's "Le peintre de la vie moderne" ("The Painter of Modern Life").

PHOTOGRAPHY

Baldus photographs the Rennes-to-Brest rail line for engineers.

Nègre moves to Nice, where he opens a commercial studio and teaches drawing at the Lycée impérial until 1878.

December: the Bisson frères declare bankruptcy.

1864

HISTORY & CULTURE

With France's support, Archduke Maximilian of Austria accepts crown of emperor of Mexico.

PAINTING

May: at the Salon, the state acquires 20 landscapes of France. Napoléon III purchases Corot's *Souvenir of Mortefontaine* (Musée du Louvre, Paris). Reform of Salon jury leads to the election of some landscape artists, Corot among them.

Late spring: Monet and Bazille paint together in the Forest of Fontainebleau and at Honfleur.

Mid-July–August: the Manet family travels to Boulogne, where the artist sketches a variety of marine subjects.

Courbet spends the entire year in his native Franche-Comté, painting the diverse topographies of the region.

PHOTOGRAPHY

Baldus creates stereographs of Lyon, Orange, Avignon, Saint-Rémy, Arles, Montmajour, Nîmes, Pont du Gard, and Aigues-Mortes.

The city of Paris commissions Marville to photograph views of Parisian streets, parks, and monuments before and after the major renovations by Napoléon III and Baron Haussmann.

1865

HISTORY & CULTURE

May 5–June 8: Emperor Napoléon III travels to Algeria.

July: the Paris branch of the International Workingman's Association is founded, which had been established in London a year before by Karl Marx andFriedrich Engels.

PAINTING

May: at the Salon, the state acquires 30 landscapes of France. Monet successfully submits 2 landscapes for the first time: *Mouth of the Seine at Honfleur* (Norton Simon Museum, Pasadena, Calif.) and *The Pointe de la Hève at Low Tide* (Kimbell Art Museum, Fort Worth).

June 10: Empress Eugénie presents the ribbon of the chevalier of the Legion of Honor to Rosa Bonheur, the first woman to receive this award.

July: Huet travels to the château of Pierrefonds to conduct research for his painting *The Château of Pierrefonds Restored* (cat. 27), commissioned by Napoléon III.

Summer: Breton visits Cernay-La Ville twice. By the fall, he leaves for Brittany, residing with his family in the fishing port of Douarnezez. He will return regularly until 1891.

1866

HISTORY & CULTURE

January: evacuation of French troops from Mexico.

July: Prussia defeats Austria at the battle of Sadowa, causing a shift in the balance of power in Europe.

Marseille's population reaches 300,000, an increase from 198,000 in 1851, making it second only to Paris in the number of inhabitants.

PAINTING

May: at the Salon, the state purchases 30 landscapes of France.

Summer: Millet travels to Auvergne for the first time; he returns in 1867 and 1868.

Dealers Paul Durand-Ruel and Hector Brame purchase unfinished paintings and studies from Rousseau.

Pissarro meets Manet, attends Émile Zola's "Thursdays," frequents the Café Guerbois in the Batignolles district, and visits Bazille's studio.

1867

HISTORY & CULTURE

February: French military withdraws from Mexico.

April 1–November 3: Exposition universelle d'art et d'industrie takes place at the Champ-de-Mars; 41 countries participate. The fair houses 52,200 exhibits and is viewed by 11 million visitors, marking the high point of the Second Empire.

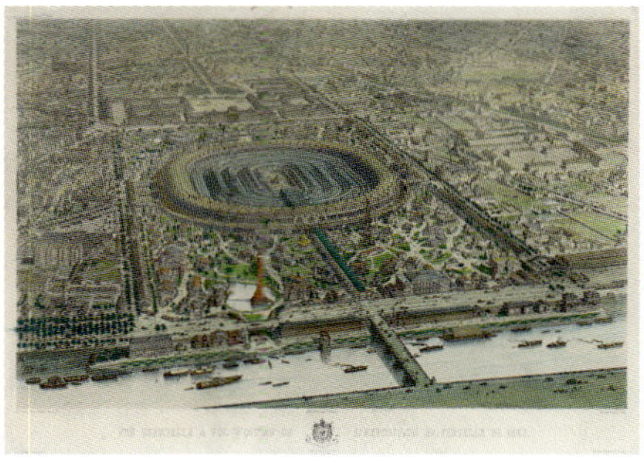

Eugène Cicéri, *Official Bird's-eye View of the Exposition Universelle of 1867*. Hand-colored lithograph. Library of Congress

June 19: Emperor Maximilian of Mexico is executed by republicans at Querétaro, further weakening the position of Napoléon III.

PAINTING

April: the Salon exhibition occurs independently but parallel to the Exposition universelle in the Palais du Champ-de-Mars. The state acquires 20 landscapes of France.

April: at the Exposition universelle, Auguste Bonheur, Rosa Bonheur, Breton, Corot, Courbet, Daubigny, Français, Harpignies, Huet, Puvis de Chavannes, Rousseau, and Troyon show works. Courbet and Manet set up independent pavilions outside the exposition site at the Pont d'Alma, at the same time as the Exposition universelle.

Summer: Monet moves from Paris to Sainte-Adresse, where he paints 20 landscapes.

Bazille produces 3 paintings of the medieval walled city of Aigues-Mortes on the Mediterranean coast (see cats. 38, 39).

June: the city of Marseille commissions Puvis de Chavannes to paint a patriotic mural, *Marseille, Gateway to the Orient* (see fig. 81), together with a pendant mural representing the city's ancient Greek history (see fig. 82).

PHOTOGRAPHY

Braun becomes a member of the SFP as well as the official photographer to Pope Pius IX.

At the Exposition universelle, Cuvelier shows views of the Forest of Fontainebleau, and Civiale shows images of the Alps. Baldus, Braun, Delondre, and Le Gray are also represented.

1868

HISTORY & CULTURE

May–June: government relaxes laws regarding press censorship, and freedom of assembly is tolerated for all nonpolitical organizations.

PAINTING

May: at the Salon, the state purchases 30 landscapes of France, 1 of which is Huet's *The Ruins of the Château of Pierrefonds* (cat. 28).

June: The Exposition maritime internationale is held in Le Havre. Manet, Boudin, Monet, Courbet, and Daubigny exhibit.

Summer: the Manet family vacations at Boulogne, where the artist sketches numerous jetties and figures on the beach. By late July or early August, he travels by steamboat to London.

Summer: Monet paints at Sainte-Adresse, Le Havre, and Étretat.

Summer: Français travels to the Alps, sketching and painting panoramic views of Mont Blanc.

July–November: Breton stays at the Hôtel du Commerce in Douarnenez, in Brittany.

PHOTOGRAPHY

August: Auguste-Rosalie Bisson makes stereoscopic view of Mont Blanc for the firm Léon et Lévy.

Braun opens a fine art publishing firm, Braun et Cie.

1869

HISTORY & CULTURE

May: Folies-Bergère, the first music hall in Paris, opens.

November 17: opening of the Suez Canal in Egypt; Empress Eugénie, the Prince of Wales, the crown prince of Prussia, and the viceroy of Egypt are present.

Le Bon Marché, the first department store in Paris, is built.

PAINTING

May: at the Salon, the state purchases 20 landscapes of France.

June: Berthe Morisot visits Brittany and paints *The Harbor at Lorient* (cat. 116).

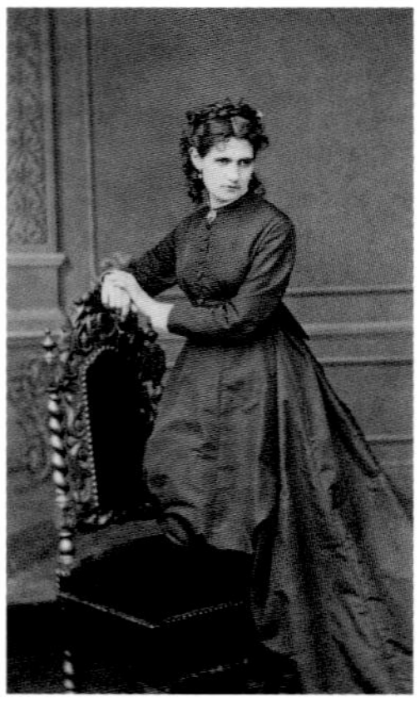

Pierre Petit, *Berthe Morisot*, 1869. Private collection / Archives Charmet

July–August: Degas returns to the Normandy coast, where he executes several pastels and paints seashore scenes.

Spring: Pissarro moves to 22, route de Versailles, Louveciennes.

July–September: Monet and Renoir paint together at La Grenouillère on the Seine and also paint barges on a boat trip along the Seine to Normandy.

PHOTOGRAPHY

Braun is invited to photograph the opening of the Suez Canal.

Baldus publishes *Palais du Louvre et des Tuileries*, his first photogravure publication using his own photographs, published in installments through 1871.

1870

HISTORY & CULTURE

January: resignation of Baron Haussmann as prefect of the Seine.

July 19: Franco-Prussian War begins when France declares war on Prussia.

September 2: Napoléon III and the French army surrender at Sedan.

September 4: Léon Gambetta proclaims France's Third Republic at the Hôtel de Ville in Paris, and General Louis-Jules Trochu becomes president.

September 19: Siege of Paris begins.

The French railway network reaches a total of 9,658 miles, a fivefold increase from its 2,018 miles in 1851.

PAINTING

May: at the Salon, the state purchases 30 landscapes of France.

June: Monet and Camille Doncieux marry in Paris and settle for the summer in Trouville, where the artist produces 9 paintings of vacationers.

Fall: Daubigny, Monet, and Pissarro flee to London for the duration of the Franco-Prussian War.

November 28: Bazille is killed in action in Beaune-la-Rolande.

Manet, Degas, Harpignies, Puvis de Chavannes, and Renoir join the National Guard in response to the outbreak of the Franco-Prussian War. Renoir is discharged due to ill health.

PHOTOGRAPHY

1870s: Baldus's *Palais de Versailles* and *Les principaux monuments de la France* are published.

1871

HISTORY & CULTURE

January 26: after siege and famine, Paris surrenders to Prussian forces.

February: the seat of government is moved to Versailles. Adolphe Thiers becomes premier.

March 18: the Commune begins in Paris, marking a brief assumption of power by the working class. The city is cut off from the rest of France.

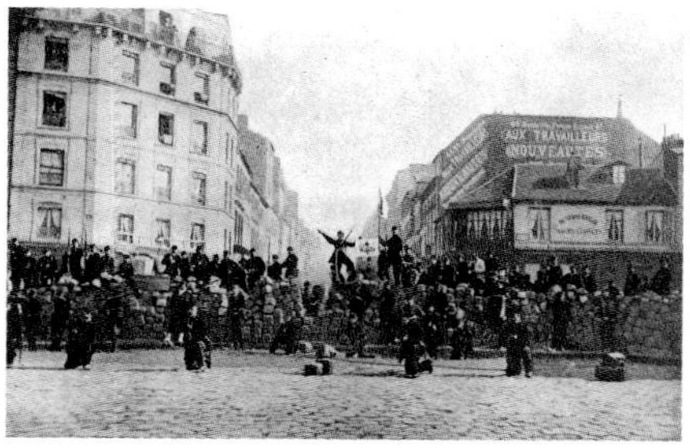

Barricade at the Faubourg Saint-Antoine during the Commune, March 18, 1871. Bibliothèque nationale de France, Paris

May 10: the Treaty of Frankfurt is signed, ending the war between France and Prussia and marking the downfall of Napoléon III and the Second Empire. France loses Alsace and Lorraine to the Prussians.

May 21–28: the Versailles government overthrows the Commune, massacring thousands of Communards.

August: Thiers is elected president of the Third Republic.

PAINTING

February–May: Puvis de Chavannes leaves Paris after the capitulation; makes small sketches and watercolors in Versailles.

April: Courbet assumes responsibility for fine arts under the Commune and participates in the destruction of the Vendôme Column, a symbol of Napoleonic rule; he is imprisoned for 6 months.

July 14: Pissarro marries Julie Vellay and returns to Louveciennes, where his studio has been sacked.

Fall: Diaz travels on doctor's orders to the Pyrenees, where he paints several views of the mountain range.

November: Monet returns to France, moving to Argenteuil with his wife and son at the end of the year. They remain until 1878.

1872

HISTORY & CULTURE

Committee for the Artistic Protection of the Forest of Fontainebleau is founded, with Millet as president of honor.

PAINTING

April–September: Corot travels on a 6-month journey around France, including visits to Beauvais, Fumay (Ardennes), Coubron, Rouen, Port-Marly, and Étretat.

August: Pissarro moves to Pontoise, near the Oise River in Normandy.

August: Cézanne establishes himself at Auvers-sur-Oise, and Pissarro recommends Cézanne to his dealer, Père Tanguy.

October–March 1873: Degas travels with his brother René to New Orleans, Louisiana.

Renoir lives in Paris and paints cityscapes.

1873

HISTORY & CULTURE

January 9: Napoléon III dies in Chislehurst, Kent, England.

May: Royalist Marshal Patrice de MacMahon replaces Thiers as president, instituting a conservative regime based on "moral order."

May 1–October 31: Weltausstellung Wien (International Exhibition, Vienna).

Repression of cafés and republican press; commemoration of July 14 banned.

PAINTING

Summer: Morisot travels to Les Petites-Dalles and Fécamp, where she paints beach scenes.

July: the Manet family stays in Berck, where the artist draws and paints *en plein air.*

July 23: Courbet goes into exile in Vevey, Switzerland.

December: the ultraclerical aristocrat the marquis Philippe de Chennevières becomes director of the École des beaux-arts and remains so until 1878, maintaining control of state patronage.

Weltausstellung Wien features landscapes by Breton, Corot, Daubigny, Diaz, Français, Harpignies, Huet, Millet, Rousseau, and Troyon.

Pissarro paints series of views of the factory building of J. Chalon et Cie in Pontoise.

PHOTOGRAPHY

Eugène Cuvelier exhibits photographs in Arras.

Weltausstellung Wien features photographs by Baldus and Braun.

1874

HISTORY & CULTURE

January: the state proclaims right to appoint mayors in all communes.

PAINTING

April: the first Impressionist exhibition takes place in Nadar's studio, at 35, boulevard des Capucines, including works by Cézanne, Degas, Monet, Morisot, Pissarro, Renoir, and Sisley. Monet exhibits *Impression, Sunrise* (Musée Marmottan Monet, Paris), the painting that gives the movement its name, and *Boulevard des Capucines* (see fig. 54).

May: at the Salon, the state buys 29 landscapes of France. Daubigny exhibits *Fields in the Month of June* (cat. 70).

August: Manet stays at Monet's villa in Argenteuil and is joined by Renoir.

December 22: marriage of Berthe Morisot and Eugène Manet.

Millet, Puvis de Chavannes, and others receive a commission to paint scenes from the life of St. Geneviève, patron saint of Paris, for the Panthéon, a prestigious official recognition.

1875

HISTORY & CULTURE

January: the Wallon Amendment affirms the republic by a majority of 1 vote.

The Paris Opéra opens.

PAINTING

Spring: Renoir paints city views of the neighborhood near his studio on the rue Saint-Georges; these include the place Saint-Georges, the Grands Boulevards, and streets near the Opéra.

Summer: Morisot spends time in West Cowes on the Isle of Wight with her husband, where she paints seascapes.

For a change of motifs, Boudin travels to Berck, Boulogne, and Calais, in northern France, and then to Holland.

1876

HISTORY & CULTURE

January–March: elections result in right-wing majority in Senate, republican majority in Chamber of Deputies.

May 10–November 10: Philadelphia World's Fair (Centennial Exhibition of 1876).

PAINTING

May: at the Salon the state buys 6 landscapes of France. Harpignies shows *A Meadow in the Bourbonnais, Morning* (cat. 56).

The second Impressionist exhibition takes place with 20 artists showing 252 works at 11, rue Le Peletier, at the Durand-Ruel galleries. Degas, Monet, Morisot, Pissarro, and Renoir are the primary participants.

Spring: Breton visits the South of France.

Summer–fall: Manet and Monet stay with the Hoschedé family at its château in Montgeron.

1877

HISTORY & CULTURE

Republicans win general elections, ending all hopes of a return to a monarchist government.

Continued repression of cafés and other locations of political opposition.

PAINTING

January: Monet rents an apartment in the rue Moncy and paints views of the Gare Saint-Lazare, some of which are shown in the third Impressionist exhibition.

April: third Impressionist exhibition takes place in the rue Le Peletier. Monet, Degas, Pissarro, Renoir, and Morisot are the primary artists represented.

May: at the Salon the state purchases 3 landscapes of France.

Breton travels to the South of France (Nice and Antibes) with his brother Émile.

1878

HISTORY & CULTURE

March: Charles de Freycinet, minister of public works, initiates a plan for massive expenditure on railways, roads, and canals.

May 20–November 10: the Exposition universelle is the largest to date, attracting close to 6 million international visitors and playing a crucial role in cementing national confidence after the Franco-Prussian War.

In celebration of the success of the Exposition universelle, the French government declares June 30 the Fête de la Paix (Celebration of Peace), a national holiday.

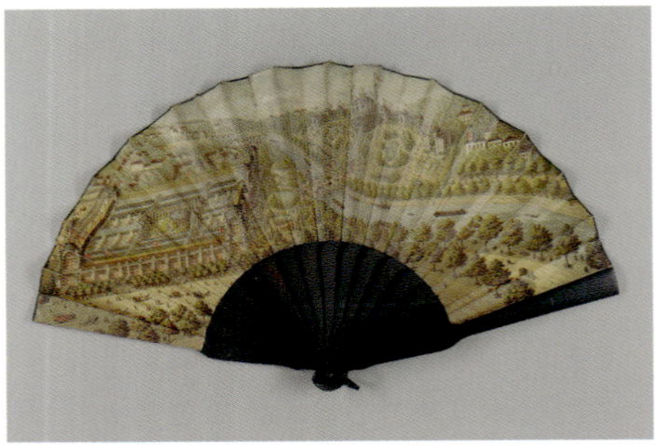

Paris Exposition Fan, 1878. Wisconsin Historical Society, gift of Elizabeth Greene Upham Davis, 1956.1671

PAINTING

May: at the Salon, the state purchases 21 landscapes of France.

May: at the Exposition universelle, Corot, Daubigny, Français, Harpignies, and Huet exhibit works.

Late summer: Monet family moves to Vétheuil, sharing a house with the Hoschedés, who have declared bankruptcy.

December: the Salon rules are revised so that 5 of 15 jurors must be landscape, animal, or still-life painters.

Art dealer Paul Durand-Ruel organizes a spectacular exhibition of 382 landscape paintings of the French school, foregrounding paintings by Millet and Courbet, whose works had been marginalized at the Exposition universelle.

1879

HISTORY & CULTURE

January: MacMahon resigns as president and is replaced by the first true republican president, Jules Grévy.

The Third Republic establishes "La Marseillaise," a Revolutionary battle song and hymn to freedom dating back to 1792, as the French national anthem.

PAINTING

April 10–May 11: the fourth Impressionist exhibition takes place at 28, avenue de l'Opéra with a catalogue of 246 works; 15,400 visitors see the display. Monet participates with 29, mostly plein air, works. Pissarro also shows 38 paintings, mostly landscapes.

May: at the Salon, statesman and republican Jules Ferry announces major shift in state art policy, giving favor to plein air painting and modern-life subjects. The state purchases 21 landscapes of France.

1880

HISTORY & CULTURE

July: the state grants amnesty to former Communards and relaxes laws controlling freedom of speech in cafés.

July 14: Bastille Day, commemorating the storming of the Bastille in 1789, is revived for the first time since 1873.

Beginning in this decade, a web of local railroad lines is built that links remote regions to the national network.

PAINTING

April 1–30: the fifth Impressionist exhibition is held at 10, rue des Pyramides; 19 participants show 232 works. Pissarro exhibits 11 paintings, mostly landscapes, and etchings of rural scenes. Morisot exhibits 15 works. Renoir, Sisley, Monet, and Cézanne do not participate.

May: Monet is admitted to the Salon with a large landscape of Lavacourt.

August: Monet submits a few canvases to the exhibition organized by the Société des amis des arts du Havre.

Select Bibliography

Anderson, Benedict. *Imagined Communities: Reflections on the Origin and Spread of Nationalism*. London: Verso, 1991.

Aubenas, Sylvie. *Gustave Le Gray, 1820–1884*. Exh. cat. Los Angeles: J. Paul Getty Museum, 2002.

———, and Paul-Louis Robert. *Primitifs de la photographie: Le calotype en France, 1843–1860*. Exh. cat. Paris: Gallimard; Bibliothèque nationale de France, 2010.

Bailey, Colin B., and Christopher Riopelle, eds. *Renoir Landscapes, 1865–1883*. Exh. cat. London: National Gallery, 2007.

Bénédité, Léonce. *Jean-Charles Cazin*. Paris: G. Baranger Fils, 1902.

Bergstein, Mary, and Maureen O'Brien, eds. *Image and Enterprise: The Photographs of Adolphe Braun*. Exh. cat. New York: Thames & Hudson in association with Museum of Art, Rhode Island School of Design, Providence, 2000.

Borcoman, James. *Charles Nègre, 1820–1880*. Exh. cat. Ottawa: National Gallery of Canada, 1976.

Brenneman, David A. *Monet: A View from the River*. Exh. cat. Atlanta: High Museum of Art, 2001.

Brettell, Richard R. *Pissarro and Pontoise: The Painter in a Landscape*. New Haven: Yale University Press, 1990.

———, and Joachim Pissarro. *Manet to Matisse: Impressionist Masters from the Marion and Henry Block Collection*. Exh. cat. Kansas City: Nelson-Atkins Museum of Art, 2008.

Breton, Jules. *The Life of an Artist*. Translated by Mary J. Serrano. New York: D. Appleton and Company, 1891.

Cusack, Tricia. *Riverscapes and National Identities*. Syracuse, N.Y.: Syracuse University Press, 2010.

Canguilhem, Denis. "André Giroux, Painter-Photographer." In *André Giroux, 1801–1879*, 175–82. Exh. cat. London: Wertheimer Foundation, 2004.

Chastel, André. "The Notion of Patrimony." In *Rethinking France: Les lieux de mémoire*, edited by Pierre Nora. Vol. 3, *Legacies*, 1–46. Chicago: University of Chicago Press, 1992.

Les frères Bisson photographes de flèche en cime, 1840–1870. Exh. cat. Paris: Bibliothèque Nationale de France; Essen: Museum Folkwang, 1999.

Civiale, M. A. *Les Alpes au point de vue de la géographie physique et de la géologie voyages photographiques dans le Dauphiné, la Savoie, le Nord d'Italie, la Suisse et le Tyrol*. Paris: J. Rothschild, 1882.

Dahlberg, Laurie. *Victor Regnault and the Advance of Photography: The Art of Avoiding Errors*. Princeton: Princeton University Press, 2005.

Daniel, Malcolm. "Édouard-Denis Baldus and the Chemin de Fer du Nord Albums." *Image* 35, nos. 3–4 (Fall–Winter 1992): 3–38.

———. *Eugène Cuvelier: Photographer in the Circle of Corot*. Exh. cat. New York: Metropolitan Museum of Art, 1996.

———. *The Photographs of Édouard Baldus*. Exh. cat. New York: Metropolitan Museum of Art; Montreal: Canadian Centre for Architecture, 1994.

Delouche, Denise. *Peintres de la Bretagne: Découverte d'une province*. Paris: Librairie C. Klincksieck, 1977.

———, and Jean-Marc Michaud. *Bretagne, terre des peintres*. Saint-Thonan: Cloître, 2003.

De Moncan, Patrice. *Les grands boulevards de Paris: De la Bastille à la Madeleine*. Paris: Les Éditions de Mécène, 1997.

De Modenard, Anne. *La Mission héliographique: Cinq photographes parcourent la France en 1851*. Paris: Centre des Monuments Nationaux; Monum, Éditions du Patrimoine, 2002.

Eisenman, Stephen F., ed. *From Corot to Monet: The Ecology of Impressionism*. Exh. cat. Milan: Skira, 2010.

Dumesnil, Henri. *Troyon: Souvenir intimes*. Paris: H. Laurens, 1888.

Fried, Michael. *Courbet's Realism*. Chicago: University of Chicago Press, 1990.

Gellner, Ernst. *Nations and Nationalism*. Ithaca, N.Y.: Cornell University Press, 1983; Oxford: Blackwell, 2006.

Gérson, Stephane. "Parisian Litterateurs, Provincial Journeys and the Construction of National Unity in Post-Revolutionary France." *Past and Present*, no. 151 (May 1996): 141–73.

———. *The Pride of Place: Local Memories and Political Culture in Nineteenth-Century France*. Ithaca, N.Y.: Cornell University Press, 2003.

Granger, Catherine. *L'empereur et les arts: La Liste Civile de Napoléon III*. Paris: École de Chartes, 2005.

Haworth-Booth, Mark. *Camille Silvy, River Scene, France*. Exh. cat. Malibu, Calif.: J. Paul Getty Museum, 1992.

Heilbrun, Françoise. *Charles Nègre, Photographe, 1820–1880*. Exh. cat. Paris: Éditions des Musées Nationaux, 1980.

Herbert, Robert L. *Impressionism: Art, Leisure and Parisian Society*. New Haven: Yale University Press, 1988.

———. *Monet on the Normandy Coast: Tourism and Painting, 1867–1888*. New Haven: Yale University Press, 1994.

House, John, ed. *Impressionists by the Sea*. Exh. cat. London: Royal Academy of Arts, 2007.

———. *Landscapes of France: Impressionism and Its Rivals*. Exh. cat. London: South Bank Centre, 1995.

Jammes, André, and Eugenia Parry Janis. *The Art of French Calotype with a Critical Dictionary of Photographers, 1845–1870*. Princeton: Princeton University Press, 1983.

Jammes, Isabelle. *Blanquart-Evrard et les origines de l'édition photographique française: Catalogue raisonné des albums photographiques édités, 1851–1855*. Paris: Librairie Droz, 1981.

———. *The Photography of Gustave Le Gray*. Exh. cat. Chicago: Art Institute of Chicago; University of Chicago Press, 1987.

———, and Josiane Sartre. *Henri Le Secq: Photographe de 1850 à 1860*. Exh. cat. Paris: Musée des Arts Décoratifs, 1986.

Jones, Kimberly, et al. *In the Forest of Fontainebleau: Painters and Photographers from Corot to Monet*. Exh. cat. Washington, D.C.: National Gallery of Art, 2008.

Jordan, David P. *Transforming Paris: The Life and Labors of Baron Haussmann*. Chicago: University of Chicago Press, 1995

Klumpke, Anna. *Rosa Bonheur: The Artist's (Auto) Biography*. Translated by Gretchen Van Slyke. Ann Arbor: University of Michigan Press, 1997.

Lacouture, Annette Bourrut. *Jules Breton: Painter of Peasant Life*. Exh. cat. New Haven: Yale University Press in association with the National Gallery of Ireland, Dublin, 2002.

McNamara, Carole, et al. *The Lens of Impressionism: Photography and Painting along the Normandy Coast, 1850–1874*. Exh. cat. Ann Arbor: University of Michigan Museum of Art in association with Hudson Hills Press, 2009.

McWilliam, Neil. "Le paysan au Salon: Critique d'art et construction d'une classe sous le Second Empire." In *La critique d'art en France, 1850–1900*, edited by Jean-Paul Bouillon, 81–94. Saint-Étienne: Université, 1989.

———, and June Hargrove, eds. *Nationalism and French Visual Culture, 1870–1914*. Studies in the

History of Art 68, Center for Advanced Study in the Visual Arts, Symposium Papers 45. Washington, D.C.: National Gallery of Art, 2005.
Menzies, Charles R. *Red Flags and Lace Coiffes: Identity and Survival in a Breton Fishing Village*. Toronto: University of Toronto Press, 2011.
Morton, Mary, and Charlotte Eyerman. *Courbet and the Modern Landscape*. Exh. cat. Los Angeles: J. Paul Getty Museum, 2006.
Nochlin, Linda. *Realism*. Harmondsworth, U.K.: Penguin, 1981.
Orton, Fred, and Griselda Pollock. "Les Données Bretonnantes: La Prairie de Représentation." In *Avant-gardes and Partisans Reviewed*, 53–88. Manchester: Manchester University Press, 1996.
Paléologue, Maurice. *Les entretiens de l'Impératice Eugénie*. Paris: Librairie Plon, 1928.
Pinckney, David H. *Napoleon III and the Rebuilding of Paris*. Princeton: Princeton University Press, 1972.
Pissarro, Joachim, and Claire Durand-Ruel Snollaerts. *Pissarro: Critical Catalogue of Paintings*. Paris: Wildenstein Institute; Milan: Skira, 2005.
Pomain, Krzysztof. "Franks and Gauls." In *Realms of Memory: Rethinking the French Past*, edited by Pierre Nora and Lawrence D. Kirtzman, 27–76. New York: Columbia University Press, 1996.
Ptacek, Robin Louis Thorne. "Bisson frères: Two Pioneers of Photography." PhD diss., University of California, Santa Barbara, 1989.
Puget, Catherine. *Peintres de la Bretagne et quête spirituelle (1860–1960)*. Exh. cat. Pont-Aven: Musée de Pont-Aven, 2006.
Reff, Theodore. *The Notebooks of Edgar Degas*. Oxford: Clarendon Press, 1976.
Rewald, John. *The Paintings of Paul Cézanne: A Catalogue Raisonné*. 2 vols. New York: Harry N. Abrams, 1996.
Rey, Jean-Dominique. *Henri Rouart, l'oeuvre peinte*. Exh. cat. Paris: Musée Marmottan Monet; Éditions Hazan, 2012.
Robb, Graham. *The Discovery of France*. London: Picador, 2007.
Roquebert, Anne. *Claude Monet, 1840–1926*. Exh. cat. Paris: Réunion des Musées Nationaux, 2010.
Roux, Nathalie, and Françoise Gilbert, eds. *Jean-François Millet: Voyages en Auverge et Bourbonnais, 1866–1868*. Exh. cat. Milan: Skira, 2002.
Rubin, James. *Impressionism and the Modern Landscape: Productivity, Technology, and Urbanization from Manet to Van Gogh*. Berkeley: University of California Press, 2008.
Salomé, Karine. *Les îles bretonnes: Une image en construction, 1750–1914*. Rennes: Presses Universitaires de France, 2003.
Schaaf, Larry J., and Russell Lord. Introduction to *Joseph, Vicomte Vigier Voyage dans les Pyrénées*, 7–15. *Sun Pictures* 16. Exh. cat. New York: Hans P. Kraus, Jr., 2007.
Schulman, Michel. *Fréderic Bazille, 1841–1870: Catalogue raisonné; Peintures, dessins, pastels, aquarelles. Sa vie, son oeuvre, sa correspondance*. Paris: Éditions de l'Amateur–Éditions des Catalogues Raisonnés, 1995.
Shaw, Jennifer L. *Dream States: Puvis de Chavannes, Modernism, and the Fantasy of France*. New Haven: Yale University Press, 2002.
Soubiran, Jean-Roger. *Le paysage provençal et l'école de Marseille avant l'impressionisme, 1845–1874*. Exh. cat. Paris: Réunion des Musées Nationaux; Toulon: Musée de Toulon, 1992.
Spate, Virginia. *Claude Monet: Life and Work*. New York: Rizzoli, 1992.
Sturges, Hollister. *Jules Breton and the French Rural Tradition*. Exh. cat. Omaha, Nebr.: Joslyn Art Museum, 1982.
Thiesse, Anne-Marie. *Ils apprenaient la France: L'exaltation des regions dans le discours patriotique*. Paris: Maison des Sciences de l'Homme, 1997.
———. *La création des identités nationales: Europe XVIIIe–XXe siècle*. Paris: Éditions du Seuil, 1999.
Thomas, Greg. *Art and Ecology in Nineteenth-Century France: The Landscapes of Théodore Rousseau*. Princeton: Princeton University Press, 2000.
Thomson, Richard, ed. *Framing France: The Representation of Landscape, 1870–1914*. Manchester: Manchester University Press, 1998.
Tucker, Paul Hayes. *Monet at Argenteuil*. New Haven: Yale University Press, 1982.
Viollet-le-Duc. Exh. cat. Paris: Éditions de la Réunion des Musées Nationaux; Ministère de la Culture et de la Communication, 1980.
Von der Bruggen, Viktoria, and Christine Peltre, eds. *L'Alsace pittoresque: L'invention d'un paysage, 1770–1870*. Exh. cat. Paris: Hazan; Colmar: Musée Unterlinden, 2011.
Weber, Eugen. *Peasants into Frenchmen: The Modernization of Rural France, 1870–1914*. Stanford: Stanford University Press, 1976.
Wildenstein, Daniel. *Claude Monet: Biographie et catalogue raisonné*. 5 vols. Lausanne and Paris: La Bibliothèque des Arts, 1974.
Wilson-Bareau, Juliet. *Manet, Monet, and the Gare Saint-Lazare*. Exh. cat. Washington, D.C.: National Gallery of Art, 1998.
———, and David Degener, eds. *Manet and the Sea*. Exh. cat. Philadelphia: Philadelphia Museum of Art, 2003.
Young, Patrick. *Enacting Brittany: Tourism and Culture in Provincial France, 1871–1939*. Farnham, U.K.: Ashgate, 2012.

Index

Italicized page references indicate illustrations. Endnotes are indicated with "n" followed by the endnote number.

DETAILS

Front cover: Claude Monet, *Boulevard des Capucines*, 1873–74, cat. 15, p. 103

Back cover: Gustave Le Gray, *Group of Ships Departing Le Havre*, ca. 1856, cat. 104, p. 273

Front endsheets: Eugène Andriveau-Goujon, *Map of the Railways and Waterways of France According to the Best Documents*, 1878, fig. 3, p. 17

Back endsheets: Jean-Joseph Mieulet. *Massif du Mont Blanc extrait des minutes de la carte de France [Document cartographique] levé par M. Mieulet, capitaine d'État major, 1865*, fig. 74, p. 252

Page 2: Édouard Manet, *The Rue Mosnier with Flags*, 1878, cat. 21, p. 113

Page 6: Gustave Le Gray, *Tree, Forest of Fontainebleau*, ca. 1856, cat. 44, p. 157

Page 14: Henri-Joseph Harpignies, *The Oaks of Château-Renard (Allier)*, 1875, fig. 20, p. 30

Page 36: Auguste-Rosalie Bisson and Louis-Auguste Bisson, *Mont-Blanc, vu du Jardin*, 1860, cat. 93, pl. 21, p. 255

Page 52: Jules Breton, *The Blessing of the Wheat in Artois*, 1857, fig. 38, p. 61

Page 66: Evariste-Vital Luminais, *The Widow* or *The Fisherman's Family*, 1865, fig. 47, p. 74

PHOTOGRAPHY CREDITS

Photographs were supplied by the owners of the works of art listed in the captions. All rights reserved, except where noted below.

Adoc-photos / Art Resource, NY: fig. 60

The Art Archive / Musée des beaux-arts d'Epinal / Kharbine-Tapabor / Photo Prud'homme: fig. 37

Photography © The Art Institute of Chicago: cats. 58, 59, 106, 107, fig. 78

Bibliothèque nationale de France, Paris: figs. 1, 8, 14, 22, 31, 68

© BnF, Dist. RMN-Grand Palais / Art Resource, NY: fig. 30

bpk, Berlin / Nationalgalerie, Staatliche Museen, Berlin, Germany / Art Resource, NY: fig. 13

The Bridgeman Art Library: cats. 29, 72, fig. 54, p. 302

Photograph © 2013 Carnegie Museum of Art, Pittsburgh: cats. 49, 86

© The Cleveland Museum of Art: cats. 2, 69, 95

© CNAP / photo: © Besançon, Musée des beaux-arts et d'archéologie–Cliché Charles CHOFFET: fig. 5

© Corbis: p. 299 (Imperial Railway Train)

© Dahesh Museum of Art, New York, USA / The Bridgeman Art Library: cat. 96

© DeA Picture Library / Art Resource, NY: p. 297 (Winterhalter, *Portrait of Napoléon III*)

© Denver Art Museum: cat. 82

Duke University Libraries, Durham, N.C. Photo: Jack Edinger: figs. 39, 40

Joshua Ferdinand: cats. 6–8, 14, 32–34, 36, 47, 53, 63–65, 74, 81, 94, 97, 105, 110, figs. 26, 27, 65

Courtesy of George Eastman House, International Museum of Photography and Film, Rochester, New York: cats. 18–20, 91, 93, figs. 10, 23, 24

Giraudon / The Bridgeman Art Library: cat. 28, figs. 20, 81, 82, p. 303

Photo: Imaging Department © President and Fellows of Harvard College: fig. 79

Photography courtesy of the Herbert F. Johnson Museum of Art, Cornell University: cat. 70

John Lamberton: back cover, cats. 35, 103, 104

Michael Lamy: cats. 48, 115

Erich Lessing / Art Resource, NY: figs. 11, 57, 73

Library of Congress: fig. 72

Tiffany Matson: cats. 22–24, 41–43, 46, 54, fig. 63

Mel McLean: cat. 68

Image copyright © The Metropolitan Museum of Art. Image source: Art Resource, NY: cats. 25, 31, 39, 90, 92, 109, fig. 77

Jamison Miller: front cover, cats. 15, 85, 87, fig. 70

© MuMa–Musée d'art moderne André Malraux, Le Havre: fig. 48

Collection Musée départemental Breton, Quimper: fig. 2

Collection Musée départemental Breton, Quimper, Cliché Musée / Serge Goarin: fig. 44

© Musée des beaux-arts et d'archéologie, Besançon—Cliché Pierre GUENAT: fig. 16

Musée du monastère royal de Brou, Bourg-en-Bresse, cliché Hugo Maertens: fig. 35

© Musée national de la Marine: fig. 9

© Musées de la Ville de Rouen / C. Lancien, C. Loisel: p. 298

Photograph © 2013 Museum of Fine Arts, Boston: fig. 46

© National Gallery, London / Art Resource, NY: fig. 55

Image courtesy of the National Gallery of Art, Washington: cats. 4, 9, 10, 38, 45, 116

Photo © NGC: fig. 71

Photography Incorporated, Toledo: cat. 101

Princeton University Art Museum / Art Resource, NY. Photo: Bruce M. White: cat. 11

© RMN-Grand Palais / Art Resource, NY: cat. 27, figs. 7, 21, 28, 33, 38, 45, 47, 50, 51, 58, 64

© RMN-Grand Palais (Musée d'Orsay) / Hervé Lewandowski: cat. 89, fig. 52

Scala / White Images / Art Resource, NY: cat. 16

David Stansbury: cat. 83

Photograph © The State Hermitage Museum / photo by Vladimir Terebenin, Leonard Kheifets, Yuri Molodkovets: fig. 18

Image © Sterling and Francine Clark Art Institute, Williamstown, Massachusetts, USA. Photo: Michael Agee: cat. 73

© Victoria and Albert Museum, London: cats. 57, 108

© Virginia Museum of Fine Arts. Photo: Katherine Wetzel: cats. 71, 79, 114

Image © Worcester Art Museum, all rights reserved: fig. 67

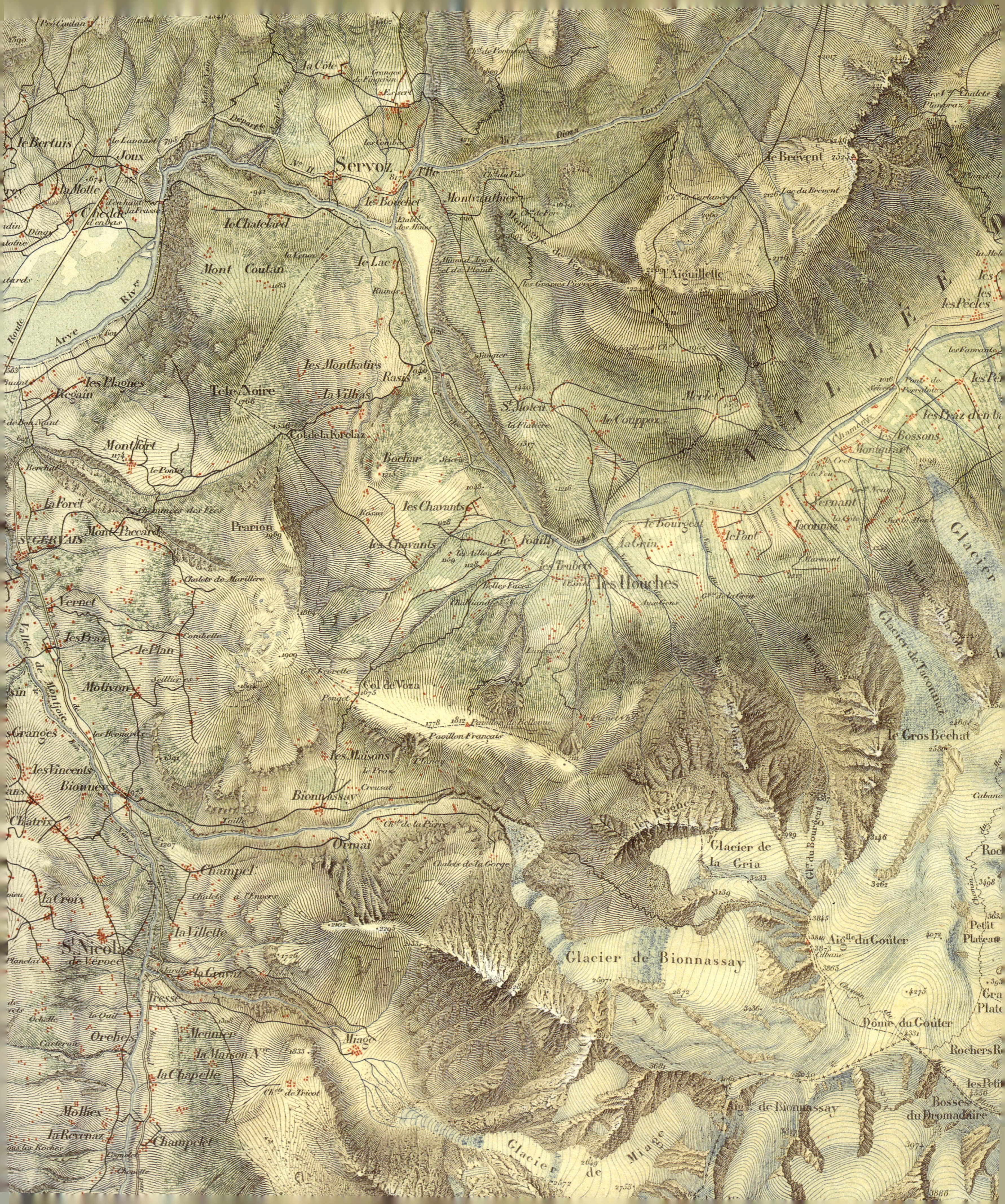
Servoz
le Bertuis
Joux
le Chatelard
Mont Coutan
le Lac
Montvauthier
le Brevent
l'Aiguillette
les Pècles
les Montkatires
Tete Noire
Col de la Forclaz
St. Moten
Merlet
le Couppoz
les Bossons
Montfort
Prarion
les Chavants
le Fouilly
les Houches
le Bourgeat
la Griaz
Taconnaz
Glacier
St. GERVAIS
Mont Paccard
Vernet
le Plan
Motivon
Col de Voza
Pavillon Français
les Maisons
Bionnassay
Glacier de Taconnaz
le Gros Bechat
les Vincents
Bionnay
Chatrix
Ormai
Champel
Glacier de la Gria
la Croix
la Villette
St. Nicolas de Véroce
Glacier de Bionnassay
Aigle du Goûter
Dôme du Goûter
Orches
la Chapelle
Miage
Molliex
la Revenaz
Champelet
Aigle de Bionnassay
Bosses du Dromadaire
Glacier de Miage